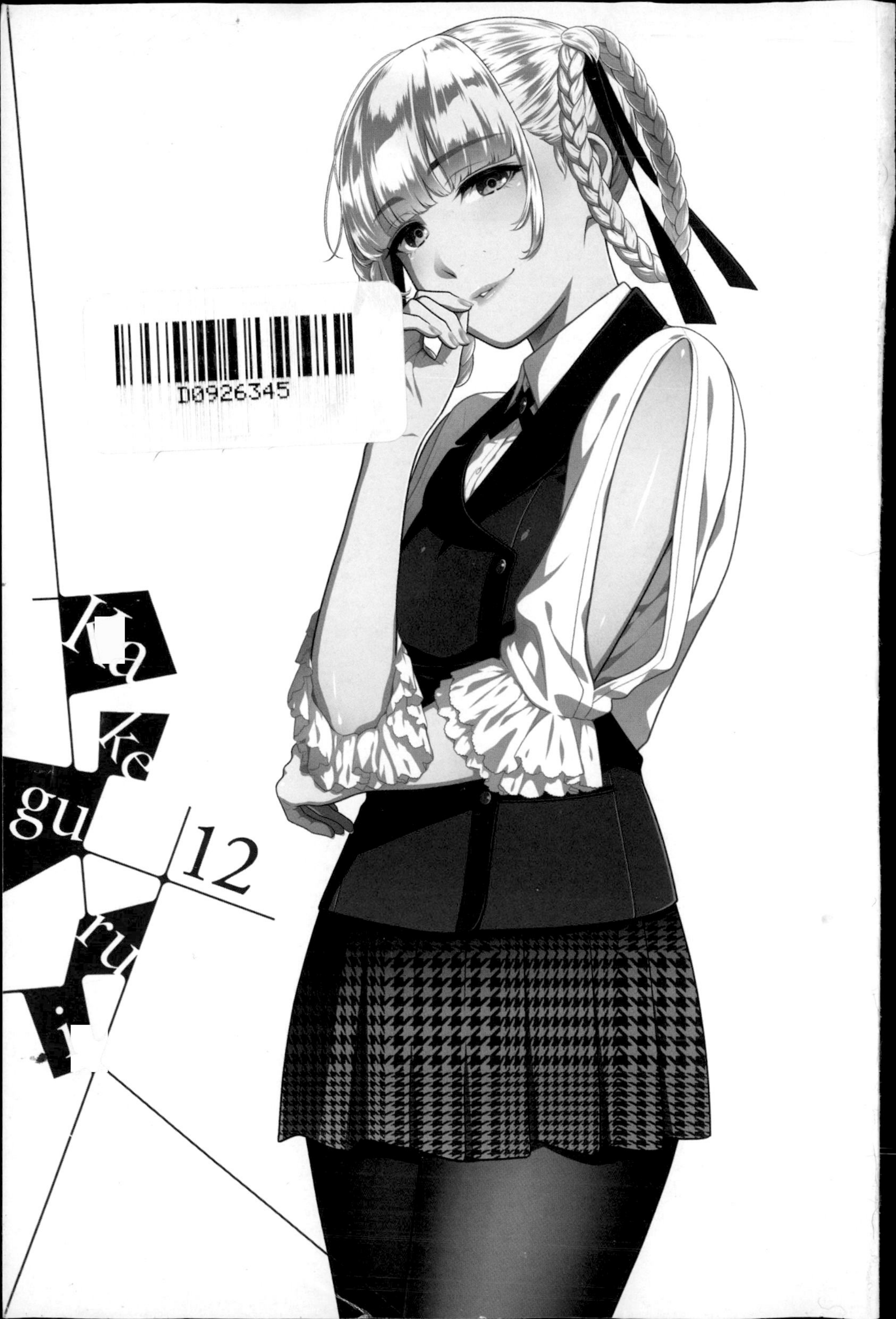
Ka
ke
gu
ru
12

⑫

KAKEGURUI

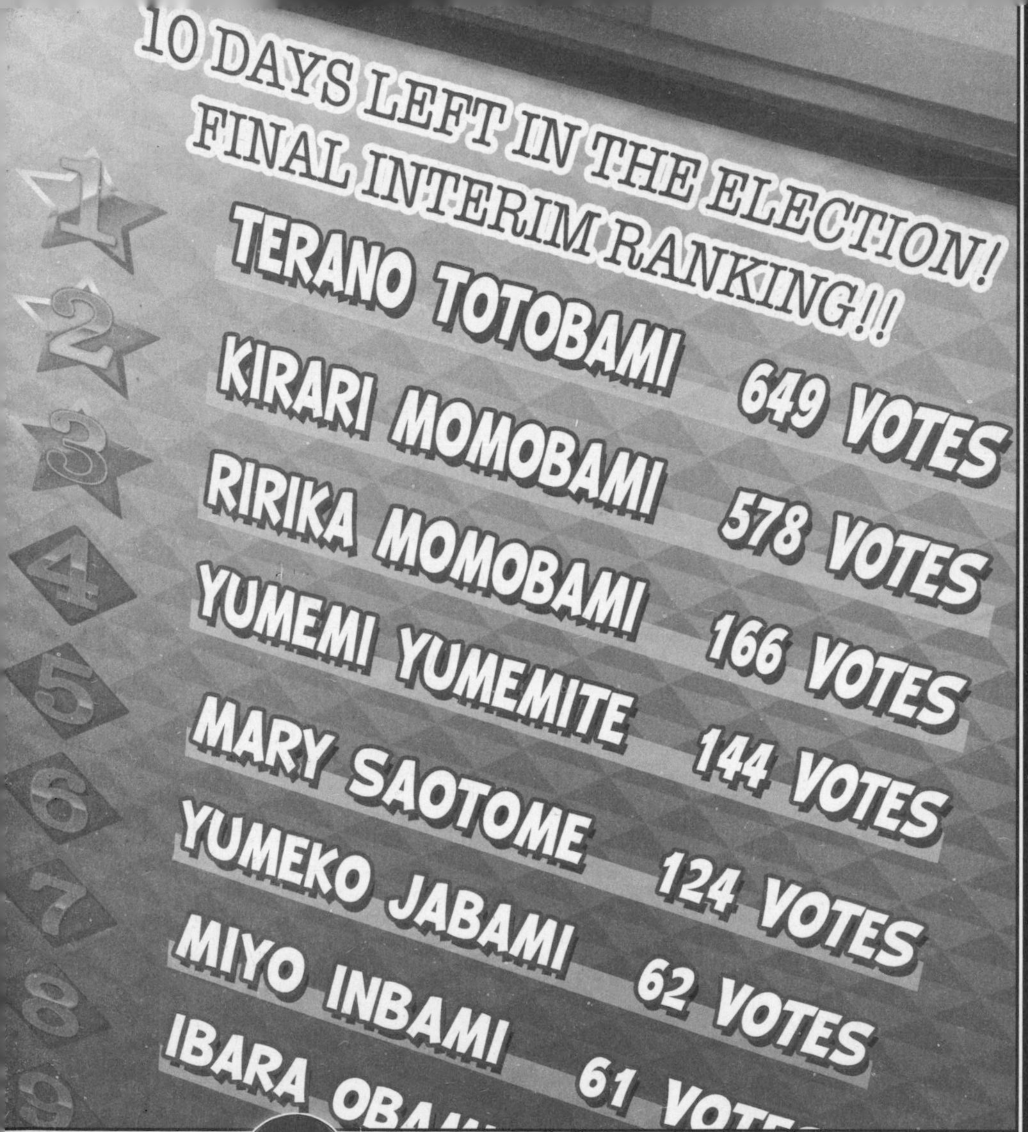
10 DAYS LEFT IN THE ELECTION!
FINAL INTERIM RANKING!!
1 TERANO TOTOBAMI 649 VOTES
2 KIRARI MOMOBAMI 578 VOTES
3 RIRIKA MOMOBAMI 166 VOTES
4 YUMEMI YUMEMITE 144 VOTES
5 MARY SAOTOME 124 VOTES
6 YUMEKO JABAMI 62 VOTES
7 MIYO INBAMI 61 VOTE
8 IBARA OBA
9

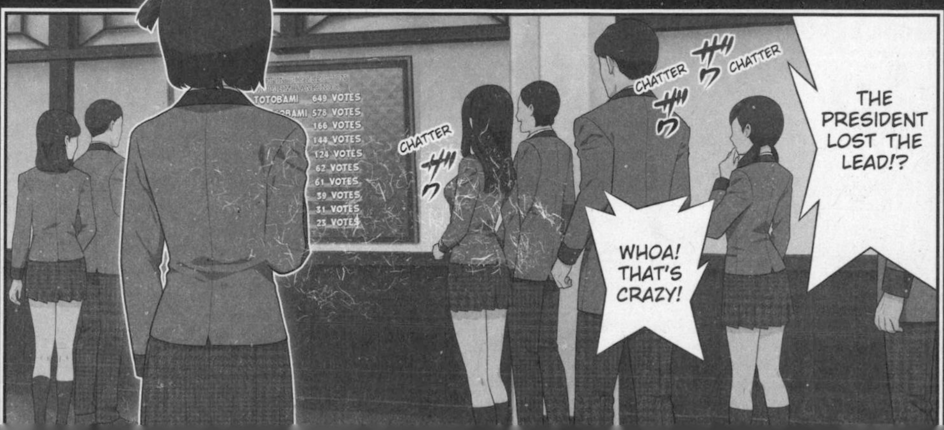
THE PRESIDENT LOST THE LEAD!?
CHATTER
CHATTER
WHOA! THAT'S CRAZY!
CHATTER

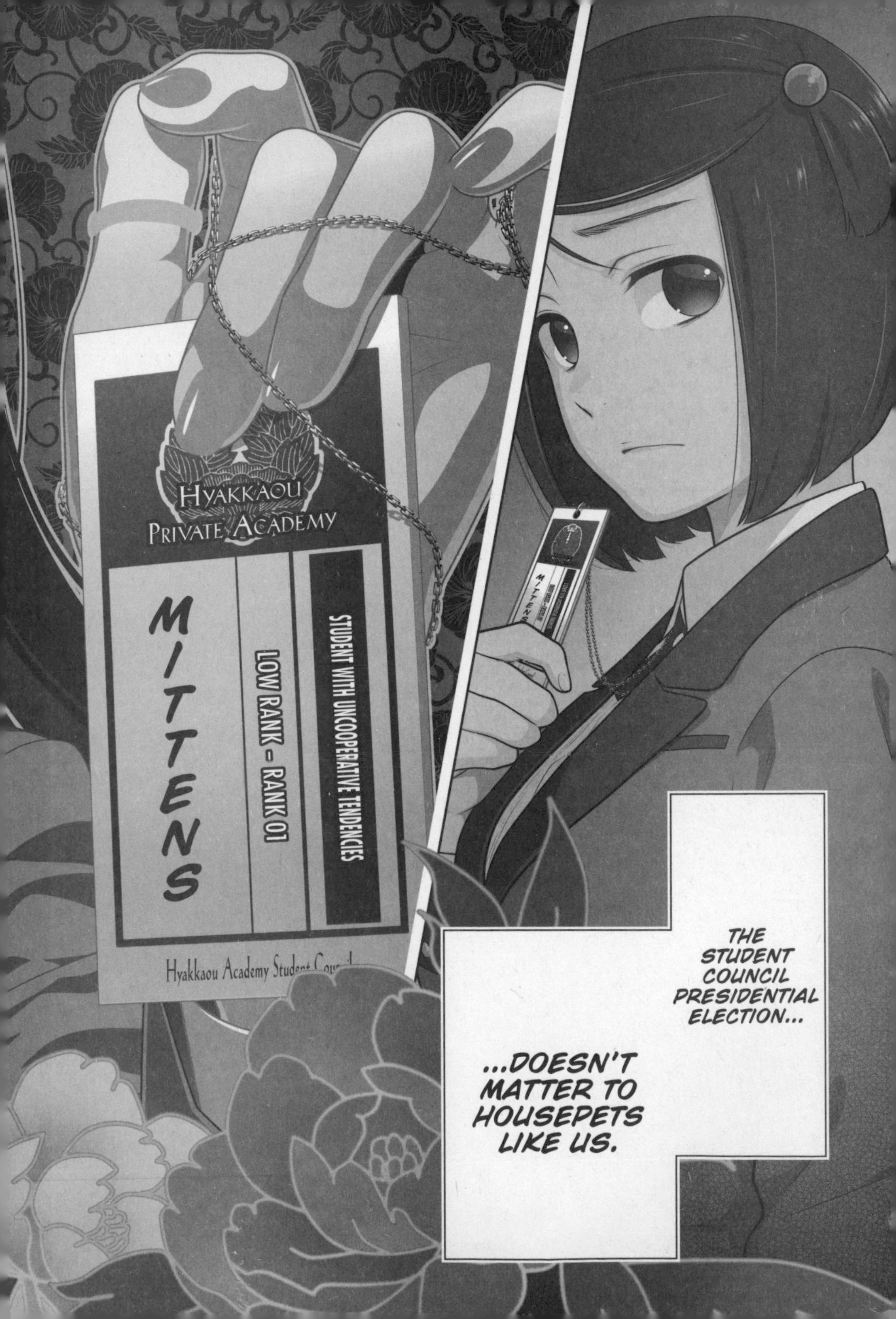
THE STUDENT COUNCIL PRESIDENTIAL ELECTION...
...DOESN'T MATTER TO HOUSEPETS LIKE US.
HYAKKAOU PRIVATE ACADEMY
MITTENS
LOW RANK - RANK 01
STUDENT WITH UNCOOPERATIVE TENDENCIES
Hyakkaou Academy Student

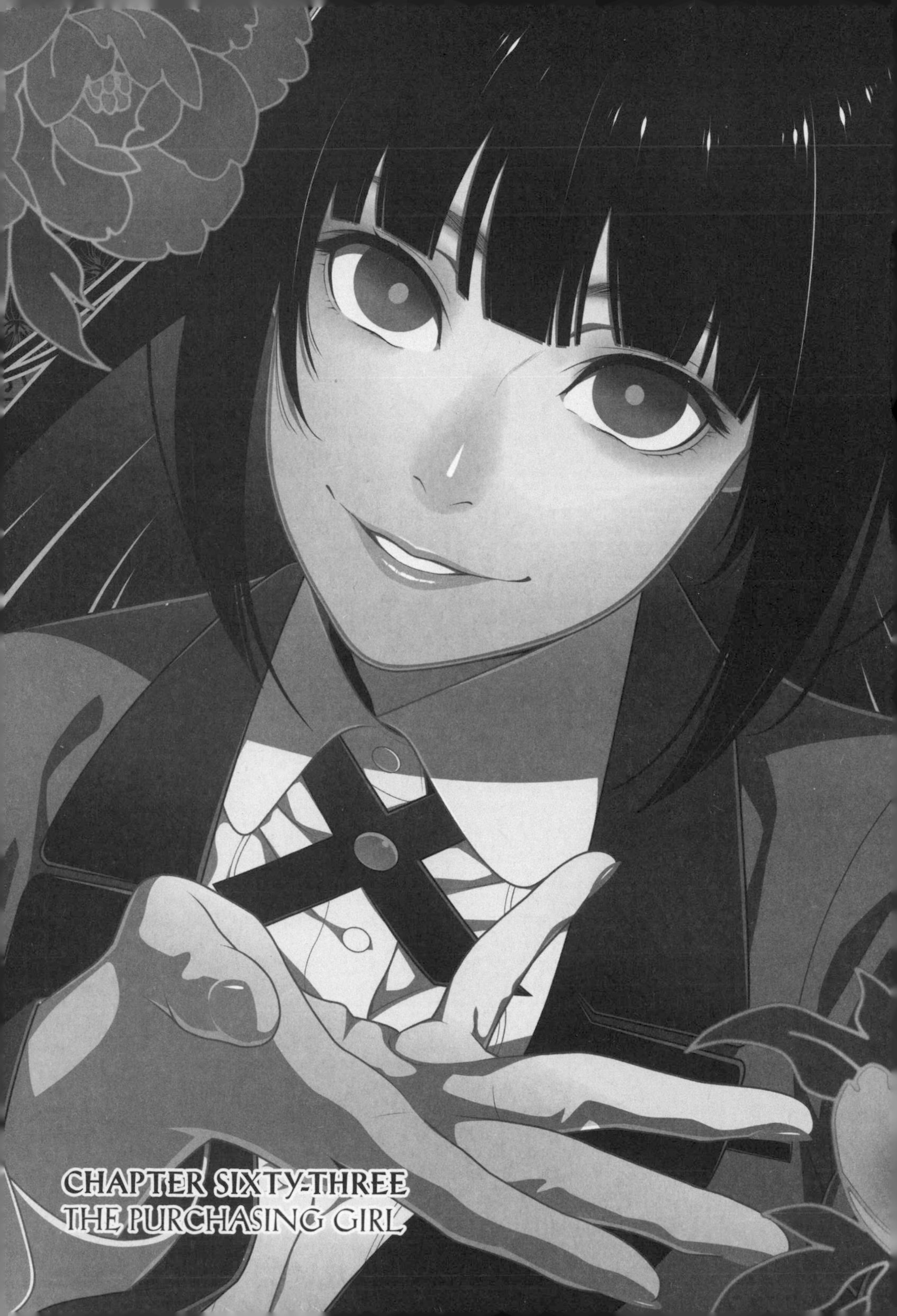

CHAPTER SIXTY-THREE
THE PURCHASING GIRL

KAKEGURUI

— Compulsive Gambler —

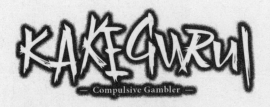

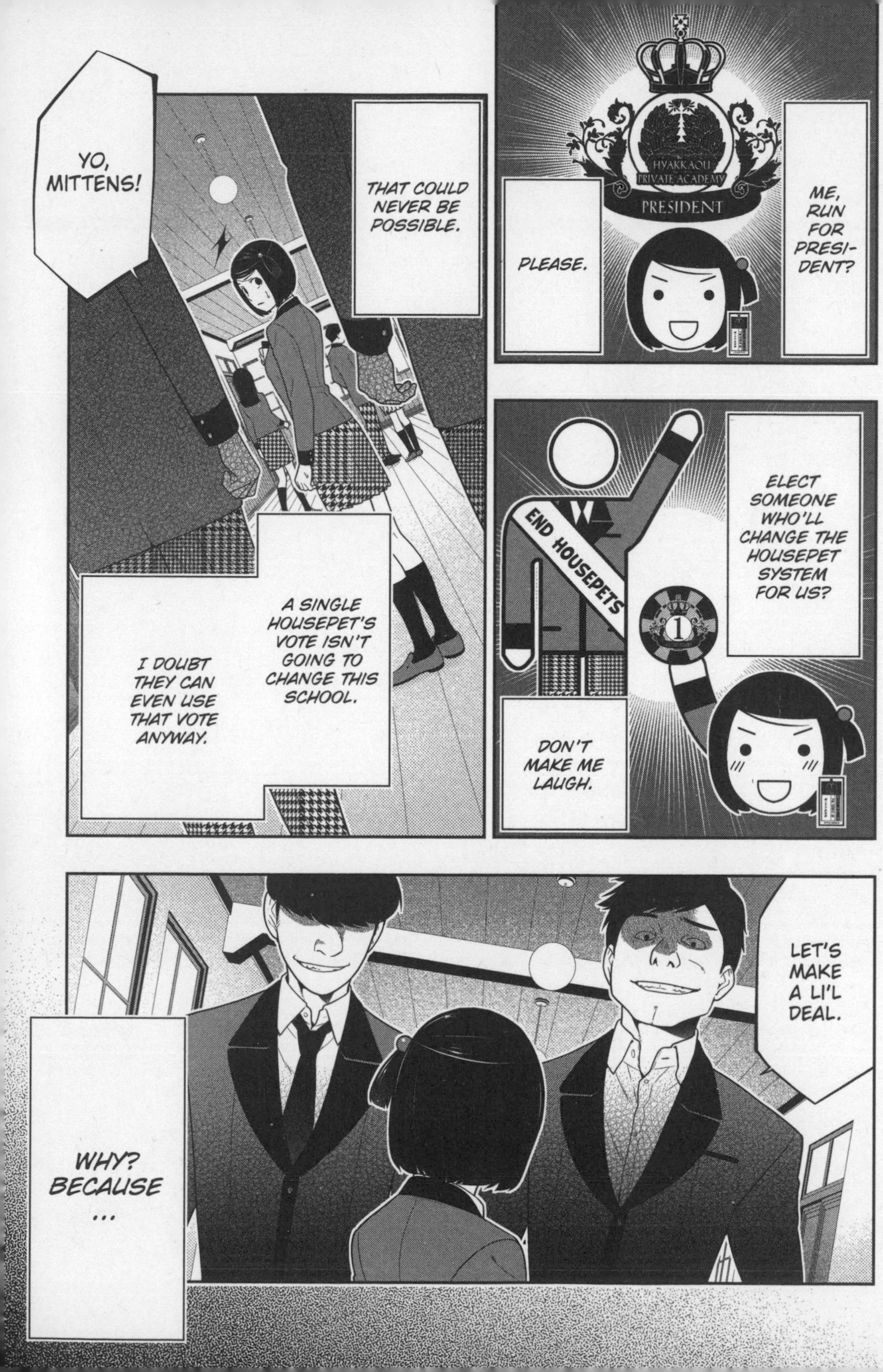
HYAKKAOU PRIVATE ACADEMY
PRESIDENT
ME, RUN FOR PRESI-DENT?
PLEASE.
ELECT SOMEONE WHO'LL CHANGE THE HOUSEPET SYSTEM FOR US?
END HOUSEPETS
DON'T MAKE ME LAUGH.
THAT COULD NEVER BE POSSIBLE.
YO, MITTENS!
A SINGLE HOUSEPET'S VOTE ISN'T GOING TO CHANGE THIS SCHOOL.
I DOUBT THEY CAN EVEN USE THAT VOTE ANYWAY.
LET'S MAKE A LI'L DEAL.
WHY? BECAUSE ...

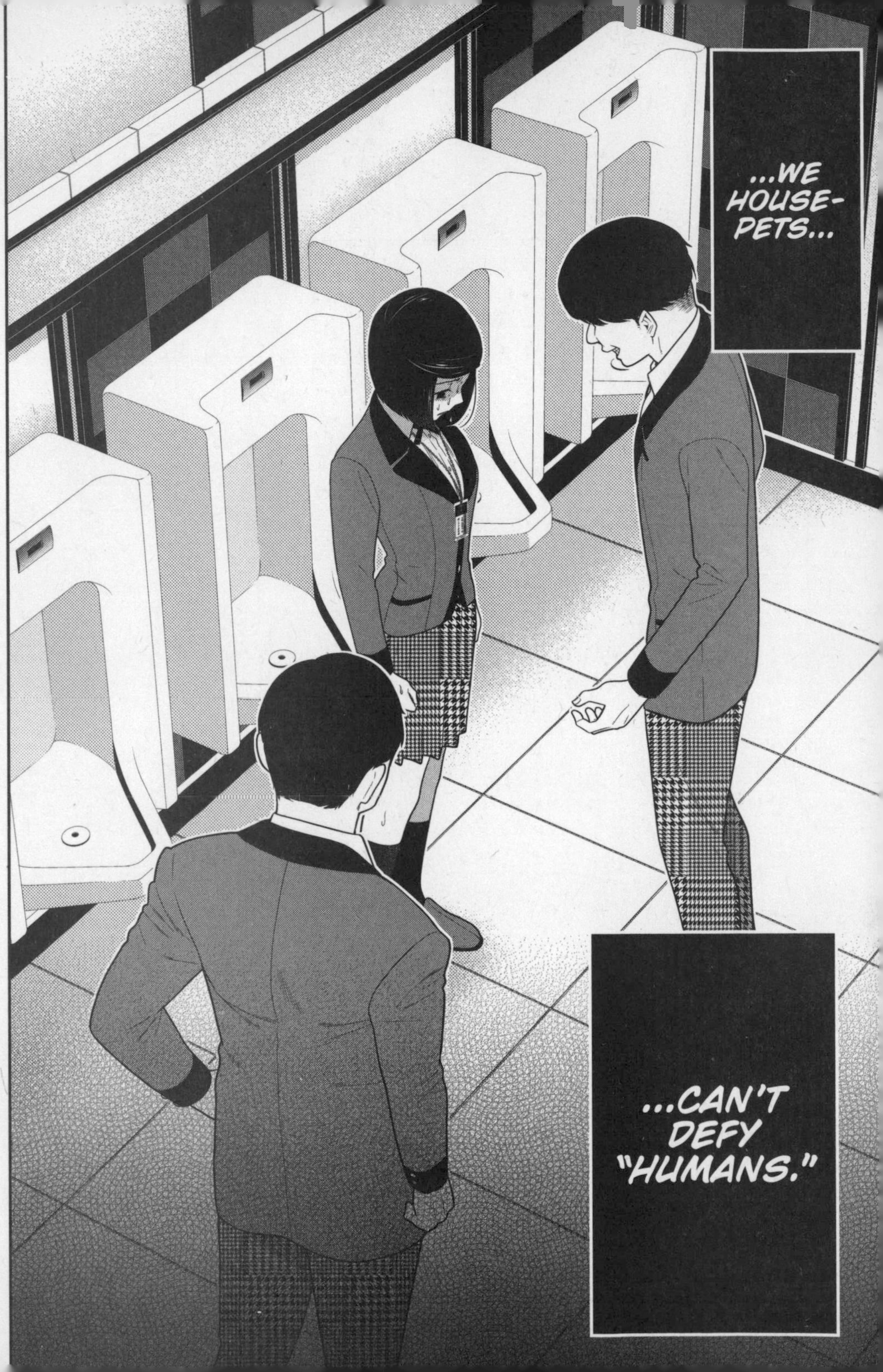
...WE HOUSE-PETS...
...CAN'T DEFY "HUMANS."

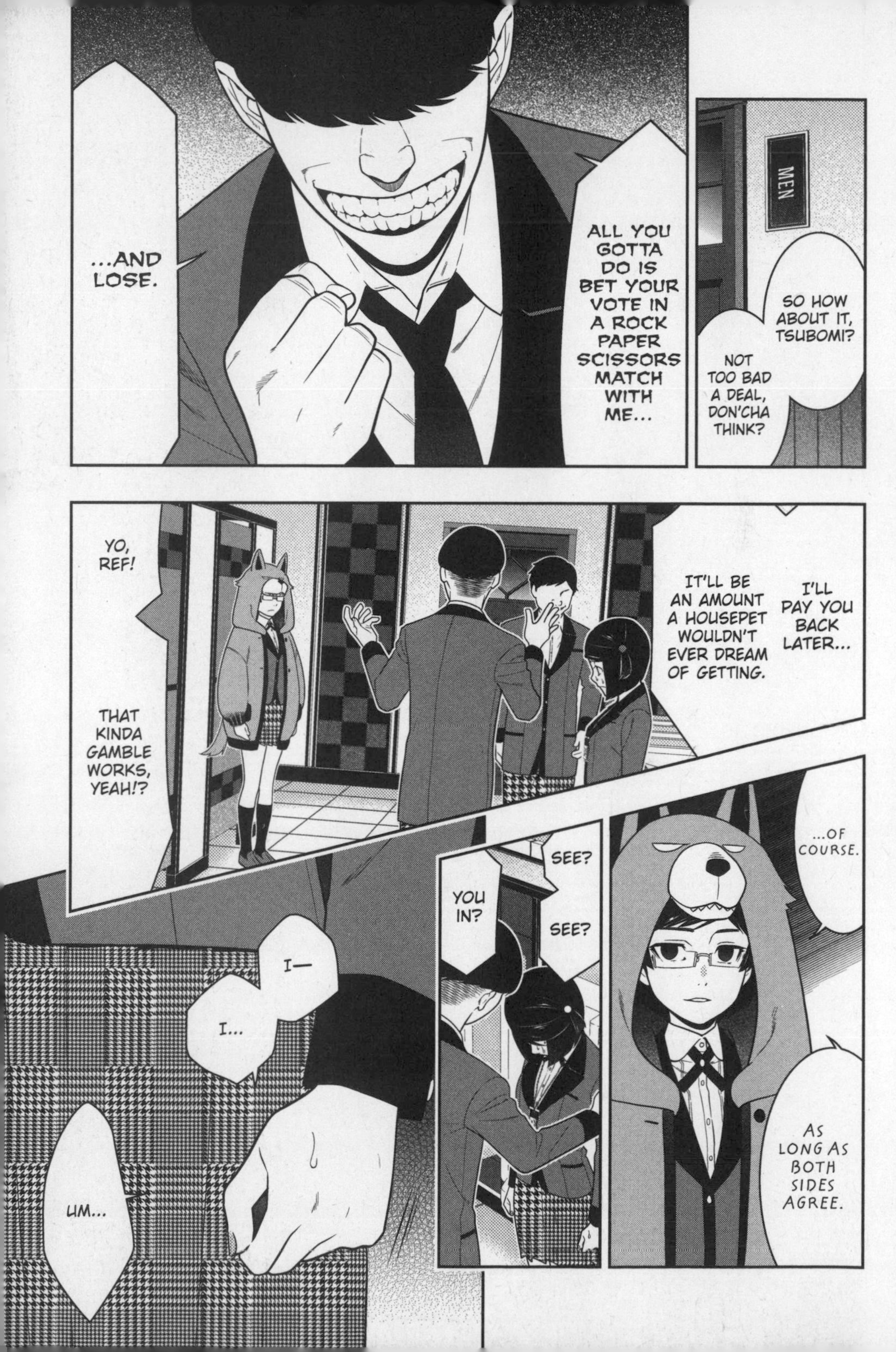
MEN
SO HOW ABOUT IT, TSUBOMI?
NOT TOO BAD A DEAL, DON'CHA THINK?
ALL YOU GOTTA DO IS BET YOUR VOTE IN A ROCK PAPER SCISSORS MATCH WITH ME...
...AND LOSE.
I'LL PAY YOU BACK LATER...
IT'LL BE AN AMOUNT A HOUSEPET WOULDN'T EVER DREAM OF GETTING.
YO, REF!
THAT KINDA GAMBLE WORKS, YEAH!?
...OF COURSE.
AS LONG AS BOTH SIDES AGREE.
SEE?
SEE?
YOU IN?
I—
I...
UM...

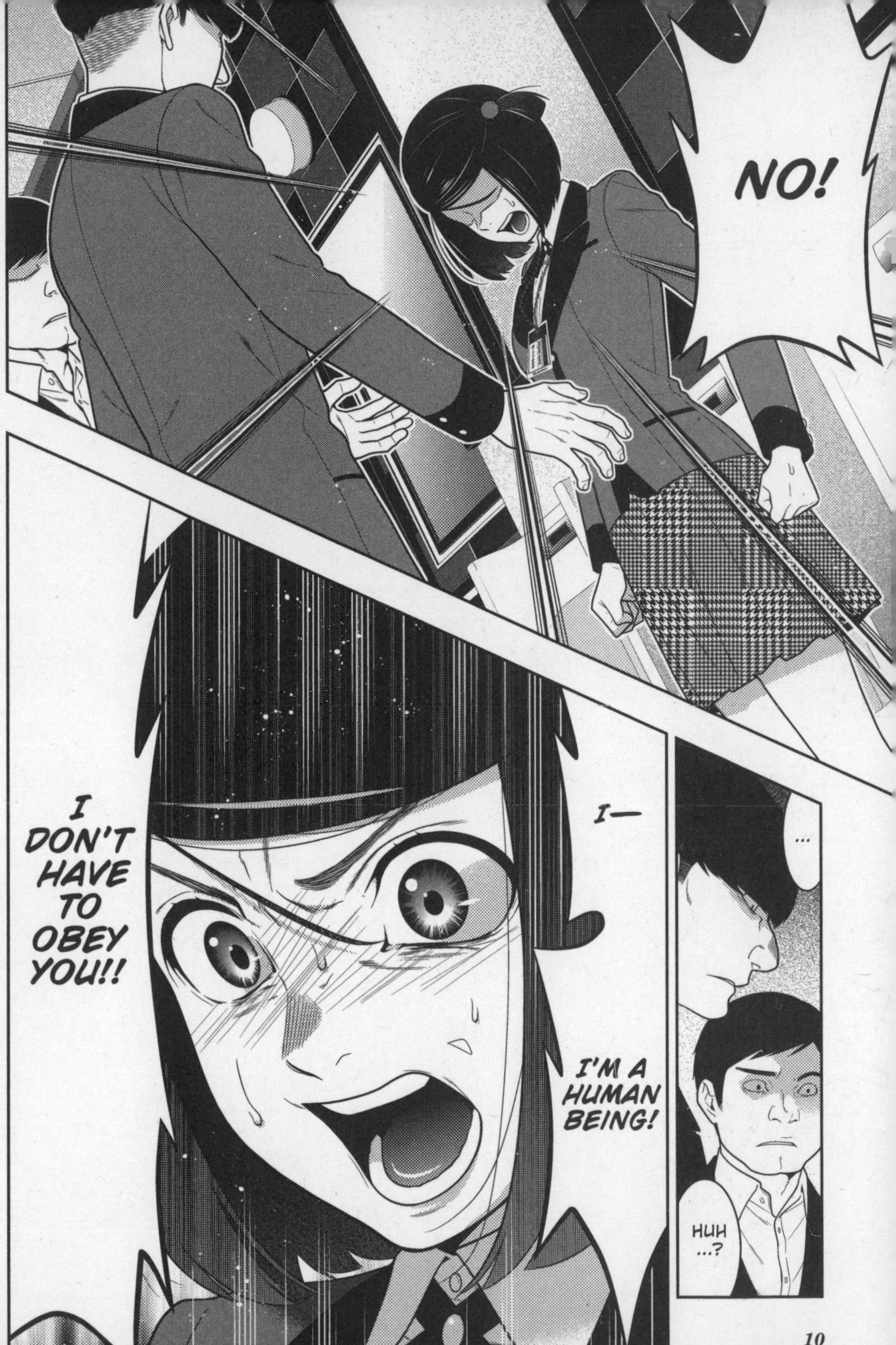
NO!
...
HUH ...?
I—
I DON'T HAVE TO OBEY YOU!!
I'M A HUMAN BEING!

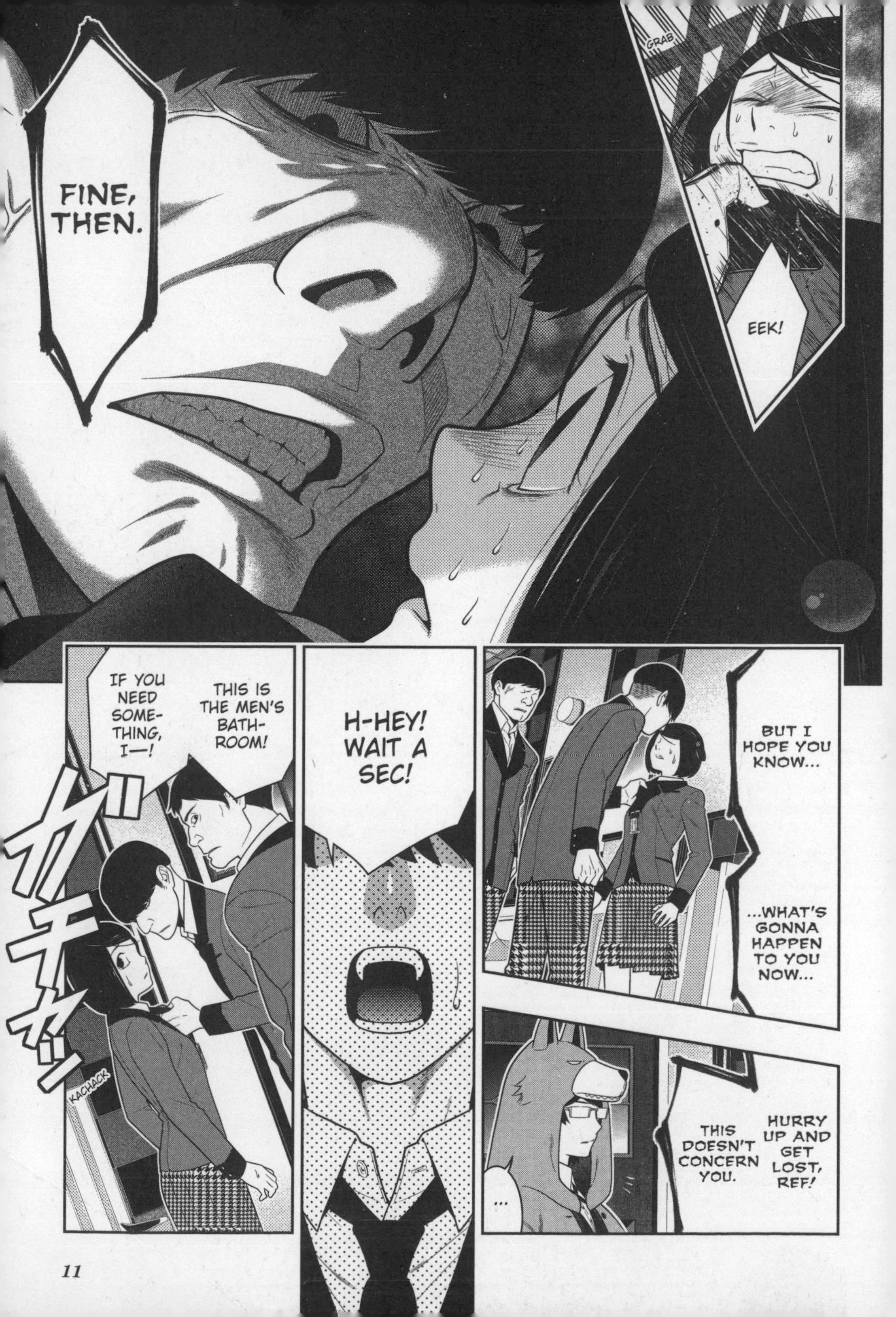
GRAB
EEK!
FINE, THEN.
BUT I HOPE YOU KNOW...
...WHAT'S GONNA HAPPEN TO YOU NOW...
HURRY UP AND GET LOST, REF!
THIS DOESN'T CONCERN YOU.
...
H-HEY! WAIT A SEC!
THIS IS THE MEN'S BATHROOM!
IF YOU NEED SOMETHING, I—!
KACHACK

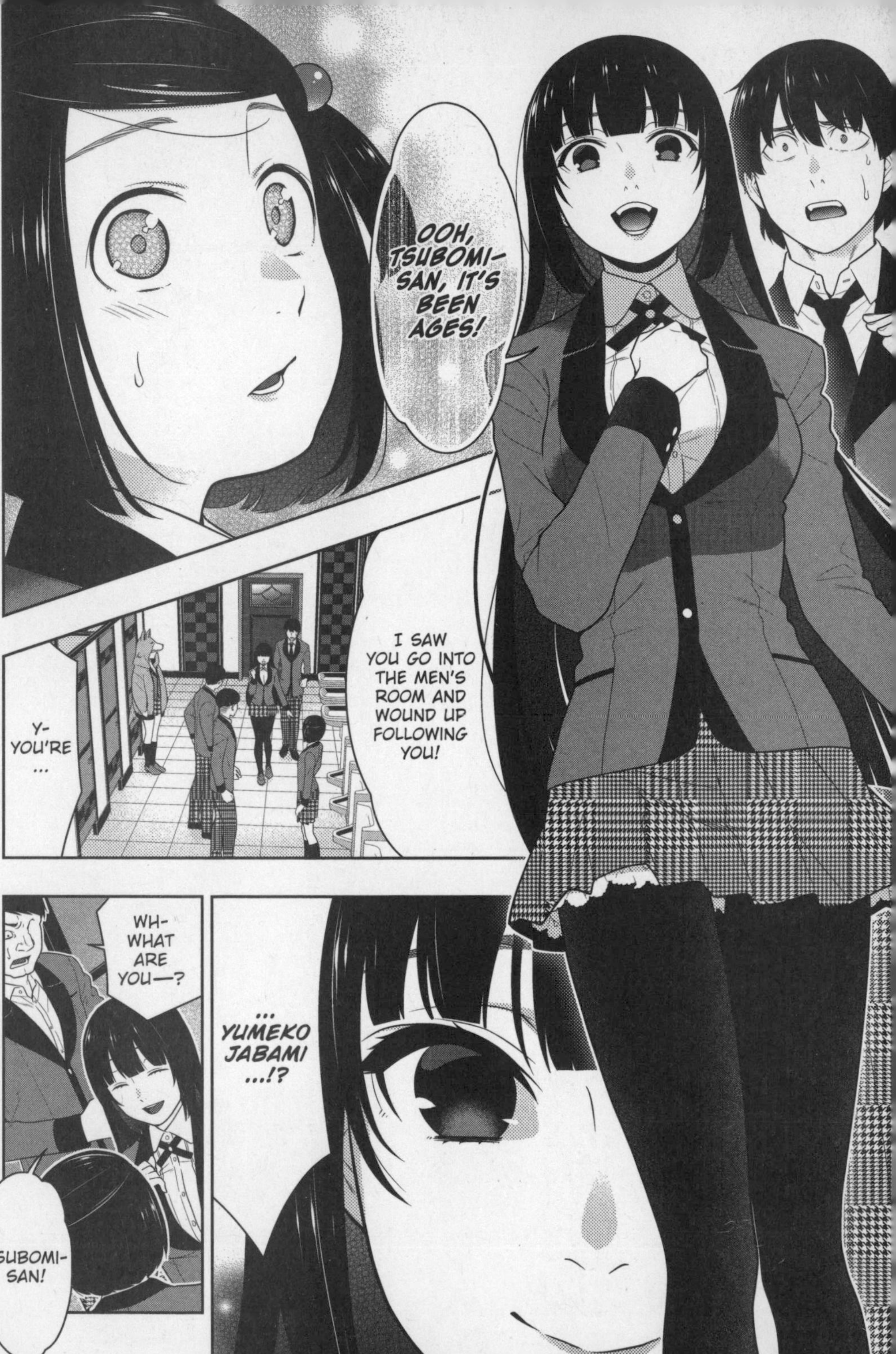
OOH, TSUBOMI-SAN, IT'S BEEN AGES!
I SAW YOU GO INTO THE MEN'S ROOM AND WOUND UP FOLLOWING YOU!
Y-YOU'RE ...
... YUMEKO JABAMI ...!?
WH-WHAT ARE YOU—?
TSUBOMI-SAN!

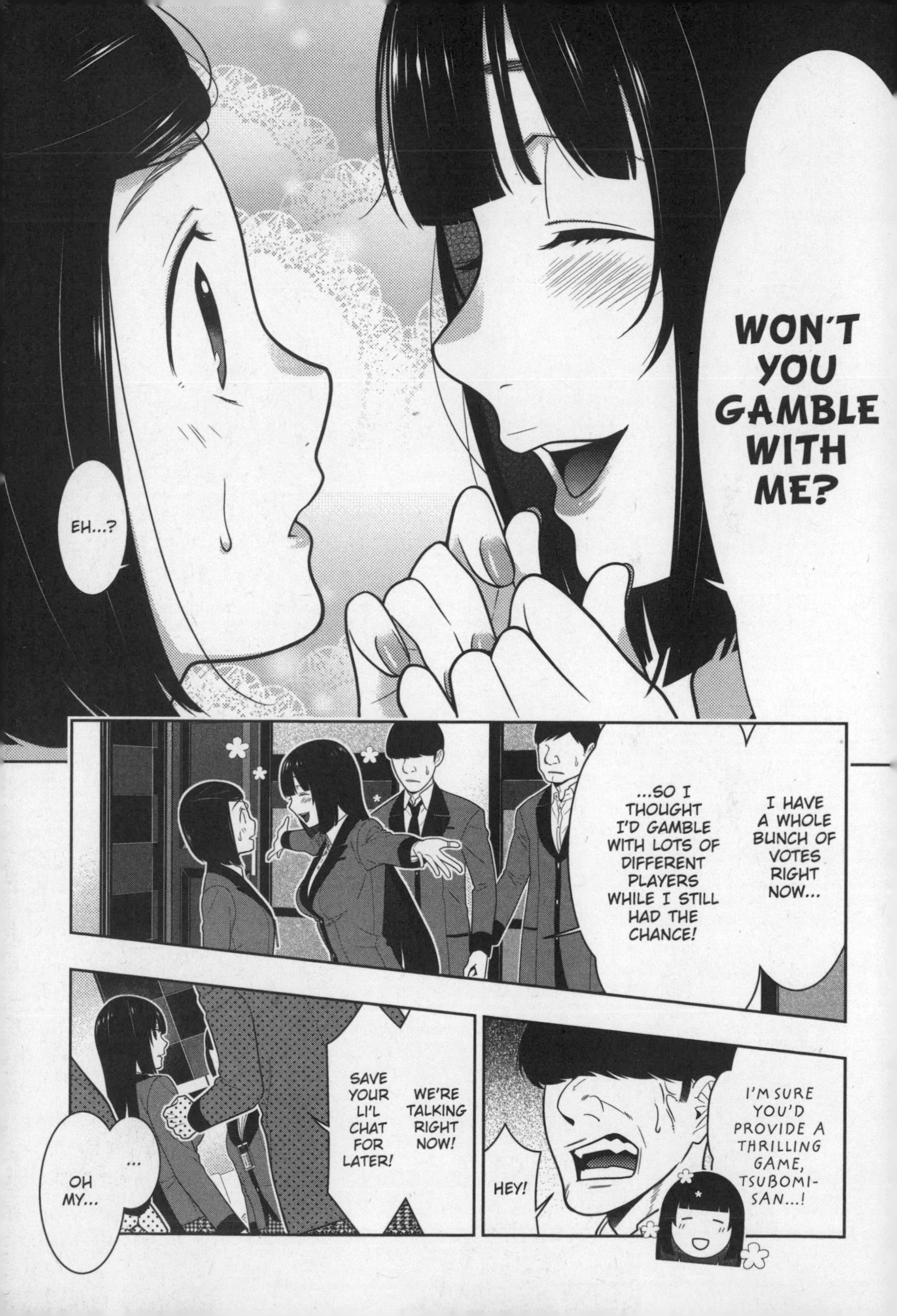
WON'T YOU GAMBLE WITH ME?
EH...?
I HAVE A WHOLE BUNCH OF VOTES RIGHT NOW...
...SO I THOUGHT I'D GAMBLE WITH LOTS OF DIFFERENT PLAYERS WHILE I STILL HAD THE CHANCE!
I'M SURE YOU'D PROVIDE A THRILLING GAME, TSUBOMI-SAN...!
HEY!
WE'RE TALKING RIGHT NOW!
SAVE YOUR LI'L CHAT FOR LATER!
... OH MY...

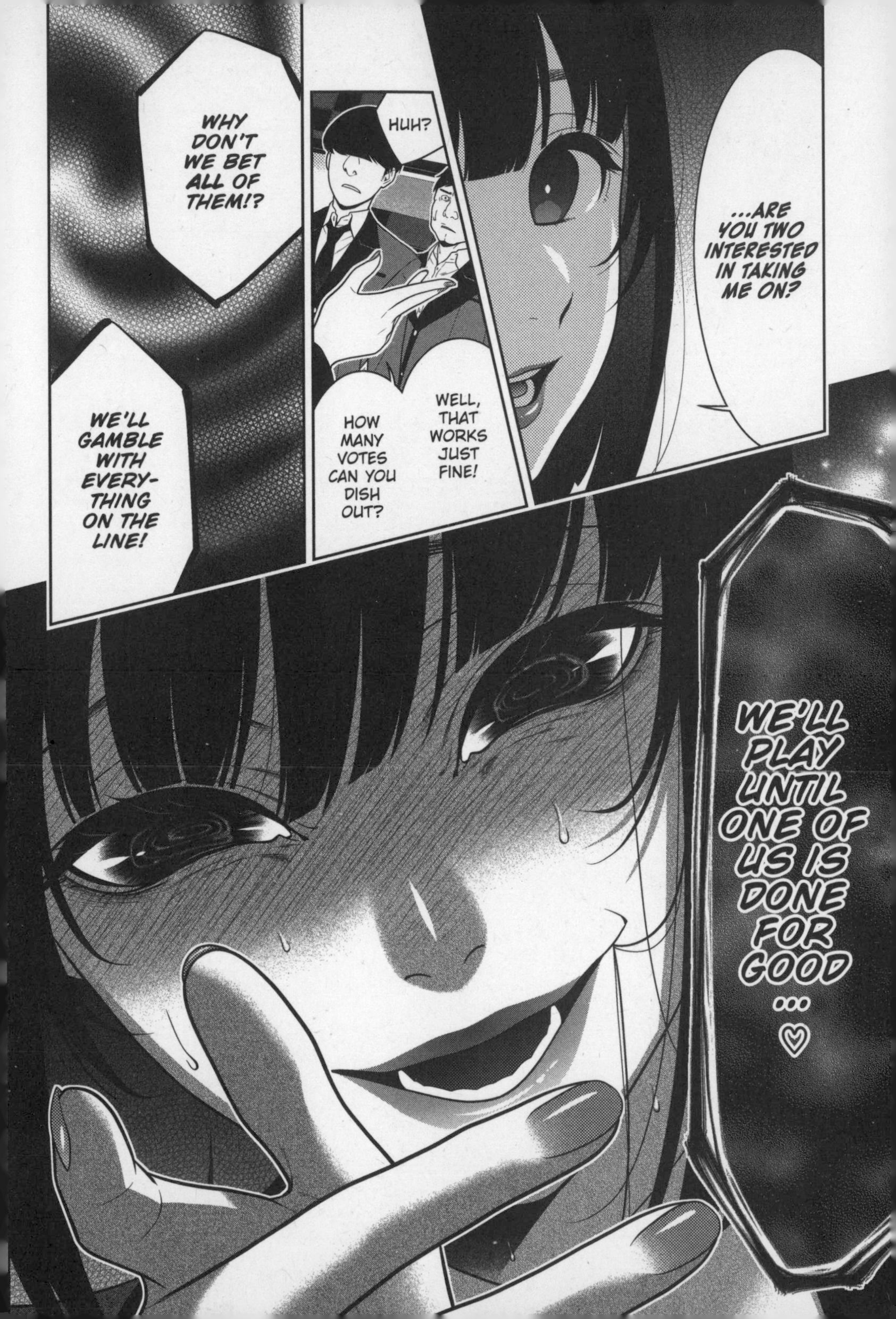
...ARE YOU TWO INTERESTED IN TAKING ME ON?
HUH?
WELL, THAT WORKS JUST FINE!
HOW MANY VOTES CAN YOU DISH OUT?
WHY DON'T WE BET ALL OF THEM!?
WE'LL GAMBLE WITH EVERY-THING ON THE LINE!
WE'LL PLAY UNTIL ONE OF US IS DONE FOR GOOD... ♡

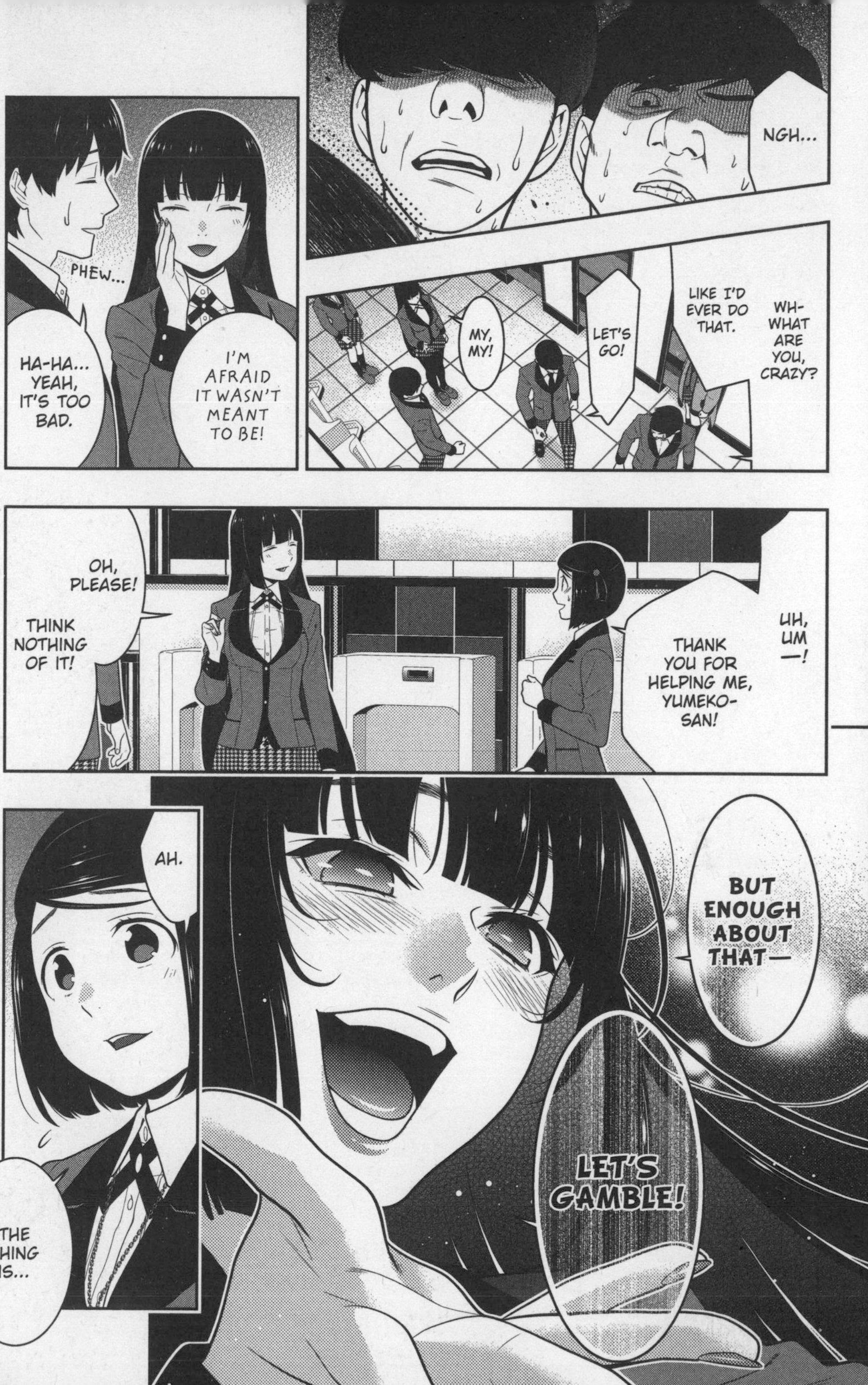
NGH...
WH-WHAT ARE YOU, CRAZY?
LIKE I'D EVER DO THAT.
LET'S GO!
MY, MY!
PHEW...
I'M AFRAID IT WASN'T MEANT TO BE!
HA-HA... YEAH, IT'S TOO BAD.
UH, UM—!
THANK YOU FOR HELPING ME, YUMEKO-SAN!
OH, PLEASE!
THINK NOTHING OF IT!
BUT ENOUGH ABOUT THAT—
LET'S GAMBLE!
AH.
THE THING IS...

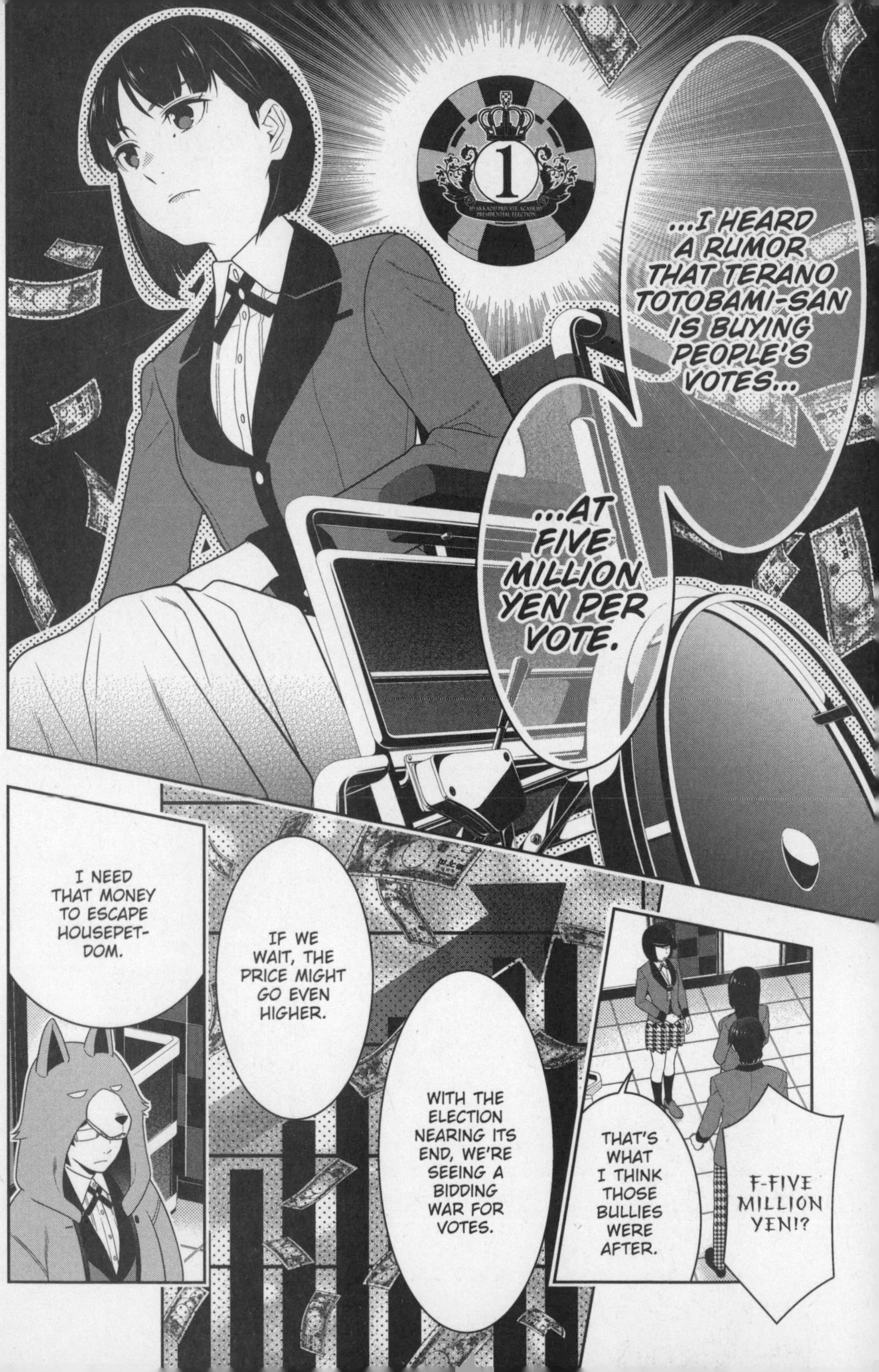
1
...I HEARD A RUMOR THAT TERANO TOTOBAMI-SAN IS BUYING PEOPLE'S VOTES...
...AT FIVE MILLION YEN PER VOTE.
F-FIVE MILLION YEN!?
THAT'S WHAT I THINK THOSE BULLIES WERE AFTER.
WITH THE ELECTION NEARING ITS END, WE'RE SEEING A BIDDING WAR FOR VOTES.
IF WE WAIT, THE PRICE MIGHT GO EVEN HIGHER.
I NEED THAT MONEY TO ESCAPE HOUSEPET-DOM.

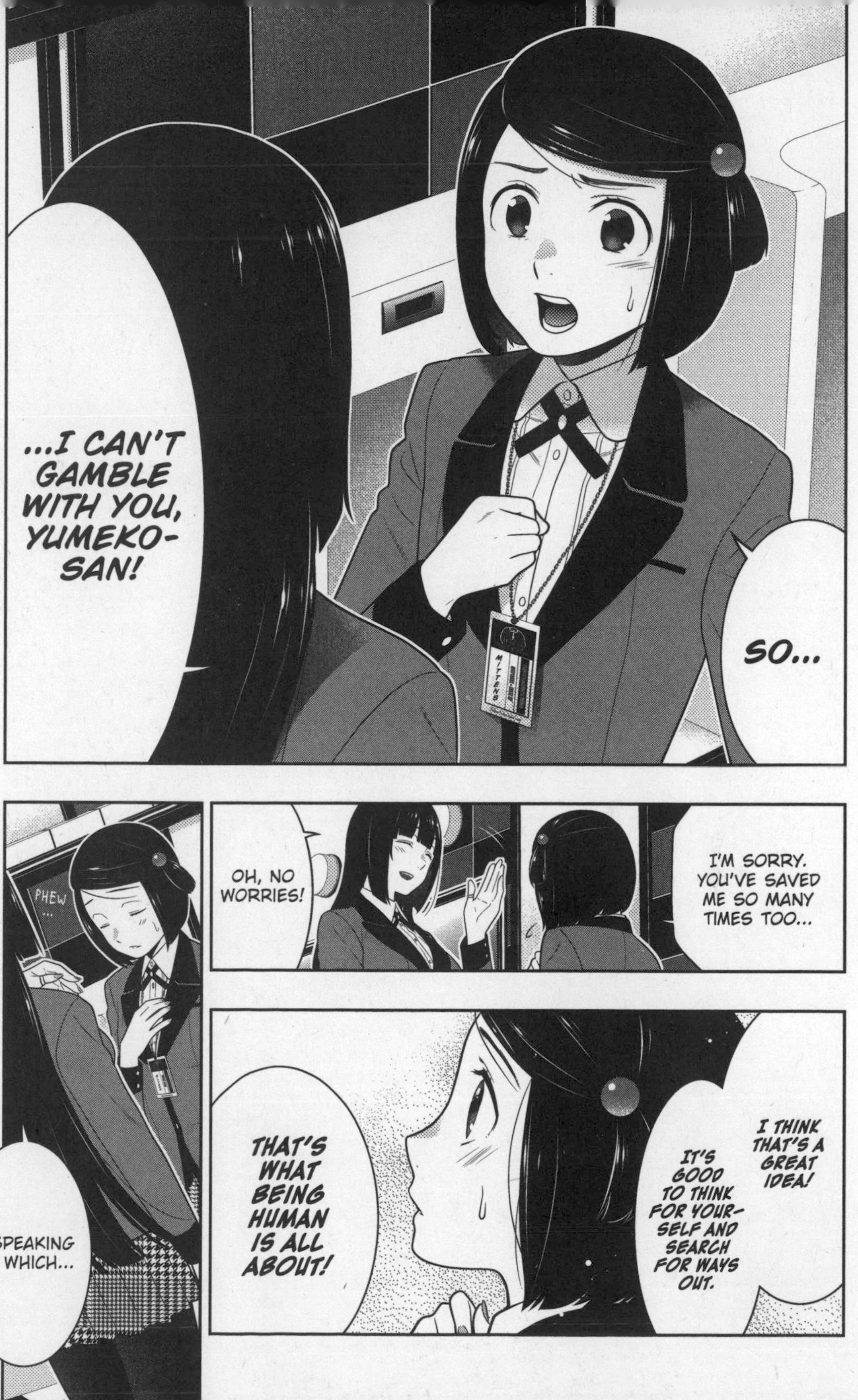
SO...
...I CAN'T GAMBLE WITH YOU, YUMEKO-SAN!
I'M SORRY. YOU'VE SAVED ME SO MANY TIMES TOO...
OH, NO WORRIES!
I THINK THAT'S A GREAT IDEA!
IT'S GOOD TO THINK FOR YOUR-SELF AND SEARCH FOR WAYS OUT.
THAT'S WHAT BEING HUMAN IS ALL ABOUT!
PHEW...
...SPEAKING OF WHICH...

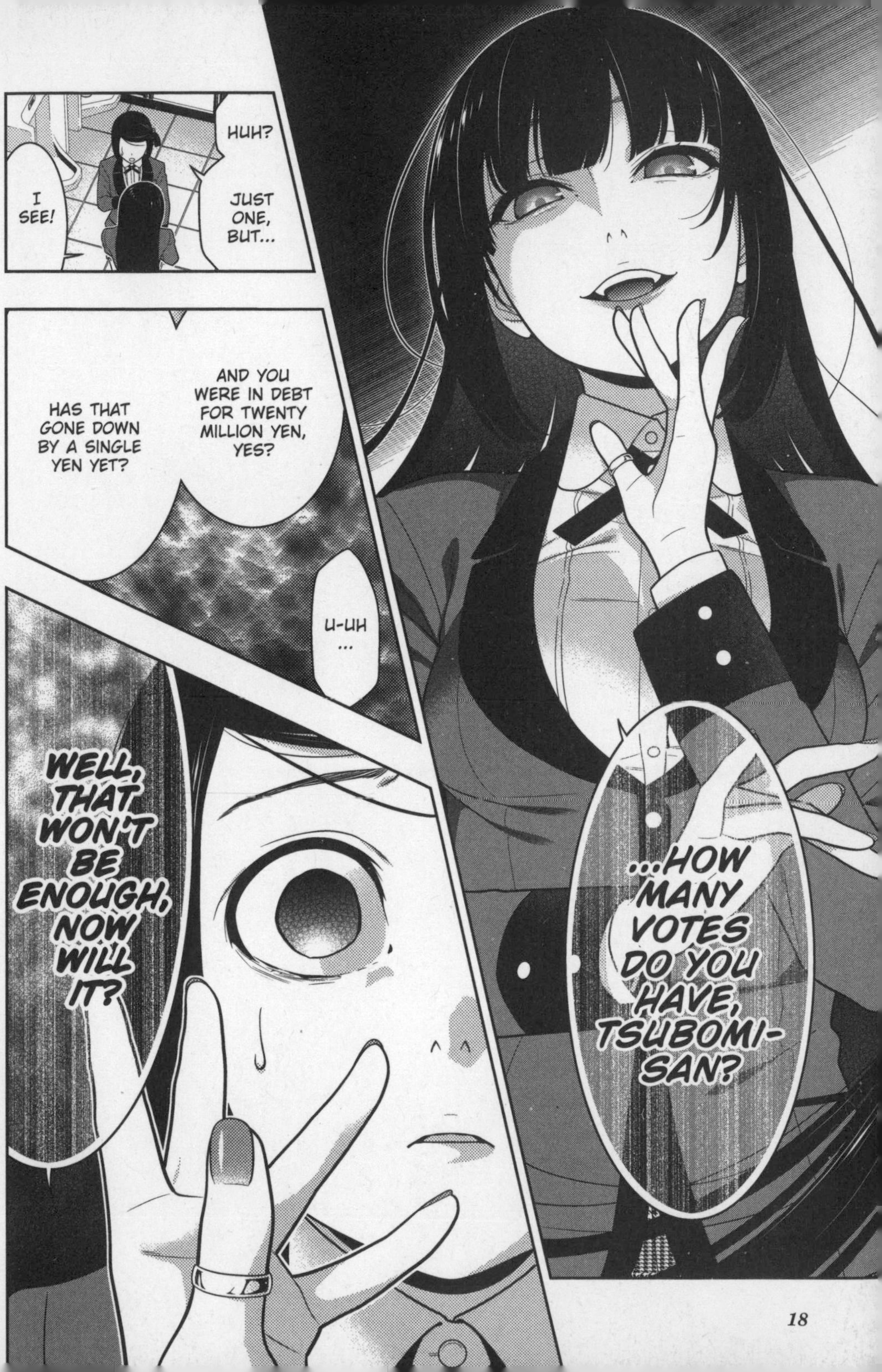
...HOW MANY VOTES DO YOU HAVE, TSUBOMI-SAN?
HUH?
JUST ONE, BUT...
I SEE!
AND YOU WERE IN DEBT FOR TWENTY MILLION YEN, YES?
HAS THAT GONE DOWN BY A SINGLE YEN YET?
U-UH...
WELL, THAT WON'T BE ENOUGH, NOW WILL IT?

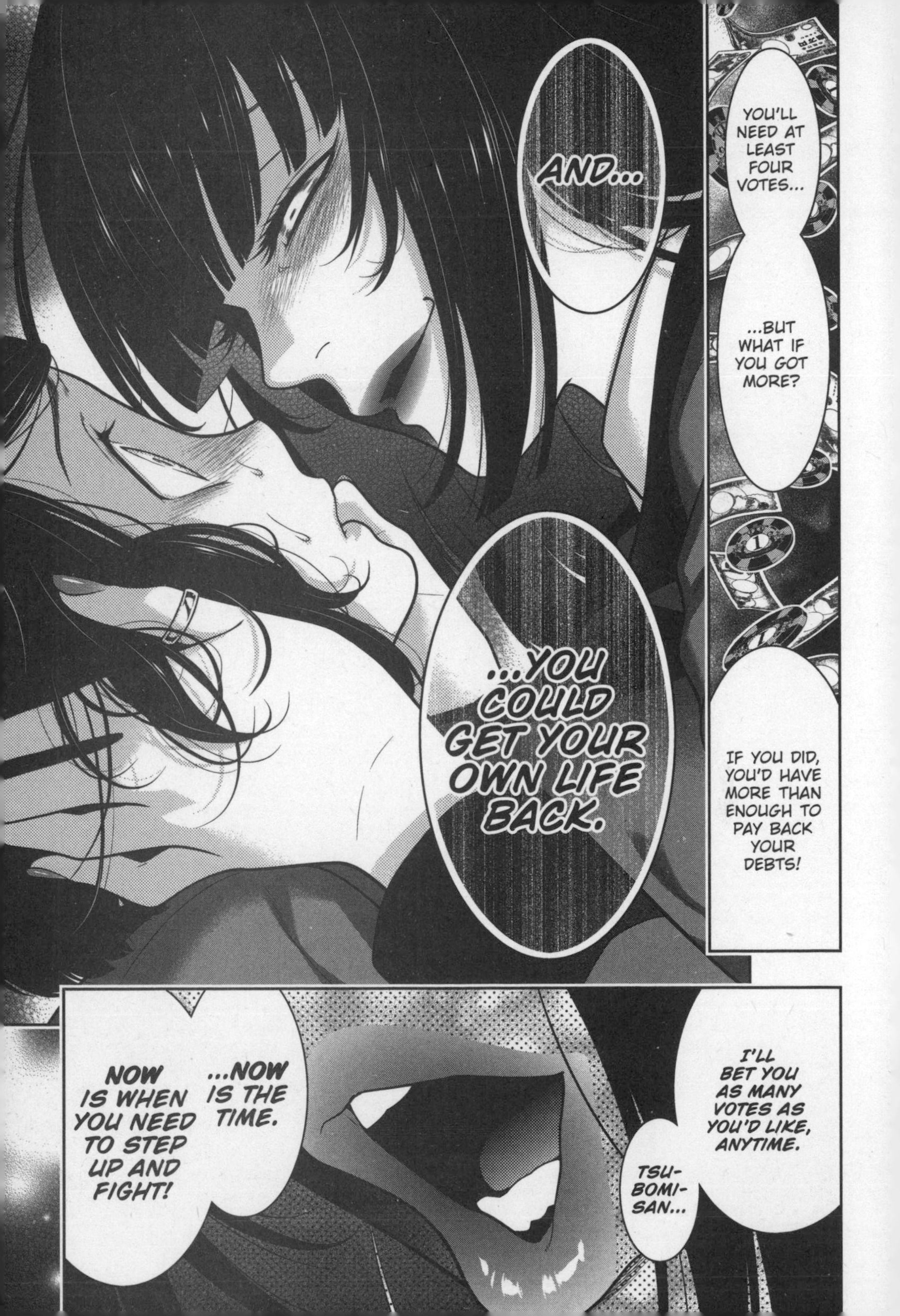
YOU'LL NEED AT LEAST FOUR VOTES...
...BUT WHAT IF YOU GOT MORE?
IF YOU DID, YOU'D HAVE MORE THAN ENOUGH TO PAY BACK YOUR DEBTS!
AND...
...YOU COULD GET YOUR OWN LIFE BACK.
I'LL BET YOU AS MANY VOTES AS YOU'D LIKE, ANYTIME.
TSU-BOMI-SAN...
...NOW IS THE TIME.
NOW IS WHEN YOU NEED TO STEP UP AND FIGHT!

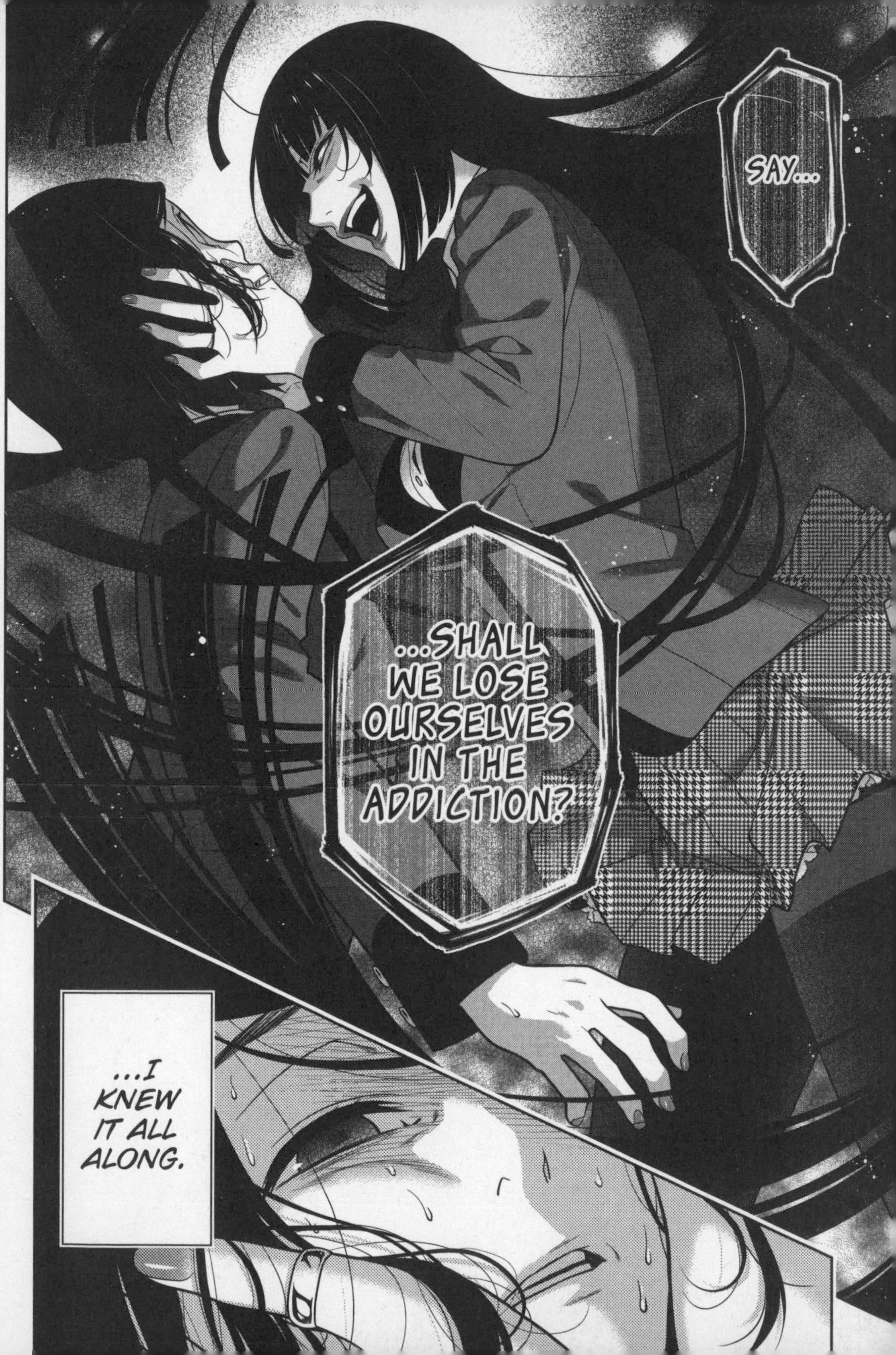
SAY...
...SHALL WE LOSE OURSELVES IN THE ADDICTION?
...I KNEW IT ALL ALONG.

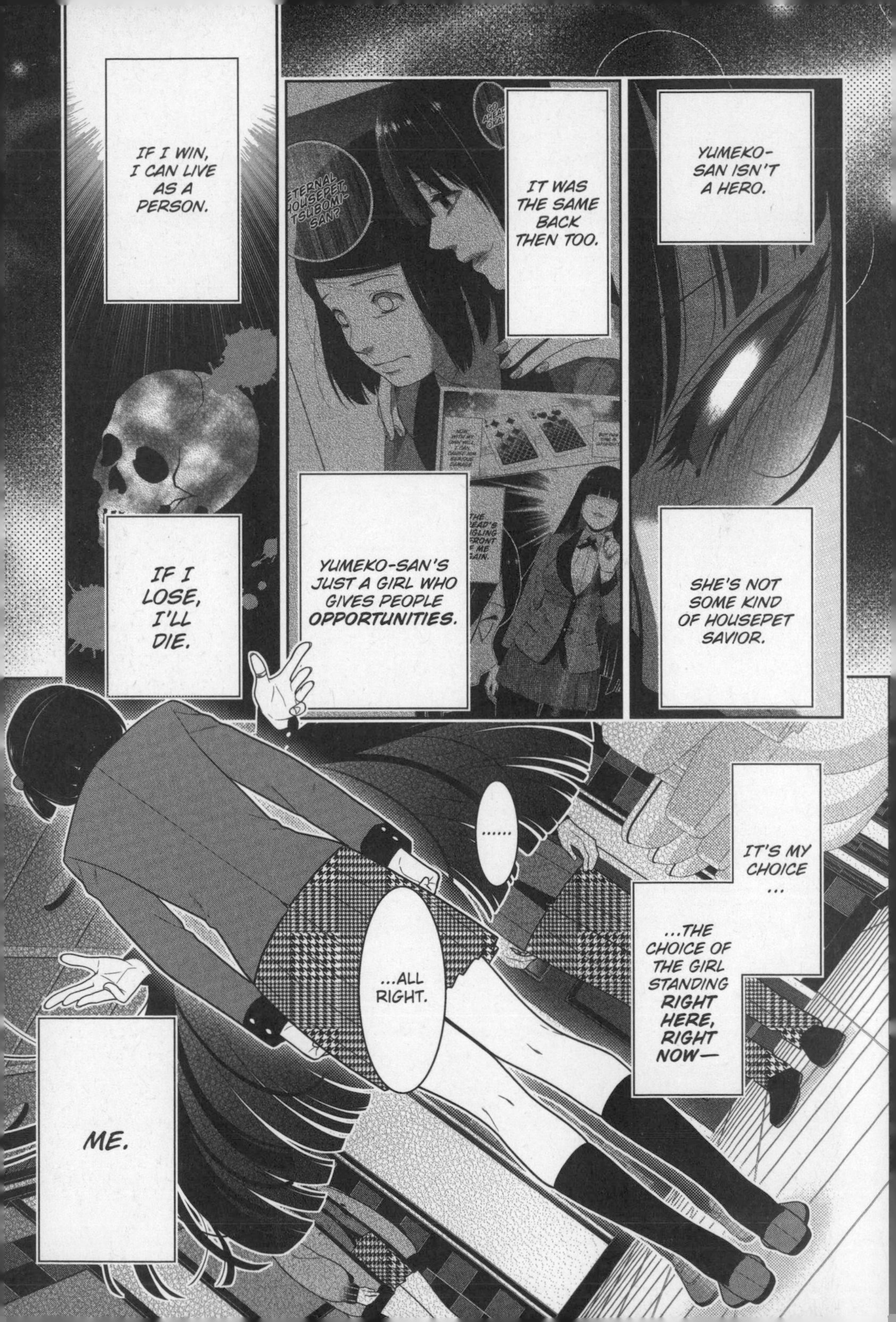

YUMEKO-SAN ISN'T A HERO.
SHE'S NOT SOME KIND OF HOUSEPET SAVIOR.
IT WAS THE SAME BACK THEN TOO.
ETERNAL HOUSEPET, TSUBOMI-SAN?
YUMEKO-SAN'S JUST A GIRL WHO GIVES PEOPLE OPPORTUNITIES.
IF I WIN, I CAN LIVE AS A PERSON.
IF I LOSE, I'LL DIE.
IT'S MY CHOICE...
...THE CHOICE OF THE GIRL STANDING RIGHT HERE, RIGHT NOW—
......
...ALL RIGHT.
ME.

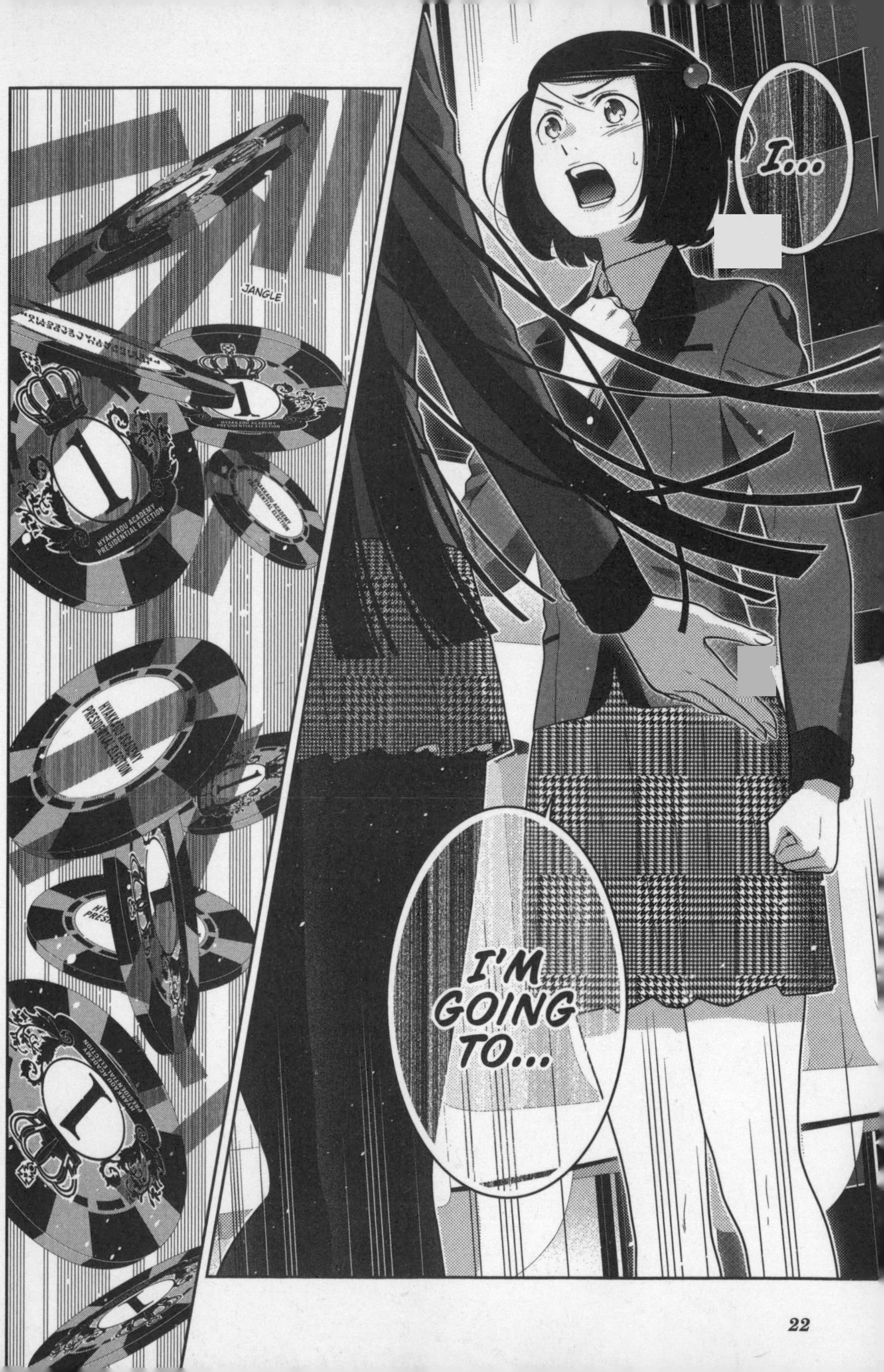
I...
I'M GOING TO...
JANGLE
HYAKKAOU ACADEMY PRESIDENTIAL ELECTION

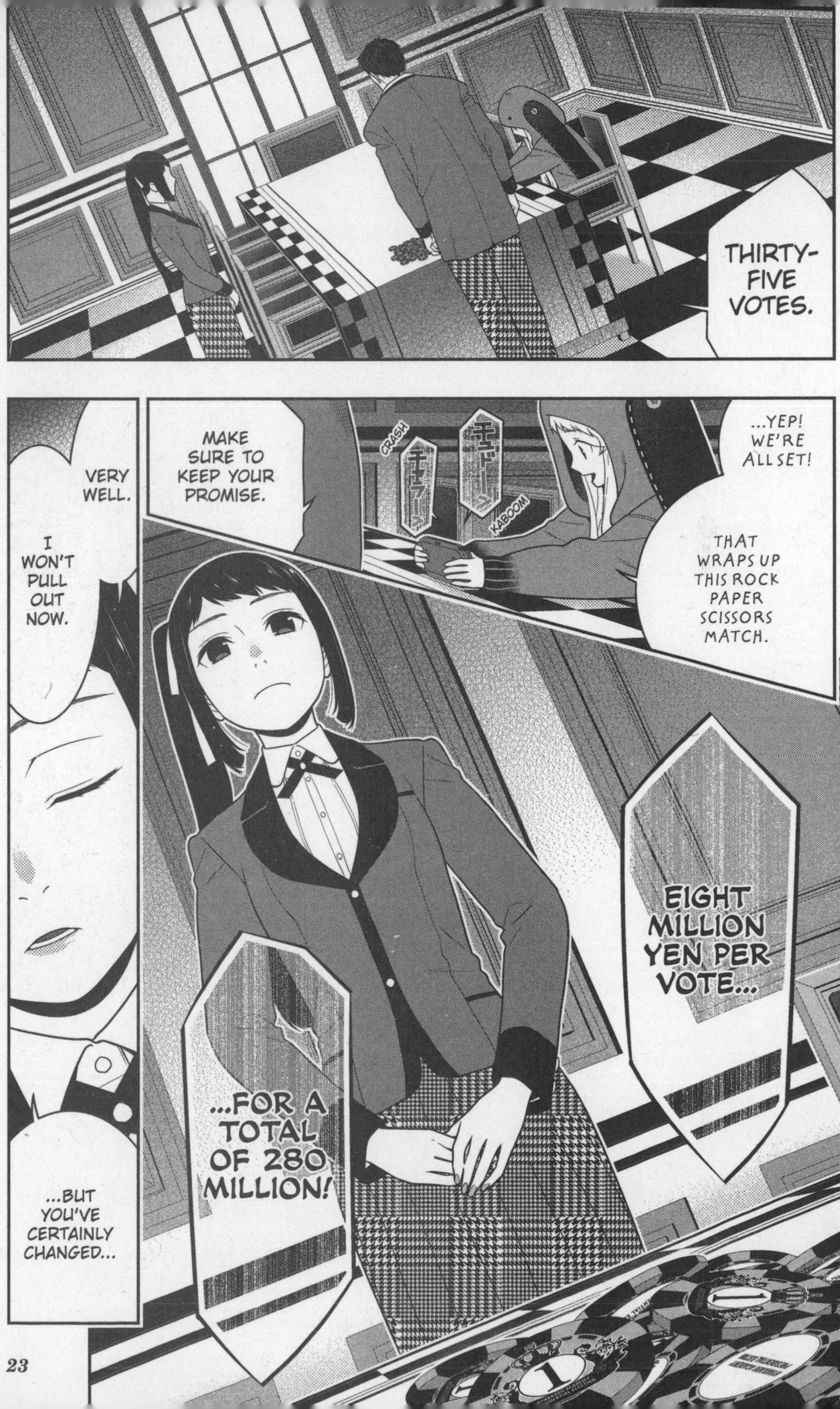
THIRTY-FIVE VOTES.
...YEP! WE'RE ALL SET!
THAT WRAPS UP THIS ROCK PAPER SCISSORS MATCH.
KABOOM
CRASH
MAKE SURE TO KEEP YOUR PROMISE.
VERY WELL.
I WON'T PULL OUT NOW.
EIGHT MILLION YEN PER VOTE...
...FOR A TOTAL OF 280 MILLION!
...BUT YOU'VE CERTAINLY CHANGED...

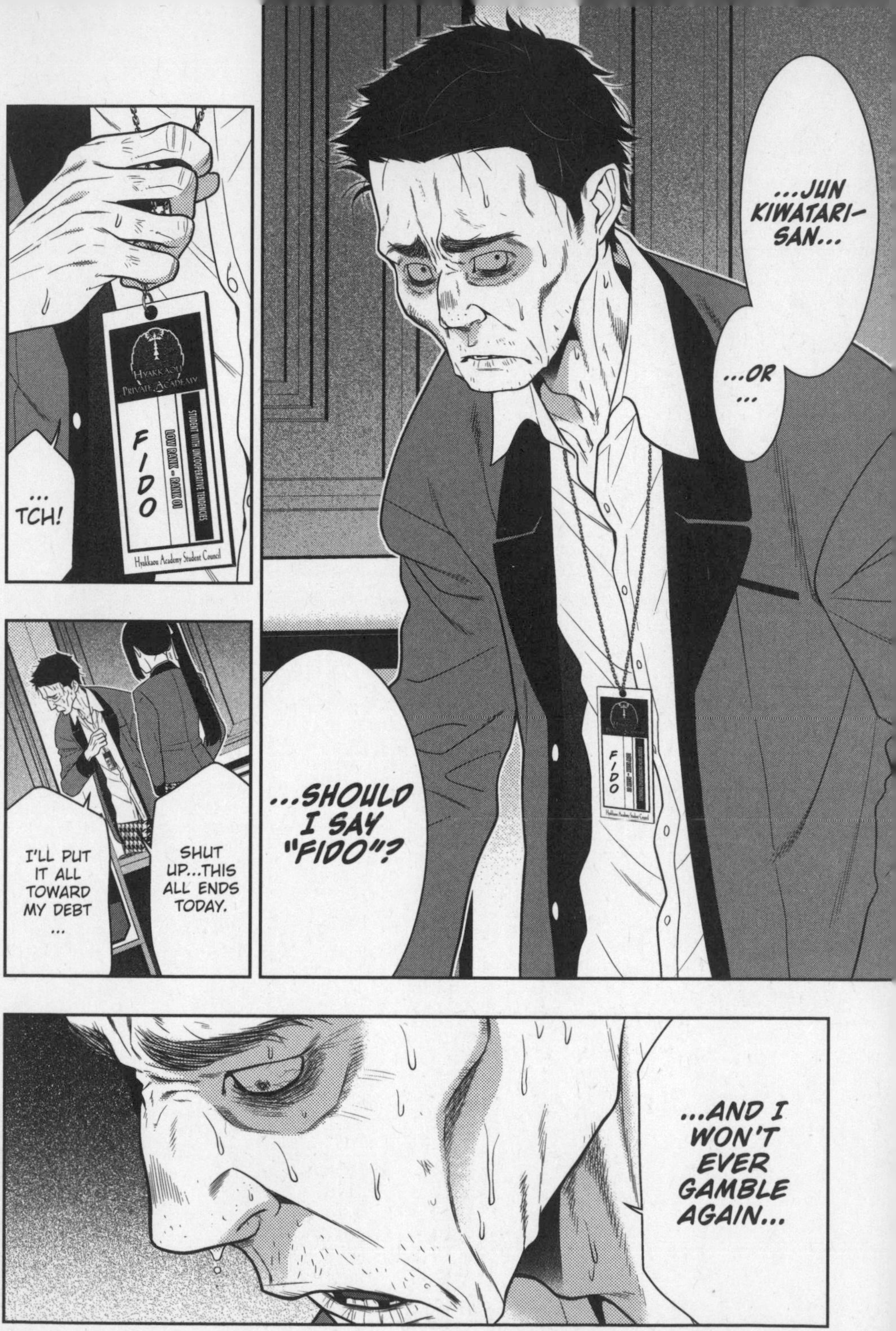
...JUN KIWATARI-SAN...
...OR ...
...SHOULD I SAY "FIDO"?
HYAKKAOU PRIVATE ACADEMY
STUDENT WITH UNCOOPERATIVE TENDENCIES
LOW RANK - RANK 01
FIDO
Hyakkaou Academy Student Council
... TCH!
SHUT UP...THIS ALL ENDS TODAY.
I'LL PUT IT ALL TOWARD MY DEBT ...
...AND I WON'T EVER GAMBLE AGAIN...

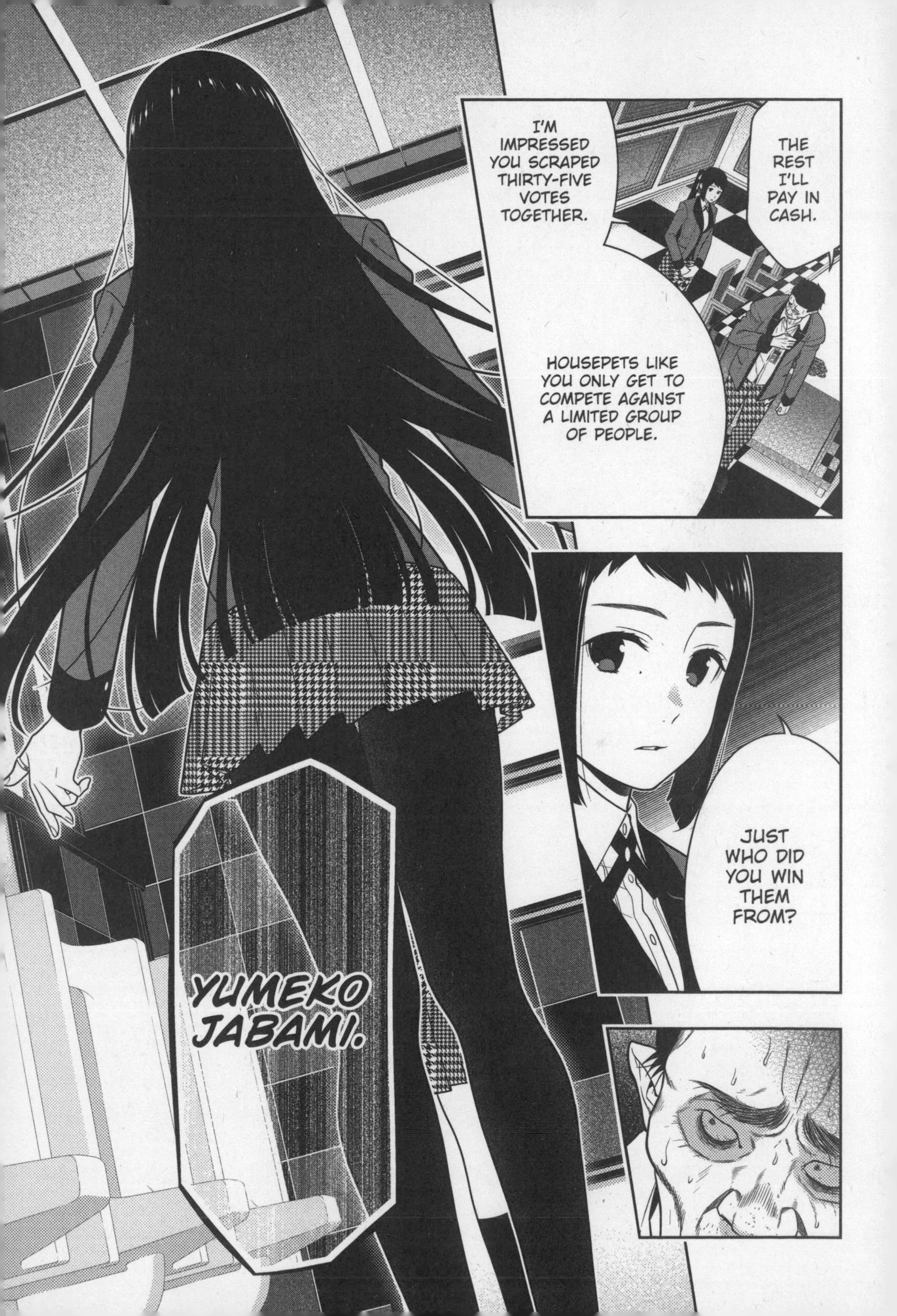
THE REST I'LL PAY IN CASH.
I'M IMPRESSED YOU SCRAPED THIRTY-FIVE VOTES TOGETHER.
HOUSEPETS LIKE YOU ONLY GET TO COMPETE AGAINST A LIMITED GROUP OF PEOPLE.
JUST WHO DID YOU WIN THEM FROM?
YUMEKO JABAMI.

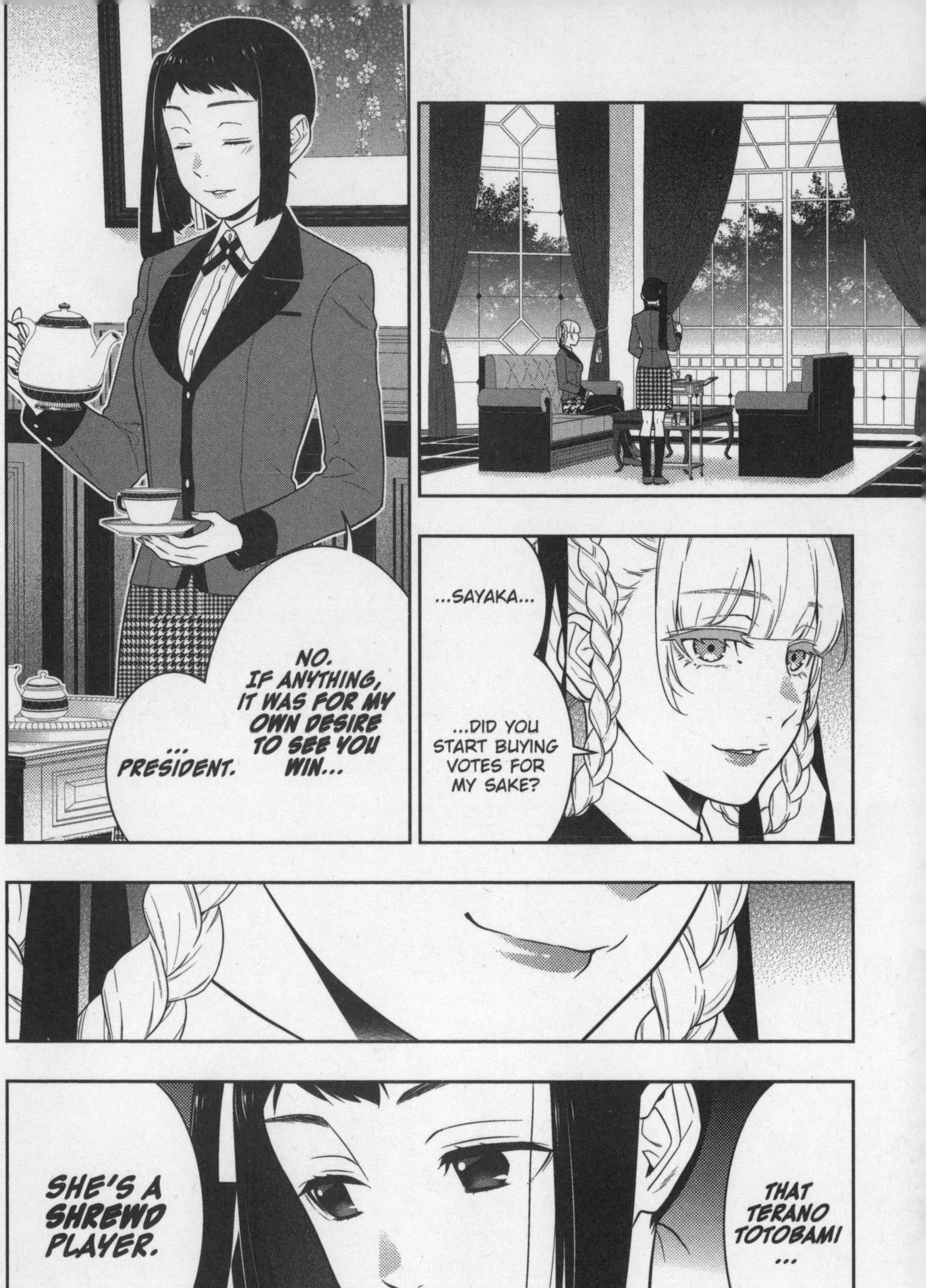
...SAYAKA...
...DID YOU START BUYING VOTES FOR MY SAKE?
NO. IF ANYTHING, IT WAS FOR MY OWN DESIRE TO SEE YOU WIN...
... PRESIDENT.
THAT TERANO TOTOBAMI ...
SHE'S A SHREWD PLAYER.

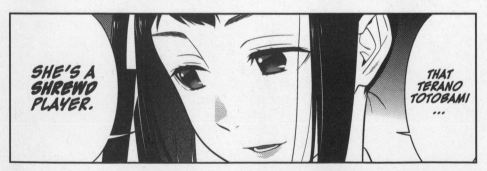

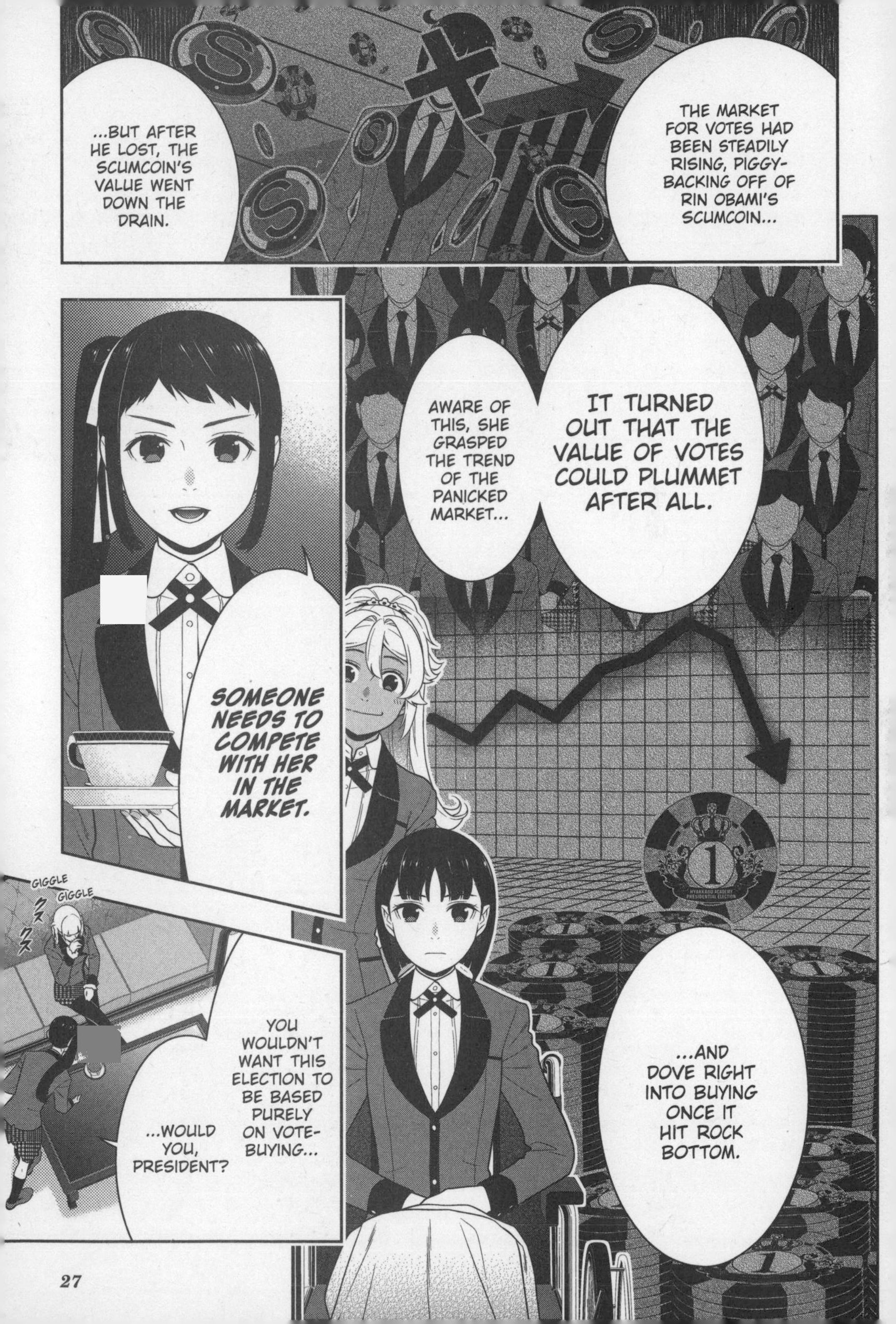
THE MARKET FOR VOTES HAD BEEN STEADILY RISING, PIGGY-BACKING OFF OF RIN OBAMI'S SCUMCOIN...
...BUT AFTER HE LOST, THE SCUMCOIN'S VALUE WENT DOWN THE DRAIN.
IT TURNED OUT THAT THE VALUE OF VOTES COULD PLUMMET AFTER ALL.
AWARE OF THIS, SHE GRASPED THE TREND OF THE PANICKED MARKET...
...AND DOVE RIGHT INTO BUYING ONCE IT HIT ROCK BOTTOM.
1
HYAKKAOU ACADEMY PRESIDENTIAL ELECTION
SOMEONE NEEDS TO COMPETE WITH HER IN THE MARKET.
GIGGLE GIGGLE
YOU WOULDN'T WANT THIS ELECTION TO BE BASED PURELY ON VOTE-BUYING...
...WOULD YOU, PRESIDENT?

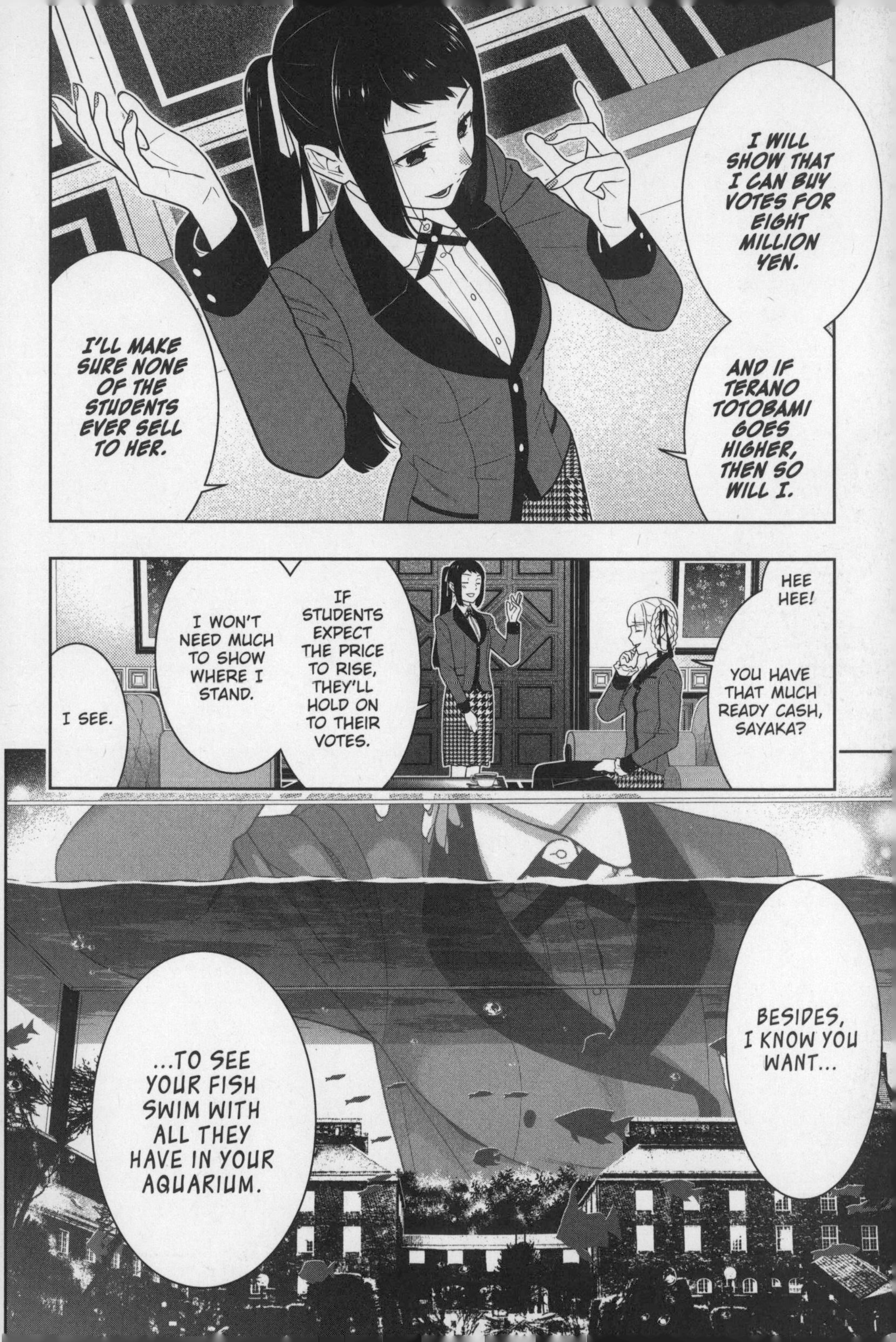
I WILL SHOW THAT I CAN BUY VOTES FOR EIGHT MILLION YEN.
AND IF TERANO TOTOBAMI GOES HIGHER, THEN SO WILL I.
I'LL MAKE SURE NONE OF THE STUDENTS EVER SELL TO HER.
HEE HEE!
YOU HAVE THAT MUCH READY CASH, SAYAKA?
IF STUDENTS EXPECT THE PRICE TO RISE, THEY'LL HOLD ON TO THEIR VOTES.
I WON'T NEED MUCH TO SHOW WHERE I STAND.
I SEE.
BESIDES, I KNOW YOU WANT...
...TO SEE YOUR FISH SWIM WITH ALL THEY HAVE IN YOUR AQUARIUM.

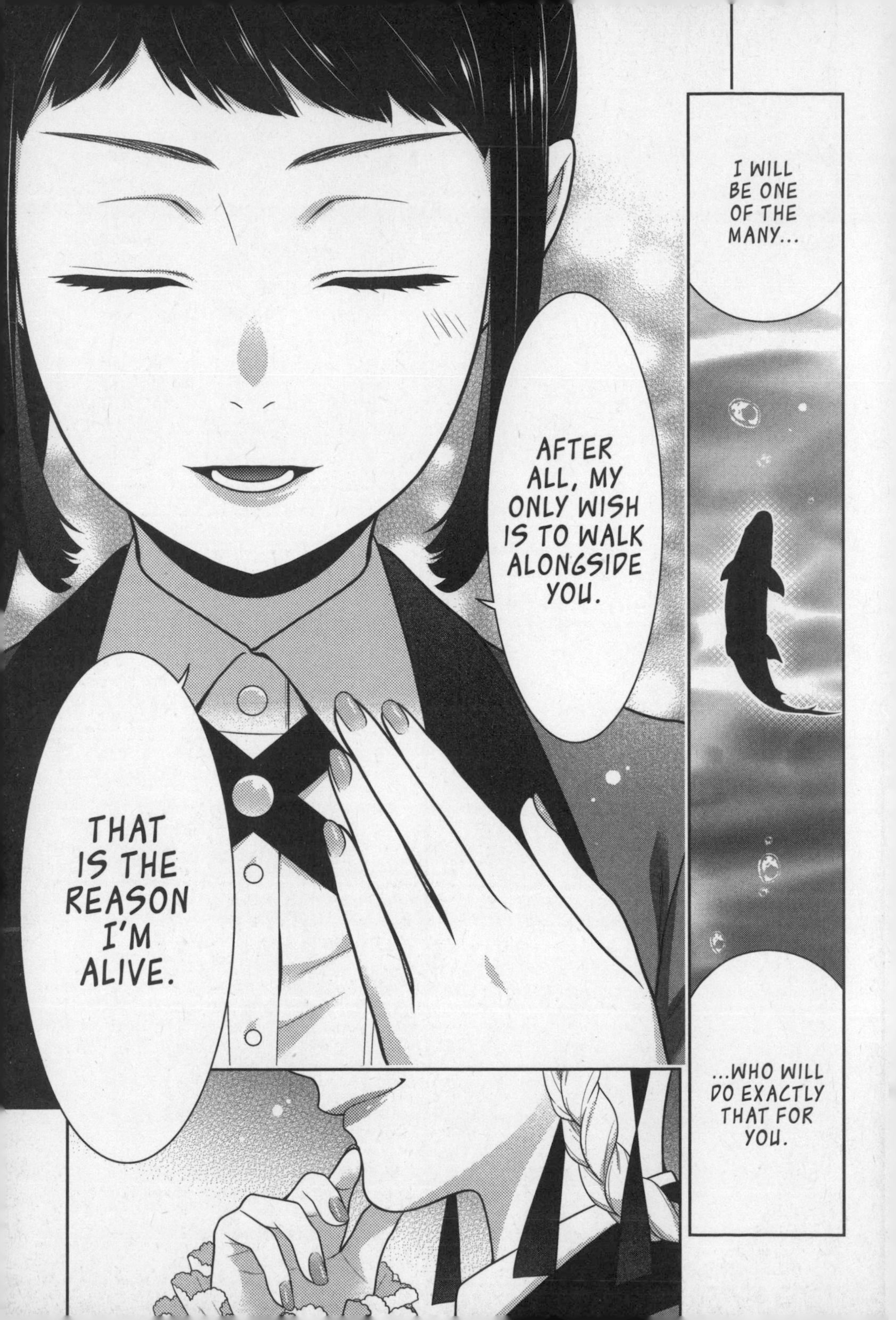
I WILL BE ONE OF THE MANY...
...WHO WILL DO EXACTLY THAT FOR YOU.
AFTER ALL, MY ONLY WISH IS TO WALK ALONGSIDE YOU.
THAT IS THE REASON I'M ALIVE.

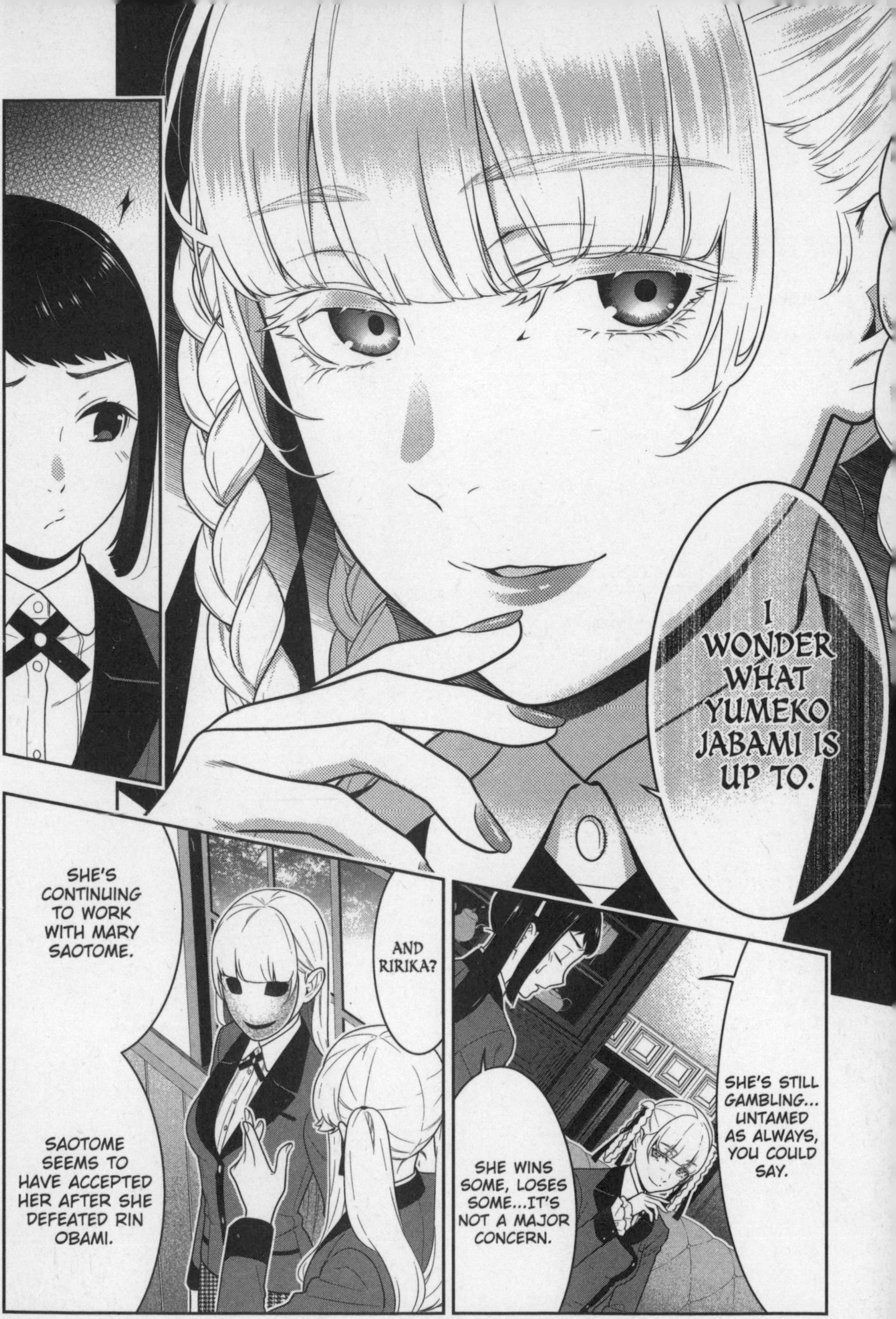
I WONDER WHAT YUMEKO JABAMI IS UP TO.
SHE'S STILL GAMBLING... UNTAMED AS ALWAYS, YOU COULD SAY.
SHE WINS SOME, LOSES SOME...IT'S NOT A MAJOR CONCERN.
AND RIRIKA?
SHE'S CONTINUING TO WORK WITH MARY SAOTOME.
SAOTOME SEEMS TO HAVE ACCEPTED HER AFTER SHE DEFEATED RIN OBAMI.

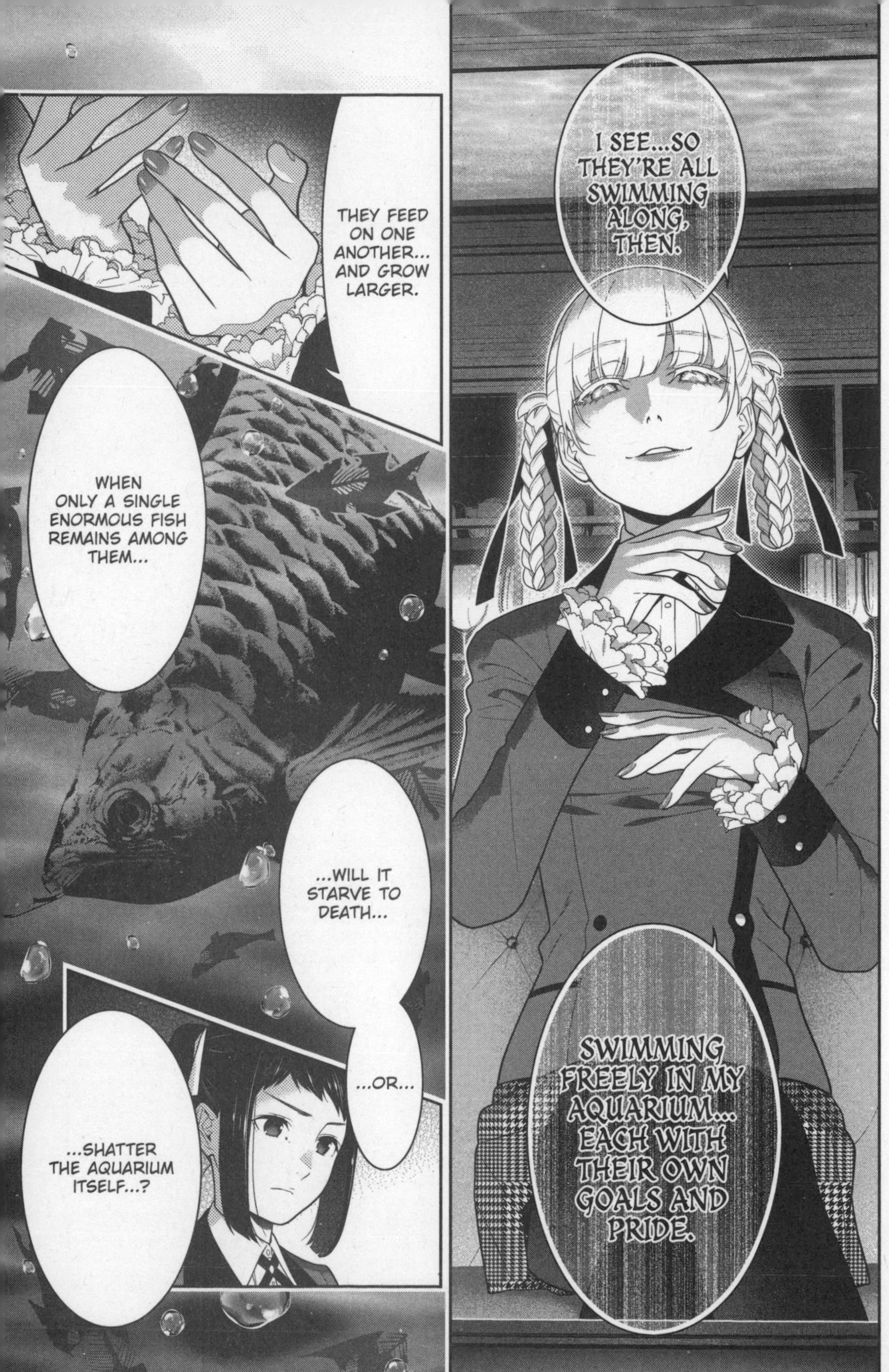
I SEE...SO THEY'RE ALL SWIMMING ALONG, THEN.
SWIMMING FREELY IN MY AQUARIUM... EACH WITH THEIR OWN GOALS AND PRIDE.
THEY FEED ON ONE ANOTHER... AND GROW LARGER.
WHEN ONLY A SINGLE ENORMOUS FISH REMAINS AMONG THEM...
...WILL IT STARVE TO DEATH...
...OR...
...SHATTER THE AQUARIUM ITSELF...?

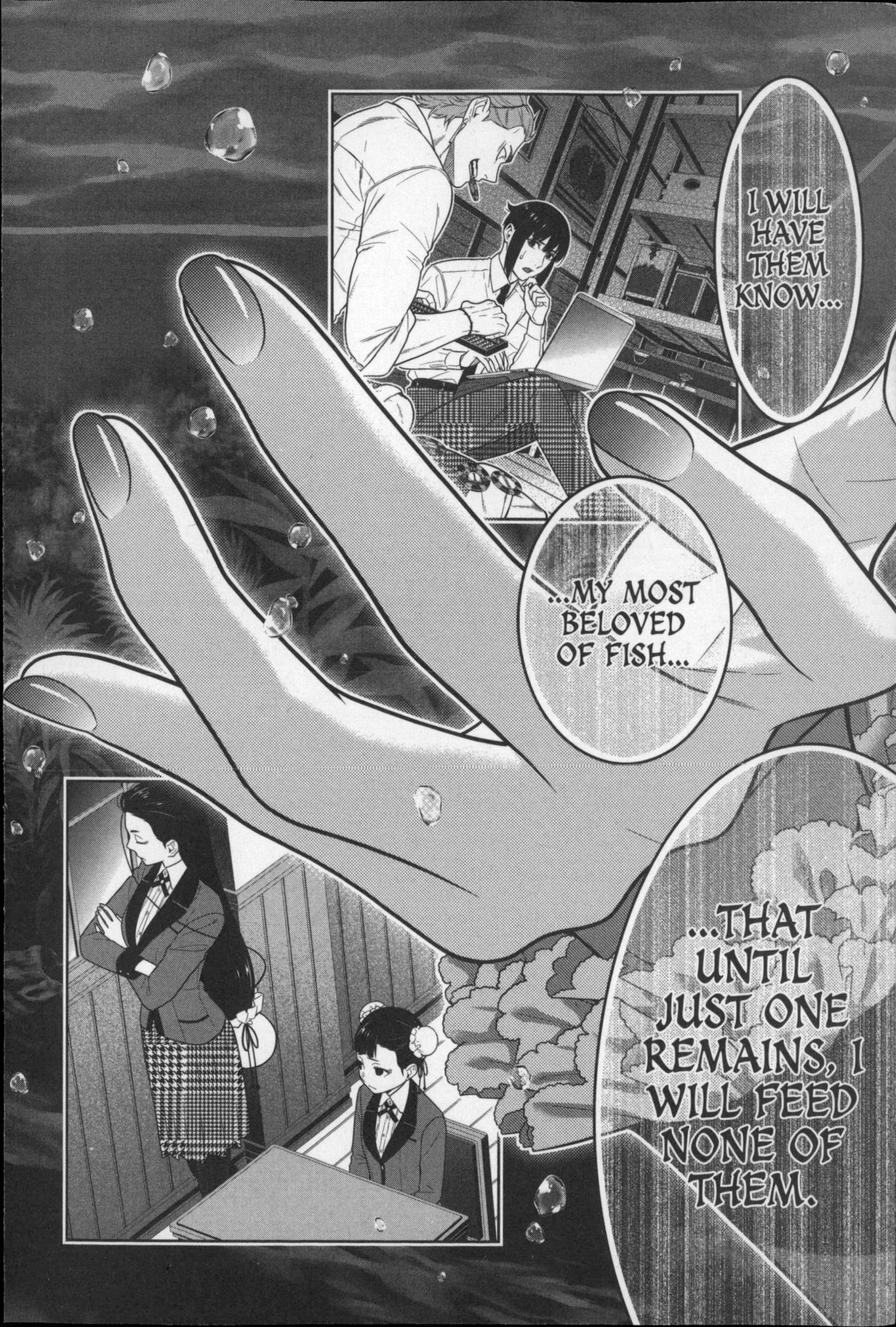
I WILL HAVE THEM KNOW...
...MY MOST BELOVED OF FISH...
...THAT UNTIL JUST ONE REMAINS, I WILL FEED NONE OF THEM.

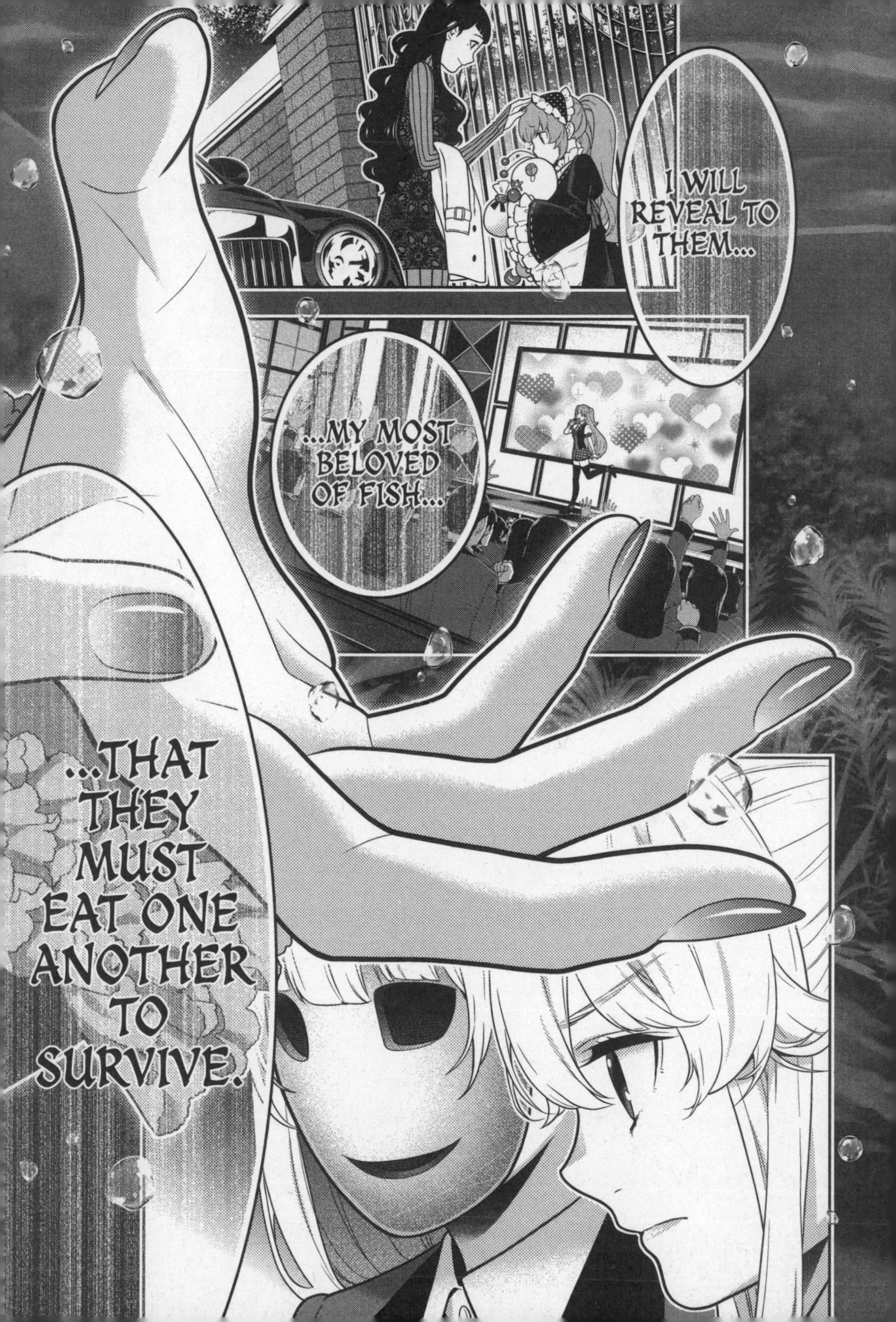
I WILL REVEAL TO THEM...
...MY MOST BELOVED OF FISH...
...THAT THEY MUST EAT ONE ANOTHER TO SURVIVE.

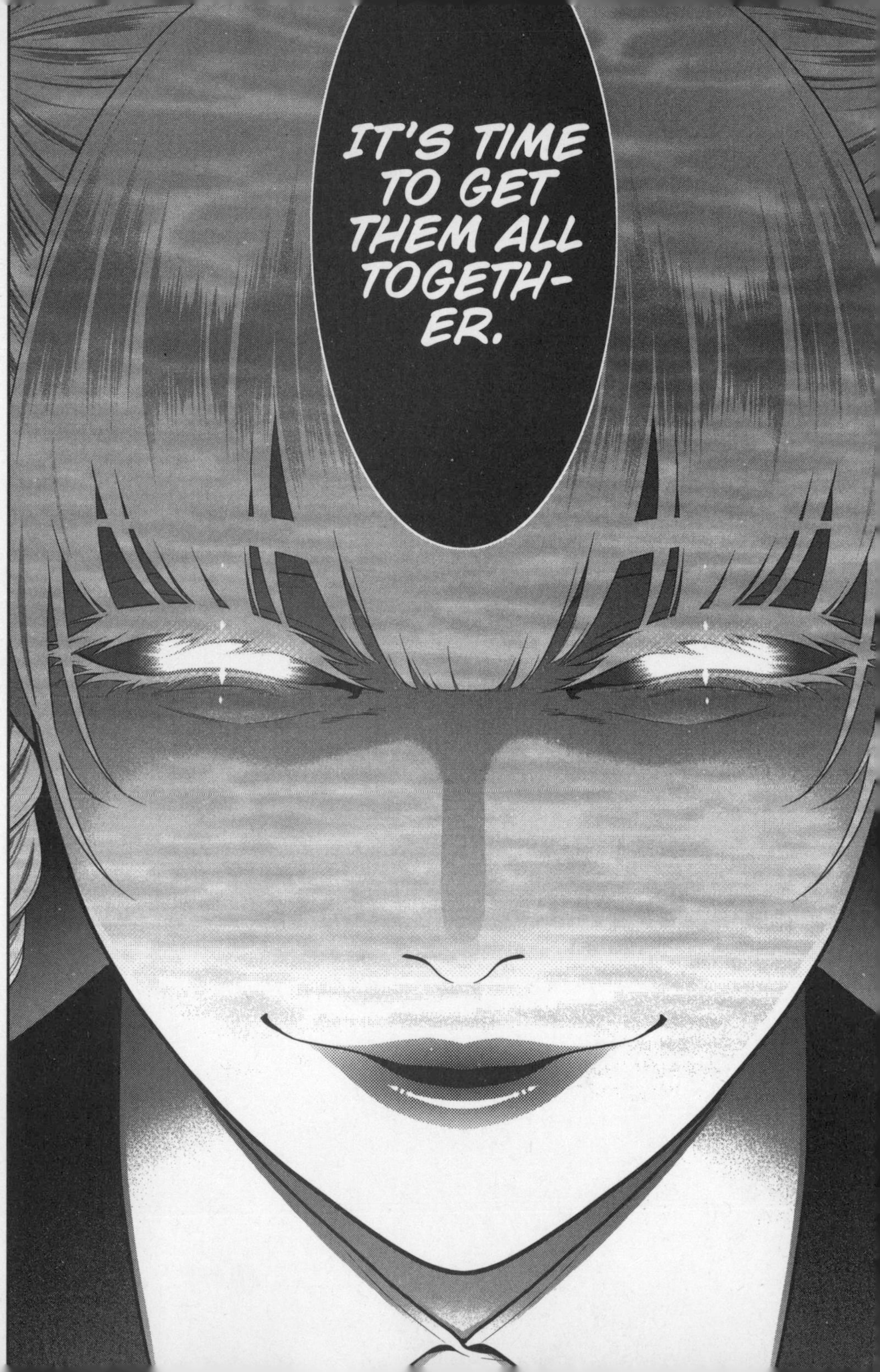
IT'S TIME TO GET THEM ALL TOGETH-ER.

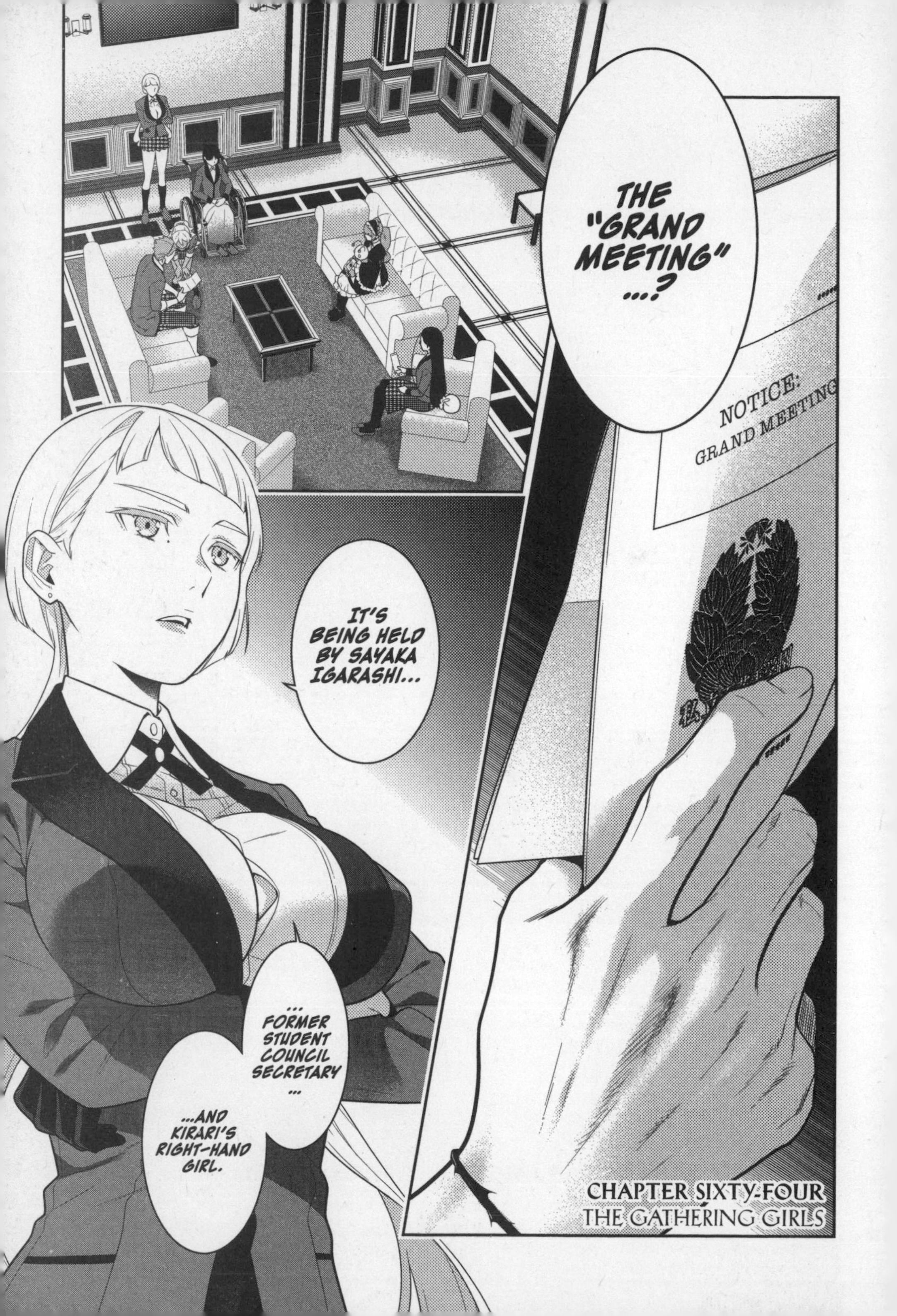
THE "GRAND MEETING" ...?
NOTICE:
GRAND MEETING
CHAPTER SIXTY-FOUR
THE GATHERING GIRLS
IT'S BEING HELD BY SAYAKA IGARASHI...
...FORMER STUDENT COUNCIL SECRETARY...
...AND KIRARI'S RIGHT-HAND GIRL.

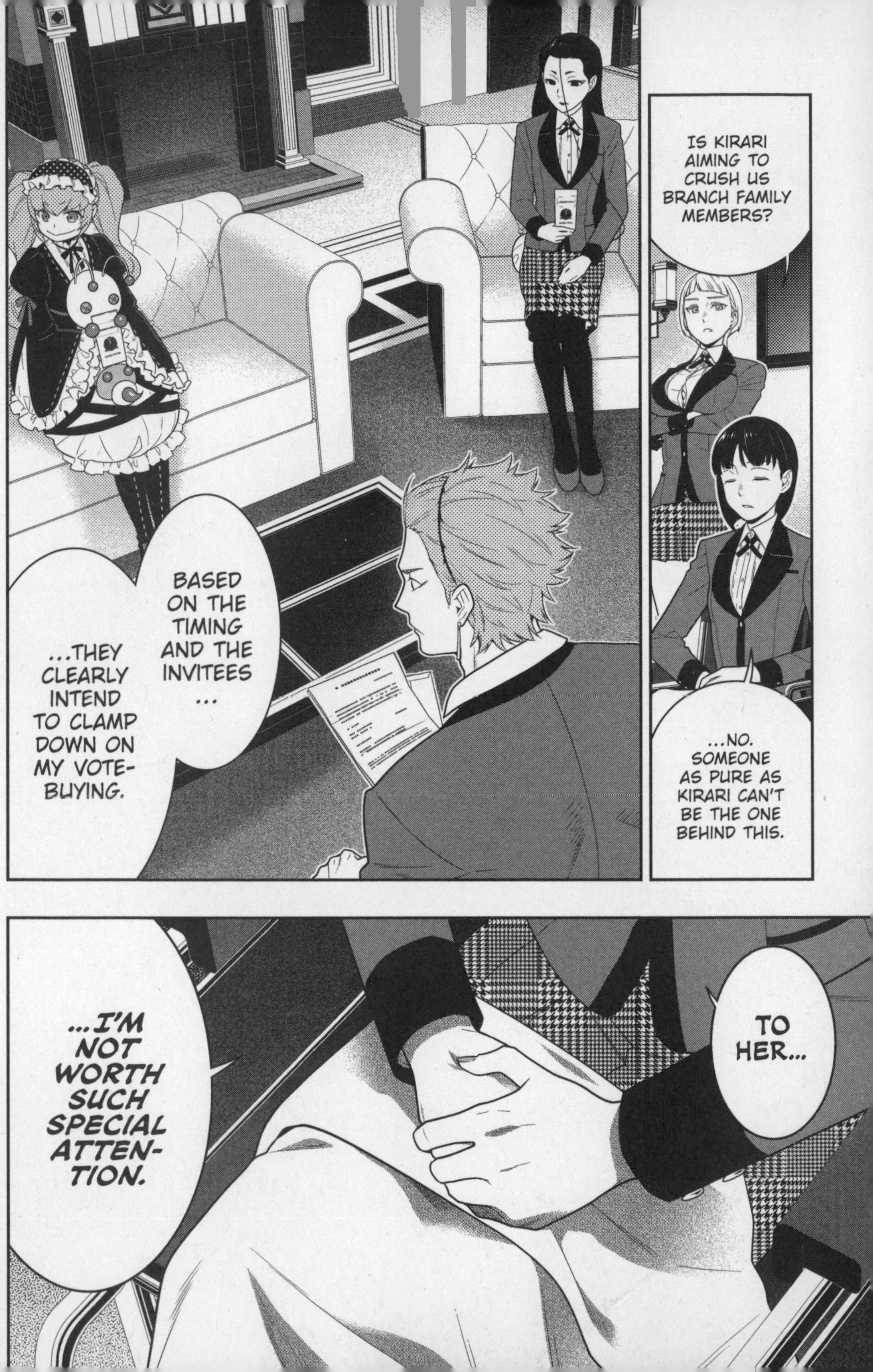
IS KIRARI AIMING TO CRUSH US BRANCH FAMILY MEMBERS?
...NO. SOMEONE AS PURE AS KIRARI CAN'T BE THE ONE BEHIND THIS.
BASED ON THE TIMING AND THE INVITEES...
...THEY CLEARLY INTEND TO CLAMP DOWN ON MY VOTE-BUYING.
TO HER...
...I'M NOT WORTH SUCH SPECIAL ATTENTION.

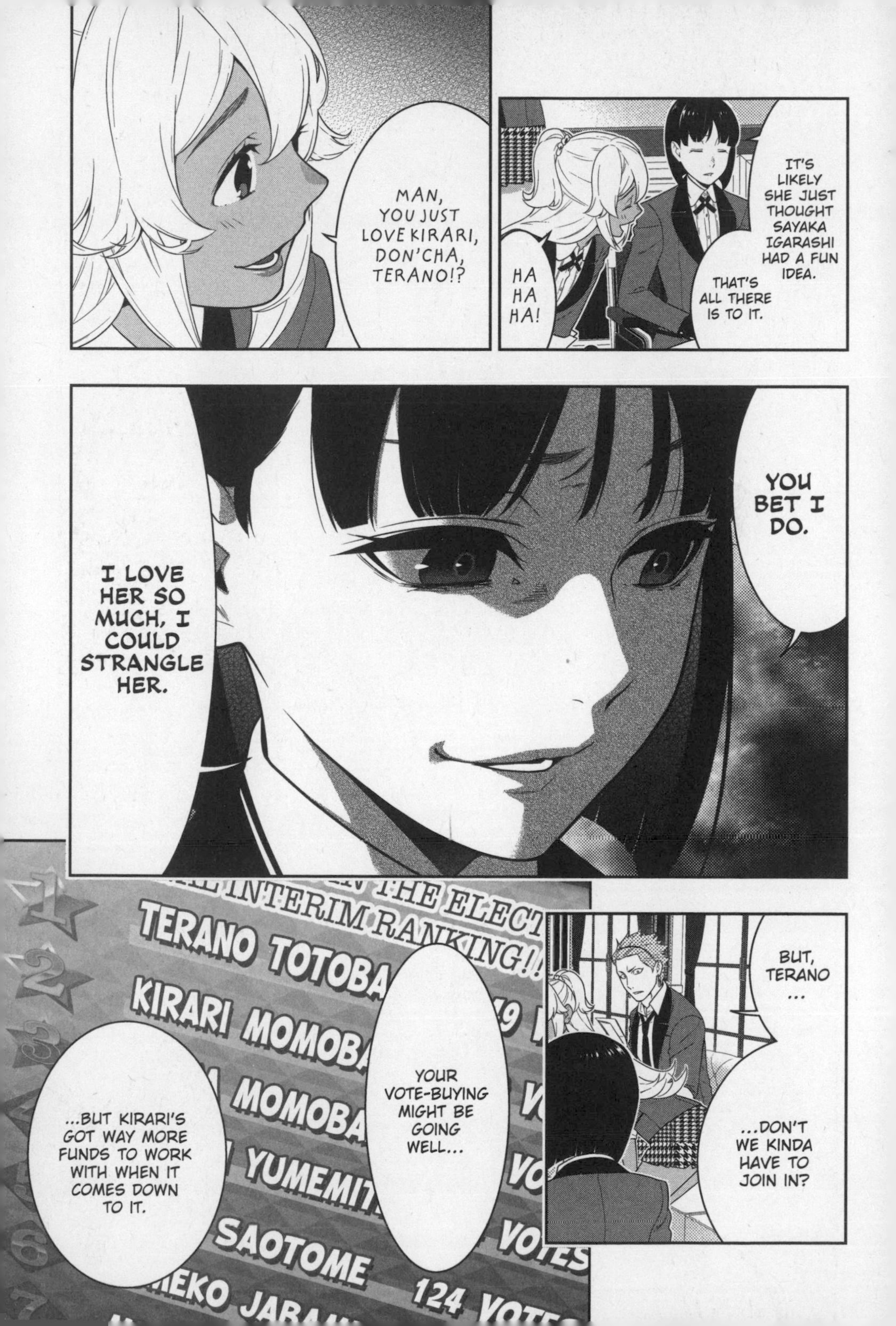
IT'S LIKELY SHE JUST THOUGHT SAYAKA IGARASHI HAD A FUN IDEA.
THAT'S ALL THERE IS TO IT.
HA HA HA!
MAN, YOU JUST LOVE KIRARI, DON'CHA, TERANO!?
YOU BET I DO.
I LOVE HER SO MUCH, I COULD STRANGLE HER.
BUT, TERANO ...
...DON'T WE KINDA HAVE TO JOIN IN?
INTERIM RANKING!!
TERANO TOTOBA
KIRARI MOMOBA
SAOTOME
124 VOTES
YOUR VOTE-BUYING MIGHT BE GOING WELL...
...BUT KIRARI'S GOT WAY MORE FUNDS TO WORK WITH WHEN IT COMES DOWN TO IT.

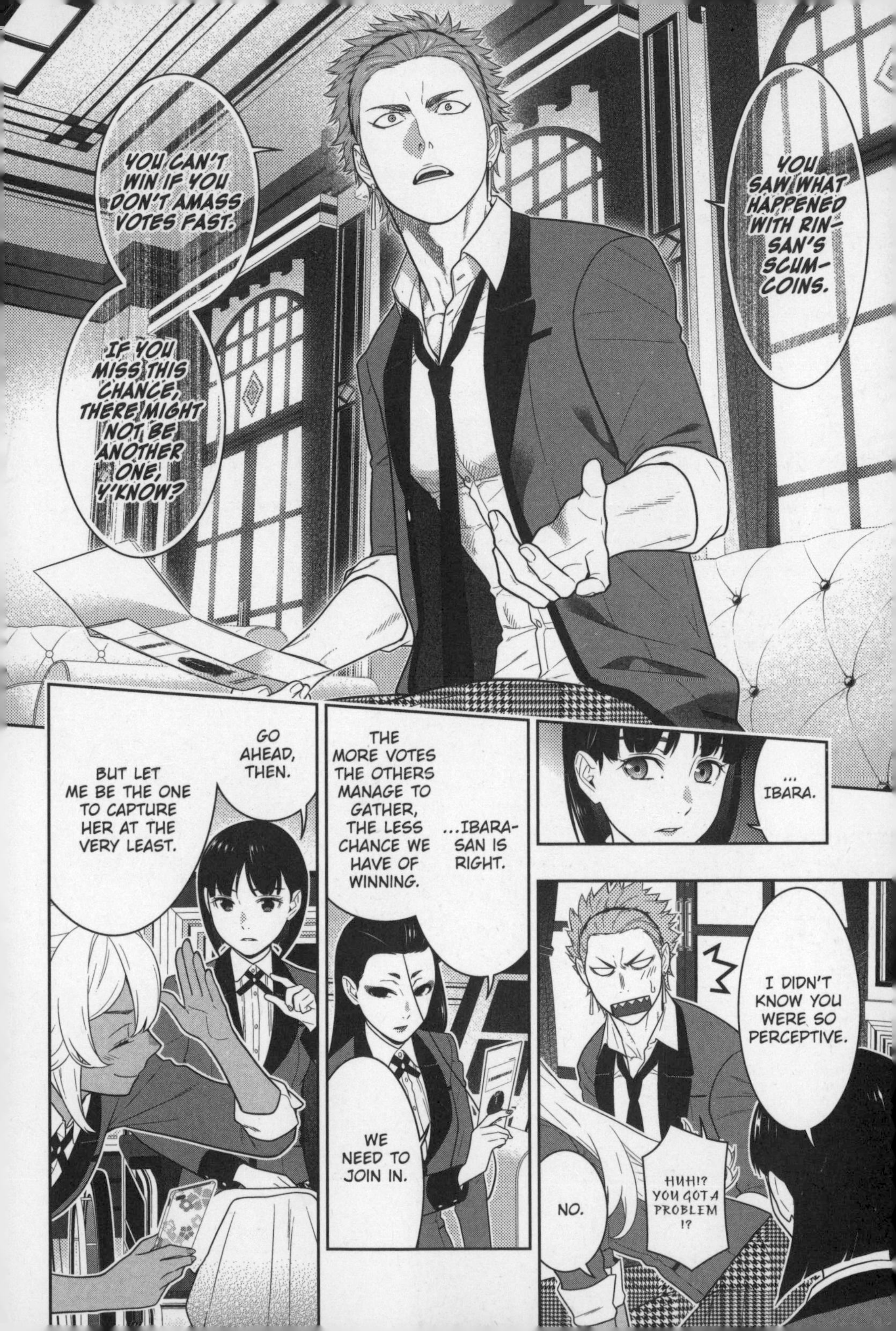
YOU SAW WHAT HAPPENED WITH RIN-SAN'S SCUM-COINS.
YOU CAN'T WIN IF YOU DON'T AMASS VOTES FAST.
IF YOU MISS THIS CHANCE, THERE MIGHT NOT BE ANOTHER ONE, Y'KNOW?
...IBARA.
I DIDN'T KNOW YOU WERE SO PERCEPTIVE.
HUH!? YOU GOT A PROBLEM!?
NO.
...IBARA-SAN IS RIGHT.
THE MORE VOTES THE OTHERS MANAGE TO GATHER, THE LESS CHANCE WE HAVE OF WINNING.
WE NEED TO JOIN IN.
GO AHEAD, THEN.
BUT LET ME BE THE ONE TO CAPTURE HER AT THE VERY LEAST.

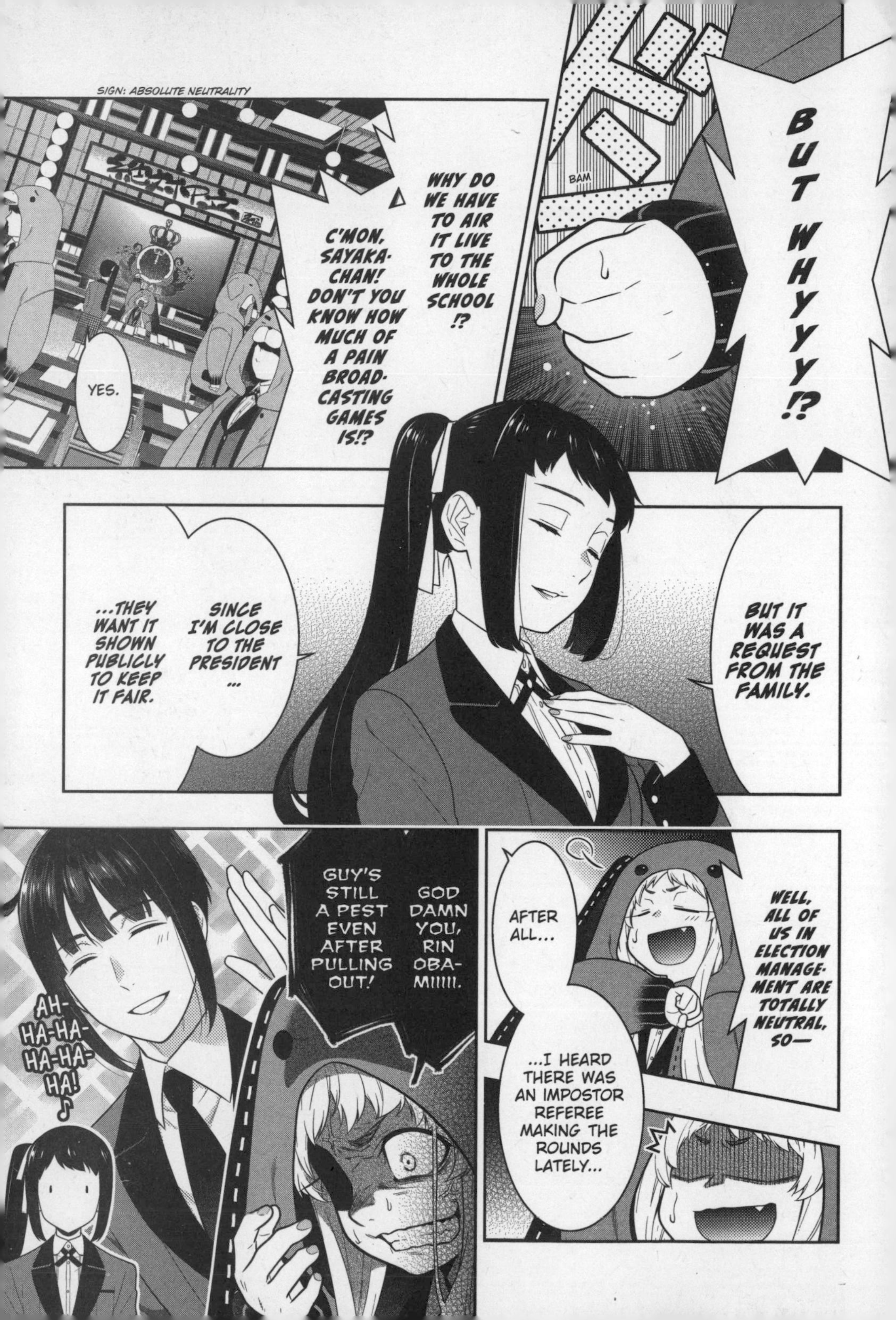
BAM
BUT WHYYYY!?
SIGN: ABSOLUTE NEUTRALITY
WHY DO WE HAVE TO AIR IT LIVE TO THE WHOLE SCHOOL!?
C'MON, SAYAKA-CHAN! DON'T YOU KNOW HOW MUCH OF A PAIN BROADCASTING GAMES IS!?
YES.
BUT IT WAS A REQUEST FROM THE FAMILY.
SINCE I'M CLOSE TO THE PRESIDENT...
...THEY WANT IT SHOWN PUBLICLY TO KEEP IT FAIR.
WELL, ALL OF US IN ELECTION MANAGEMENT ARE TOTALLY NEUTRAL, SO—
AFTER ALL...
...I HEARD THERE WAS AN IMPOSTOR REFEREE MAKING THE ROUNDS LATELY...
GOD DAMN YOU, RIN OBAMIIIII.
GUY'S STILL A PEST EVEN AFTER PULLING OUT!
AH-HA-HA-HA-HA-HA!♪

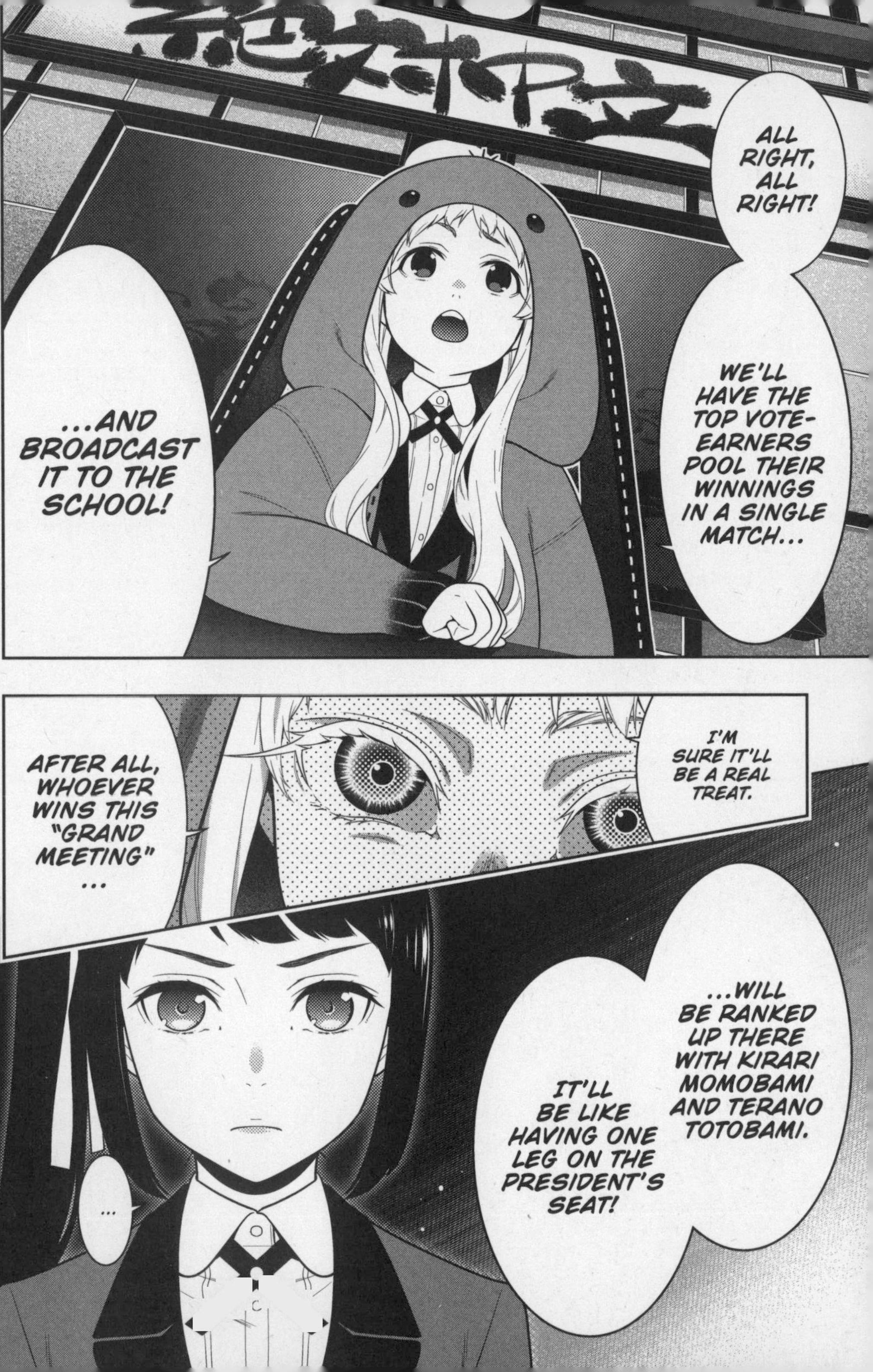
ALL RIGHT, ALL RIGHT!
WE'LL HAVE THE TOP VOTE-EARNERS POOL THEIR WINNINGS IN A SINGLE MATCH...
...AND BROADCAST IT TO THE SCHOOL!
I'M SURE IT'LL BE A REAL TREAT.
AFTER ALL, WHOEVER WINS THIS "GRAND MEETING"...
...WILL BE RANKED UP THERE WITH KIRARI MOMOBAMI AND TERANO TOTOBAMI.
IT'LL BE LIKE HAVING ONE LEG ON THE PRESIDENT'S SEAT!
...

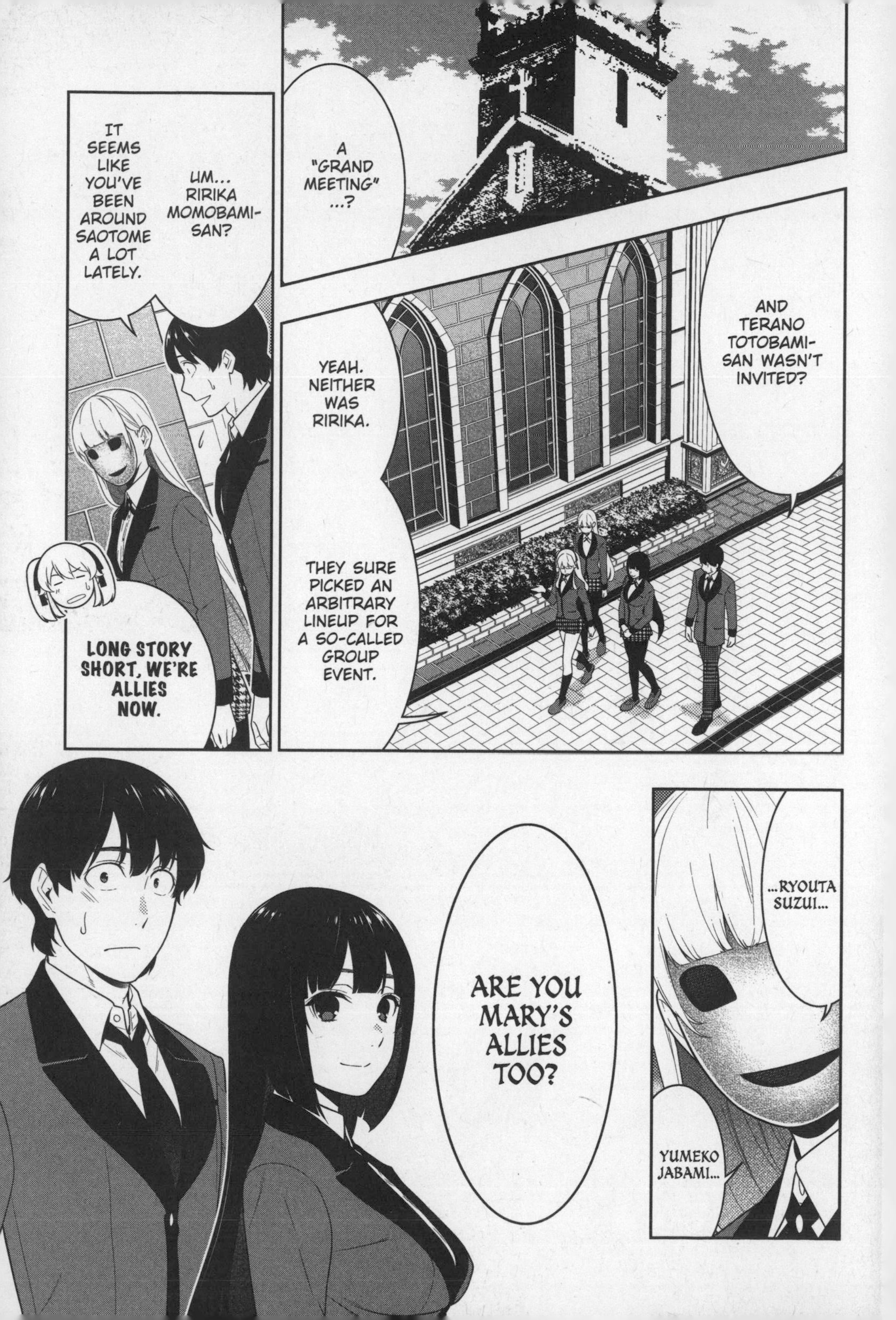
A "GRAND MEETING" ...?
AND TERANO TOTOBAMI-SAN WASN'T INVITED?
YEAH. NEITHER WAS RIRIKA.
THEY SURE PICKED AN ARBITRARY LINEUP FOR A SO-CALLED GROUP EVENT.
UM... RIRIKA MOMOBAMI-SAN?
IT SEEMS LIKE YOU'VE BEEN AROUND SAOTOME A LOT LATELY.
LONG STORY SHORT, WE'RE ALLIES NOW.
...RYOUTA SUZUI...
YUMEKO JABAMI...
ARE YOU MARY'S ALLIES TOO?

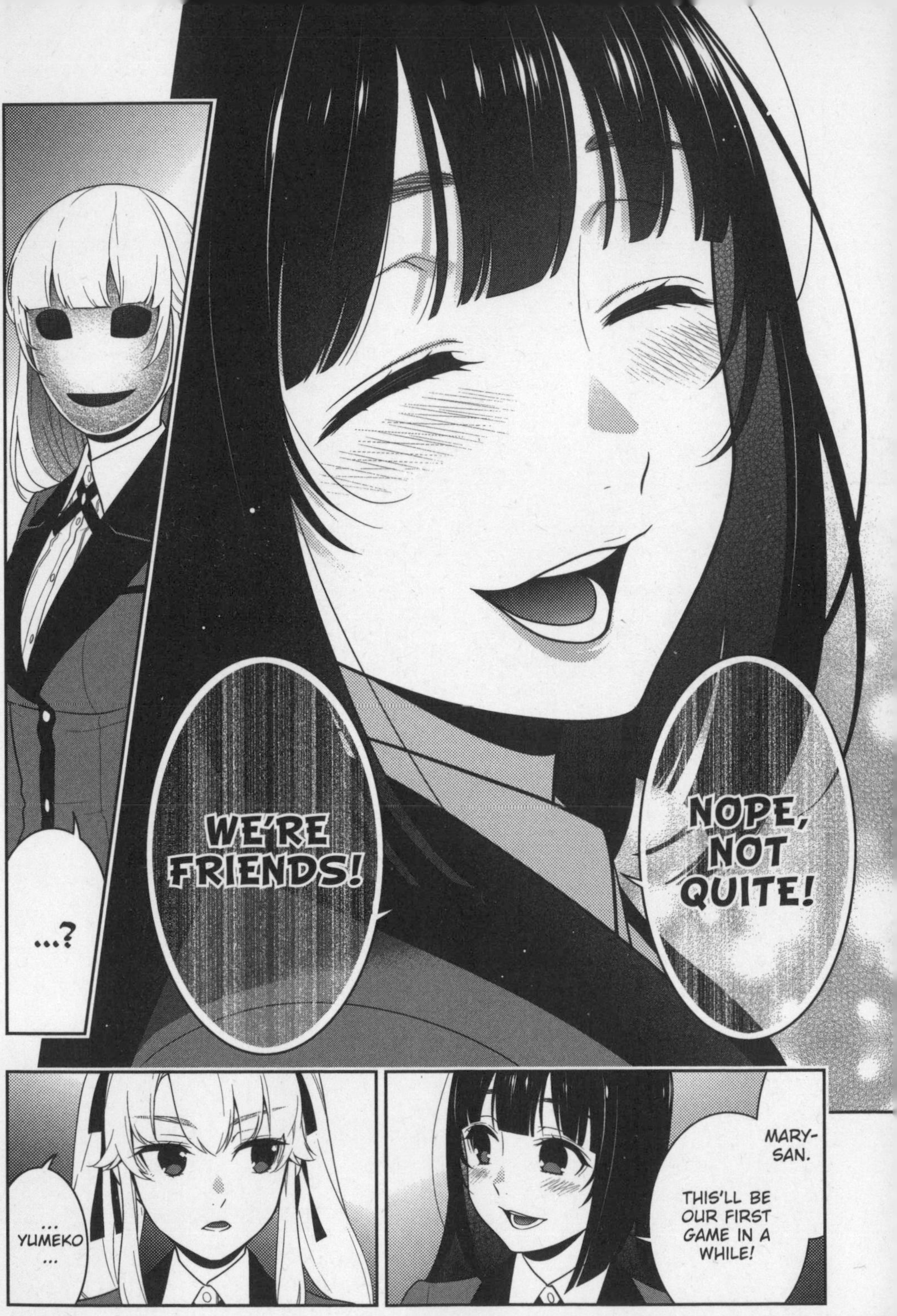
NOPE, NOT QUITE!
WE'RE FRIENDS!
...?
MARY-SAN.
THIS'LL BE OUR FIRST GAME IN A WHILE!
... YUMEKO ...

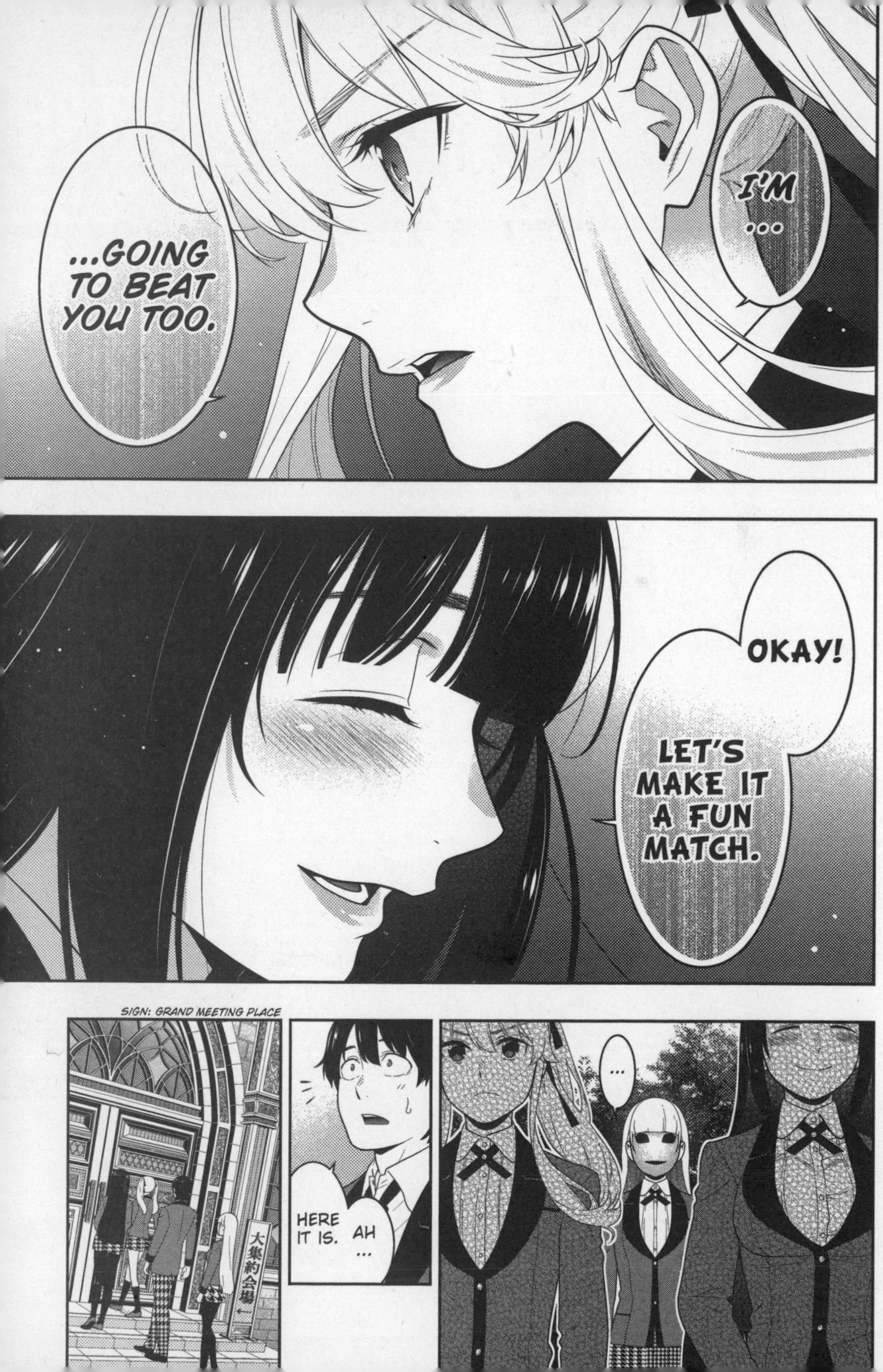
I'M ...
...GOING TO BEAT YOU TOO.
OKAY!
LET'S MAKE IT A FUN MATCH.
...
HERE IT IS. AH ...
SIGN: GRAND MEETING PLACE
大集約会場

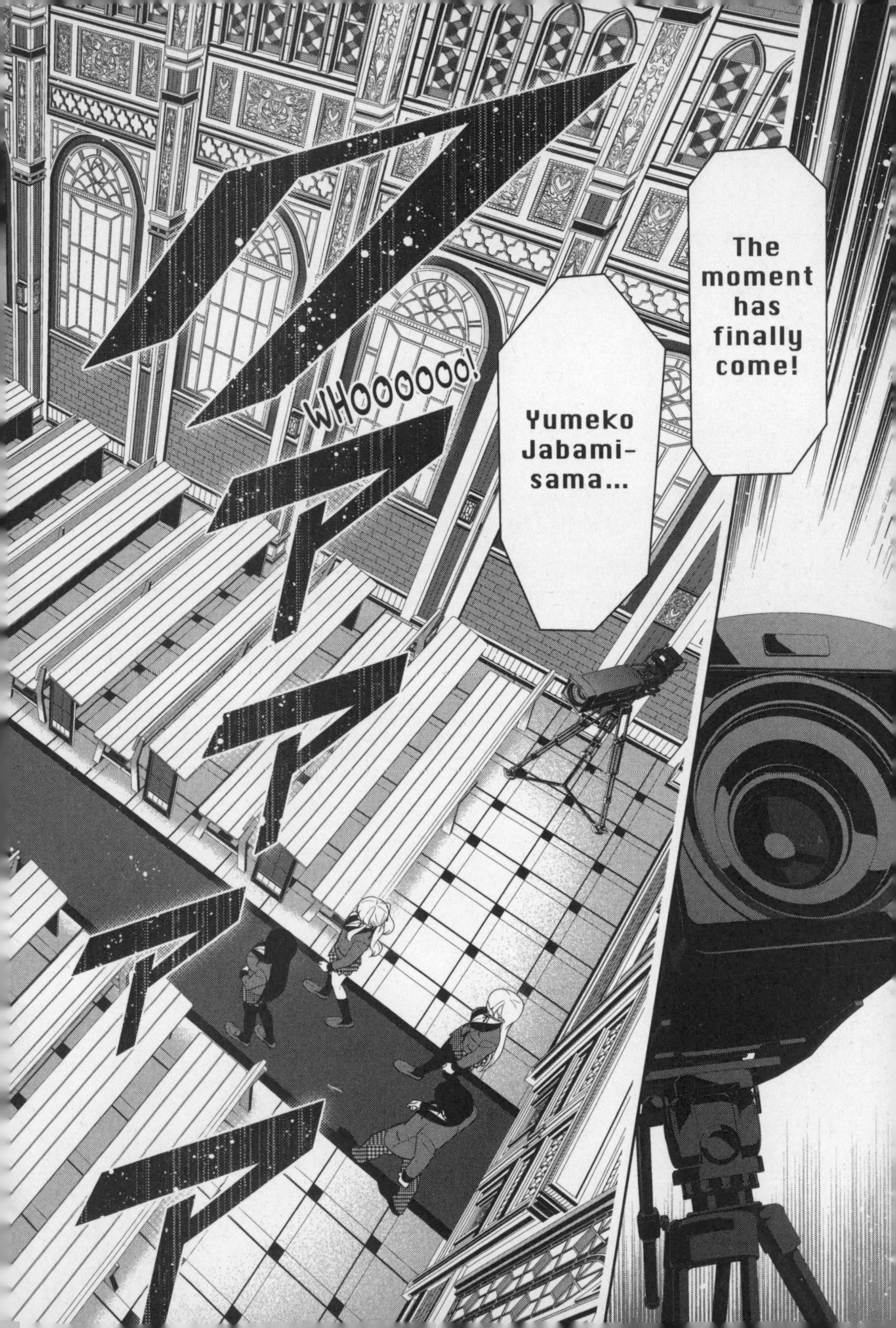
The moment has finally come!
Yumeko Jabami-sama...
WHOOOOOO!

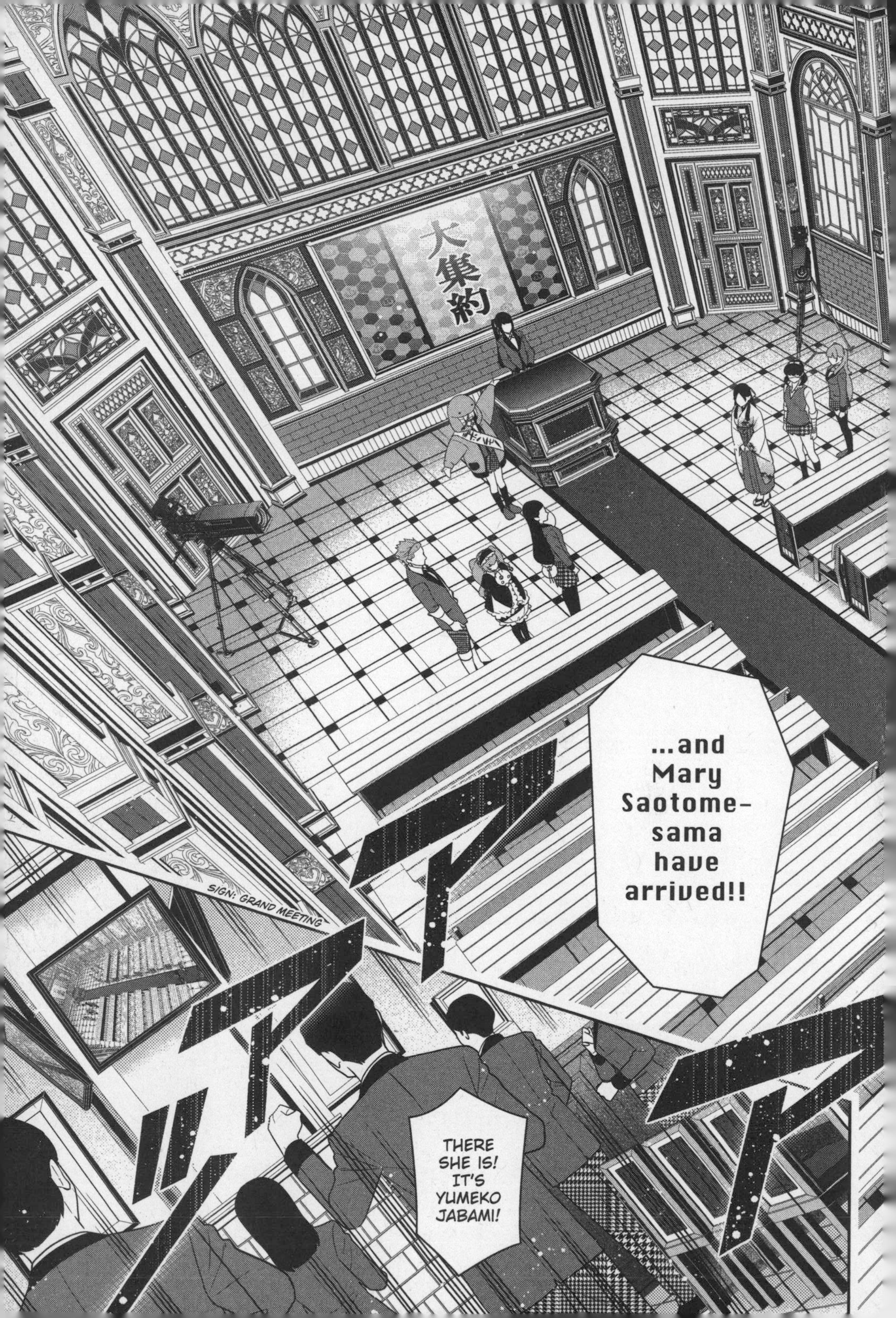
大集約
...and Mary Saotome-sama have arrived!!
SIGN: GRAND MEETING
THERE SHE IS! IT'S YUMEKO JABAMI!

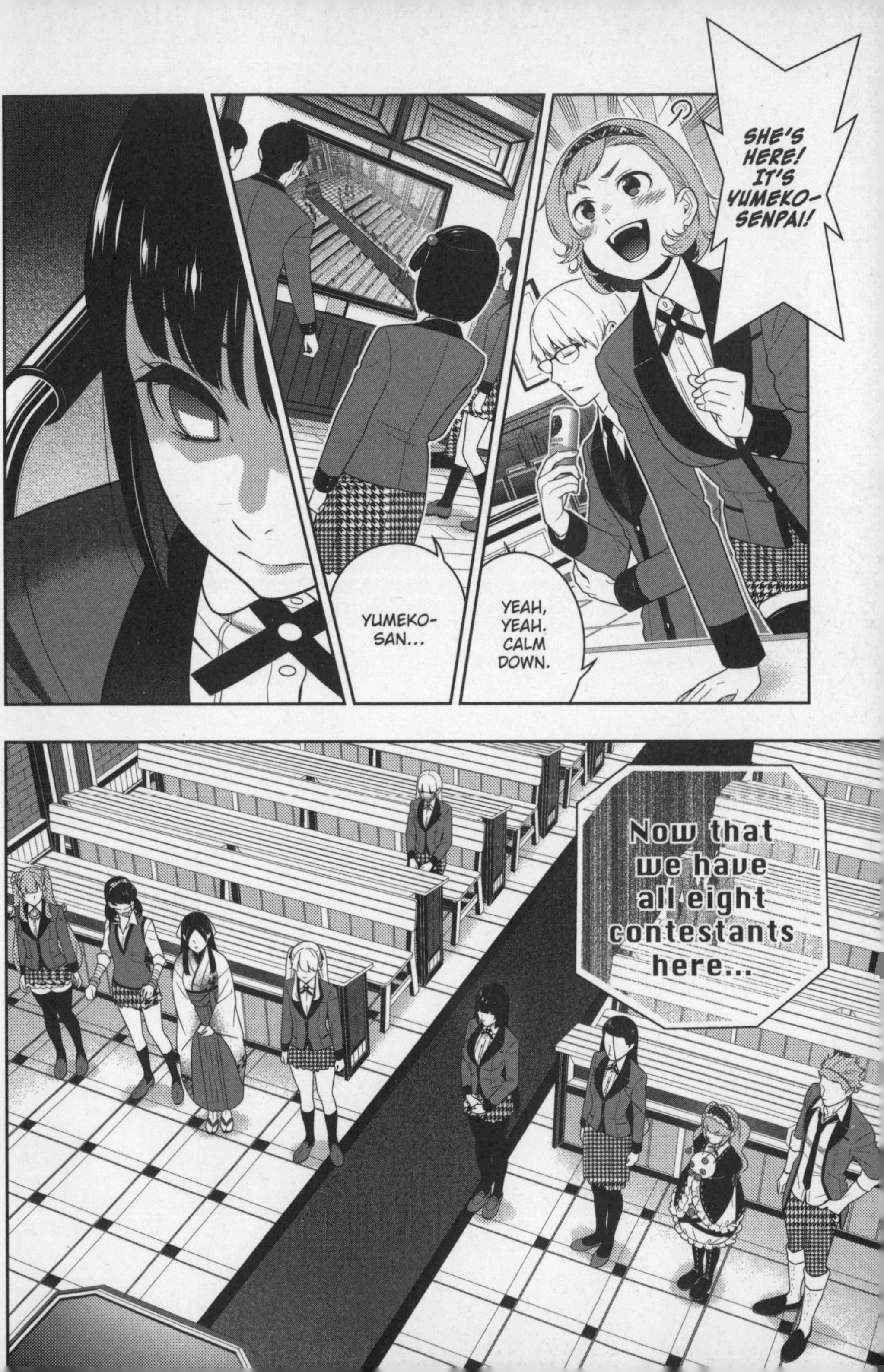
SHE'S HERE! IT'S YUMEKO-SENPAI!
YEAH, YEAH. CALM DOWN.
YUMEKO-SAN...
Now that we have all eight contestants here...

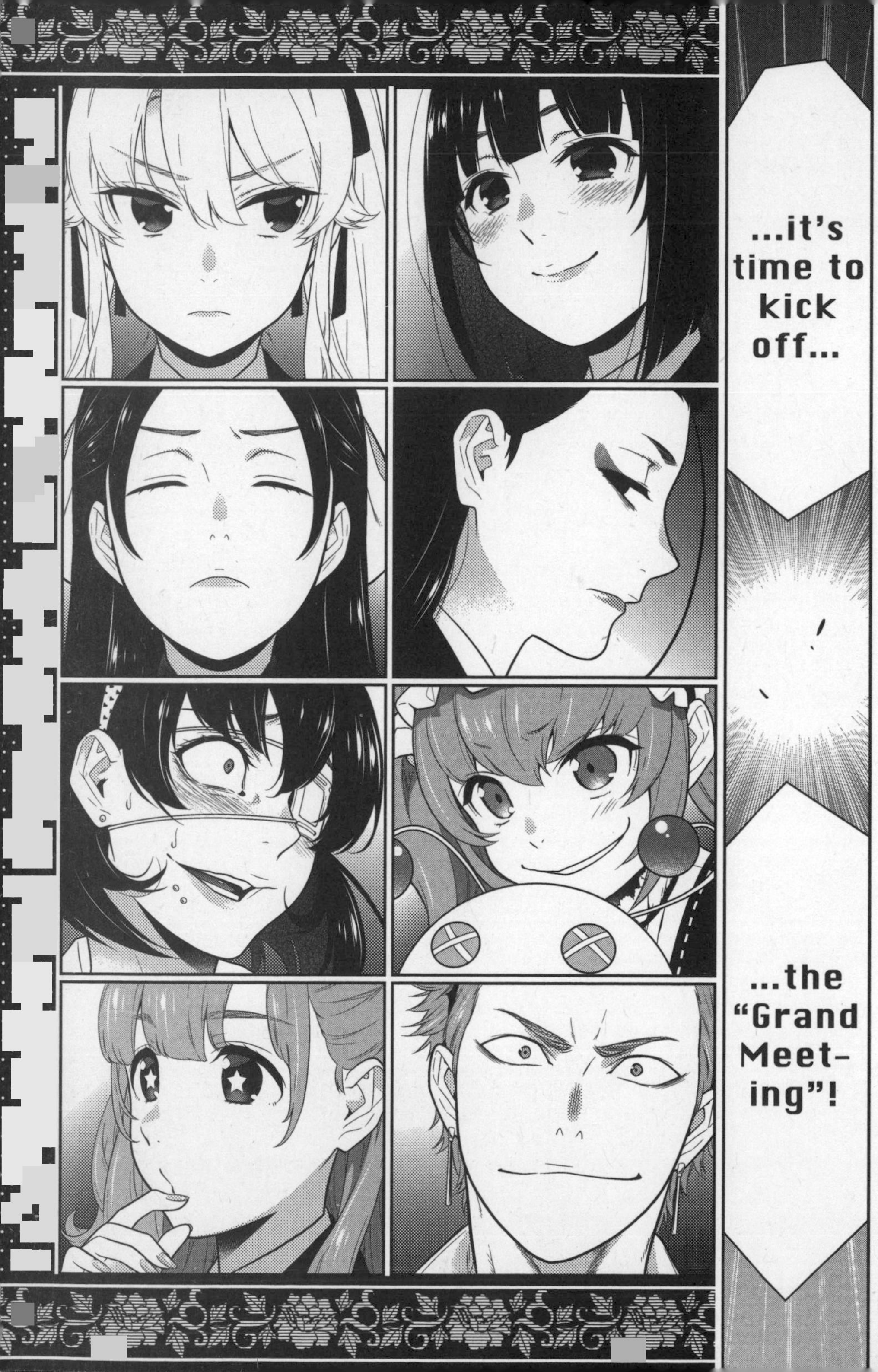
...it's time to kick off...
...the "Grand Meeting"!

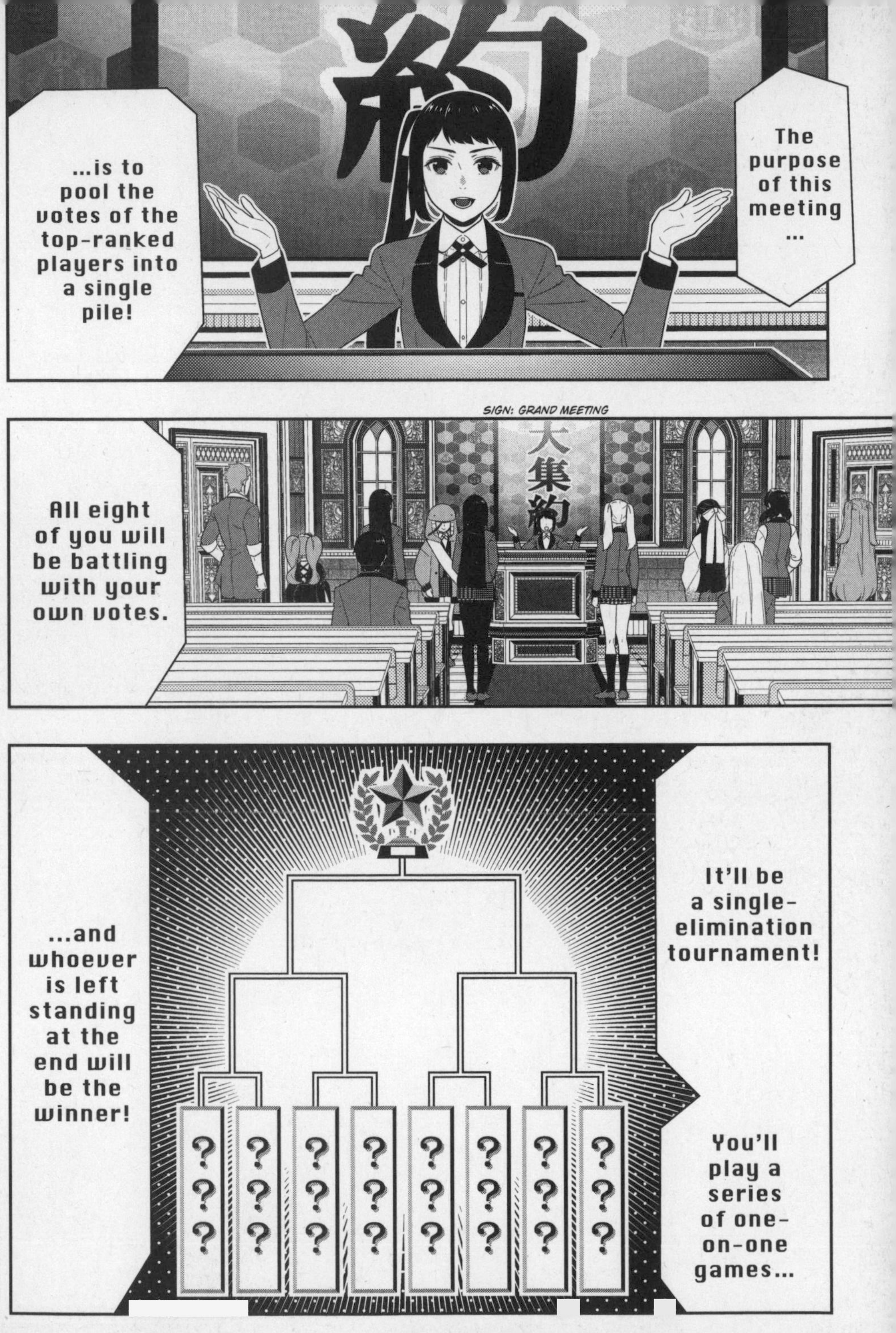
The purpose of this meeting ...
...is to pool the votes of the top-ranked players into a single pile!
SIGN: GRAND MEETING
大集約
All eight of you will be battling with your own votes.
It'll be a single-elimination tournament!
You'll play a series of one-on-one games...
...and whoever is left standing at the end will be the winner!

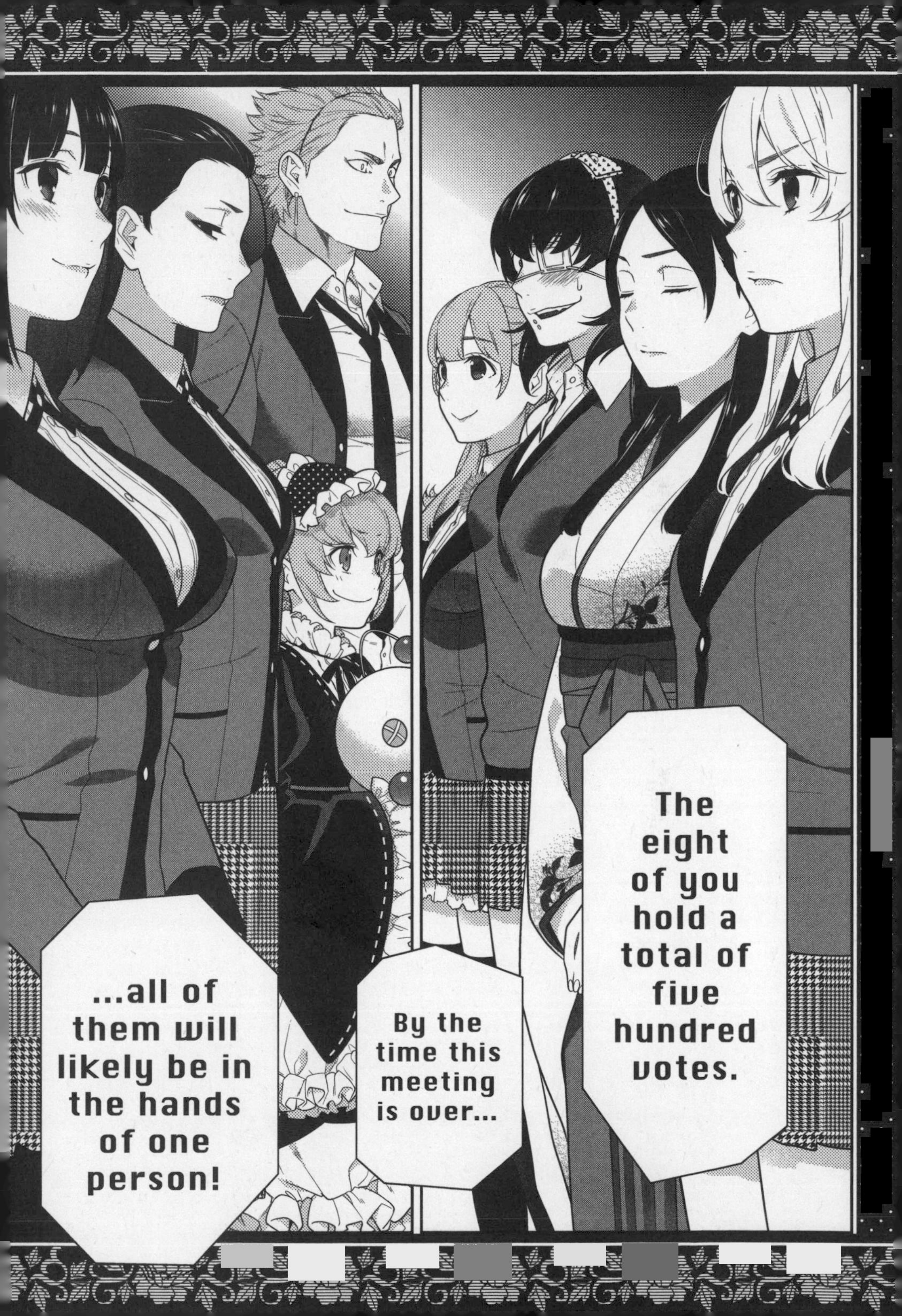
The eight of you hold a total of five hundred votes.
By the time this meeting is over...
...all of them will likely be in the hands of one person!

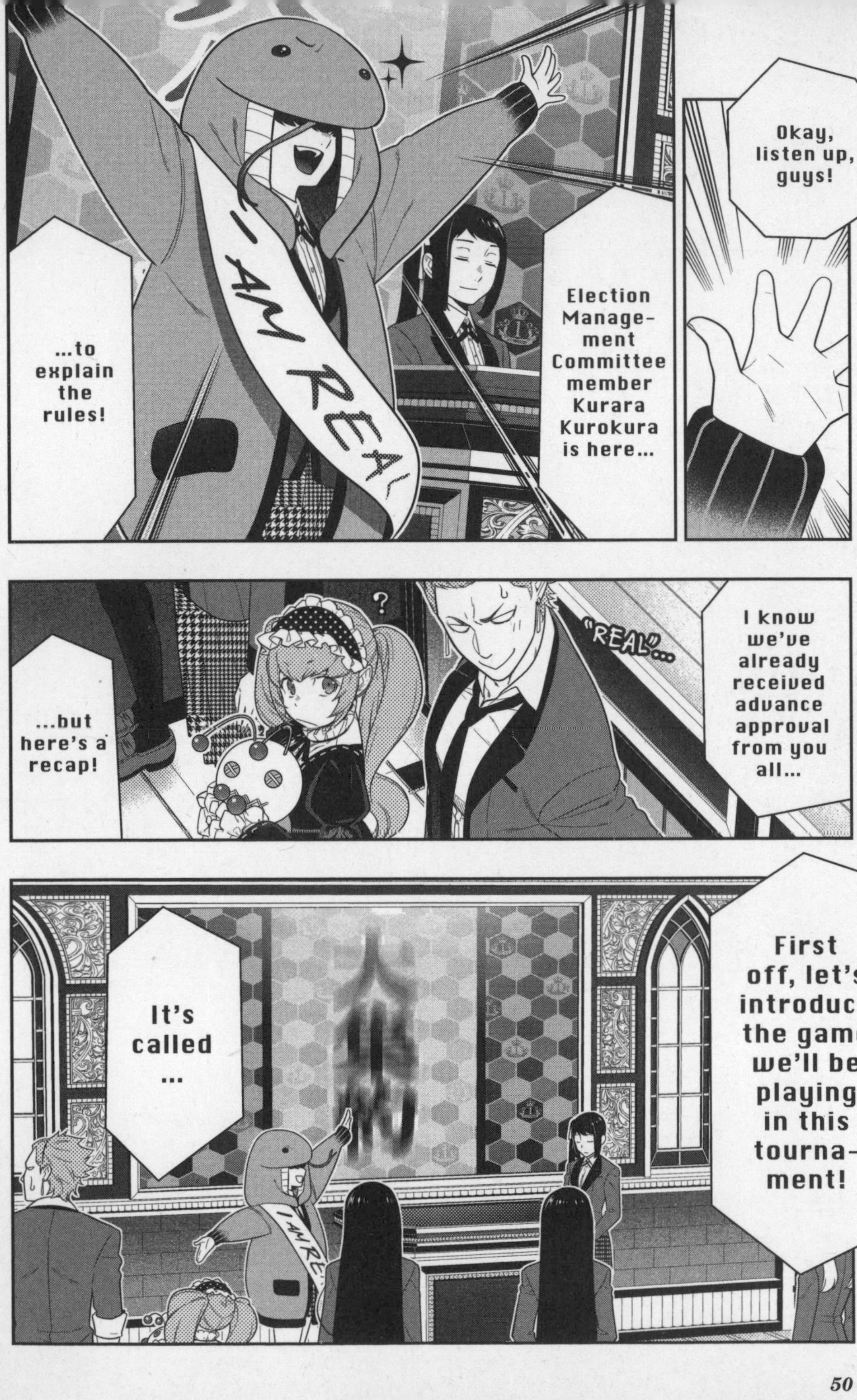
Okay, listen up, guys!
Election Management Committee member Kurara Kurokura is here...
...to explain the rules!
I AM REAL
I know we've already received advance approval from you all...
"REAL"...
?
...but here's a recap!
First off, let's introduce the game we'll be playing in this tournament!
It's called ...
I AM RE

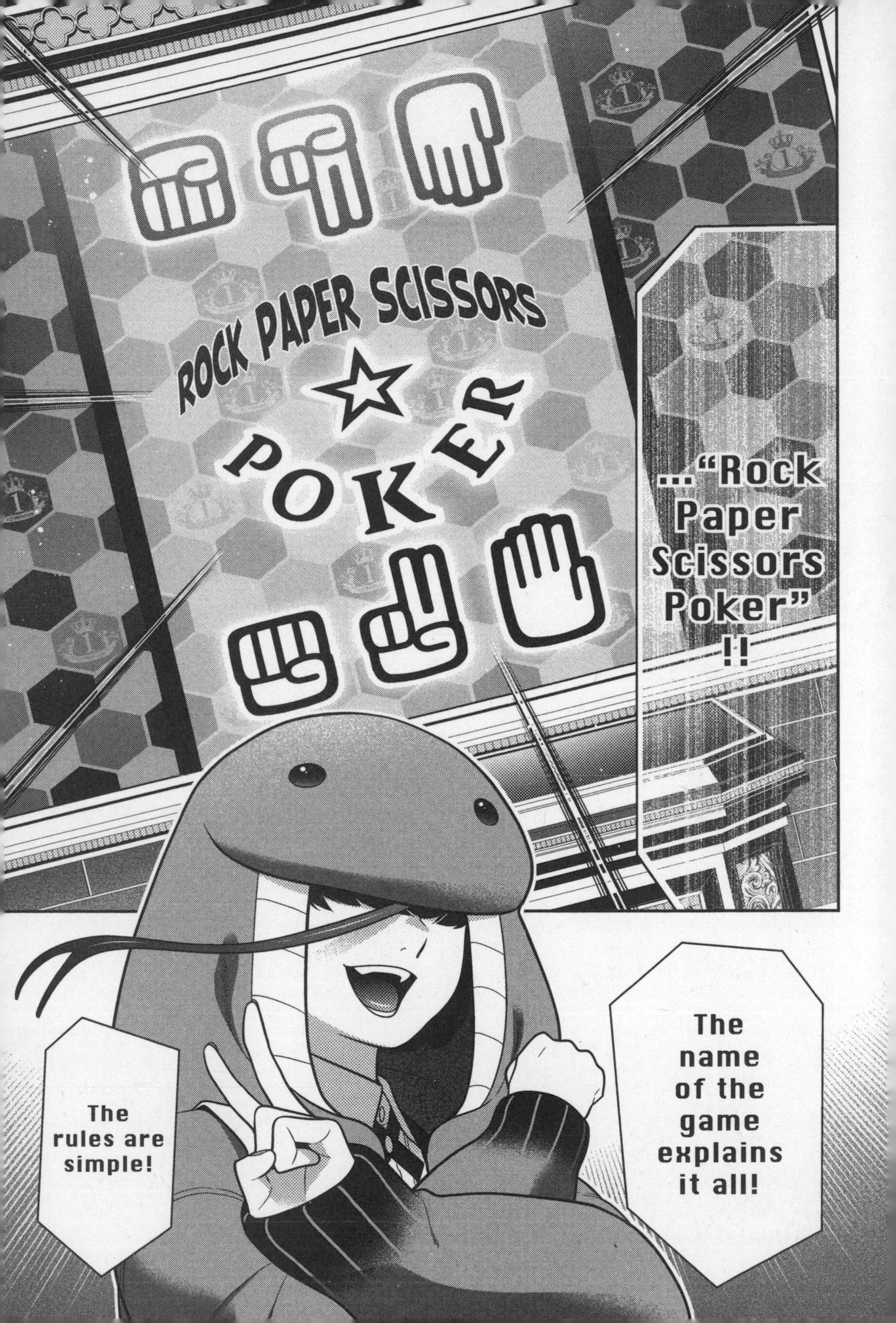
ROCK PAPER SCISSORS ☆ POKER
..."Rock Paper Scissors Poker"!!
The name of the game explains it all!
The rules are simple!

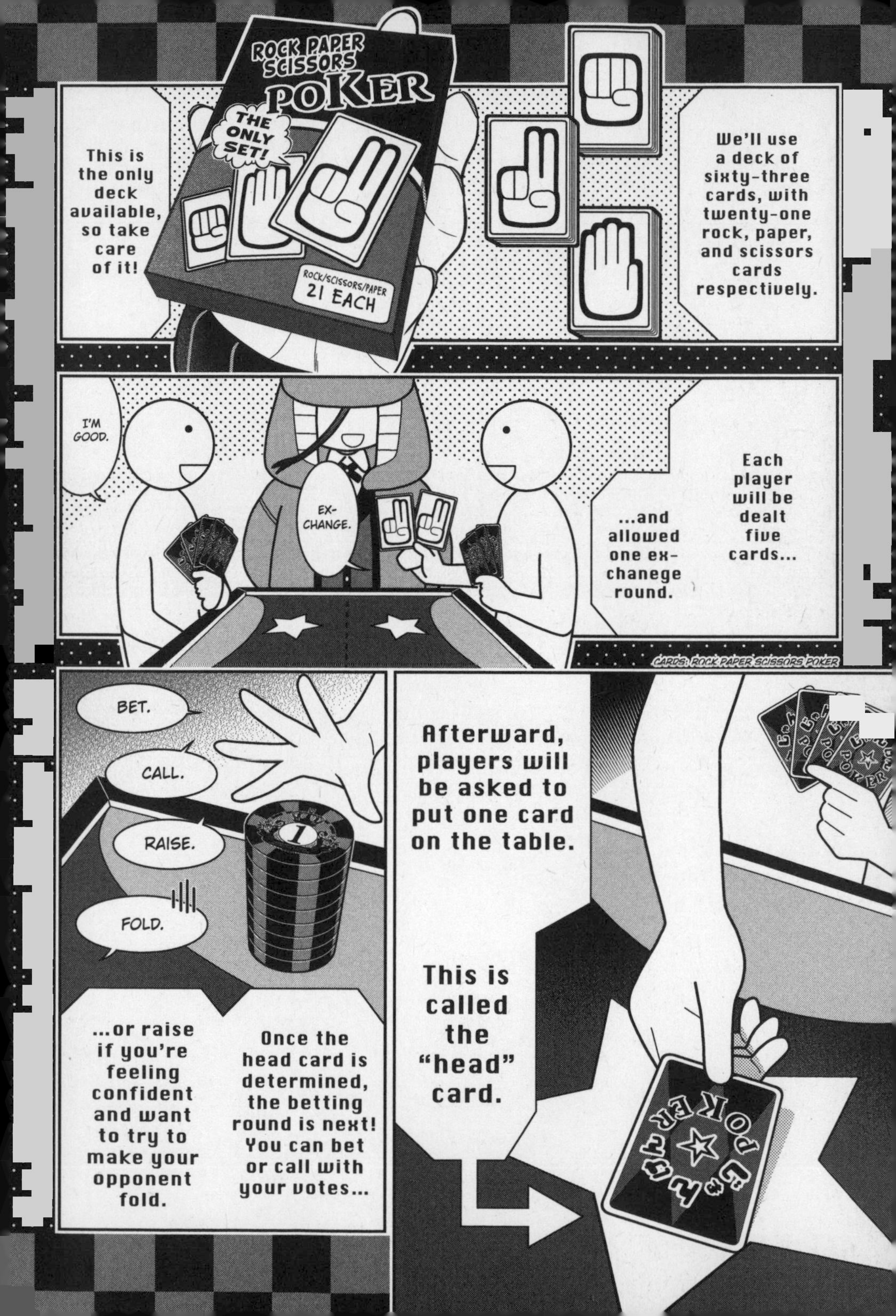
We'll use a deck of sixty-three cards, with twenty-one rock, paper, and scissors cards respectively.
ROCK PAPER SCISSORS POKER
THE ONLY SET!
ROCK/SCISSORS/PAPER 21 EACH
This is the only deck available, so take care of it!
Each player will be dealt five cards...
...and allowed one ex-chanege round.
EX-CHANGE.
I'M GOOD.
CARDS: ROCK PAPER SCISSORS POKER
Afterward, players will be asked to put one card on the table.
This is called the "head" card.
BET.
CALL.
RAISE.
FOLD.
Once the head card is determined, the betting round is next! You can bet or call with your votes...
...or raise if you're feeling confident and want to try to make your opponent fold.

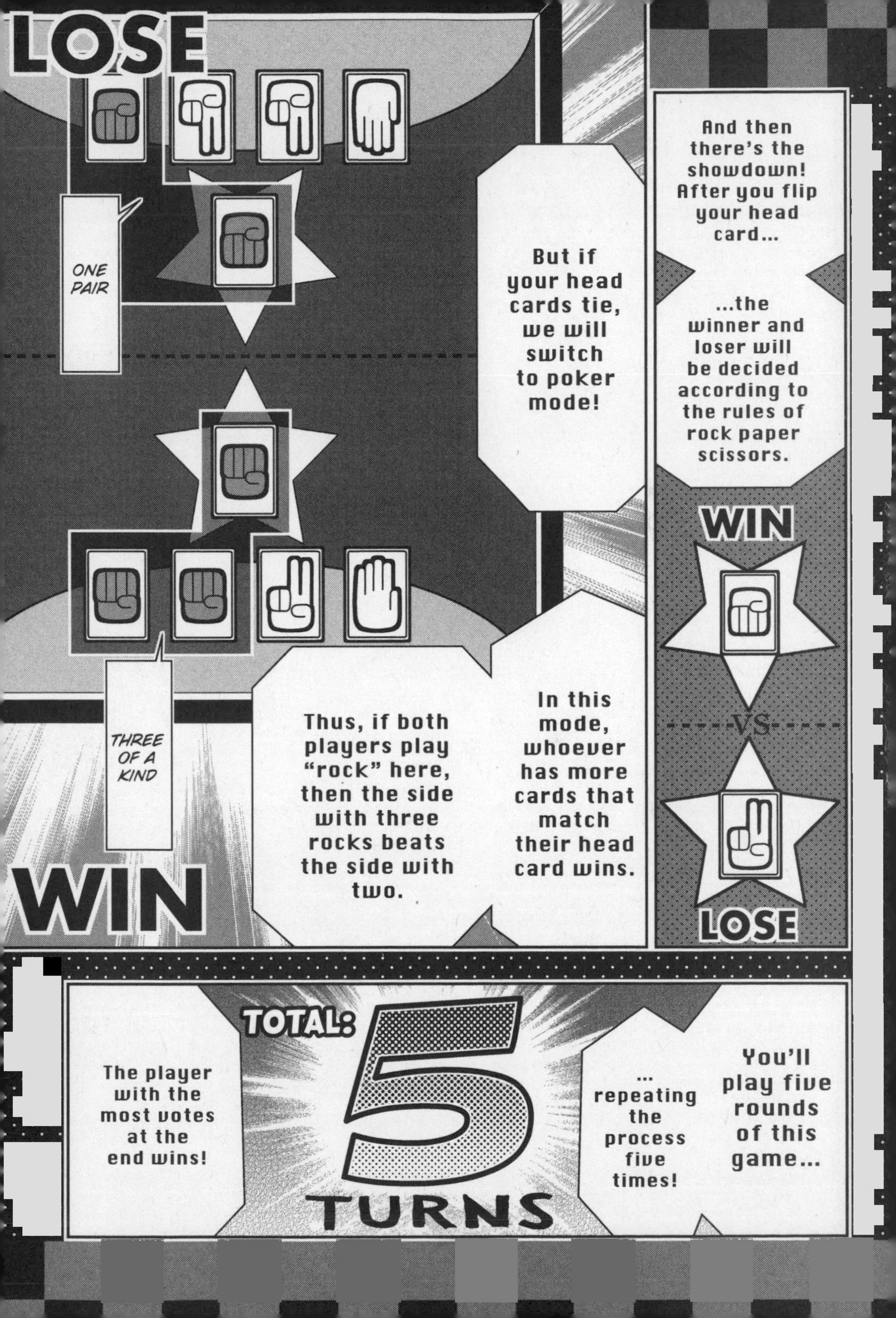

And then there's the showdown! After you flip your head card...
...the winner and loser will be decided according to the rules of rock paper scissors.
WIN
VS
LOSE
LOSE
But if your head cards tie, we will switch to poker mode!
ONE PAIR
In this mode, whoever has more cards that match their head card wins.
Thus, if both players play "rock" here, then the side with three rocks beats the side with two.
THREE OF A KIND
WIN
You'll play five rounds of this game...
...repeating the process five times!
TOTAL: 5 TURNS
The player with the most votes at the end wins!

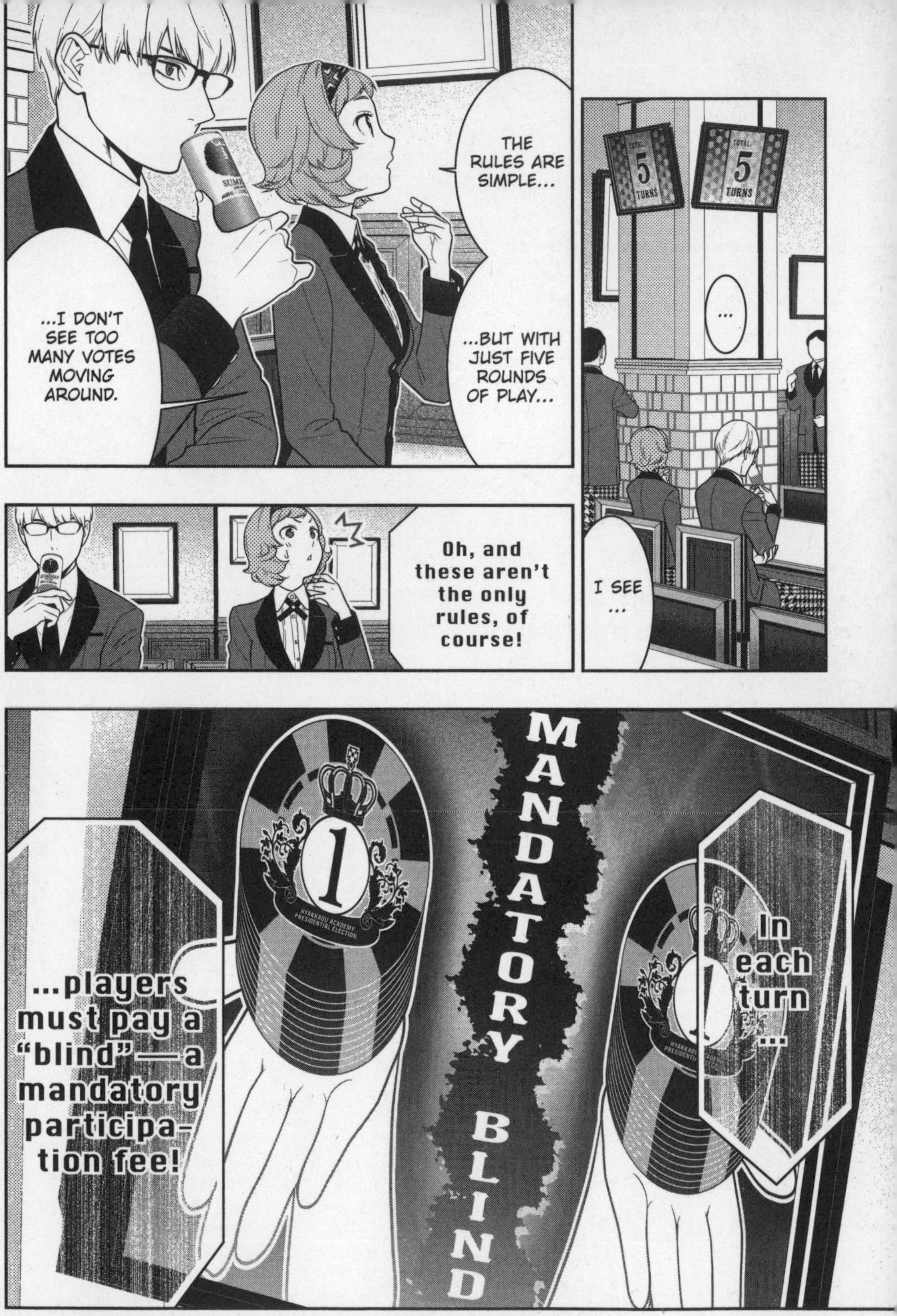
TOTAL: 5 TURNS
TOTAL: 5 TURNS
...
I SEE ...
THE RULES ARE SIMPLE...
...BUT WITH JUST FIVE ROUNDS OF PLAY...
...I DON'T SEE TOO MANY VOTES MOVING AROUND.
Oh, and these aren't the only rules, of course!
In each turn ...
MANDATORY BLIND
HYAKKAOU ACADEMY PRESIDENTIAL ELECTION
...players must pay a "blind"—a mandatory participation fee!

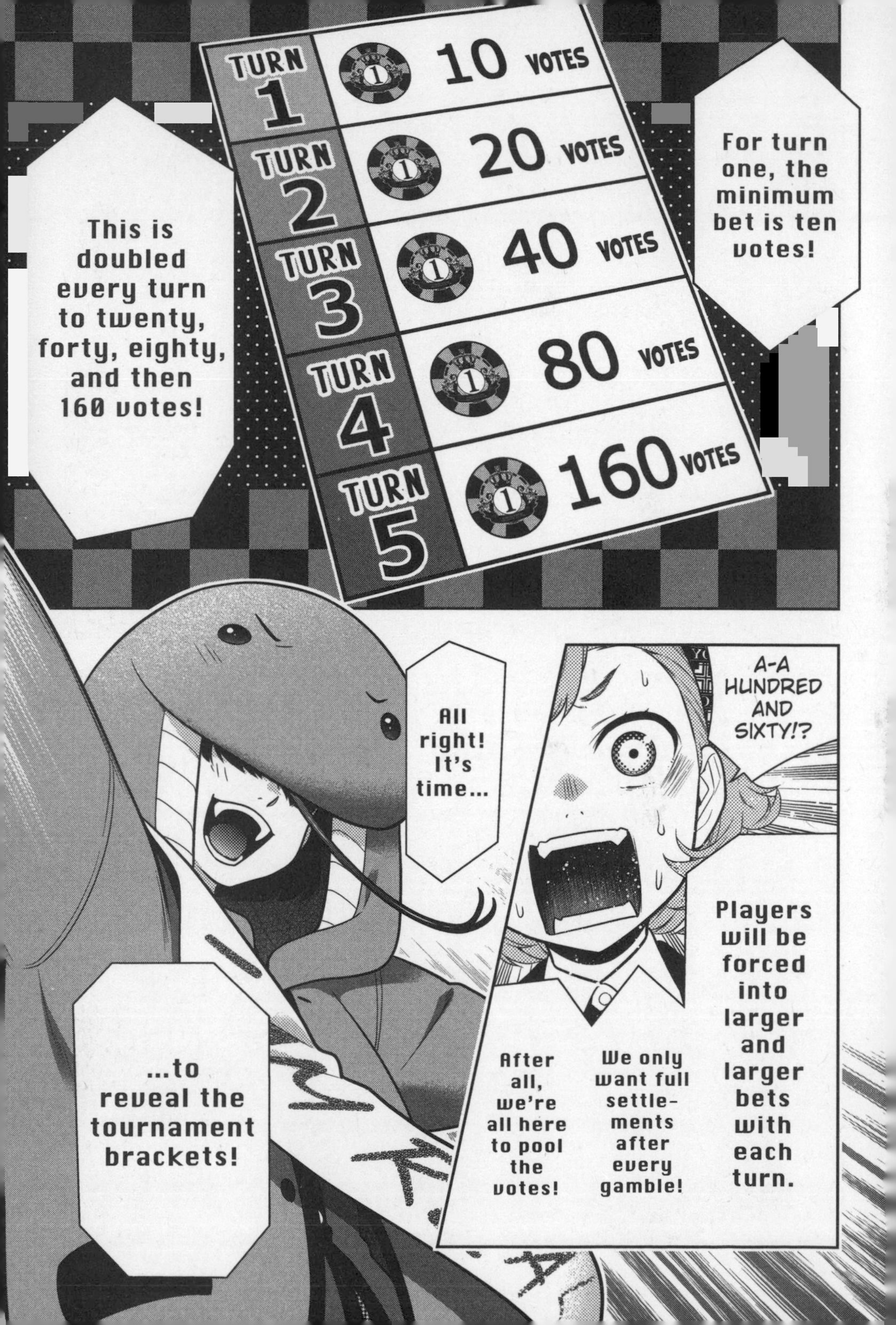
For turn one, the minimum bet is ten votes!
TURN 1 10 VOTES
TURN 2 20 VOTES
TURN 3 40 VOTES
TURN 4 80 VOTES
TURN 5 160 VOTES
This is doubled every turn to twenty, forty, eighty, and then 160 votes!
A-A HUNDRED AND SIXTY!?
Players will be forced into larger and larger bets with each turn.
We only want full settle-ments after every gamble!
After all, we're all here to pool the votes!
All right! It's time...
...to reveal the tournament brackets!

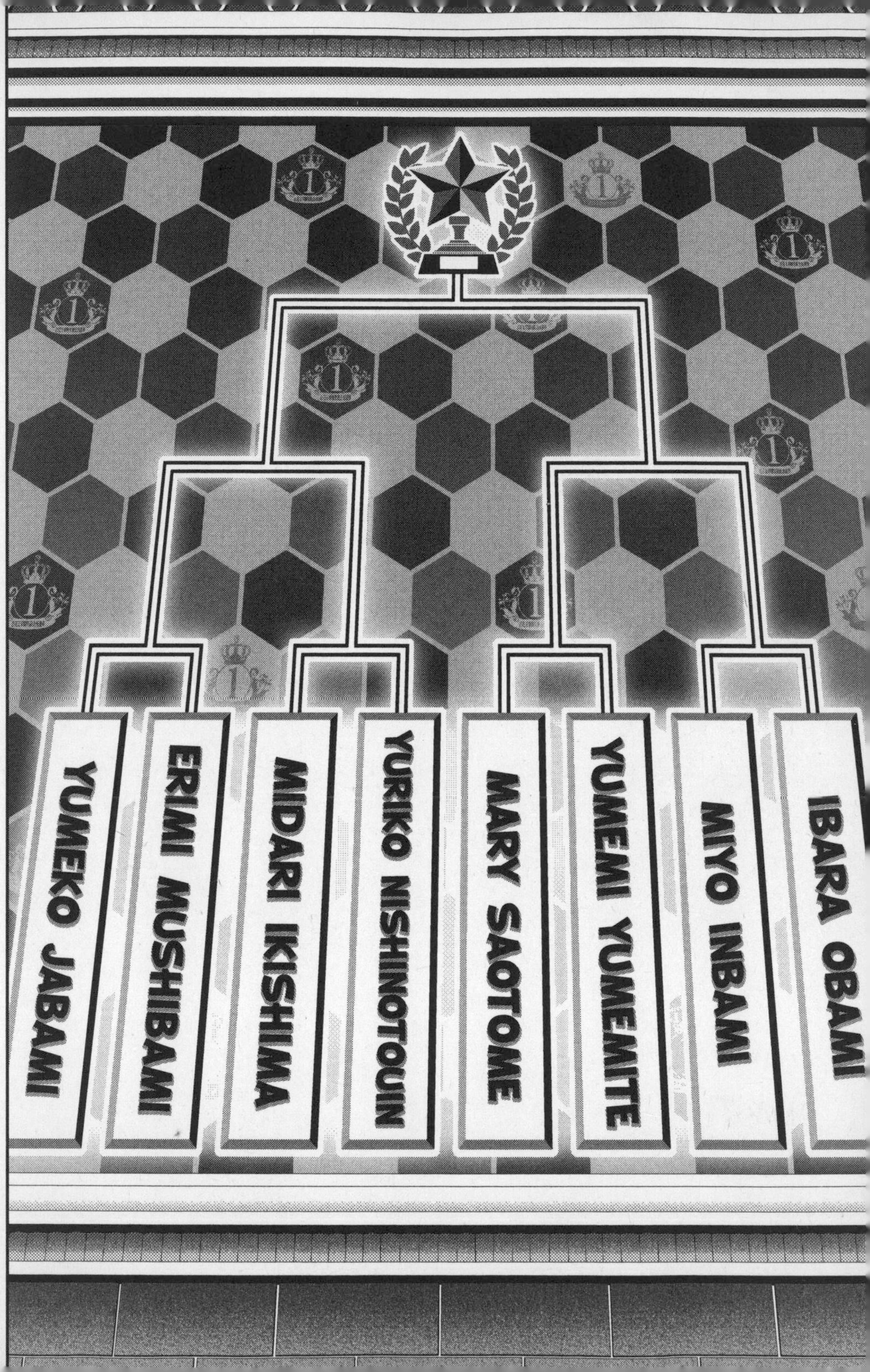
YUMEKO JABAMI
ERIMI MUSHIBAMI
MIDARI IKISHIMA
YURIKO NISHINOTOUIN
MARY SAOTOME
YUMEMI YUMEMITE
MIYO INBAMI
IBARA OBAMI

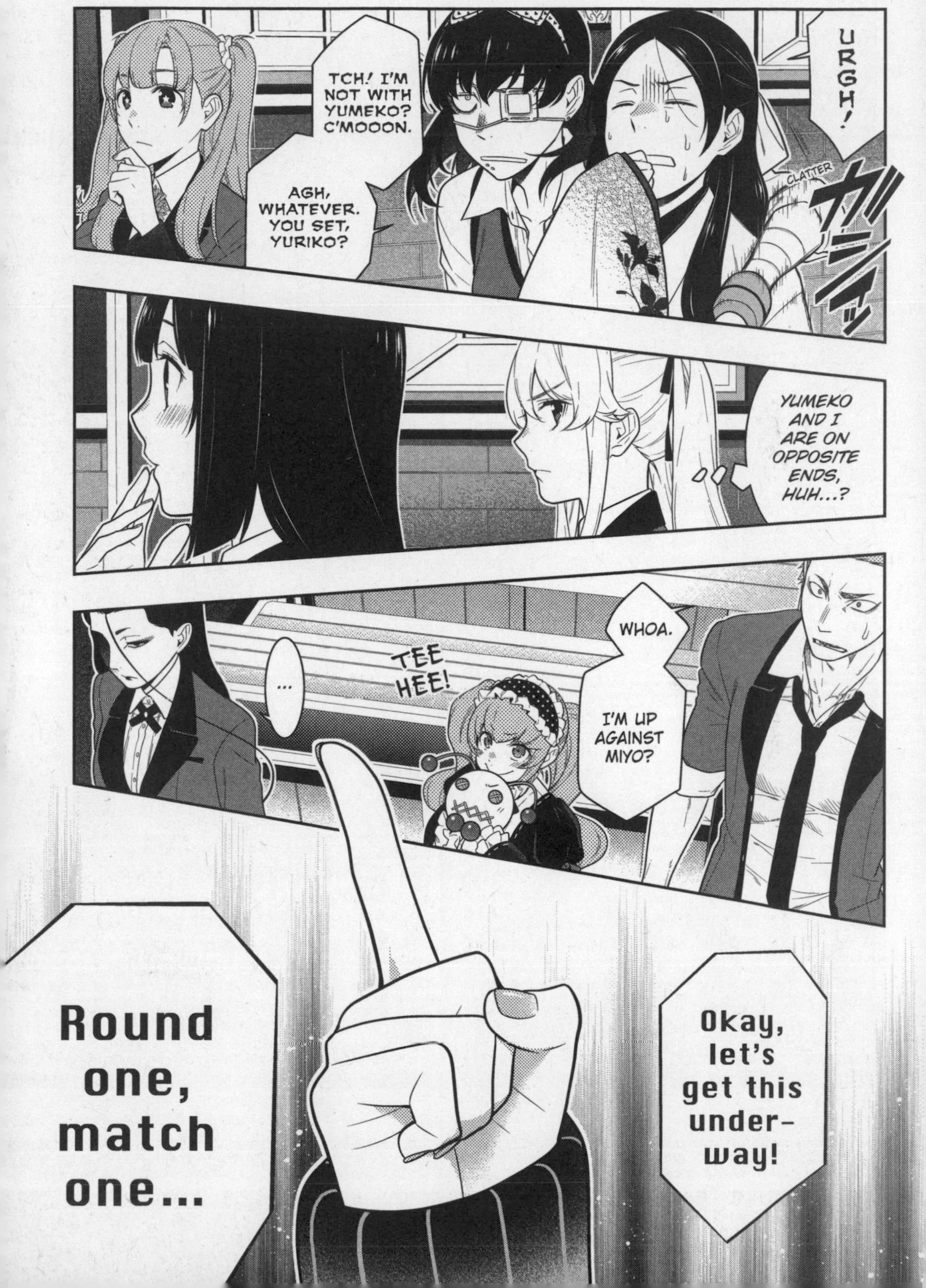
URGH!
CLATTER
TCH! I'M NOT WITH YUMEKO? C'MOOON.
AGH, WHATEVER. YOU SET, YURIKO?
YUMEKO AND I ARE ON OPPOSITE ENDS, HUH...?
WHOA.
I'M UP AGAINST MIYO?
TEE HEE!
...
Okay, let's get this under-way!
Round one, match one...

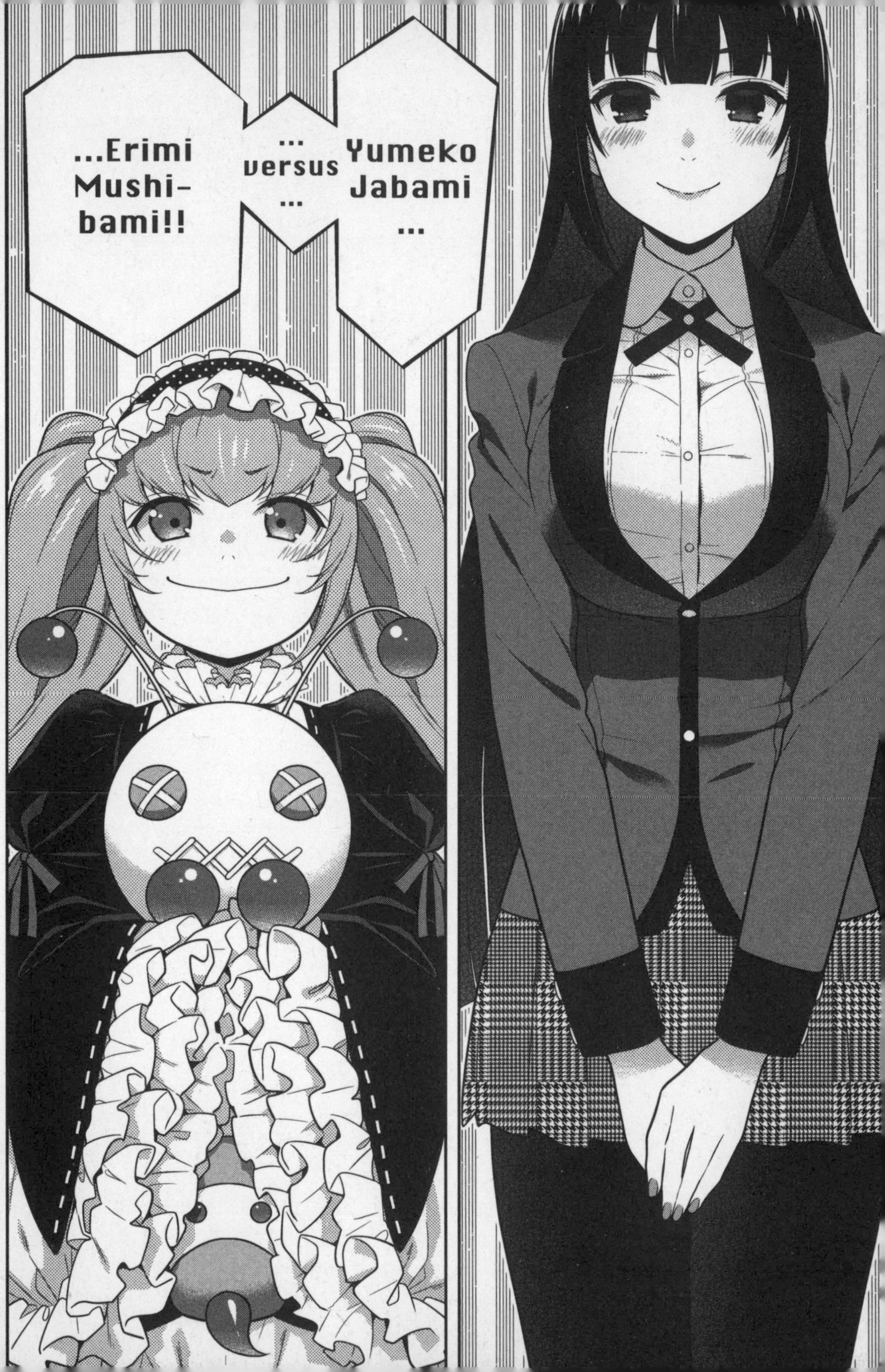
Yumeko Jabami ...
... versus ...
...Erimi Mushi-bami!!

KAKEGURUI
— Compulsive Gambler —

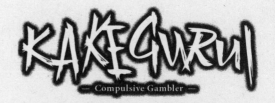

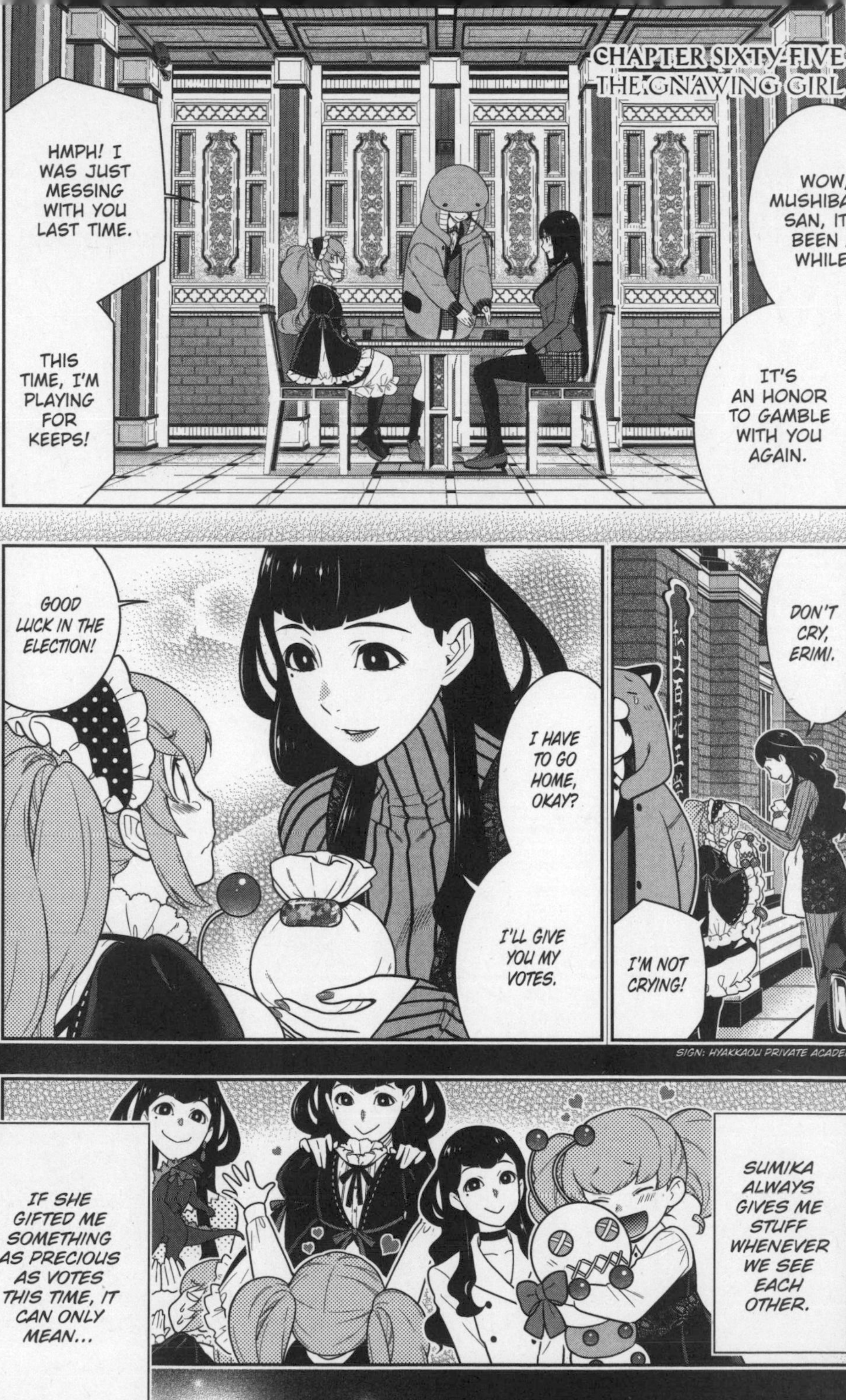
CHAPTER SIXTY-FIVE
THE GNAWING GIRL
WOW, MUSHIBAMI-SAN, IT'S BEEN A WHILE!
IT'S AN HONOR TO GAMBLE WITH YOU AGAIN.
HMPH! I WAS JUST MESSING WITH YOU LAST TIME.
THIS TIME, I'M PLAYING FOR KEEPS!
DON'T CRY, ERIMI.
I'M NOT CRYING!
I HAVE TO GO HOME, OKAY?
I'LL GIVE YOU MY VOTES.
GOOD LUCK IN THE ELECTION!
SIGN: HYAKKAOU PRIVATE ACADEMY
SUMIKA ALWAYS GIVES ME STUFF WHENEVER WE SEE EACH OTHER.
IF SHE GIFTED ME SOMETHING AS PRECIOUS AS VOTES THIS TIME, IT CAN ONLY MEAN...

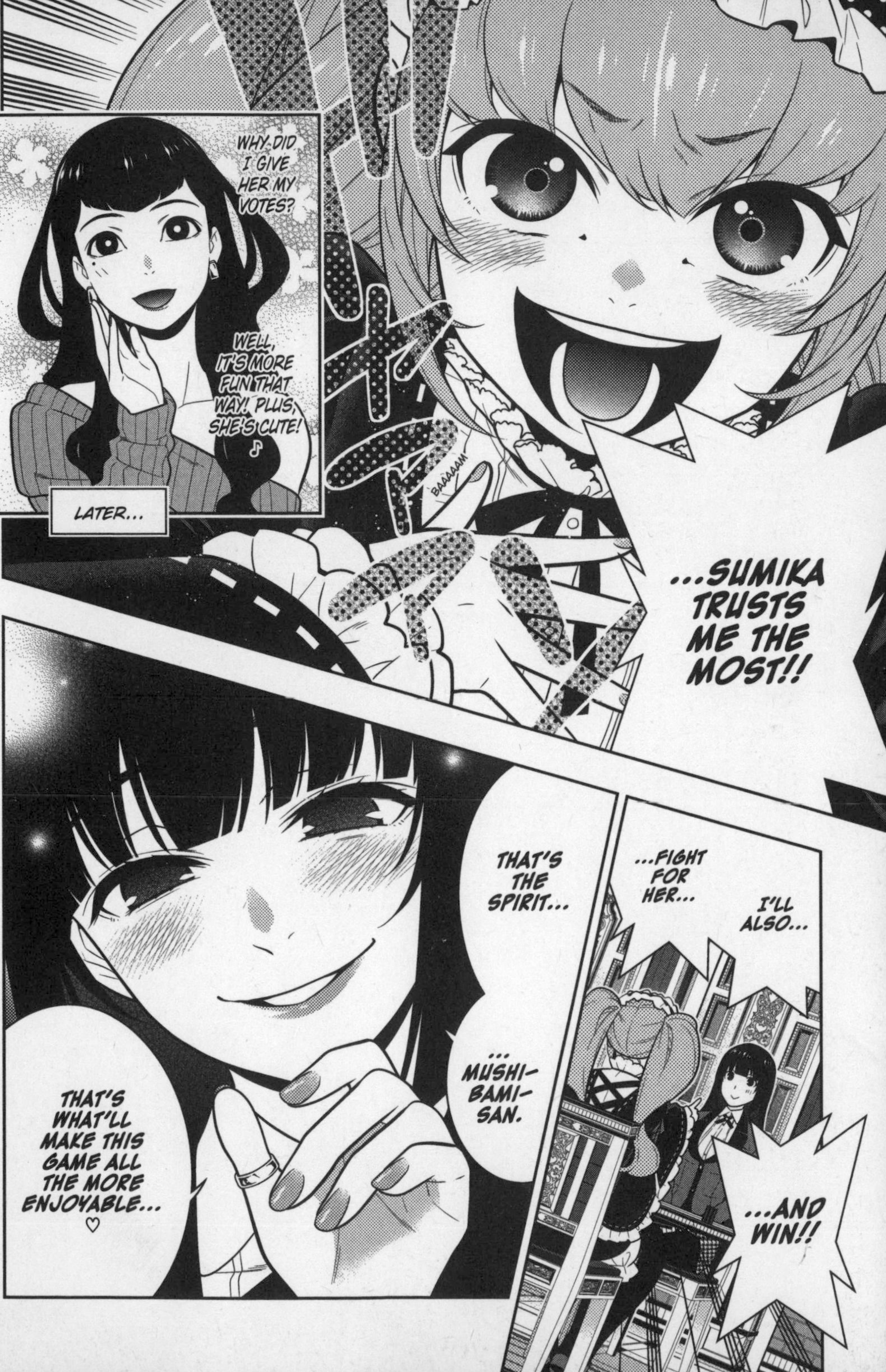

...SUMIKA TRUSTS ME THE MOST!!
BAAAAAM
WHY DID I GIVE HER MY VOTES?
WELL, IT'S MORE FUN THAT WAY! PLUS, SHE'S CUTE! ♪
LATER...
I'LL ALSO...
...FIGHT FOR HER...
...AND WIN!!
... MUSHI-BAMI-SAN.
THAT'S THE SPIRIT...
THAT'S WHAT'LL MAKE THIS GAME ALL THE MORE ENJOYABLE... ♡

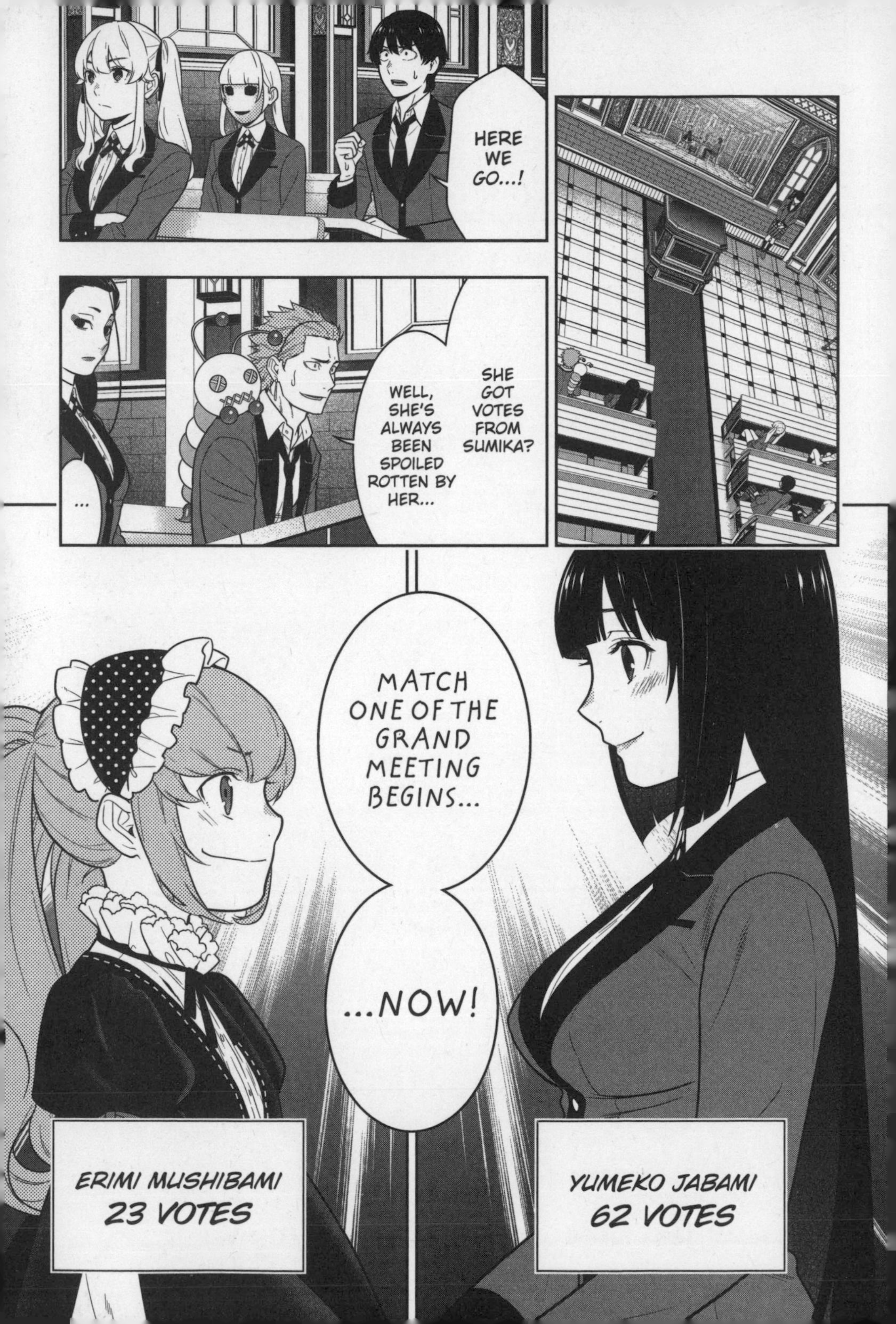
HERE WE GO...!
SHE GOT VOTES FROM SUMIKA?
WELL, SHE'S ALWAYS BEEN SPOILED ROTTEN BY HER...
...
MATCH ONE OF THE GRAND MEETING BEGINS...
...NOW!
YUMEKO JABAMI 62 VOTES
ERIMI MUSHIBAMI 23 VOTES

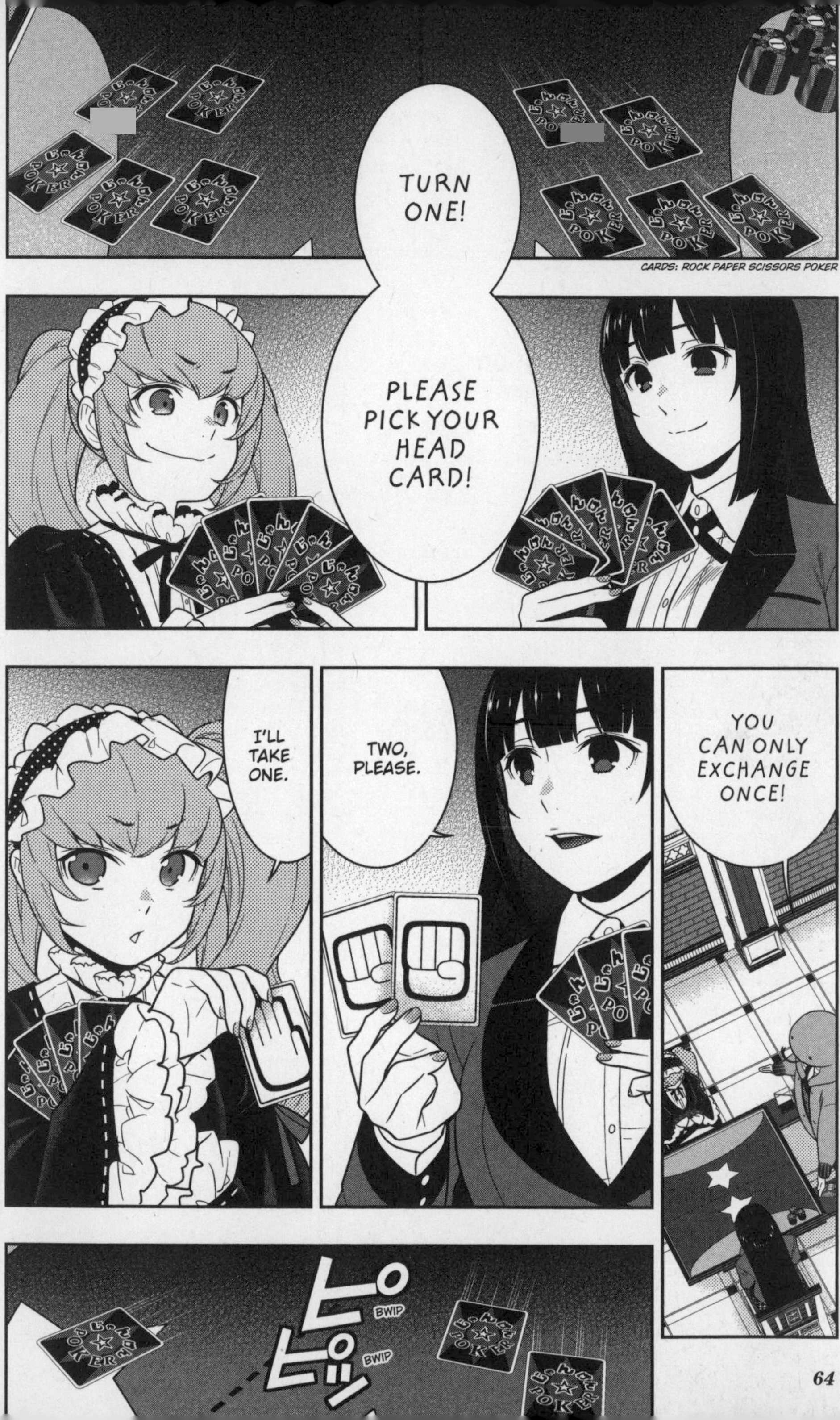
TURN ONE!
CARDS: ROCK PAPER SCISSORS POKER
PLEASE PICK YOUR HEAD CARD!
YOU CAN ONLY EXCHANGE ONCE!
TWO, PLEASE.
I'LL TAKE ONE.
BWIP
BWIP

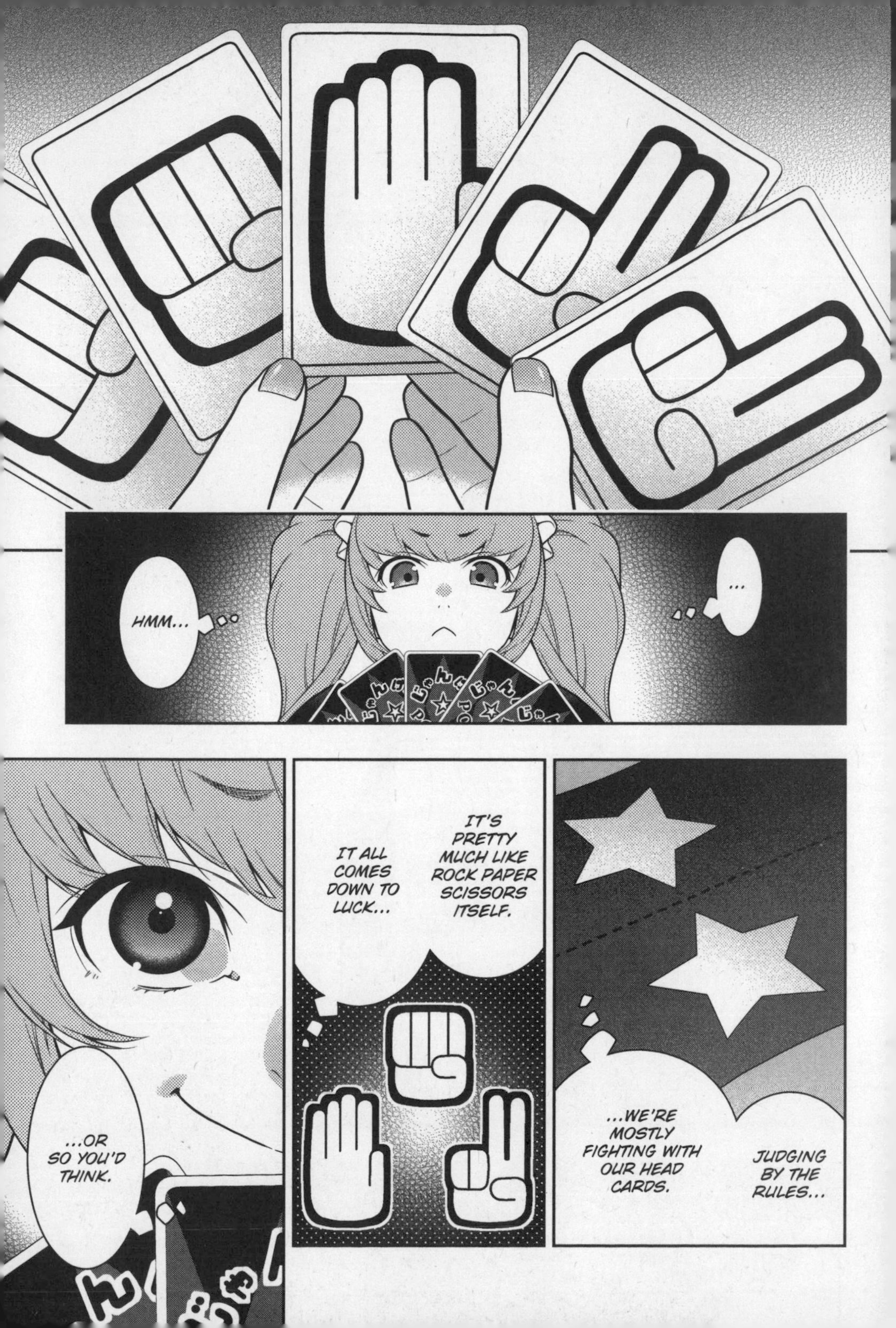
...
HMM...
JUDGING BY THE RULES...
...WE'RE MOSTLY FIGHTING WITH OUR HEAD CARDS.
IT'S PRETTY MUCH LIKE ROCK PAPER SCISSORS ITSELF.
IT ALL COMES DOWN TO LUCK...
...OR SO YOU'D THINK.

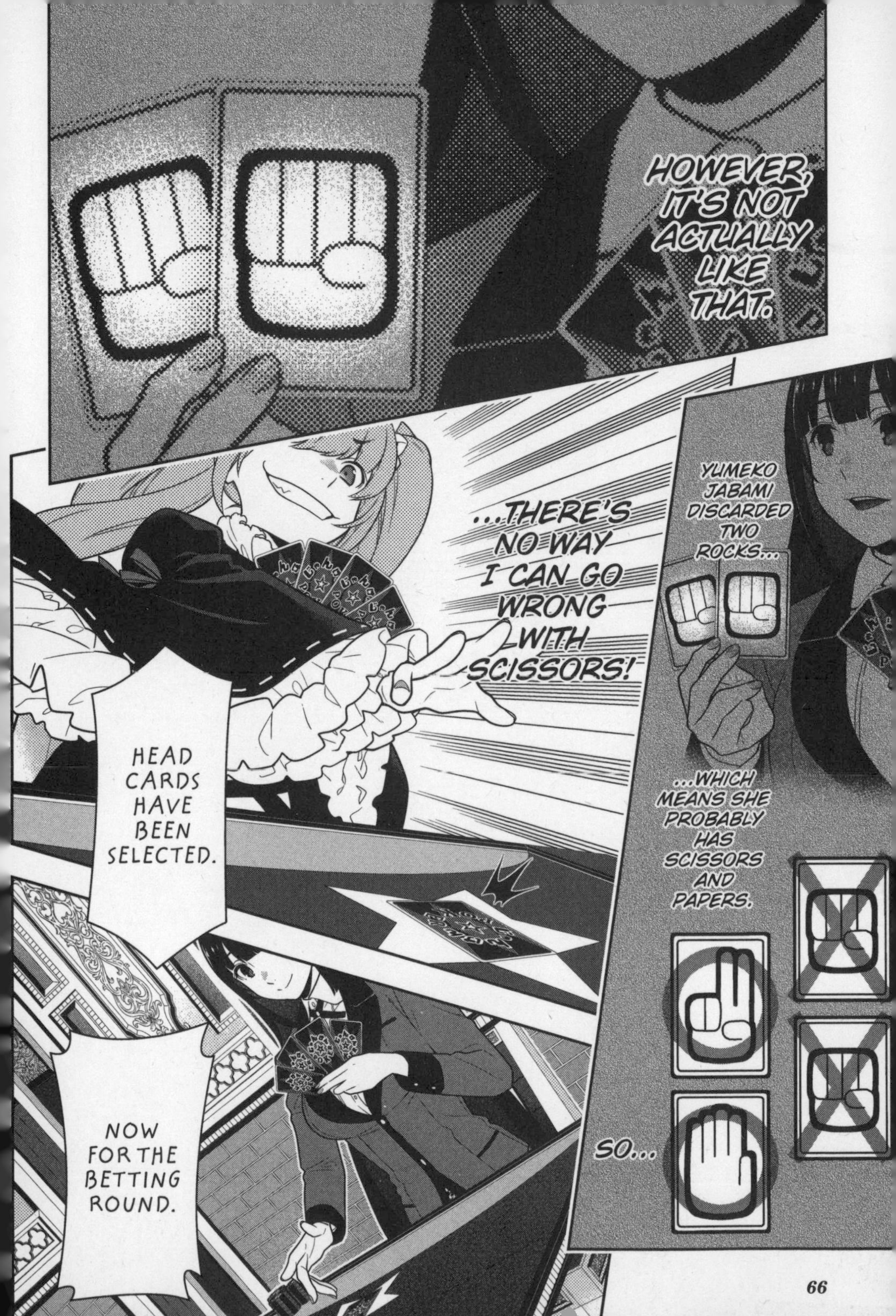
HOWEVER, IT'S NOT ACTUALLY LIKE THAT.
YUMEKO JABAMI DISCARDED TWO ROCKS...
...WHICH MEANS SHE PROBABLY HAS SCISSORS AND PAPERS.
SO...
...THERE'S NO WAY I CAN GO WRONG WITH SCISSORS!
HEAD CARDS HAVE BEEN SELECTED.
NOW FOR THE BETTING ROUND.

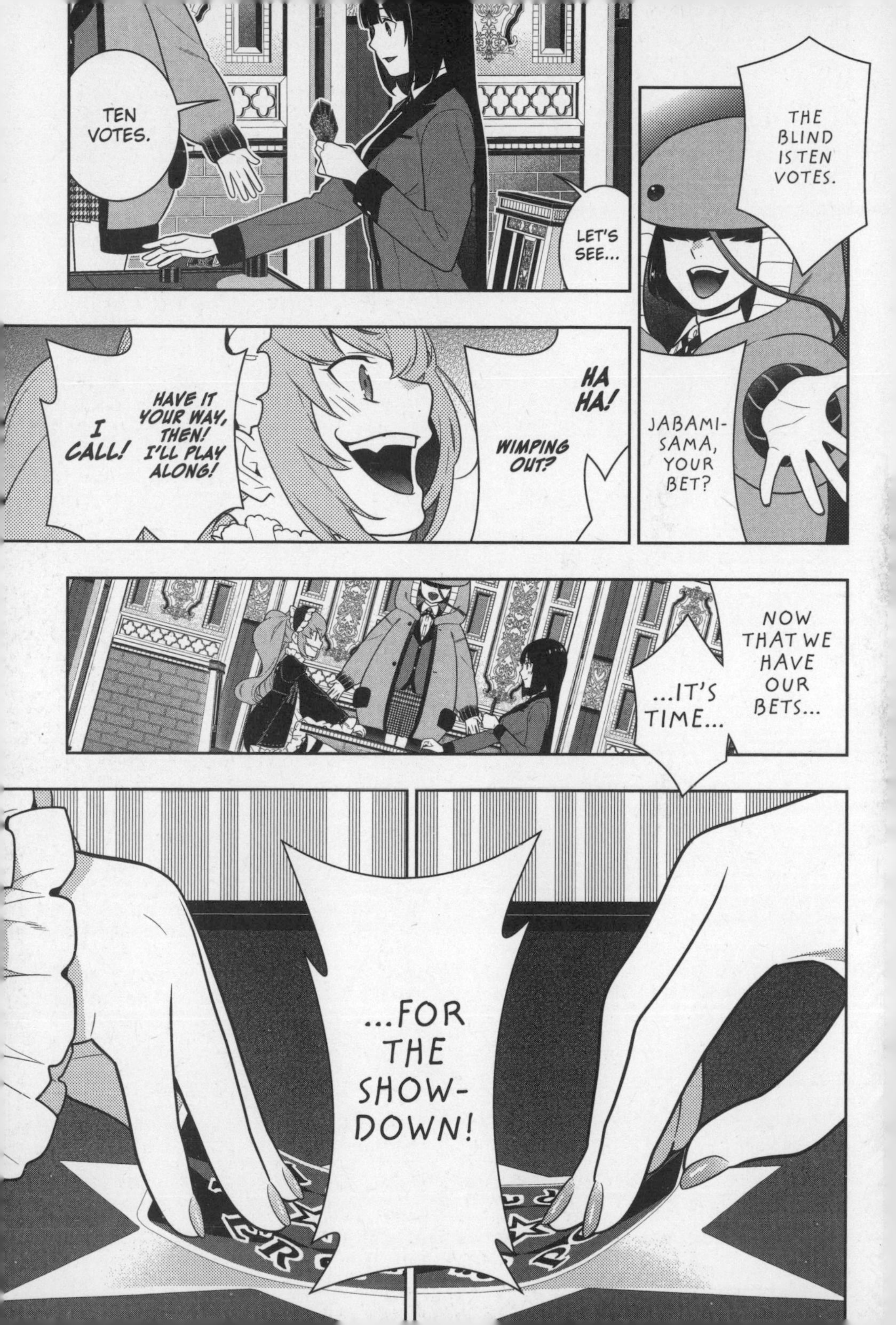
THE BLIND IS TEN VOTES.
JABAMI-SAMA, YOUR BET?
LET'S SEE...
TEN VOTES.
HA HA!
WIMPING OUT?
HAVE IT YOUR WAY, THEN! I'LL PLAY ALONG!
I CALL!
NOW THAT WE HAVE OUR BETS...
...IT'S TIME...
...FOR THE SHOW-DOWN!

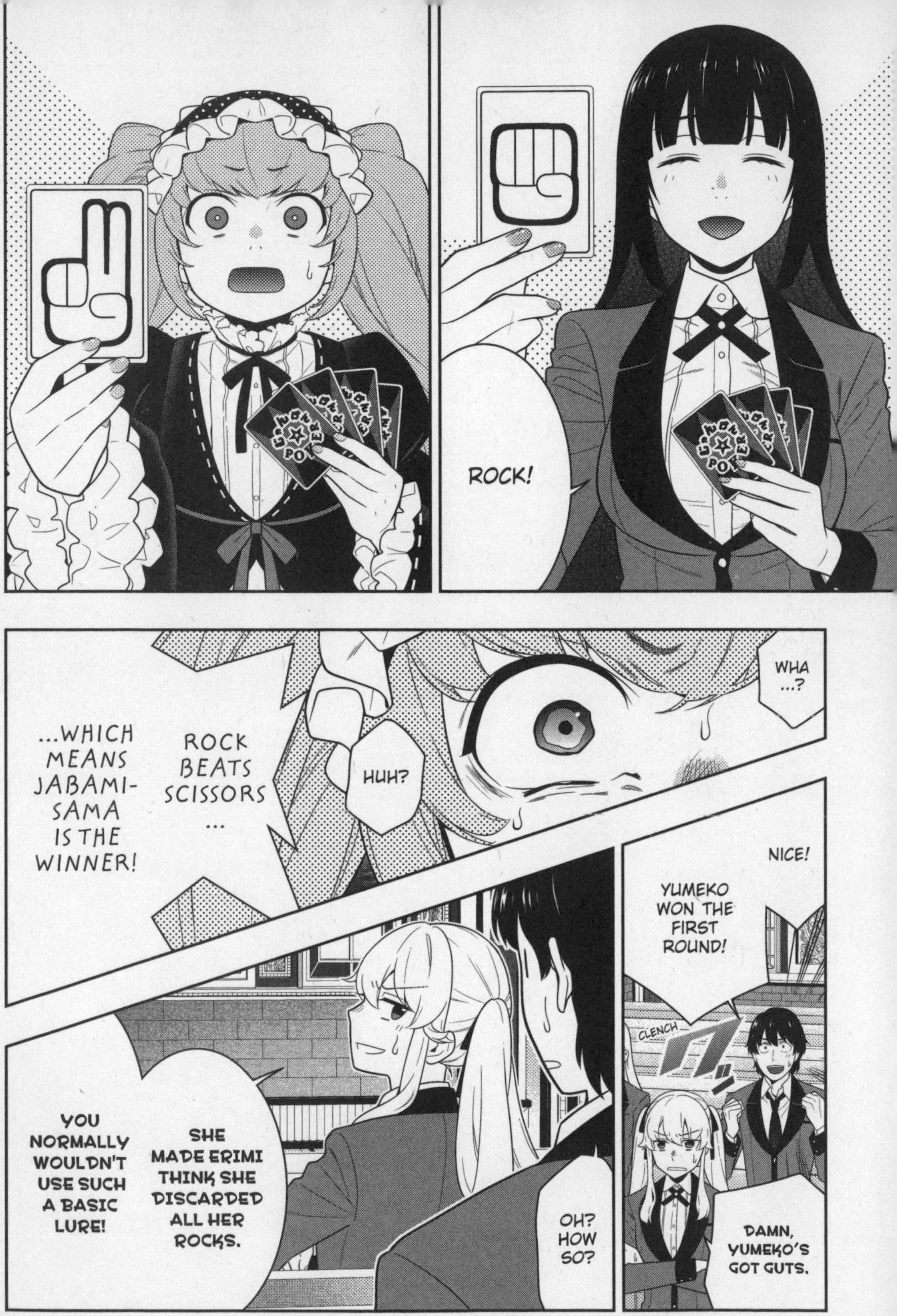
ROCK!
WHA ...?
HUH?
ROCK BEATS SCISSORS ...
...WHICH MEANS JABAMI-SAMA IS THE WINNER!
NICE!
YUMEKO WON THE FIRST ROUND!
CLENCH
DAMN, YUMEKO'S GOT GUTS.
OH? HOW SO?
SHE MADE ERIMI THINK SHE DISCARDED ALL HER ROCKS.
YOU NORMALLY WOULDN'T USE SUCH A BASIC LURE!

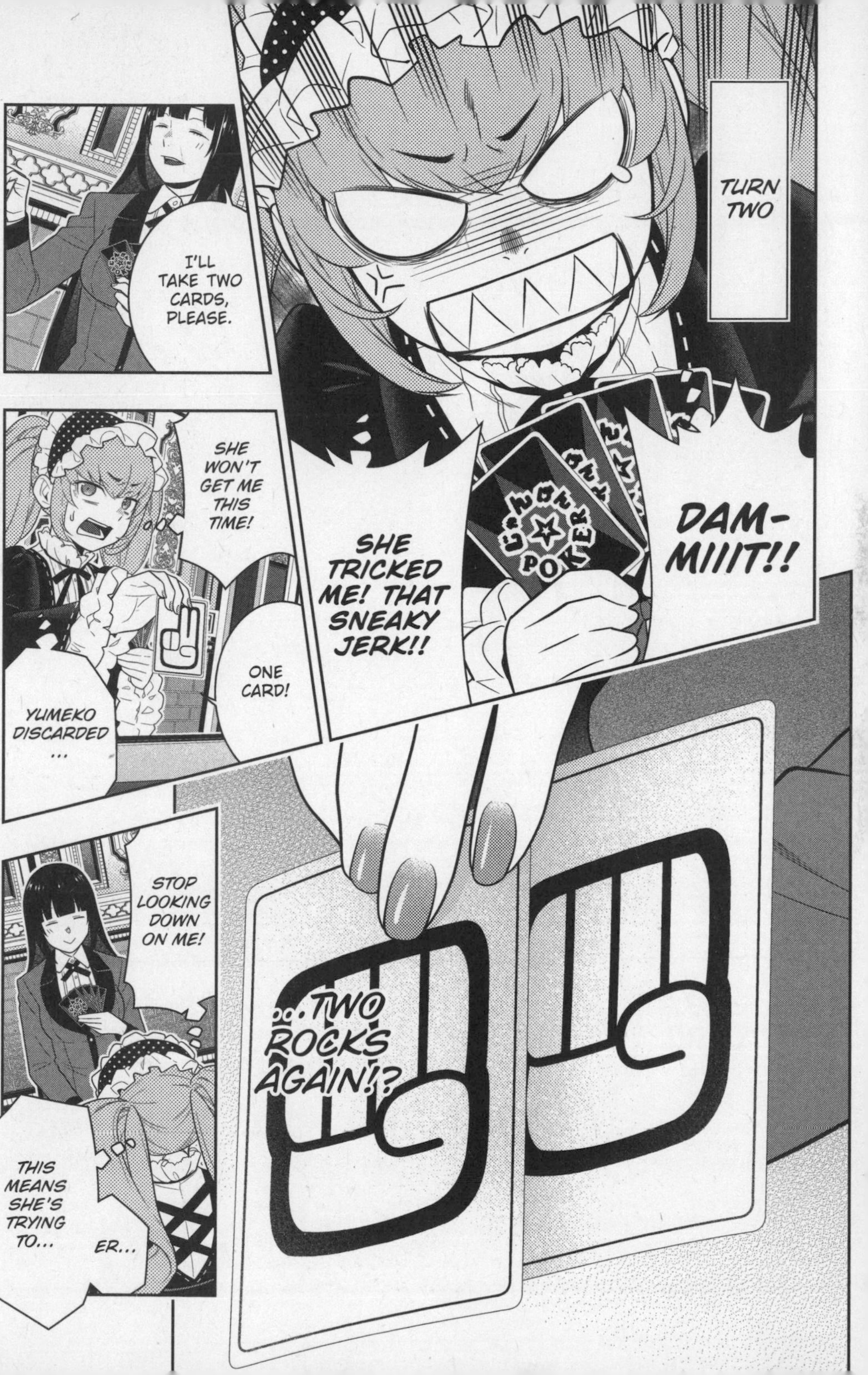
TURN TWO
DAM-MIIIT!!
SHE TRICKED ME! THAT SNEAKY JERK!!
I'LL TAKE TWO CARDS, PLEASE.
SHE WON'T GET ME THIS TIME!
ONE CARD!
YUMEKO DISCARDED ...
...TWO ROCKS AGAIN!?
STOP LOOKING DOWN ON ME!
THIS MEANS SHE'S TRYING TO...
ER...

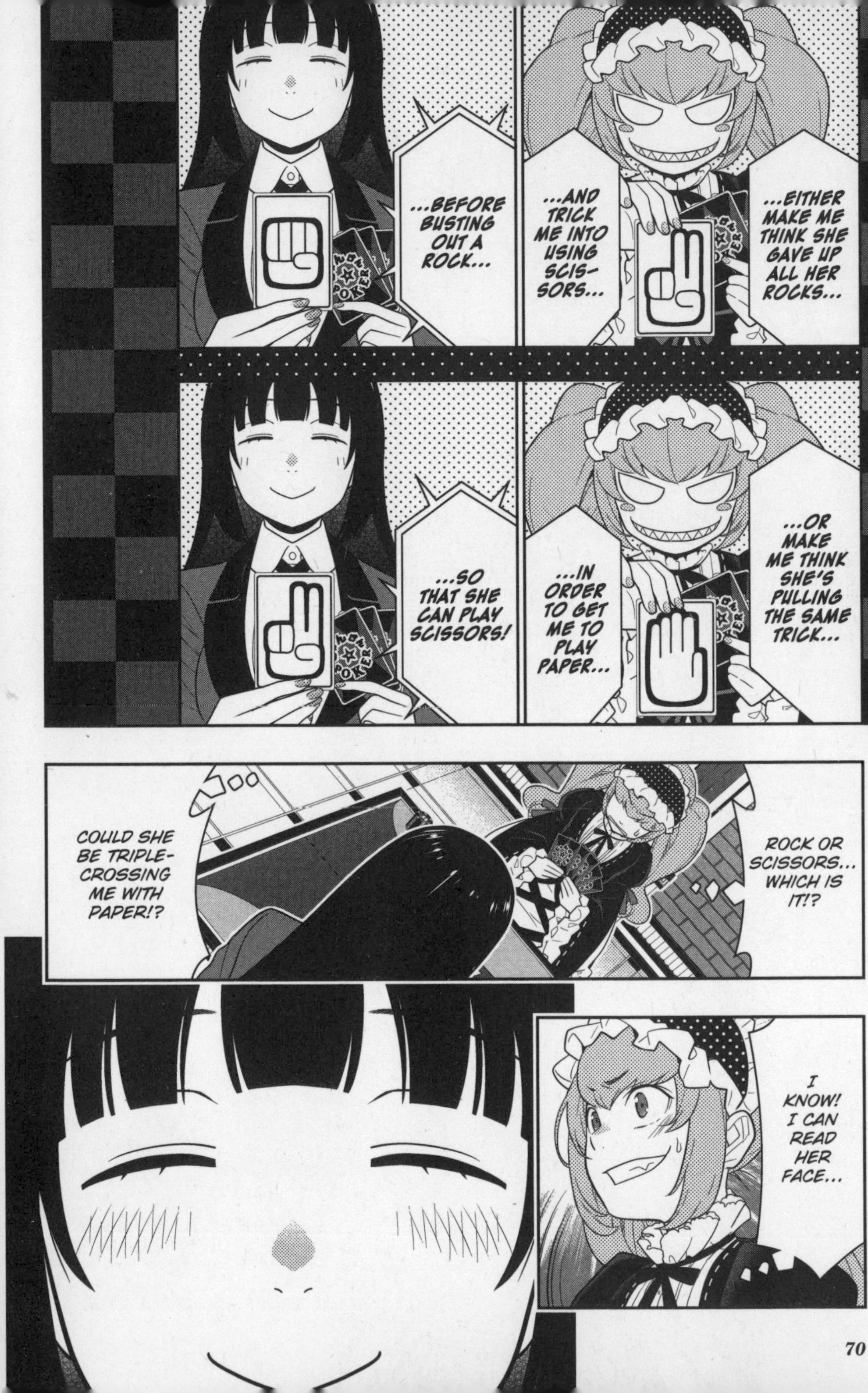
...EITHER MAKE ME THINK SHE GAVE UP ALL HER ROCKS...
...AND TRICK ME INTO USING SCIS-SORS...
...BEFORE BUSTING OUT A ROCK...
POKER
...OR MAKE ME THINK SHE'S PULLING THE SAME TRICK...
...IN ORDER TO GET ME TO PLAY PAPER...
...SO THAT SHE CAN PLAY SCISSORS!
ROCK OR SCISSORS... WHICH IS IT!?
COULD SHE BE TRIPLE-CROSSING ME WITH PAPER!?
I KNOW! I CAN READ HER FACE...

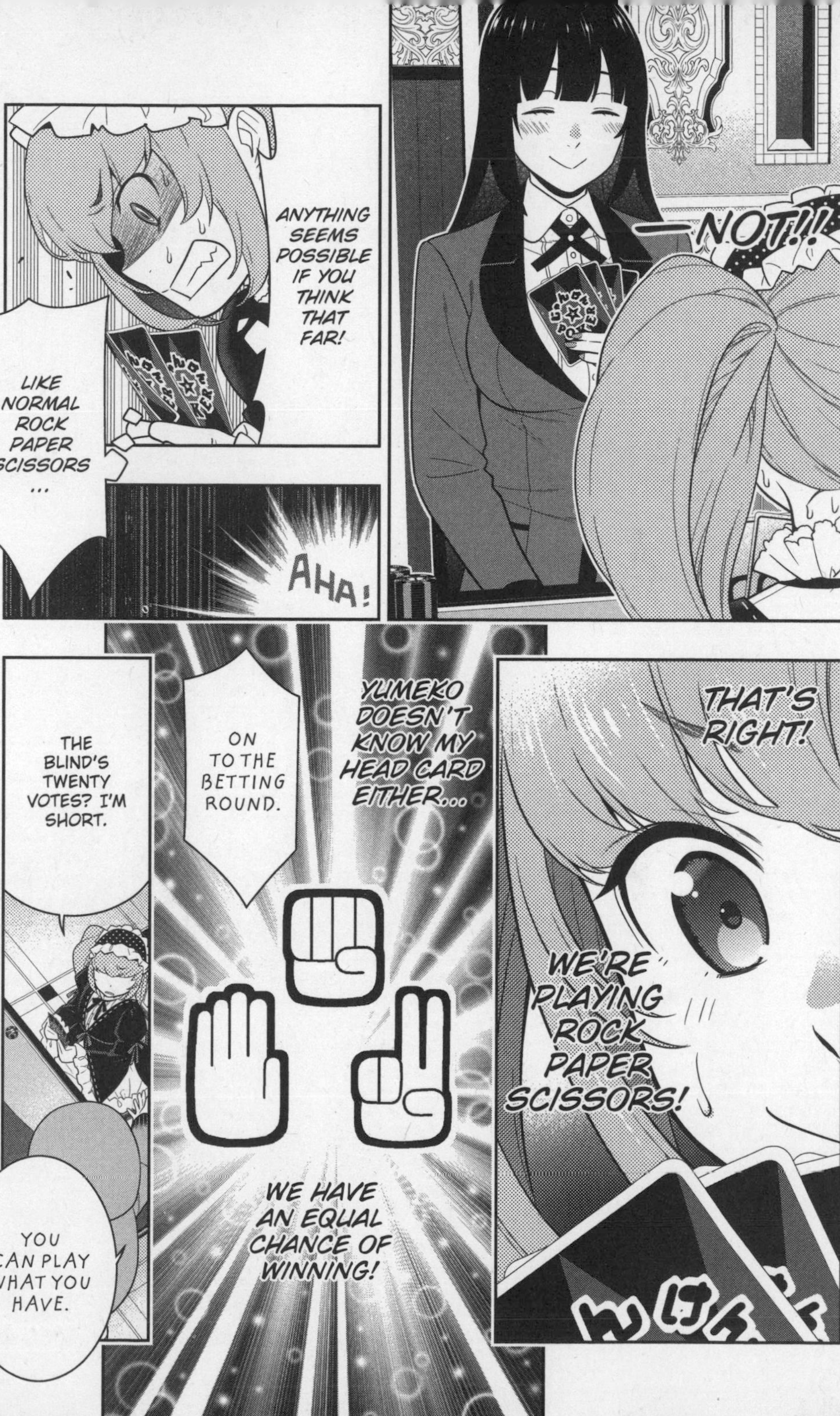
—NOT!!!
ANYTHING SEEMS POSSIBLE IF YOU THINK THAT FAR!
LIKE NORMAL ROCK PAPER SCISSORS...
AHA!
THAT'S RIGHT!
WE'RE PLAYING ROCK PAPER SCISSORS!
YUMEKO DOESN'T KNOW MY HEAD CARD EITHER...
ON TO THE BETTING ROUND.
WE HAVE AN EQUAL CHANCE OF WINNING!
THE BLIND'S TWENTY VOTES? I'M SHORT.
YOU CAN PLAY WHAT YOU HAVE.

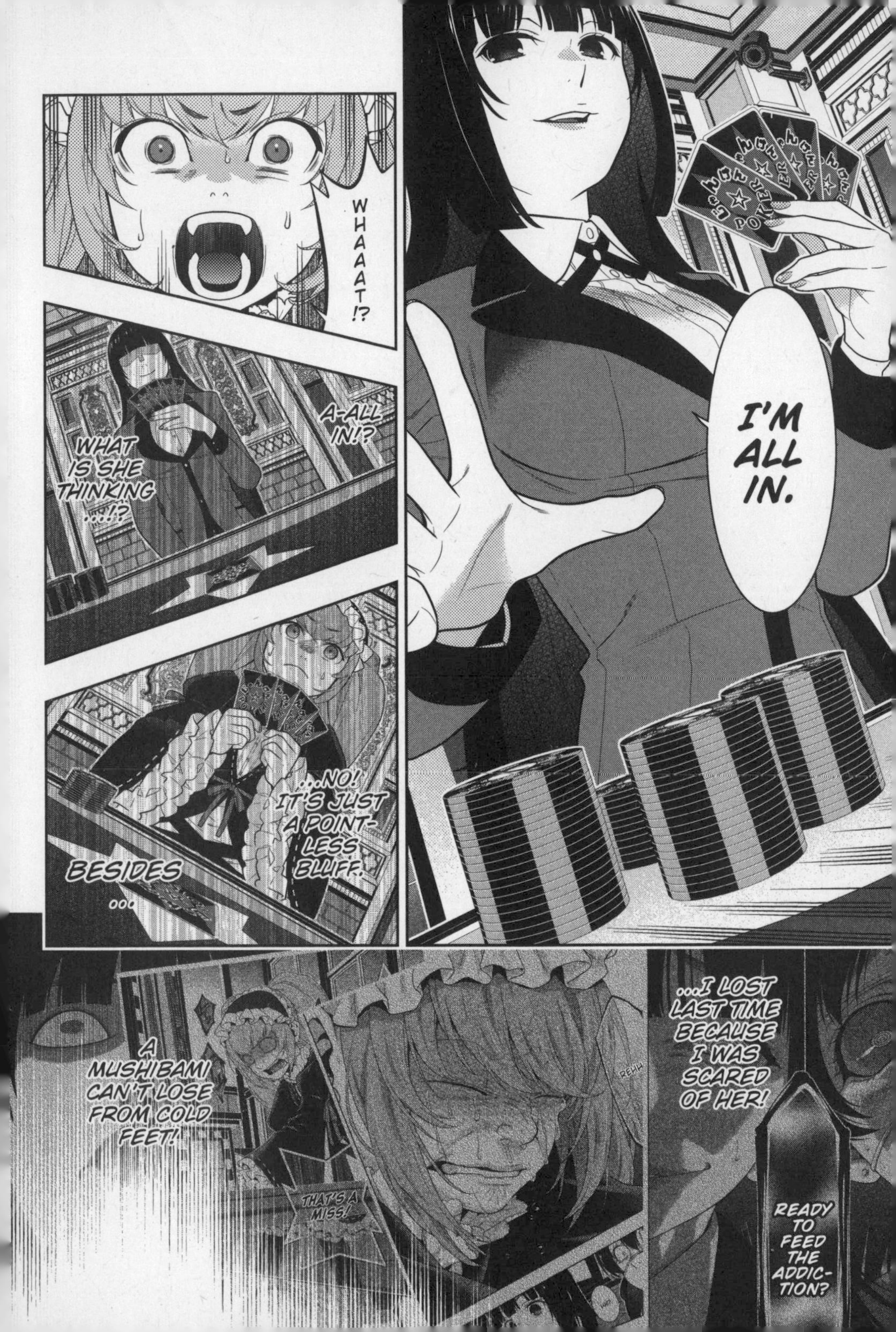
I'M ALL IN.
WHAAAT!?
A-ALL IN!?
WHAT IS SHE THINKING ...!?
...NO! IT'S JUST A POINTLESS BLUFF.
BESIDES ...
...I LOST LAST TIME BECAUSE I WAS SCARED OF HER!
READY TO FEED THE ADDICTION?
THAT'S A MISS!
A MUSHIBAMI CAN'T LOSE FROM COLD FEET!

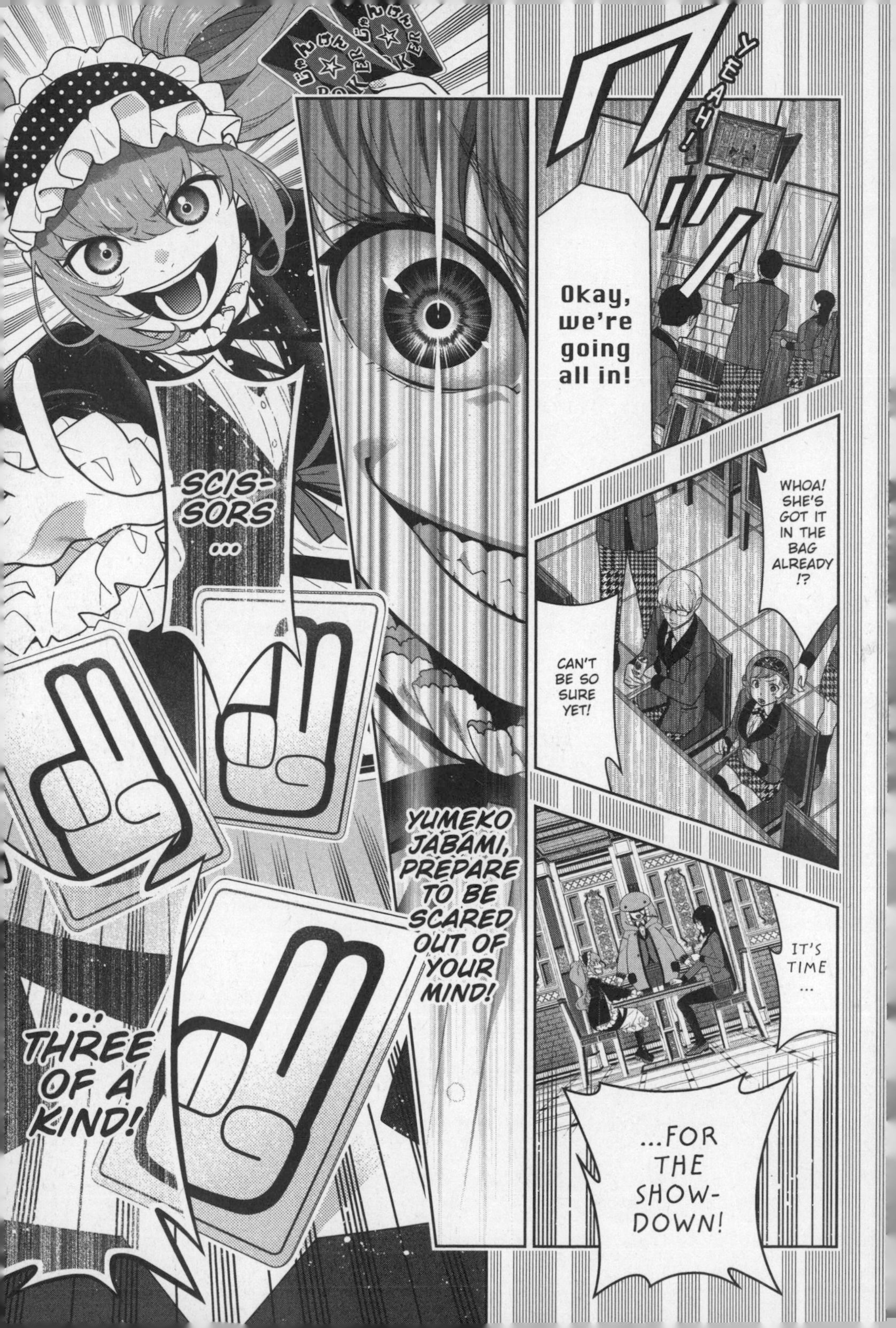
YEAH!!
Okay, we're going all in!
WHOA! SHE'S GOT IT IN THE BAG ALREADY!?
CAN'T BE SO SURE YET!
IT'S TIME...
...FOR THE SHOW-DOWN!
YUMEKO JABAMI, PREPARE TO BE SCARED OUT OF YOUR MIND!
SCIS-SORS...
...THREE OF A KIND!

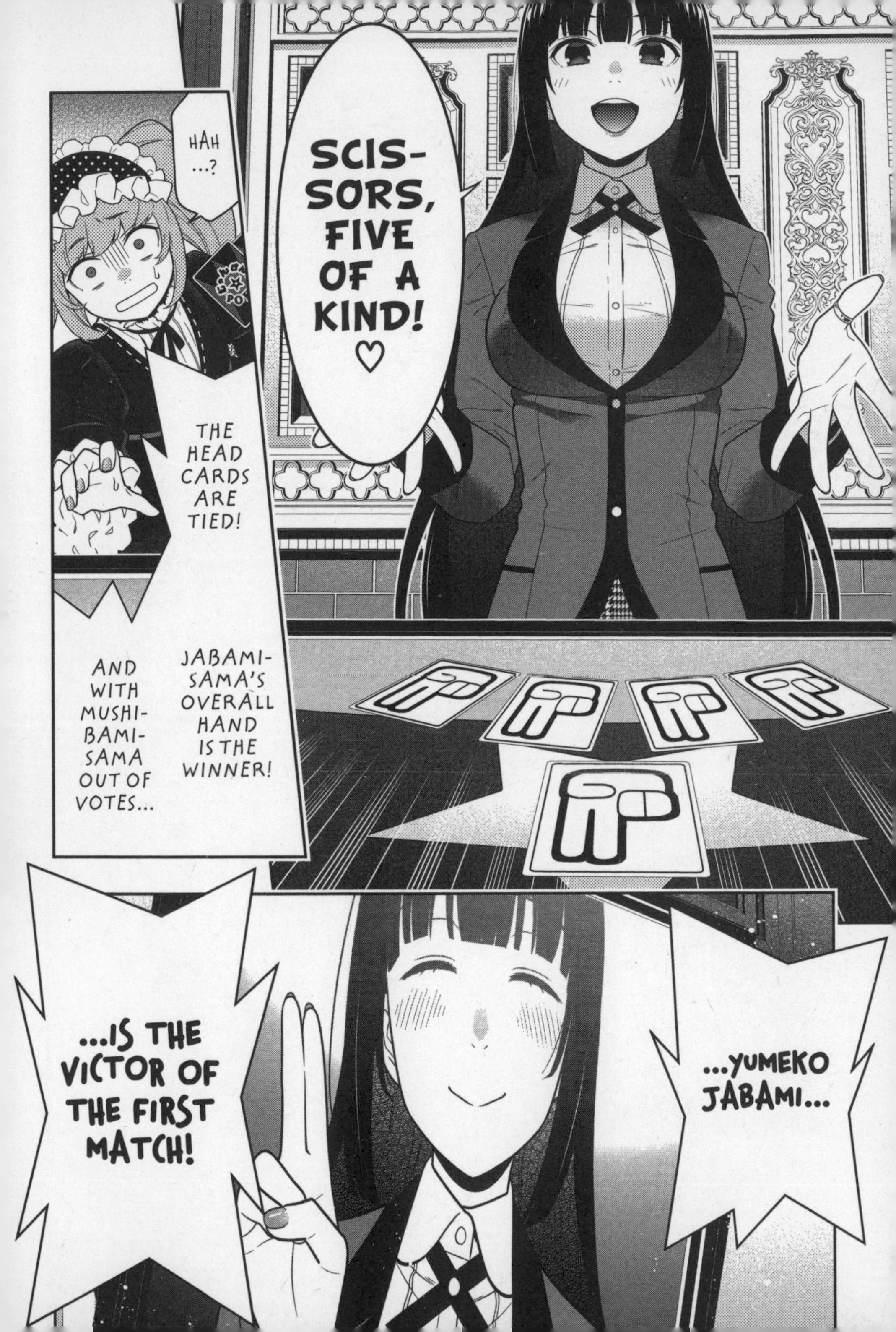
SCIS-SORS, FIVE OF A KIND! ♡
HAH ...?
THE HEAD CARDS ARE TIED!
JABAMI-SAMA'S OVERALL HAND IS THE WINNER!
AND WITH MUSHI-BAMI-SAMA OUT OF VOTES...
...YUMEKO JABAMI...
...IS THE VICTOR OF THE FIRST MATCH!

CHAPTER SIXTY-SIX THE FIGHTING GIRLS

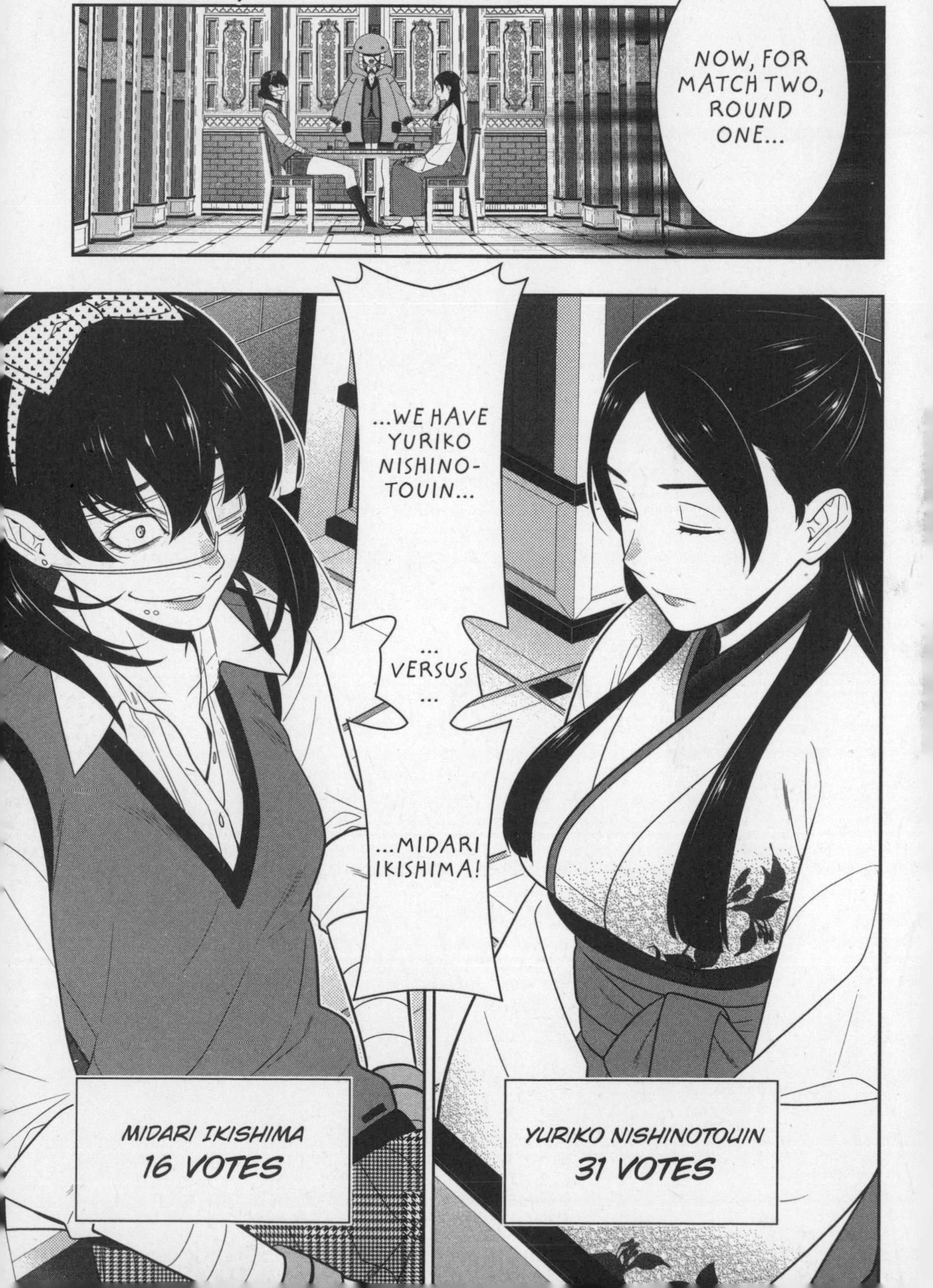
NOW, FOR MATCH TWO, ROUND ONE...
...WE HAVE YURIKO NISHINO-TOUIN...
...VERSUS...
...MIDARI IKISHIMA!
YURIKO NISHINOTOUIN 31 VOTES
MIDARI IKISHIMA 16 VOTES

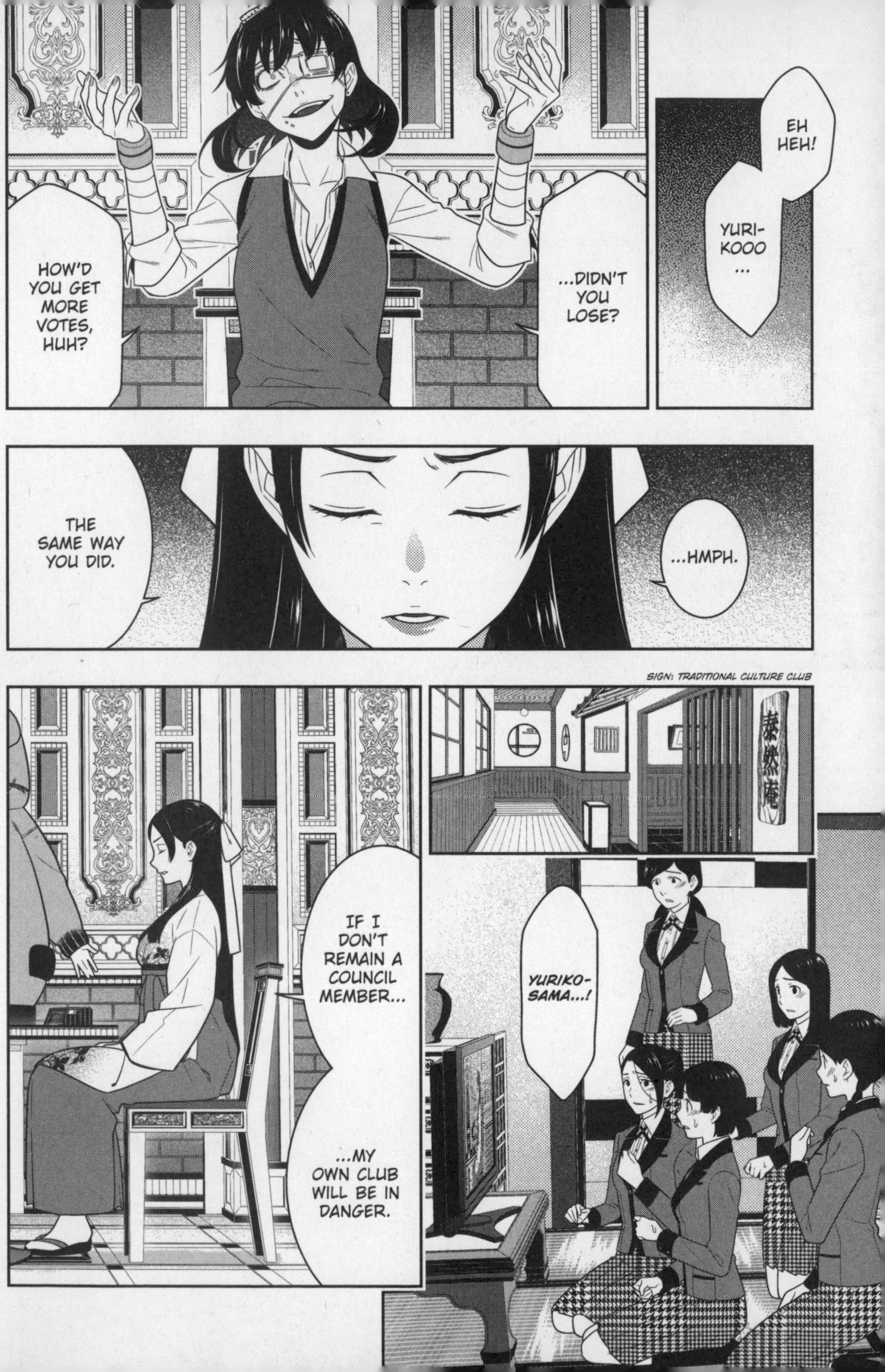
EH HEH!
YURI-KOOO ...
...DIDN'T YOU LOSE?
HOW'D YOU GET MORE VOTES, HUH?
...HMPH.
THE SAME WAY YOU DID.
SIGN: TRADITIONAL CULTURE CLUB
泰然庵
YURIKO-SAMA...!
IF I DON'T REMAIN A COUNCIL MEMBER...
...MY OWN CLUB WILL BE IN DANGER.

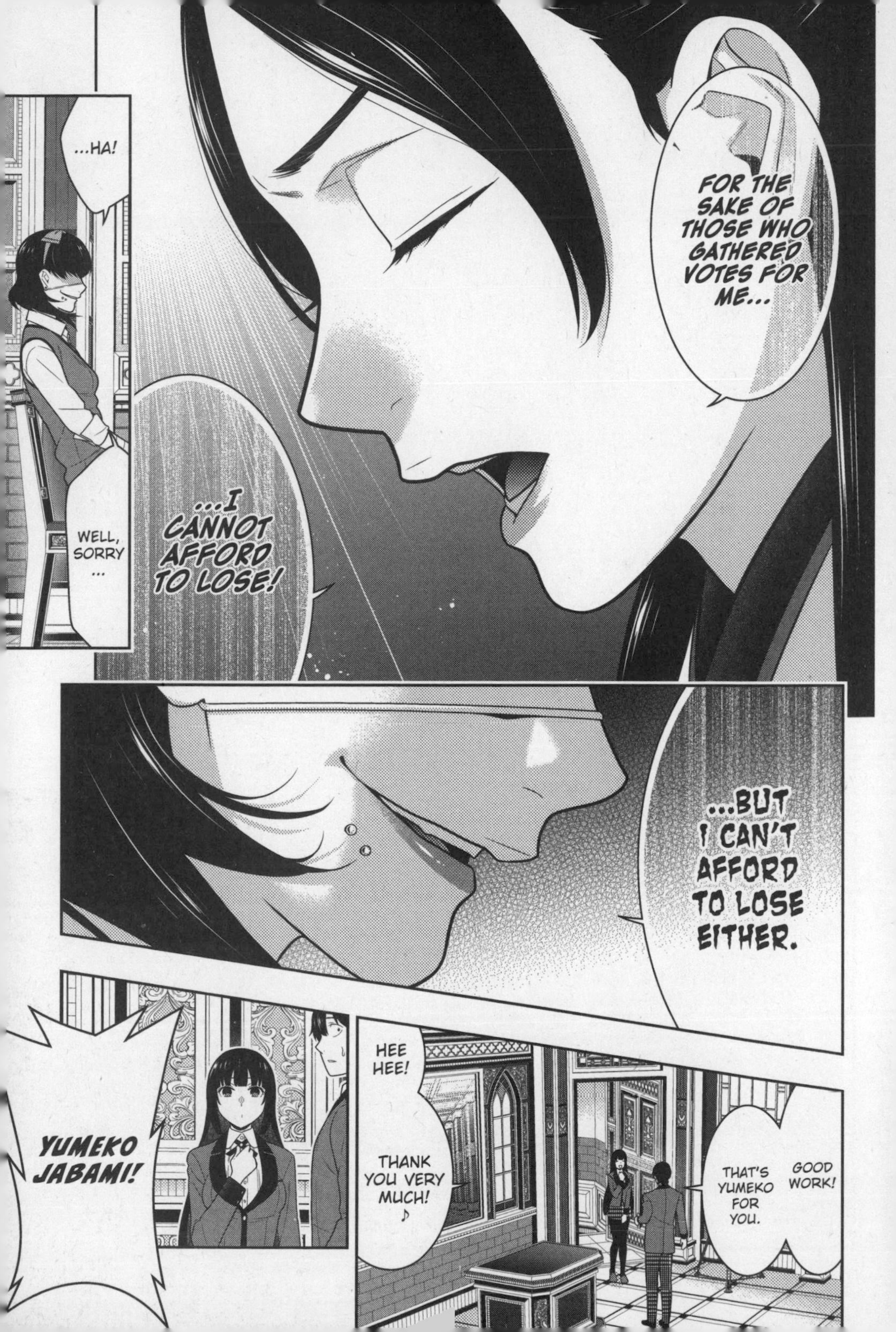
FOR THE SAKE OF THOSE WHO GATHERED VOTES FOR ME...
...I CANNOT AFFORD TO LOSE!
...HA!
WELL, SORRY ...
...BUT I CAN'T AFFORD TO LOSE EITHER.
GOOD WORK!
THAT'S YUMEKO FOR YOU.
HEE HEE!
THANK YOU VERY MUCH! ♪
YUMEKO JABAMI!

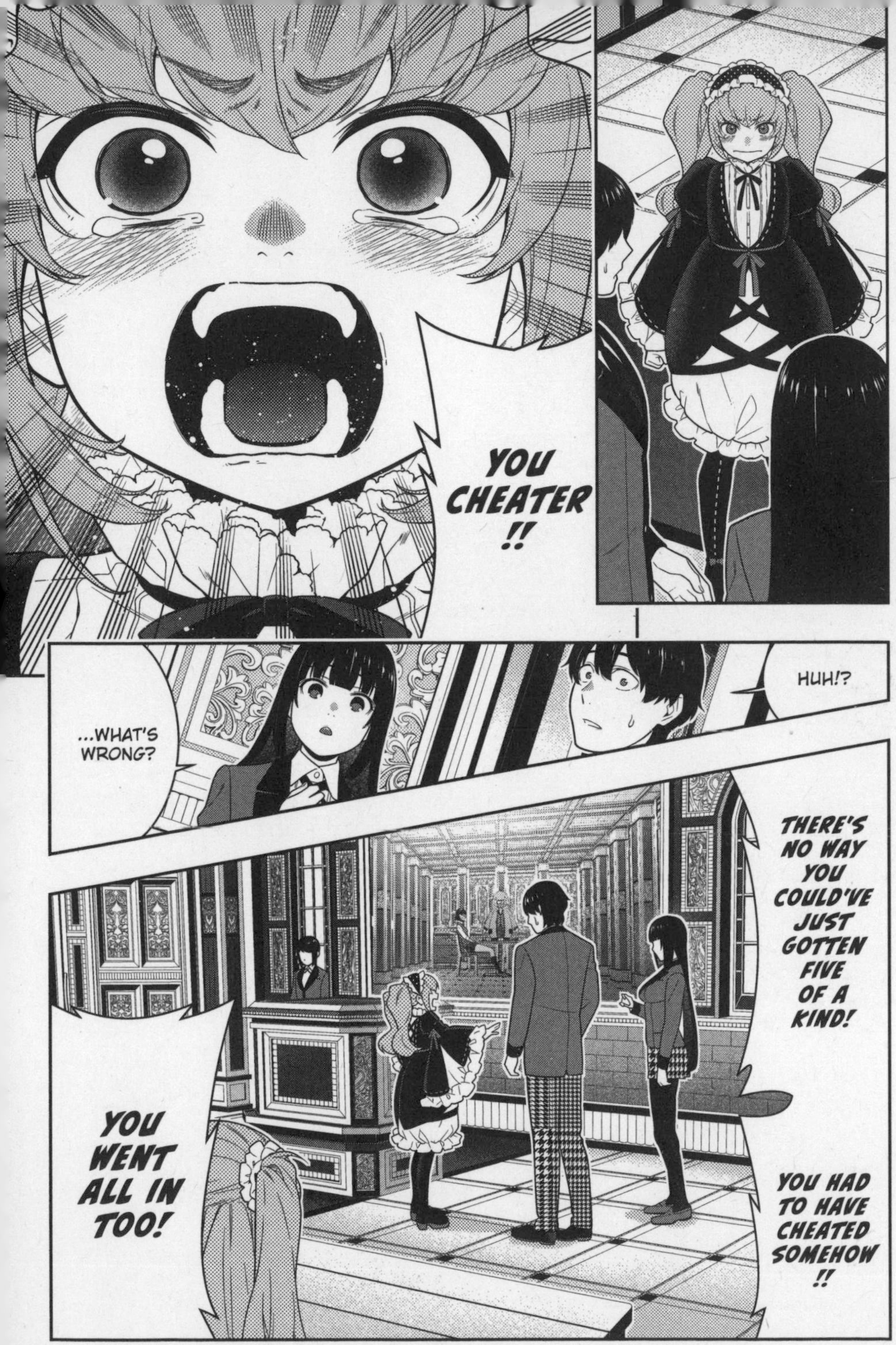
YOU CHEATER!!
HUH!?
...WHAT'S WRONG?
THERE'S NO WAY YOU COULD'VE JUST GOTTEN FIVE OF A KIND!
YOU WENT ALL IN TOO!
YOU HAD TO HAVE CHEATED SOMEHOW!!

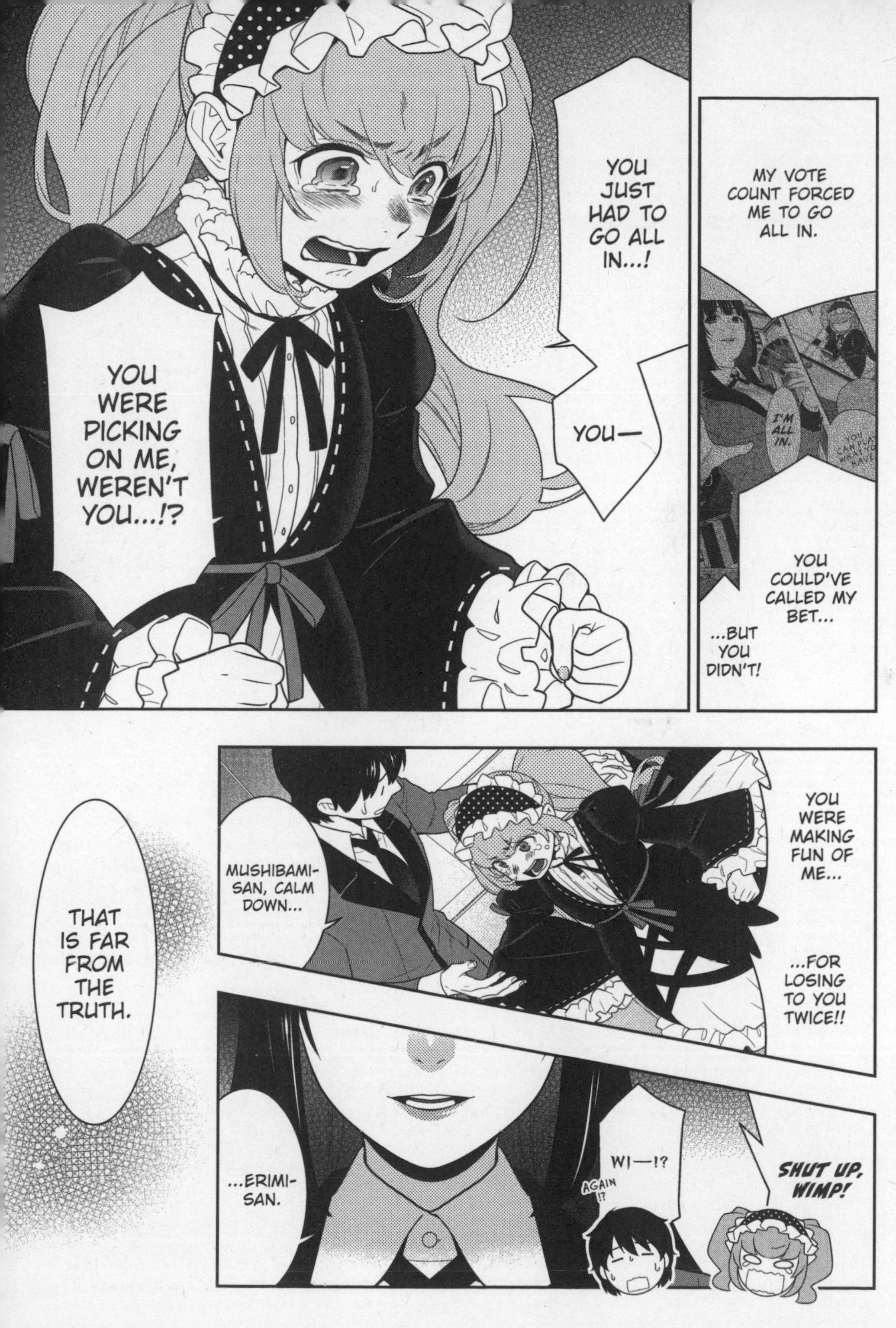
MY VOTE COUNT FORCED ME TO GO ALL IN.
I'M ALL IN.
YOU COULD'VE CALLED MY BET...
...BUT YOU DIDN'T!
YOU JUST HAD TO GO ALL IN...!
YOU—
YOU WERE PICKING ON ME, WEREN'T YOU...!?
YOU WERE MAKING FUN OF ME...
...FOR LOSING TO YOU TWICE!!
MUSHIBAMI-SAN, CALM DOWN...
SHUT UP, WIMP!
WI—!?
AGAIN !?
THAT IS FAR FROM THE TRUTH.
...ERIMI-SAN.

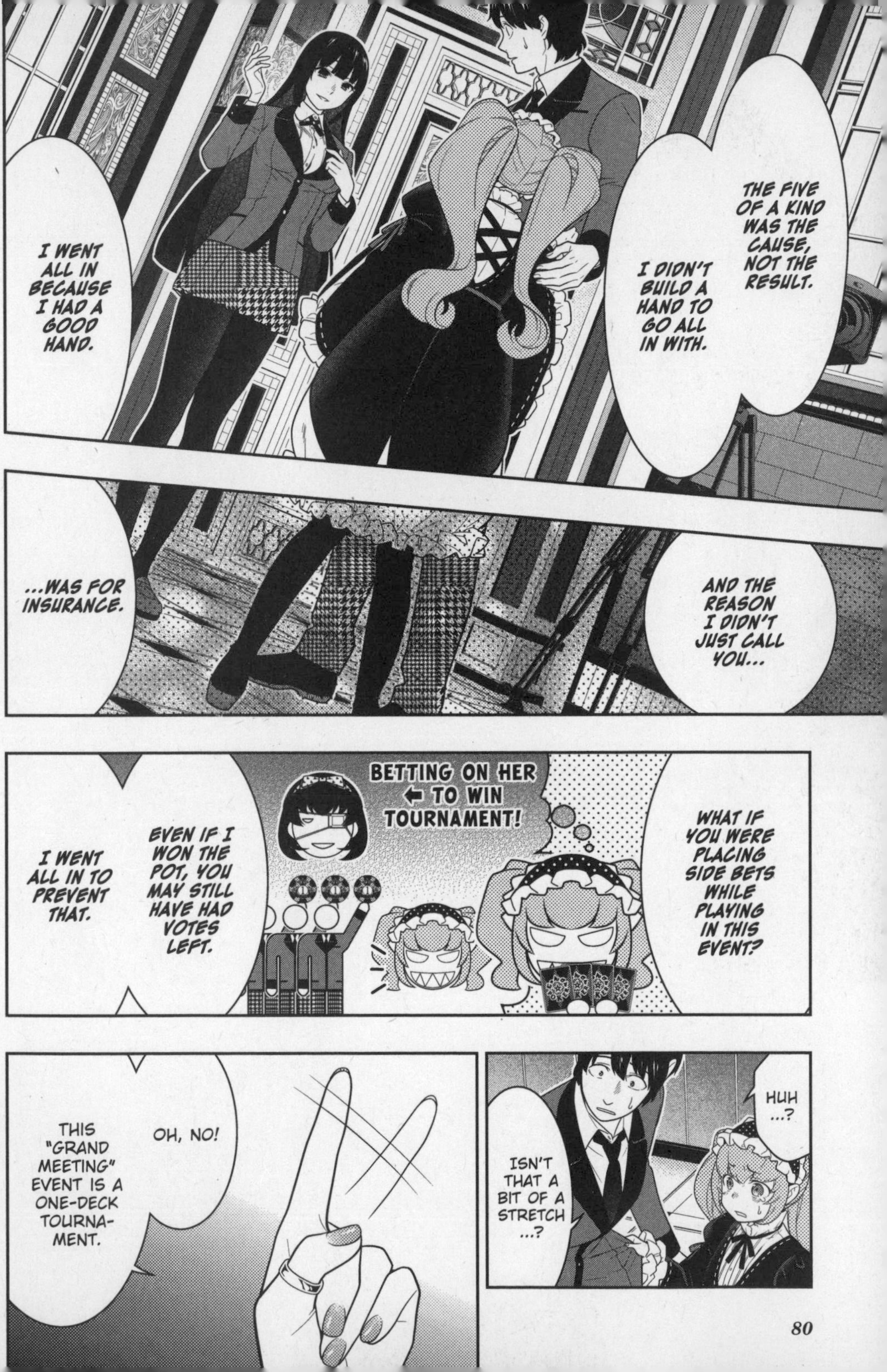
THE FIVE OF A KIND WAS THE CAUSE, NOT THE RESULT.
I DIDN'T BUILD A HAND TO GO ALL IN WITH.
I WENT ALL IN BECAUSE I HAD A GOOD HAND.
AND THE REASON I DIDN'T JUST CALL YOU...
...WAS FOR INSURANCE.
WHAT IF YOU WERE PLACING SIDE BETS WHILE PLAYING IN THIS EVENT?
BETTING ON HER ← TO WIN TOURNAMENT!
EVEN IF I WON THE POT, YOU MAY STILL HAVE HAD VOTES LEFT.
I WENT ALL IN TO PREVENT THAT.
HUH ...?
ISN'T THAT A BIT OF A STRETCH ...?
OH, NO!
THIS "GRAND MEETING" EVENT IS A ONE-DECK TOURNAMENT.

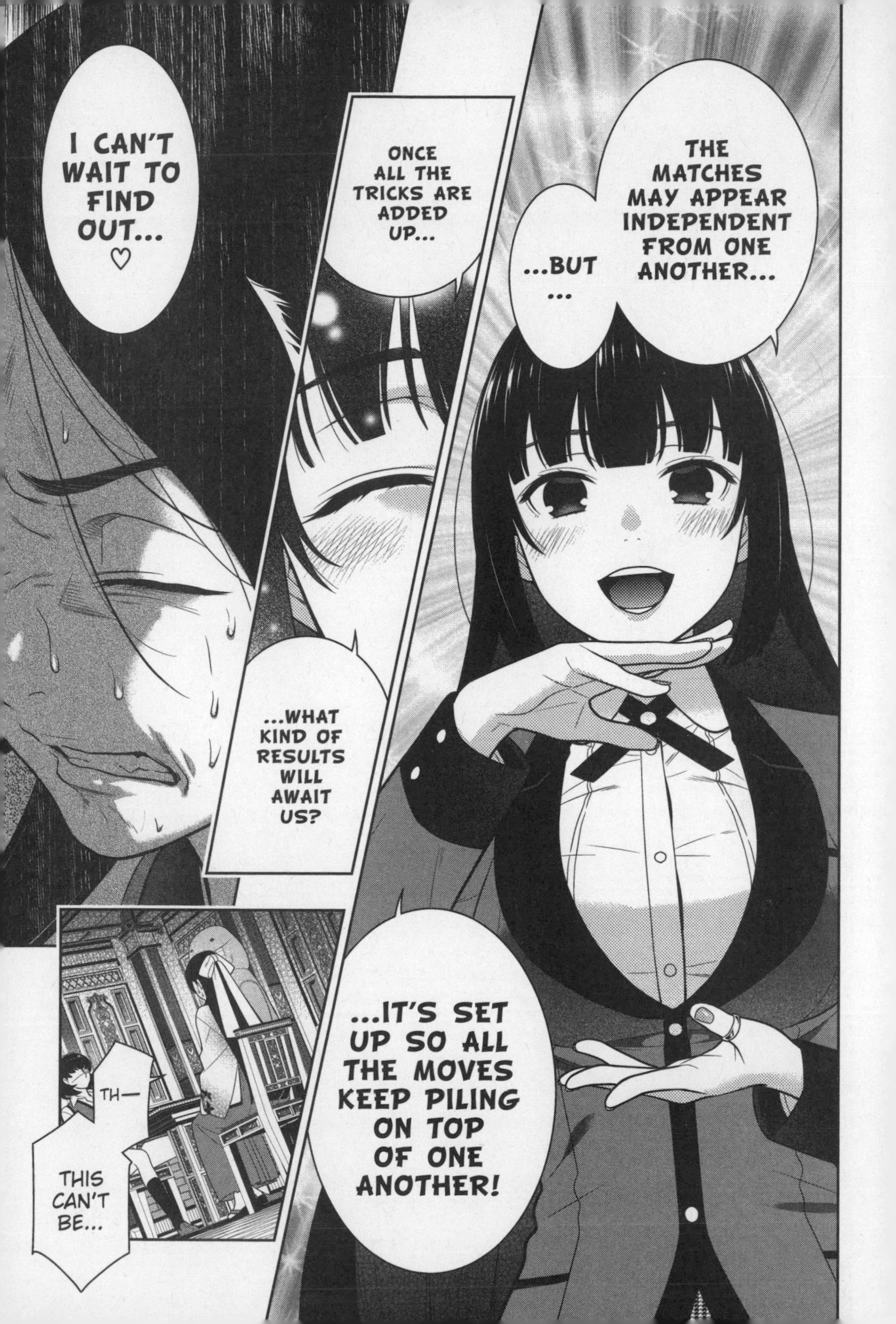
THE MATCHES MAY APPEAR INDEPENDENT FROM ONE ANOTHER...
...BUT ...
...IT'S SET UP SO ALL THE MOVES KEEP PILING ON TOP OF ONE ANOTHER!
ONCE ALL THE TRICKS ARE ADDED UP...
...WHAT KIND OF RESULTS WILL AWAIT US?
I CAN'T WAIT TO FIND OUT... ♡
TH—
THIS CAN'T BE...

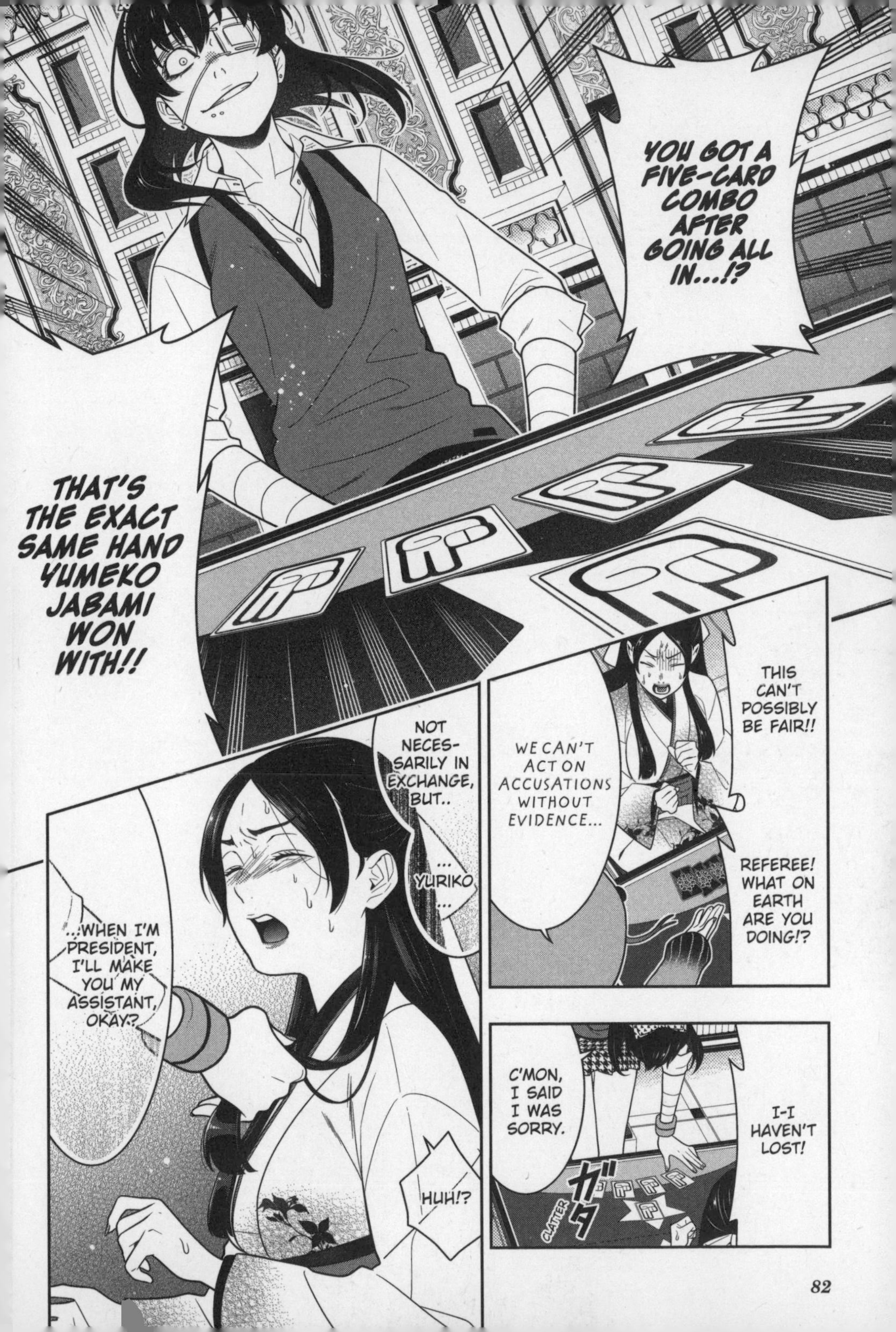
YOU GOT A FIVE-CARD COMBO AFTER GOING ALL IN...!?
THAT'S THE EXACT SAME HAND YUMEKO JABAMI WON WITH!!
THIS CAN'T POSSIBLY BE FAIR!!
REFEREE! WHAT ON EARTH ARE YOU DOING!?
WE CAN'T ACT ON ACCUSATIONS WITHOUT EVIDENCE...
I-I HAVEN'T LOST!
C'MON, I SAID I WAS SORRY.
CLATTER
NOT NECES-SARILY IN EXCHANGE, BUT..
...YURIKO...
...WHEN I'M PRESIDENT, I'LL MAKE YOU MY ASSISTANT, OKAY?
HUH!?

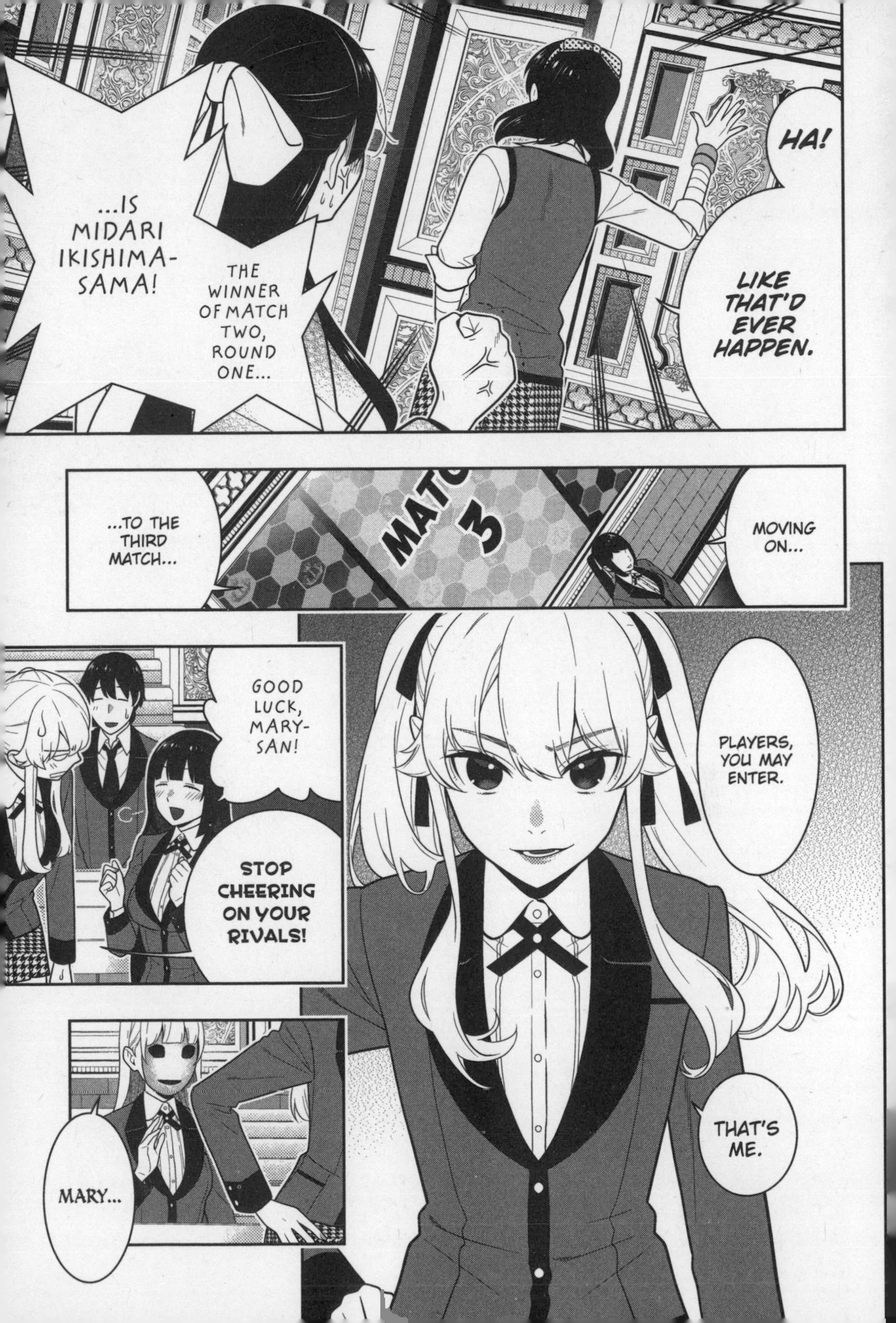
HA!
LIKE THAT'D EVER HAPPEN.
THE WINNER OF MATCH TWO, ROUND ONE...
...IS MIDARI IKISHIMA-SAMA!
MATC
3
MOVING ON...
...TO THE THIRD MATCH...
PLAYERS, YOU MAY ENTER.
THAT'S ME.
GOOD LUCK, MARY-SAN!
STOP CHEERING ON YOUR RIVALS!
MARY...

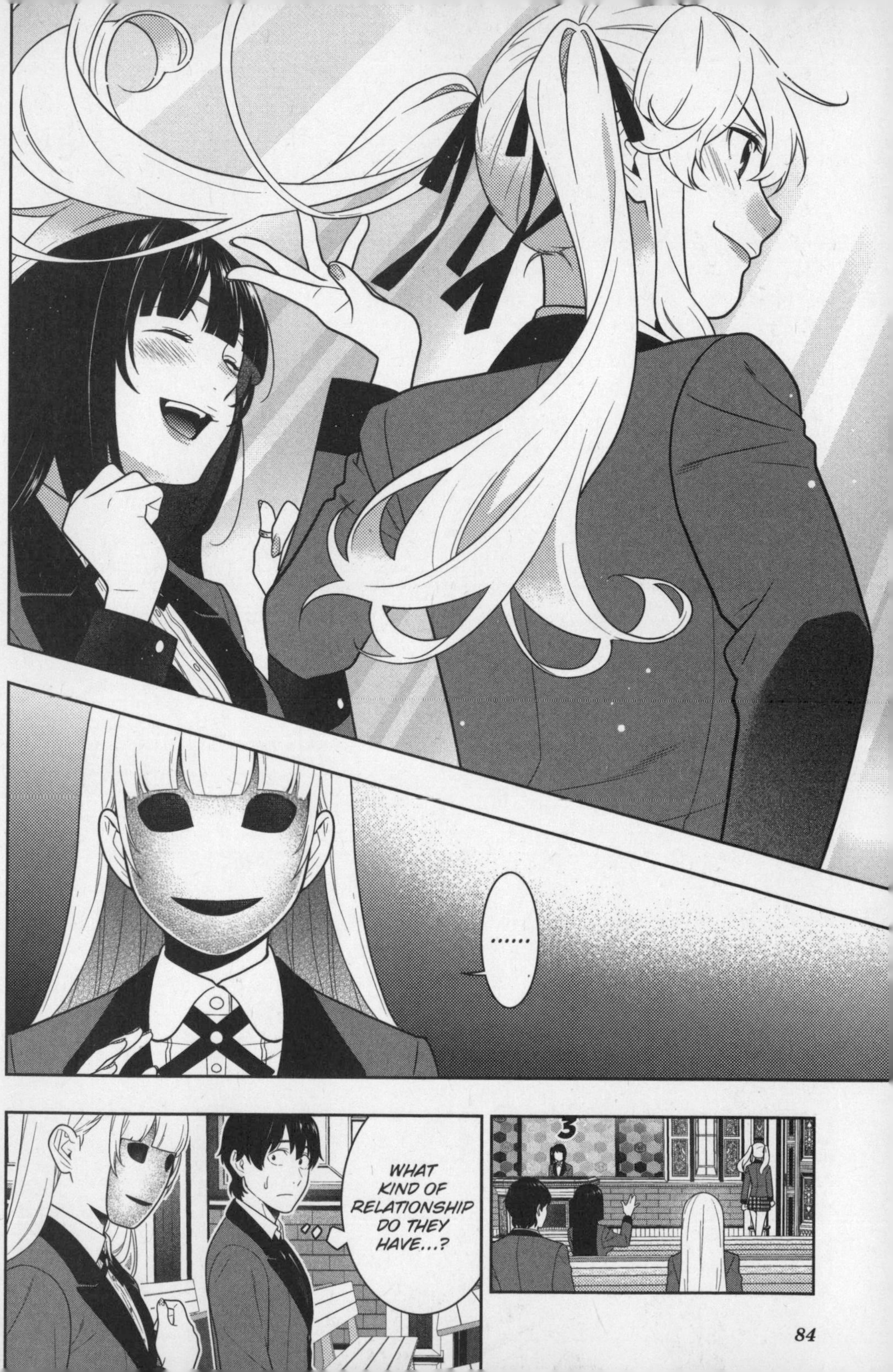
……
3
WHAT KIND OF RELATIONSHIP DO THEY HAVE…?

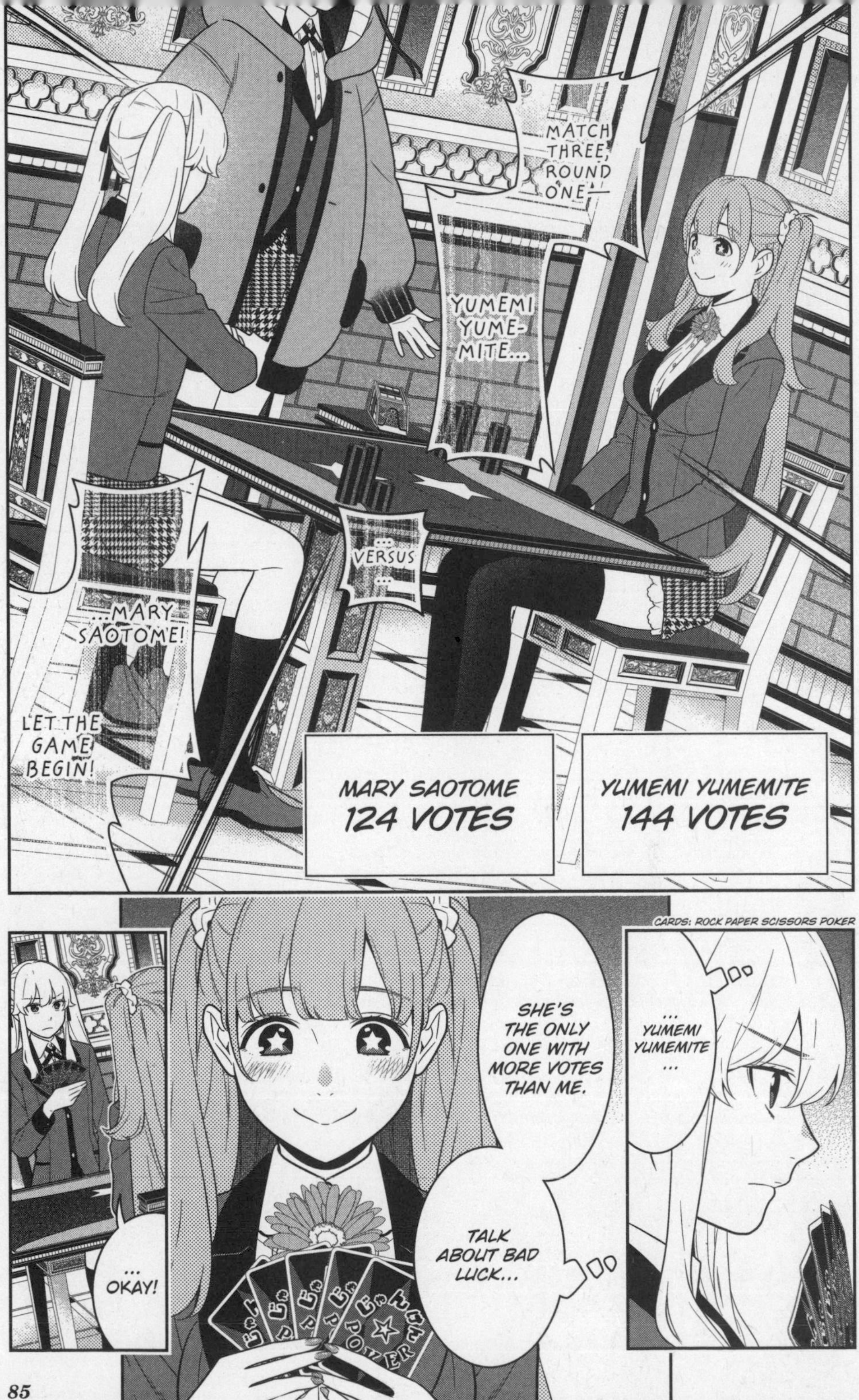
MATCH THREE, ROUND ONE
YUMEMI YUMEMITE...
...VERSUS...
...MARY SAOTOME!
LET THE GAME BEGIN!
YUMEMI YUMEMITE 144 VOTES
MARY SAOTOME 124 VOTES
CARDS: ROCK PAPER SCISSORS POKER
...YUMEMI YUMEMITE...
SHE'S THE ONLY ONE WITH MORE VOTES THAN ME.
TALK ABOUT BAD LUCK...
...OKAY!

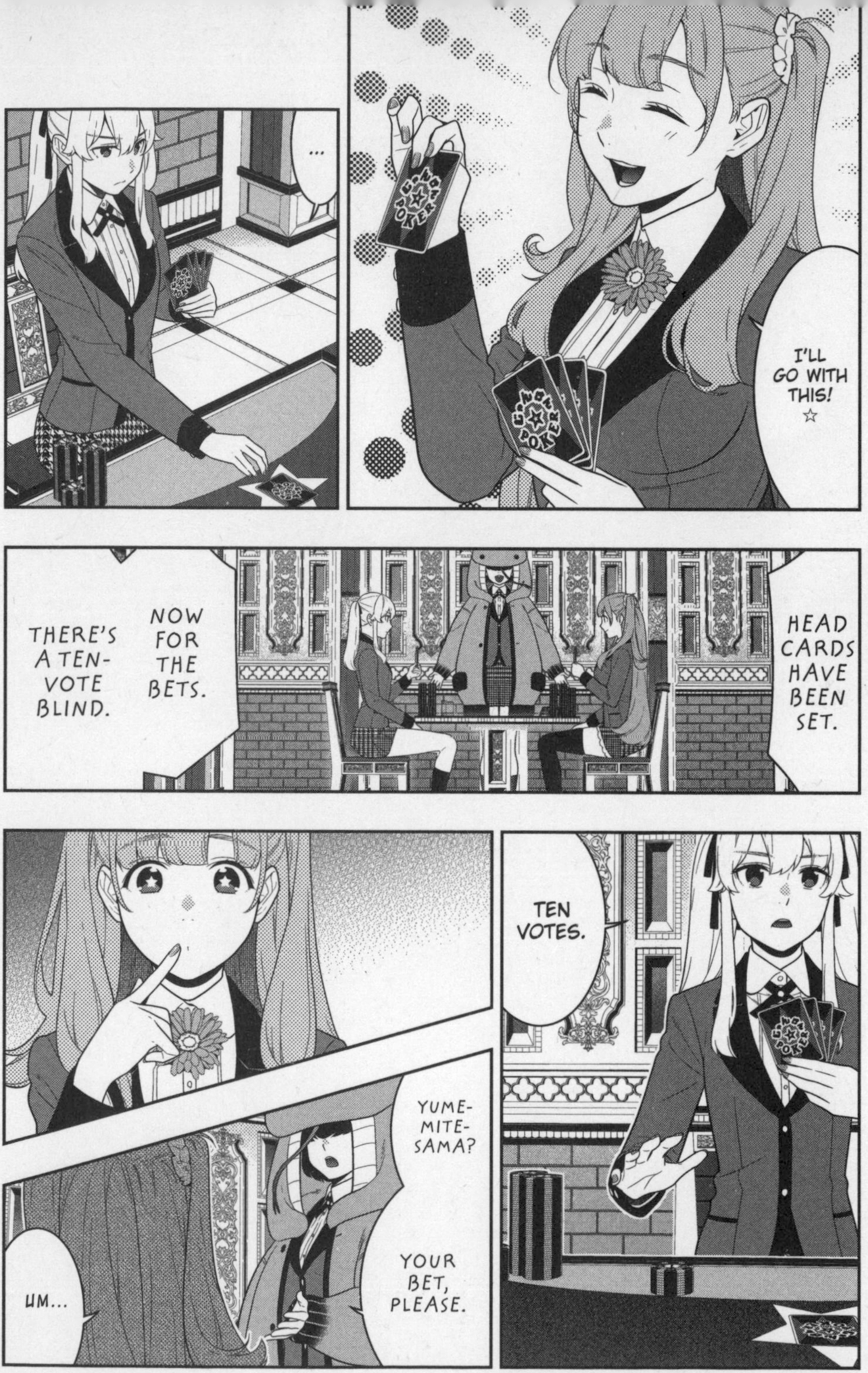
I'LL GO WITH THIS! ☆
...
HEAD CARDS HAVE BEEN SET.
NOW FOR THE BETS.
THERE'S A TEN-VOTE BLIND.
TEN VOTES.
YUME-MITE-SAMA?
YOUR BET, PLEASE.
UM...

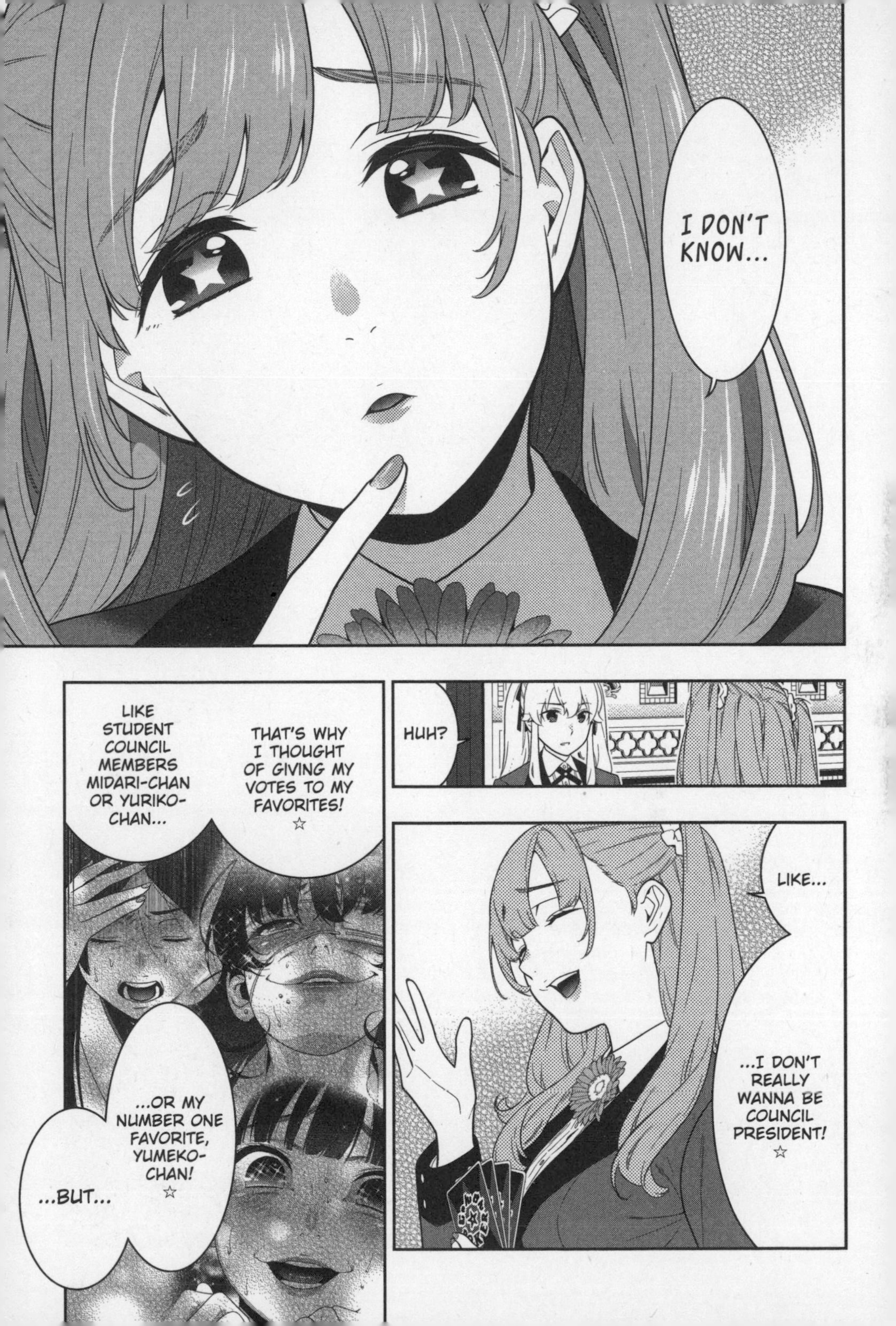
I DON'T KNOW...
HUH?
LIKE...
...I DON'T REALLY WANNA BE COUNCIL PRESIDENT! ☆
THAT'S WHY I THOUGHT OF GIVING MY VOTES TO MY FAVORITES! ☆
LIKE STUDENT COUNCIL MEMBERS MIDARI-CHAN OR YURIKO-CHAN...
...OR MY NUMBER ONE FAVORITE, YUMEKO-CHAN! ☆
...BUT...

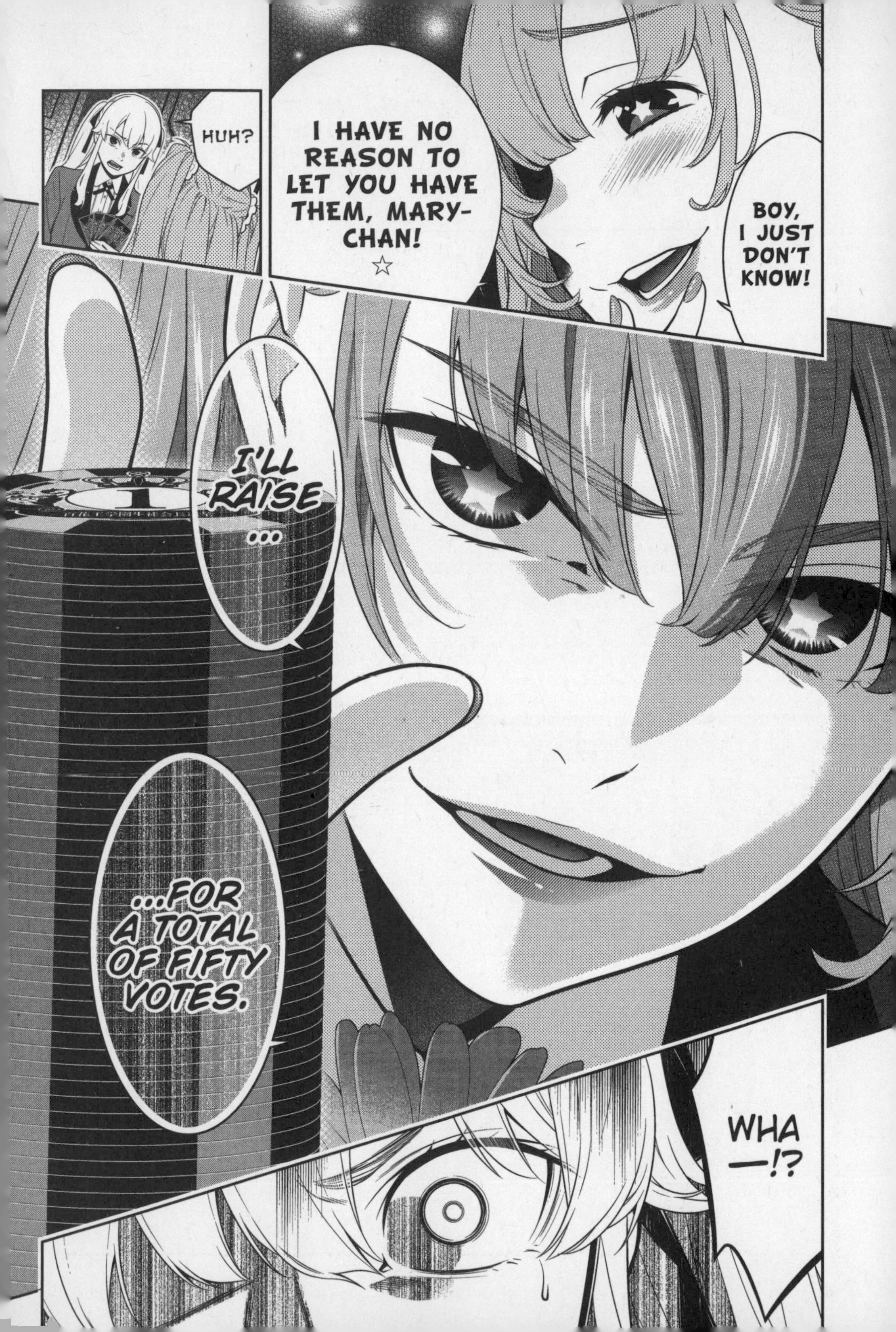
BOY, I JUST DON'T KNOW!
I HAVE NO REASON TO LET YOU HAVE THEM, MARY-CHAN! ☆
HUH?
I'LL RAISE ...
...FOR A TOTAL OF FIFTY VOTES.
WHA—!?

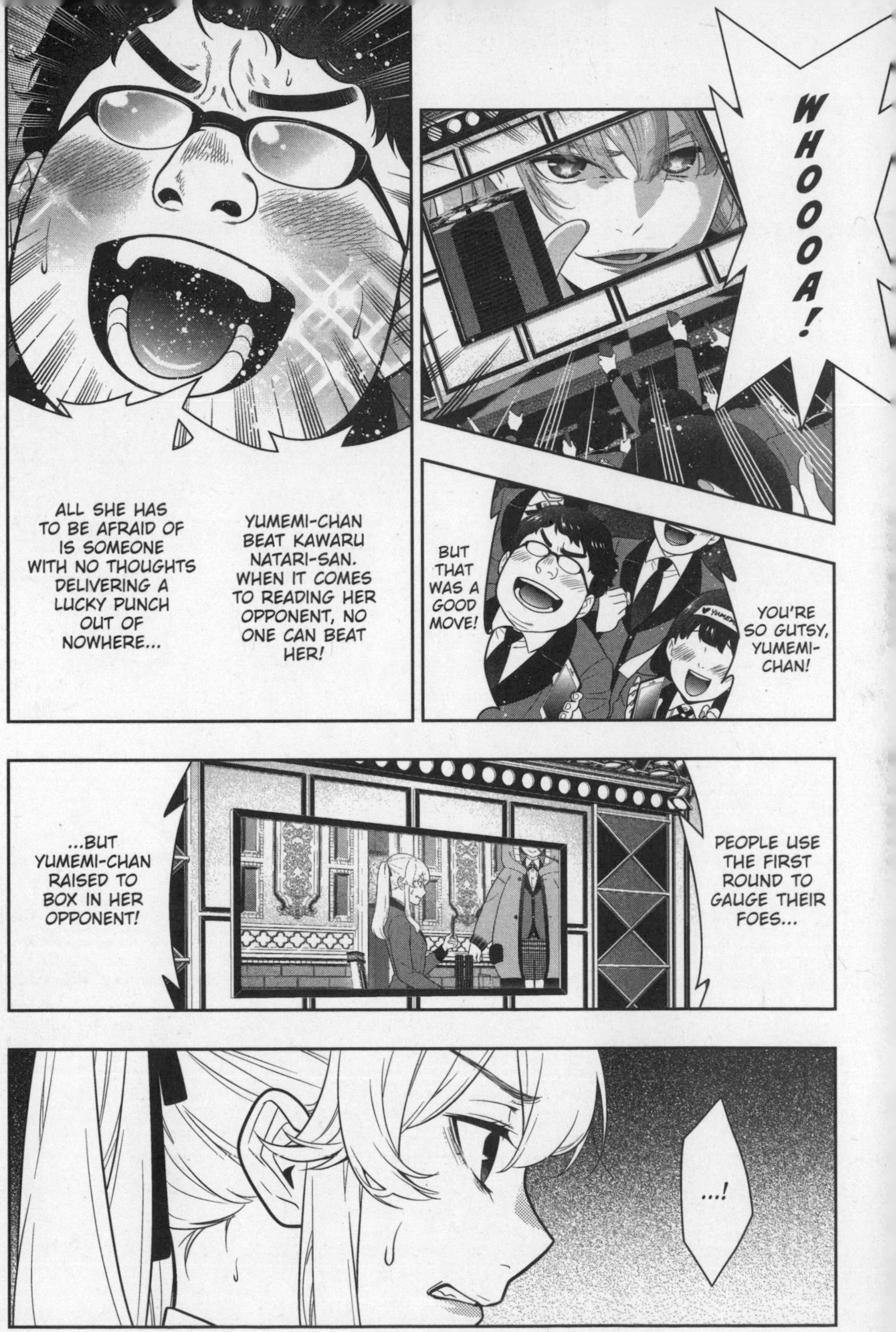
WHOOOA!
YOU'RE SO GUTSY, YUMEMI-CHAN!
BUT THAT WAS A GOOD MOVE!
YUMEMI-CHAN BEAT KAWARU NATARI-SAN. WHEN IT COMES TO READING HER OPPONENT, NO ONE CAN BEAT HER!
ALL SHE HAS TO BE AFRAID OF IS SOMEONE WITH NO THOUGHTS DELIVERING A LUCKY PUNCH OUT OF NOWHERE...
PEOPLE USE THE FIRST ROUND TO GAUGE THEIR FOES...
...BUT YUMEMI-CHAN RAISED TO BOX IN HER OPPONENT!
...!

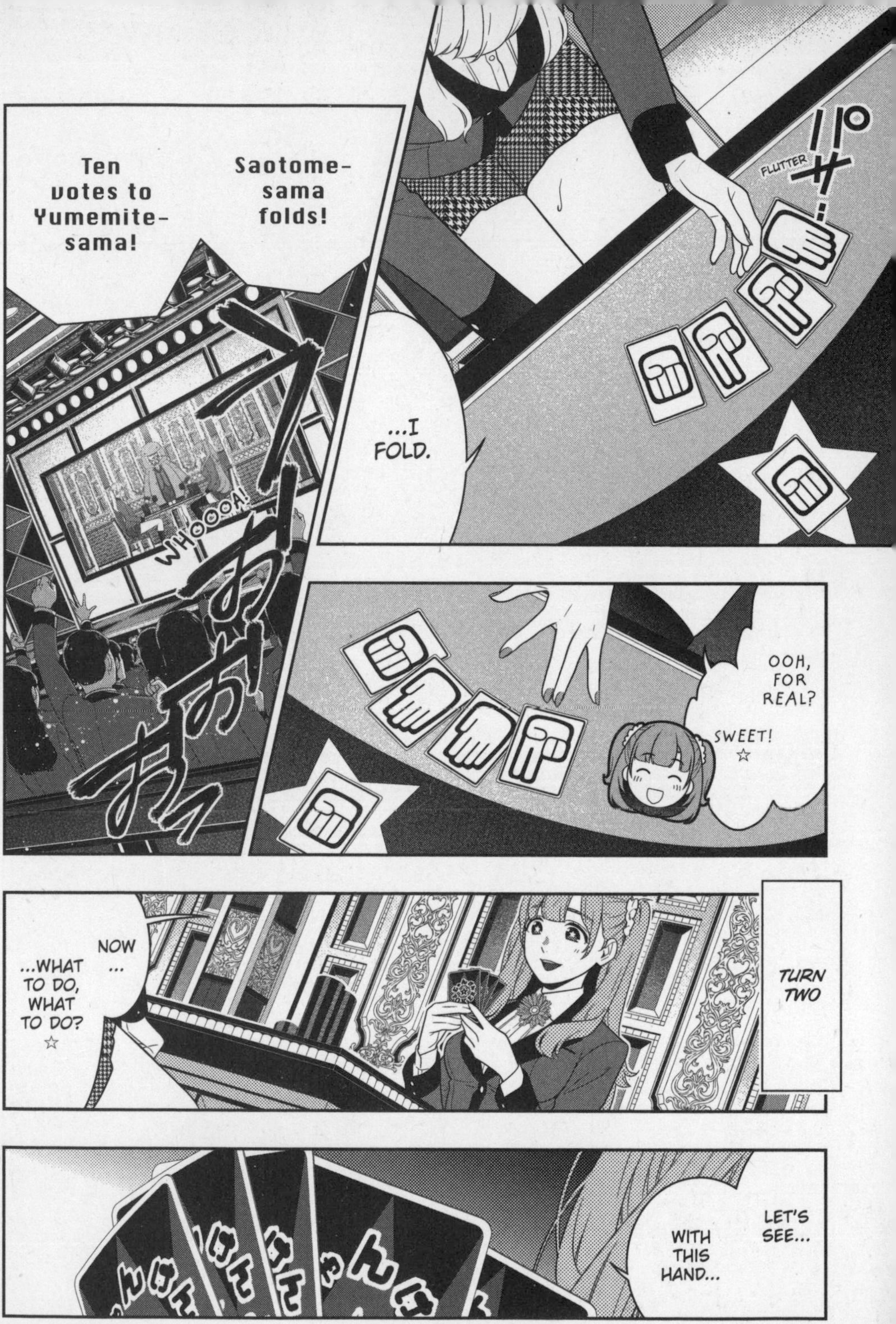
FLUTTER
...I FOLD.
OOH, FOR REAL?
SWEET! ☆
Saotome-sama folds!
Ten votes to Yumemite-sama!
WHOOOA!
TURN TWO
NOW...
...WHAT TO DO, WHAT TO DO? ☆
LET'S SEE...
WITH THIS HAND...

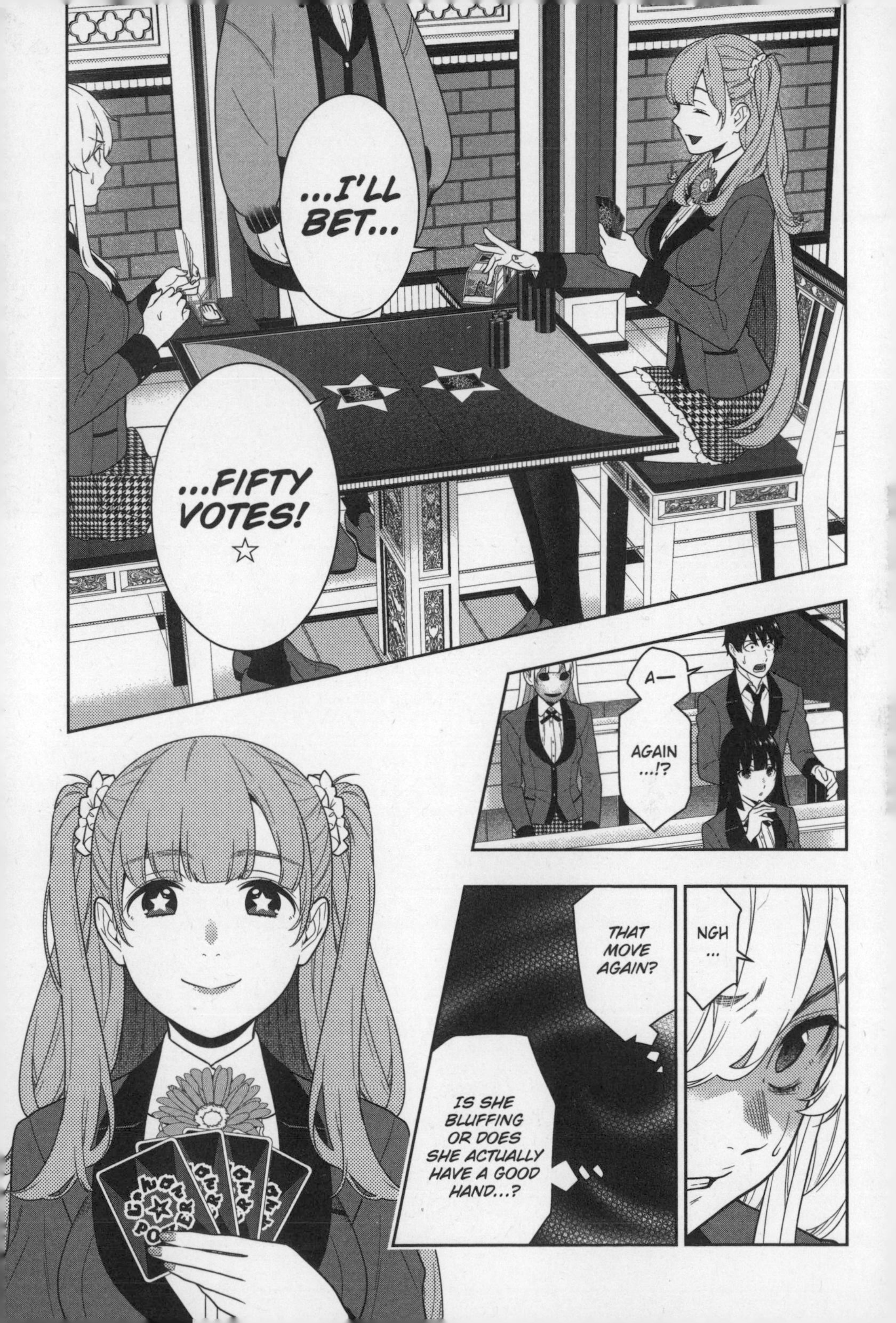
...I'LL BET...
...FIFTY VOTES! ☆
A—
AGAIN ...!?
NGH ...
THAT MOVE AGAIN?
IS SHE BLUFFING OR DOES SHE ACTUALLY HAVE A GOOD HAND...?

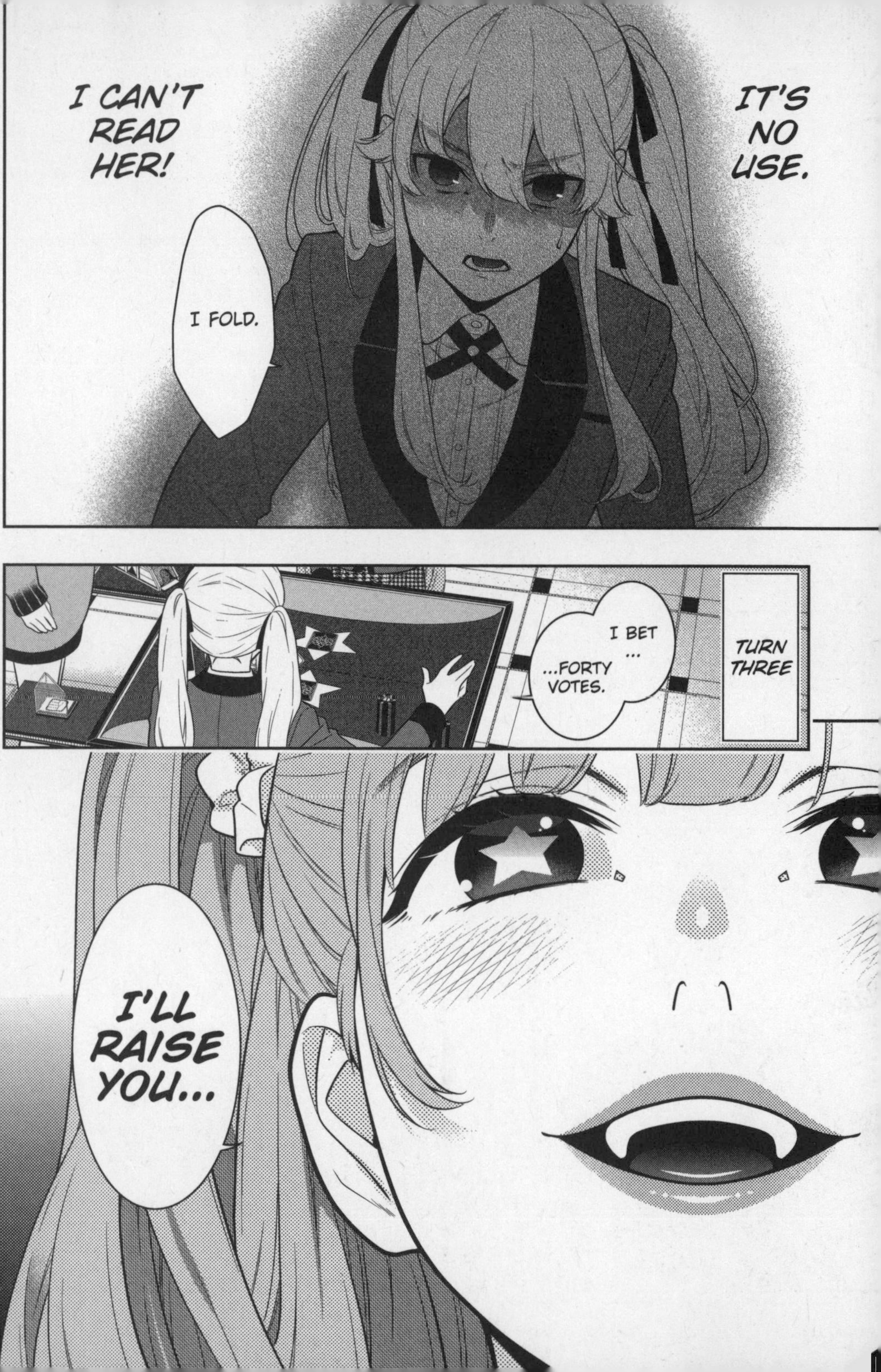
IT'S NO USE.
I CAN'T READ HER!
I FOLD.
TURN THREE
I BET ... ...FORTY VOTES.
I'LL RAISE YOU...

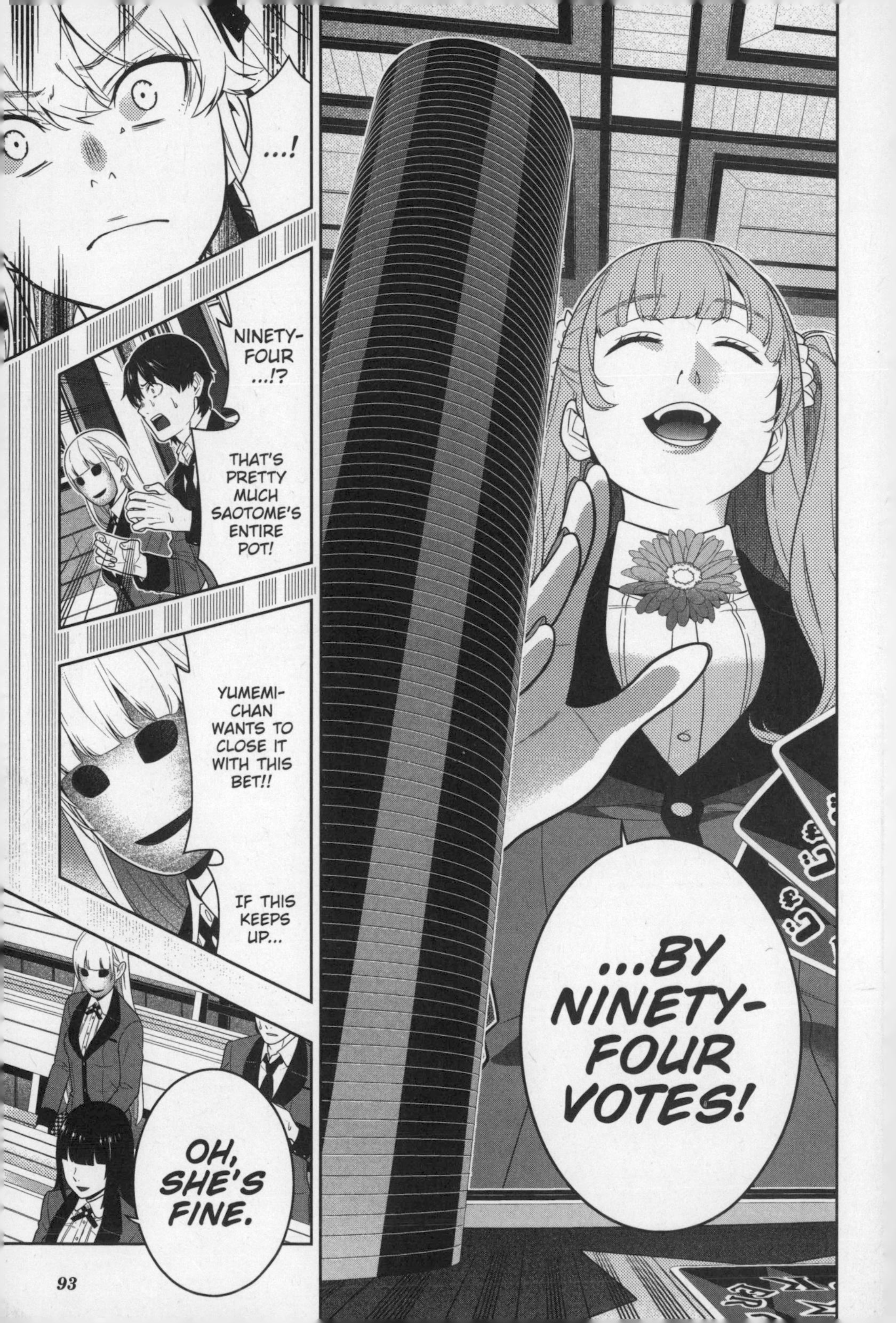
...BY NINETY-FOUR VOTES!
...!
NINETY-FOUR ...!?
THAT'S PRETTY MUCH SAOTOME'S ENTIRE POT!
YUMEMI-CHAN WANTS TO CLOSE IT WITH THIS BET!!
IF THIS KEEPS UP...
OH, SHE'S FINE.

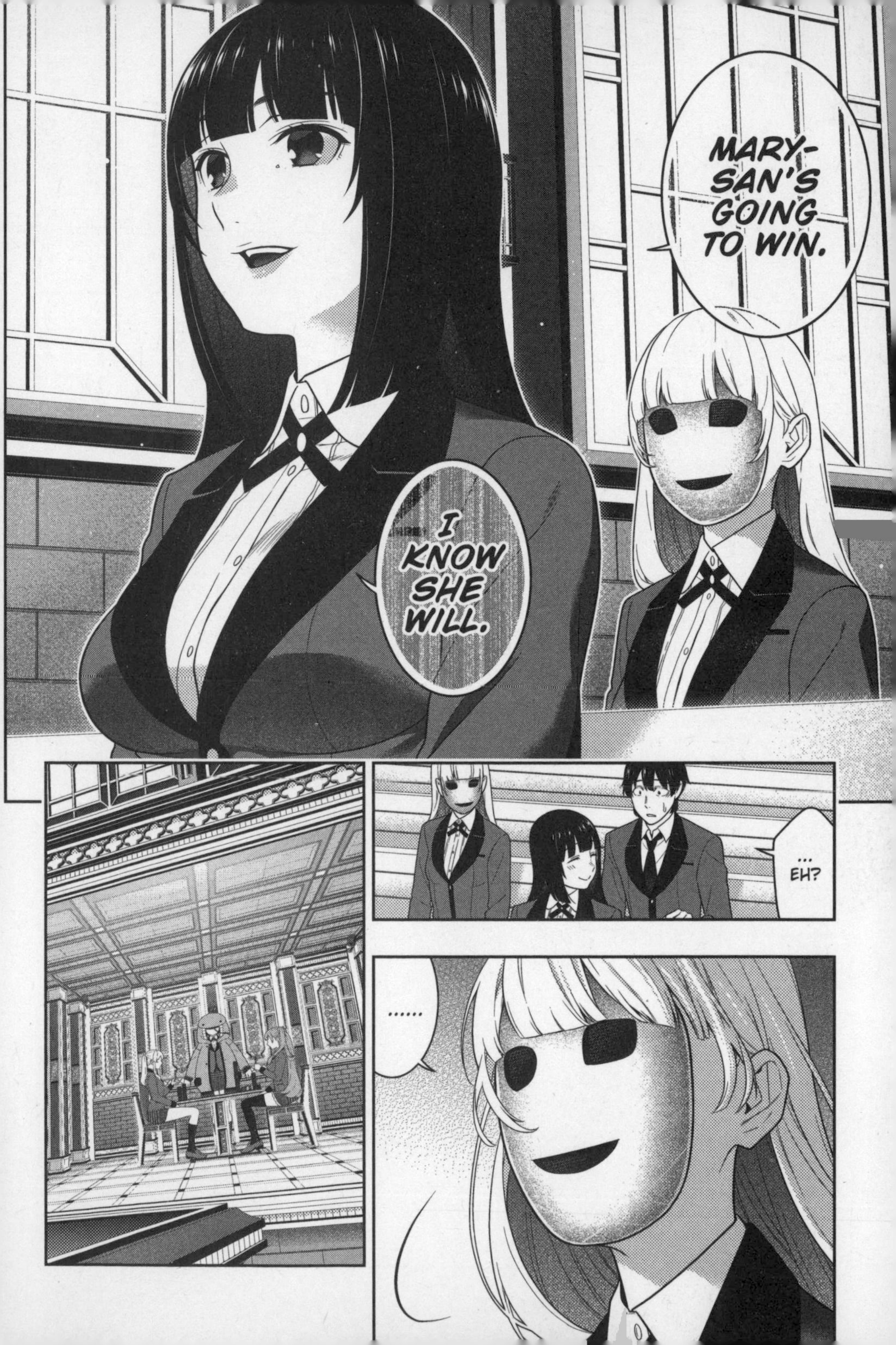
MARY-SAN'S GOING TO WIN.
I KNOW SHE WILL.
...EH?
......

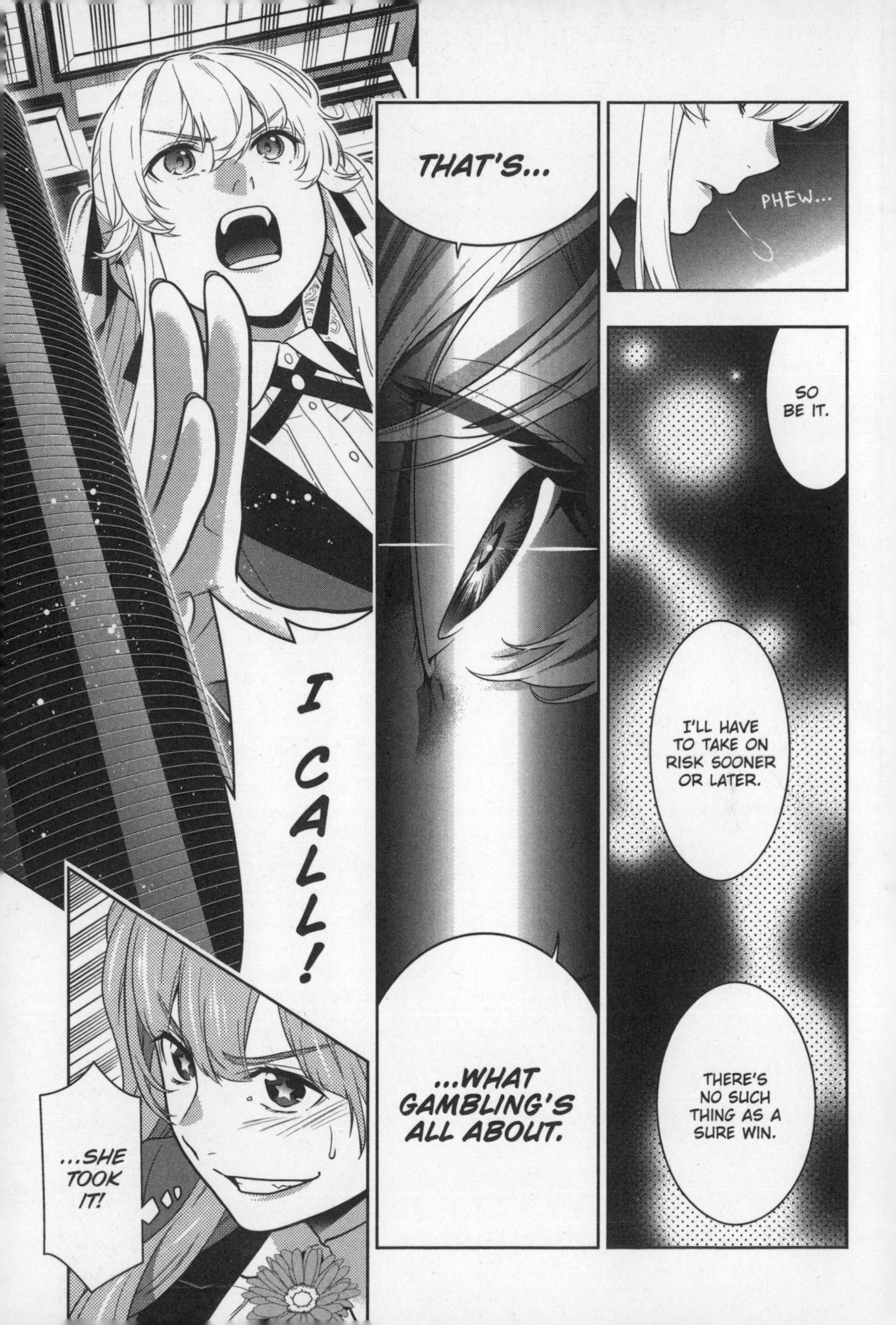
PHEW...
SO BE IT.
I'LL HAVE TO TAKE ON RISK SOONER OR LATER.
THERE'S NO SUCH THING AS A SURE WIN.
THAT'S...
...WHAT GAMBLING'S ALL ABOUT.
I CALL!
...SHE TOOK IT!

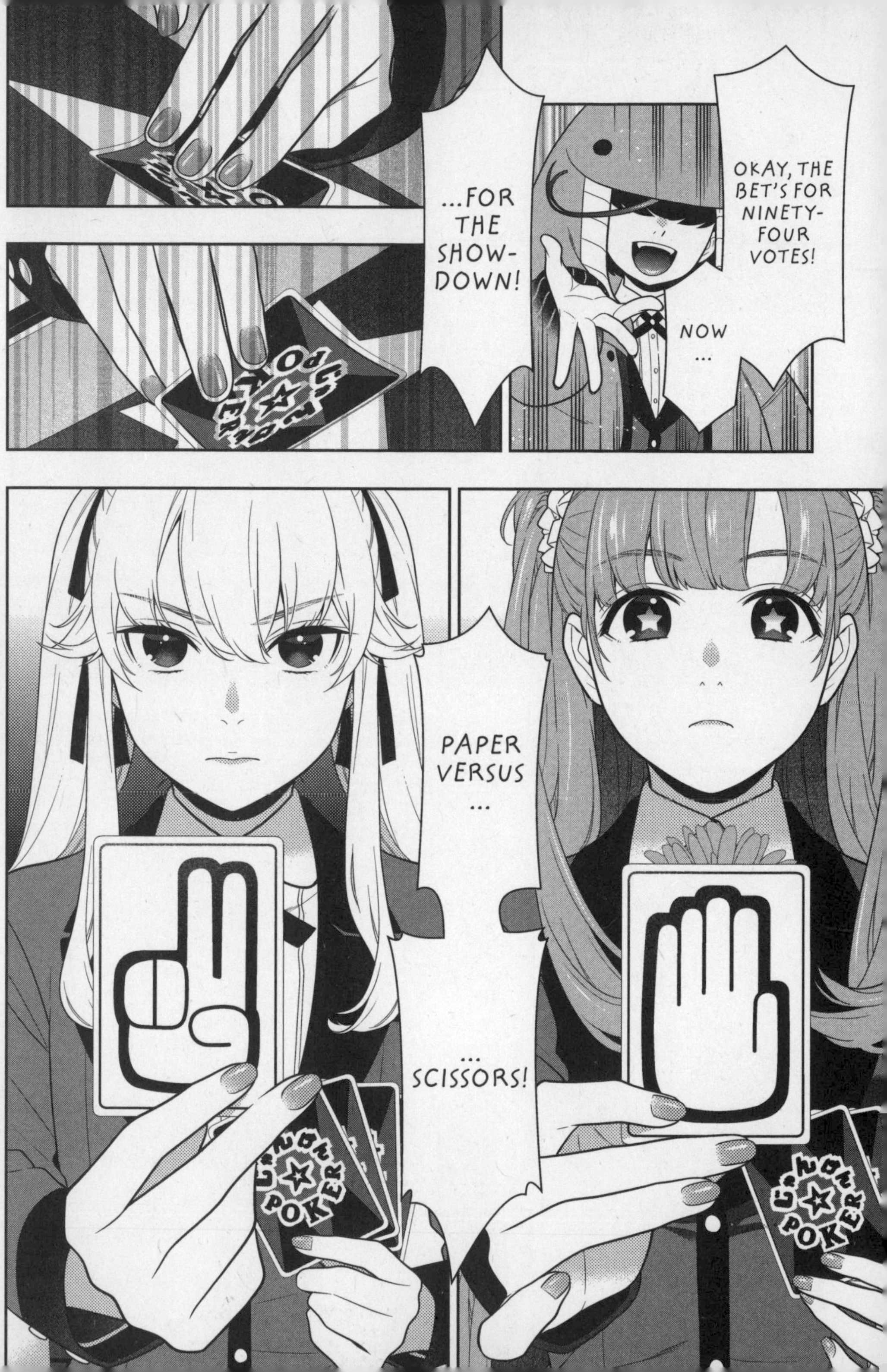
OKAY, THE BET'S FOR NINETY-FOUR VOTES!
NOW ...
...FOR THE SHOWDOWN!
PAPER VERSUS ...
... SCISSORS!

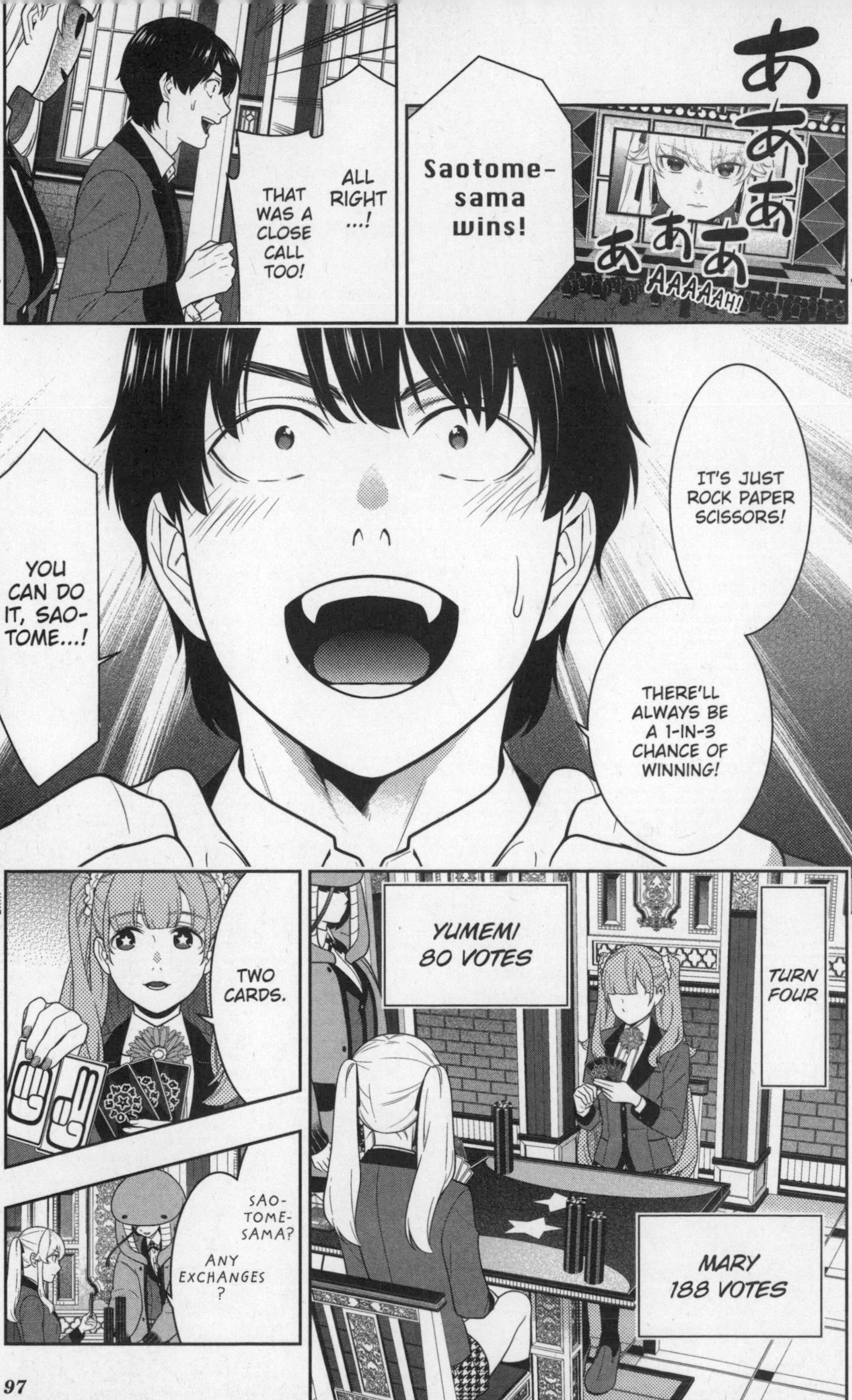

Saotome-sama wins!
ああああああ
AAAAAAH!
ALL RIGHT...!
THAT WAS A CLOSE CALL TOO!
IT'S JUST ROCK PAPER SCISSORS!
THERE'LL ALWAYS BE A 1-IN-3 CHANCE OF WINNING!
YOU CAN DO IT, SAO-TOME...!
TURN FOUR
YUMEMI 80 VOTES
MARY 188 VOTES
TWO CARDS.
SAO-TOME-SAMA? ANY EXCHANGES?

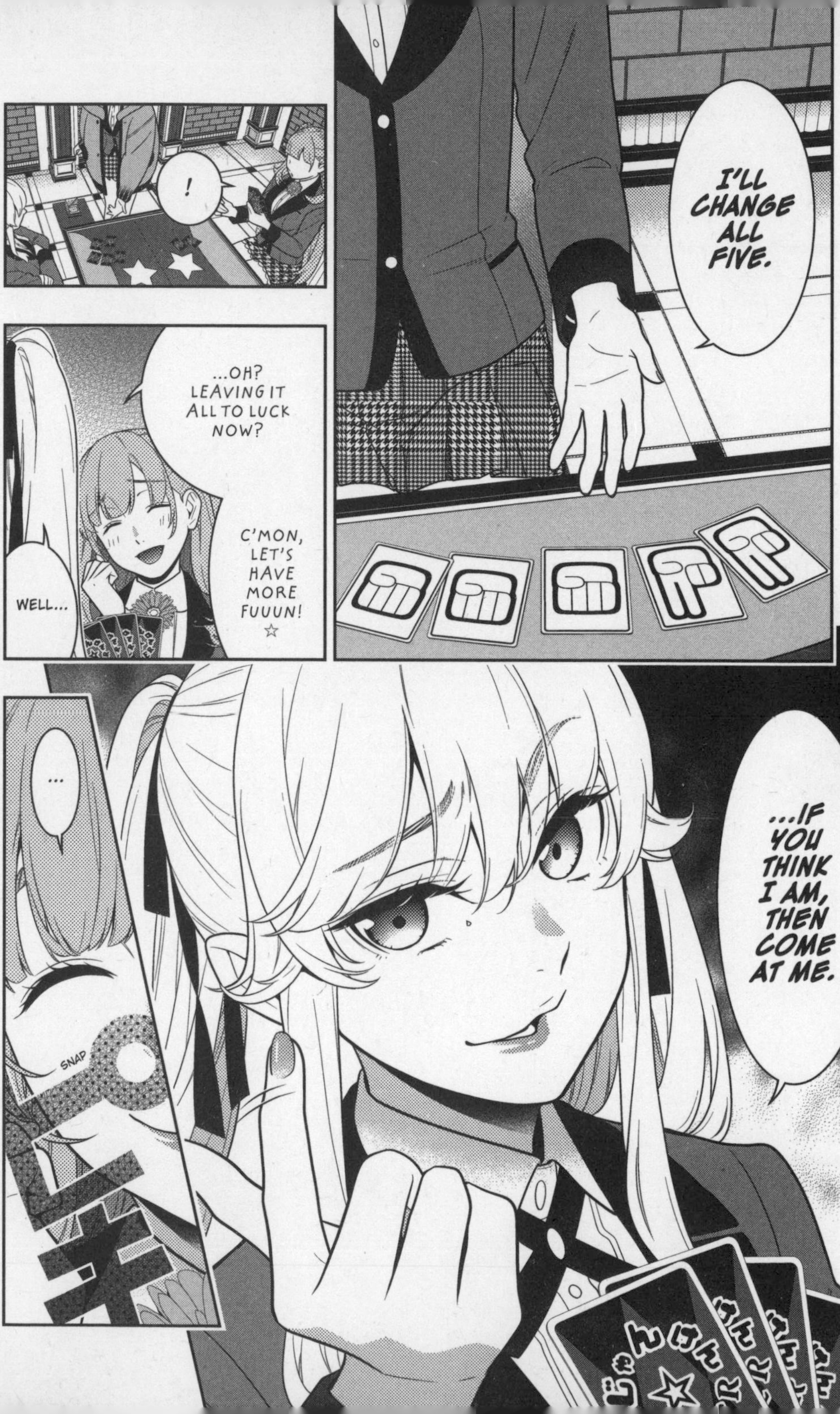
I'LL CHANGE ALL FIVE.
!
...OH? LEAVING IT ALL TO LUCK NOW?
C'MON, LET'S HAVE MORE FUUUN! ☆
WELL...
...IF YOU THINK I AM, THEN COME AT ME.
...
SNAP

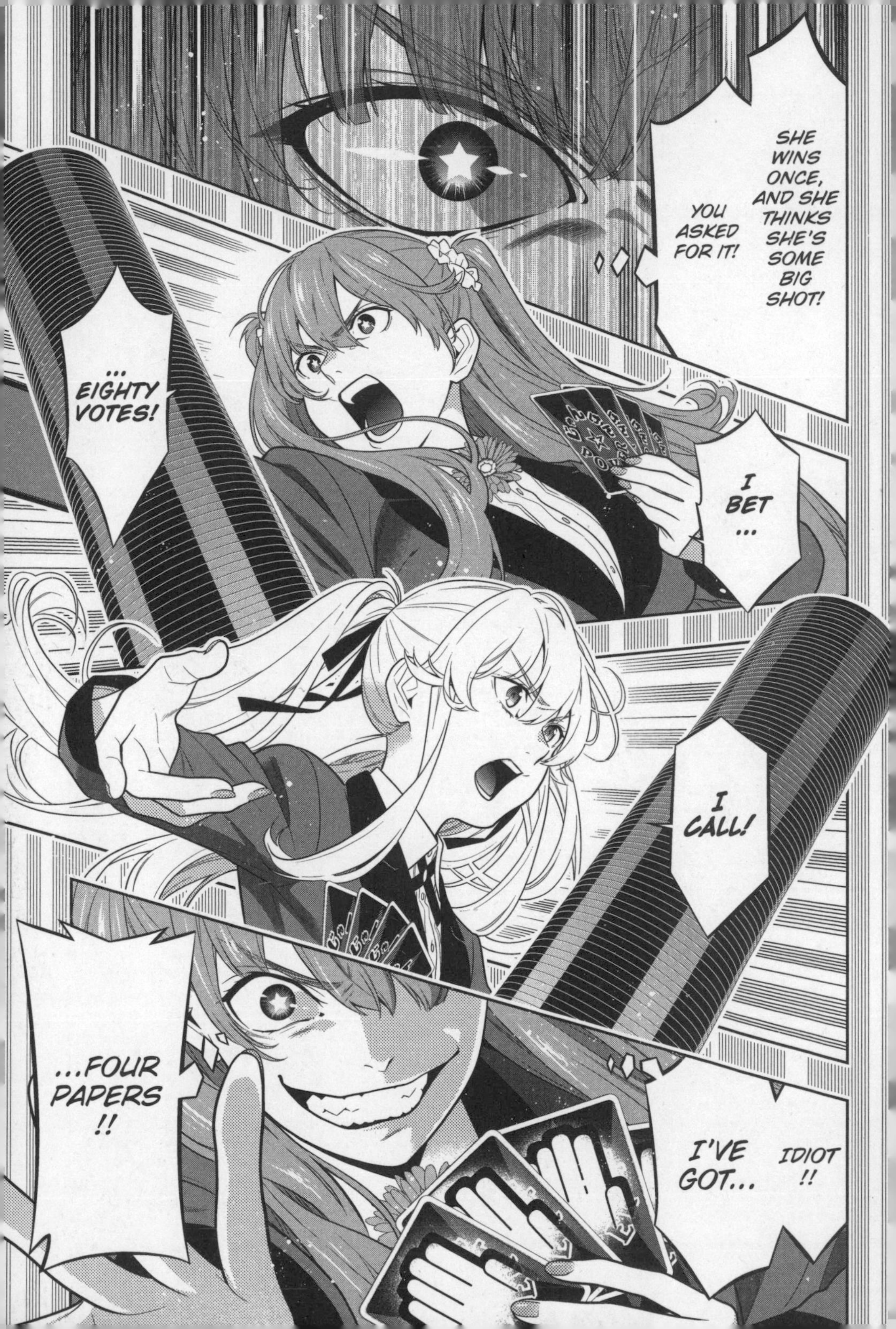
SHE WINS ONCE, AND SHE THINKS SHE'S SOME BIG SHOT!
YOU ASKED FOR IT!
I BET...
...EIGHTY VOTES!
I CALL!
IDIOT!!
I'VE GOT...
...FOUR PAPERS!!

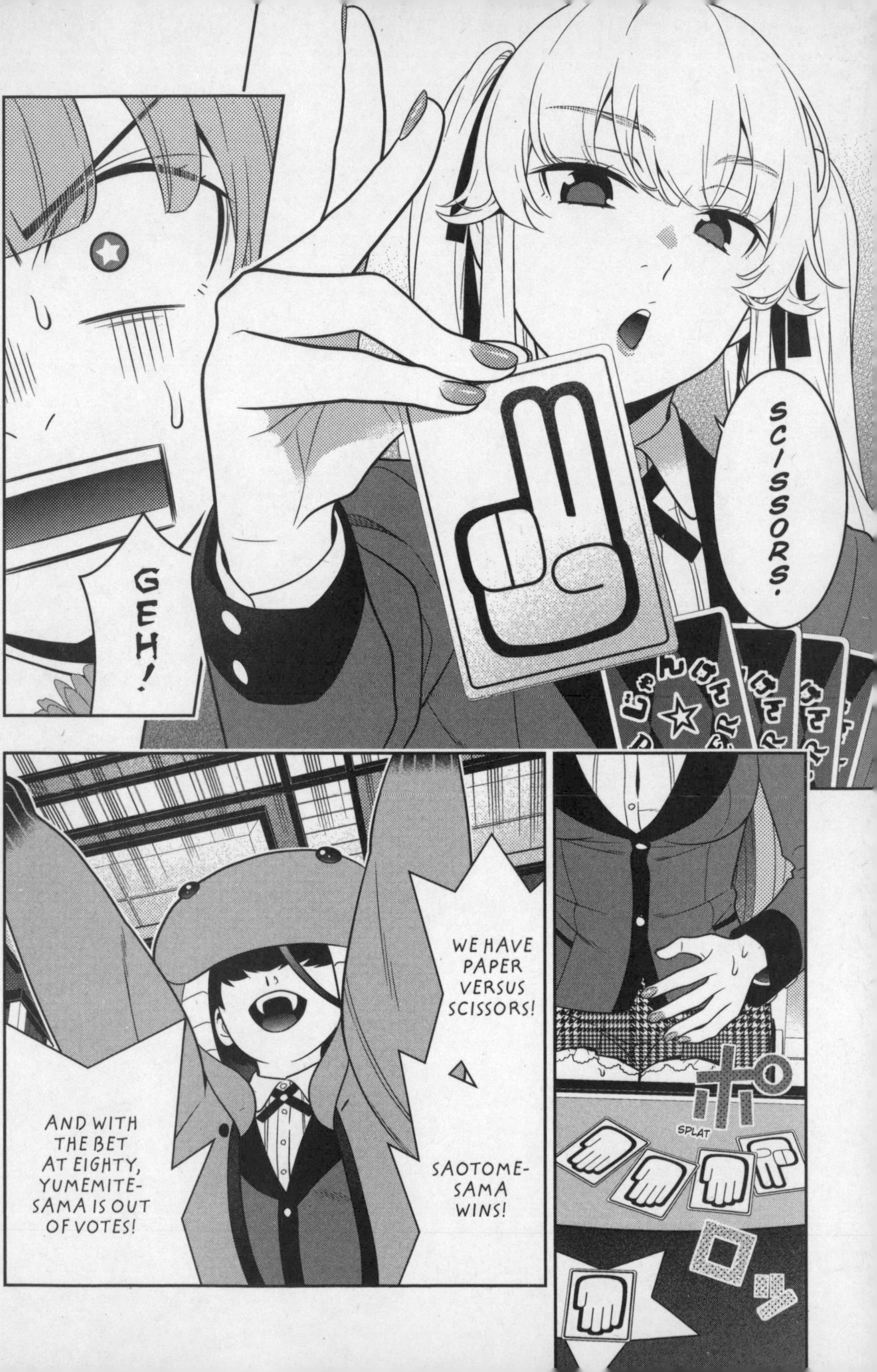
SCISSORS.
GEH!
ポ
SPLAT
ロッ
WE HAVE PAPER VERSUS SCISSORS!
SAOTOME-SAMA WINS!
AND WITH THE BET AT EIGHTY, YUMEMITE-SAMA IS OUT OF VOTES!

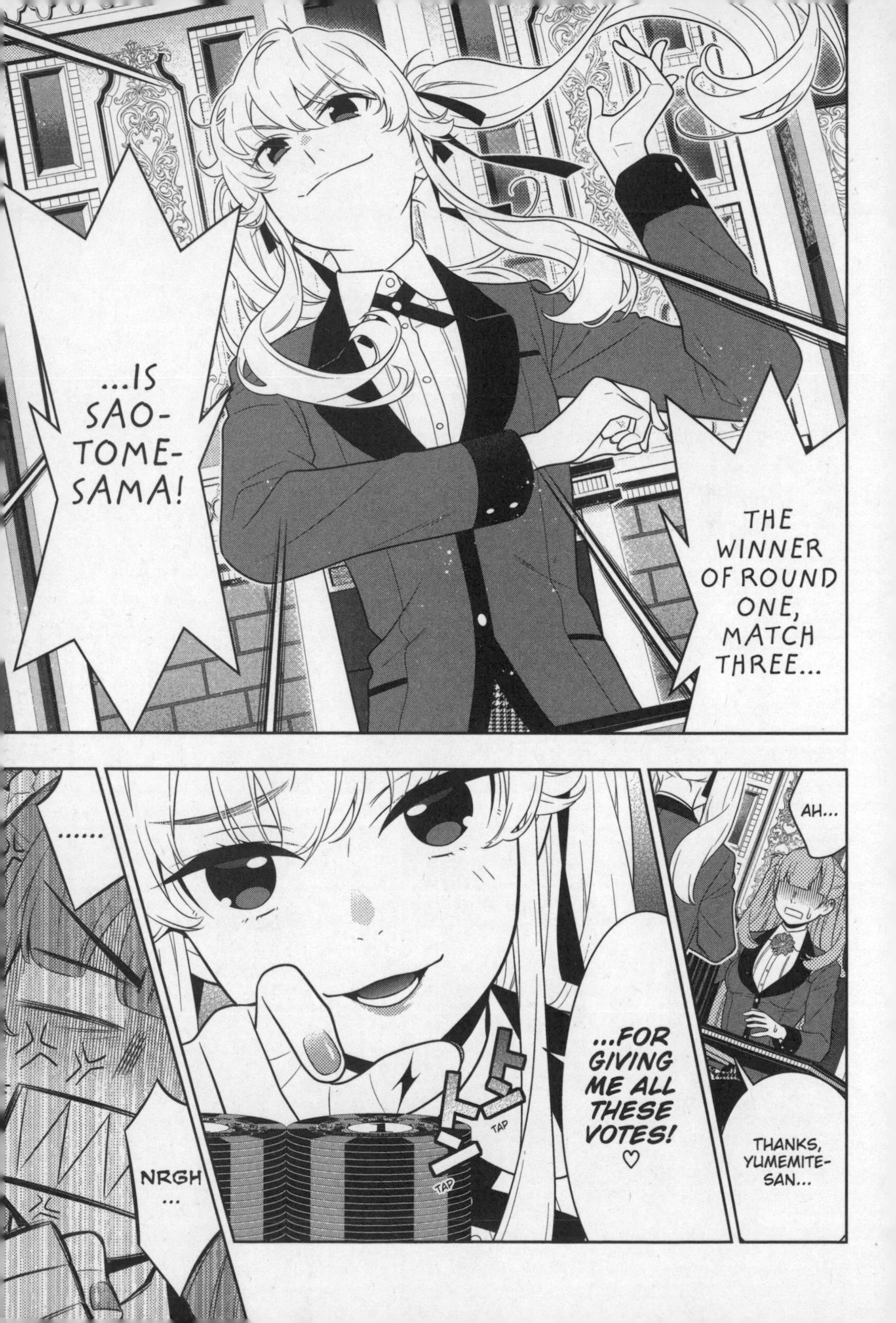
THE WINNER OF ROUND ONE, MATCH THREE...
...IS SAO-TOME-SAMA!
AH...
THANKS, YUMEMITE-SAN...
...FOR GIVING ME ALL THESE VOTES! ♡
TAP
TAP
......
NRGH ...

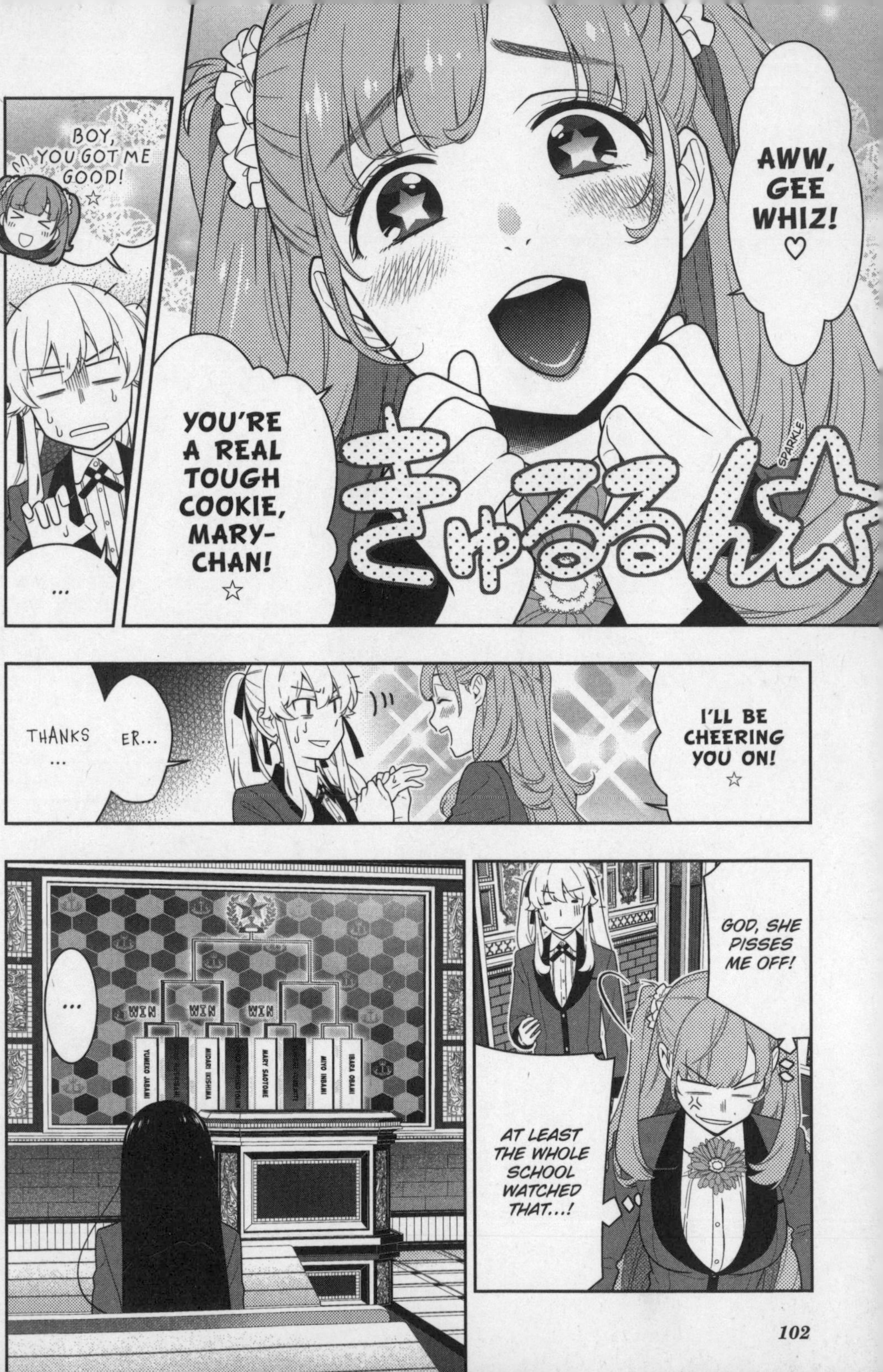
AWW, GEE WHIZ! ♡
YOU'RE A REAL TOUGH COOKIE, MARY-CHAN! ☆
きゅるるん☆
SPARKLE
BOY, YOU GOT ME GOOD! ☆
...
I'LL BE CHEERING YOU ON! ☆
ER...
THANKS ...
GOD, SHE PISSES ME OFF!
AT LEAST THE WHOLE SCHOOL WATCHED THAT...!
...
WIN
WIN
WIN
YUMEKO JABAMI
MIDARI IKISHIMA
MARY SAOTOME
MIYO INBAMI
IBARA OBAMI

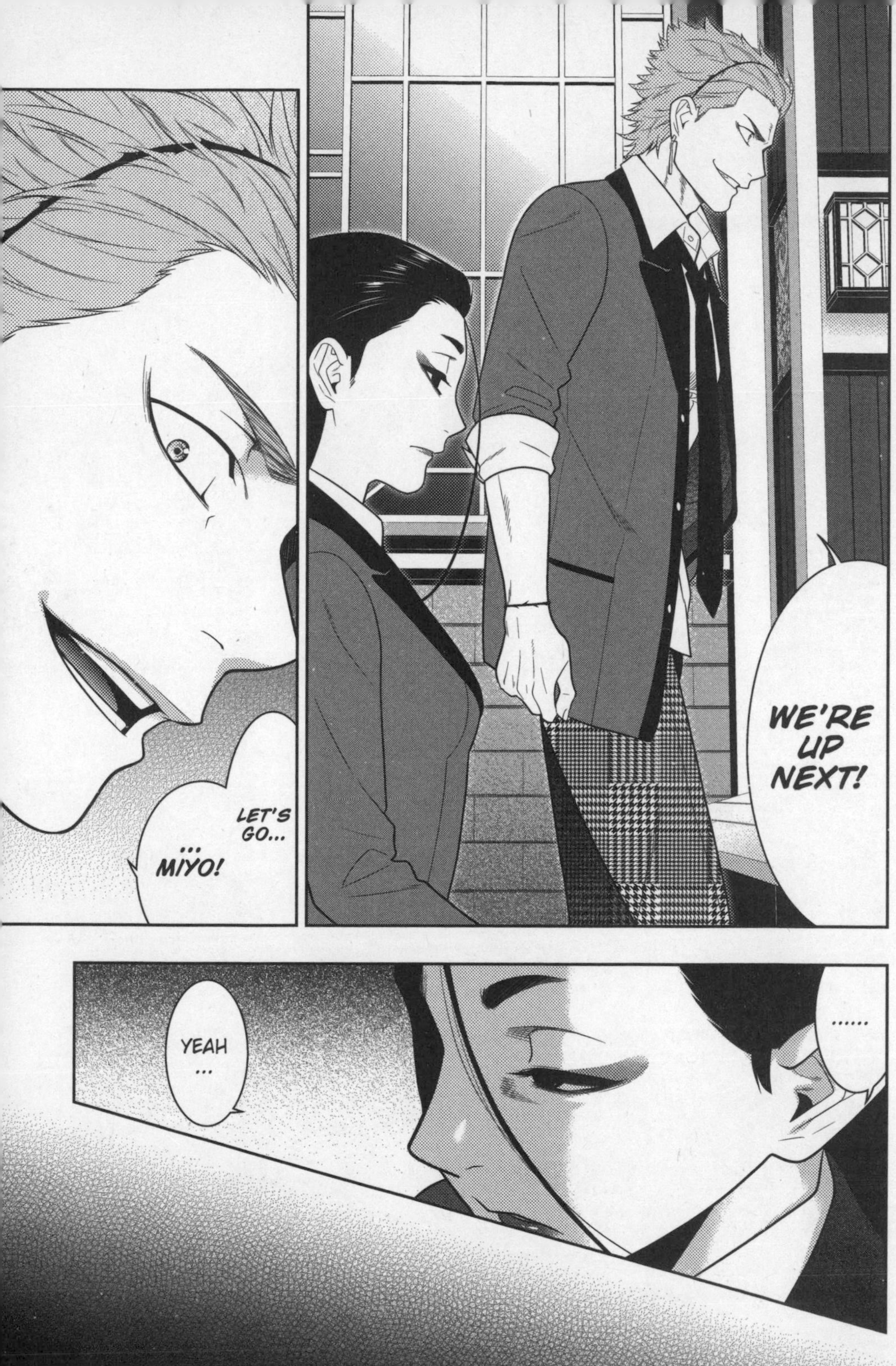
WE'RE UP NEXT!
LET'S GO... ...MIYO!
......
YEAH ...

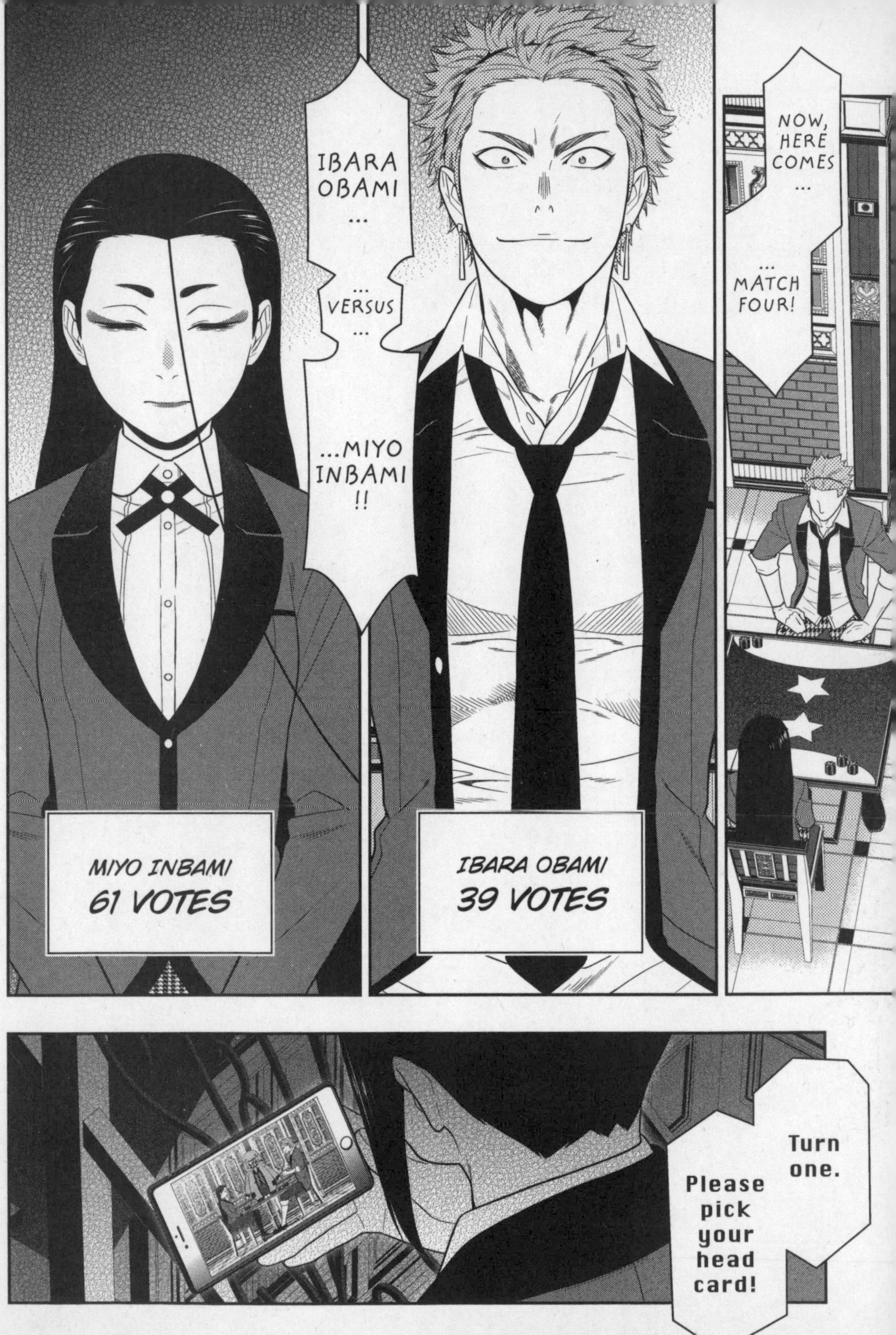
NOW, HERE COMES ...
... MATCH FOUR!
IBARA OBAMI ...
... VERSUS ...
...MIYO INBAMI !!
IBARA OBAMI
39 VOTES
MIYO INBAMI
61 VOTES
Turn one.
Please pick your head card!

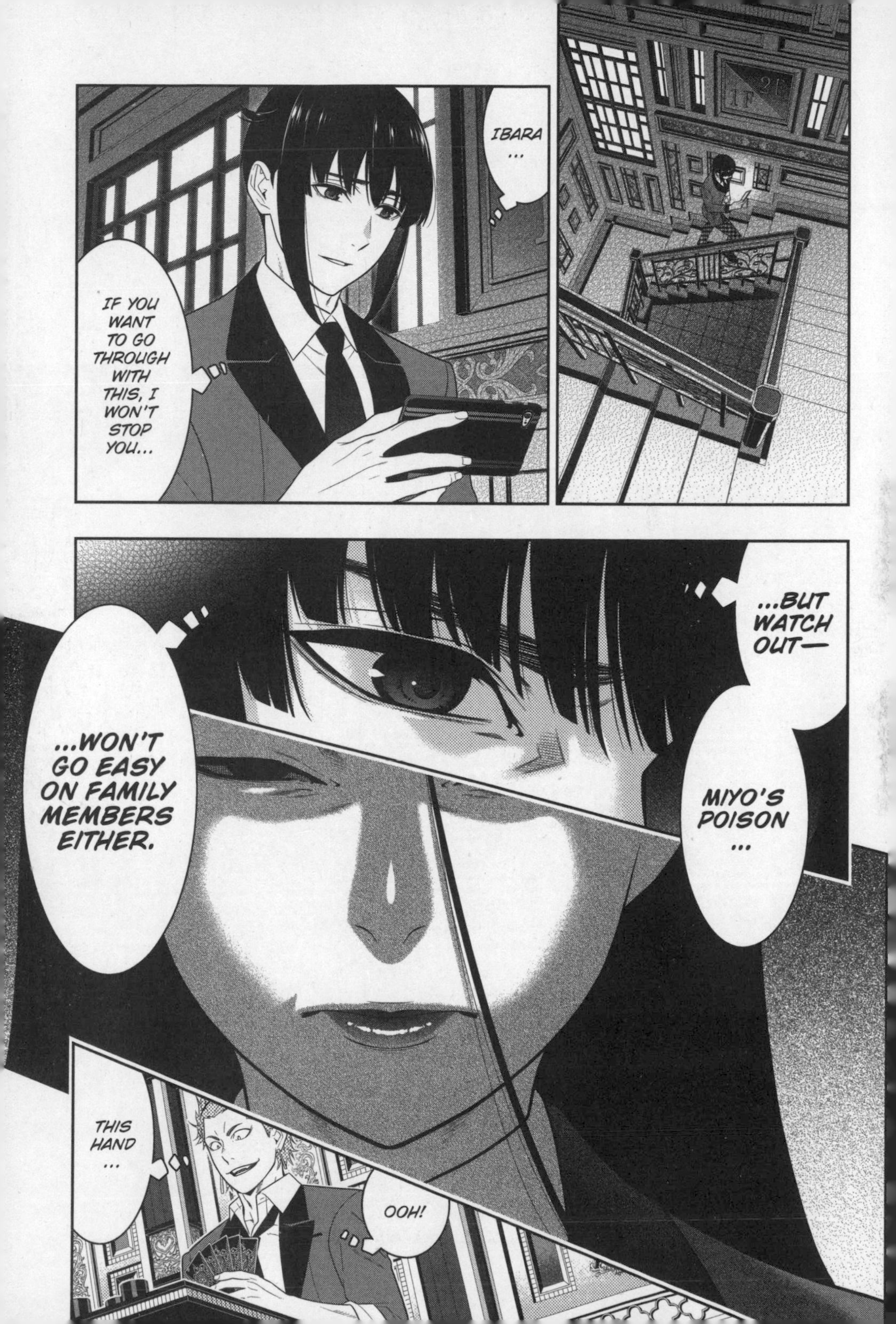
IBARA ...
IF YOU WANT TO GO THROUGH WITH THIS, I WON'T STOP YOU...
...BUT WATCH OUT—
MIYO'S POISON ...
...WON'T GO EASY ON FAMILY MEMBERS EITHER.
OOH!
THIS HAND ...

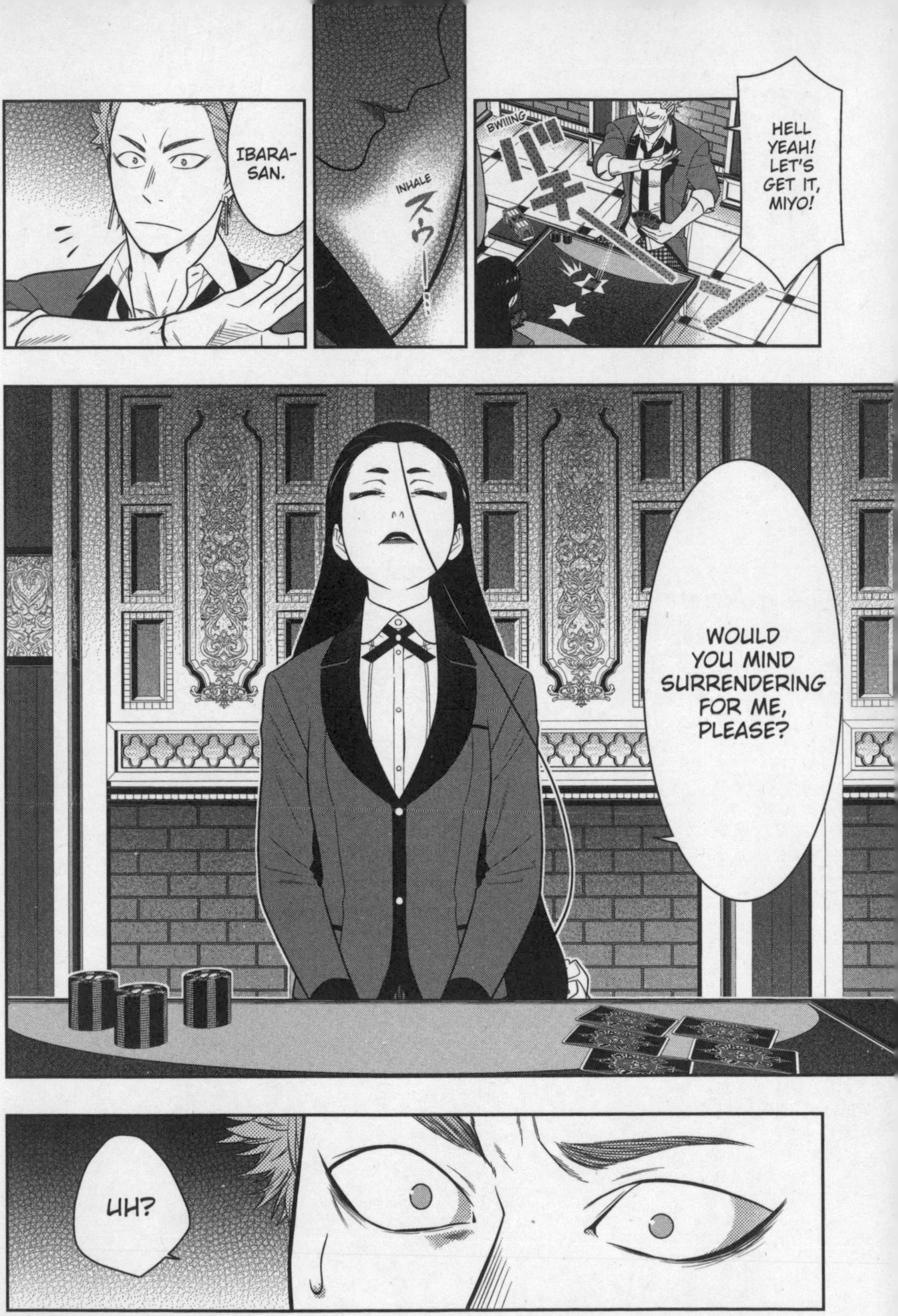

BWIIING
HELL YEAH! LET'S GET IT, MIYO!
INHALE
スウー
IBARA-SAN.
WOULD YOU MIND SURRENDERING FOR ME, PLEASE?
UH?

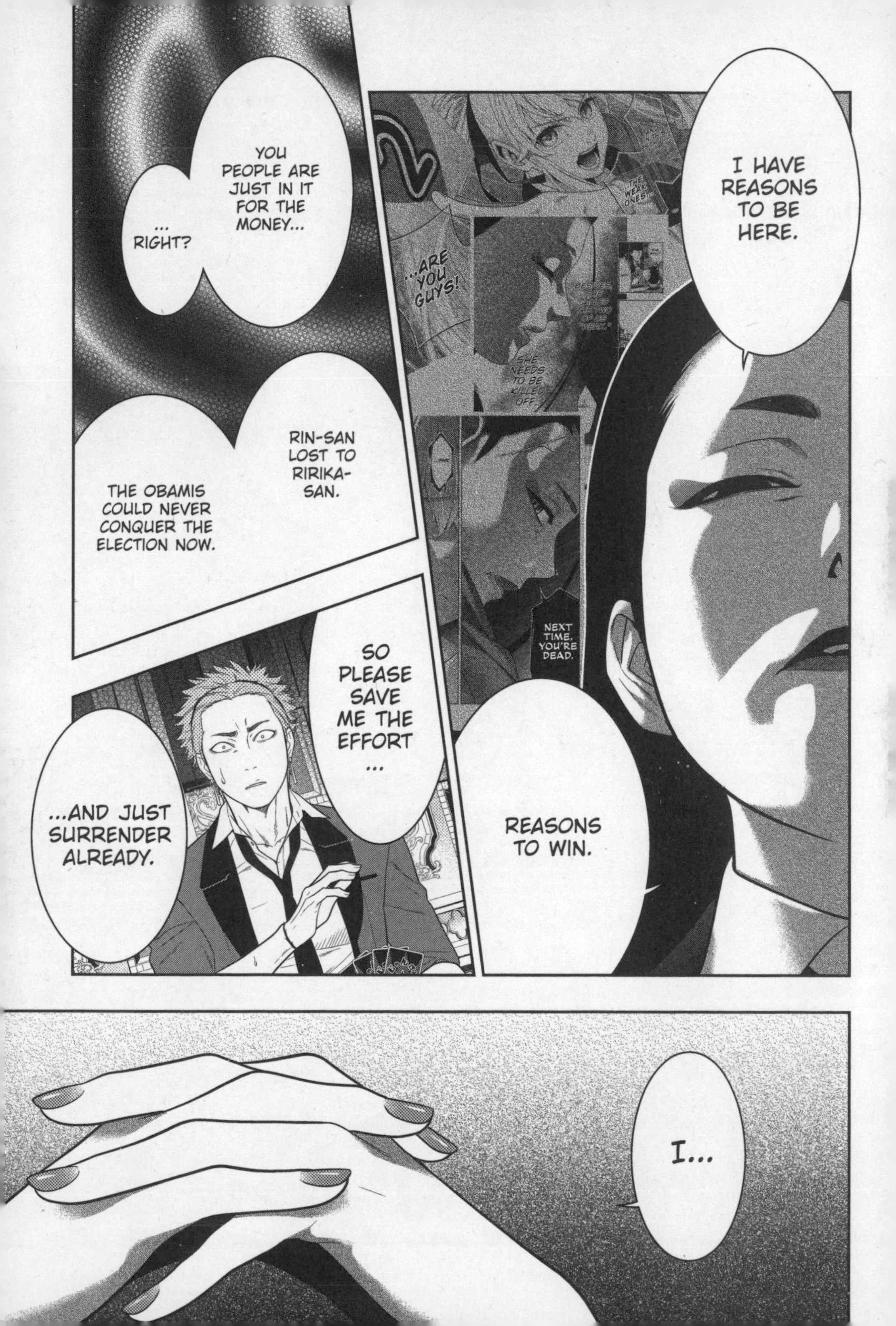
I HAVE REASONS TO BE HERE.
...THE WEAK ONES...
...ARE YOU GUYS!
SHE NEEDS TO BE KILLED OFF.
NEXT TIME, YOU'RE DEAD.
REASONS TO WIN.
YOU PEOPLE ARE JUST IN IT FOR THE MONEY...
...RIGHT?
RIN-SAN LOST TO RIRIKA-SAN.
THE OBAMIS COULD NEVER CONQUER THE ELECTION NOW.
SO PLEASE SAVE ME THE EFFORT...
...AND JUST SURRENDER ALREADY.
I...

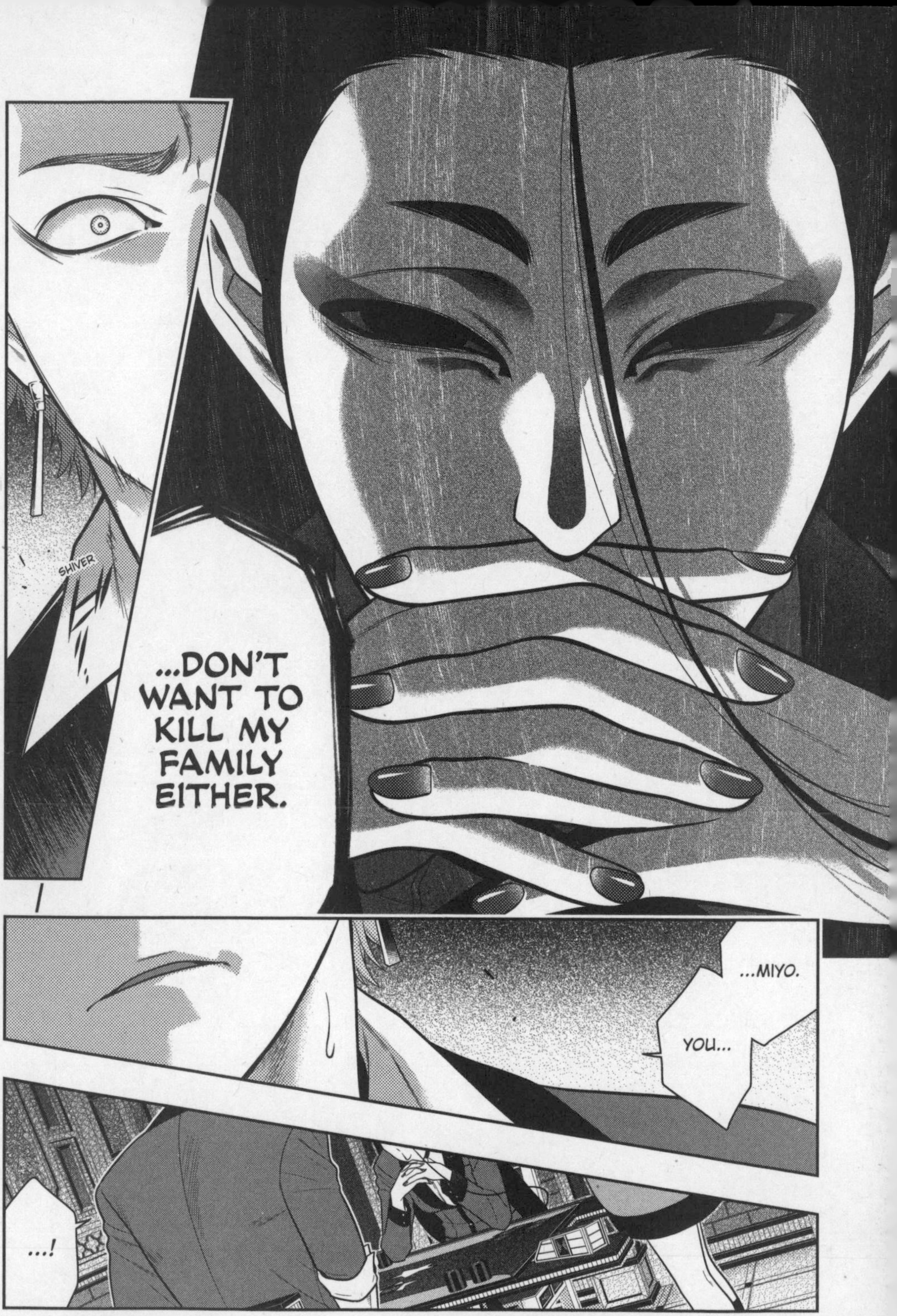
...DON'T WANT TO KILL MY FAMILY EITHER.
SHIVER
...MIYO.
YOU...
...!

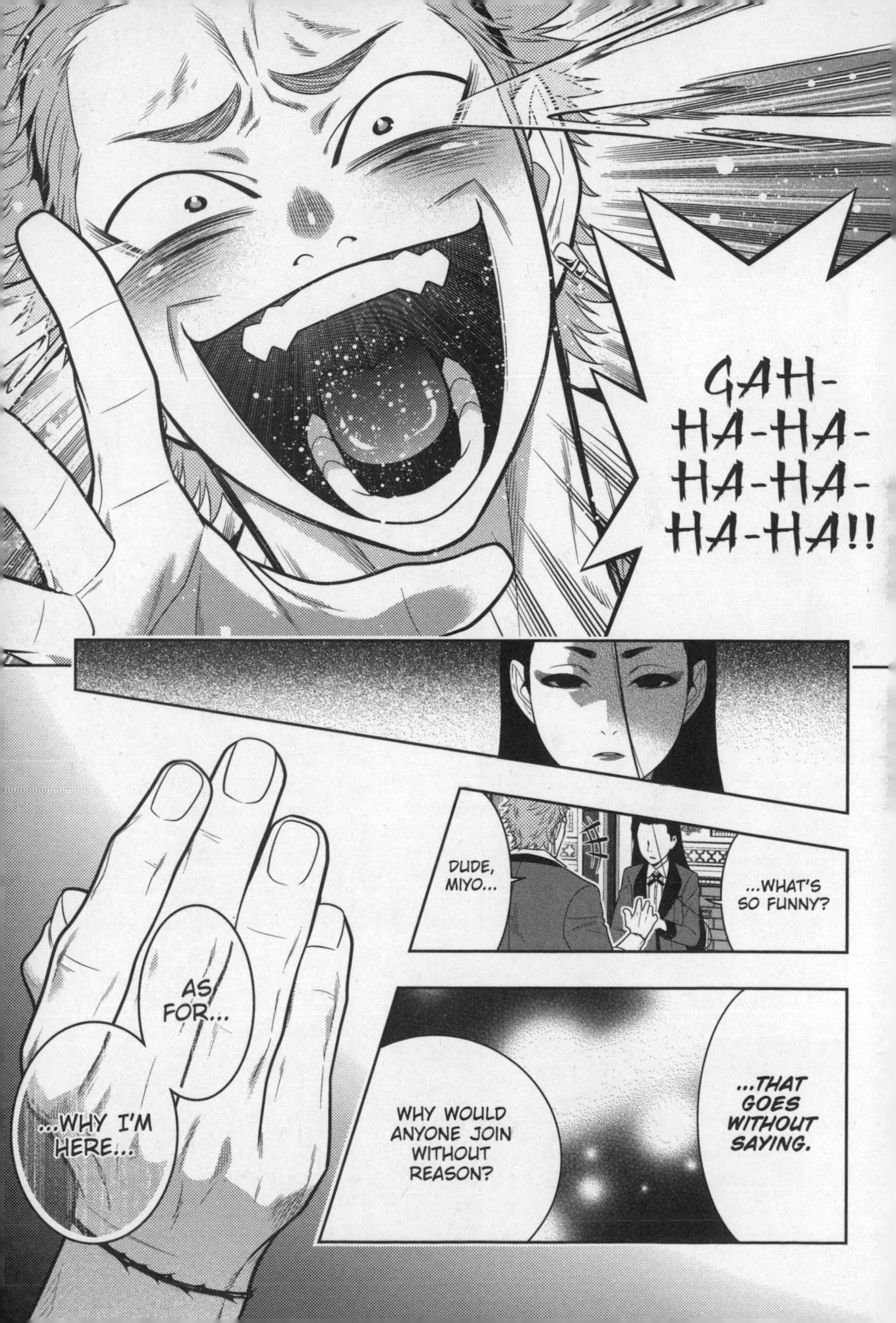
GAH-HA-HA-HA-HA-HA-HA-HA!!
DUDE, MIYO...
...WHAT'S SO FUNNY?
...THAT GOES WITHOUT SAYING.
WHY WOULD ANYONE JOIN WITHOUT REASON?
AS FOR...
...WHY I'M HERE...

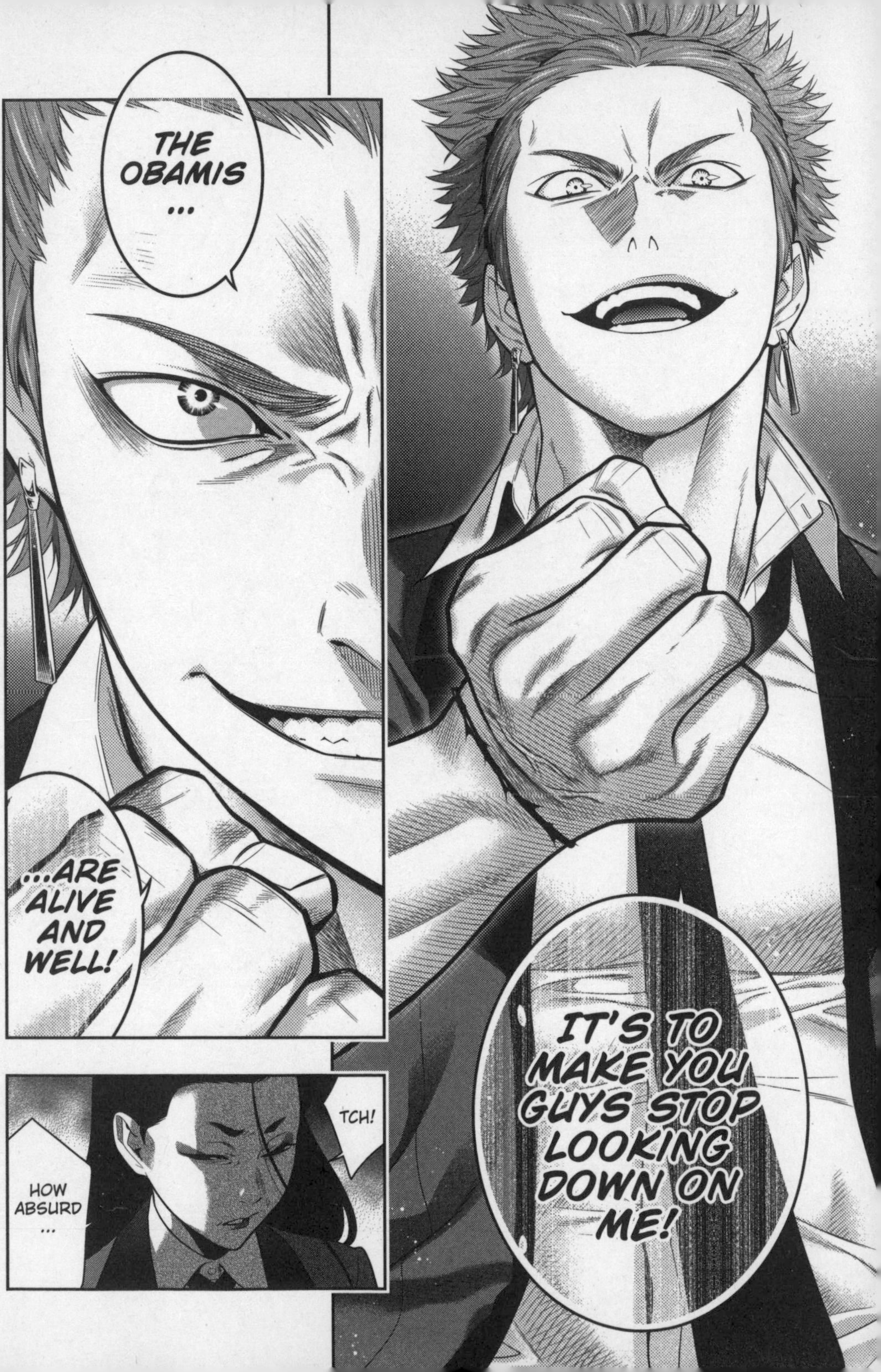
IT'S TO MAKE YOU GUYS STOP LOOKING DOWN ON ME!
THE OBAMIS ...
...ARE ALIVE AND WELL!
TCH!
HOW ABSURD ...

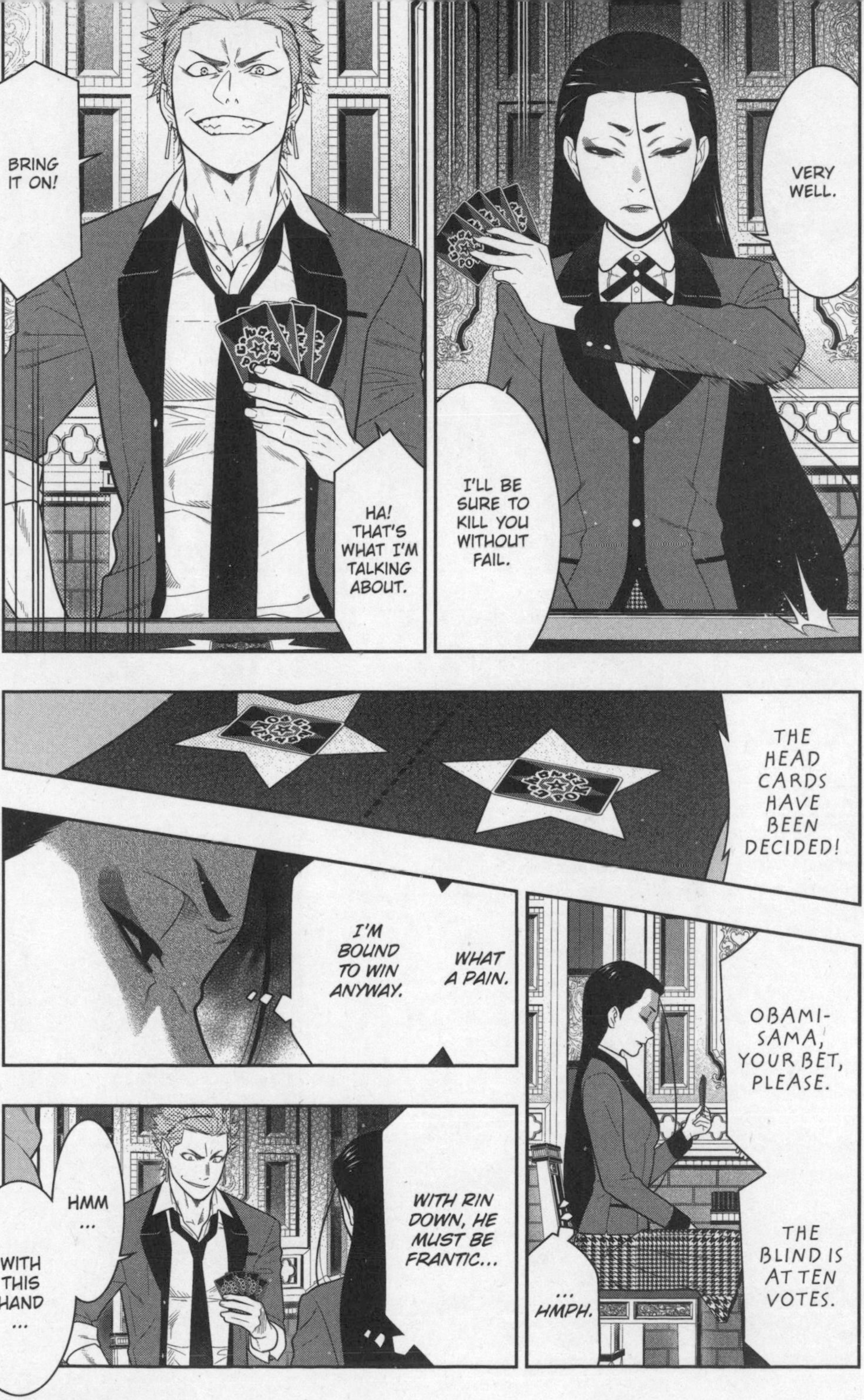
VERY WELL.
I'LL BE SURE TO KILL YOU WITHOUT FAIL.
BRING IT ON!
HA! THAT'S WHAT I'M TALKING ABOUT.
THE HEAD CARDS HAVE BEEN DECIDED!
OBAMI-SAMA, YOUR BET, PLEASE.
THE BLIND IS AT TEN VOTES.
... HMPH.
WHAT A PAIN.
I'M BOUND TO WIN ANYWAY.
WITH RIN DOWN, HE MUST BE FRANTIC...
HMM ...
WITH THIS HAND ...

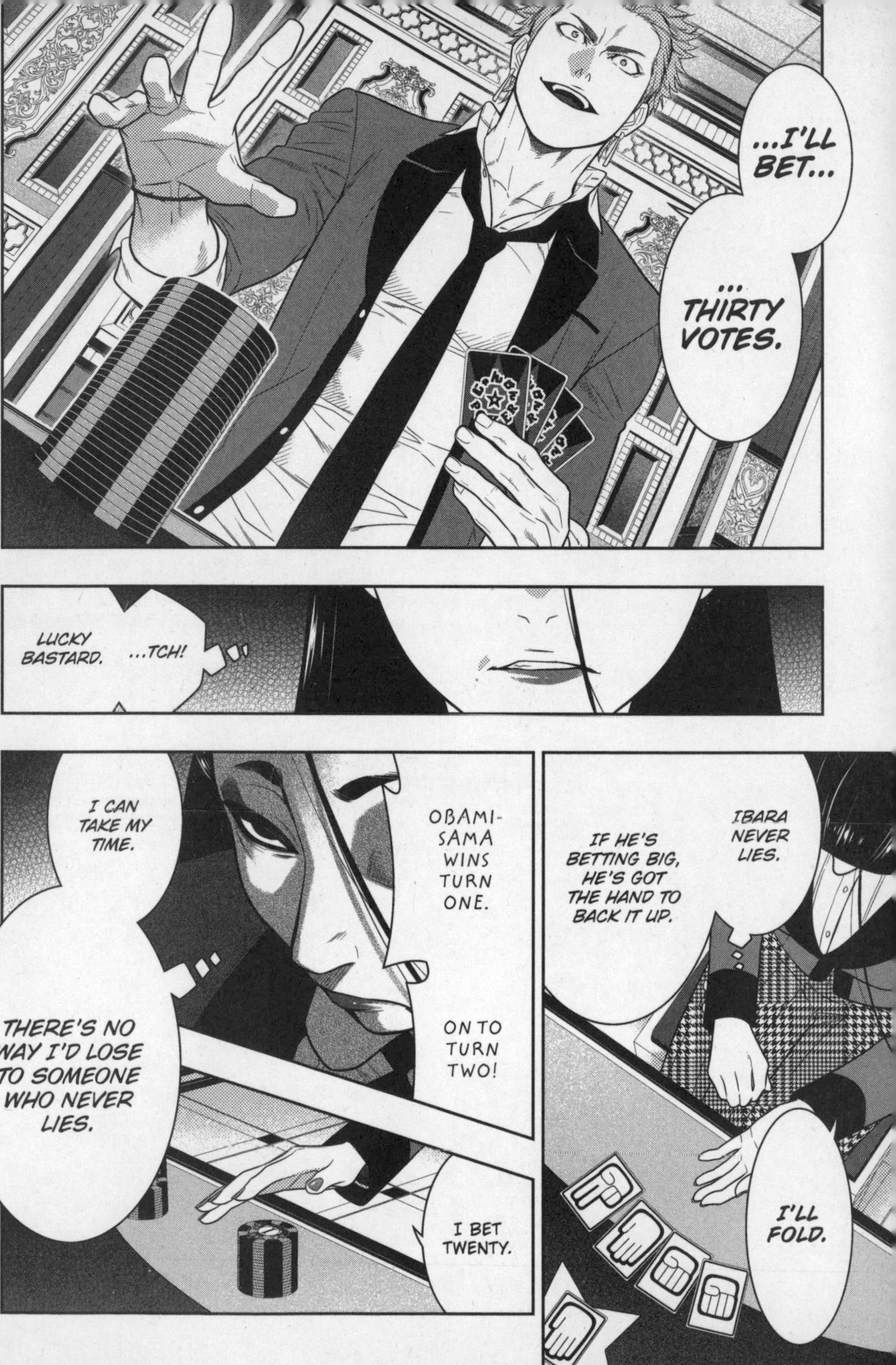
...I'LL BET...
... THIRTY VOTES.
...TCH!
LUCKY BASTARD.
IBARA NEVER LIES.
IF HE'S BETTING BIG, HE'S GOT THE HAND TO BACK IT UP.
I'LL FOLD.
OBAMI-SAMA WINS TURN ONE.
ON TO TURN TWO!
I BET TWENTY.
I CAN TAKE MY TIME.
THERE'S NO WAY I'D LOSE TO SOMEONE WHO NEVER LIES.

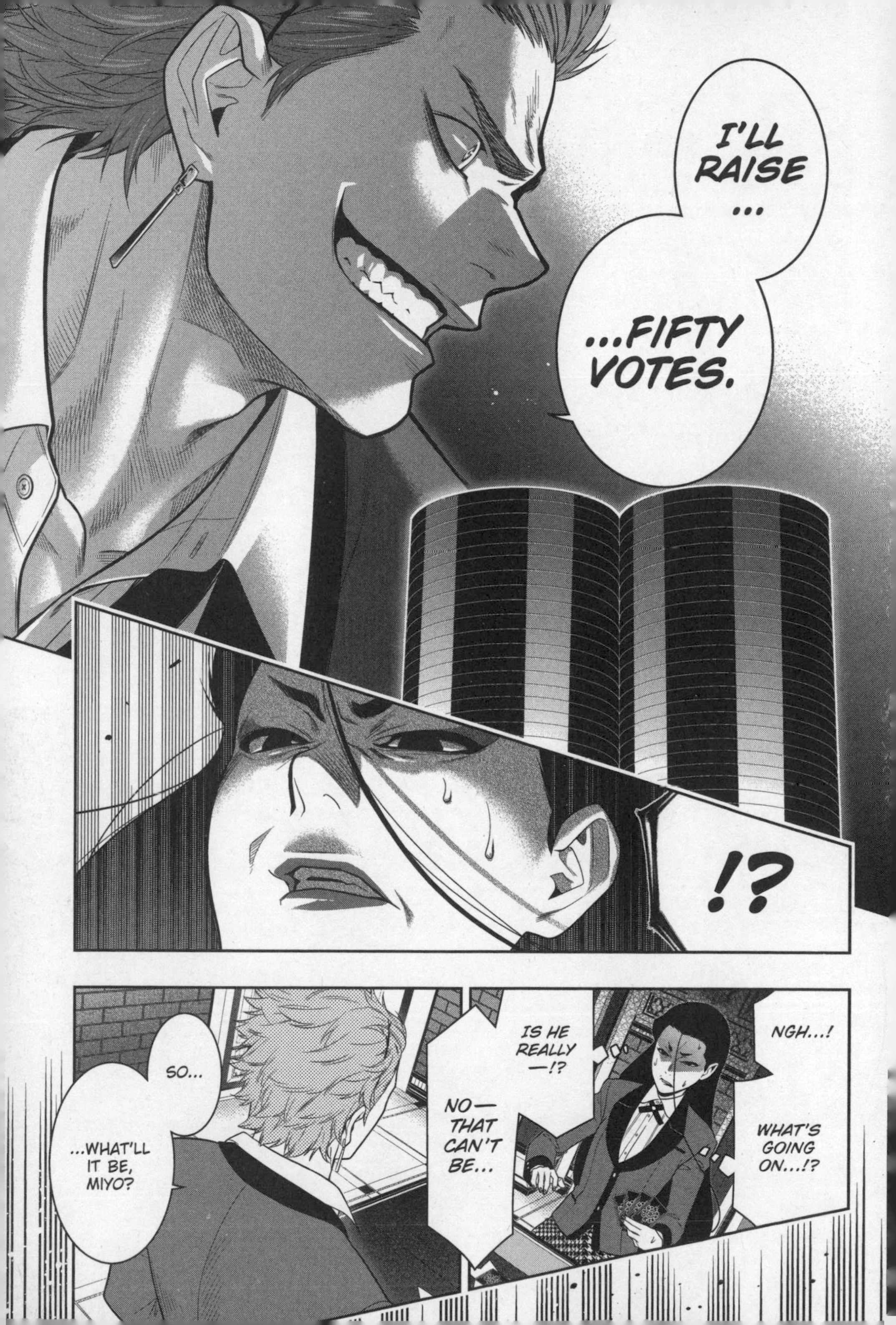
I'LL RAISE ...
...FIFTY VOTES.
!?
NGH...!
IS HE REALLY—!?
WHAT'S GOING ON...!?
NO—THAT CAN'T BE...
SO...
...WHAT'LL IT BE, MIYO?

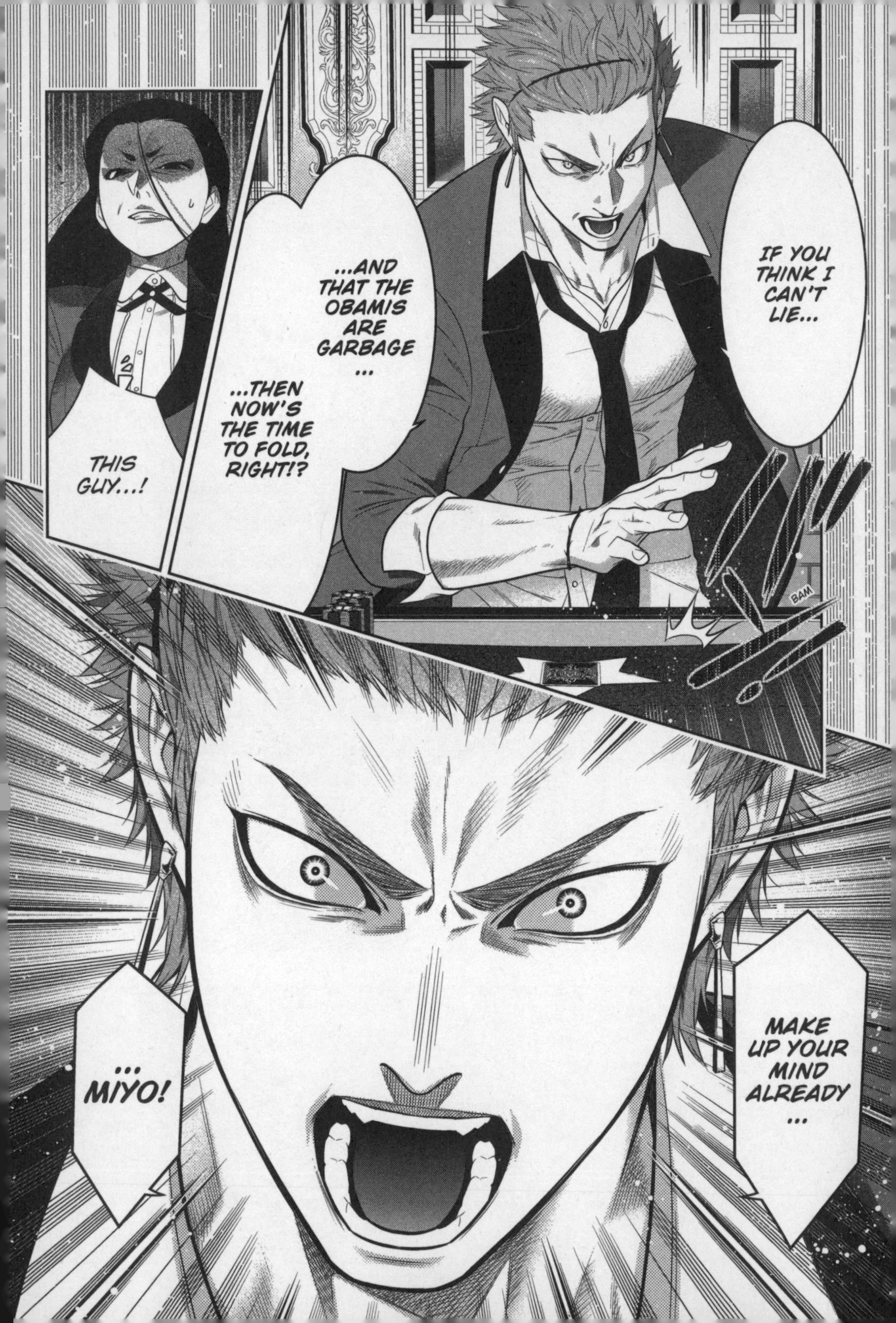
IF YOU THINK I CAN'T LIE...
...AND THAT THE OBAMIS ARE GARBAGE ...
...THEN NOW'S THE TIME TO FOLD, RIGHT!?
THIS GUY...!
BAM
MAKE UP YOUR MIND ALREADY ...
... MIYO!

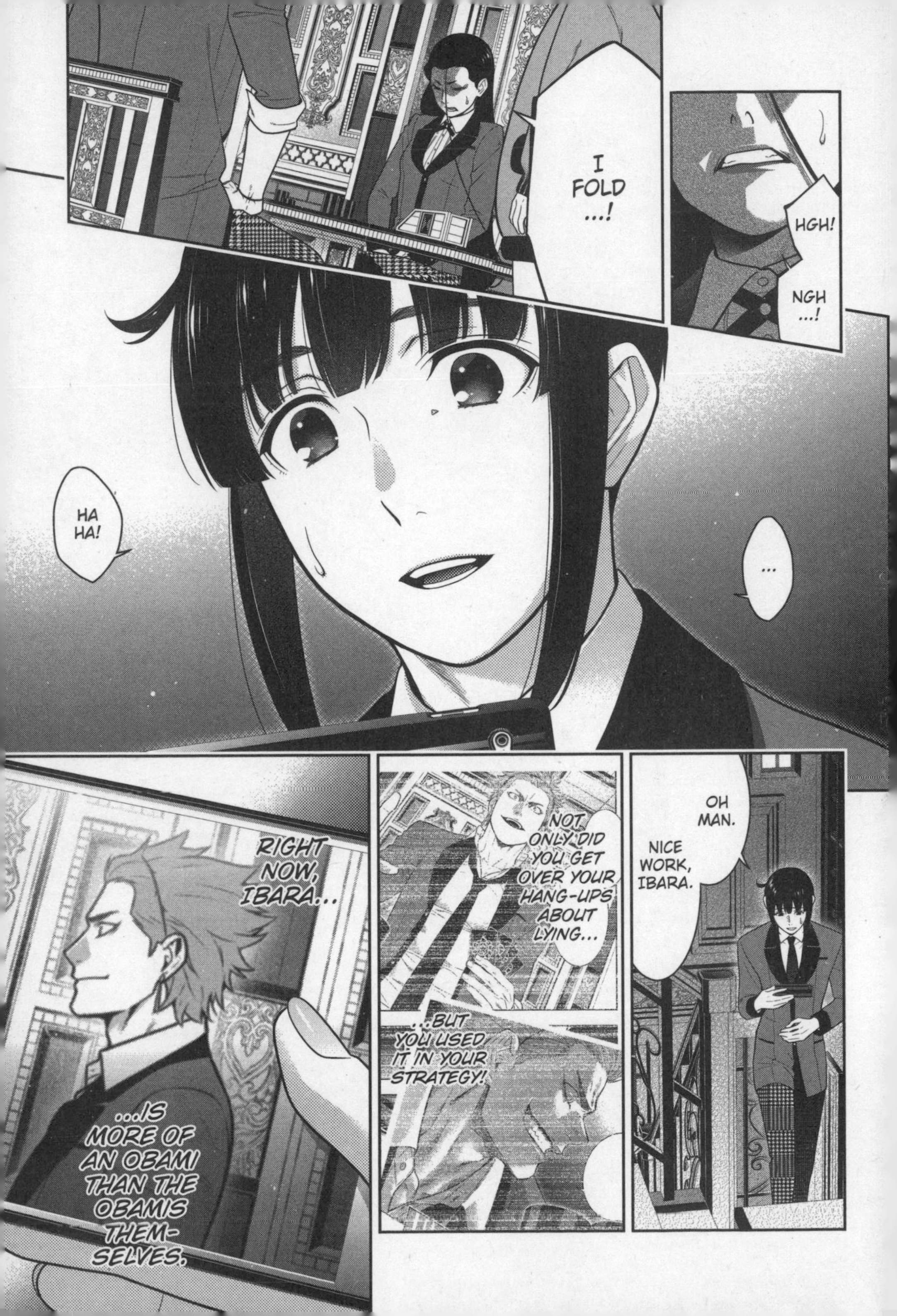
HGH!
NGH ...!
I FOLD ...!
...
HA HA!
OH MAN.
NICE WORK, IBARA.
NOT ONLY DID YOU GET OVER YOUR HANG-UPS ABOUT LYING...
...BUT YOU USED IT IN YOUR STRATEGY!
RIGHT NOW, IBARA...
...IS MORE OF AN OBAMI THAN THE OBAMIS THEM-SELVES.

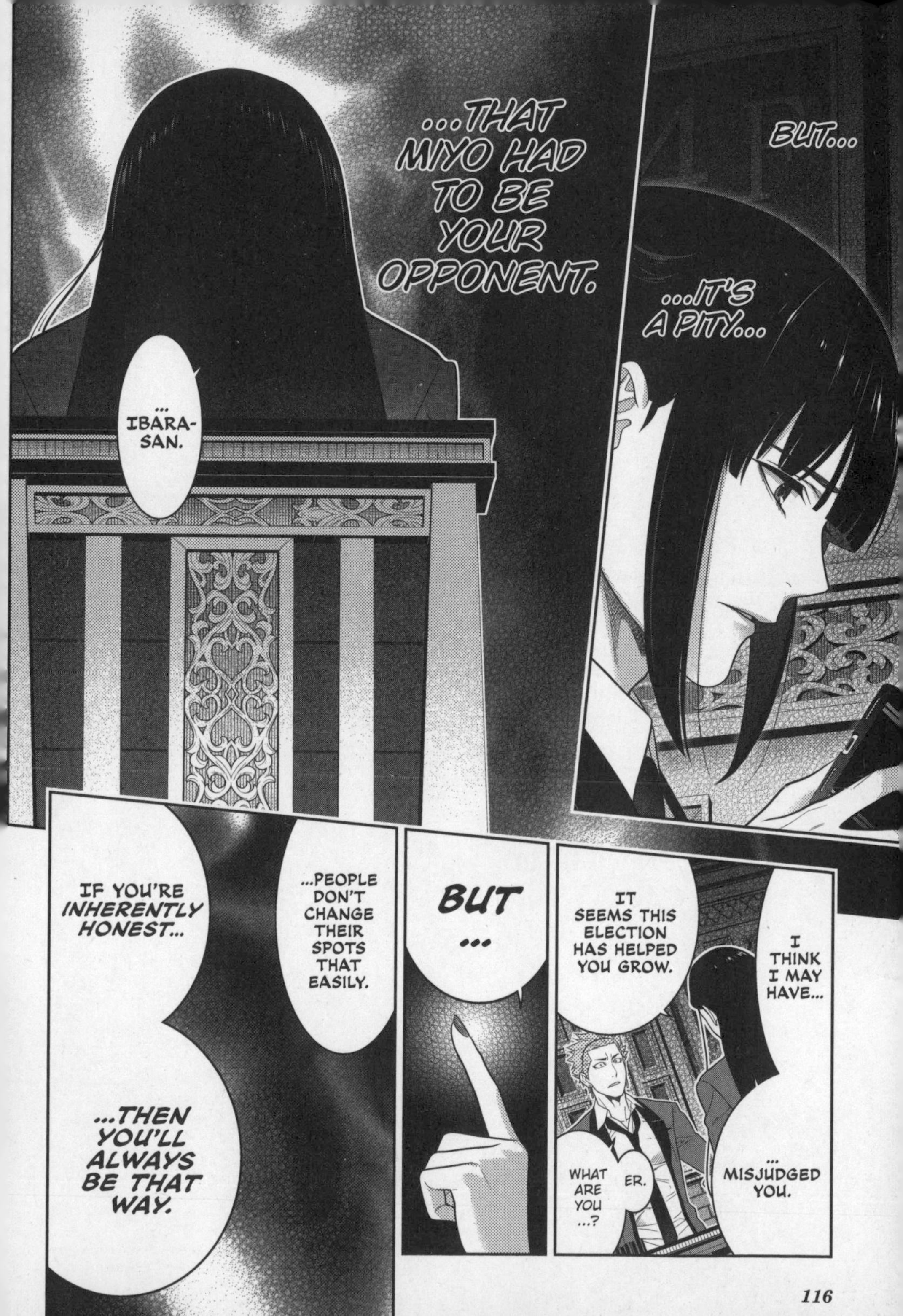

BUT...
...IT'S A PITY...
...THAT MIYO HAD TO BE YOUR OPPONENT.
... IBARA-SAN.
I THINK I MAY HAVE...
... MISJUDGED YOU.
IT SEEMS THIS ELECTION HAS HELPED YOU GROW.
ER.
WHAT ARE YOU ...?
BUT ...
...PEOPLE DON'T CHANGE THEIR SPOTS THAT EASILY.
IF YOU'RE *INHERENTLY* HONEST...
...THEN YOU'LL ALWAYS BE THAT WAY.

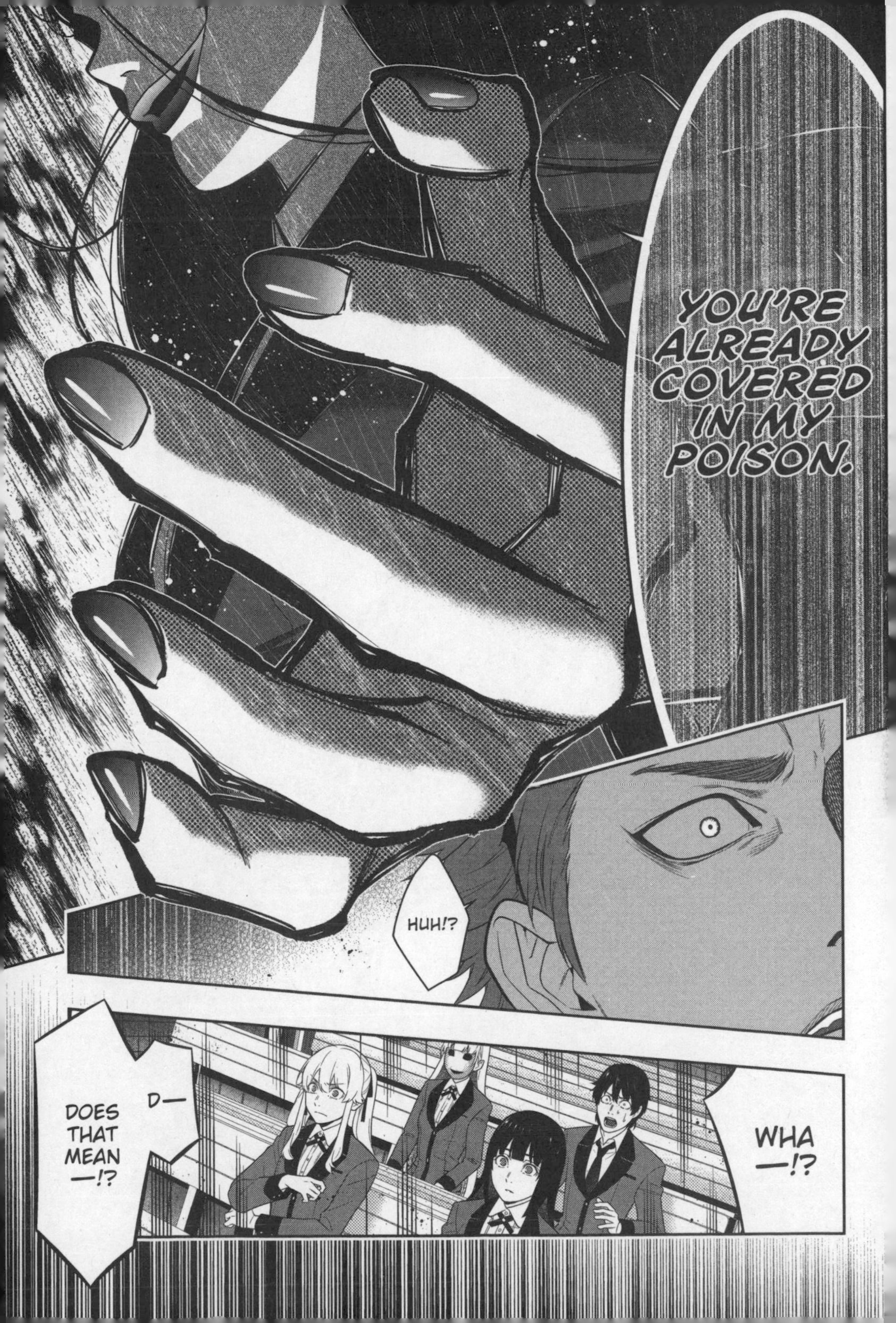
YOU'RE ALREADY COVERED IN MY POISON.
HUH!?
WHA—!?
D—
DOES THAT MEAN—!?

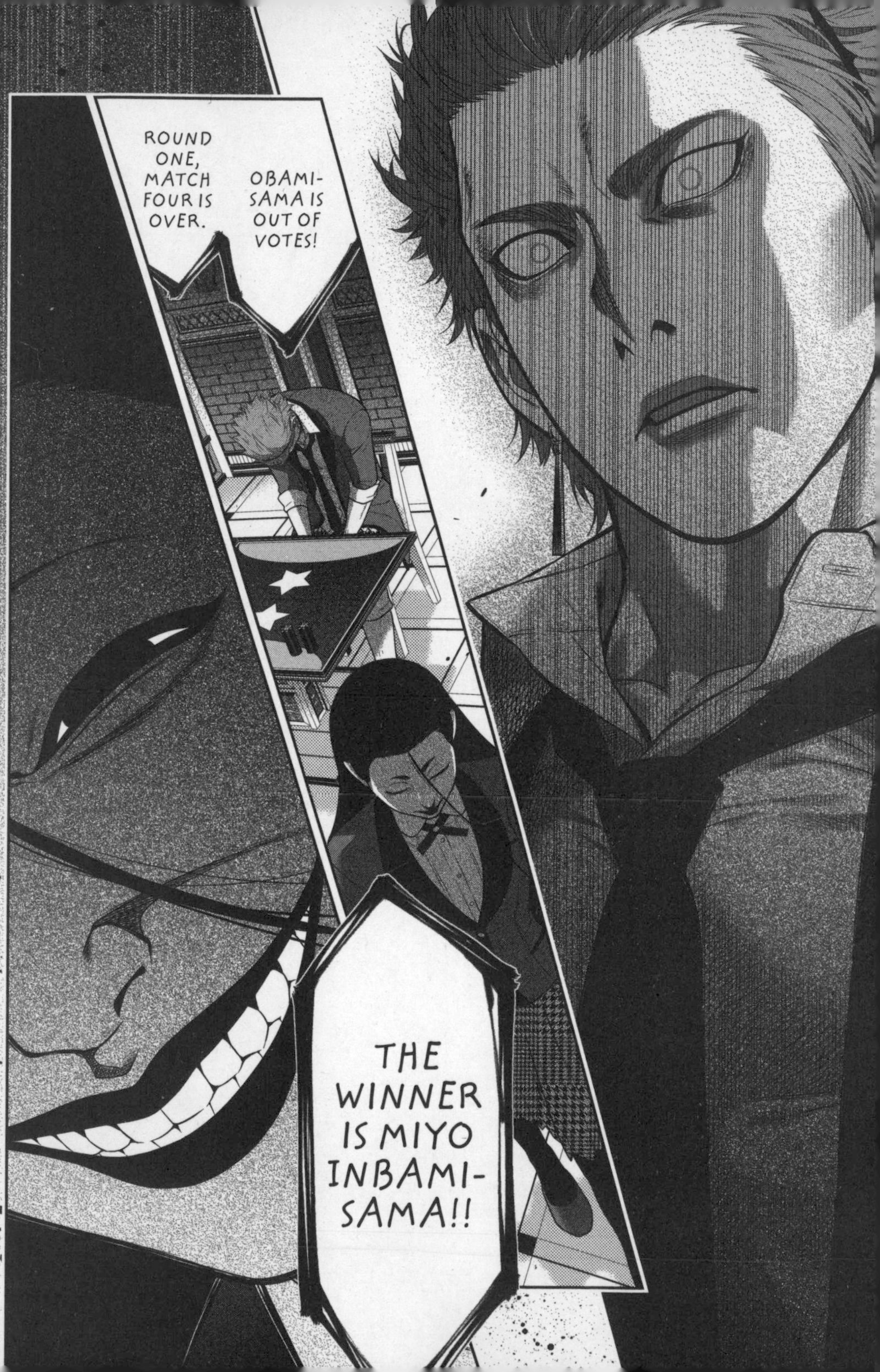
ROUND ONE, MATCH FOUR IS OVER.
OBAMI-SAMA IS OUT OF VOTES!
THE WINNER IS MIYO INBAMI-SAMA!!

CHAPTER SIXTY-SEVEN
THE GIRL WHO CAN ONLY SMILE

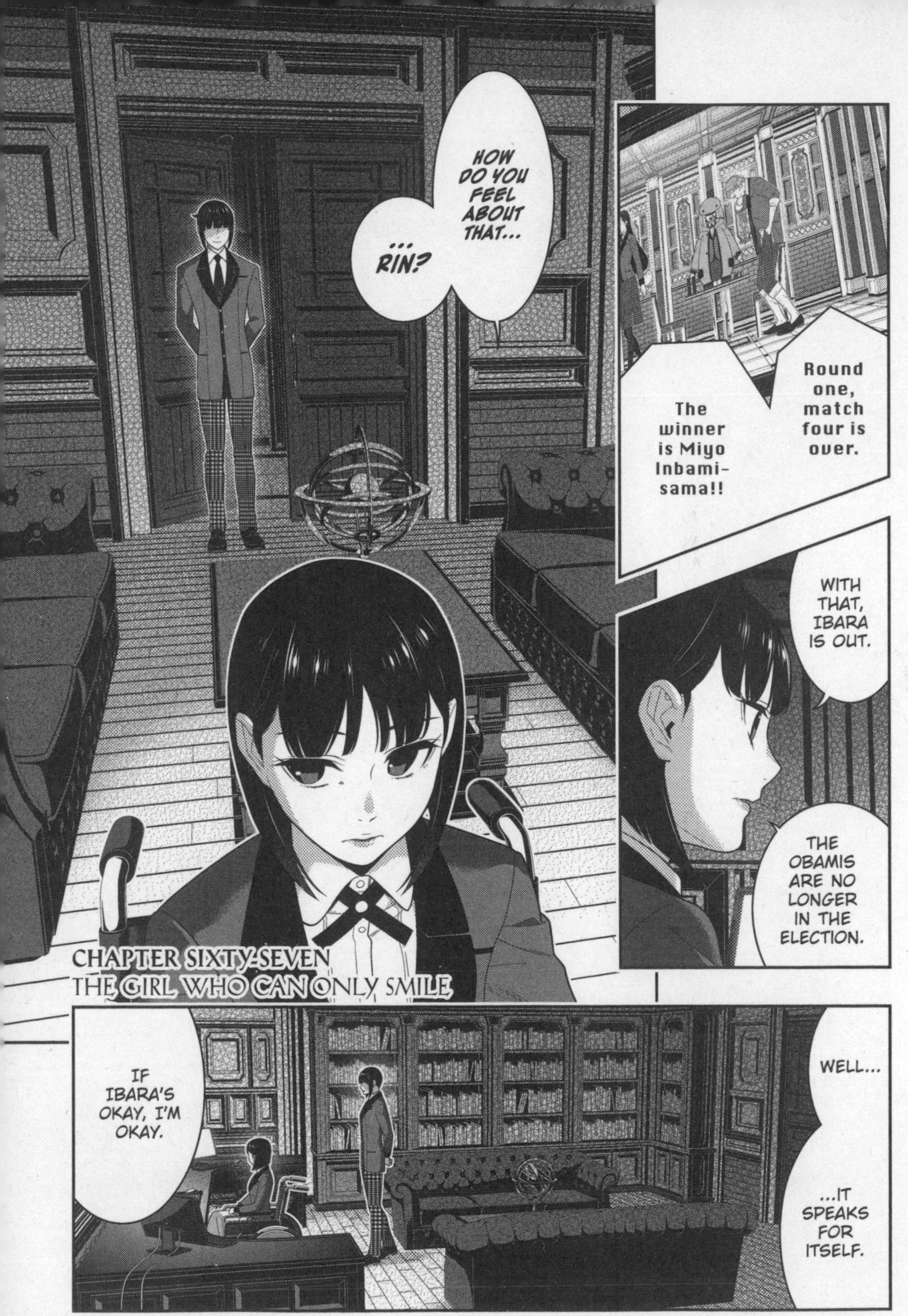
Round one, match four is over.
The winner is Miyo Inbami-sama!!
WITH THAT, IBARA IS OUT.
THE OBAMIS ARE NO LONGER IN THE ELECTION.
HOW DO YOU FEEL ABOUT THAT...
...RIN?
WELL...
...IT SPEAKS FOR ITSELF.
IF IBARA'S OKAY, I'M OKAY.

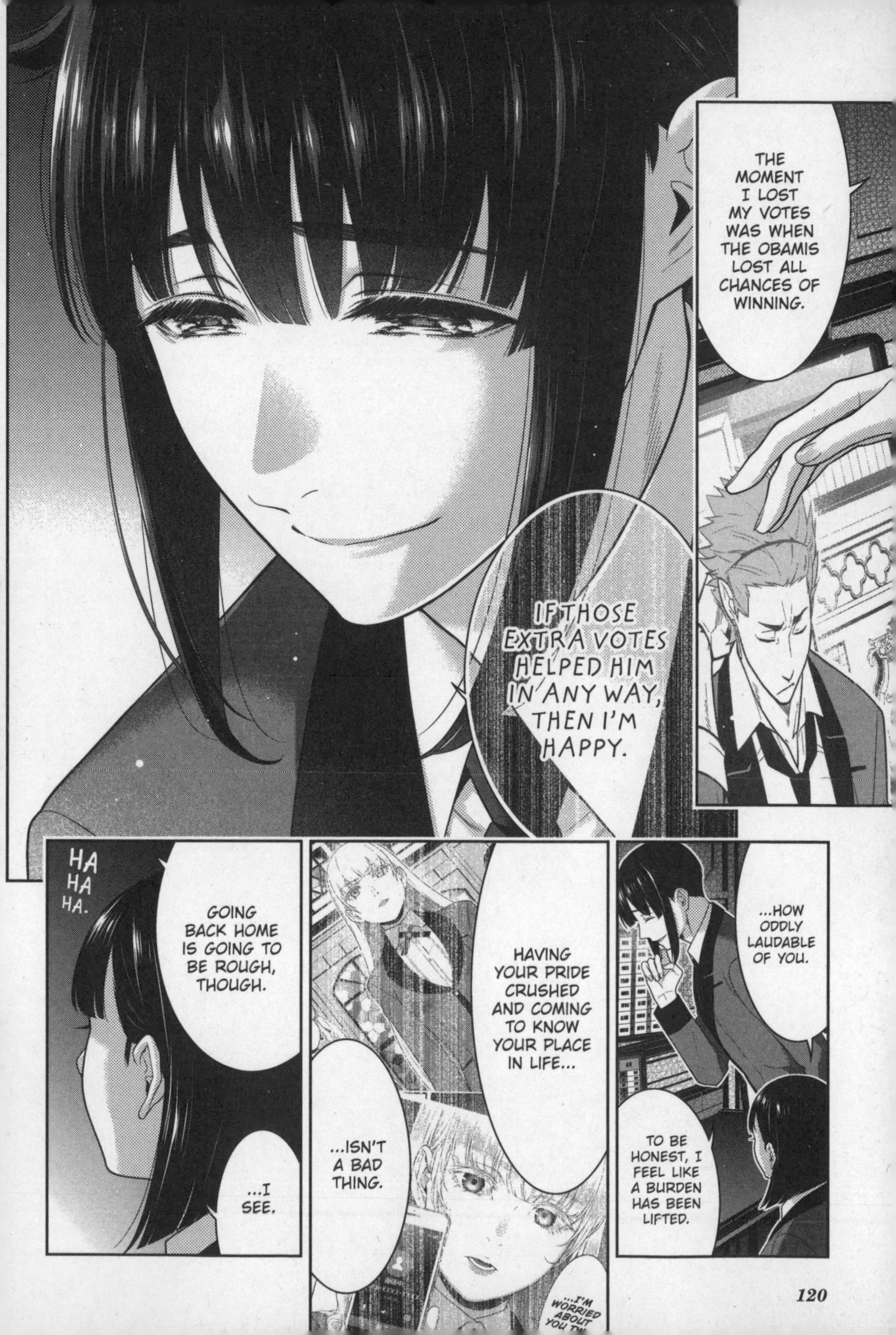
THE MOMENT I LOST MY VOTES WAS WHEN THE OBAMIS LOST ALL CHANCES OF WINNING.
IF THOSE EXTRA VOTES HELPED HIM IN ANY WAY, THEN I'M HAPPY.
...HOW ODDLY LAUDABLE OF YOU.
TO BE HONEST, I FEEL LIKE A BURDEN HAS BEEN LIFTED.
HAVING YOUR PRIDE CRUSHED AND COMING TO KNOW YOUR PLACE IN LIFE...
...ISN'T A BAD THING.
...I'M WORRIED ABOUT YOU
GOING BACK HOME IS GOING TO BE ROUGH, THOUGH.
HA HA HA.
...I SEE.

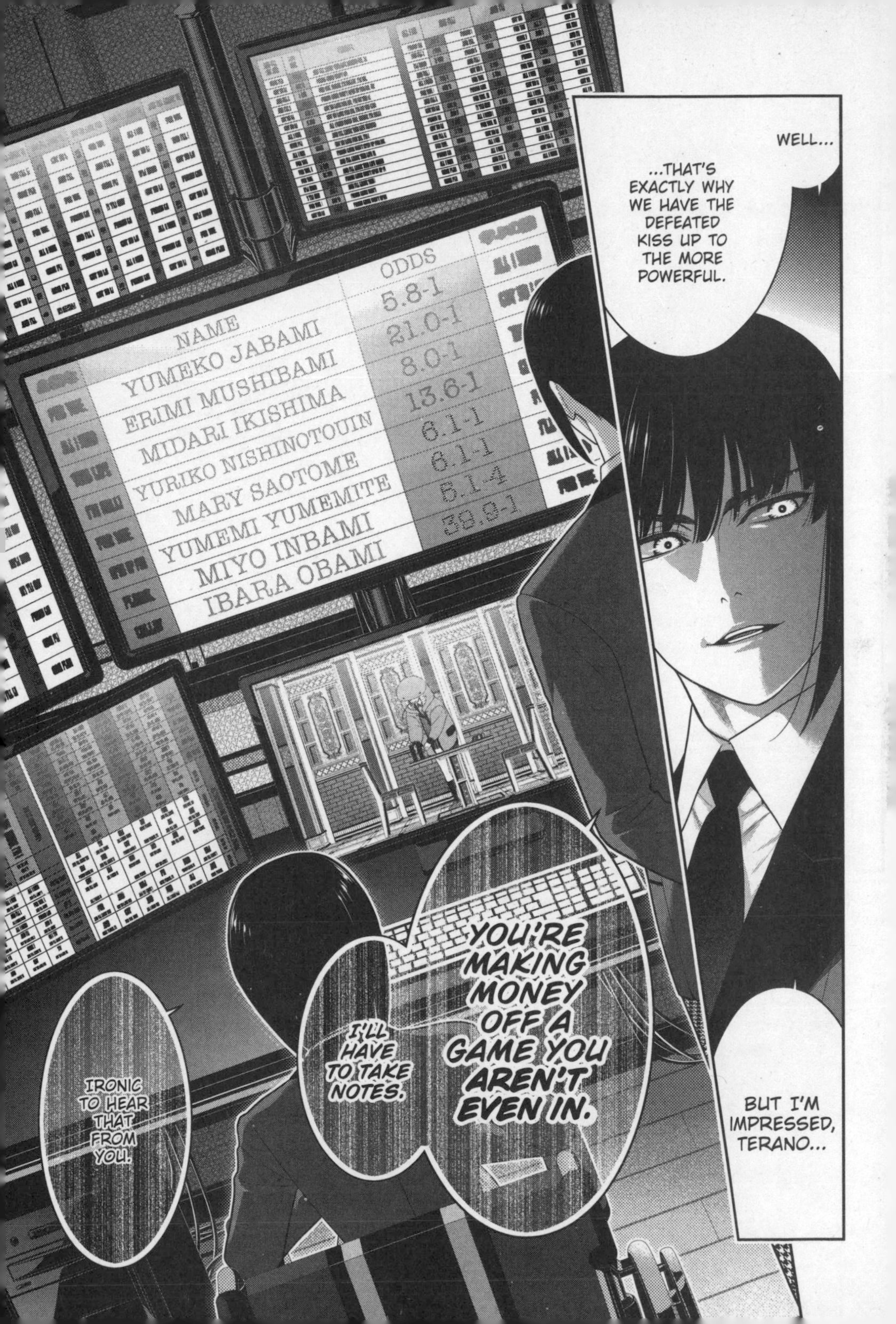
WELL...
...THAT'S EXACTLY WHY WE HAVE THE DEFEATED KISS UP TO THE MORE POWERFUL.
BUT I'M IMPRESSED, TERANO...
NAME
ODDS
YUMEKO JABAMI 5.8-1
ERIMI MUSHIBAMI 21.0-1
MIDARI IKISHIMA 8.0-1
YURIKO NISHINOTOUIN 13.6-1
MARY SAOTOME 6.1-1
YUMEMI YUMEMITE 6.1-1
MIYO INBAMI 5.1-4
IBARA OBAMI 39.9-1
YOU'RE MAKING MONEY OFF A GAME YOU AREN'T EVEN IN.
I'LL HAVE TO TAKE NOTES.
IRONIC TO HEAR THAT FROM YOU.

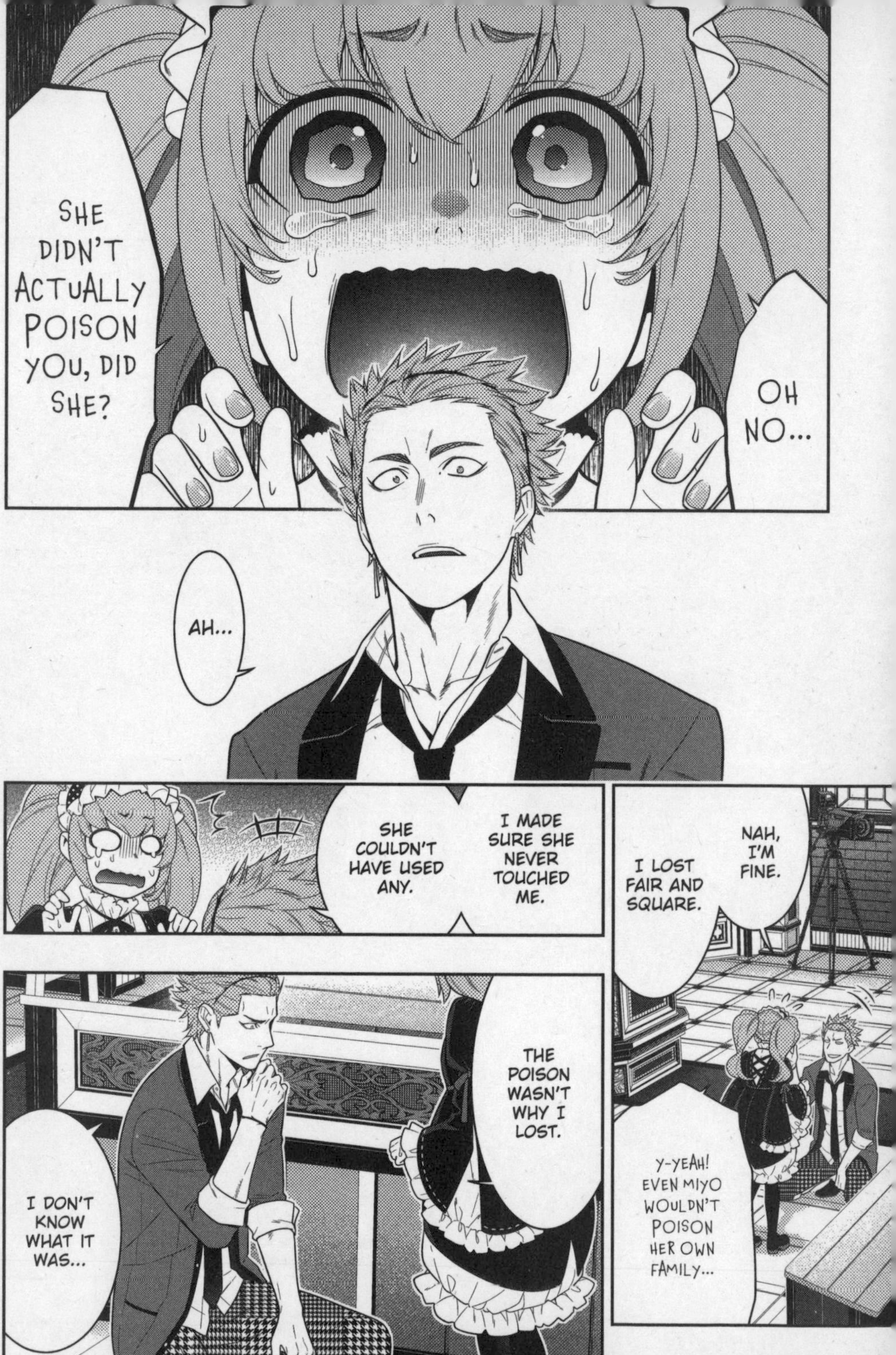
OH NO...
SHE DIDN'T ACTUALLY POISON YOU, DID SHE?
AH...
NAH, I'M FINE.
I LOST FAIR AND SQUARE.
Y-YEAH! EVEN MIYO WOULDN'T POISON HER OWN FAMILY...
I MADE SURE SHE NEVER TOUCHED ME.
SHE COULDN'T HAVE USED ANY.
THE POISON WASN'T WHY I LOST.
I DON'T KNOW WHAT IT WAS...

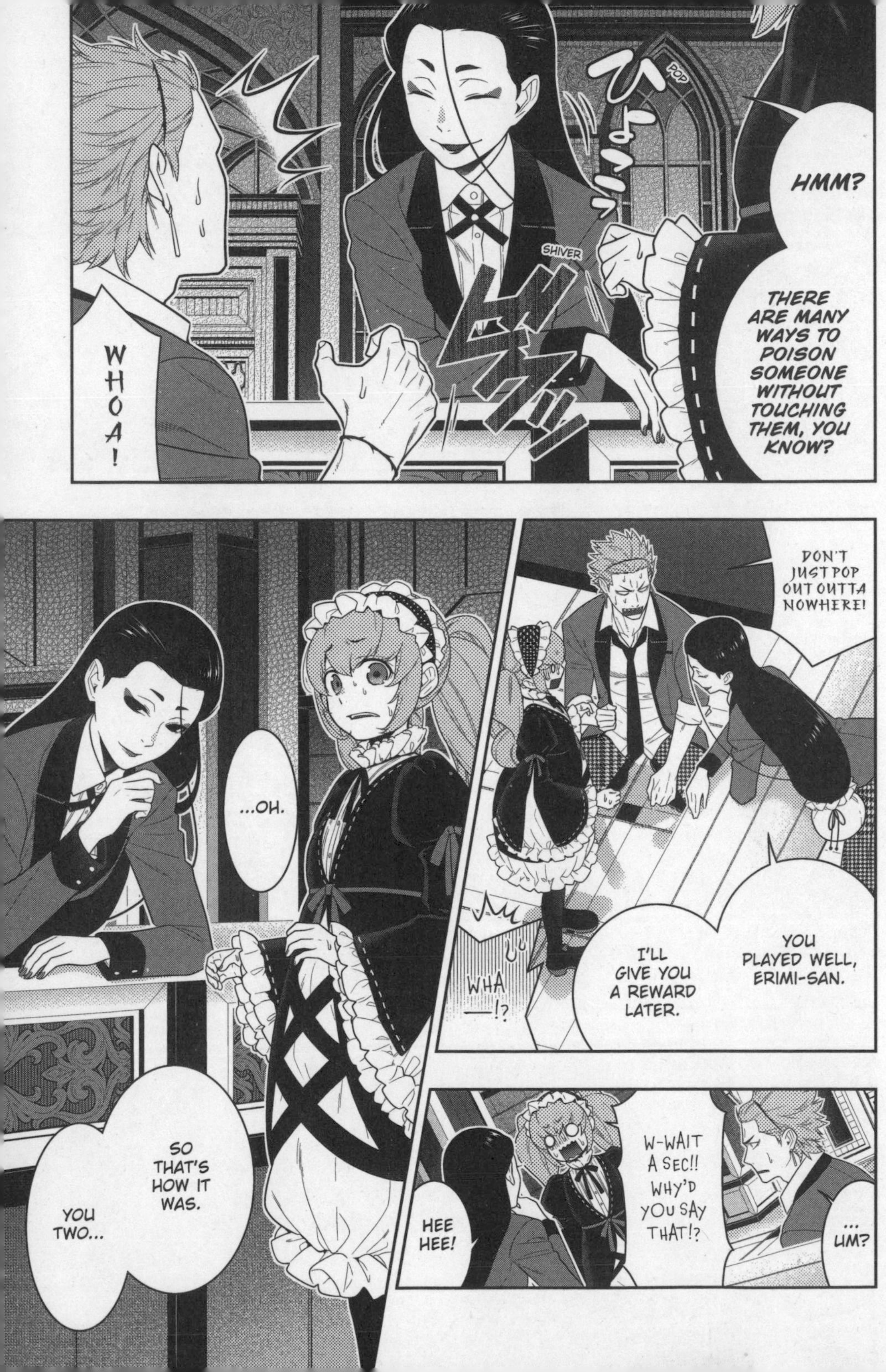
HMM?
POP
THERE ARE MANY WAYS TO POISON SOMEONE WITHOUT TOUCHING THEM, YOU KNOW?
SHIVER
WHOA!
DON'T JUST POP OUT OUTTA NOWHERE!
YOU PLAYED WELL, ERIMI-SAN.
I'LL GIVE YOU A REWARD LATER.
WHA—!?
...UM?
W-WAIT A SEC!! WHY'D YOU SAY THAT!?
HEE HEE!
...OH.
SO THAT'S HOW IT WAS.
YOU TWO...

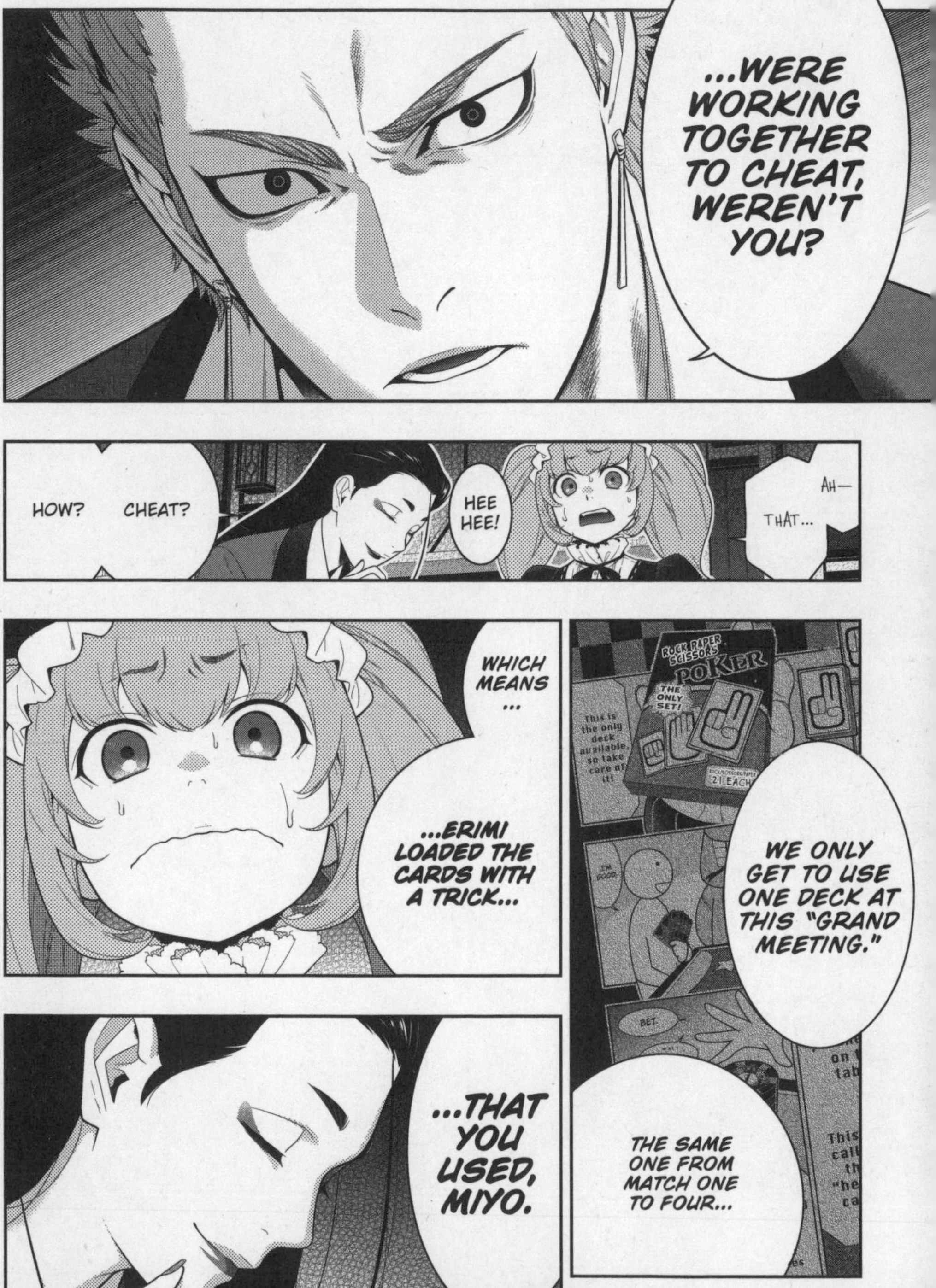
...WERE WORKING TOGETHER TO CHEAT, WEREN'T YOU?
AH— THAT...
HEE HEE!
HOW? CHEAT?
ROCK PAPER SCISSORS POKER
THE ONLY SET!
This is the only deck available, so take care of it!
21 EACH
I'M GOOD.
BET.
WE ONLY GET TO USE ONE DECK AT THIS "GRAND MEETING."
THE SAME ONE FROM MATCH ONE TO FOUR...
WHICH MEANS ...
...ERIMI LOADED THE CARDS WITH A TRICK...
...THAT YOU USED, MIYO.

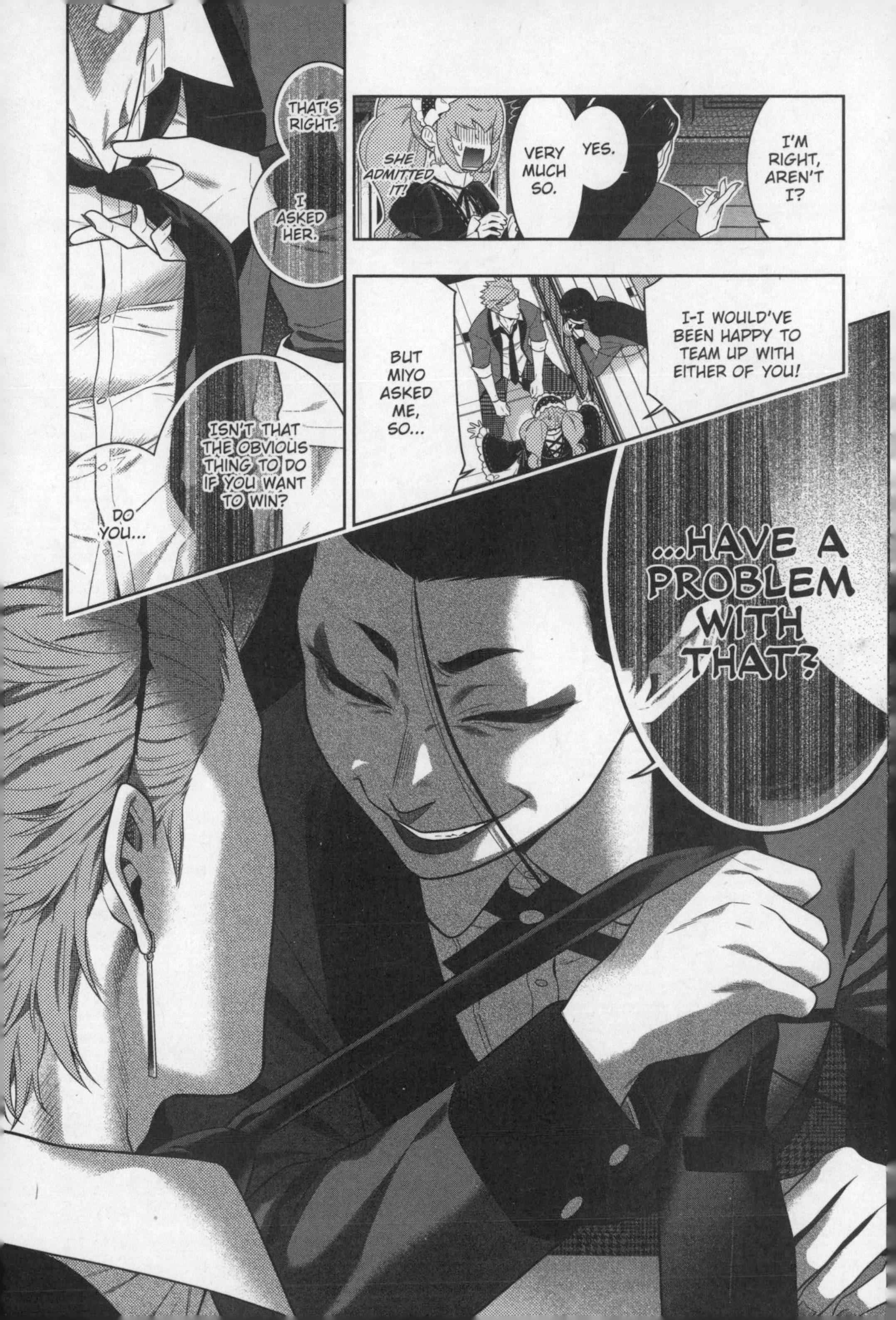
I'M RIGHT, AREN'T I?
YES.
VERY MUCH SO.
SHE ADMITTED IT!
I-I WOULD'VE BEEN HAPPY TO TEAM UP WITH EITHER OF YOU!
BUT MIYO ASKED ME, SO...
THAT'S RIGHT.
I ASKED HER.
ISN'T THAT THE OBVIOUS THING TO DO IF YOU WANT TO WIN?
DO YOU...
...HAVE A PROBLEM WITH THAT?

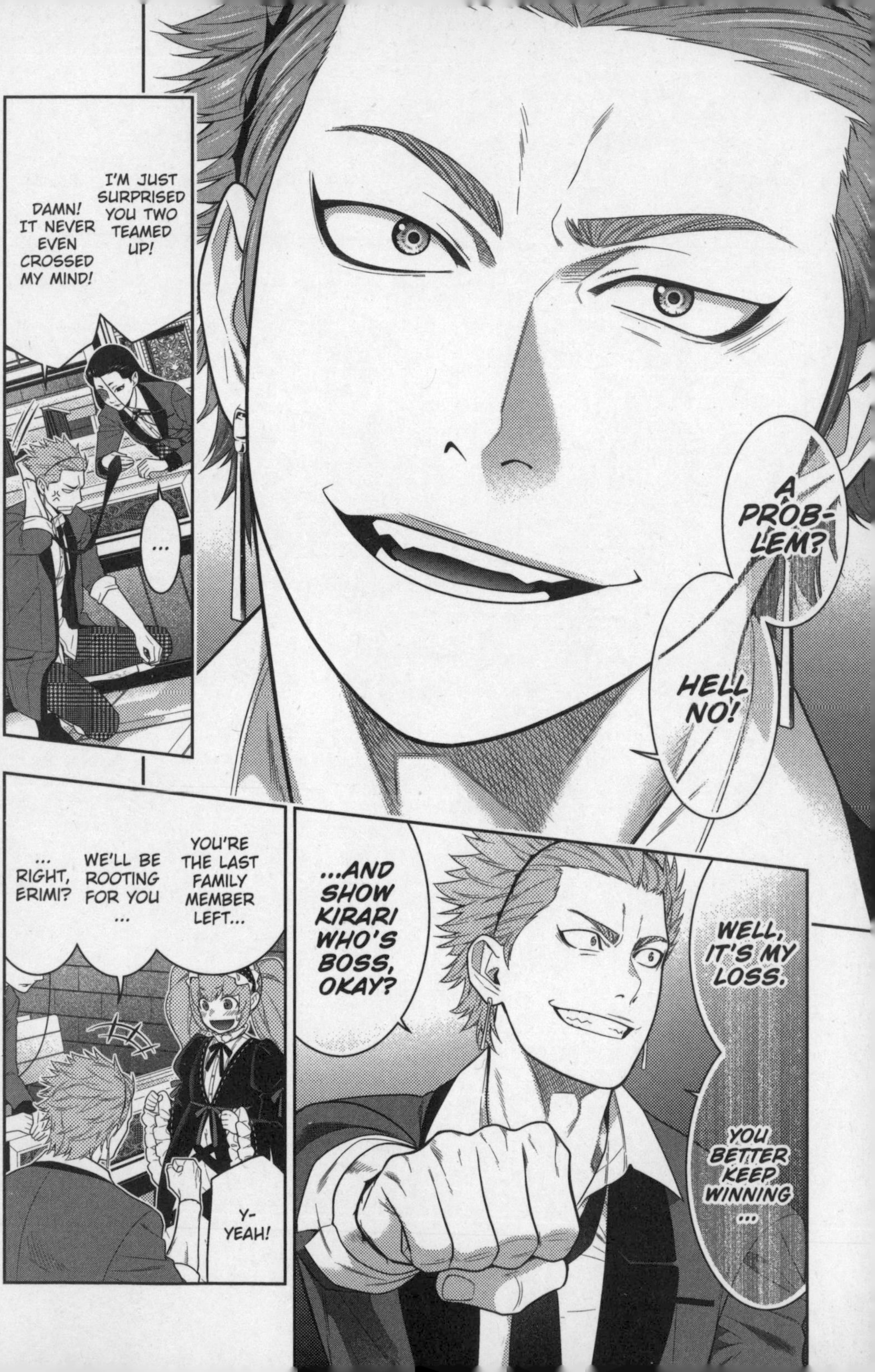
A PROB-LEM?
HELL NO!
I'M JUST SURPRISED YOU TWO TEAMED UP!
DAMN! IT NEVER EVEN CROSSED MY MIND!
...
WELL, IT'S MY LOSS.
YOU BETTER KEEP WINNING...
...AND SHOW KIRARI WHO'S BOSS, OKAY?
YOU'RE THE LAST FAMILY MEMBER LEFT...
WE'LL BE ROOTING FOR YOU...
...RIGHT, ERIMI?
Y-YEAH!

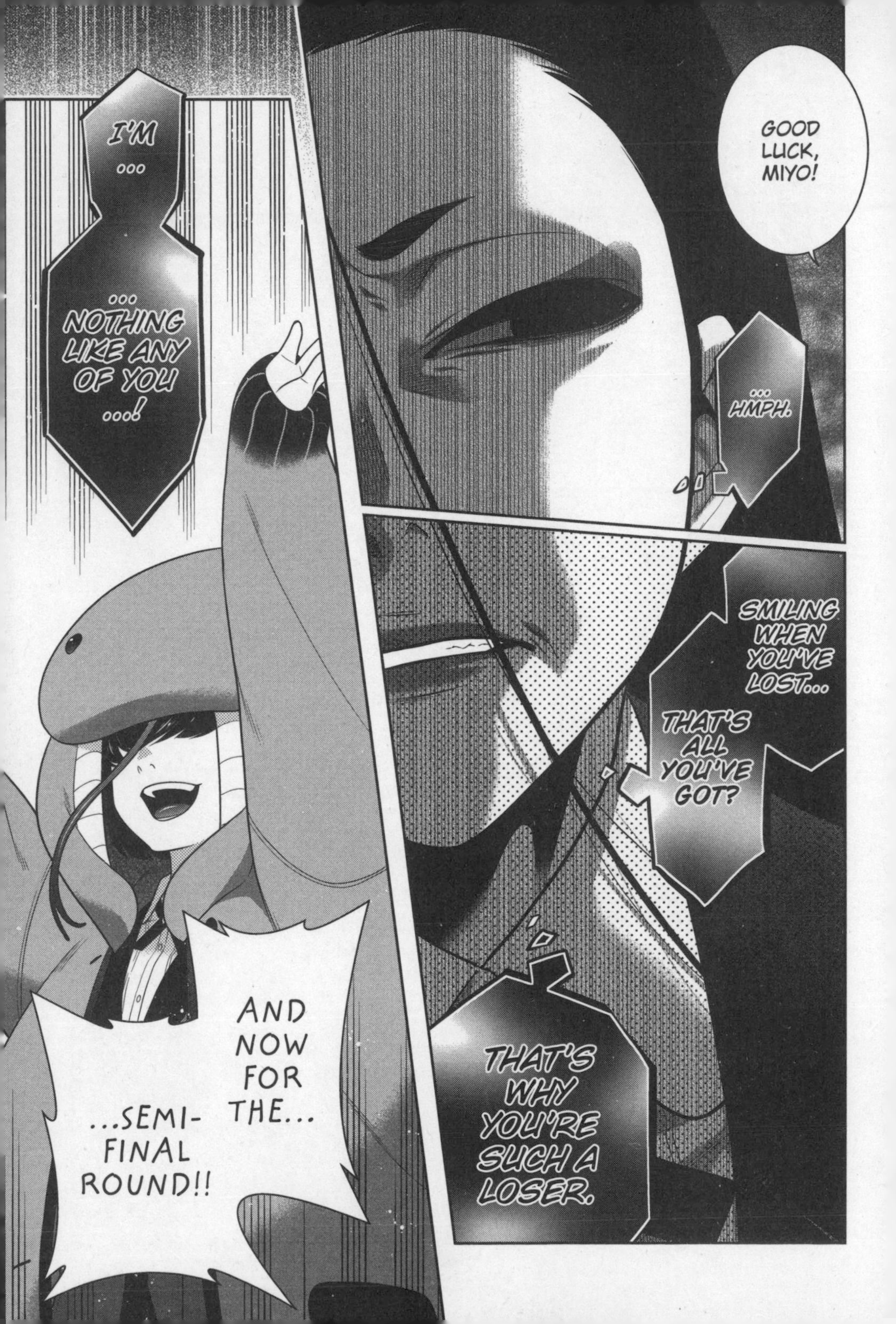
GOOD LUCK, MIYO!
...HMPH.
SMILING WHEN YOU'VE LOST...
THAT'S ALL YOU'VE GOT?
THAT'S WHY YOU'RE SUCH A LOSER.
I'M ...
...NOTHING LIKE ANY OF YOU ...!
AND NOW FOR THE... ...SEMI-FINAL ROUND!!

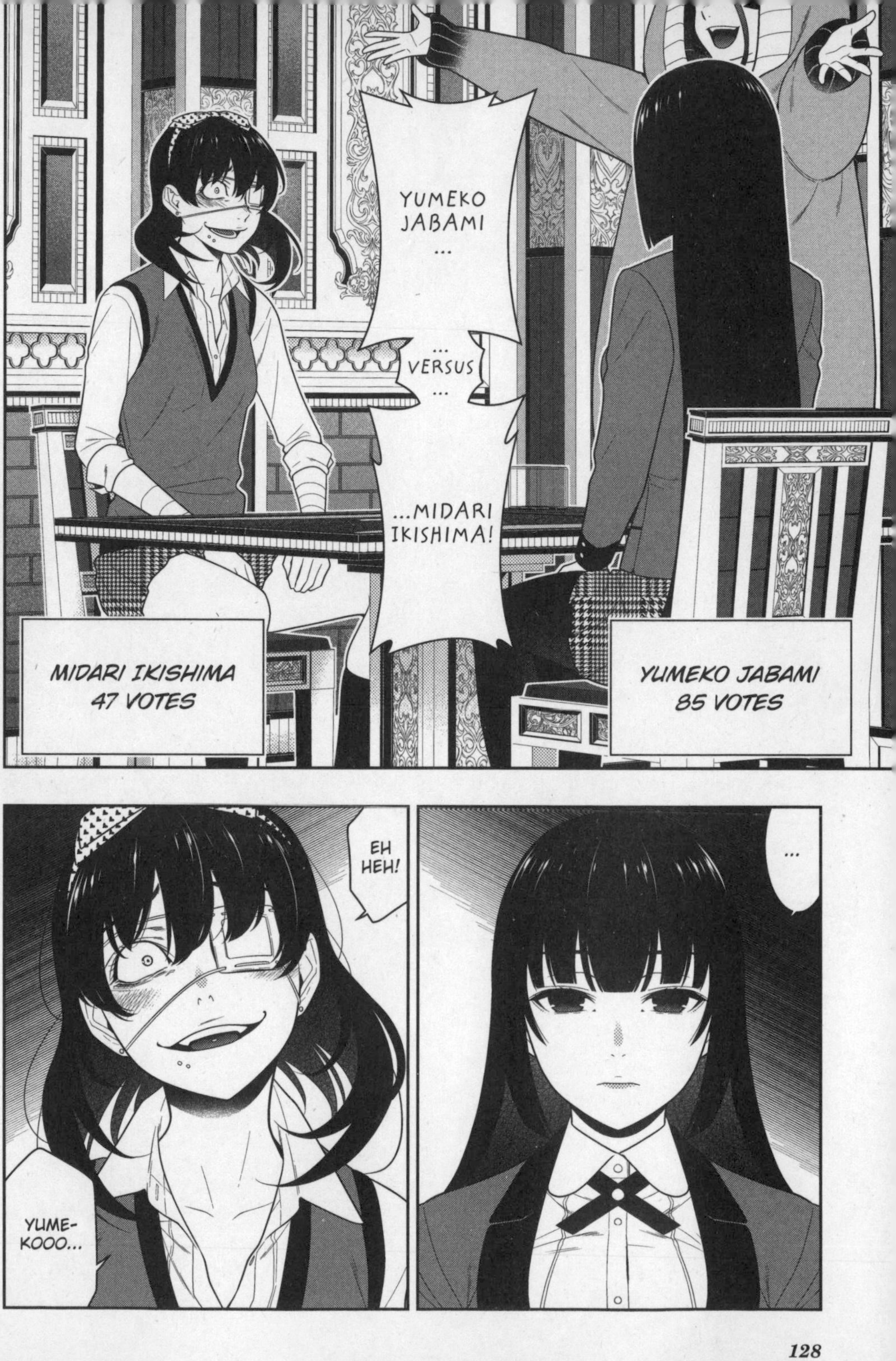
YUMEKO JABAMI ...
... VERSUS ...
...MIDARI IKISHIMA!
YUMEKO JABAMI 85 VOTES
MIDARI IKISHIMA 47 VOTES
...
EH HEH!
YUME-KOOO...

CARDS: ROCK PAPER SCISSORS POKER

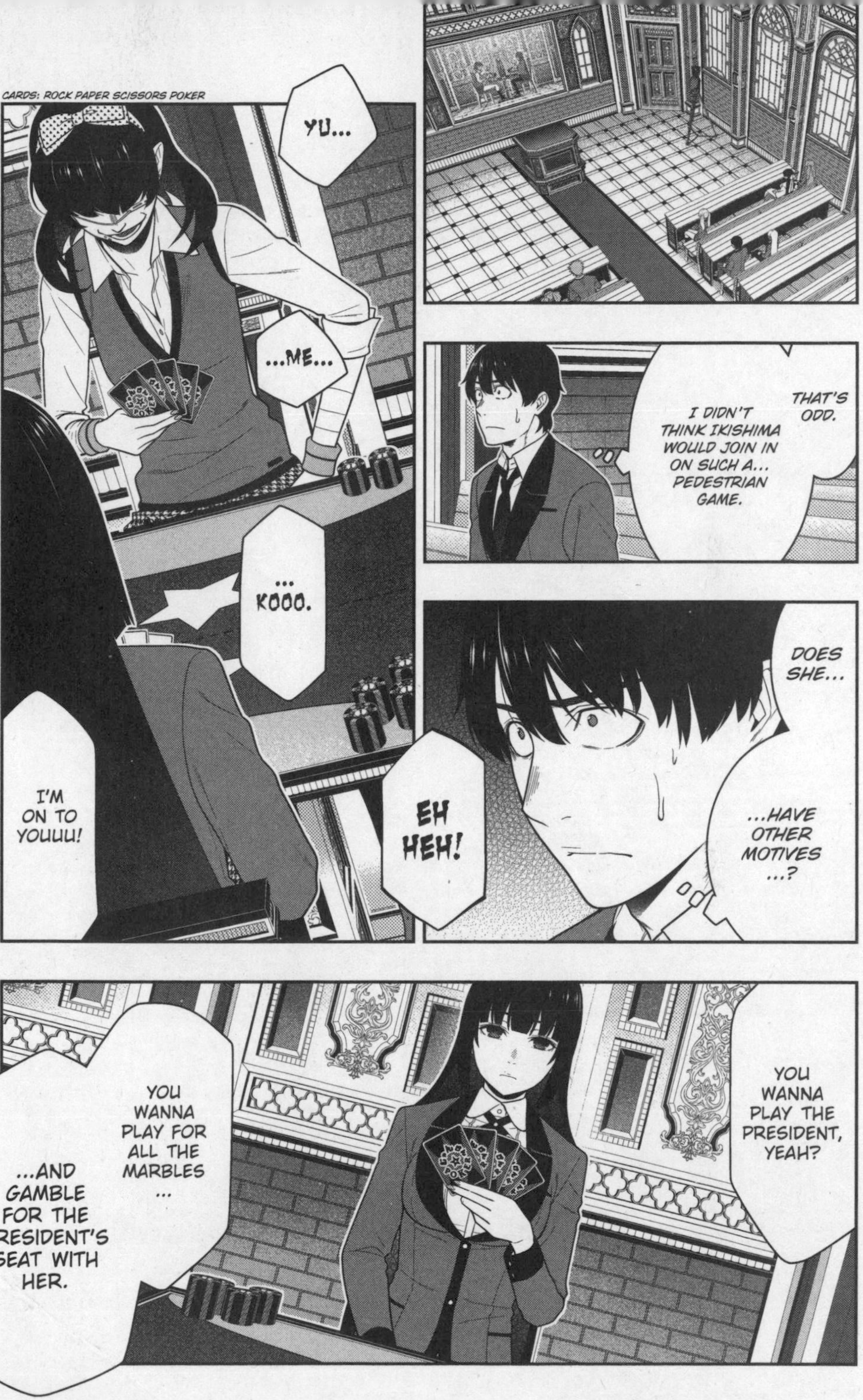
THAT'S ODD.
I DIDN'T THINK IKISHIMA WOULD JOIN IN ON SUCH A... PEDESTRIAN GAME.
DOES SHE...
...HAVE OTHER MOTIVES ...?
YU...
...ME...
... KOOO.
EH HEH!
I'M ON TO YOUUU!
YOU WANNA PLAY THE PRESIDENT, YEAH?
YOU WANNA PLAY FOR ALL THE MARBLES ...
...AND GAMBLE FOR THE PRESIDENT'S SEAT WITH HER.

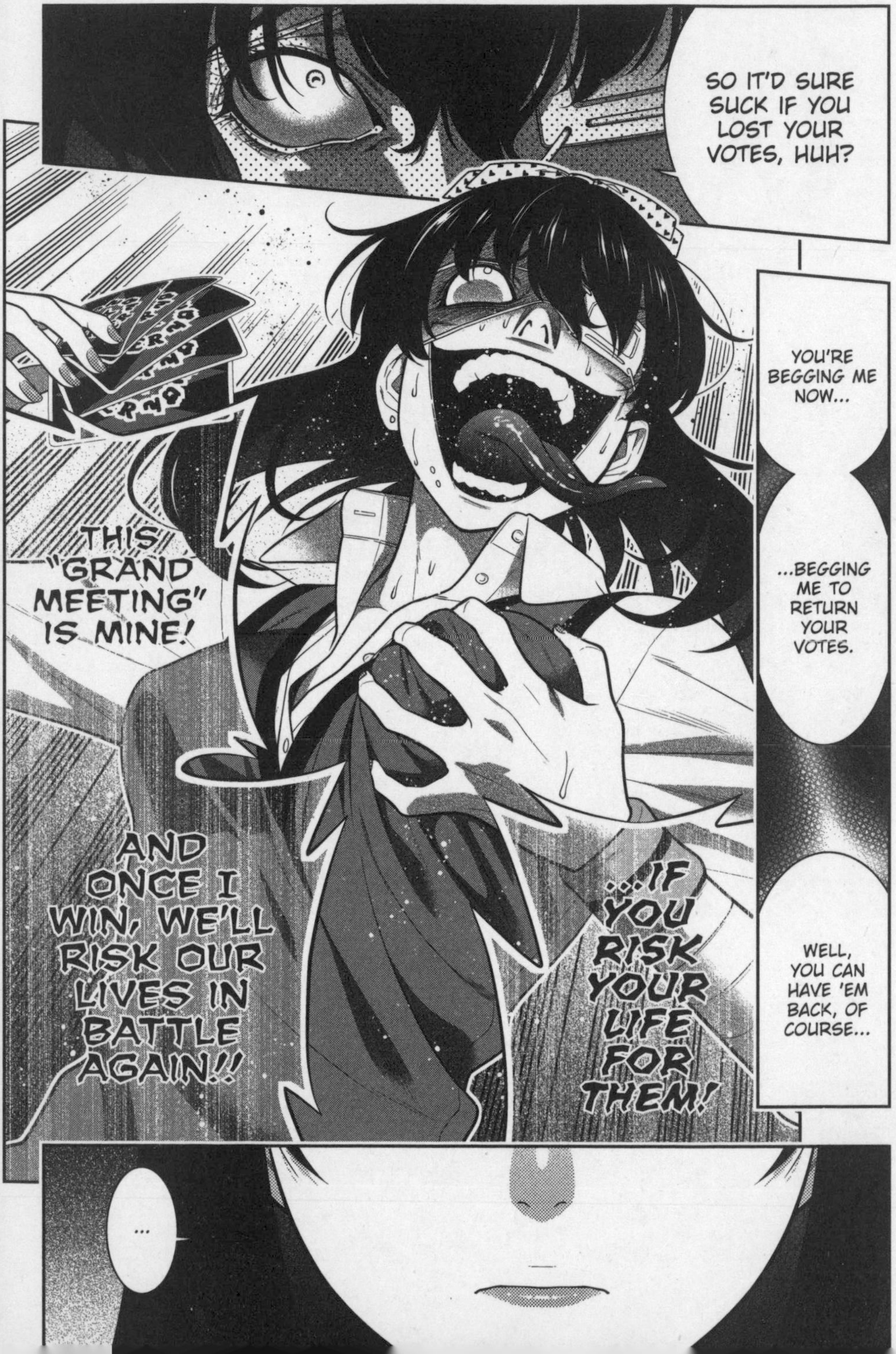
SO IT'D SURE SUCK IF YOU LOST YOUR VOTES, HUH?
YOU'RE BEGGING ME NOW...
...BEGGING ME TO RETURN YOUR VOTES.
WELL, YOU CAN HAVE 'EM BACK, OF COURSE...
...IF YOU RISK YOUR LIFE FOR THEM!
THIS "GRAND MEETING" IS MINE!
AND ONCE I WIN, WE'LL RISK OUR LIVES IN BATTLE AGAIN!!
...

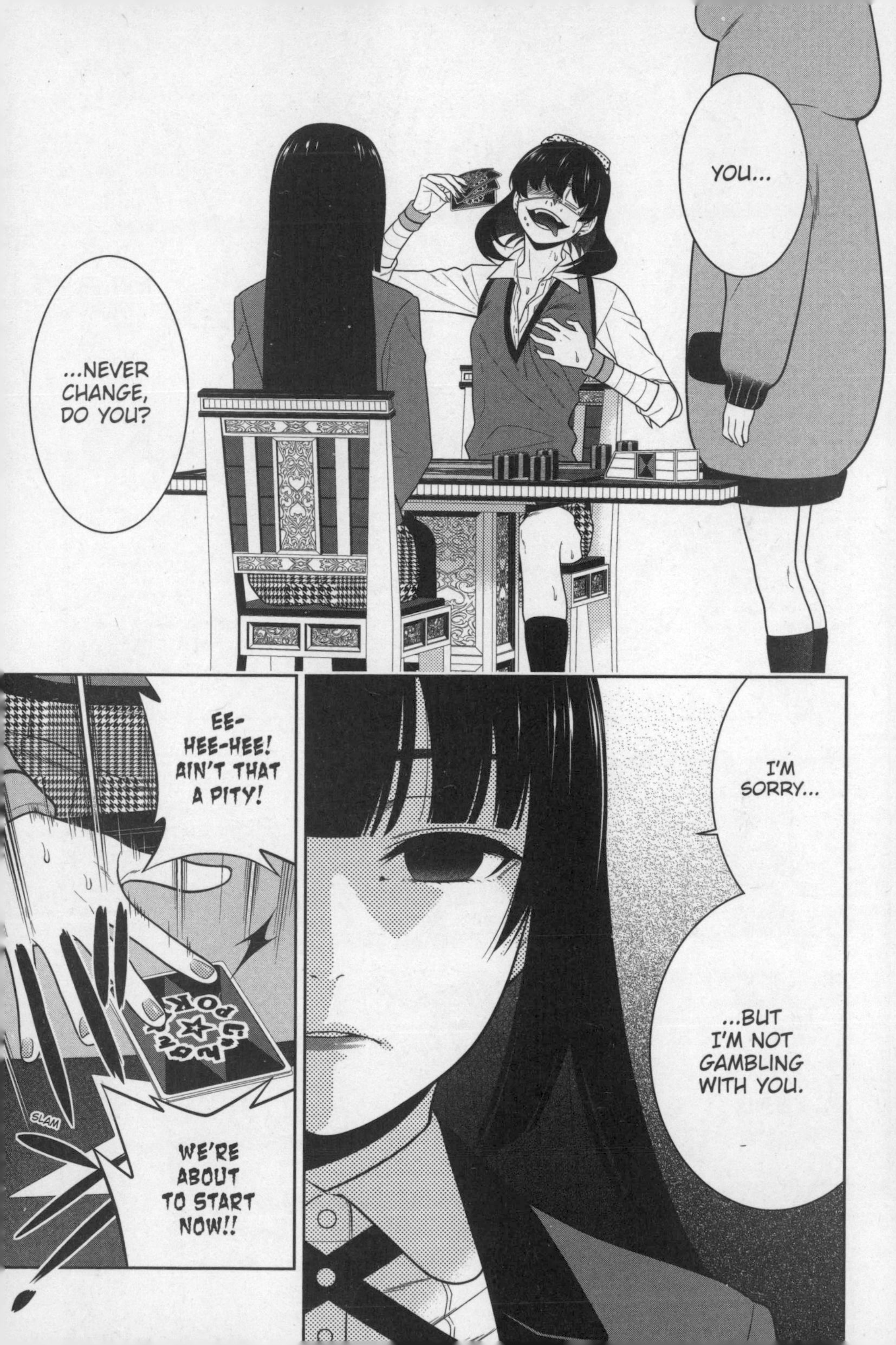
YOU...
...NEVER CHANGE, DO YOU?
I'M SORRY...
...BUT I'M NOT GAMBLING WITH YOU.
EE-HEE-HEE! AIN'T THAT A PITY!
SLAM
WE'RE ABOUT TO START NOW!!

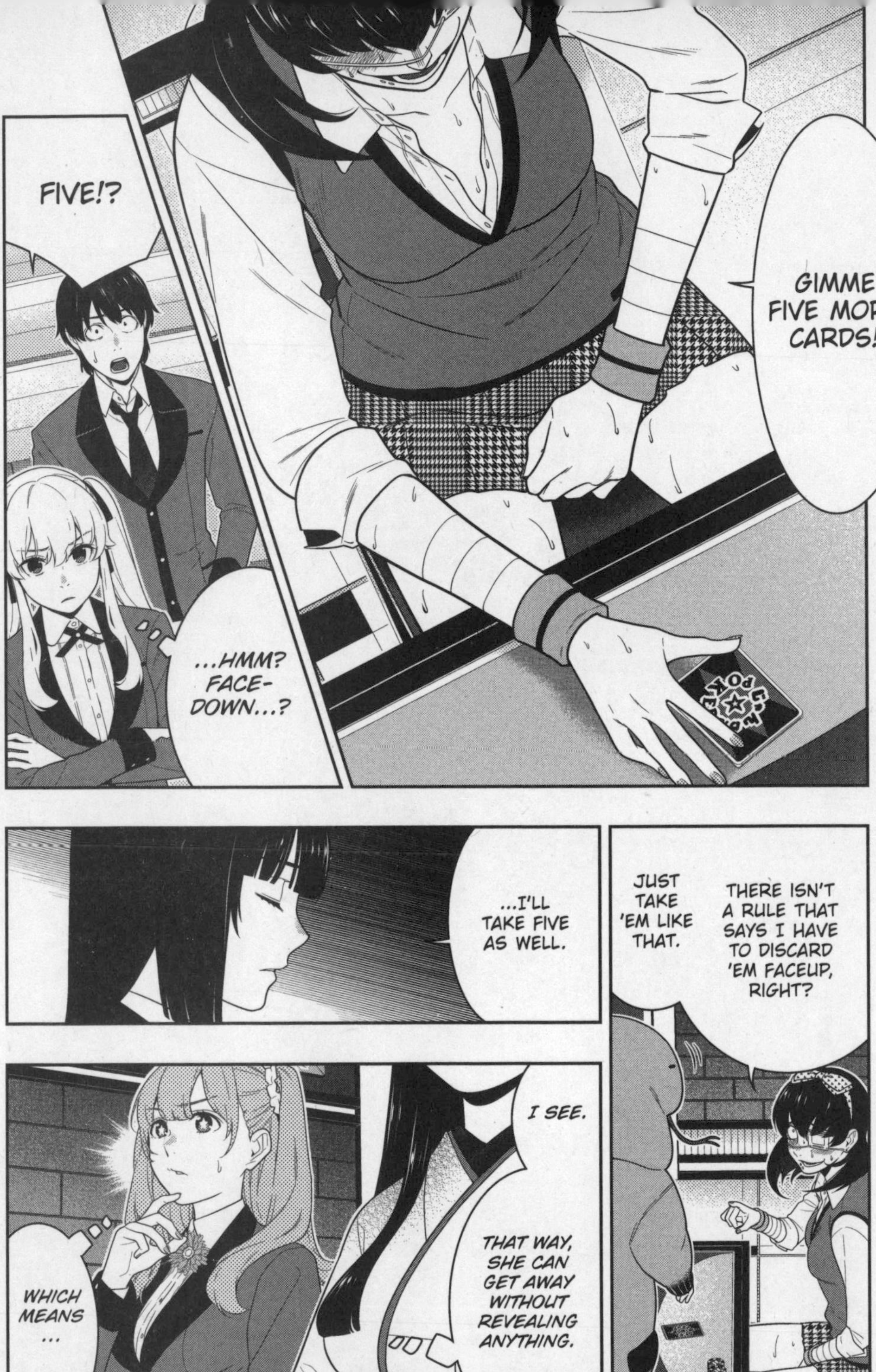
GIMME FIVE MORE CARDS!
FIVE!?
...HMM? FACE-DOWN...?
THERE ISN'T A RULE THAT SAYS I HAVE TO DISCARD 'EM FACEUP, RIGHT?
JUST TAKE 'EM LIKE THAT.
...I'LL TAKE FIVE AS WELL.
I SEE.
THAT WAY, SHE CAN GET AWAY WITHOUT REVEALING ANYTHING.
WHICH MEANS ...

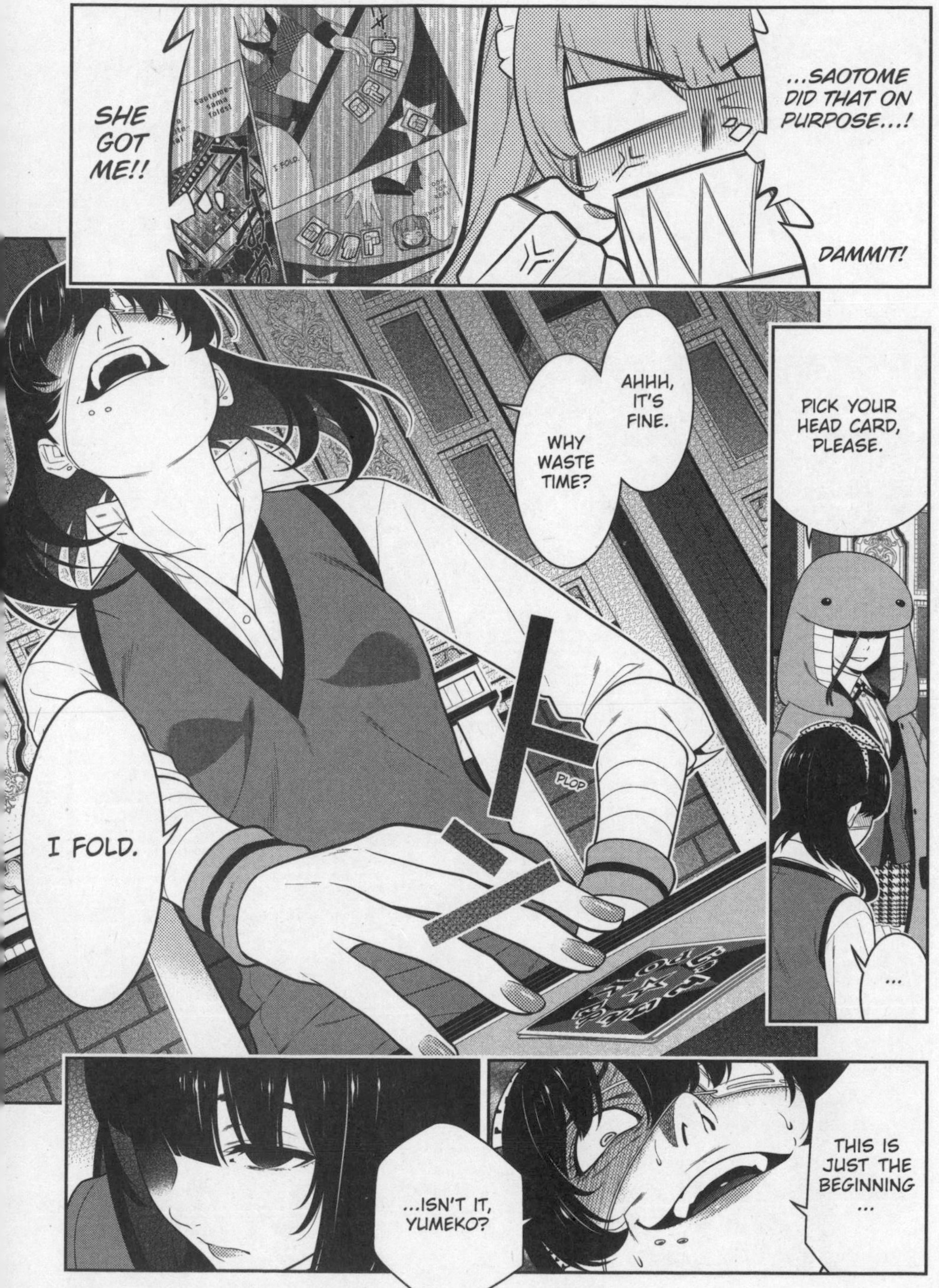
...SAOTOME DID THAT ON PURPOSE...!
DAMMIT!
SHE GOT ME!!
PICK YOUR HEAD CARD, PLEASE.
...
AHHH, IT'S FINE.
WHY WASTE TIME?
PLOP
I FOLD.
THIS IS JUST THE BEGINNING ...
...ISN'T IT, YUMEKO?

GIMME FIVE.

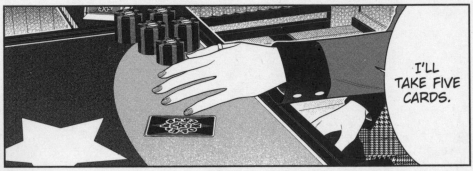

I'LL TAKE FIVE CARDS.

WHO KNOWS?

WHAT I CAN SAY...

WHAT HAS YUMEKO BEEN DOING THIS WHOLE TIME...?

EXCHANGING FIVE CARDS DOESN'T GIVE HER A BETTER HAND.

SHE DOESN'T NEED TO FOLLOW IKISHIMA'S LEAD...

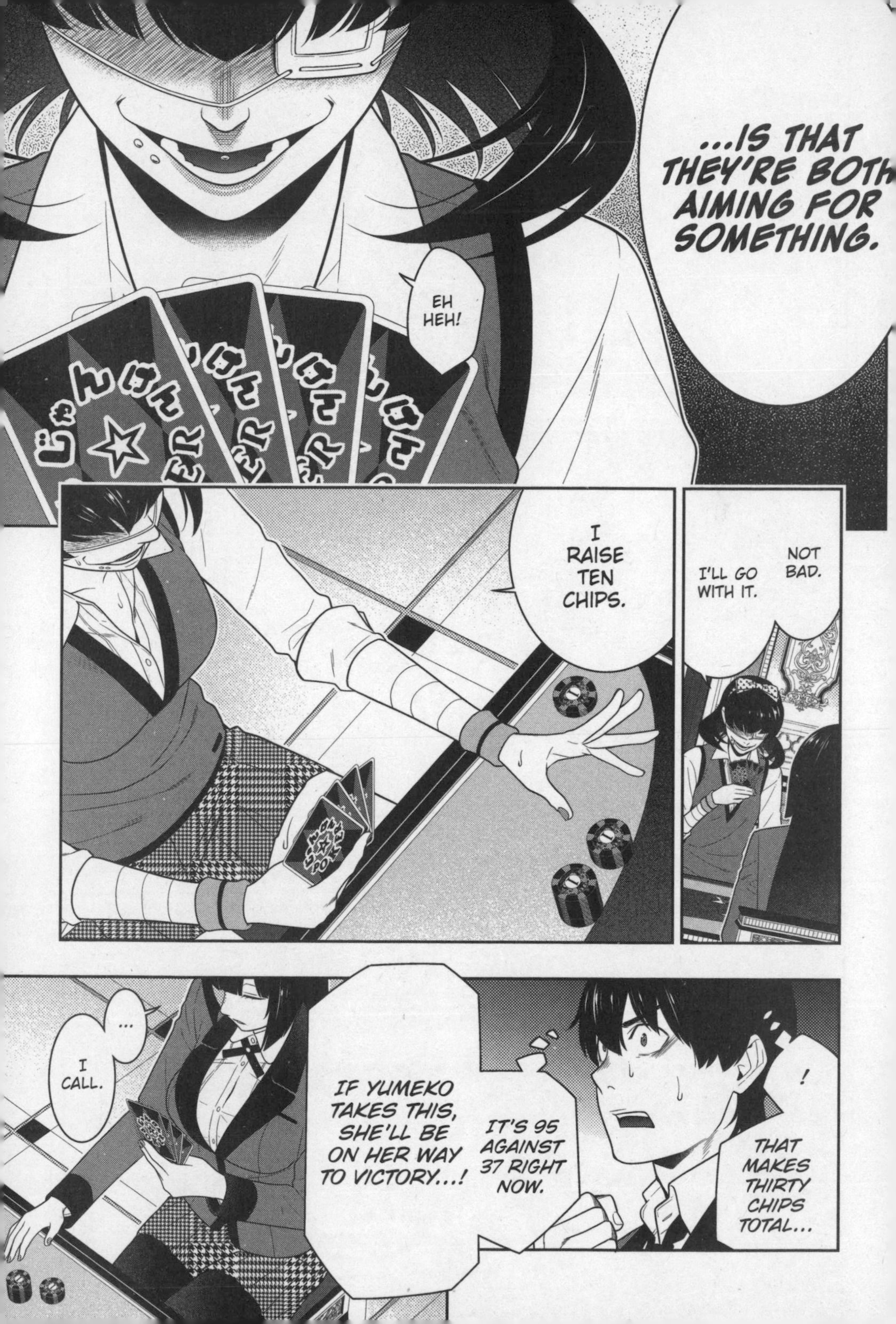
...IS THAT THEY'RE BOTH AIMING FOR SOMETHING.
EH HEH!
NOT BAD.
I'LL GO WITH IT.
I RAISE TEN CHIPS.
!
THAT MAKES THIRTY CHIPS TOTAL...
IT'S 95 AGAINST 37 RIGHT NOW.
IF YUMEKO TAKES THIS, SHE'LL BE ON HER WAY TO VICTORY...!
...
I CALL.

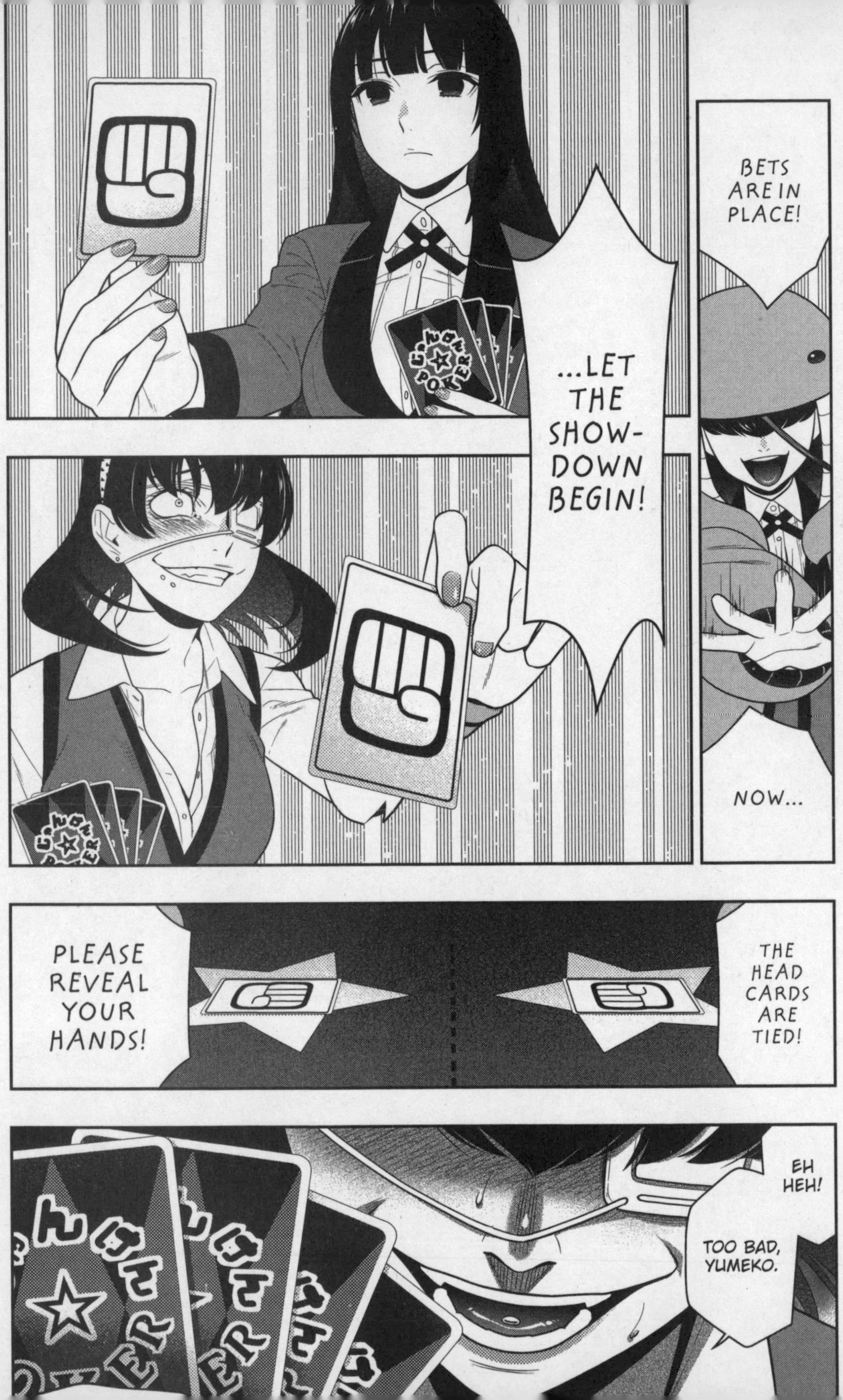
BETS ARE IN PLACE!
NOW...
...LET THE SHOW-DOWN BEGIN!
THE HEAD CARDS ARE TIED!
PLEASE REVEAL YOUR HANDS!
EH HEH!
TOO BAD, YUMEKO.

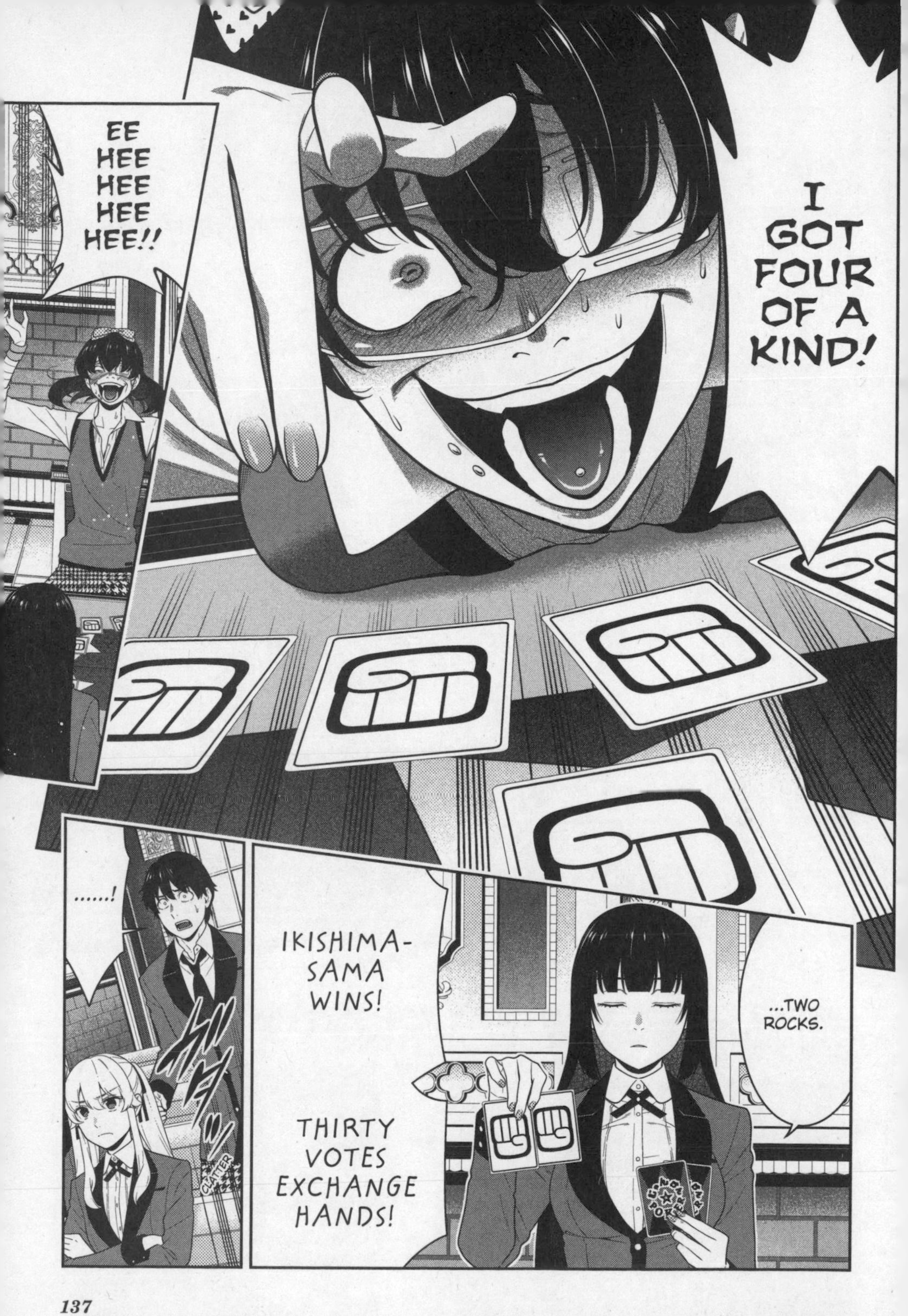
I GOT FOUR OF A KIND!
EE HEE HEE HEE HEE!!
...TWO ROCKS.
IKISHIMA-SAMA WINS!
THIRTY VOTES EXCHANGE HANDS!
......!
CLATTER

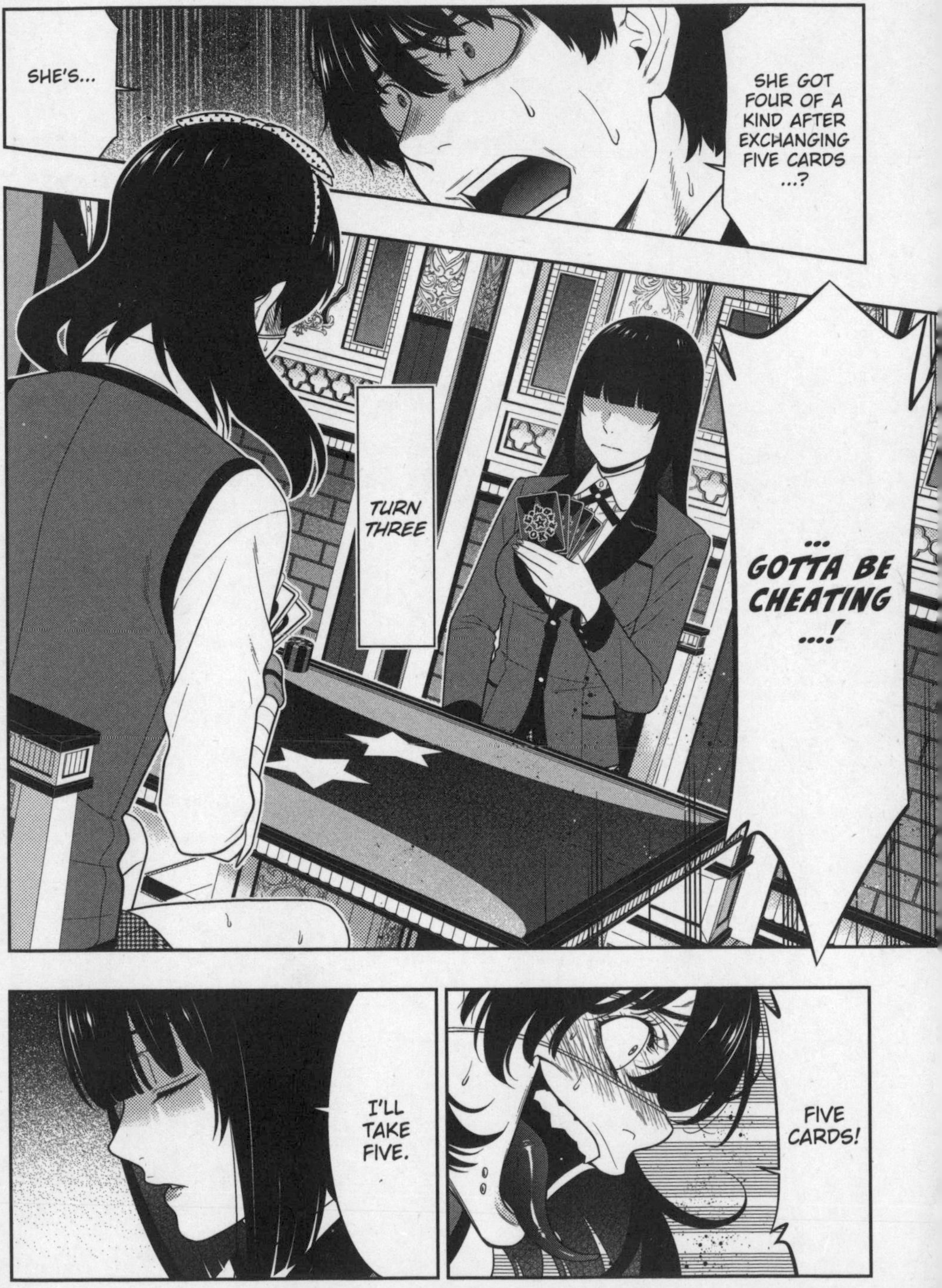
SHE GOT FOUR OF A KIND AFTER EXCHANGING FIVE CARDS ...?
SHE'S...
...GOTTA BE CHEATING ...!
TURN THREE
FIVE CARDS!
I'LL TAKE FIVE.

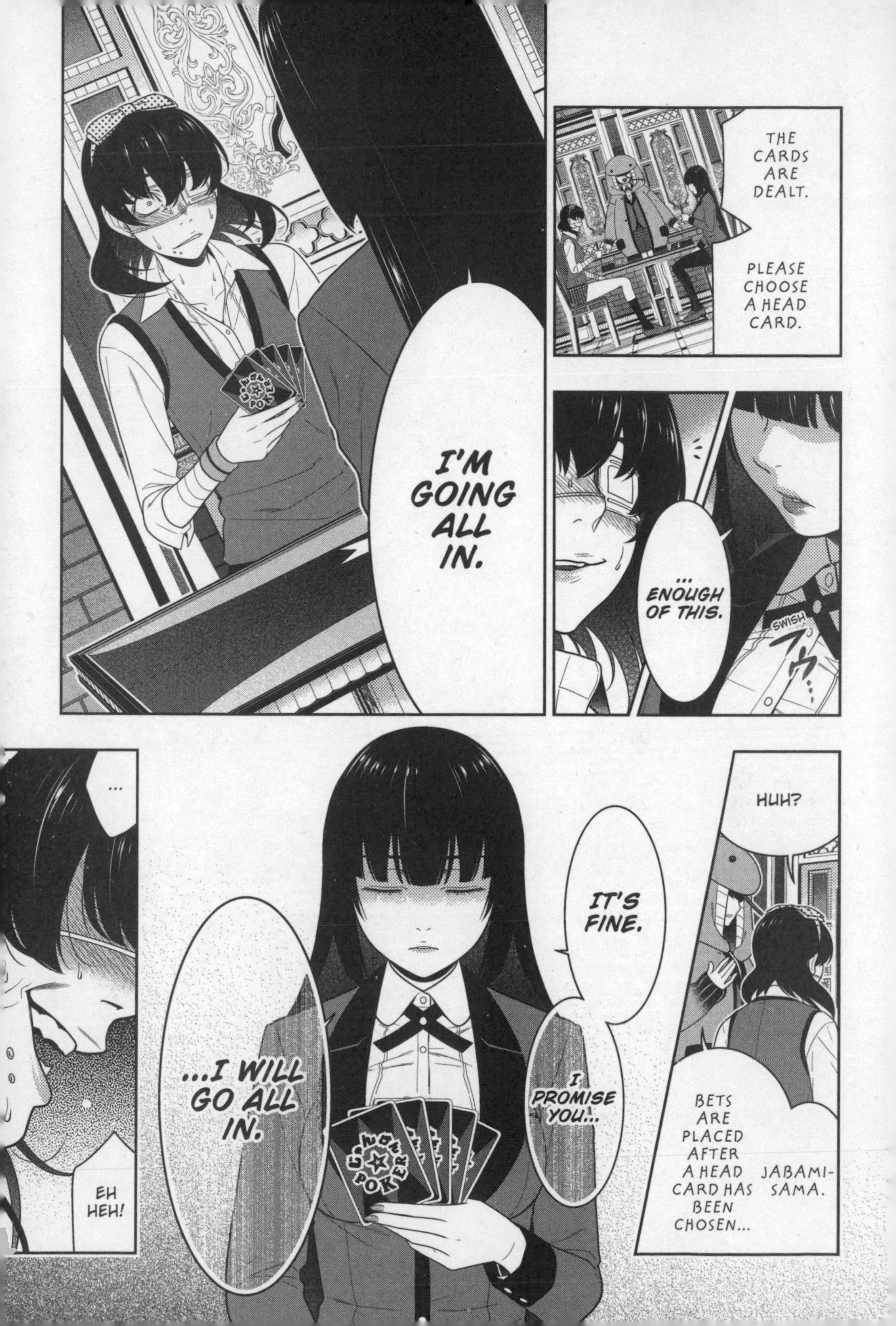
THE CARDS ARE DEALT.
PLEASE CHOOSE A HEAD CARD.
...ENOUGH OF THIS.
SWISH
I'M GOING ALL IN.
HUH?
BETS ARE PLACED AFTER A HEAD CARD HAS BEEN CHOSEN...
JABAMI-SAMA.
IT'S FINE.
I PROMISE YOU...
...I WILL GO ALL IN.
...
EH HEH!

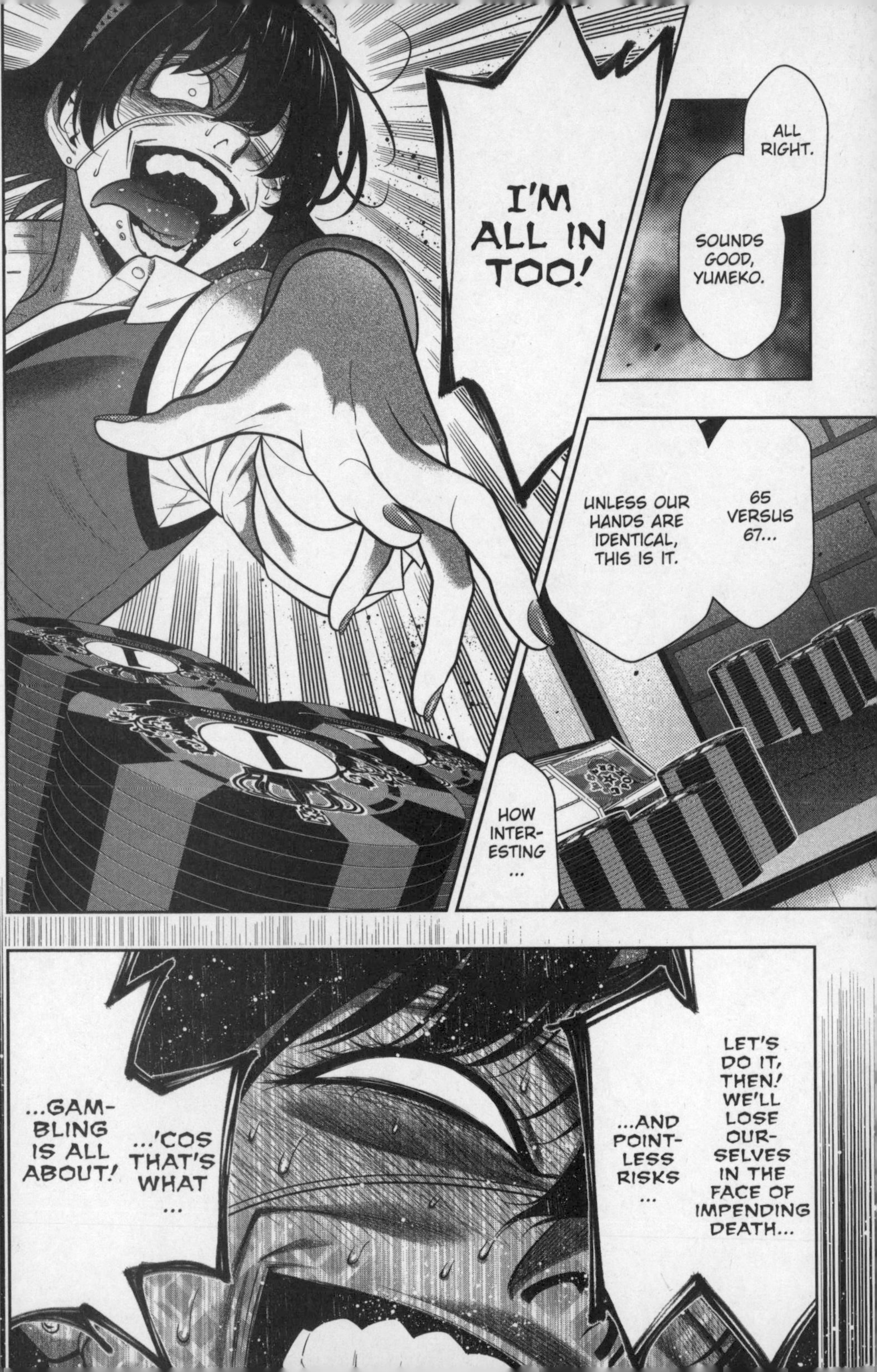
ALL RIGHT.
SOUNDS GOOD, YUMEKO.
65 VERSUS 67...
UNLESS OUR HANDS ARE IDENTICAL, THIS IS IT.
HOW INTERESTING...
I'M ALL IN TOO!
LET'S DO IT, THEN! WE'LL LOSE OURSELVES IN THE FACE OF IMPENDING DEATH...
...AND POINTLESS RISKS...
...'COS THAT'S WHAT...
...GAMBLING IS ALL ABOUT!

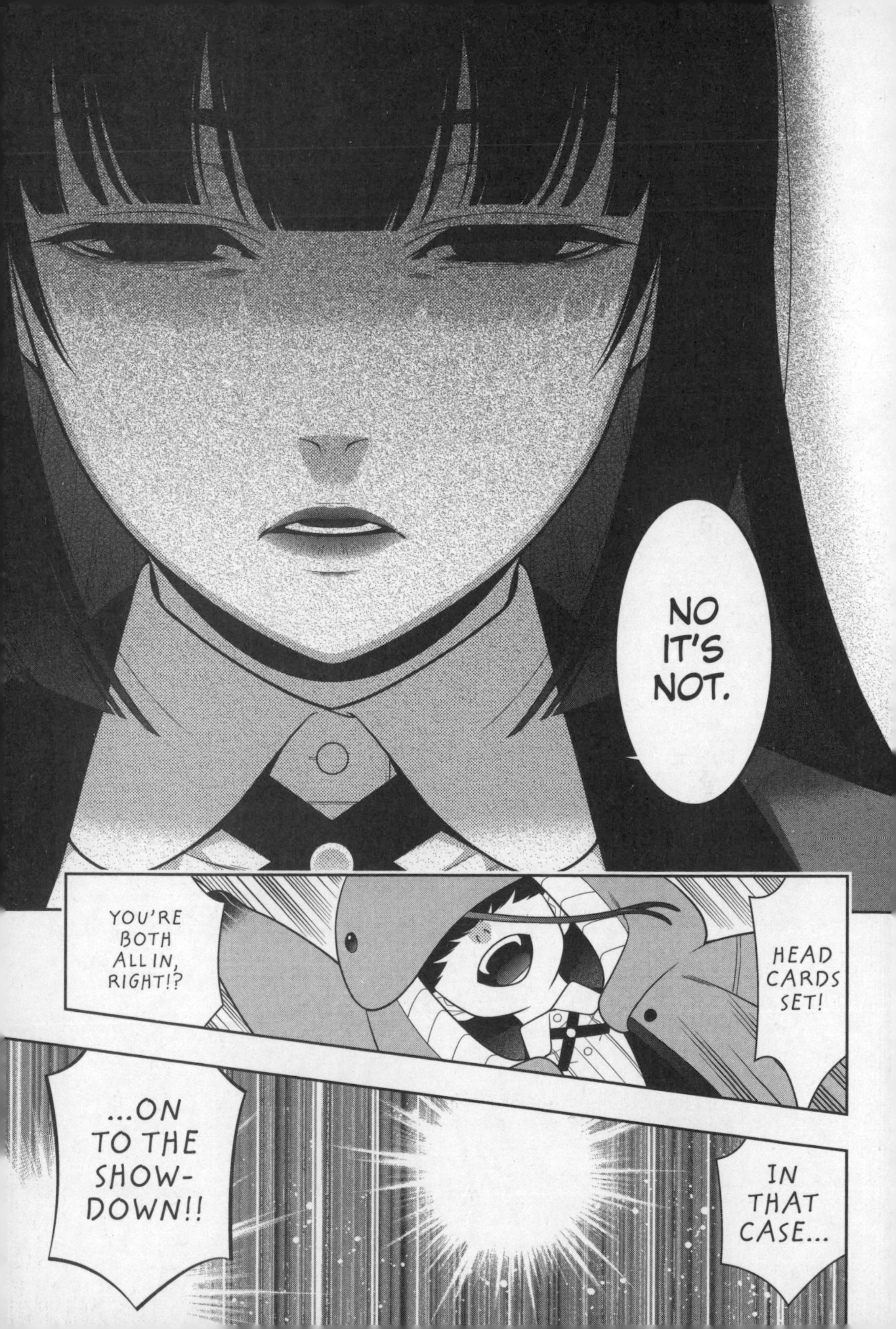
NO IT'S NOT.
HEAD CARDS SET!
YOU'RE BOTH ALL IN, RIGHT!?
IN THAT CASE...
...ON TO THE SHOW-DOWN!!

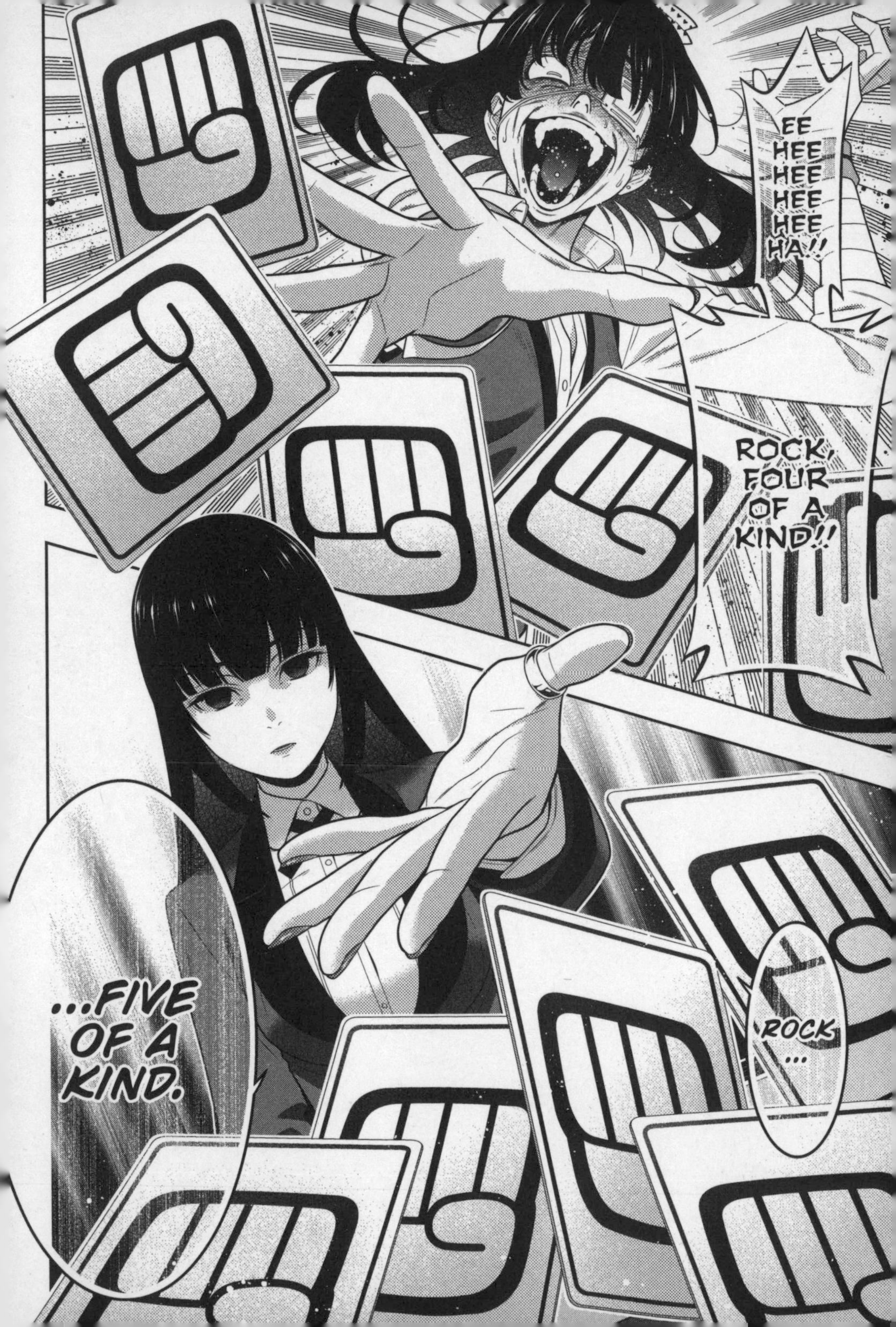
EE HEE HEE HEE HEE HA!!
ROCK, FOUR OF A KIND!!
ROCK...
...FIVE OF A KIND.

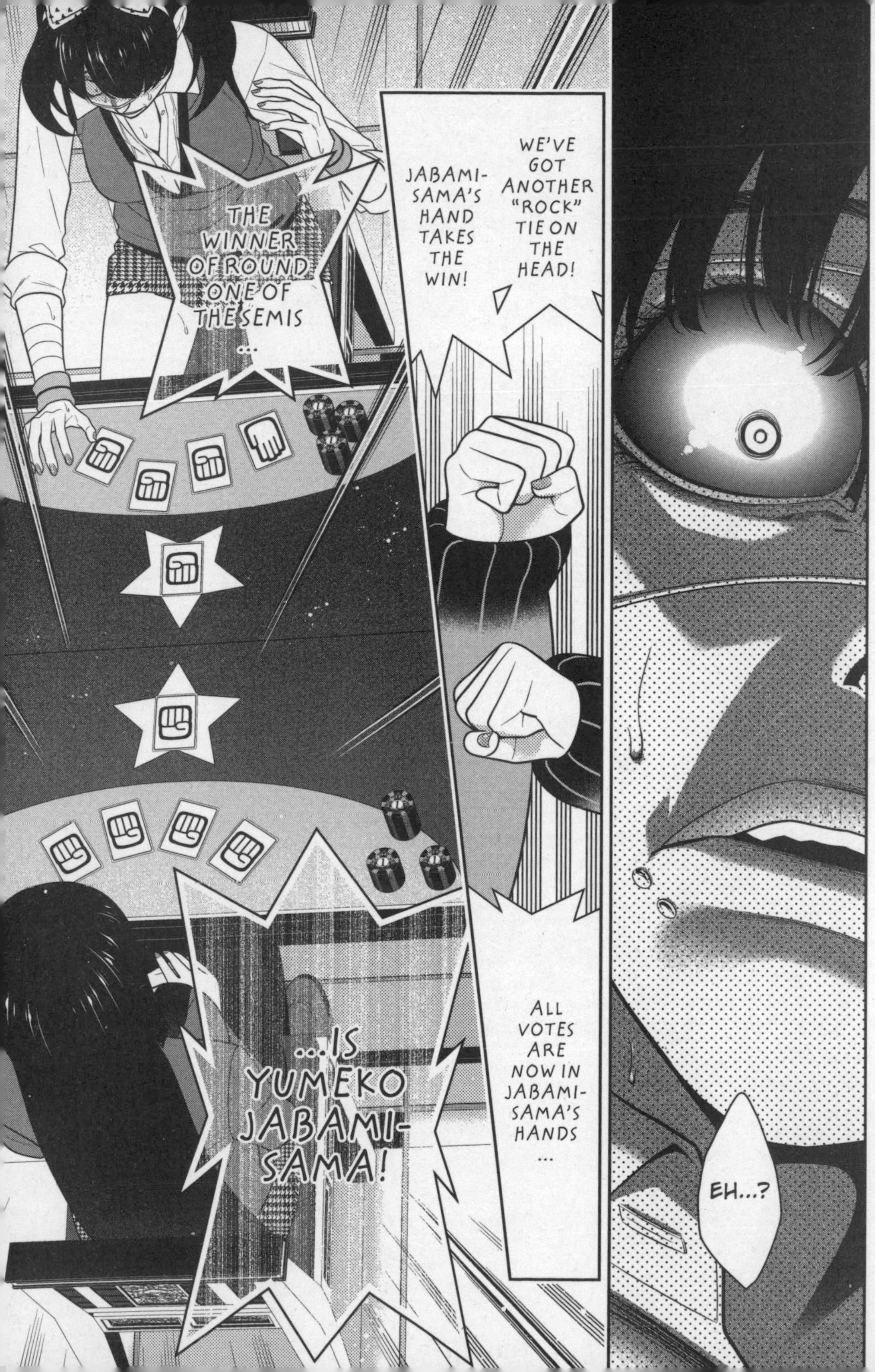
EH...?
WE'VE GOT ANOTHER "ROCK" TIE ON THE HEAD!
JABAMI-SAMA'S HAND TAKES THE WIN!
ALL VOTES ARE NOW IN JABAMI-SAMA'S HANDS...
THE WINNER OF ROUND ONE OF THE SEMIS...
...IS YUMEKO JABAMI-SAMA!

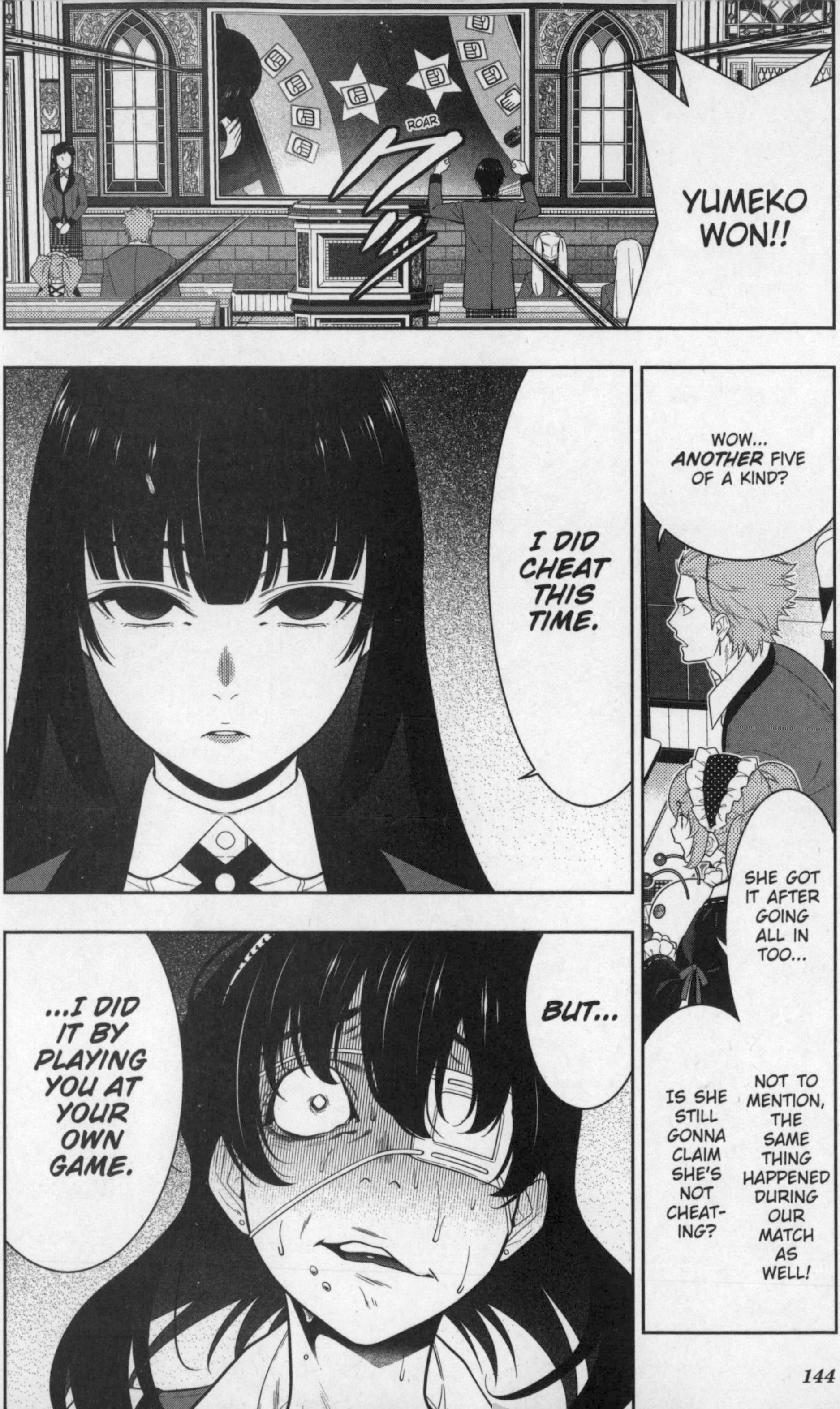
ROAR
YUMEKO WON!!
WOW... ANOTHER FIVE OF A KIND?
SHE GOT IT AFTER GOING ALL IN TOO...
NOT TO MENTION, THE SAME THING HAPPENED DURING OUR MATCH AS WELL!
IS SHE STILL GONNA CLAIM SHE'S NOT CHEAT-ING?
I DID CHEAT THIS TIME.
BUT...
...I DID IT BY PLAYING YOU AT YOUR OWN GAME.

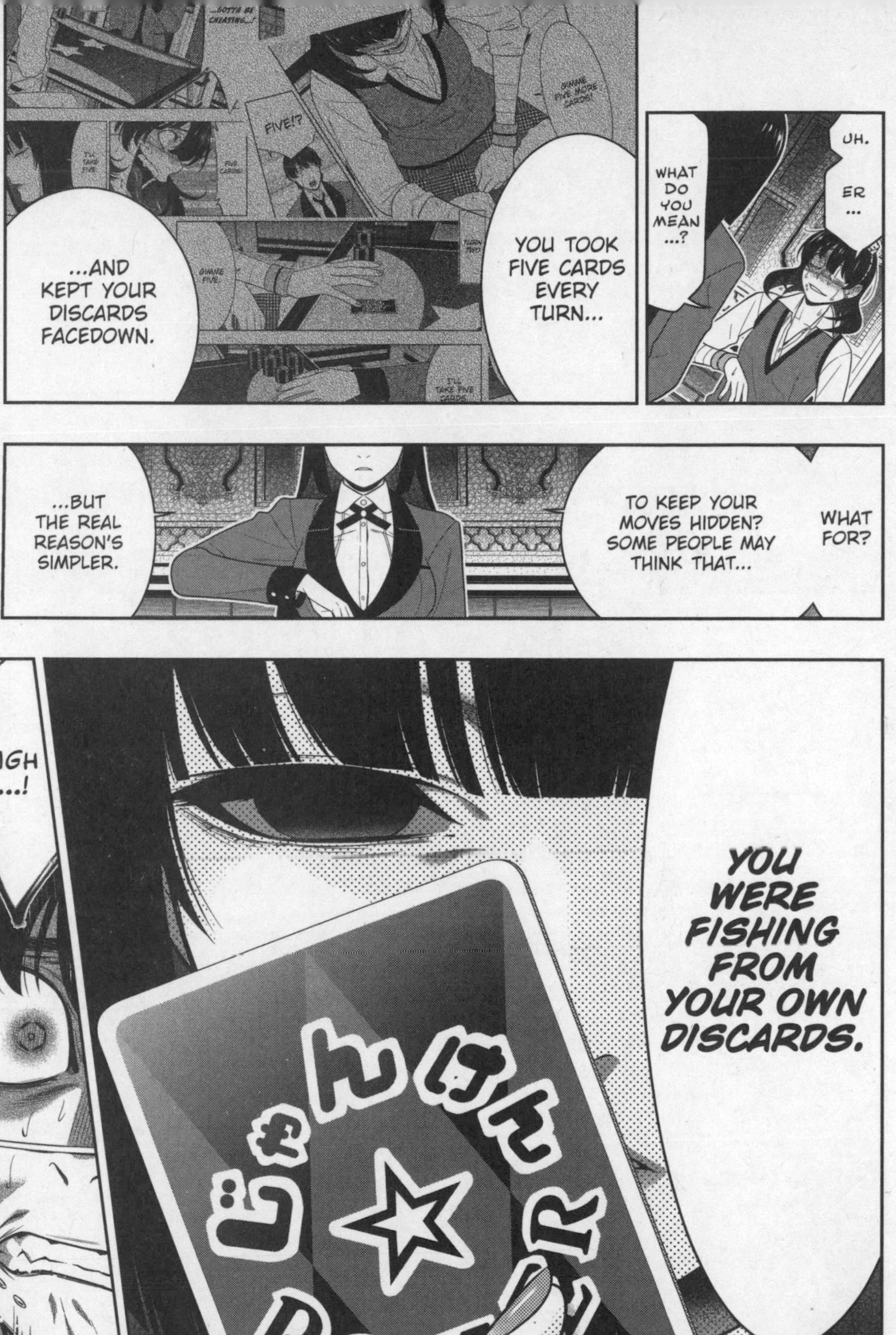

UH.
ER ...
WHAT DO YOU MEAN ...?
YOU TOOK FIVE CARDS EVERY TURN...
...GOTTA BE CHEATING...!
GIMME FIVE MORE CARDS!
FIVE!?
FIVE CARDS!
I'LL TAKE FIVE
TURN TWO
GIMME FIVE!
I'LL TAKE FIVE CARDS
...AND KEPT YOUR DISCARDS FACEDOWN.
WHAT FOR?
TO KEEP YOUR MOVES HIDDEN? SOME PEOPLE MAY THINK THAT...
...BUT THE REAL REASON'S SIMPLER.
YOU WERE FISHING FROM YOUR OWN DISCARDS.
NGH ...!

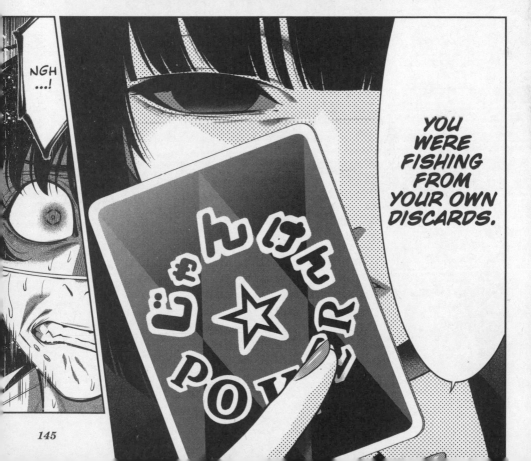

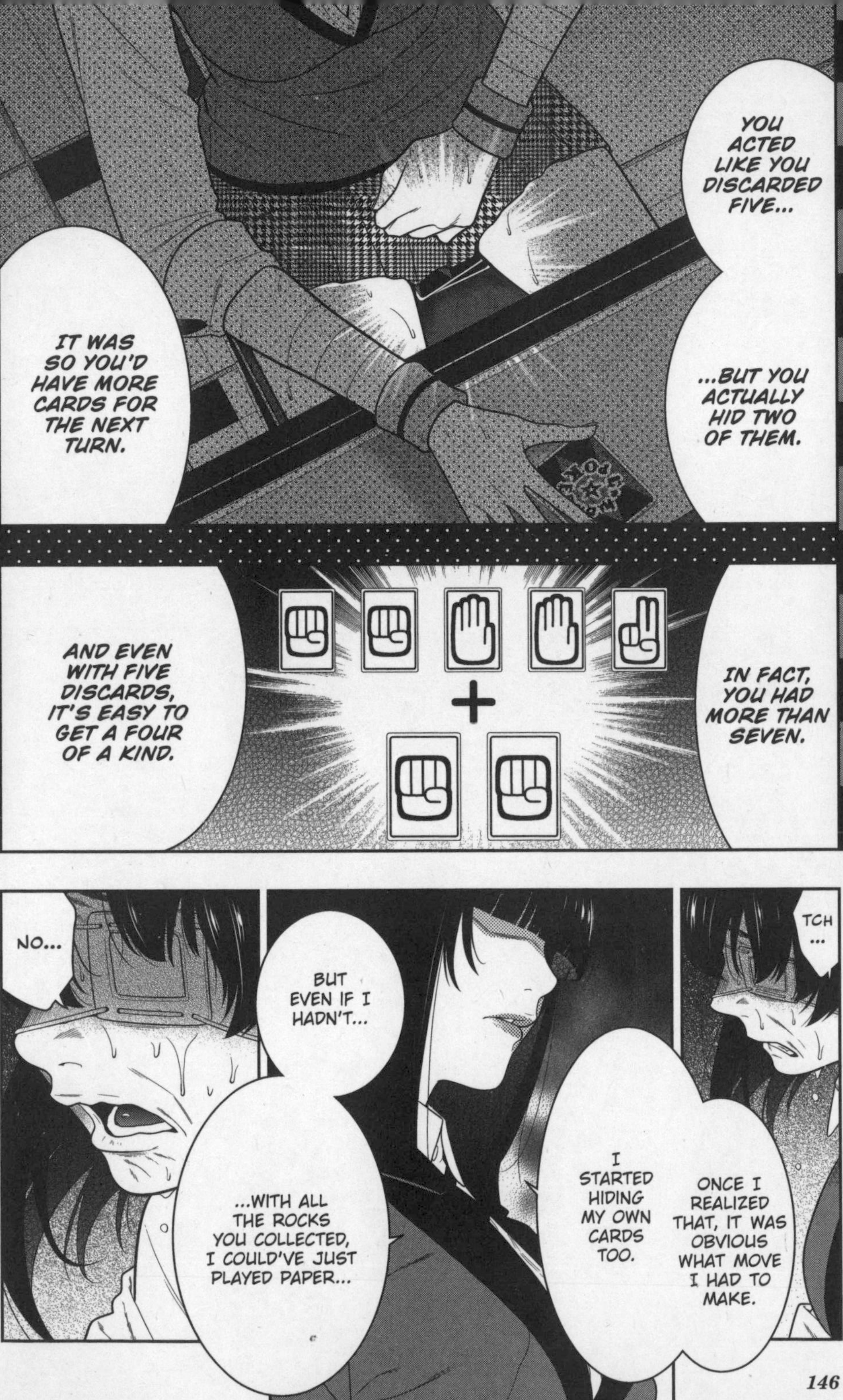
YOU ACTED LIKE YOU DISCARDED FIVE...
...BUT YOU ACTUALLY HID TWO OF THEM.
IT WAS SO YOU'D HAVE MORE CARDS FOR THE NEXT TURN.
IN FACT, YOU HAD MORE THAN SEVEN.
AND EVEN WITH FIVE DISCARDS, IT'S EASY TO GET A FOUR OF A KIND.
TCH ...
ONCE I REALIZED THAT, IT WAS OBVIOUS WHAT MOVE I HAD TO MAKE.
I STARTED HIDING MY OWN CARDS TOO.
BUT EVEN IF I HADN'T...
...WITH ALL THE ROCKS YOU COLLECTED, I COULD'VE JUST PLAYED PAPER...
NO...

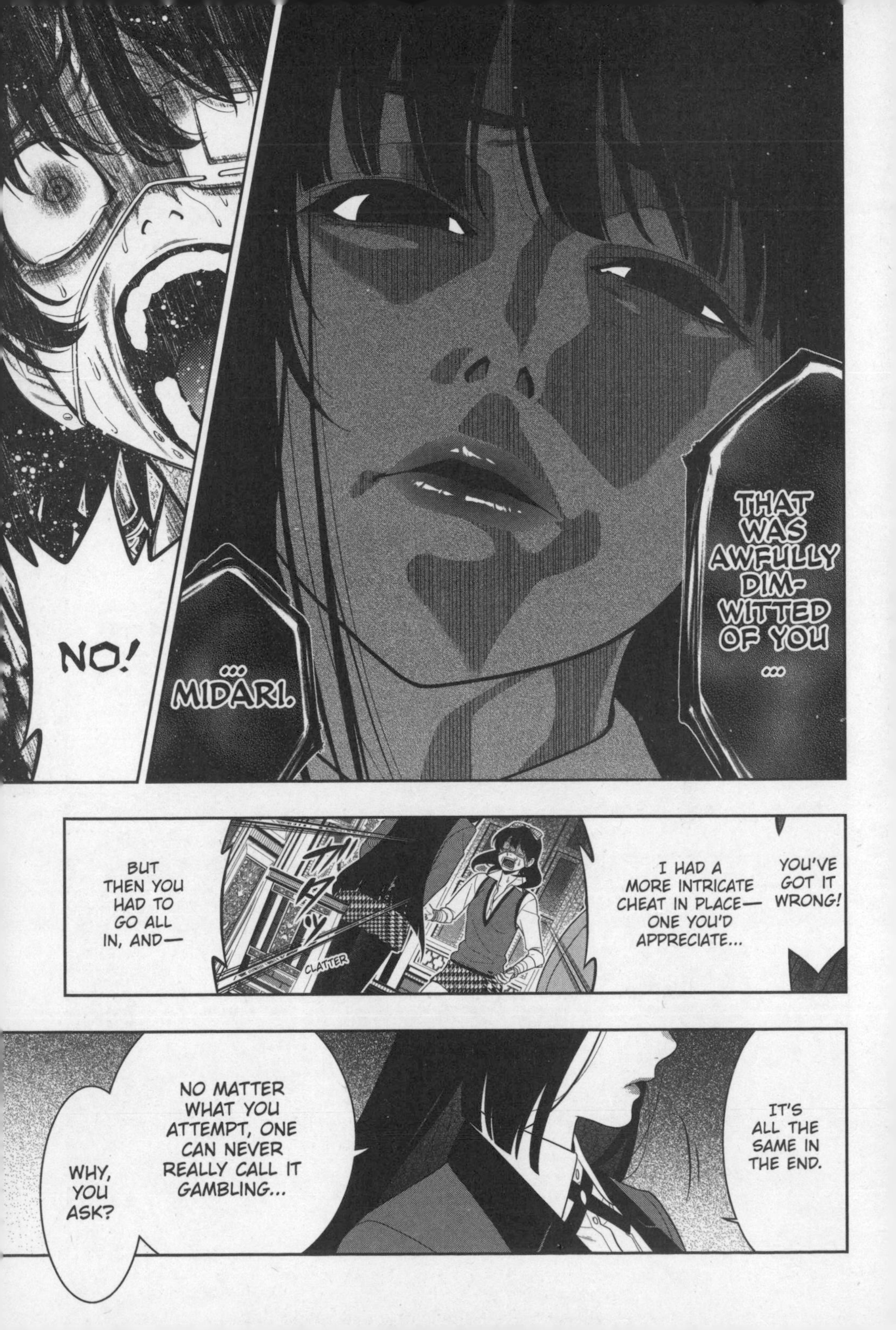
THAT WAS AWFULLY DIM-WITTED OF YOU ...
... MIDARI.
NO!
YOU'VE GOT IT WRONG!
I HAD A MORE INTRICATE CHEAT IN PLACE— ONE YOU'D APPRECIATE...
BUT THEN YOU HAD TO GO ALL IN, AND—
CLATTER
IT'S ALL THE SAME IN THE END.
NO MATTER WHAT YOU ATTEMPT, ONE CAN NEVER REALLY CALL IT GAMBLING...
WHY, YOU ASK?

BECAUSE TO YOU, GAMBLING IS JUST A MEANS TO AN END.

I CAN'T GAMBLE WITH SOMEONE WHO DOESN'T GET THAT.

GOOD-BYE.

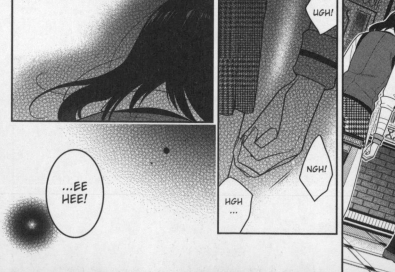

...EE HEE!

UGH!

NGH!

HGH...

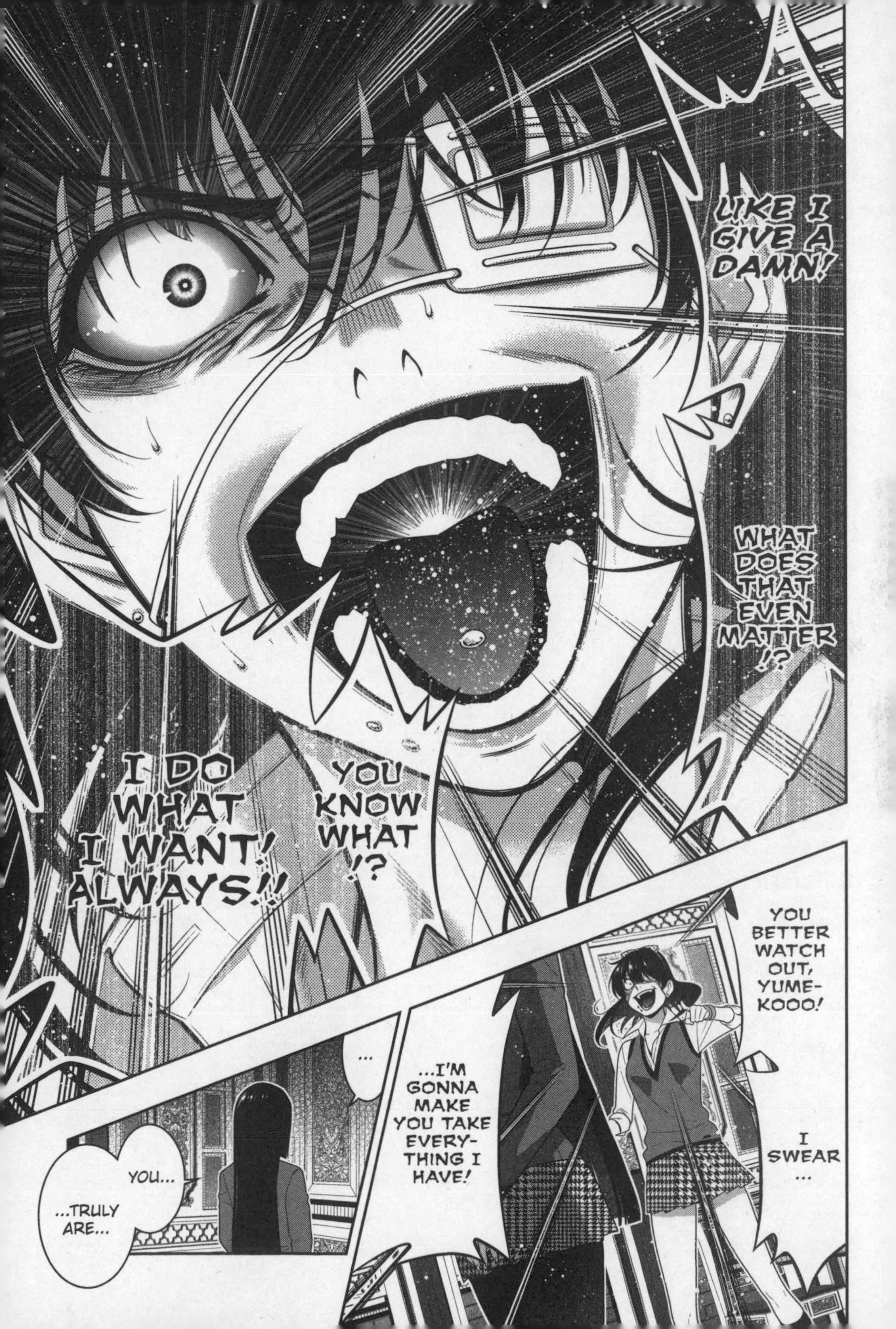
LIKE I GIVE A DAMN!
WHAT DOES THAT EVEN MATTER!?
YOU KNOW WHAT!?
I DO WHAT I WANT! ALWAYS!!
YOU BETTER WATCH OUT, YUME-KOOO!
I SWEAR...
...I'M GONNA MAKE YOU TAKE EVERY-THING I HAVE!
...
YOU...
...TRULY ARE...

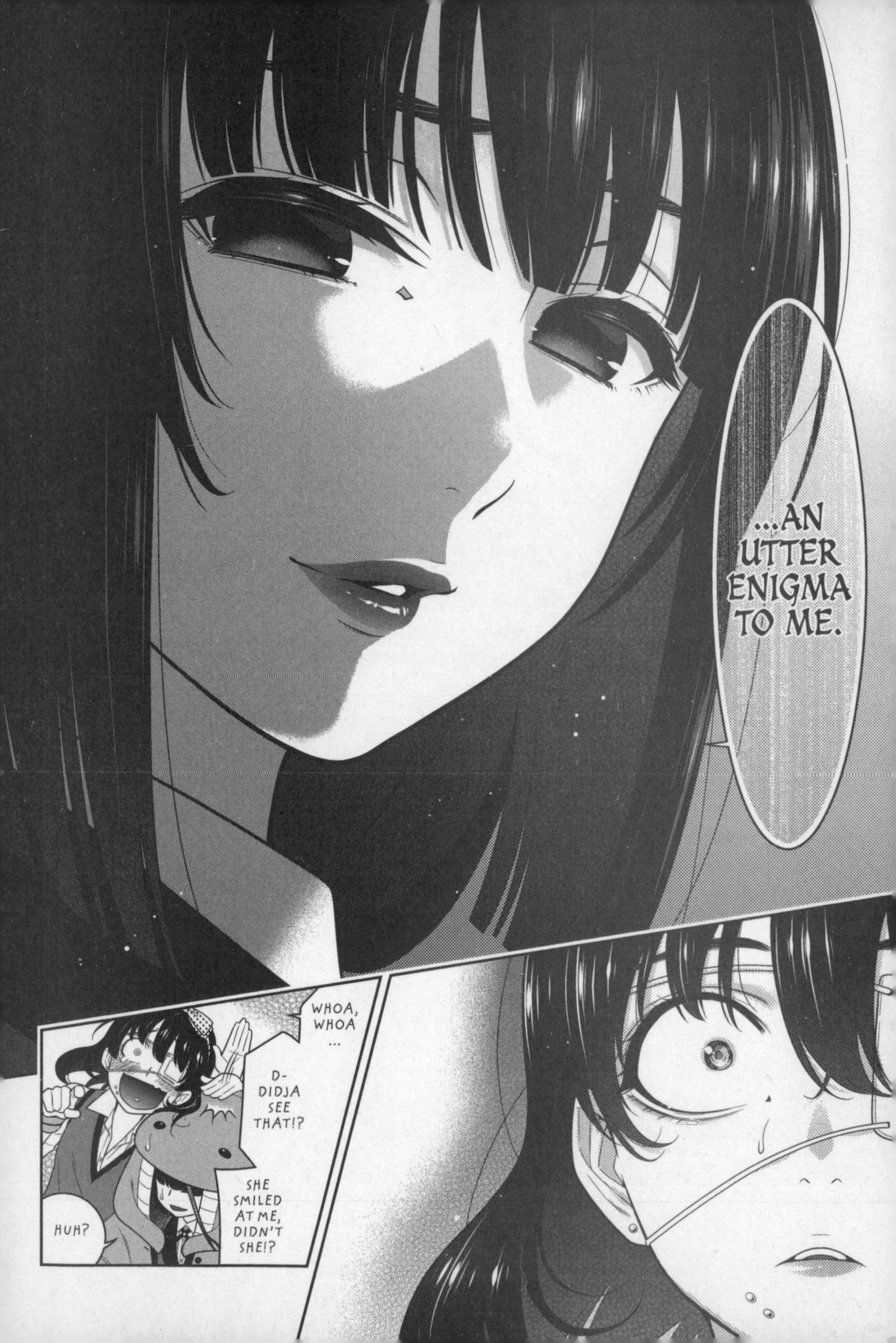
...AN UTTER ENIGMA TO ME.
WHOA, WHOA ...
D-DIDJA SEE THAT!?
SHE SMILED AT ME, DIDN'T SHE!?
HUH?

KAKEGURUI

— Compulsive Gambler —

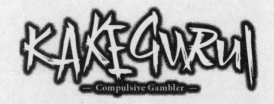

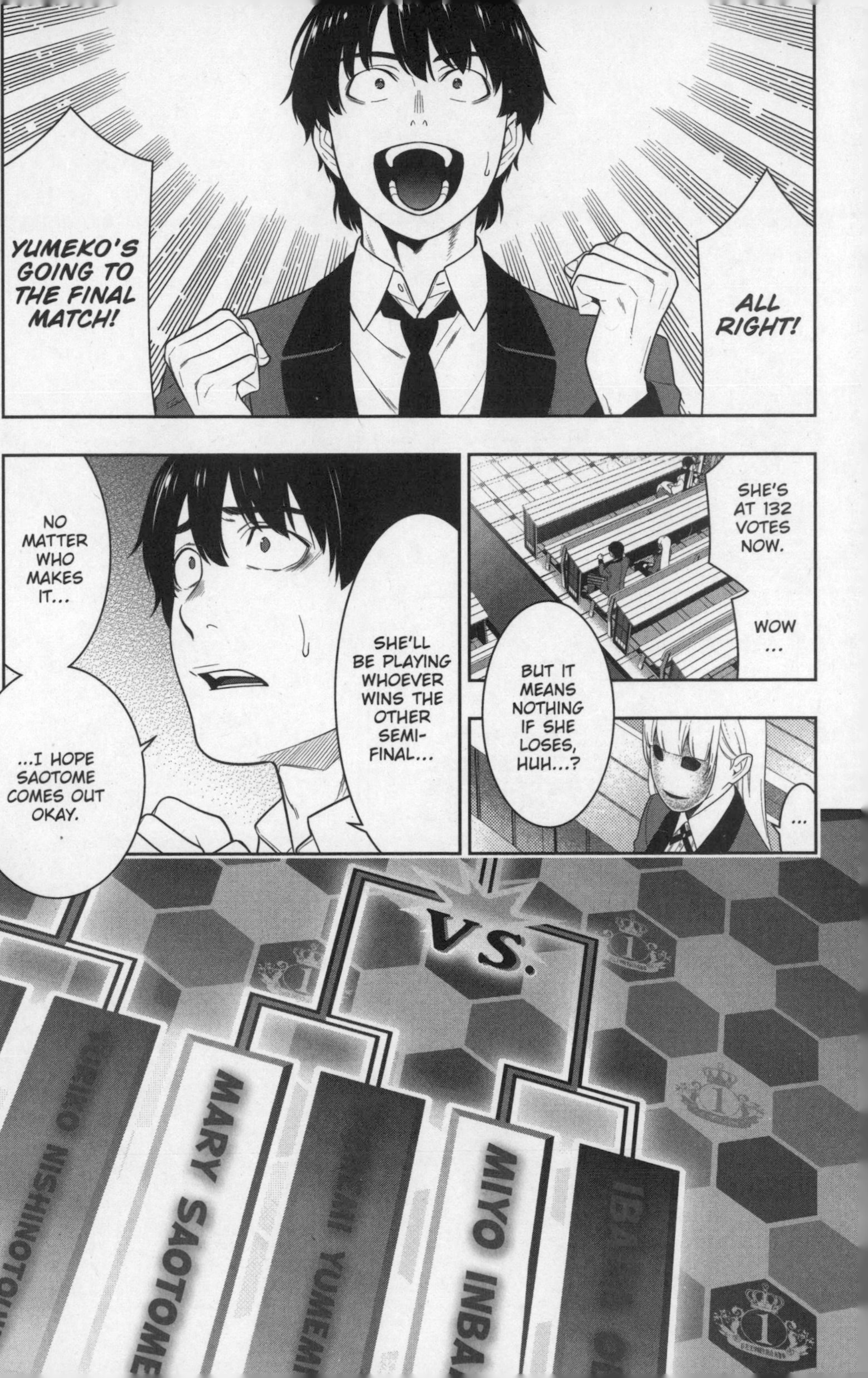
ALL RIGHT!
YUMEKO'S GOING TO THE FINAL MATCH!
SHE'S AT 132 VOTES NOW.
WOW ...
BUT IT MEANS NOTHING IF SHE LOSES, HUH...?
...
SHE'LL BE PLAYING WHOEVER WINS THE OTHER SEMI-FINAL...
NO MATTER WHO MAKES IT...
...I HOPE SAOTOME COMES OUT OKAY.
VS.
MIYO INBA
MARY SAOTOME
YURIKO NISHINOTOUIN

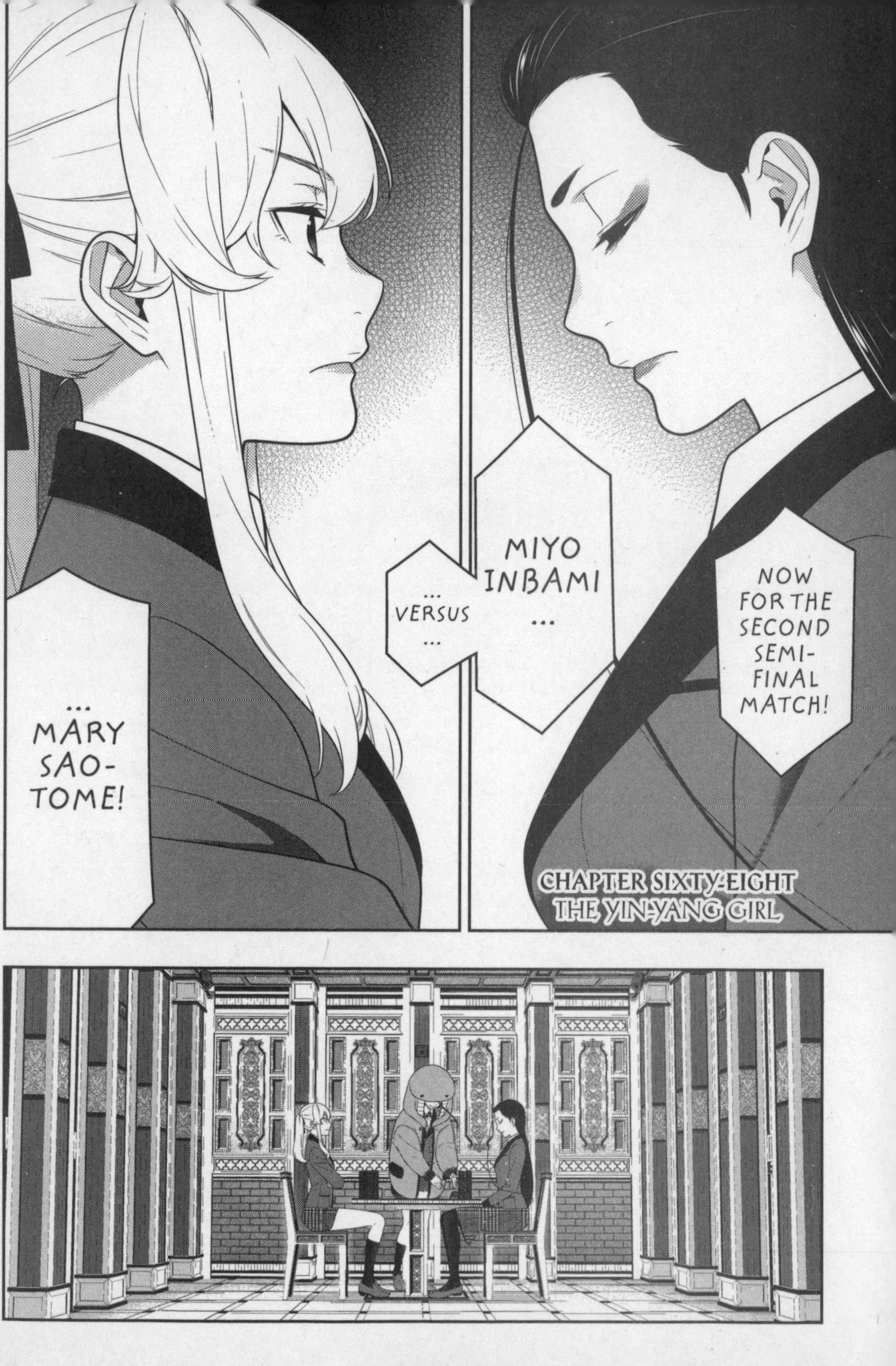
NOW FOR THE SECOND SEMI-FINAL MATCH!
MIYO INBAMI ...
... VERSUS ...
CHAPTER SIXTY-EIGHT THE YIN-YANG GIRL
... MARY SAO-TOME!

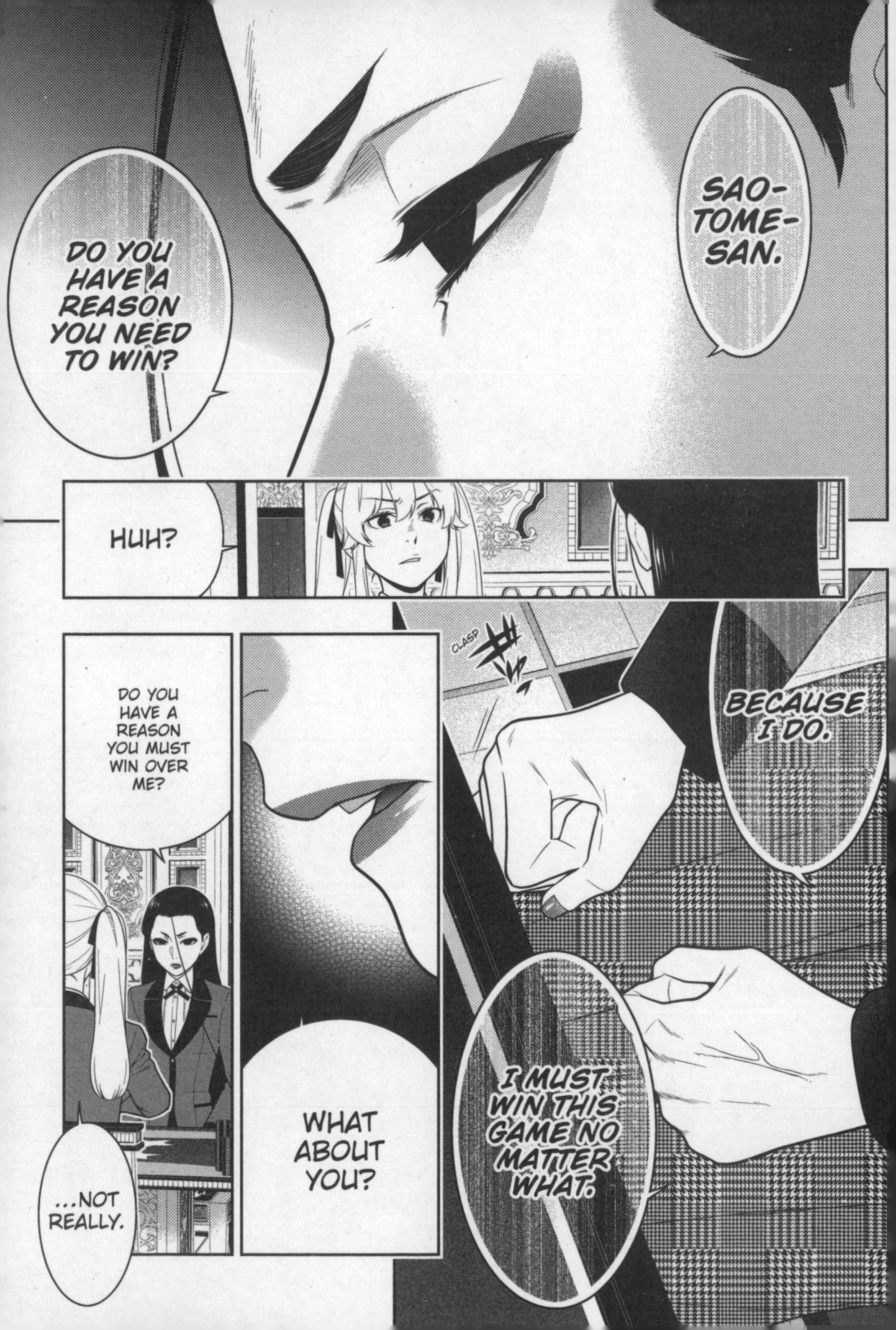

SAO-TOME-SAN.
DO YOU HAVE A REASON YOU NEED TO WIN?
HUH?
CLASP
BECAUSE I DO.
I MUST WIN THIS GAME NO MATTER WHAT.
WHAT ABOUT YOU?
DO YOU HAVE A REASON YOU MUST WIN OVER ME?
...NOT REALLY.

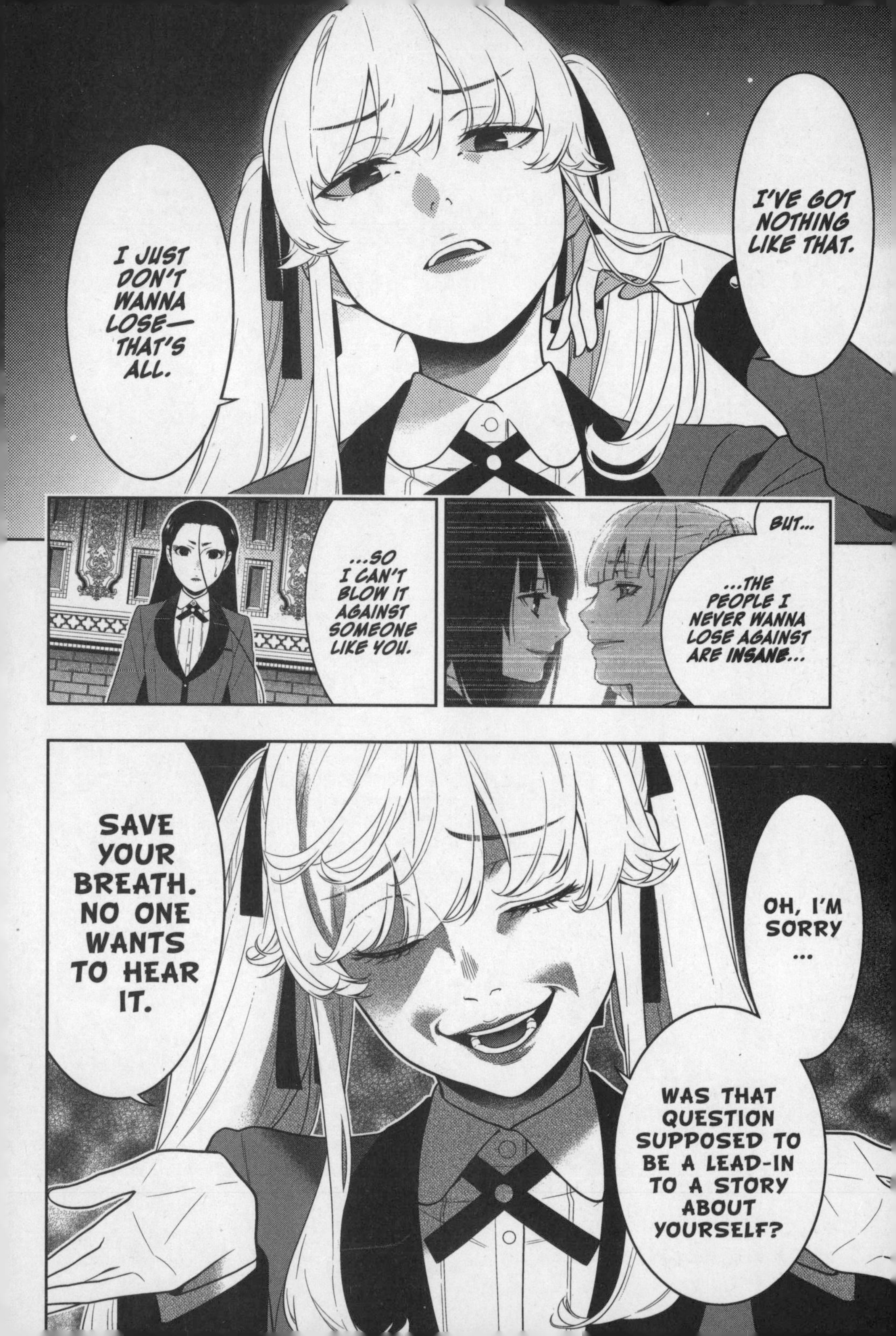
I'VE GOT NOTHING LIKE THAT.
I JUST DON'T WANNA LOSE—THAT'S ALL.
BUT...
...THE PEOPLE I NEVER WANNA LOSE AGAINST ARE INSANE...
...SO I CAN'T BLOW IT AGAINST SOMEONE LIKE YOU.
OH, I'M SORRY ...
WAS THAT QUESTION SUPPOSED TO BE A LEAD-IN TO A STORY ABOUT YOURSELF?
SAVE YOUR BREATH. NO ONE WANTS TO HEAR IT.

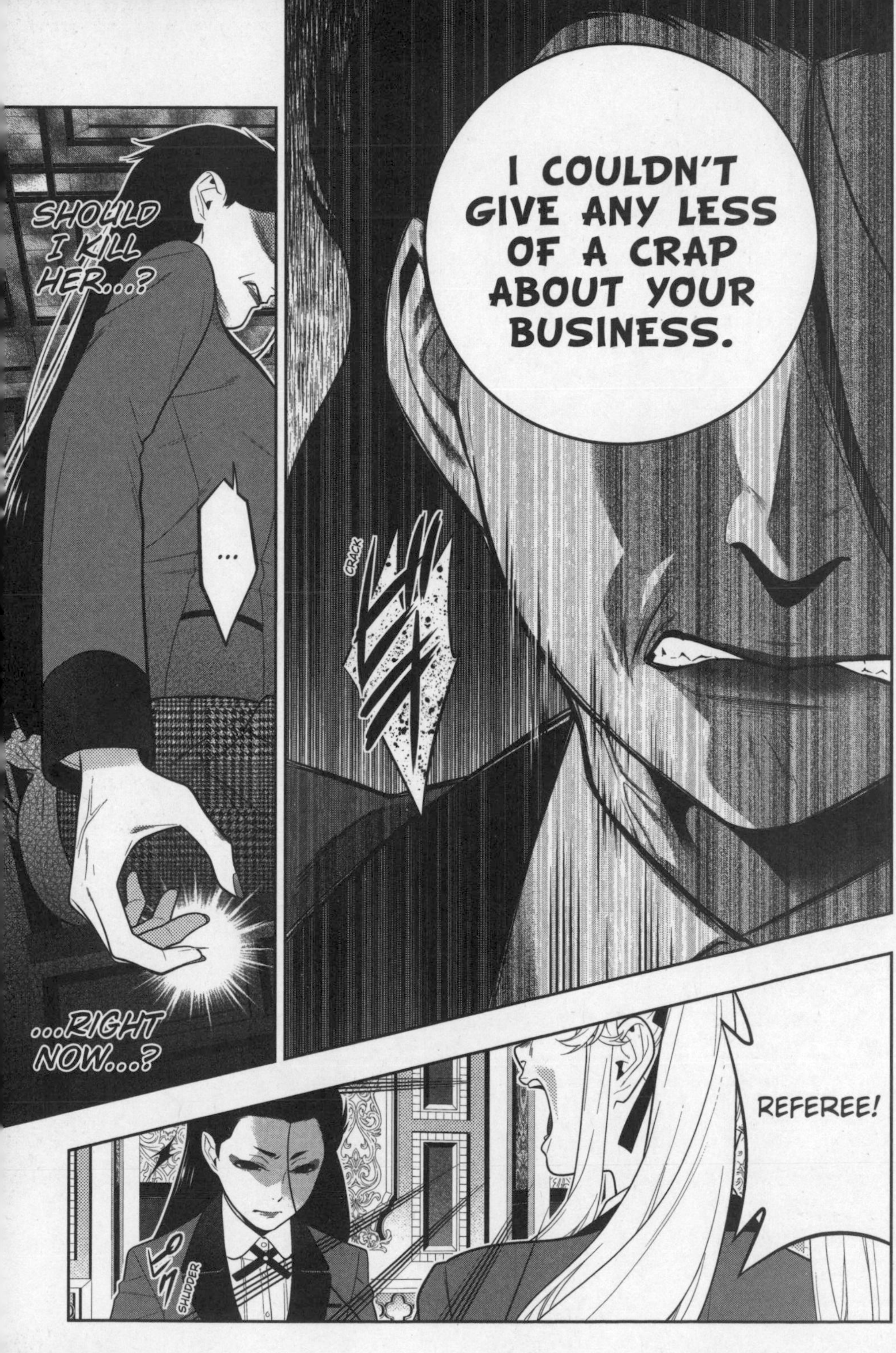
I COULDN'T GIVE ANY LESS OF A CRAP ABOUT YOUR BUSINESS.
CRACK
SHOULD I KILL HER...?
...
...RIGHT NOW...?
REFEREE!
SHUDDER

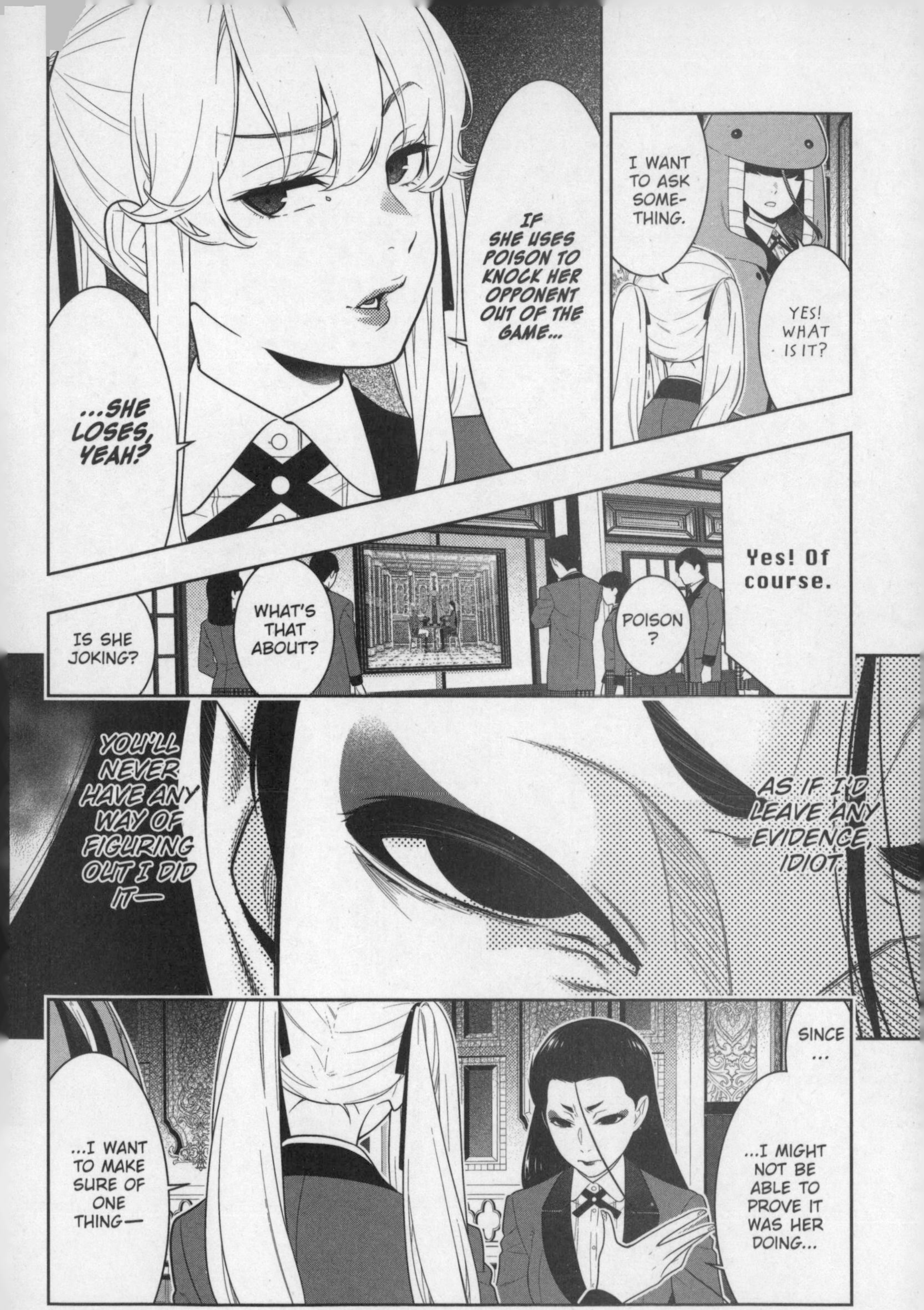
I WANT TO ASK SOME-THING.
YES! WHAT IS IT?
IF SHE USES POISON TO KNOCK HER OPPONENT OUT OF THE GAME...
...SHE LOSES, YEAH?
Yes! Of course.
POISON?
WHAT'S THAT ABOUT?
IS SHE JOKING?
AS IF I'D LEAVE ANY EVIDENCE, IDIOT.
YOU'LL NEVER HAVE ANY WAY OF FIGURING OUT I DID IT—
SINCE ...
...I MIGHT NOT BE ABLE TO PROVE IT WAS HER DOING...
...I WANT TO MAKE SURE OF ONE THING—

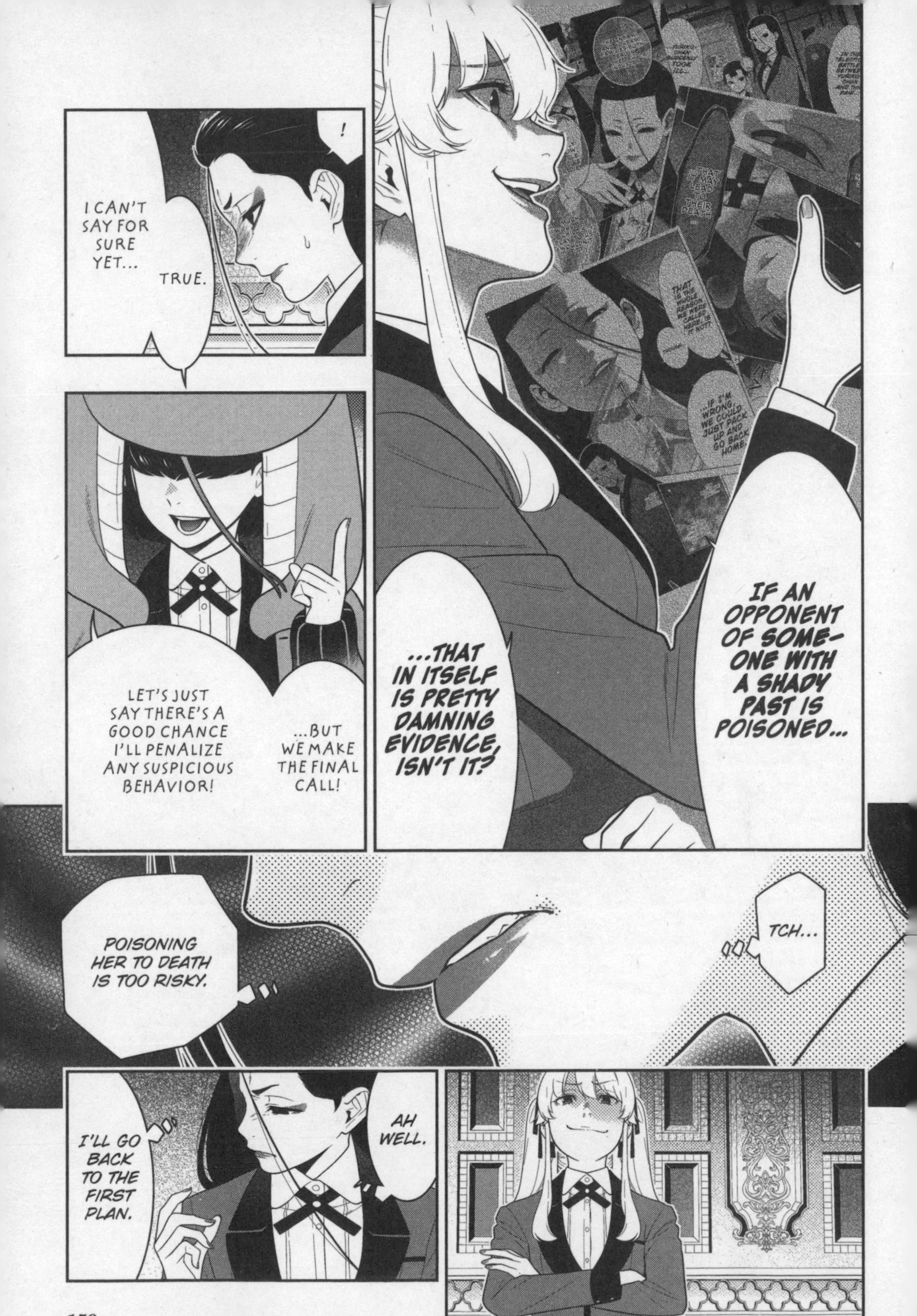
THAT IT MAY LEAD TO THEIR DEATH.
THAT IS THE WHOLE REASON WE WERE CALLED HERE, IS IT NOT?
...IF I'M WRONG, WE COULD JUST PACK UP AND GO BACK HOME.
IF AN OPPONENT OF SOME-ONE WITH A SHADY PAST IS POISONED...
...THAT IN ITSELF IS PRETTY DAMNING EVIDENCE, ISN'T IT?
!
I CAN'T SAY FOR SURE YET...
TRUE.
...BUT WE MAKE THE FINAL CALL!
LET'S JUST SAY THERE'S A GOOD CHANCE I'LL PENALIZE ANY SUSPICIOUS BEHAVIOR!
TCH...
POISONING HER TO DEATH IS TOO RISKY.
AH WELL.
I'LL GO BACK TO THE FIRST PLAN.

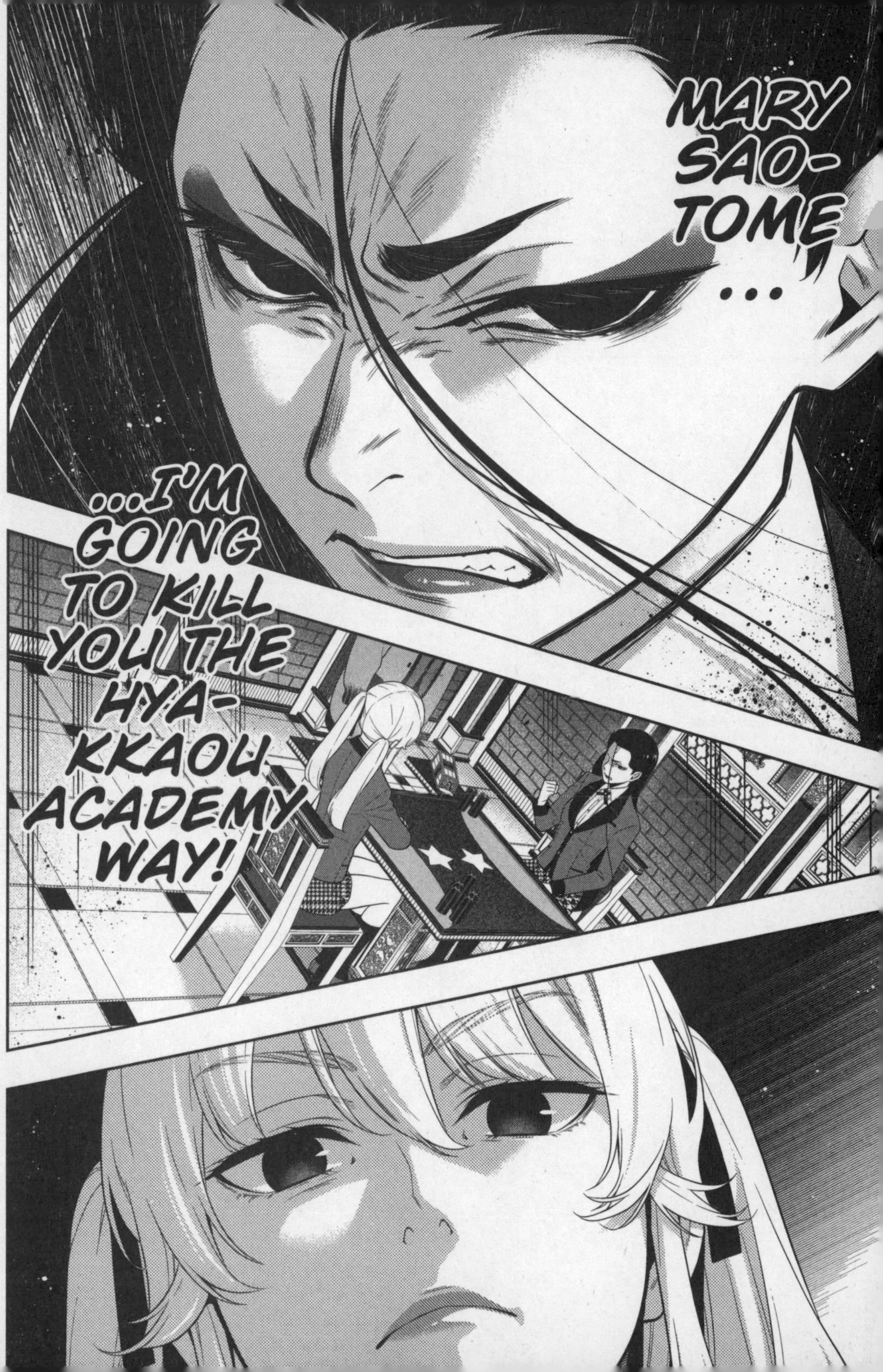
MARY SAO-TOME ...
...I'M GOING TO KILL YOU THE HYA-KKAOU ACADEMY WAY!

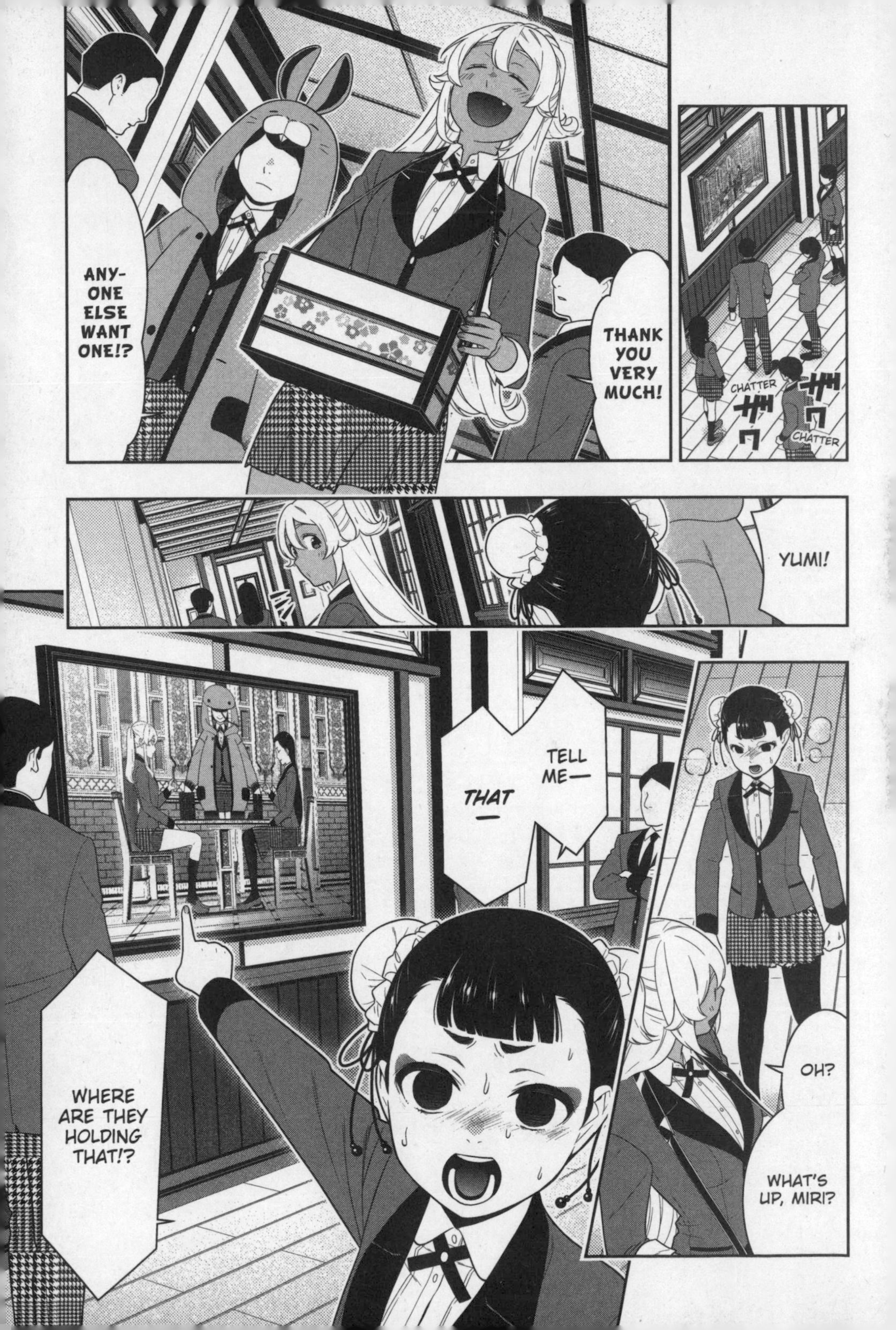
CHATTER
CHATTER
THANK YOU VERY MUCH!
ANY-ONE ELSE WANT ONE!?
YUMI!
OH?
WHAT'S UP, MIRI?
TELL ME—
THAT—
WHERE ARE THEY HOLDING THAT!?

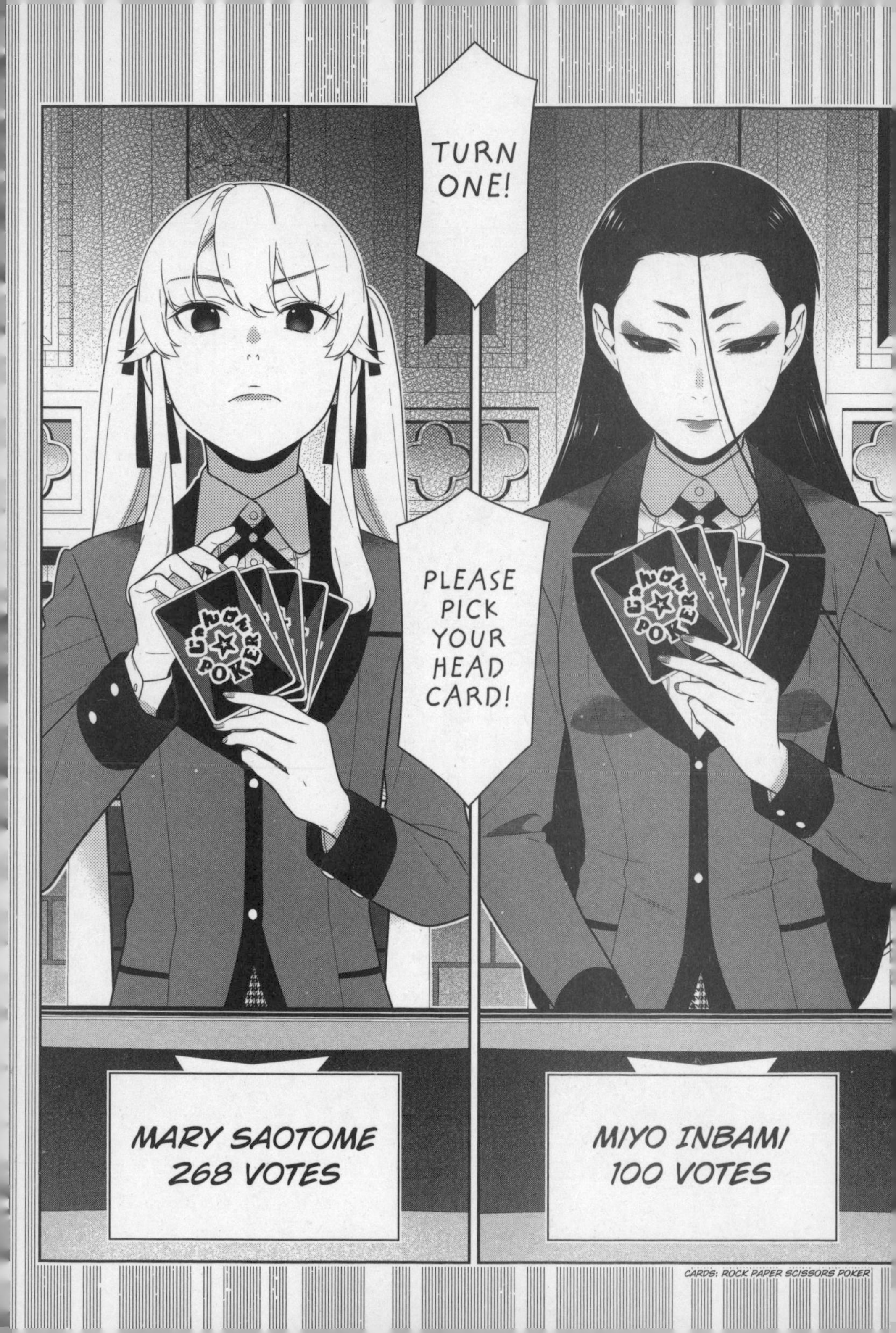
TURN ONE!
PLEASE PICK YOUR HEAD CARD!
MIYO INBAMI
100 VOTES
MARY SAOTOME
268 VOTES
CARDS: ROCK PAPER SCISSORS POKER

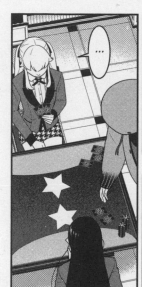

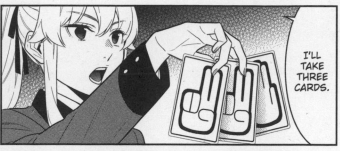

I'LL TAKE THREE CARDS.
...TWO CARDS.
...
FOR NOW...
...I GUESS I'LL JUST WAIT AND SEE.
THE HEAD CARDS HAVE BEEN PLACED.
NEXT UP—THE BETTING ROUND!

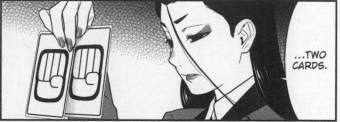

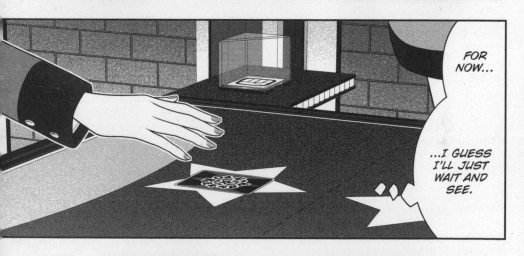

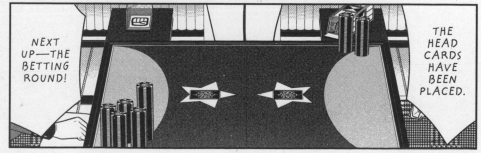

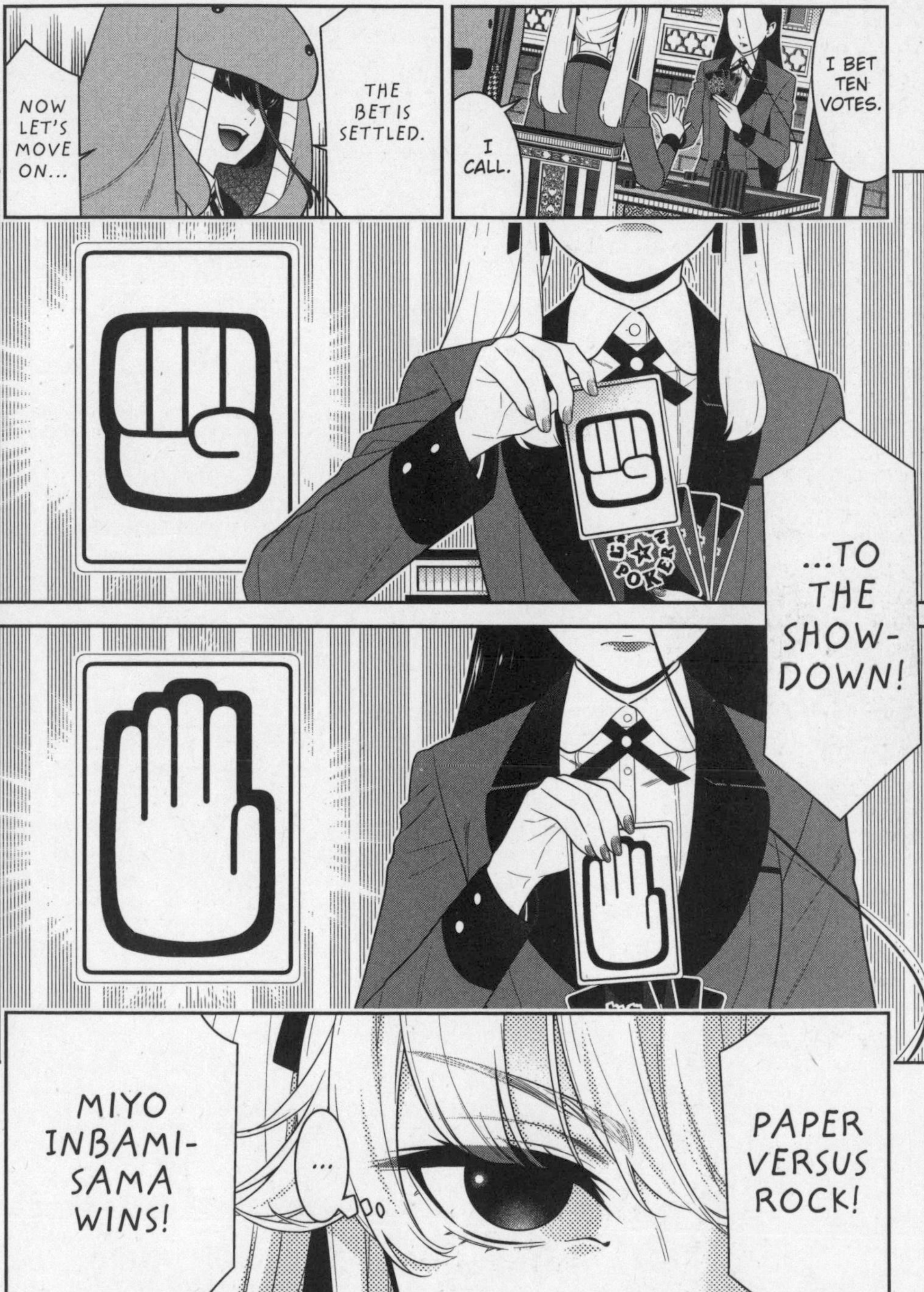
I BET TEN VOTES.
I CALL.
THE BET IS SETTLED.
NOW LET'S MOVE ON...
...TO THE SHOWDOWN!
PAPER VERSUS ROCK!
...
MIYO INBAMI-SAMA WINS!

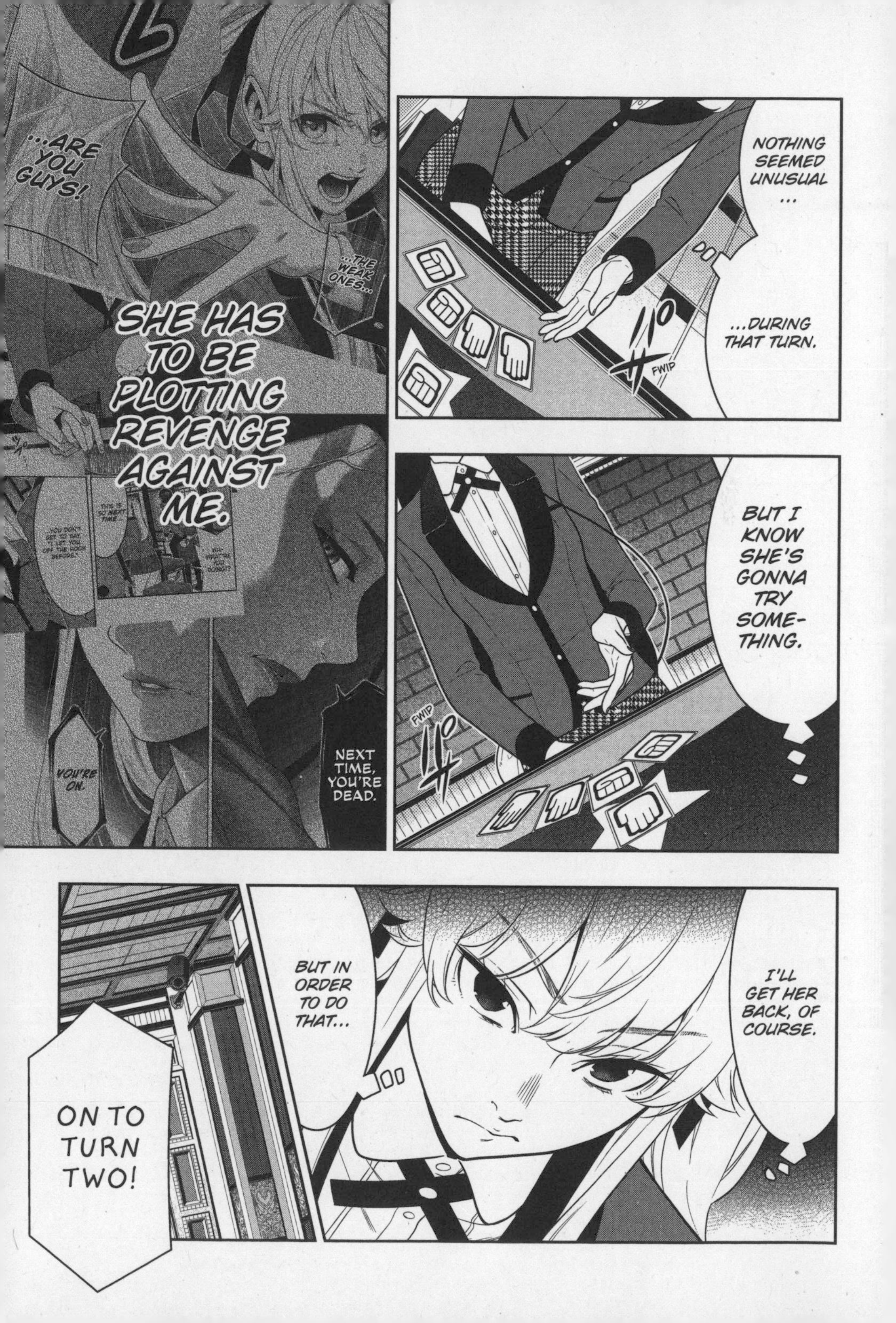
NOTHING SEEMED UNUSUAL...
...DURING THAT TURN.
FWIP
BUT I KNOW SHE'S GONNA TRY SOME-THING.
FWIP
...THE WEAK ONES...
...ARE YOU GUYS!
SHE HAS TO BE PLOTTING REVENGE AGAINST ME.
NEXT TIME, YOU'RE DEAD.
YOU'RE ON.
I'LL GET HER BACK, OF COURSE.
BUT IN ORDER TO DO THAT...
ON TO TURN TWO!

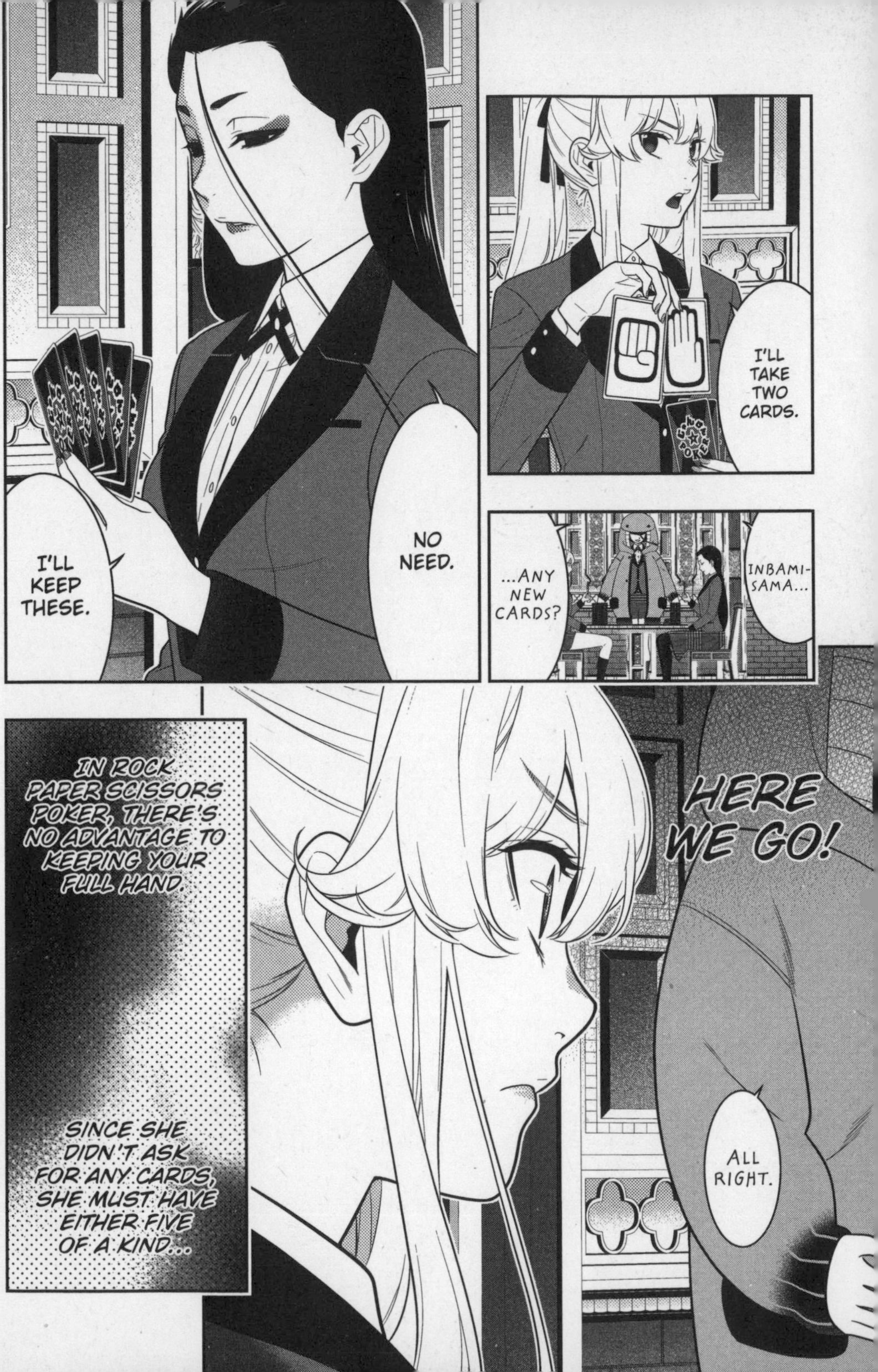
I'LL TAKE TWO CARDS.
INBAMI-SAMA...
...ANY NEW CARDS?
NO NEED.
I'LL KEEP THESE.
HERE WE GO!
IN ROCK PAPER SCISSORS POKER, THERE'S NO ADVANTAGE TO KEEPING YOUR FULL HAND.
ALL RIGHT.
SINCE SHE DIDN'T ASK FOR ANY CARDS, SHE MUST HAVE EITHER FIVE OF A KIND...

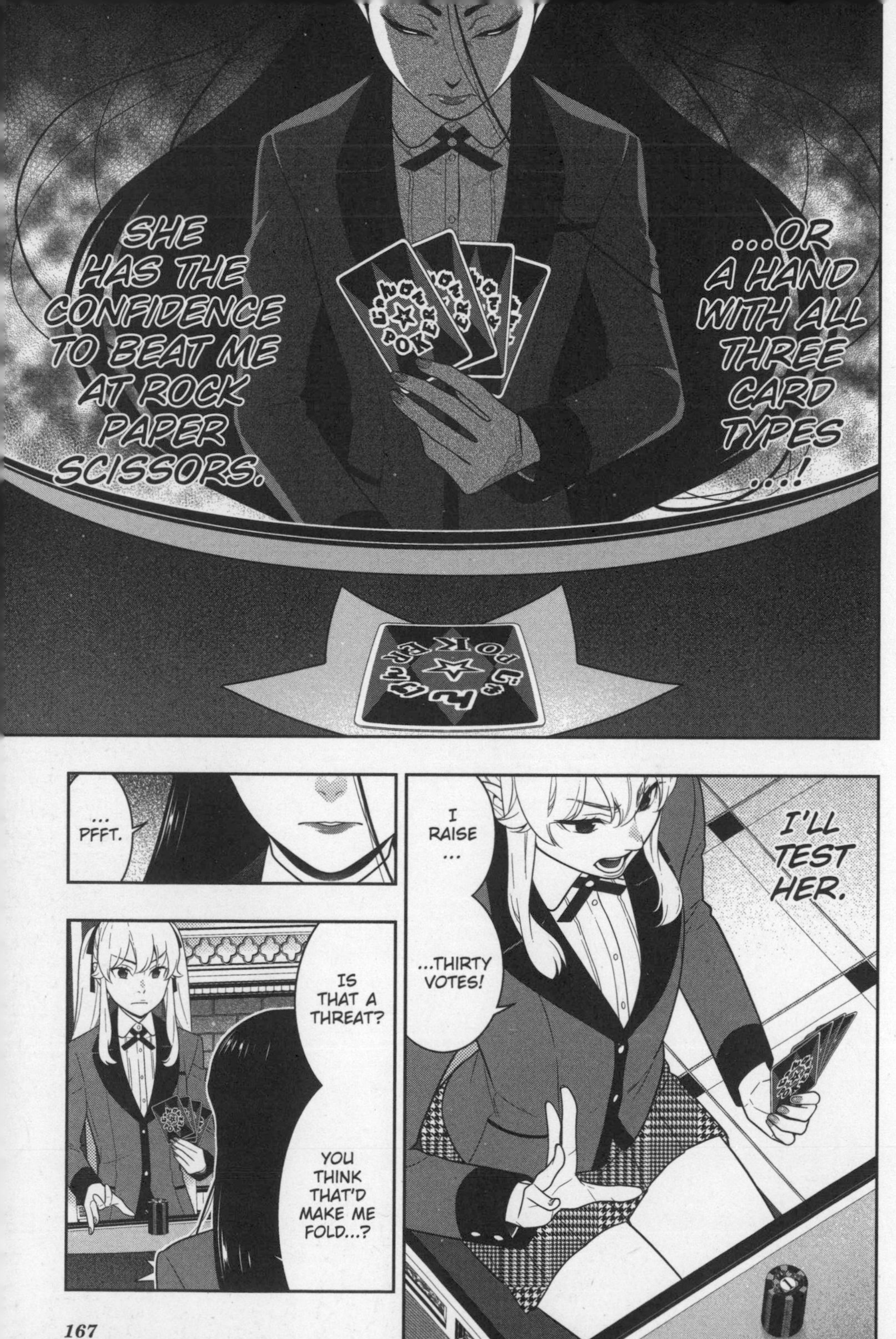
SHE HAS THE CONFIDENCE TO BEAT ME AT ROCK PAPER SCISSORS.
...OR A HAND WITH ALL THREE CARD TYPES ...!
I'LL TEST HER.
I RAISE ...
...THIRTY VOTES!
... PFFT.
IS THAT A THREAT?
YOU THINK THAT'D MAKE ME FOLD...?

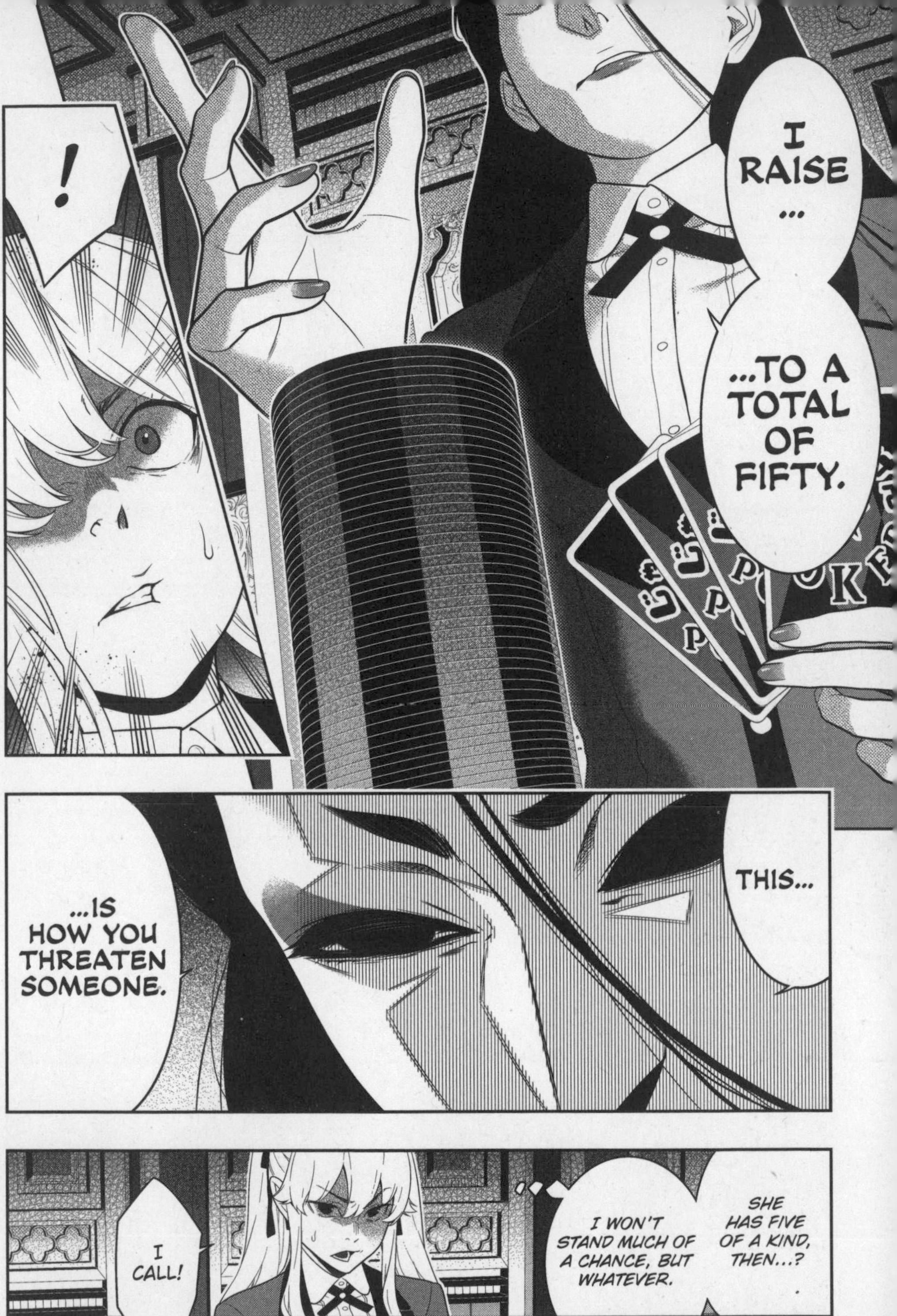
I RAISE...
...TO A TOTAL OF FIFTY.
!
THIS...
...IS HOW YOU THREATEN SOMEONE.
SHE HAS FIVE OF A KIND, THEN...?
I WON'T STAND MUCH OF A CHANCE, BUT WHATEVER.
I CALL!

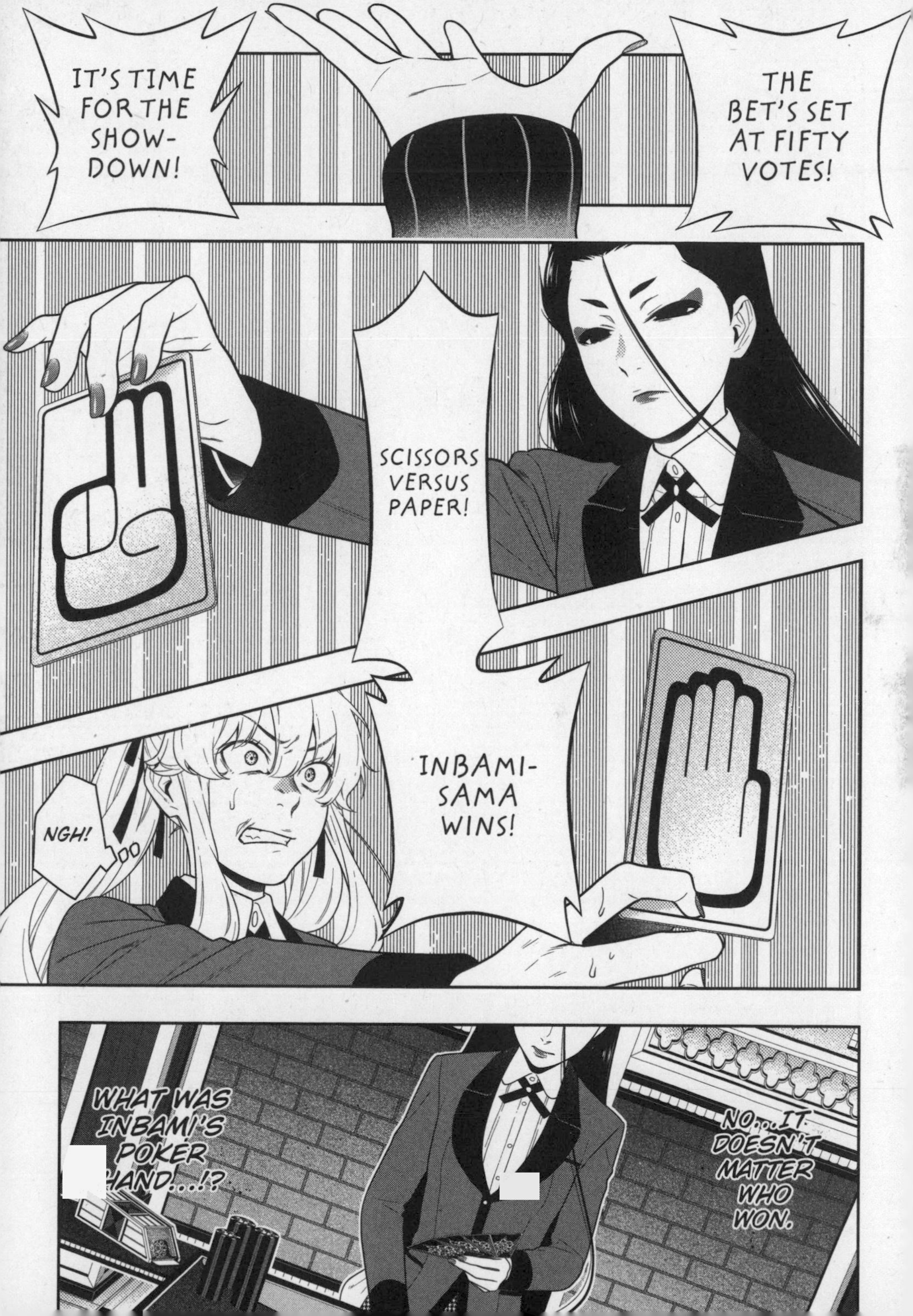
THE BET'S SET AT FIFTY VOTES!
IT'S TIME FOR THE SHOW-DOWN!
SCISSORS VERSUS PAPER!
INBAMI-SAMA WINS!
NGH!
NO... IT DOESN'T MATTER WHO WON.
WHAT WAS INBAMI'S POKER HAND...!?

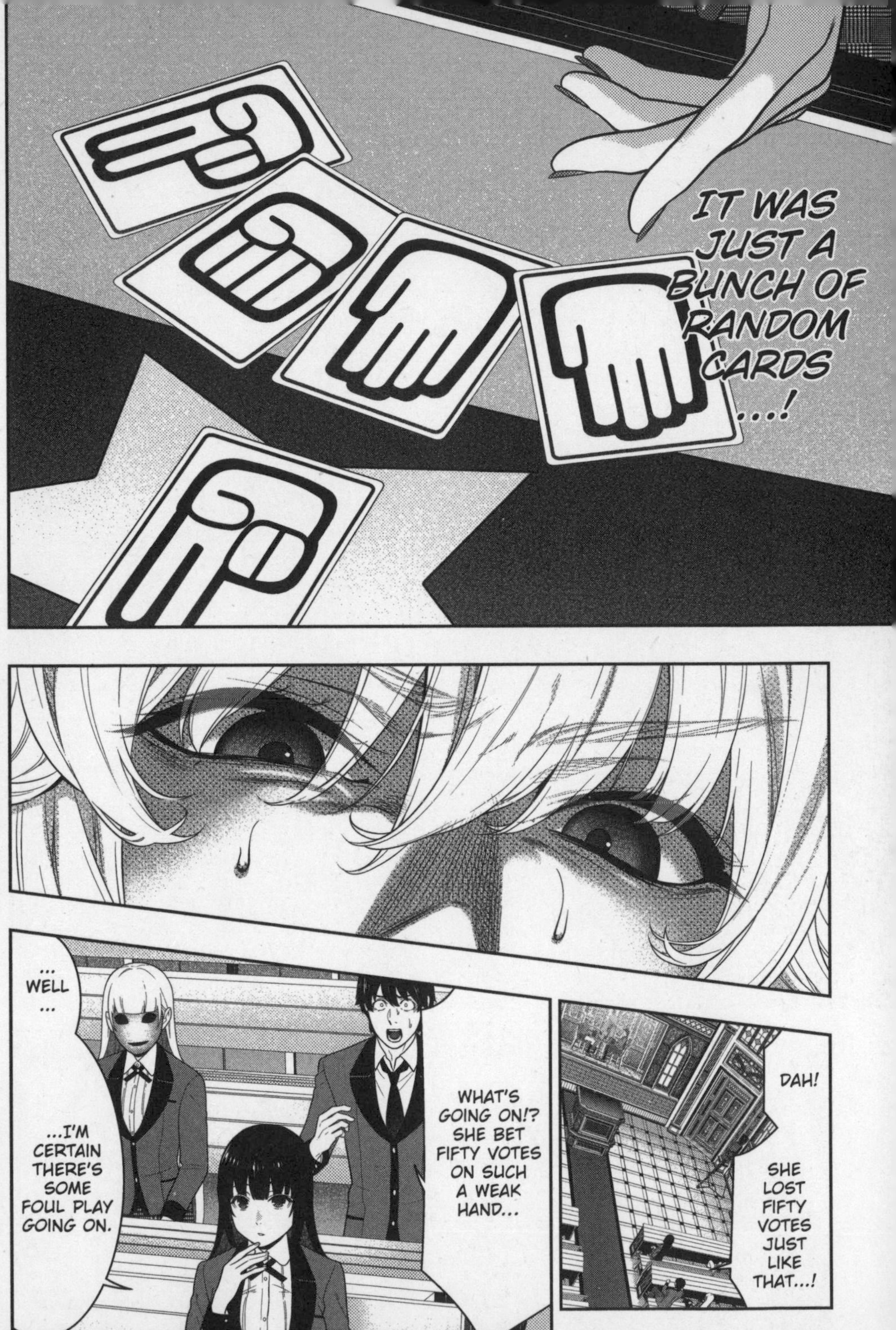
IT WAS JUST A BUNCH OF RANDOM CARDS ...!
DAH!
SHE LOST FIFTY VOTES JUST LIKE THAT...!
WHAT'S GOING ON!? SHE BET FIFTY VOTES ON SUCH A WEAK HAND...
... WELL ...
...I'M CERTAIN THERE'S SOME FOUL PLAY GOING ON.

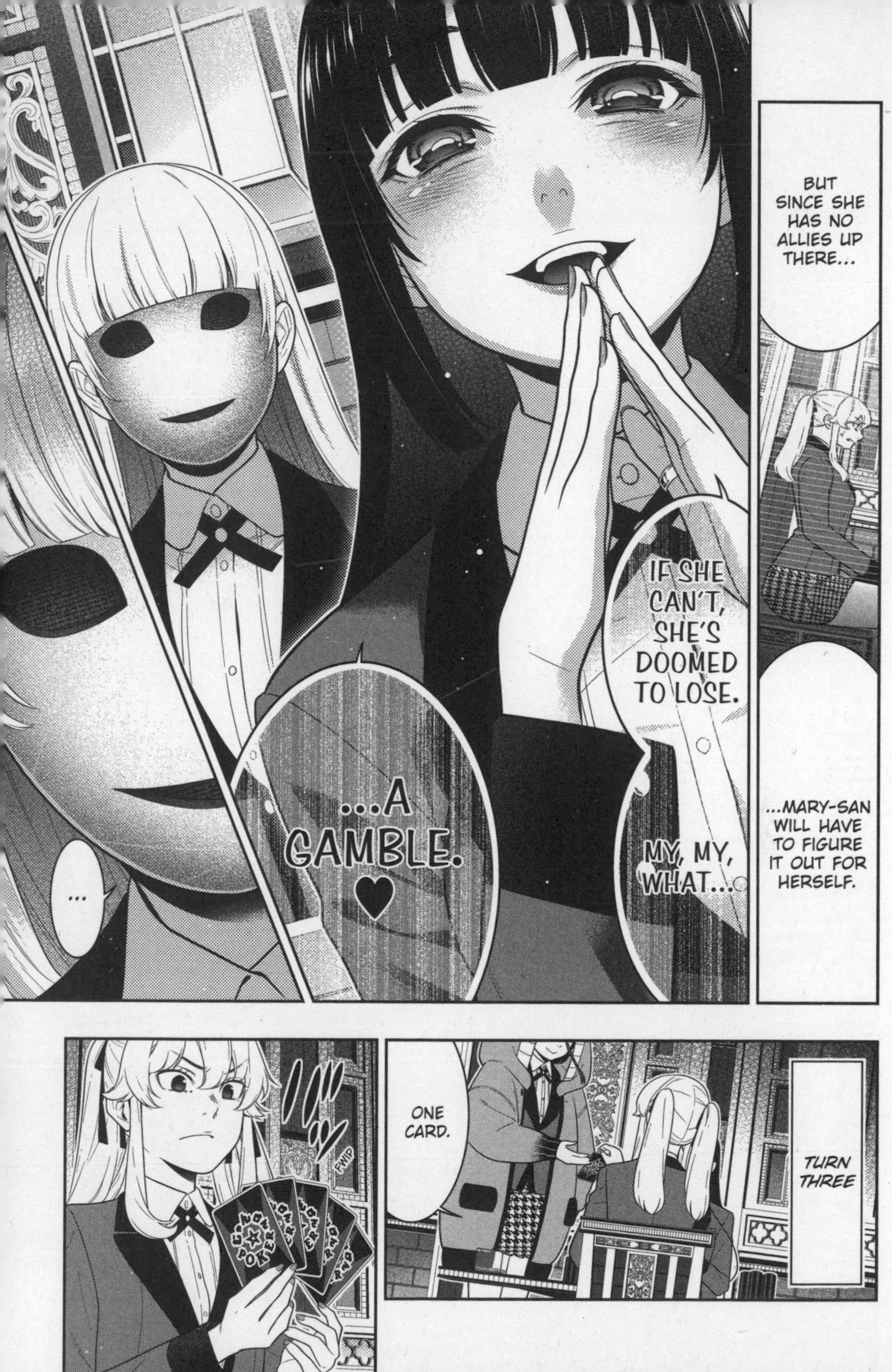
BUT SINCE SHE HAS NO ALLIES UP THERE...
...MARY-SAN WILL HAVE TO FIGURE IT OUT FOR HERSELF.
IF SHE CAN'T, SHE'S DOOMED TO LOSE.
MY, MY, WHAT...
...A GAMBLE. ♥
...
TURN THREE
ONE CARD.
FWIP

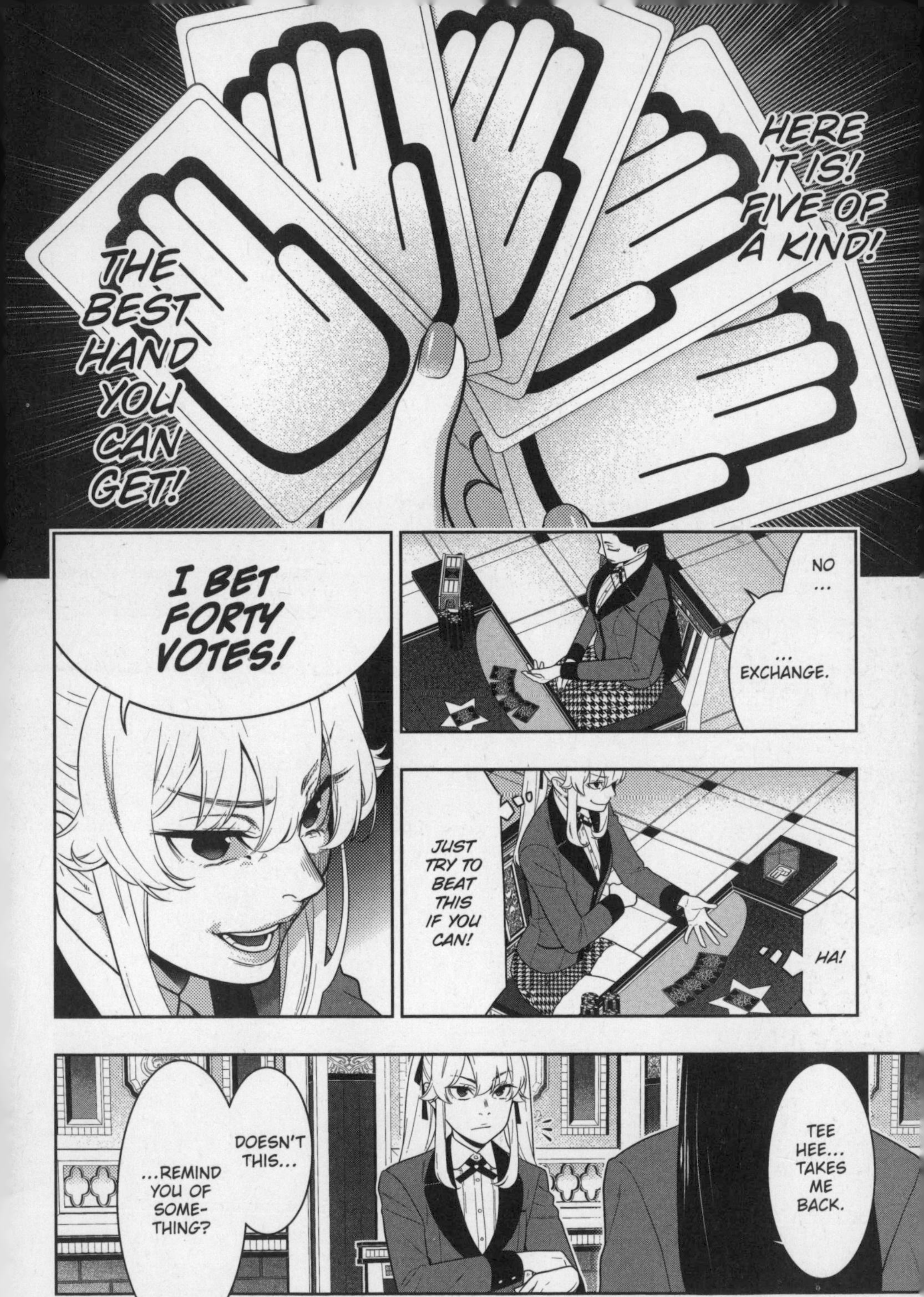
HERE IT IS! FIVE OF A KIND!
THE BEST HAND YOU CAN GET!
NO ...
... EXCHANGE.
JUST TRY TO BEAT THIS IF YOU CAN!
HA!
I BET FORTY VOTES!
TEE HEE... TAKES ME BACK.
DOESN'T THIS...
...REMIND YOU OF SOME-THING?

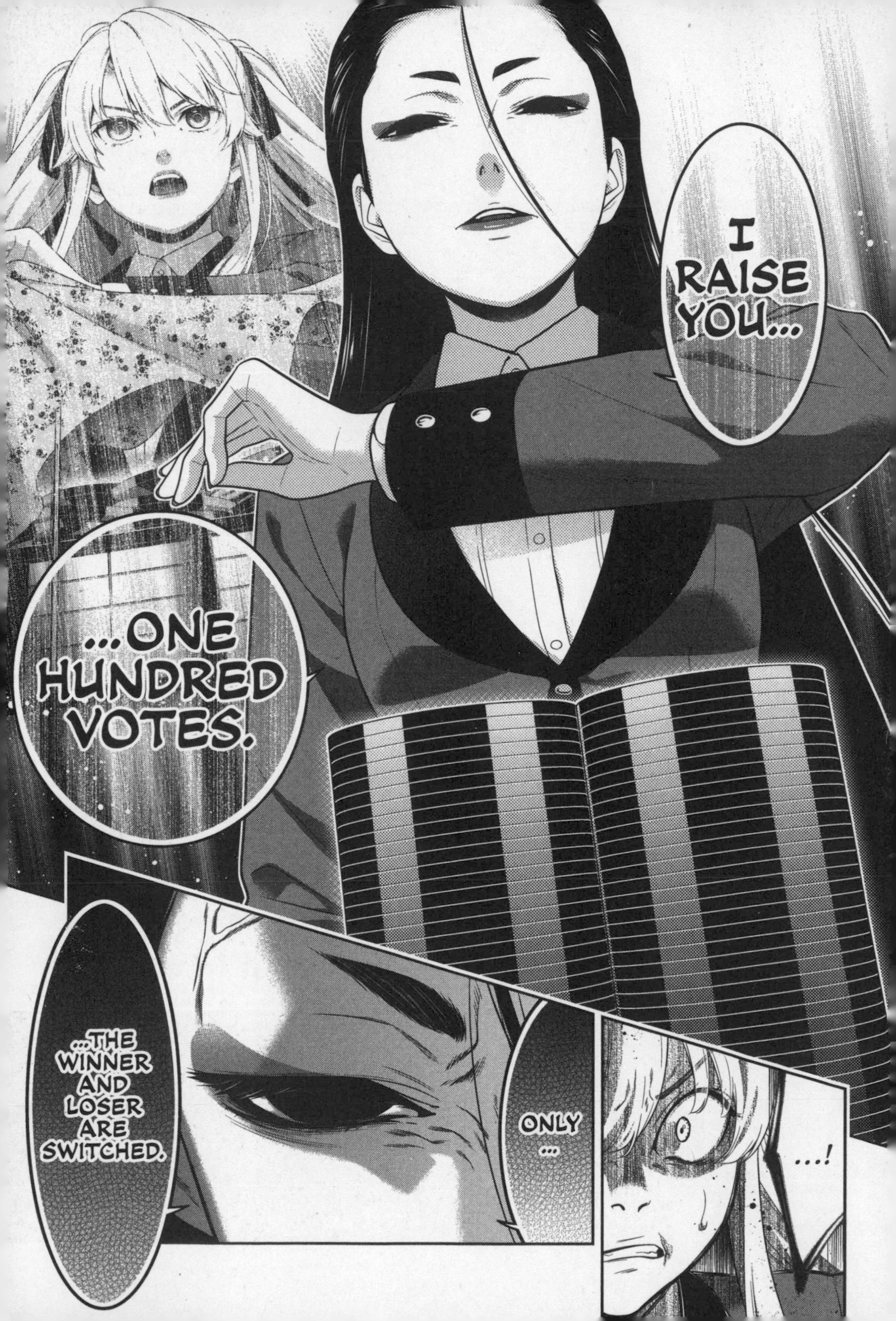
I RAISE YOU...
...ONE HUNDRED VOTES.
...!
ONLY ...
...THE WINNER AND LOSER ARE SWITCHED.

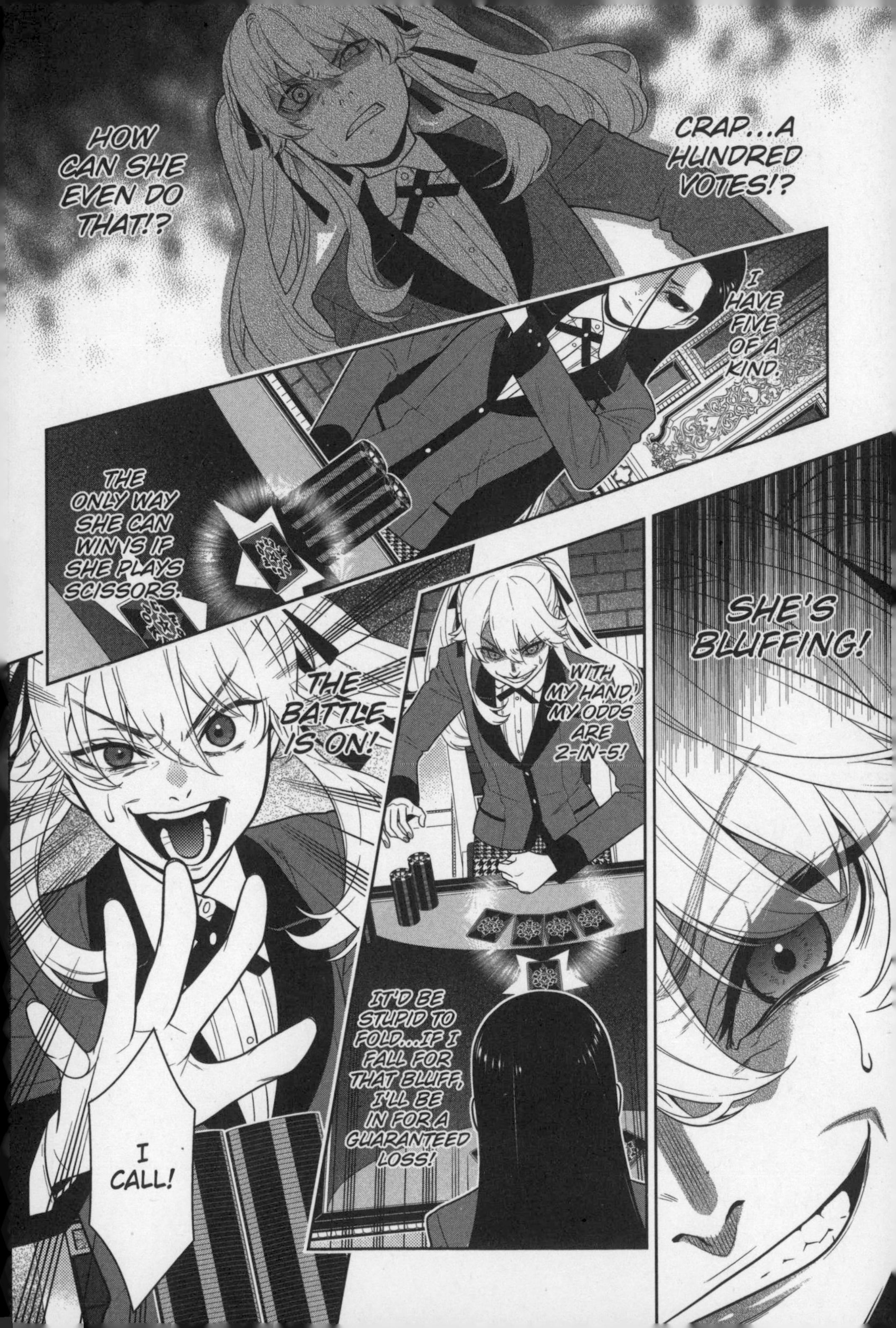
CRAP...A HUNDRED VOTES!?
HOW CAN SHE EVEN DO THAT!?
I HAVE FIVE OF A KIND.
THE ONLY WAY SHE CAN WIN IS IF SHE PLAYS SCISSORS.
SHE'S BLUFFING!
WITH MY HAND, MY ODDS ARE 2-IN-5!
IT'D BE STUPID TO FOLD...IF I FALL FOR THAT BLUFF, I'LL BE IN FOR A GUARANTEED LOSS!
THE BATTLE IS ON!
I CALL!

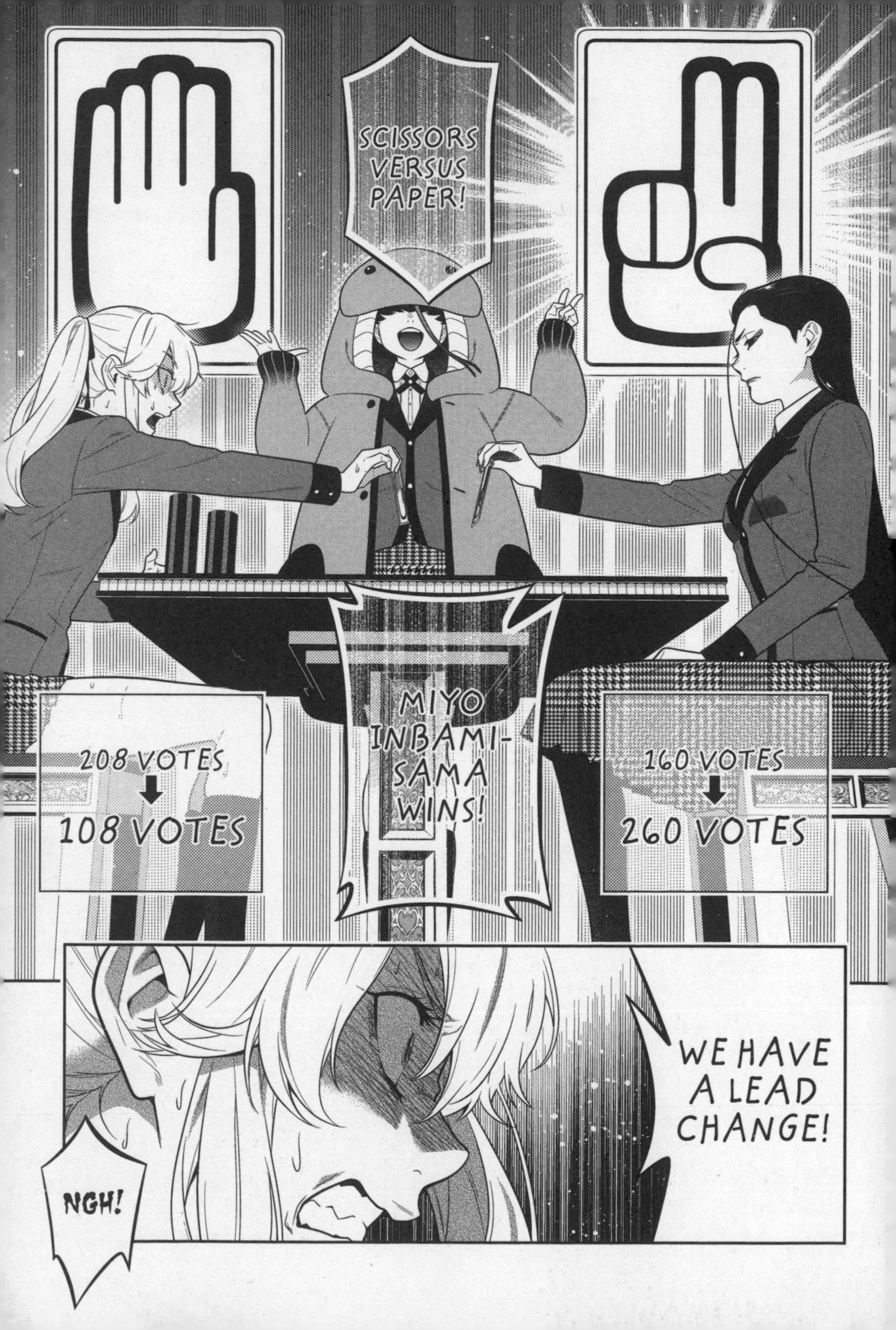
SCISSORS VERSUS PAPER!
MIYO INBAMI-SAMA WINS!
160 VOTES ↓ 260 VOTES
208 VOTES ↓ 108 VOTES
WE HAVE A LEAD CHANGE!
NGH!

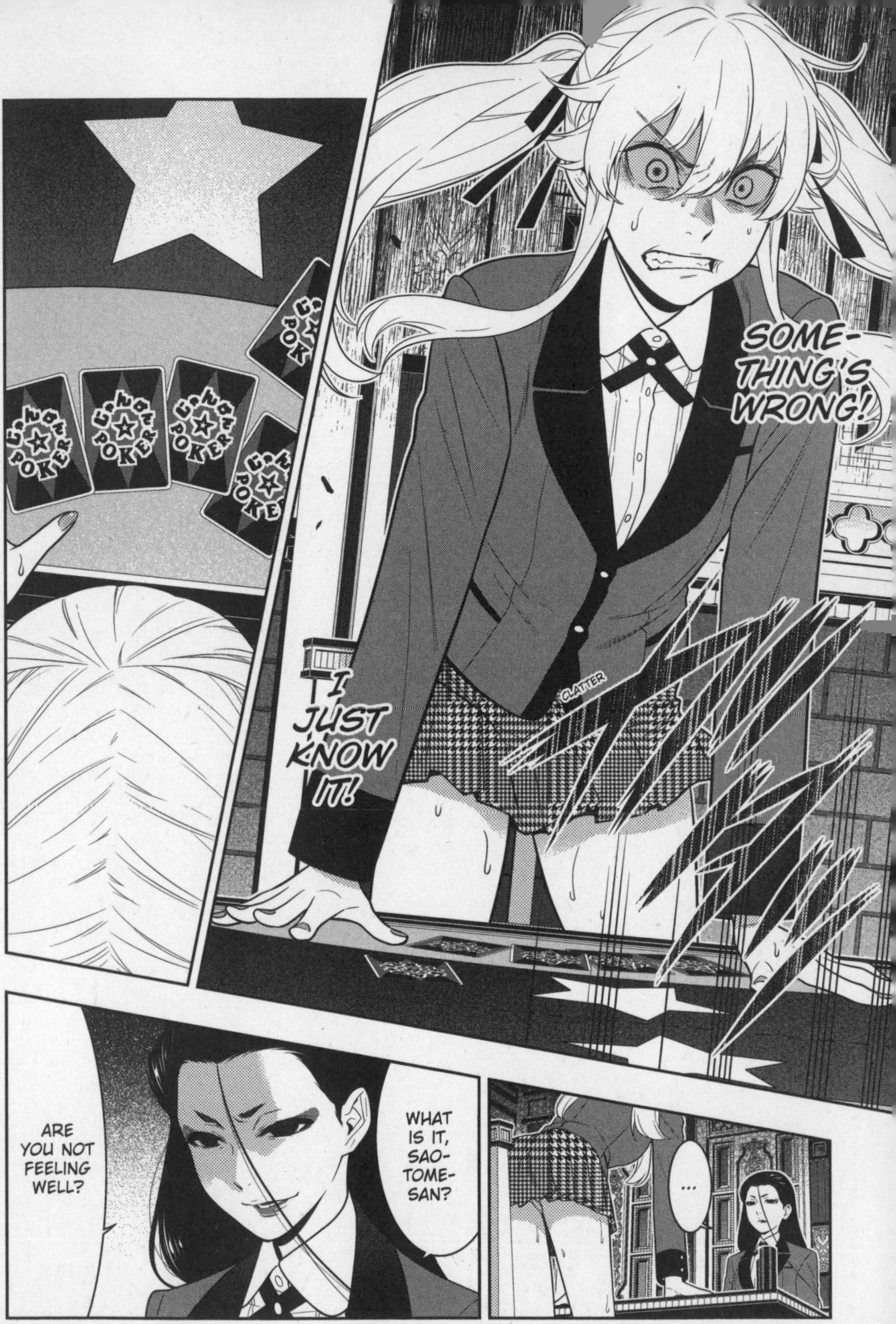
SOME-THING'S WRONG!
I JUST KNOW IT!
CLATTER
...
WHAT IS IT, SAO-TOME-SAN?
ARE YOU NOT FEELING WELL?

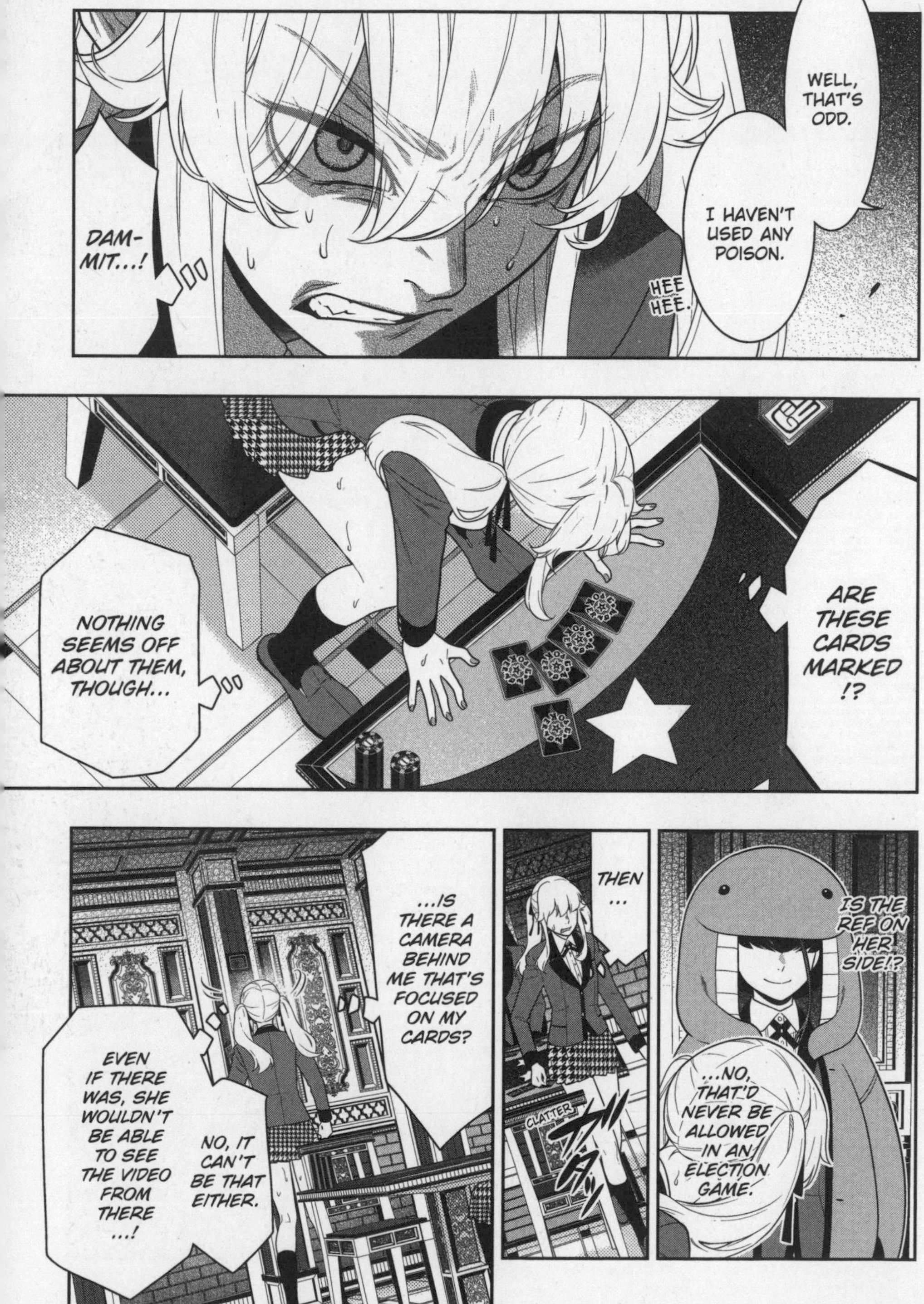
WELL, THAT'S ODD.
I HAVEN'T USED ANY POISON.
HEE HEE.
DAM-MIT...!
ARE THESE CARDS MARKED!?
NOTHING SEEMS OFF ABOUT THEM, THOUGH...
IS THE REF ON HER SIDE!?
...NO, THAT'D NEVER BE ALLOWED IN AN ELECTION GAME.
THEN...
CLATTER
...IS THERE A CAMERA BEHIND ME THAT'S FOCUSED ON MY CARDS?
EVEN IF THERE WAS, SHE WOULDN'T BE ABLE TO SEE THE VIDEO FROM THERE...!
NO, IT CAN'T BE THAT EITHER.

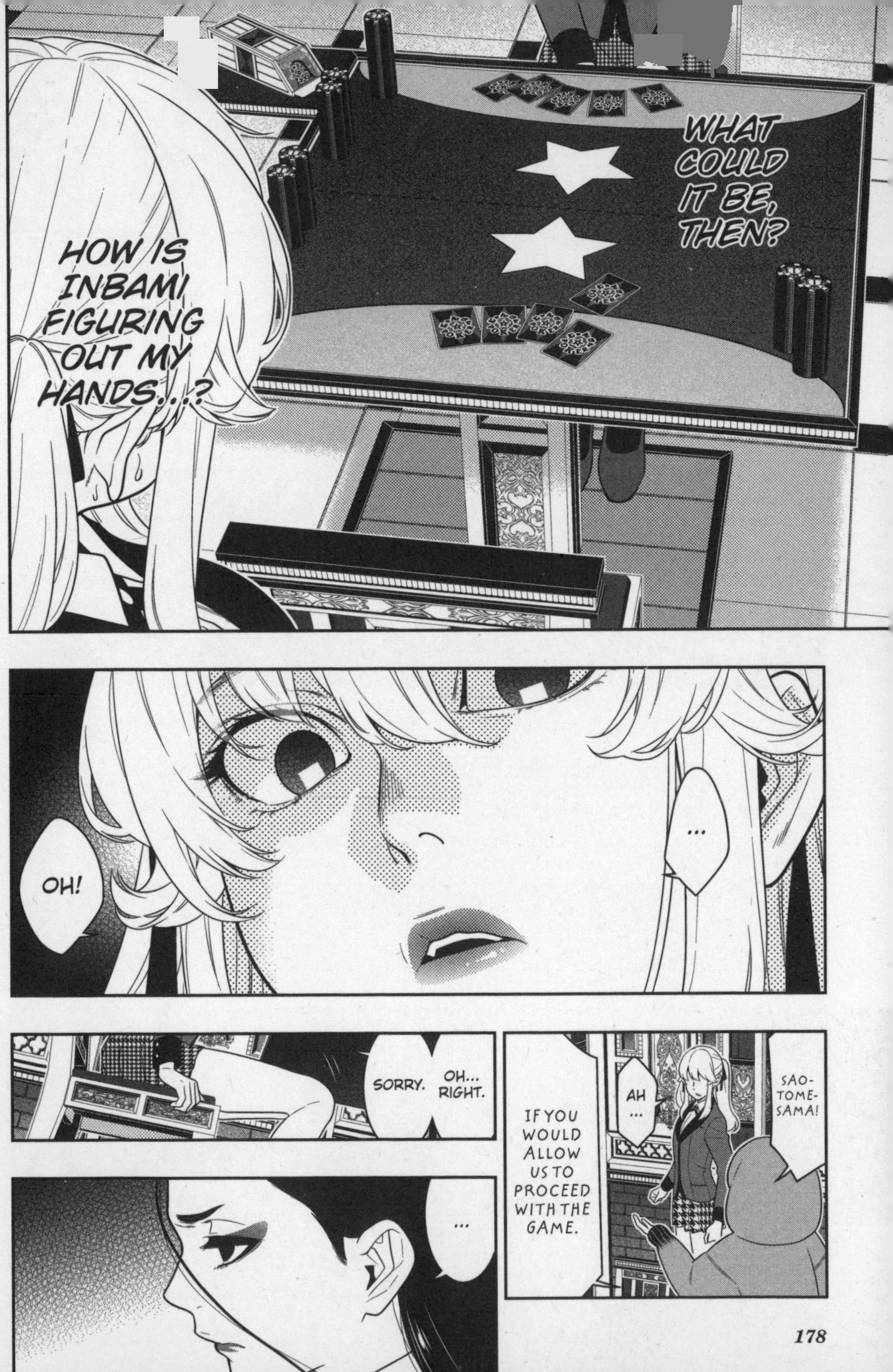

WHAT COULD IT BE, THEN?
HOW IS INBAMI FIGURING OUT MY HANDS...?
...
OH!
SAOTOME-SAMA!
AH...
IF YOU WOULD ALLOW US TO PROCEED WITH THE GAME.
OH... RIGHT.
SORRY.
...

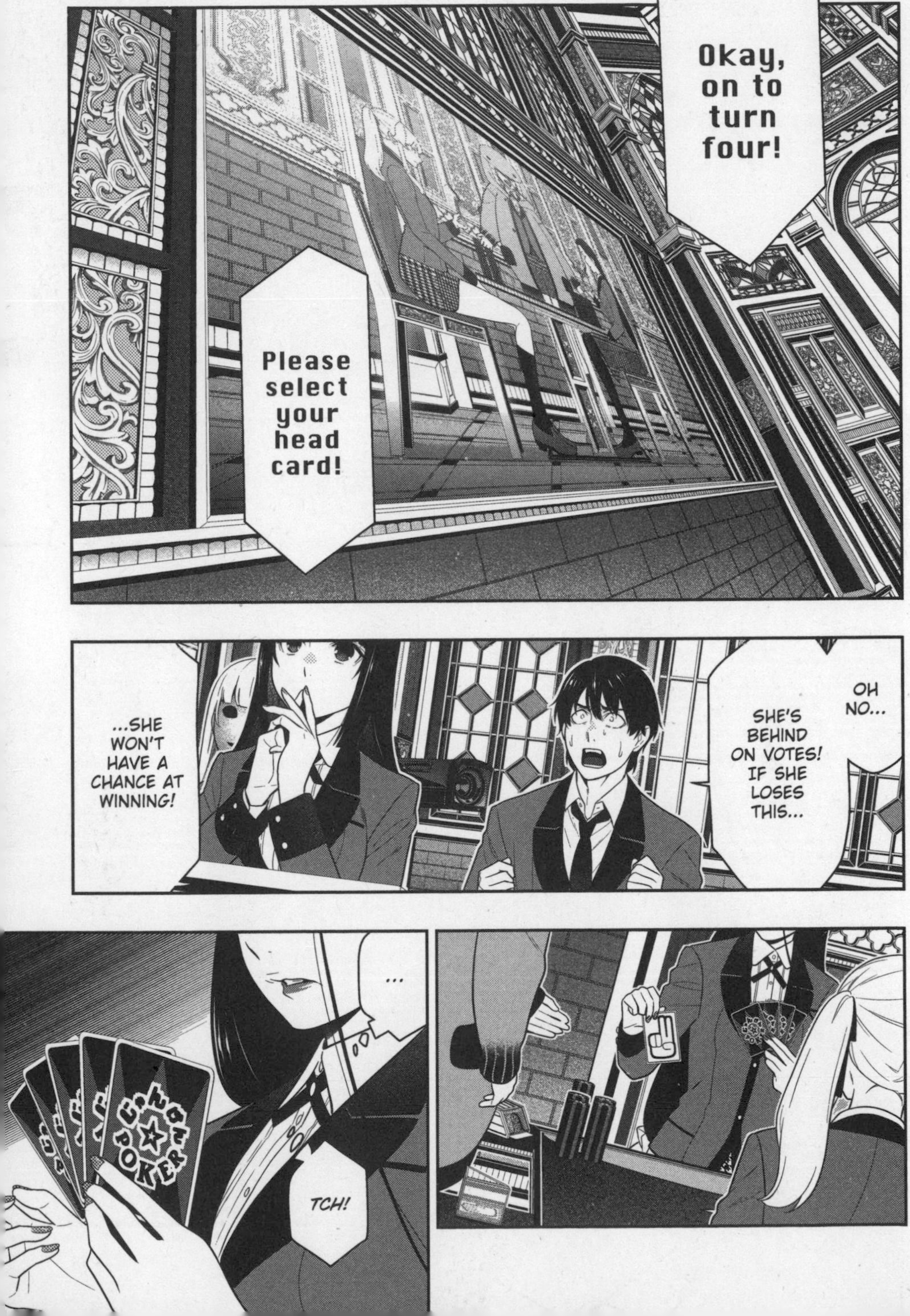

Okay, on to turn four!
Please select your head card!
OH NO...
SHE'S BEHIND ON VOTES! IF SHE LOSES THIS...
...SHE WON'T HAVE A CHANCE AT WINNING!
...
TCH!

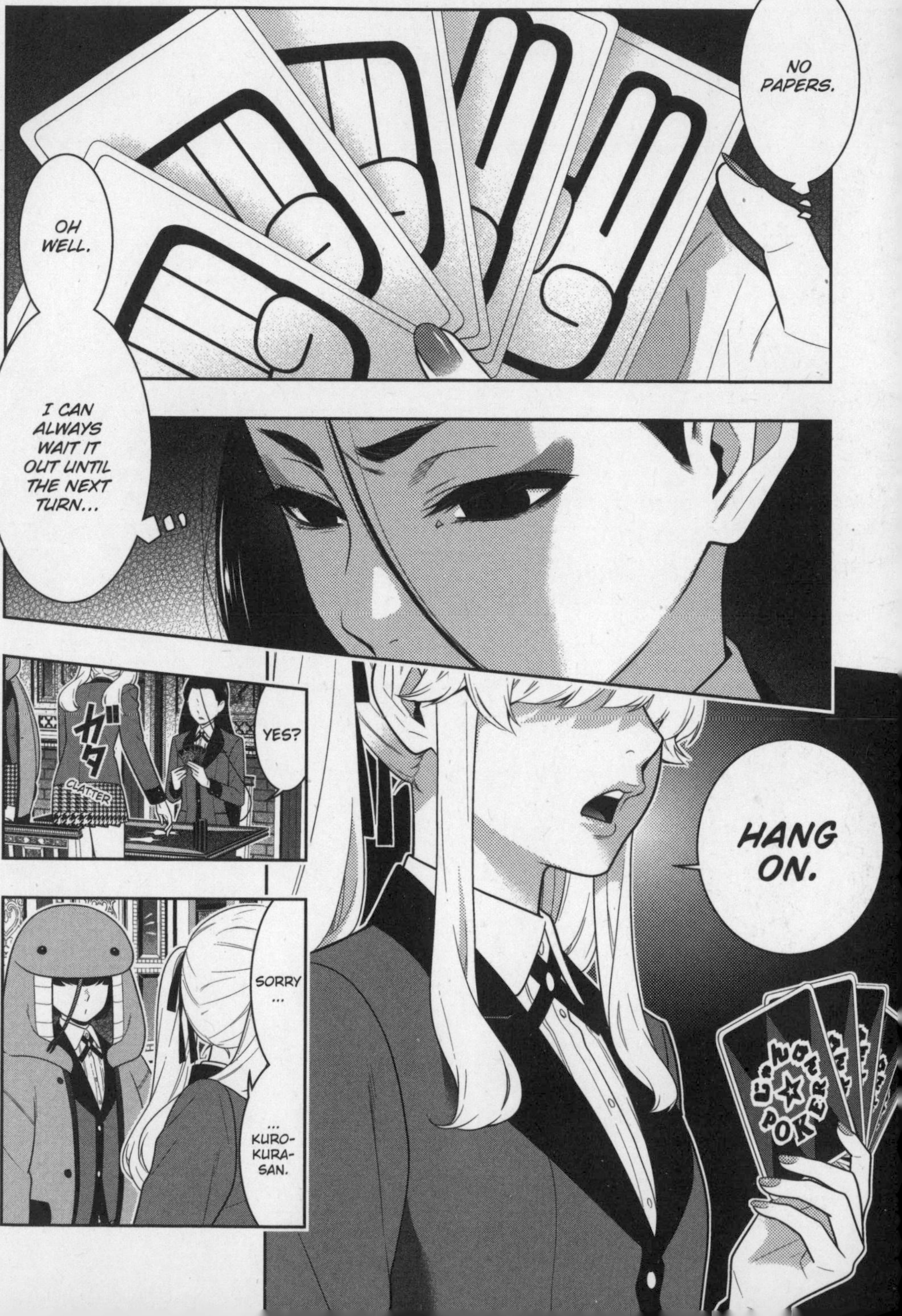
NO PAPERS.
OH WELL.
I CAN ALWAYS WAIT IT OUT UNTIL THE NEXT TURN...
HANG ON.
YES?
CLATTER
SORRY ... ... KURO-KURA-SAN.
POKER

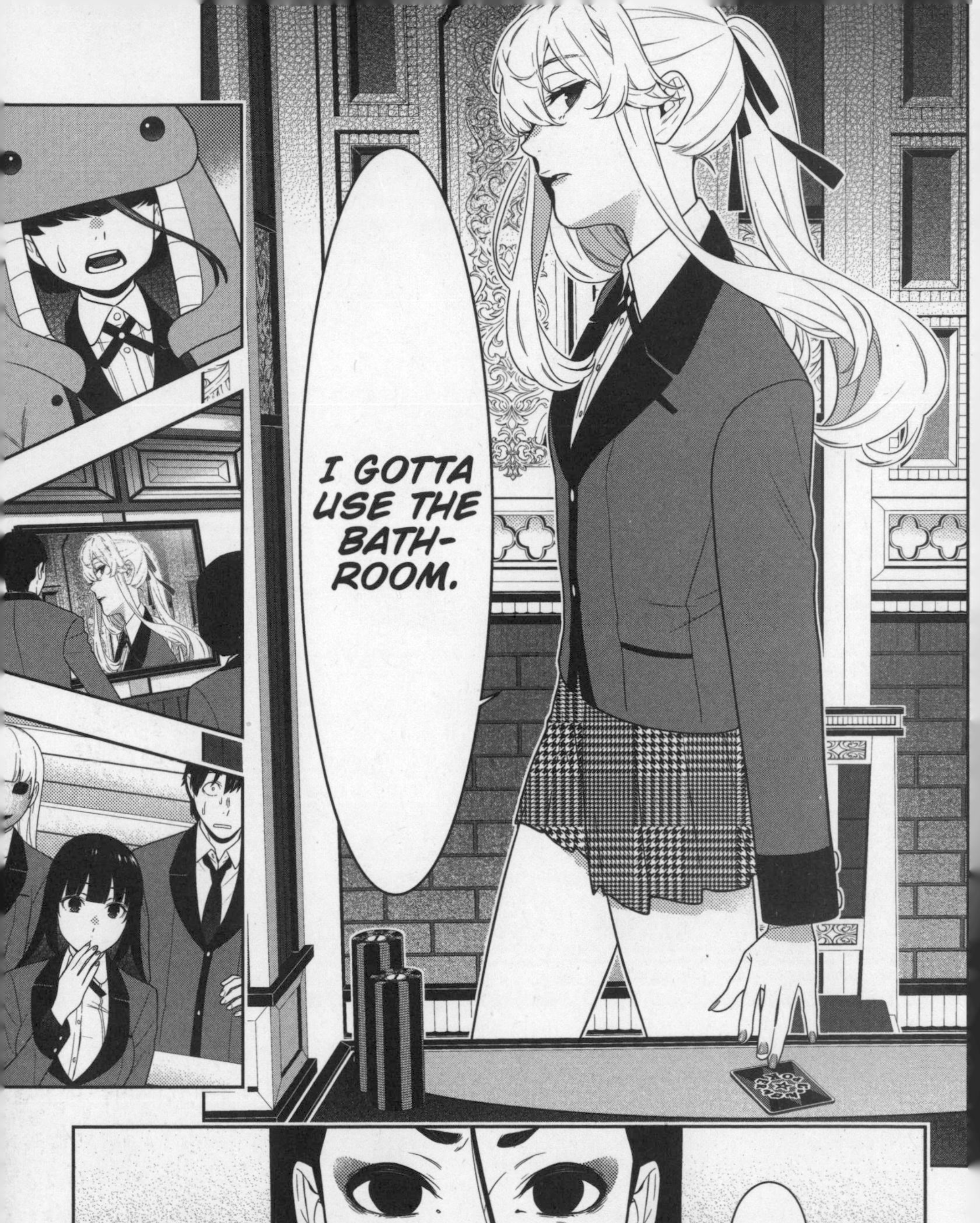
I GOTTA USE THE BATH-ROOM.
WHAT ...?

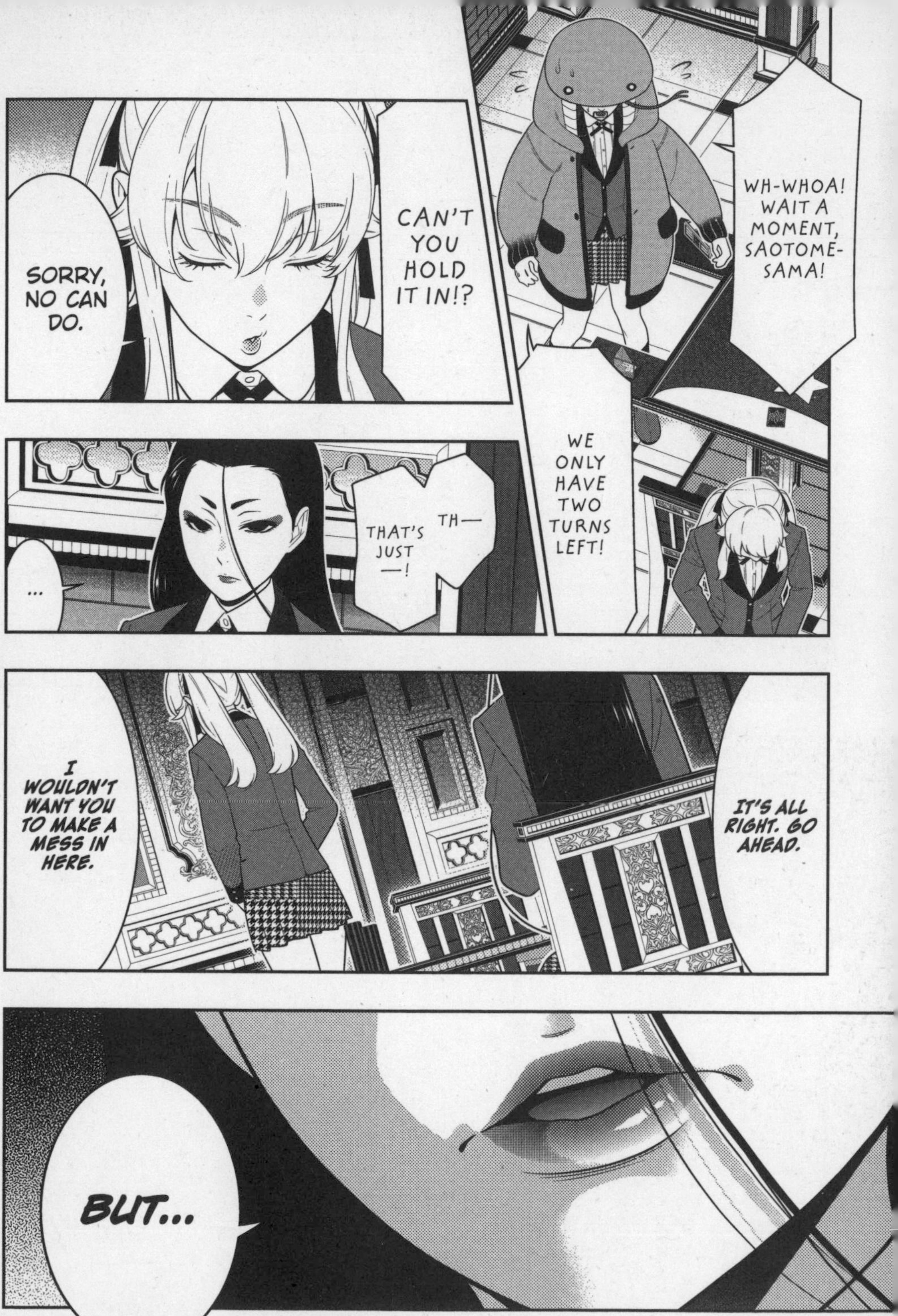
WH-WHOA! WAIT A MOMENT, SAOTOME-SAMA!
WE ONLY HAVE TWO TURNS LEFT!
CAN'T YOU HOLD IT IN!?
SORRY, NO CAN DO.
TH—
THAT'S JUST —!
...
IT'S ALL RIGHT. GO AHEAD.
I WOULDN'T WANT YOU TO MAKE A MESS IN HERE.
BUT...

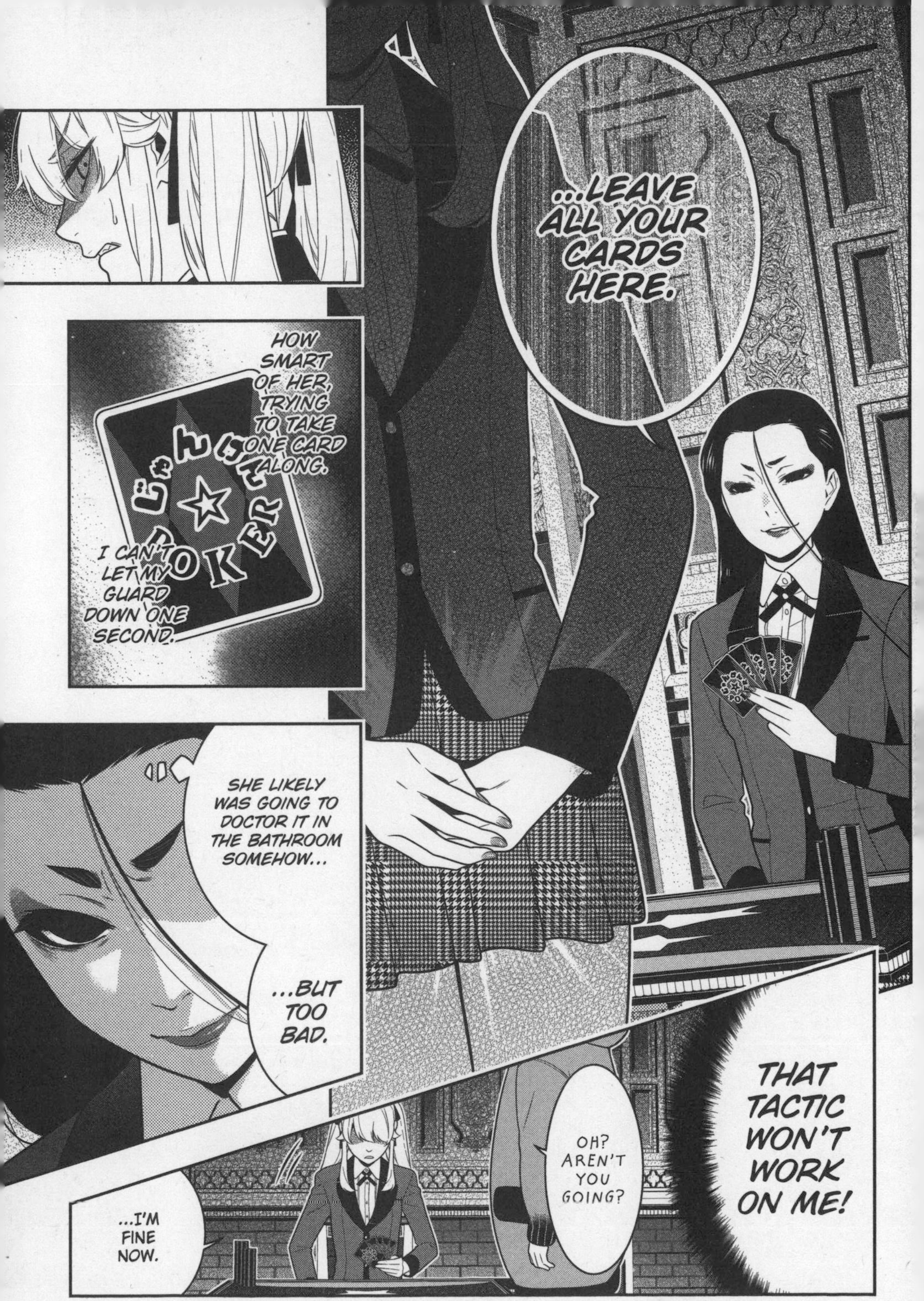
...LEAVE ALL YOUR CARDS HERE.
HOW SMART OF HER, TRYING TO TAKE ONE CARD ALONG.
I CAN'T LET MY GUARD DOWN ONE SECOND.
JOKER
SHE LIKELY WAS GOING TO DOCTOR IT IN THE BATHROOM SOMEHOW...
...BUT TOO BAD.
THAT TACTIC WON'T WORK ON ME!
OH? AREN'T YOU GOING?
...I'M FINE NOW.

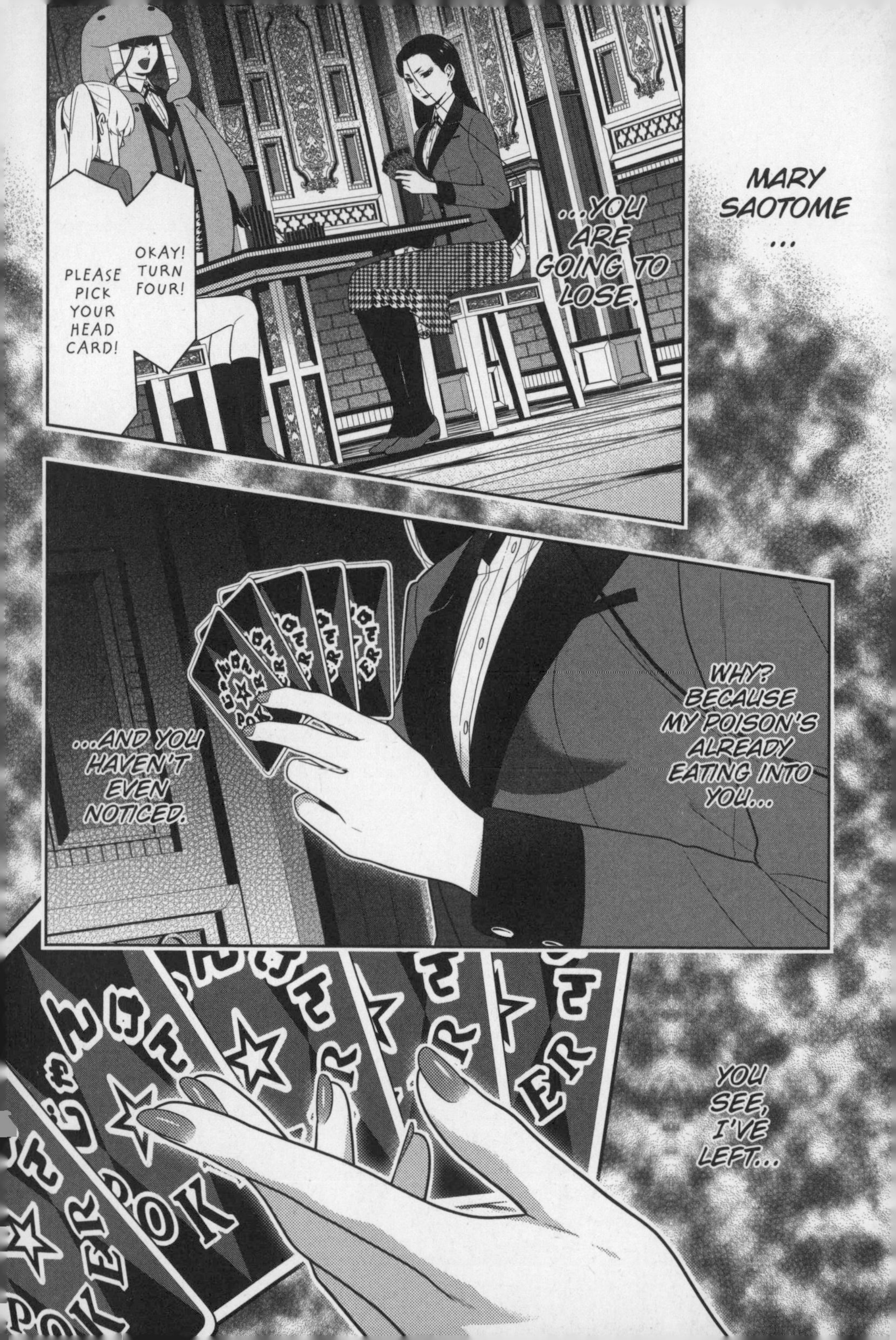
MARY SAOTOME ...
...YOU ARE GOING TO LOSE.
OKAY! TURN FOUR!
PLEASE PICK YOUR HEAD CARD!
WHY? BECAUSE MY POISON'S ALREADY EATING INTO YOU...
...AND YOU HAVEN'T EVEN NOTICED.
YOU SEE, I'VE LEFT...

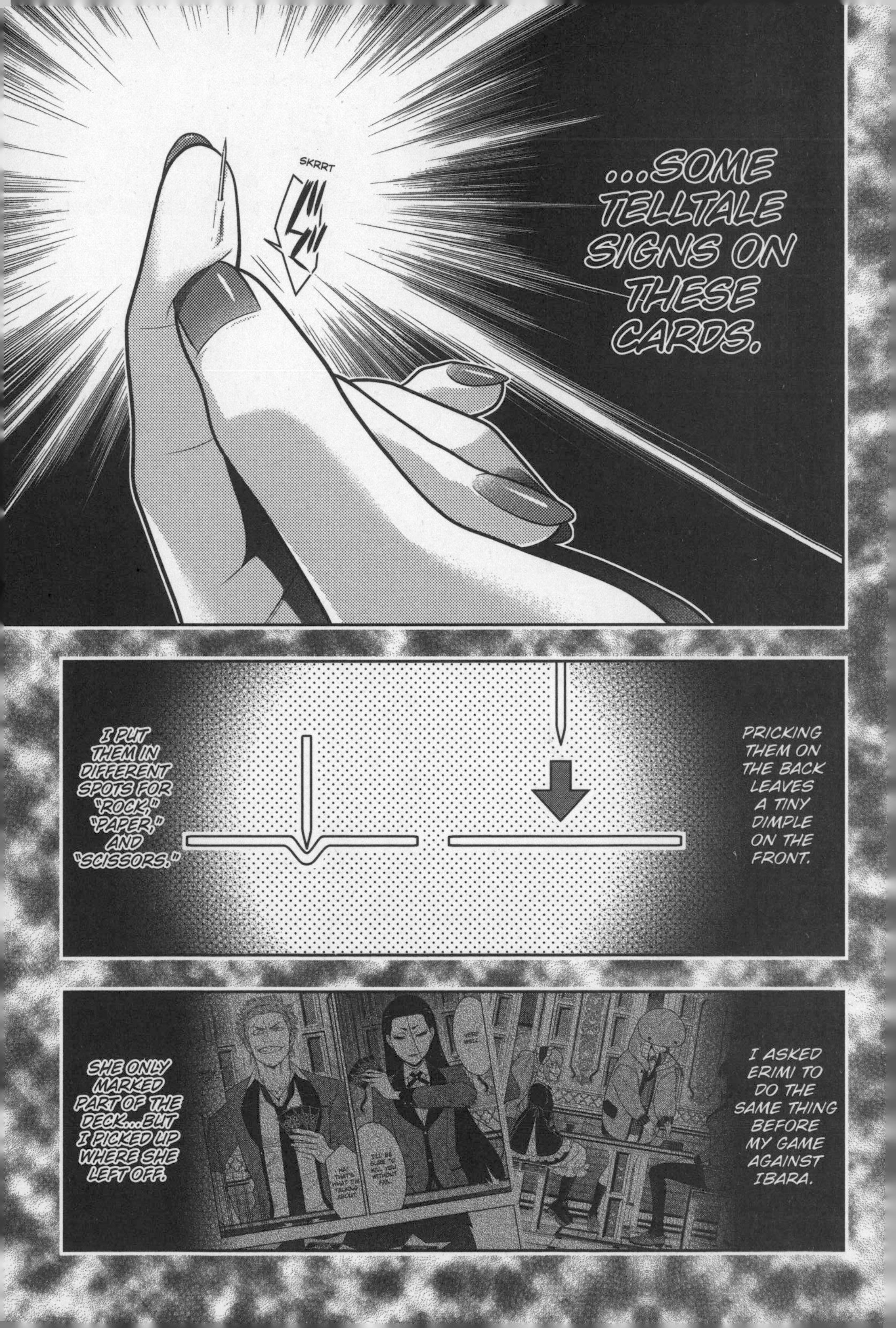
SKRRT
...SOME TELLTALE SIGNS ON THESE CARDS.
PRICKING THEM ON THE BACK LEAVES A TINY DIMPLE ON THE FRONT.
I PUT THEM IN DIFFERENT SPOTS FOR "ROCK," "PAPER," AND "SCISSORS."
I ASKED ERIMI TO DO THE SAME THING BEFORE MY GAME AGAINST IBARA.
SHE ONLY MARKED PART OF THE DECK...BUT I PICKED UP WHERE SHE LEFT OFF.

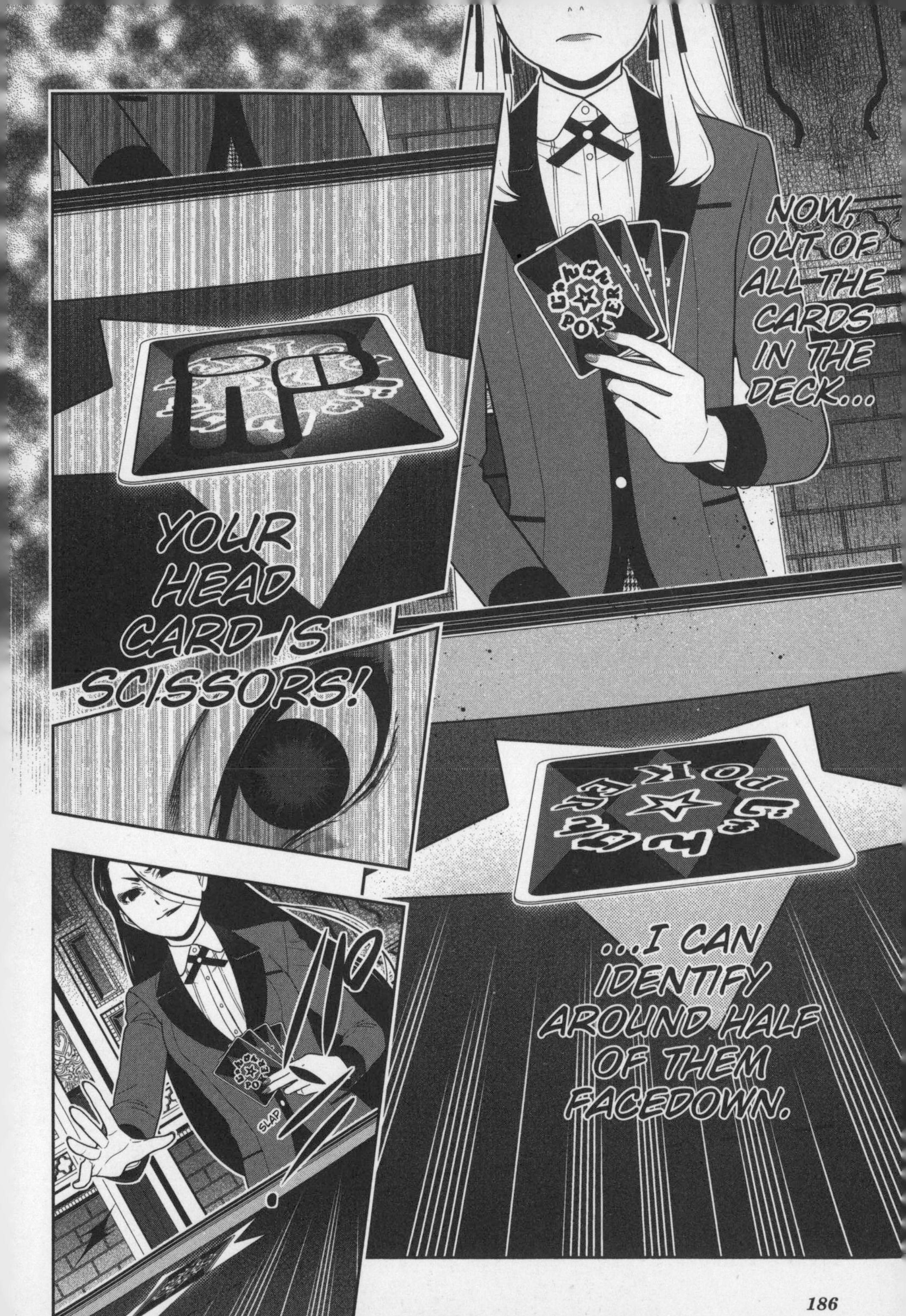
NOW, OUT OF ALL THE CARDS IN THE DECK...
YOUR HEAD CARD IS SCISSORS!
...I CAN IDENTIFY AROUND HALF OF THEM FACEDOWN.
SLAP

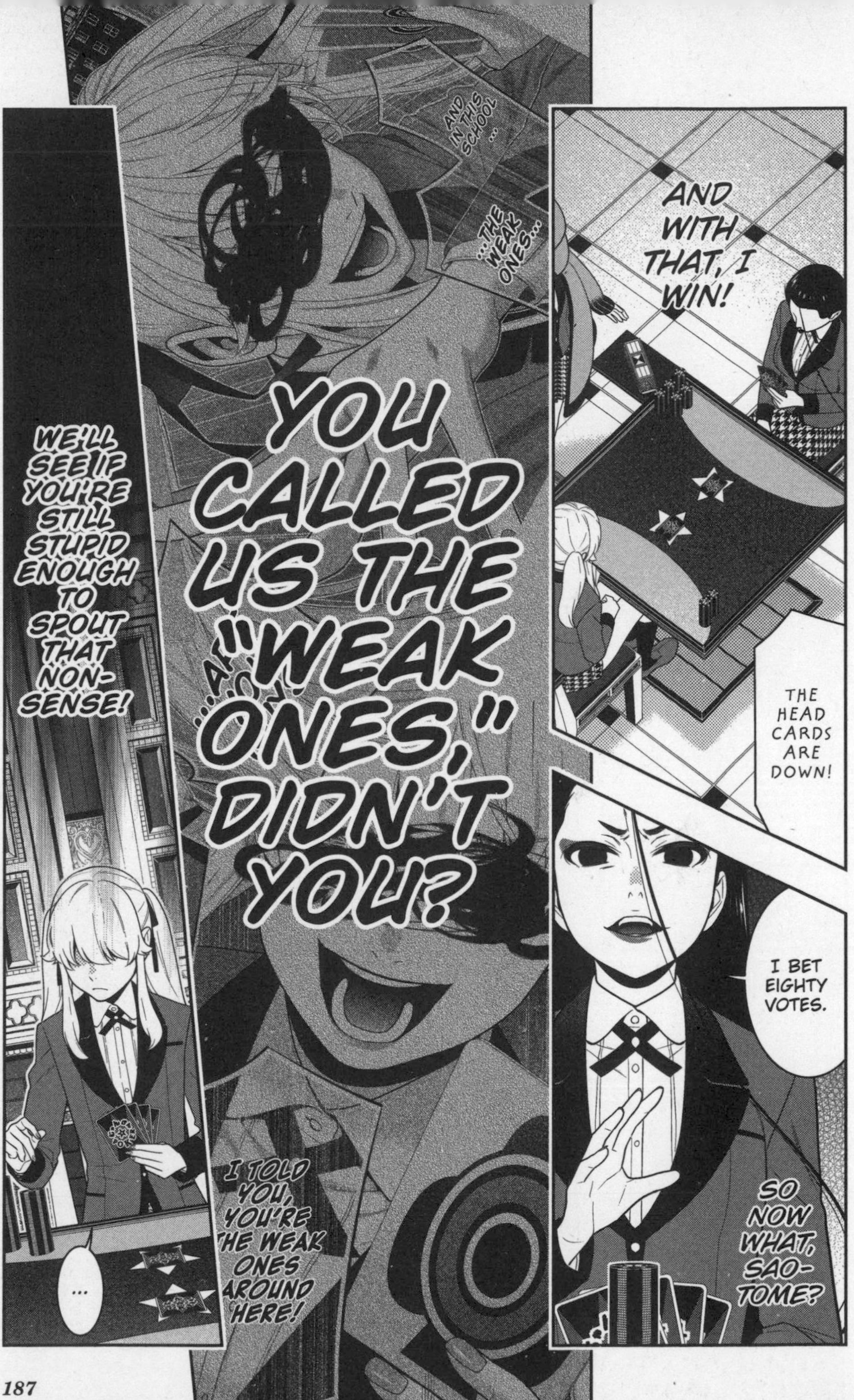
AND WITH THAT, I WIN!
THE HEAD CARDS ARE DOWN!
I BET EIGHTY VOTES.
SO NOW WHAT, SAOTOME?
AND IN THIS SCHOOL...
...THE WEAK ONES...
YOU CALLED US THE "WEAK ONES," DIDN'T YOU?
I TOLD YOU, YOU'RE THE WEAK ONES AROUND HERE!
WE'LL SEE IF YOU'RE STILL STUPID ENOUGH TO SPOUT THAT NONSENSE!
...

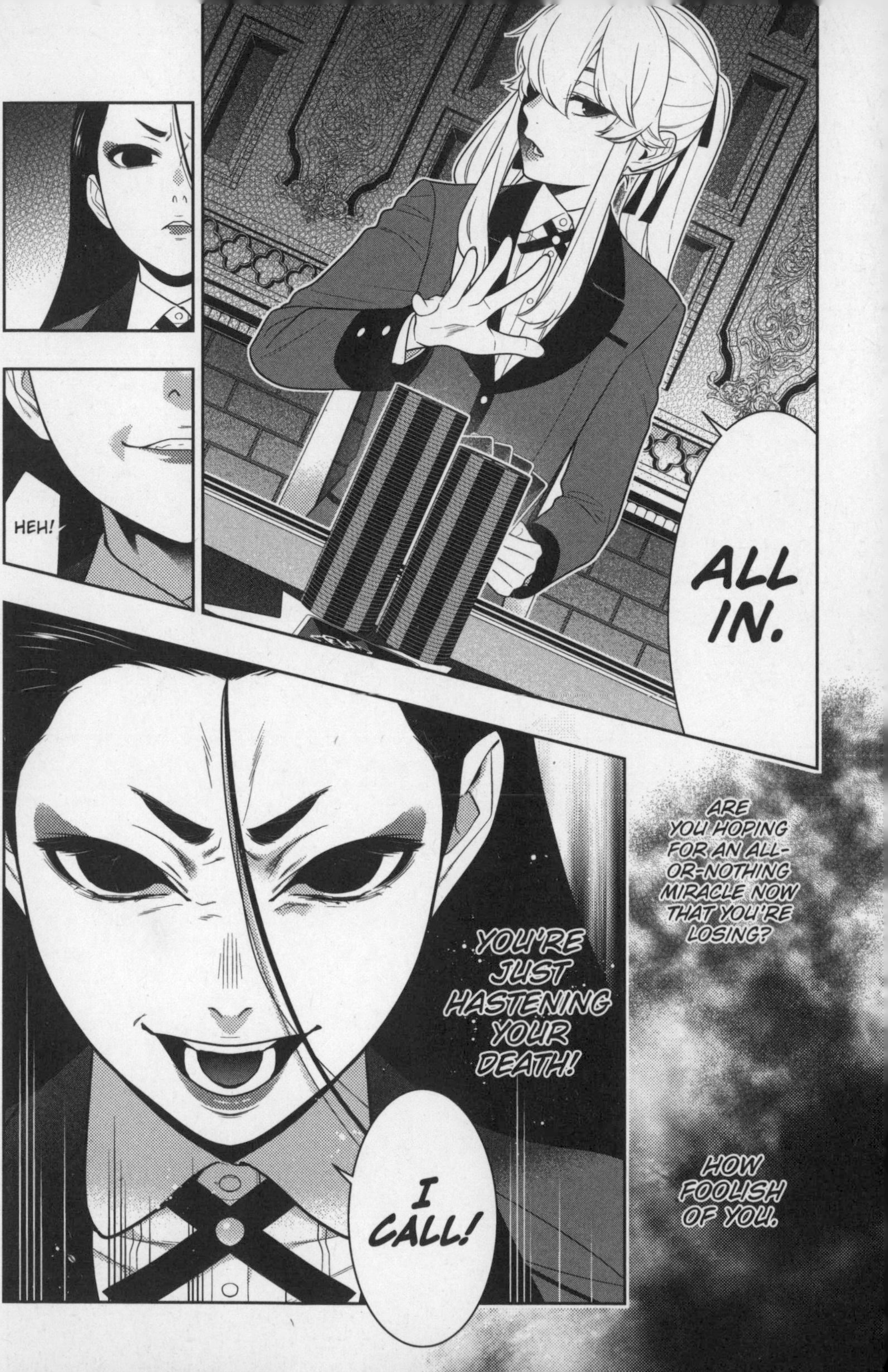
ALL IN.
HEH!
ARE YOU HOPING FOR AN ALL-OR-NOTHING MIRACLE NOW THAT YOU'RE LOSING?
YOU'RE JUST HASTENING YOUR DEATH!
HOW FOOLISH OF YOU.
I CALL!

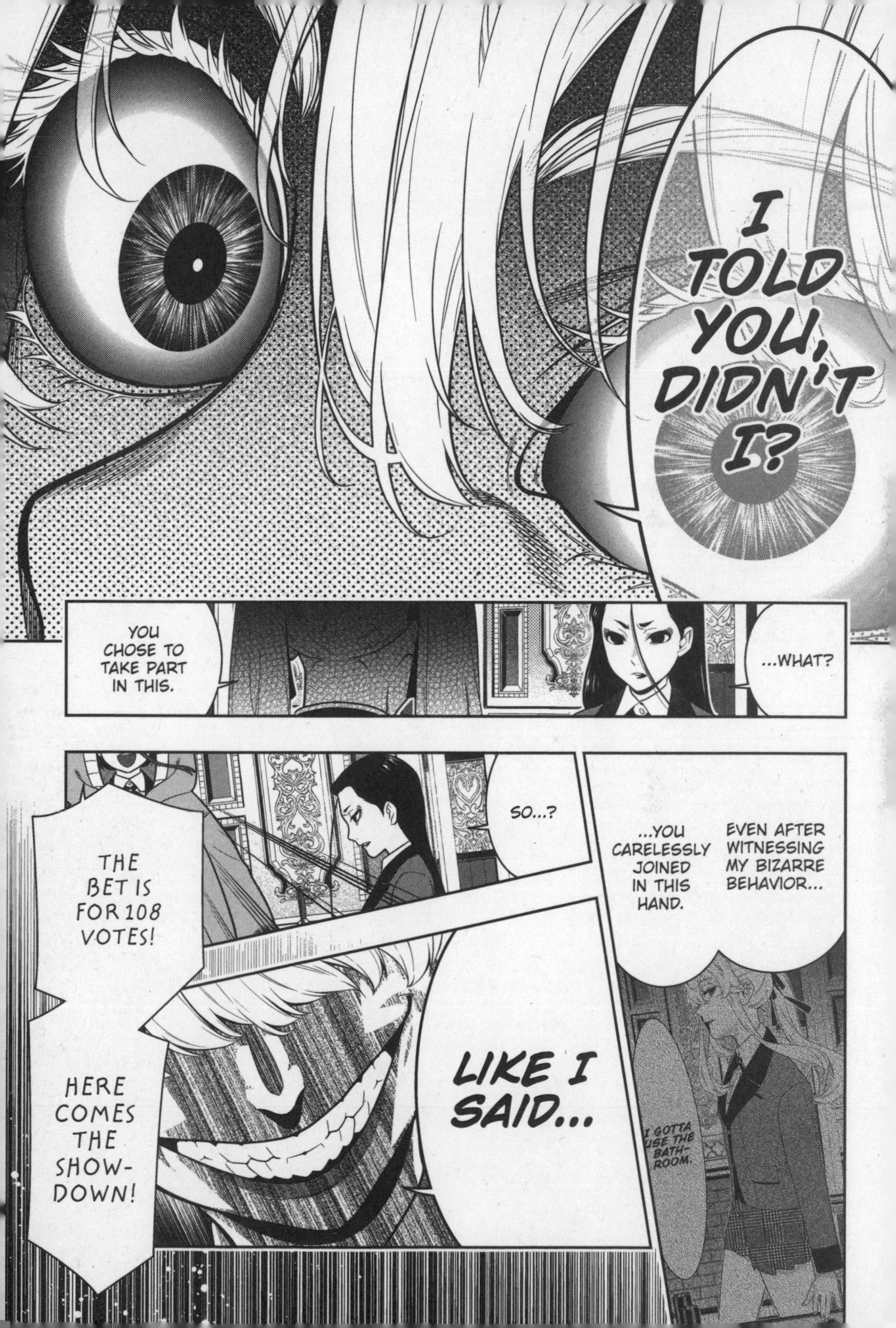
I TOLD YOU, DIDN'T I?
...WHAT?
YOU CHOSE TO TAKE PART IN THIS.
EVEN AFTER WITNESSING MY BIZARRE BEHAVIOR...
...YOU CARELESSLY JOINED IN THIS HAND.
I GOTTA USE THE BATH-ROOM.
SO...?
LIKE I SAID...
THE BET IS FOR 108 VOTES!
HERE COMES THE SHOW-DOWN!

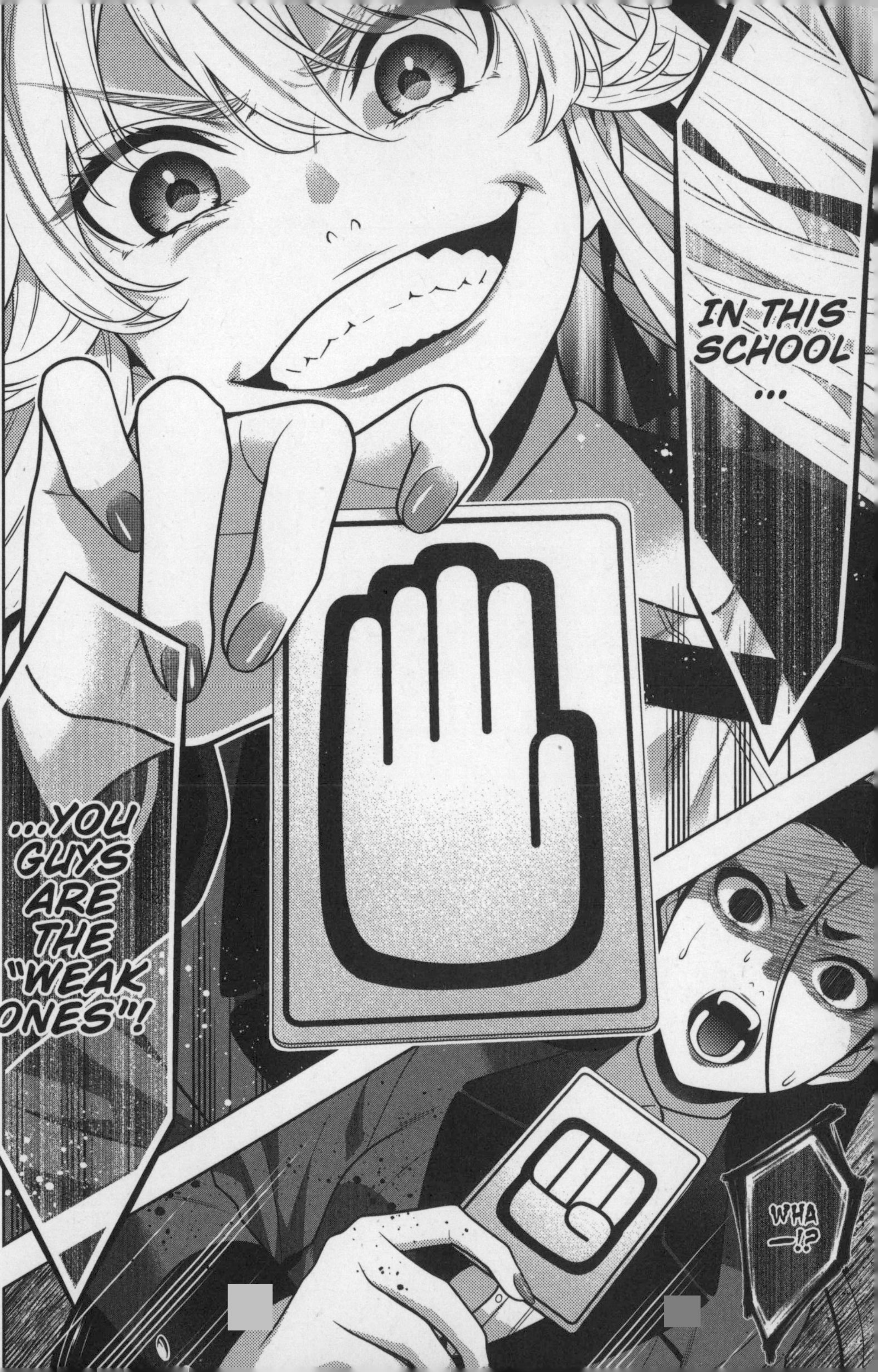
IN THIS SCHOOL ...
...YOU GUYS ARE THE "WEAK ONES"!
WHA—!?

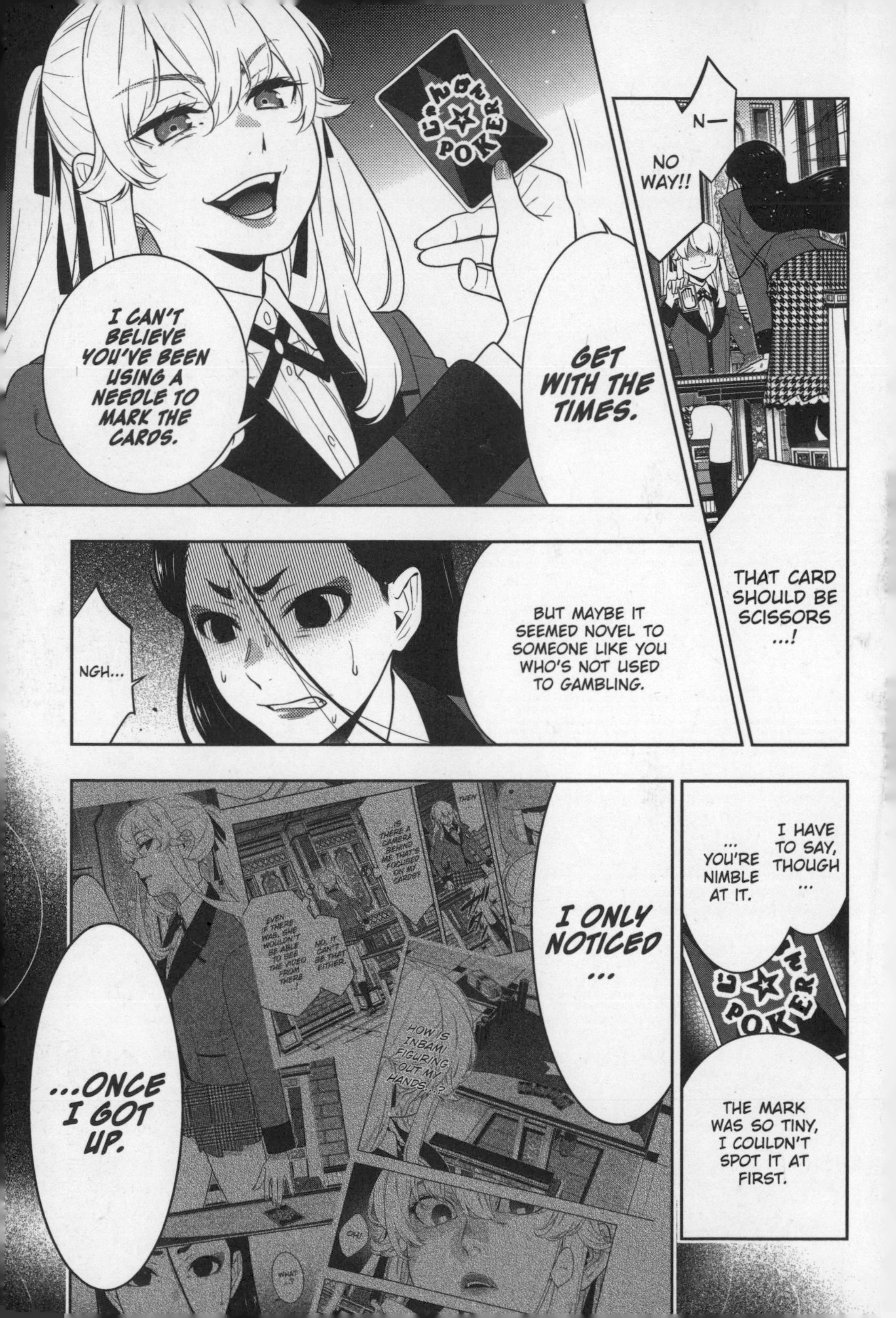
N—
NO WAY!!
POKER
I CAN'T BELIEVE YOU'VE BEEN USING A NEEDLE TO MARK THE CARDS.
GET WITH THE TIMES.
THAT CARD SHOULD BE SCISSORS ...!
BUT MAYBE IT SEEMED NOVEL TO SOMEONE LIKE YOU WHO'S NOT USED TO GAMBLING.
NGH...
I HAVE TO SAY, THOUGH ...
... YOU'RE NIMBLE AT IT.
POKER
THE MARK WAS SO TINY, I COULDN'T SPOT IT AT FIRST.
I ONLY NOTICED ...
THEN
...IS THERE A CAMERA BEHIND ME THAT'S FOCUSED ON MY CARDS?
EVEN IF THERE WAS, SHE WOULDN'T BE ABLE TO SEE THE VIDEO FROM THERE ...
NO, IT CAN'T BE THAT EITHER.
HOW IS INBAMI FIGURING OUT MY HANDS...?
OH!
WHAT ...?
...ONCE I GOT UP.

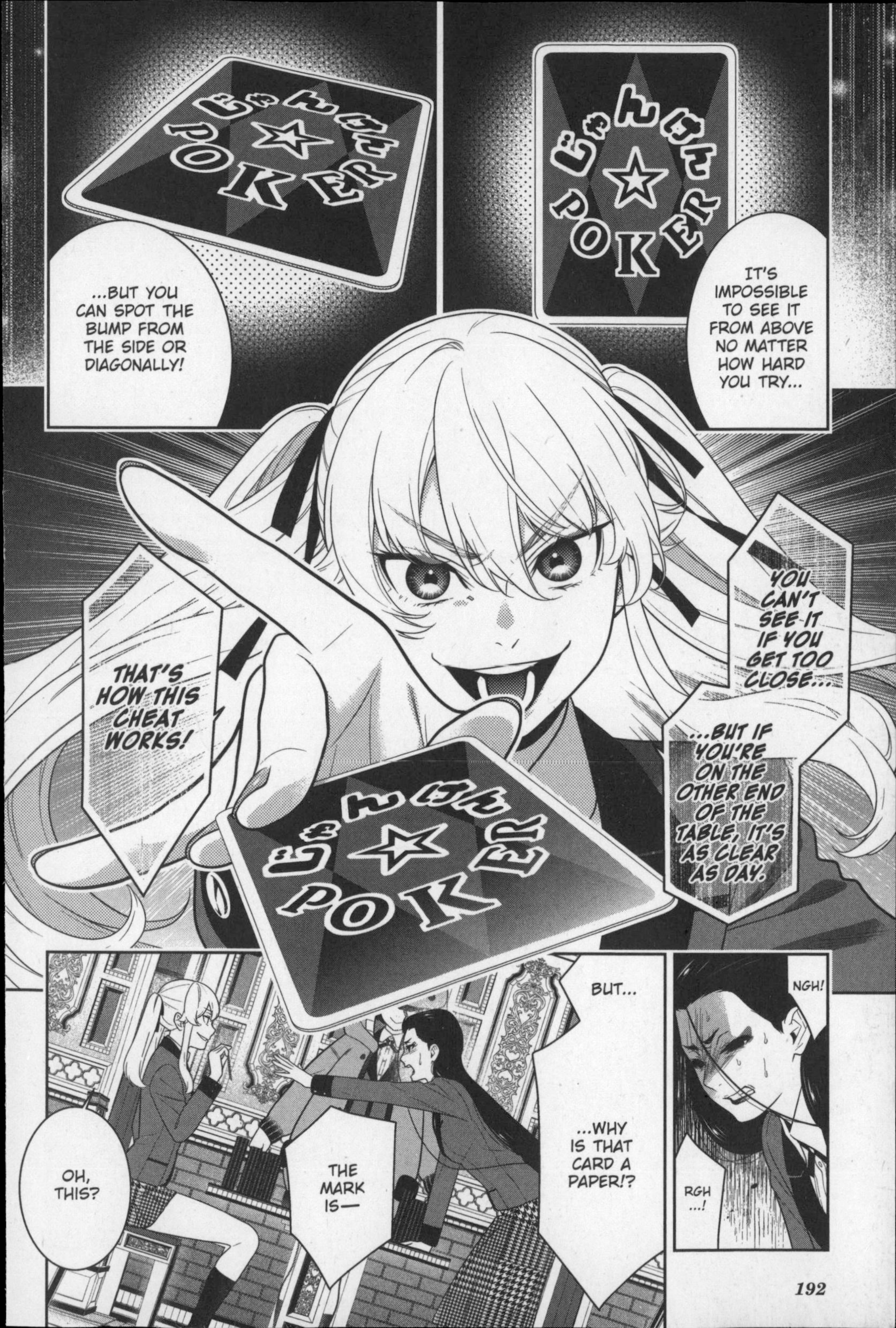

じゃんけん★POKER
IT'S IMPOSSIBLE TO SEE IT FROM ABOVE NO MATTER HOW HARD YOU TRY...
じゃんけん★POKER
...BUT YOU CAN SPOT THE BUMP FROM THE SIDE OR DIAGONALLY!
YOU CAN'T SEE IT IF YOU GET TOO CLOSE...
...BUT IF YOU'RE ON THE OTHER END OF THE TABLE, IT'S AS CLEAR AS DAY.
THAT'S HOW THIS CHEAT WORKS!
じゃんけん★POKER
NGH!
RGH ...!
BUT...
...WHY IS THAT CARD A PAPER!?
THE MARK IS—
OH, THIS?

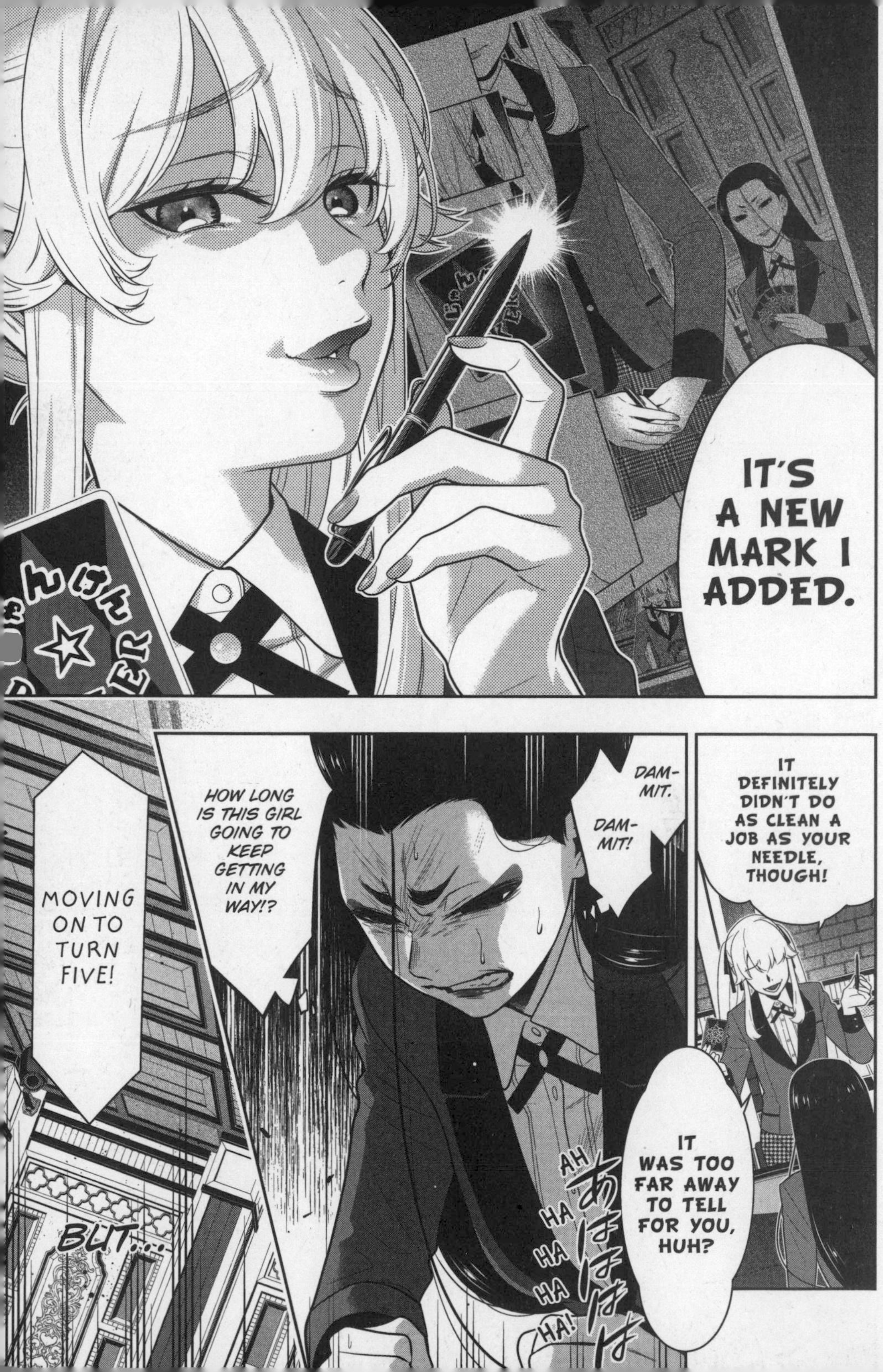
IT'S A NEW MARK I ADDED.
IT DEFINITELY DIDN'T DO AS CLEAN A JOB AS YOUR NEEDLE, THOUGH!
IT WAS TOO FAR AWAY TO TELL FOR YOU, HUH?
AH HA HA HA HA!
あははは
DAM-MIT.
DAM-MIT!
HOW LONG IS THIS GIRL GOING TO KEEP GETTING IN MY WAY!?
MOVING ON TO TURN FIVE!
BUT...

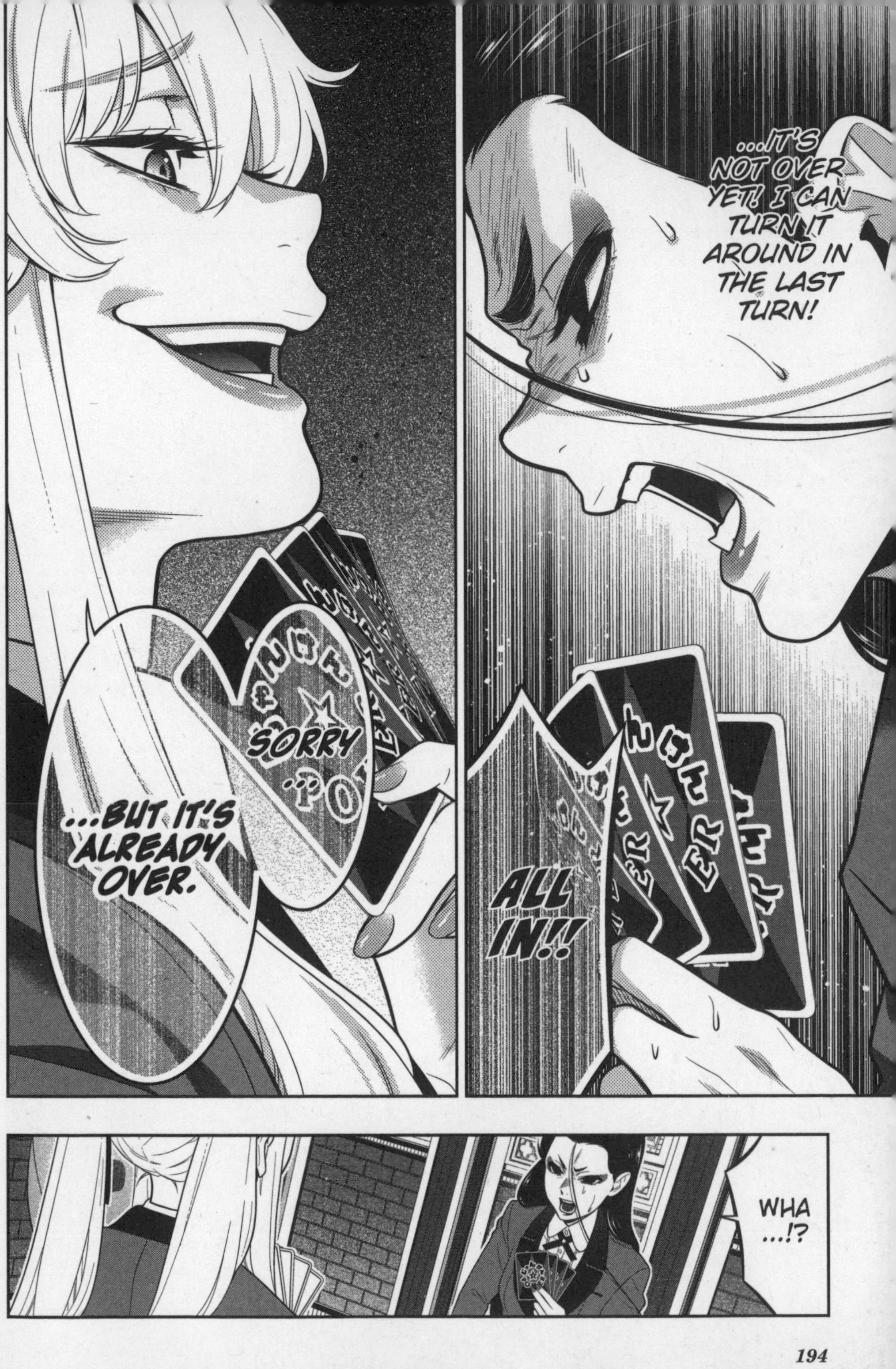
...IT'S NOT OVER YET! I CAN TURN IT AROUND IN THE LAST TURN!
ALL IN!!
SORRY
...BUT IT'S ALREADY OVER.
WHA ...!?

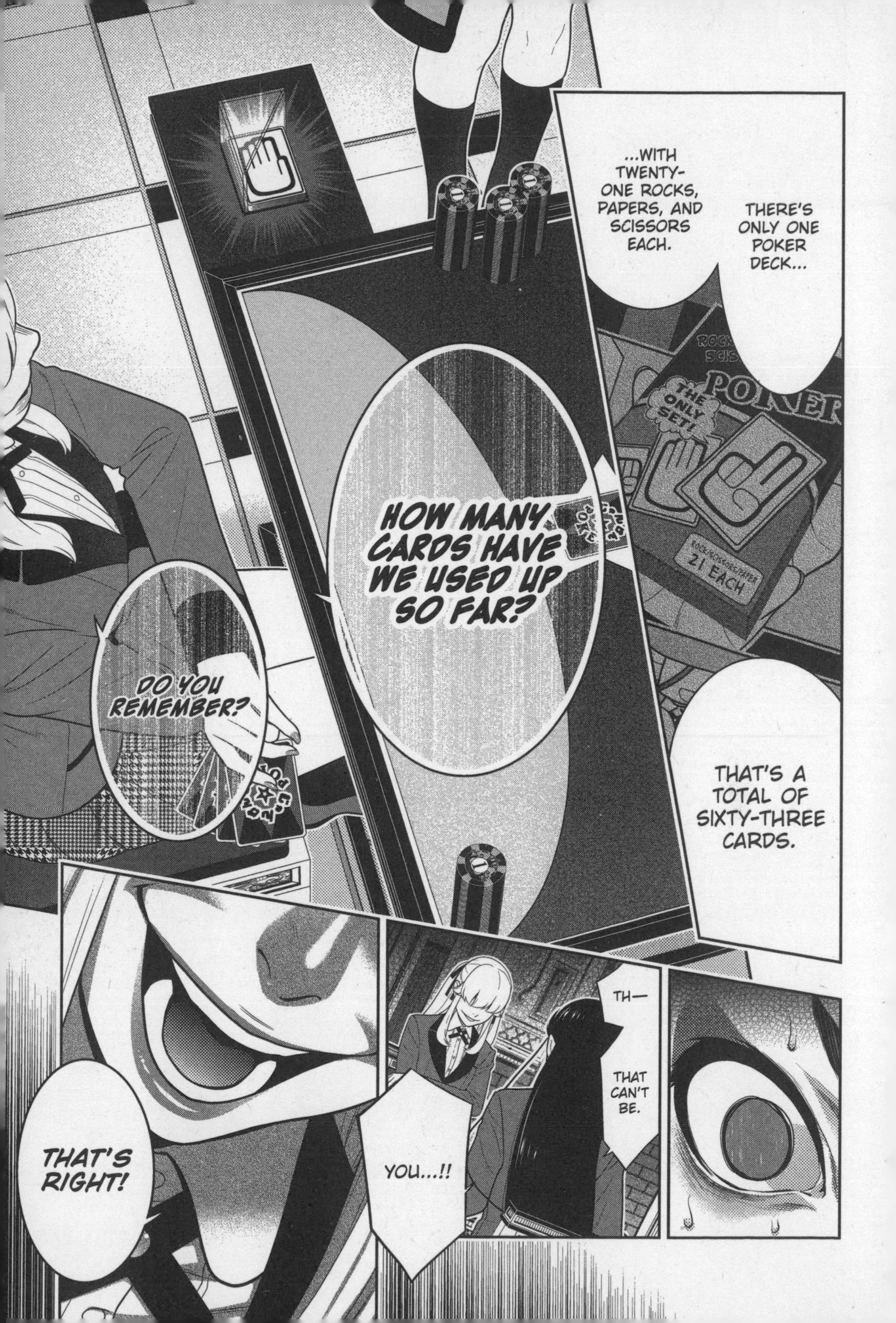
THERE'S ONLY ONE POKER DECK...
...WITH TWENTY-ONE ROCKS, PAPERS, AND SCISSORS EACH.
POKER
THE ONLY SET!
ROCK/SCISSORS/PAPER 21 EACH
THAT'S A TOTAL OF SIXTY-THREE CARDS.
HOW MANY CARDS HAVE WE USED UP SO FAR?
DO YOU REMEMBER?
TH—
THAT CAN'T BE.
YOU...!!
THAT'S RIGHT!

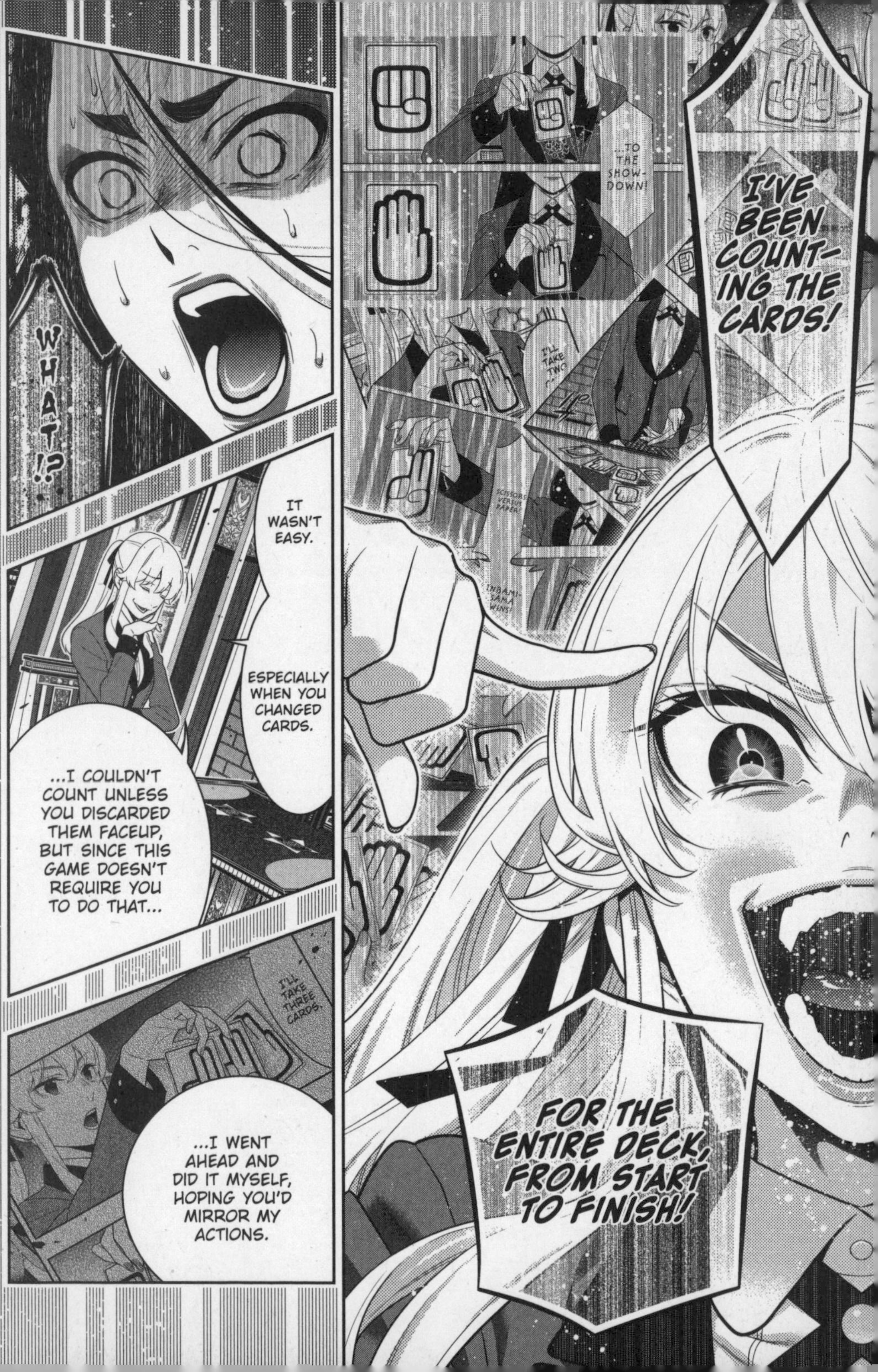
...TO THE SHOW-DOWN!
I'VE BEEN COUNTING THE CARDS!
I'LL TAKE TWO.
SCISSORS VERSUS PAPER!
INBAMI-SAMA WINS!
FOR THE ENTIRE DECK, FROM START TO FINISH!
WHAT!?
IT WASN'T EASY.
ESPECIALLY WHEN YOU CHANGED CARDS.
...I COULDN'T COUNT UNLESS YOU DISCARDED THEM FACEUP, BUT SINCE THIS GAME DOESN'T REQUIRE YOU TO DO THAT...
I'LL TAKE THREE CARDS.
...I WENT AHEAD AND DID IT MYSELF, HOPING YOU'D MIRROR MY ACTIONS.

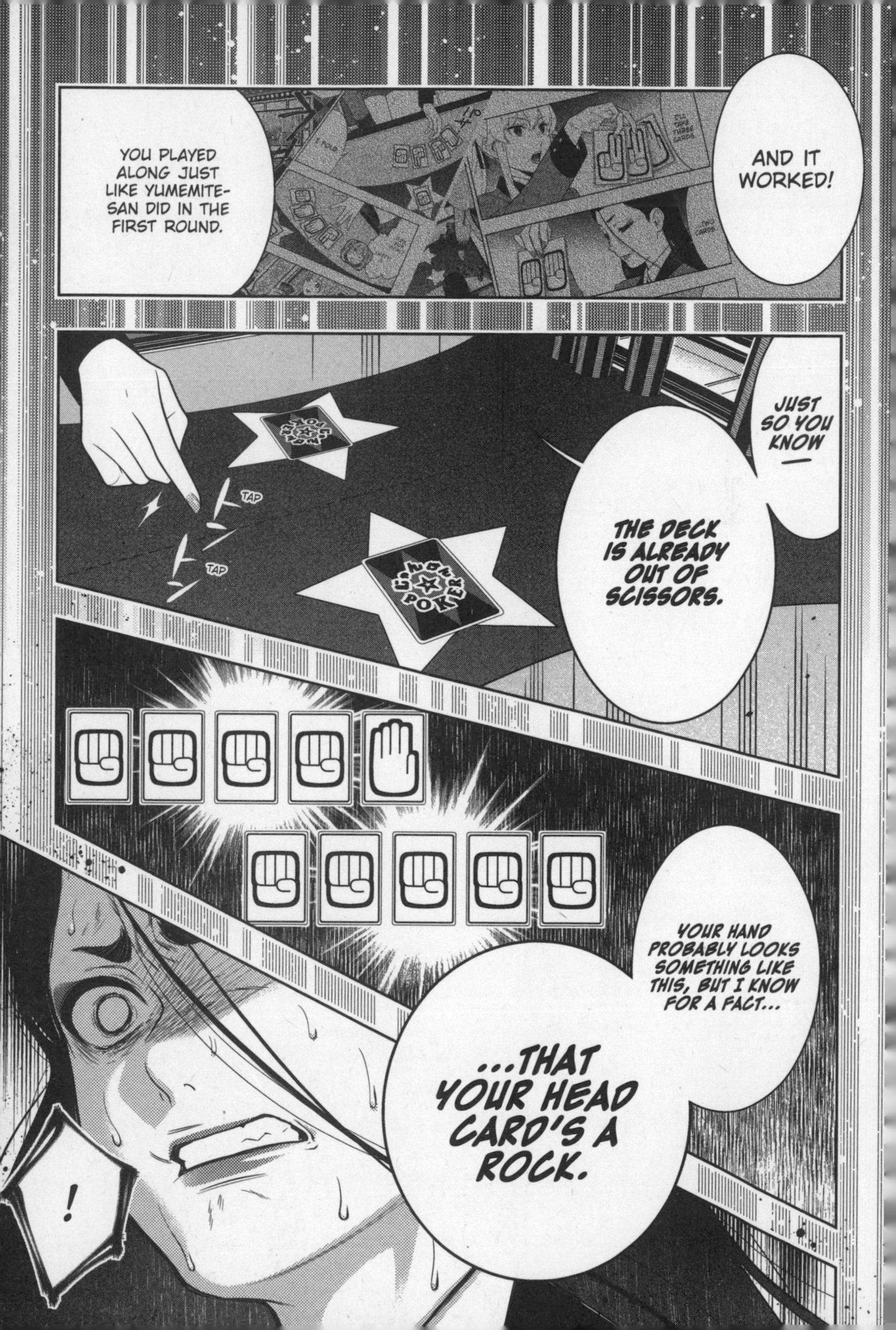
AND IT WORKED!
YOU PLAYED ALONG JUST LIKE YUMEMITE-SAN DID IN THE FIRST ROUND.
JUST SO YOU KNOW—
THE DECK IS ALREADY OUT OF SCISSORS.
TAP
TAP
YOUR HAND PROBABLY LOOKS SOMETHING LIKE THIS, BUT I KNOW FOR A FACT...
...THAT YOUR HEAD CARD'S A ROCK.
!

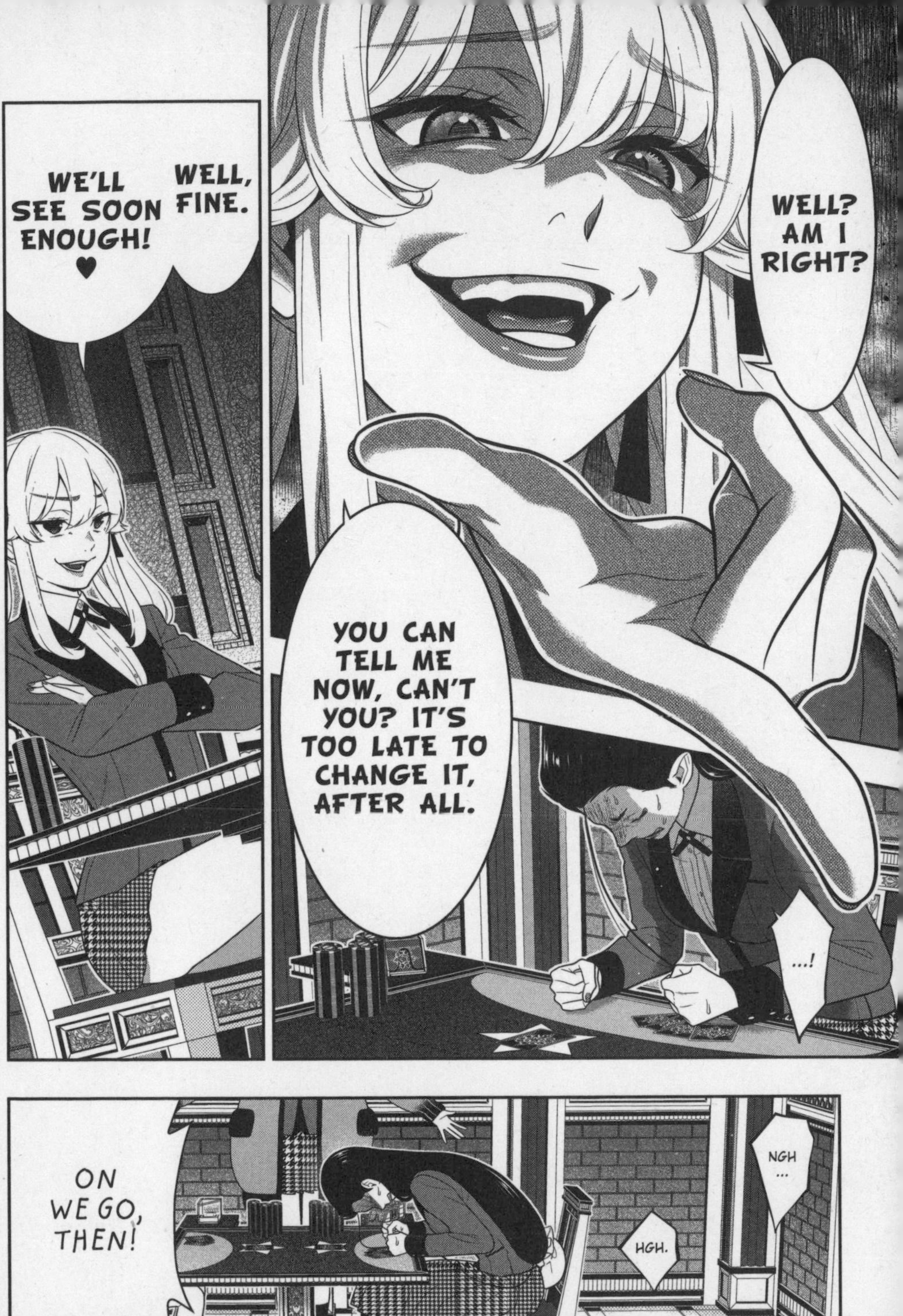
WELL? AM I RIGHT?
YOU CAN TELL ME NOW, CAN'T YOU? IT'S TOO LATE TO CHANGE IT, AFTER ALL.
...!
WELL, FINE.
WE'LL SEE SOON ENOUGH! ♥
NGH ...
HGH.
ON WE GO, THEN!

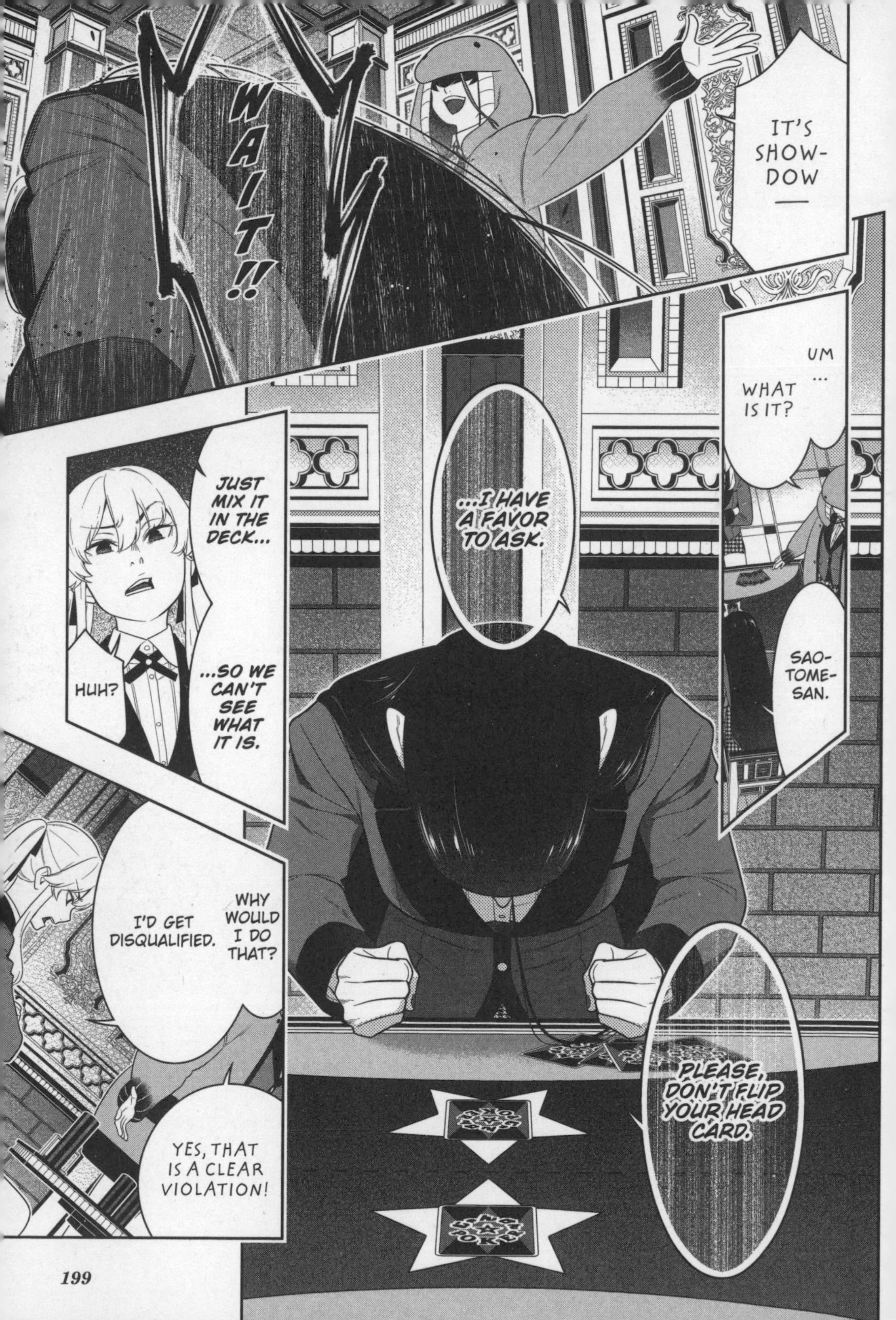
IT'S SHOW-DOW —
WAIT!!
UM ...
WHAT IS IT?
SAO-TOME-SAN.
...I HAVE A FAVOR TO ASK.
PLEASE, DON'T FLIP YOUR HEAD CARD.
JUST MIX IT IN THE DECK...
...SO WE CAN'T SEE WHAT IT IS.
HUH?
WHY WOULD I DO THAT?
I'D GET DISQUALIFIED.
YES, THAT IS A CLEAR VIOLATION!

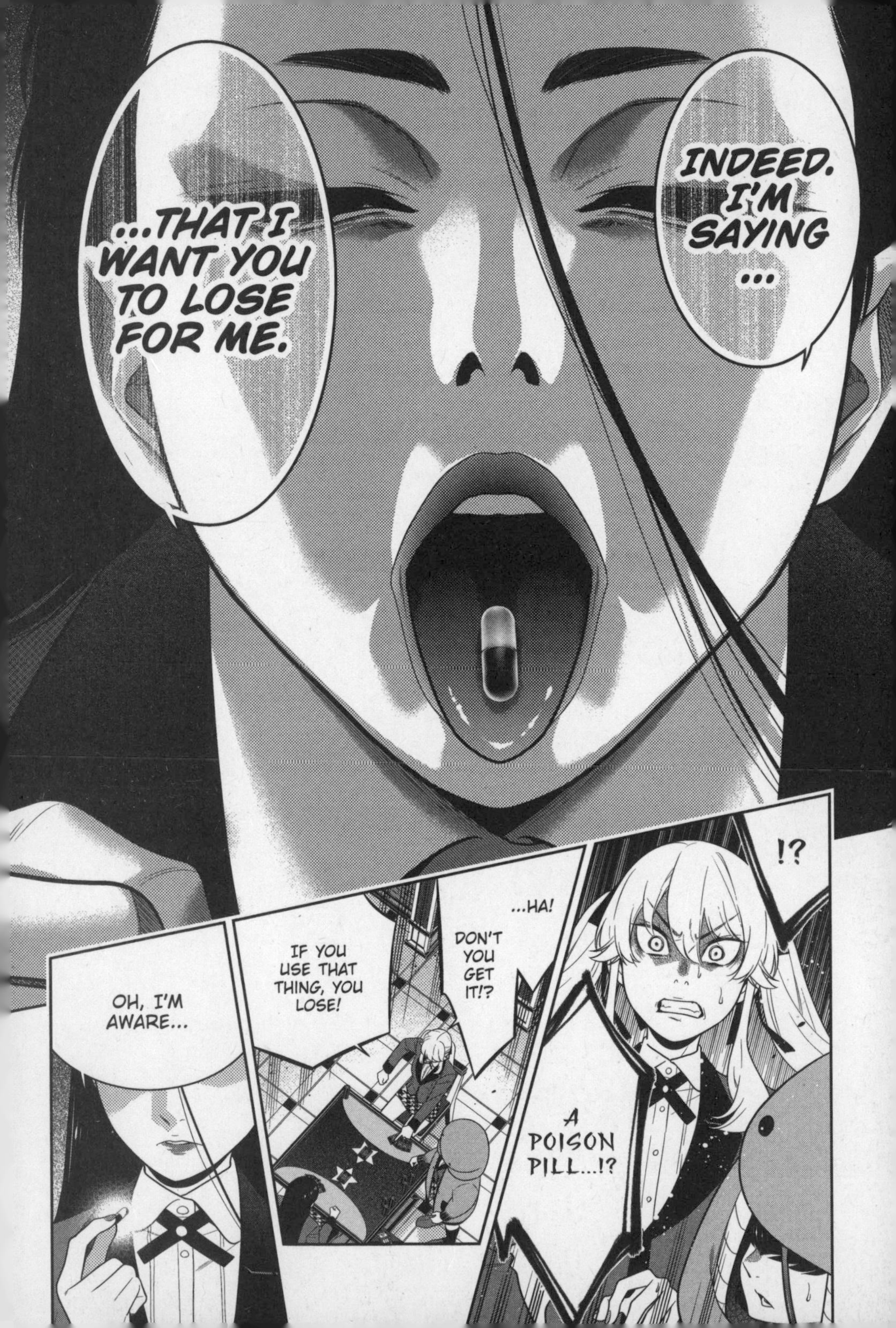
INDEED. I'M SAYING ...
...THAT I WANT YOU TO LOSE FOR ME.
!?
A POISON PILL...!?
...HA!
DON'T YOU GET IT!?
IF YOU USE THAT THING, YOU LOSE!
OH, I'M AWARE...

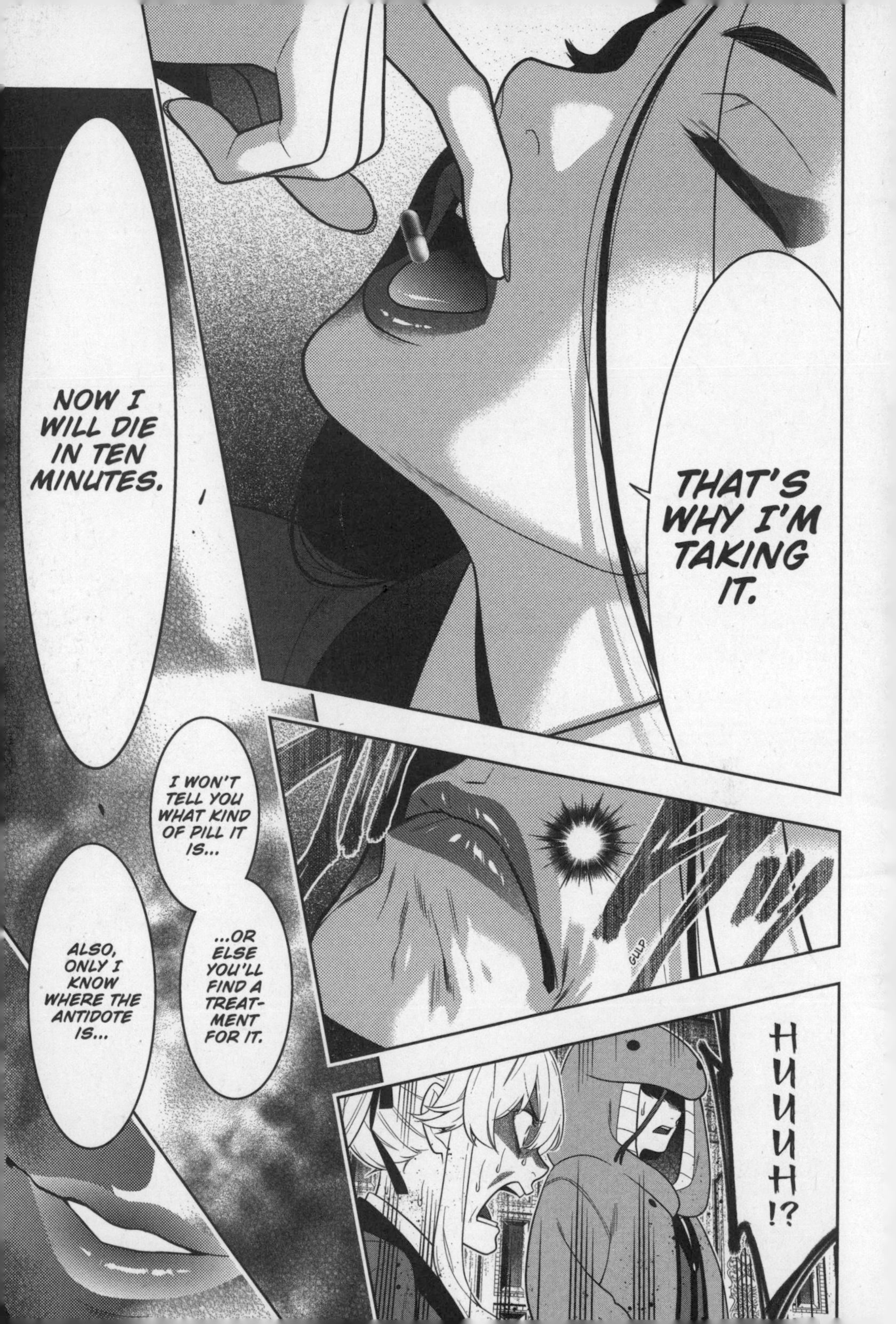
THAT'S WHY I'M TAKING IT.
NOW I WILL DIE IN TEN MINUTES.
I WON'T TELL YOU WHAT KIND OF PILL IT IS...
...OR ELSE YOU'LL FIND A TREAT-MENT FOR IT.
ALSO, ONLY I KNOW WHERE THE ANTIDOTE IS...
GULP
HUUUH!?

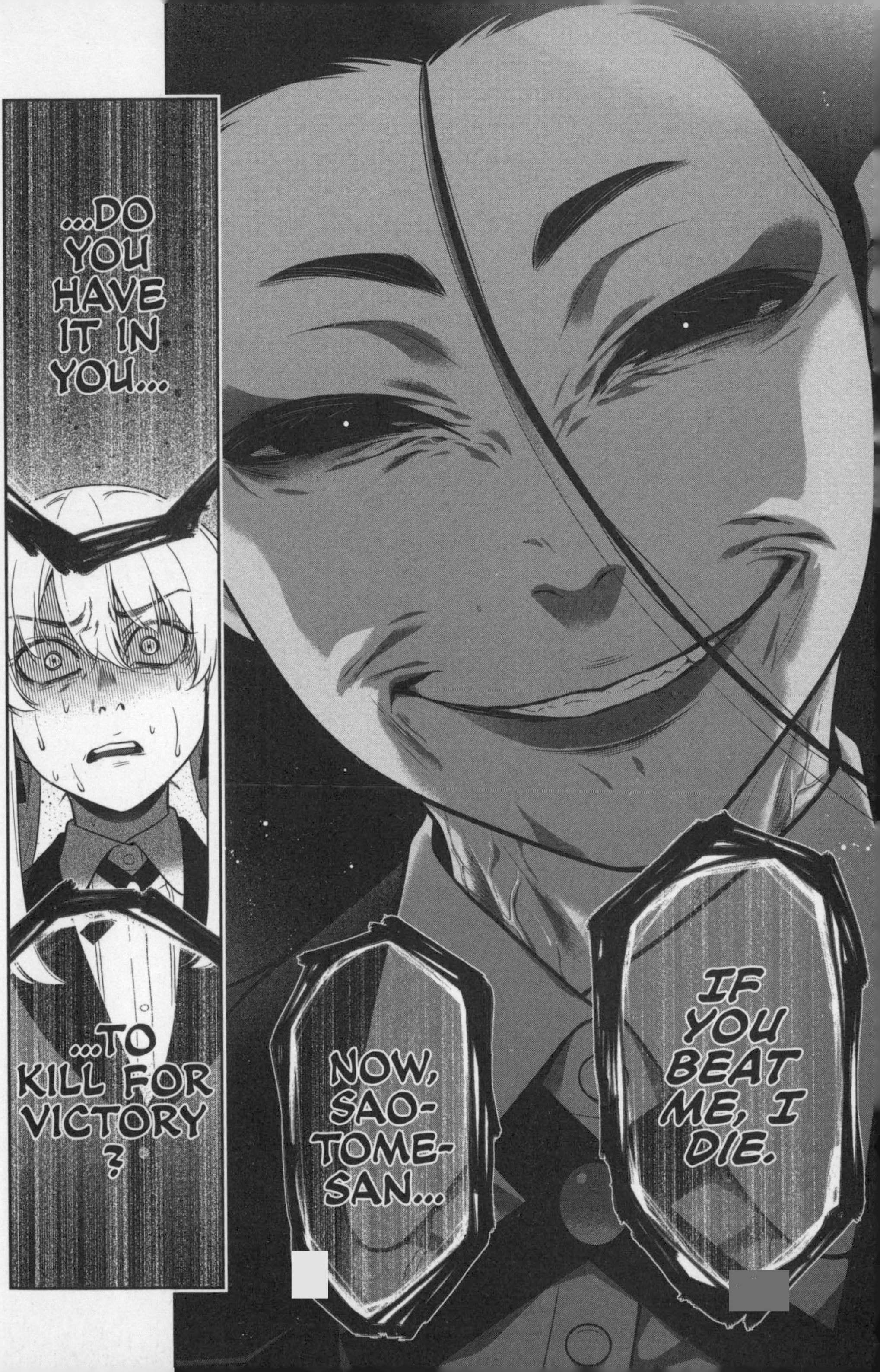
IF YOU BEAT ME, I DIE.
NOW, SAO-TOME-SAN...
...DO YOU HAVE IT IN YOU...
...TO KILL FOR VICTORY?

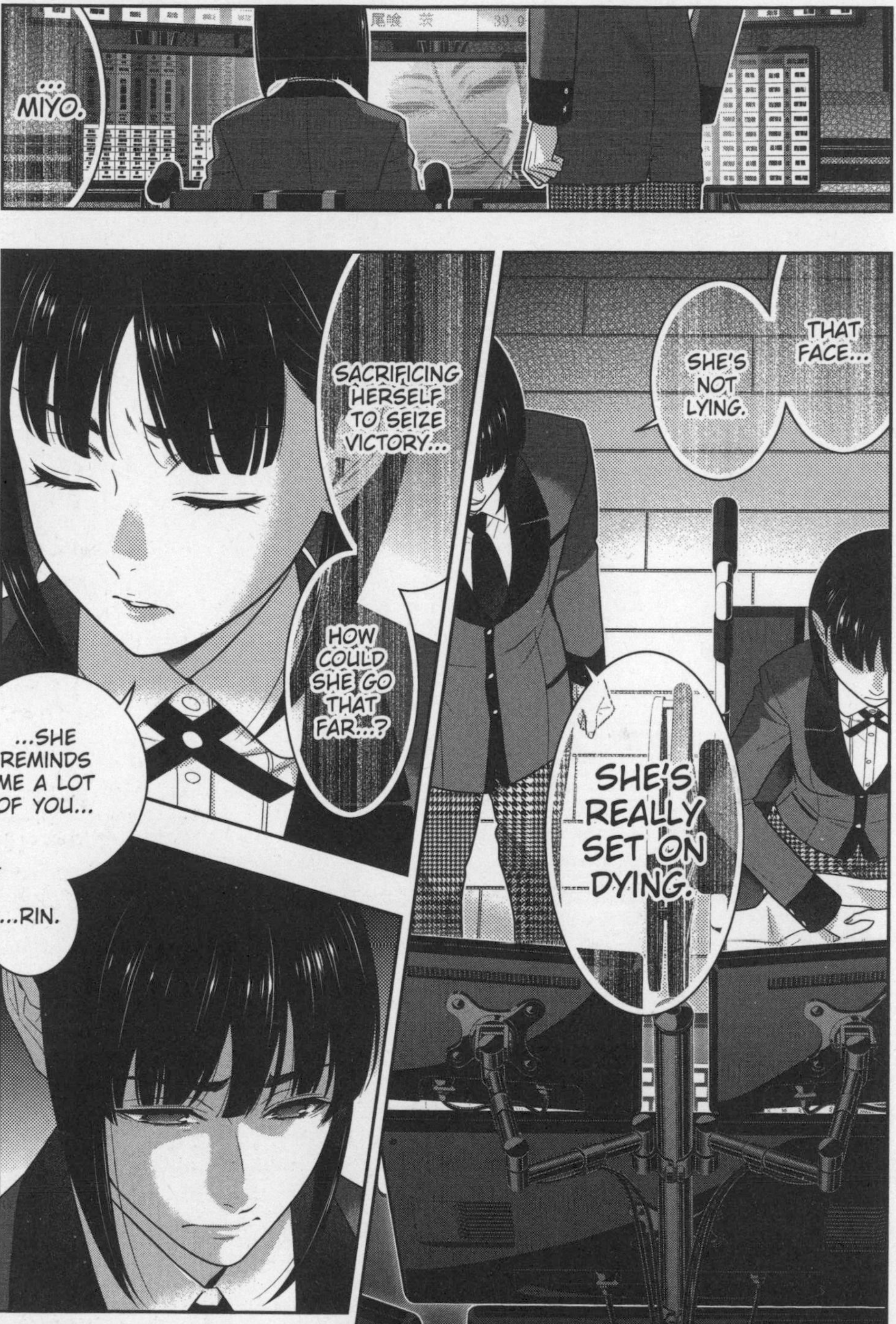
...MIYO.
THAT FACE...
SHE'S NOT LYING.
SHE'S REALLY SET ON DYING.
SACRIFICING HERSELF TO SEIZE VICTORY...
HOW COULD SHE GO THAT FAR...?
...SHE REMINDS ME A LOT OF YOU...
...RIN.

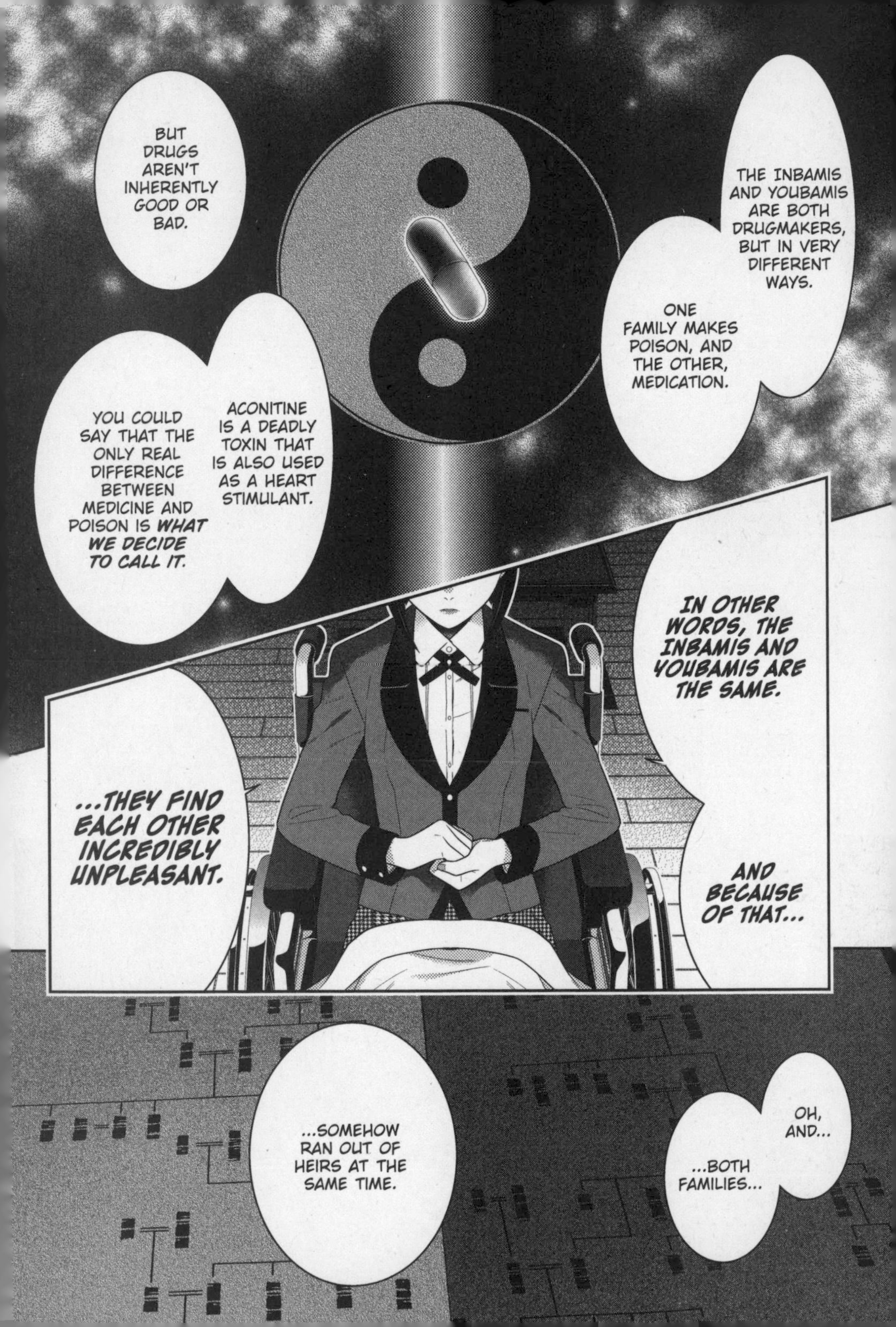
THE INBAMIS AND YOUBAMIS ARE BOTH DRUGMAKERS, BUT IN VERY DIFFERENT WAYS.
ONE FAMILY MAKES POISON, AND THE OTHER, MEDICATION.
BUT DRUGS AREN'T INHERENTLY GOOD OR BAD.
ACONITINE IS A DEADLY TOXIN THAT IS ALSO USED AS A HEART STIMULANT.
YOU COULD SAY THAT THE ONLY REAL DIFFERENCE BETWEEN MEDICINE AND POISON IS *WHAT WE DECIDE TO CALL IT.*
IN OTHER WORDS, THE INBAMIS AND YOUBAMIS ARE THE SAME.
AND BECAUSE OF THAT...
...THEY FIND EACH OTHER INCREDIBLY UNPLEASANT.
OH, AND...
...BOTH FAMILIES...
...SOMEHOW RAN OUT OF HEIRS AT THE SAME TIME.

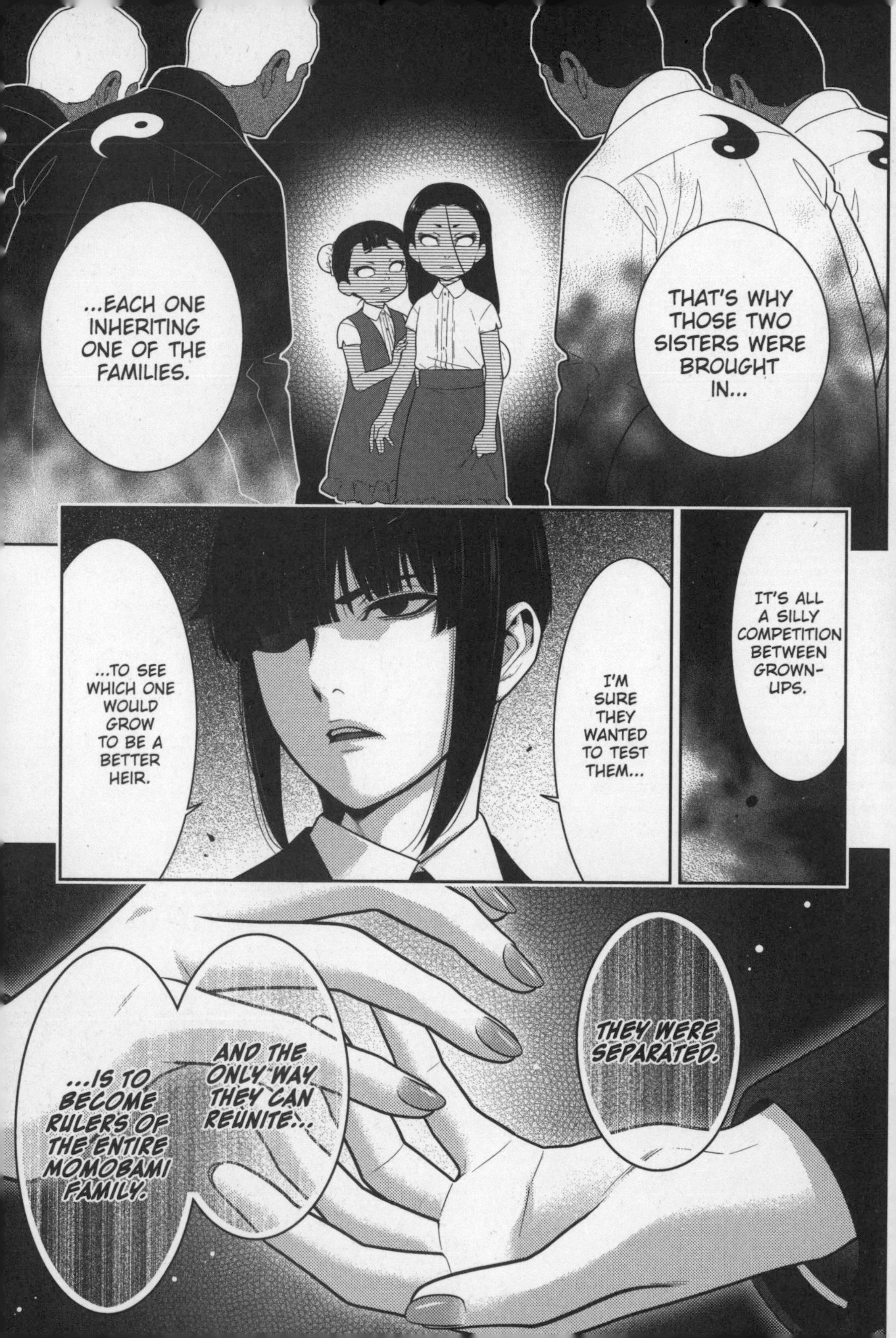
THAT'S WHY THOSE TWO SISTERS WERE BROUGHT IN...
...EACH ONE INHERITING ONE OF THE FAMILIES.
IT'S ALL A SILLY COMPETITION BETWEEN GROWN-UPS.
I'M SURE THEY WANTED TO TEST THEM...
...TO SEE WHICH ONE WOULD GROW TO BE A BETTER HEIR.
THEY WERE SEPARATED.
AND THE ONLY WAY THEY CAN REUNITE...
...IS TO BECOME RULERS OF THE ENTIRE MOMOBAMI FAMILY.

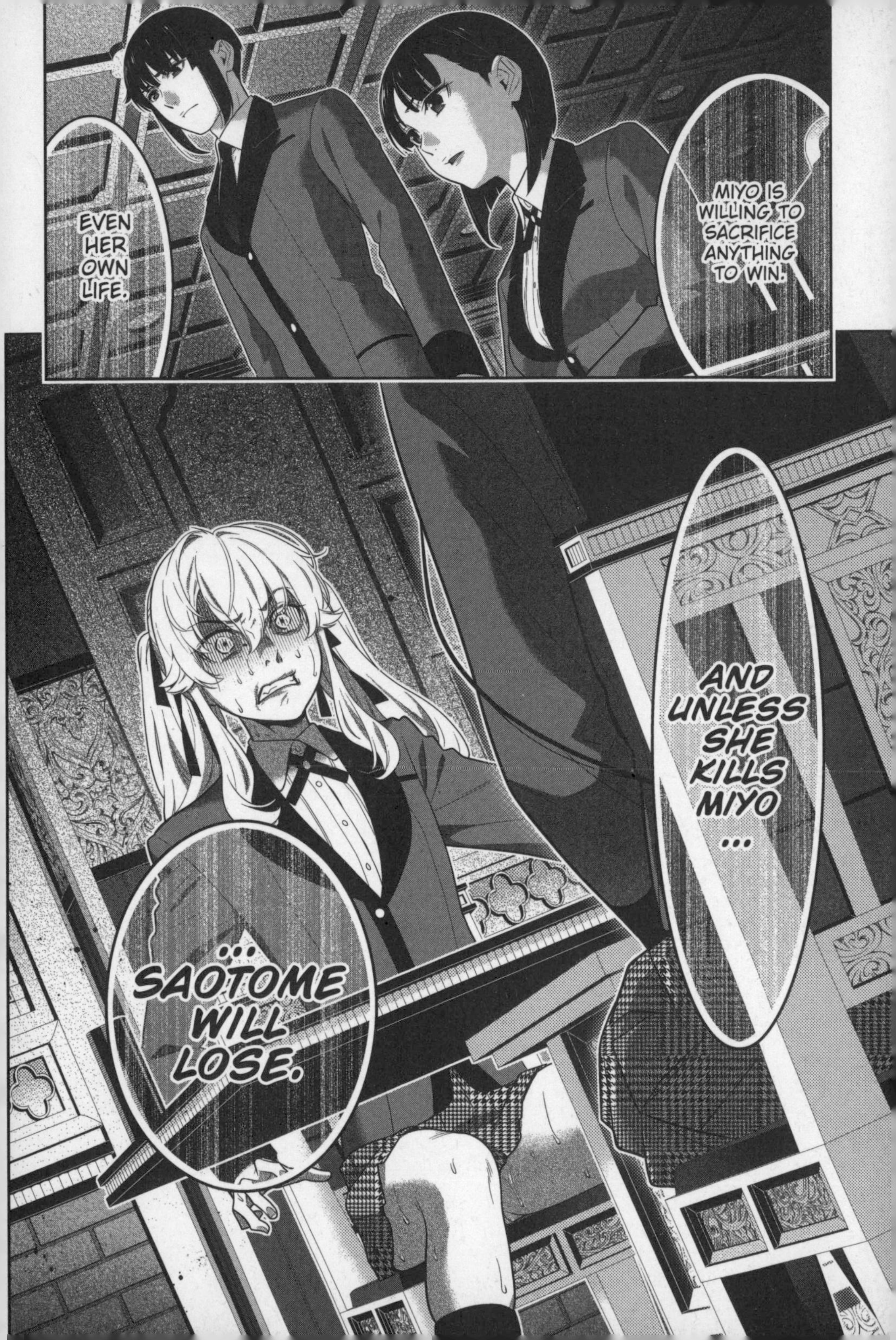
MIYO IS WILLING TO SACRIFICE ANYTHING TO WIN.
EVEN HER OWN LIFE.
AND UNLESS SHE KILLS MIYO...
...SAOTOME WILL LOSE.

KAKEGURUI

— Compulsive Gambler —

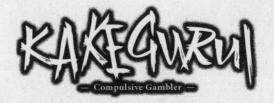

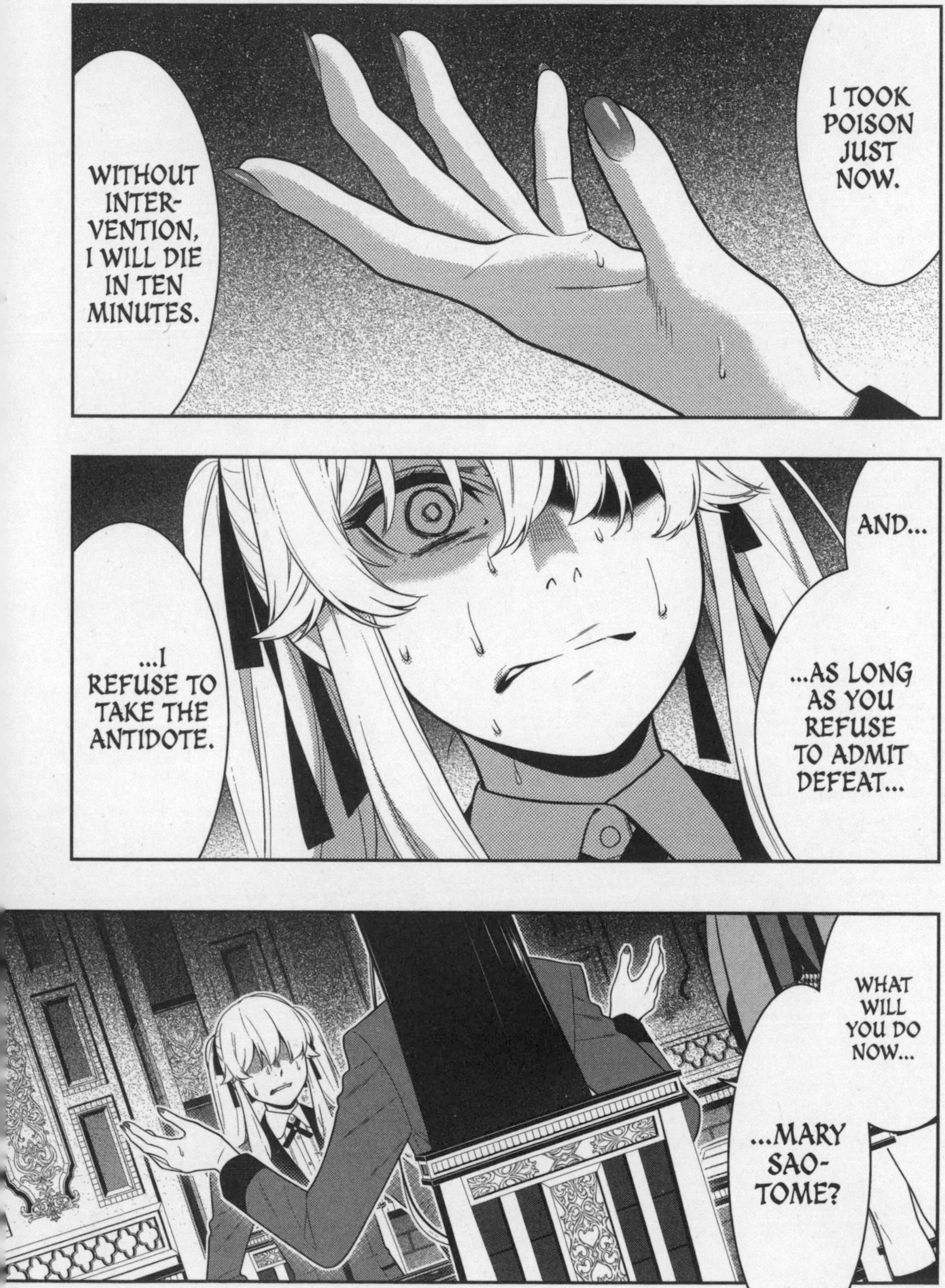
I TOOK POISON JUST NOW.
WITHOUT INTER-VENTION, I WILL DIE IN TEN MINUTES.
AND...
...AS LONG AS YOU REFUSE TO ADMIT DEFEAT...
...I REFUSE TO TAKE THE ANTIDOTE.
WHAT WILL YOU DO NOW...
...MARY SAO-TOME?

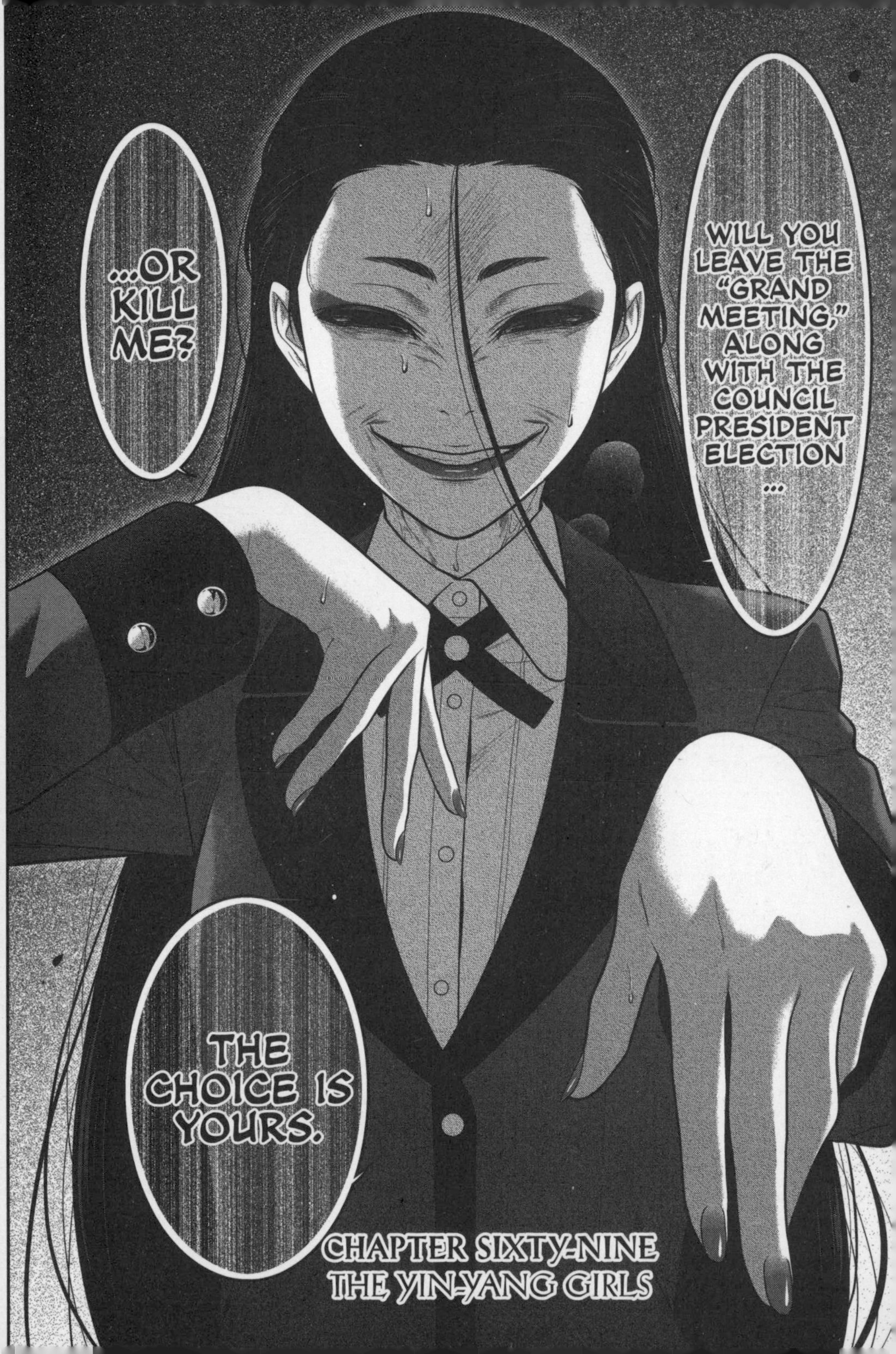

CHAPTER SIXTY-NINE
THE YIN-YANG GIRLS

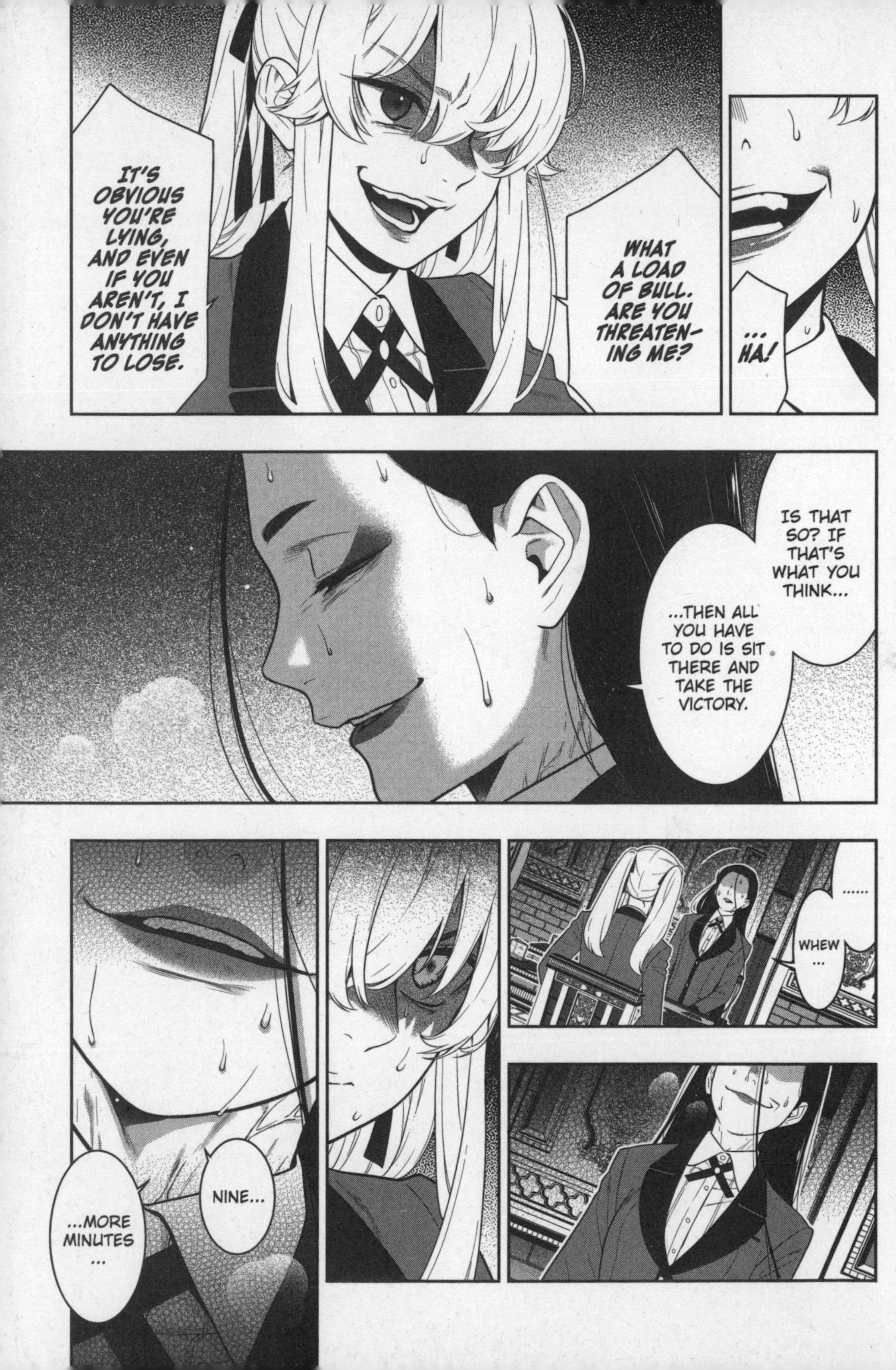
...HA!
WHAT A LOAD OF BULL. ARE YOU THREATEN-ING ME?
IT'S OBVIOUS YOU'RE LYING, AND EVEN IF YOU AREN'T, I DON'T HAVE ANYTHING TO LOSE.
IS THAT SO? IF THAT'S WHAT YOU THINK...
...THEN ALL YOU HAVE TO DO IS SIT THERE AND TAKE THE VICTORY.
......
WHEW...
NINE...
...MORE MINUTES...

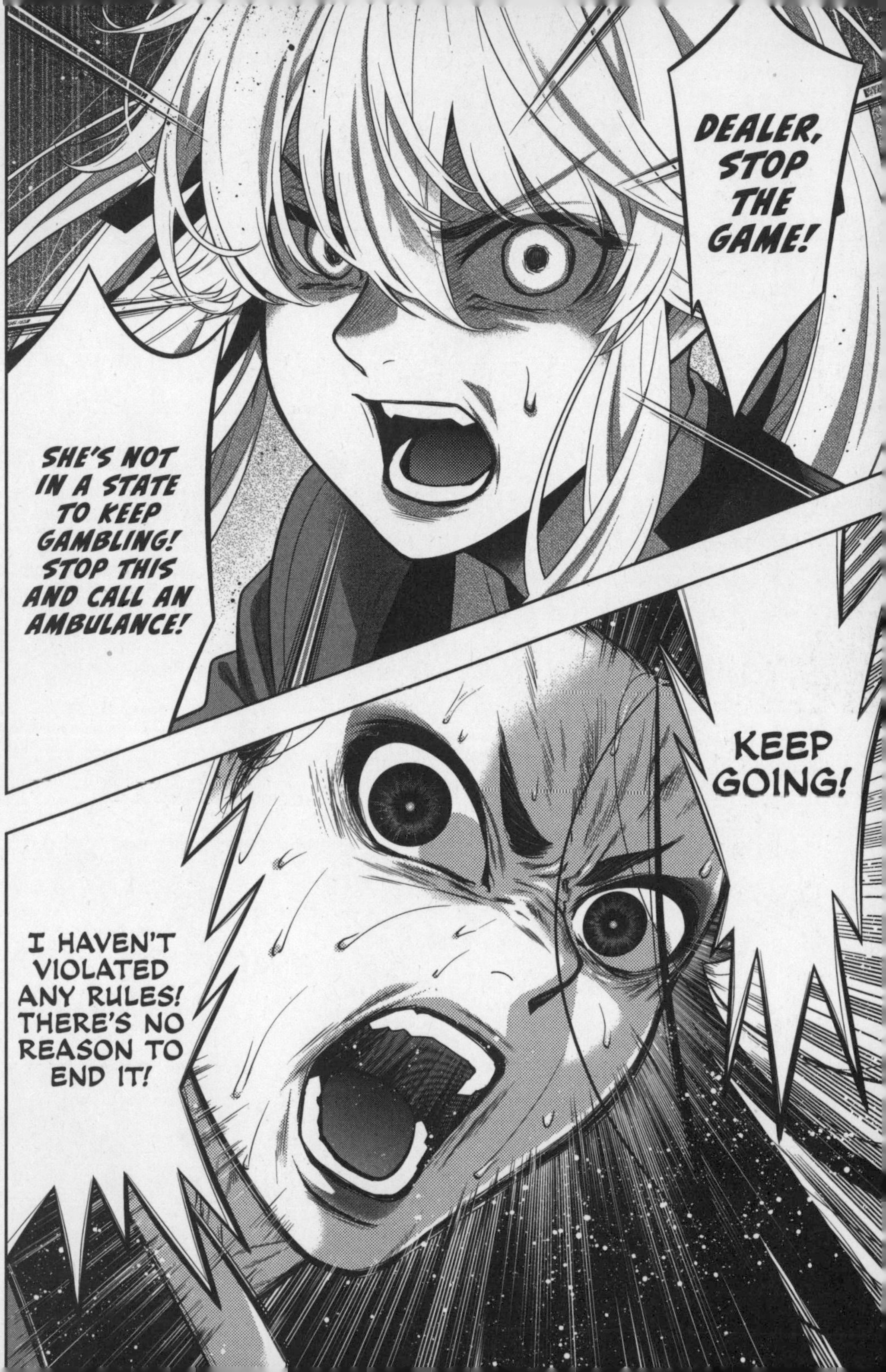
DEALER, STOP THE GAME!
SHE'S NOT IN A STATE TO KEEP GAMBLING! STOP THIS AND CALL AN AMBULANCE!
KEEP GOING!
I HAVEN'T VIOLATED ANY RULES! THERE'S NO REASON TO END IT!

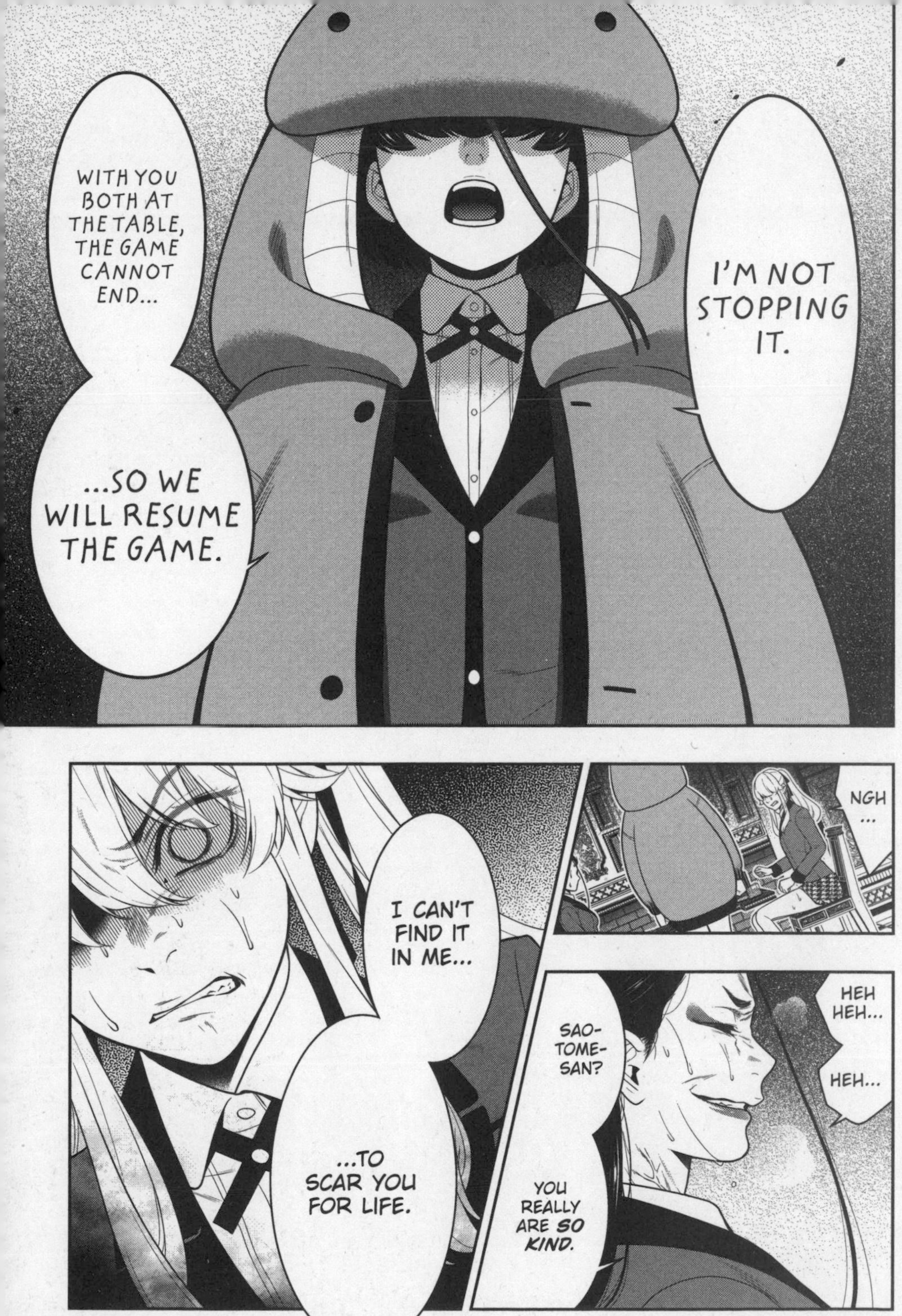
I'M NOT STOPPING IT.
WITH YOU BOTH AT THE TABLE, THE GAME CANNOT END...
...SO WE WILL RESUME THE GAME.
NGH...
HEH HEH...
HEH...
SAOTOME-SAN?
YOU REALLY ARE *SO KIND*.
I CAN'T FIND IT IN ME...
...TO SCAR YOU FOR LIFE.

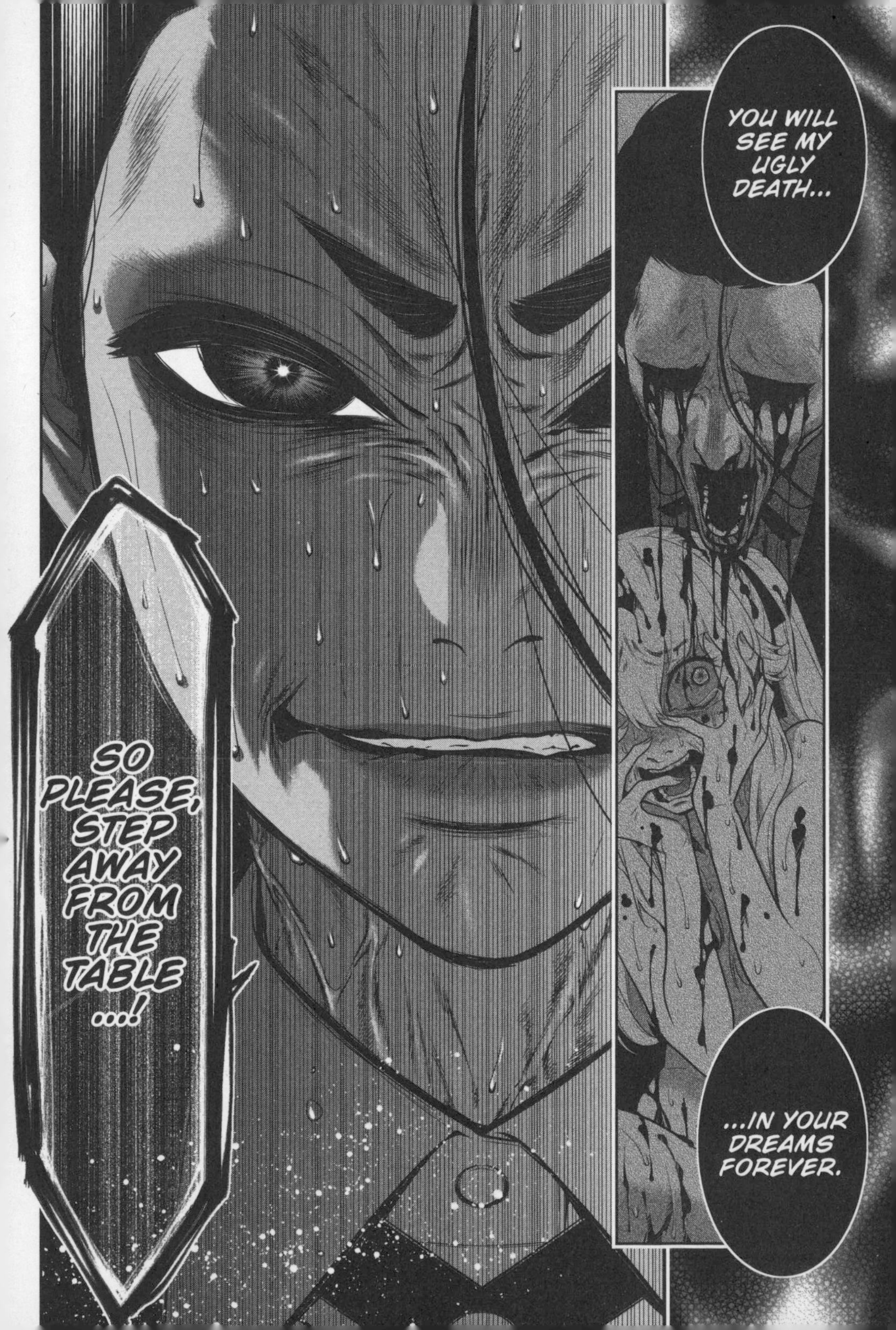
YOU WILL SEE MY UGLY DEATH...
...IN YOUR DREAMS FOREVER.
SO PLEASE, STEP AWAY FROM THE TABLE ...!

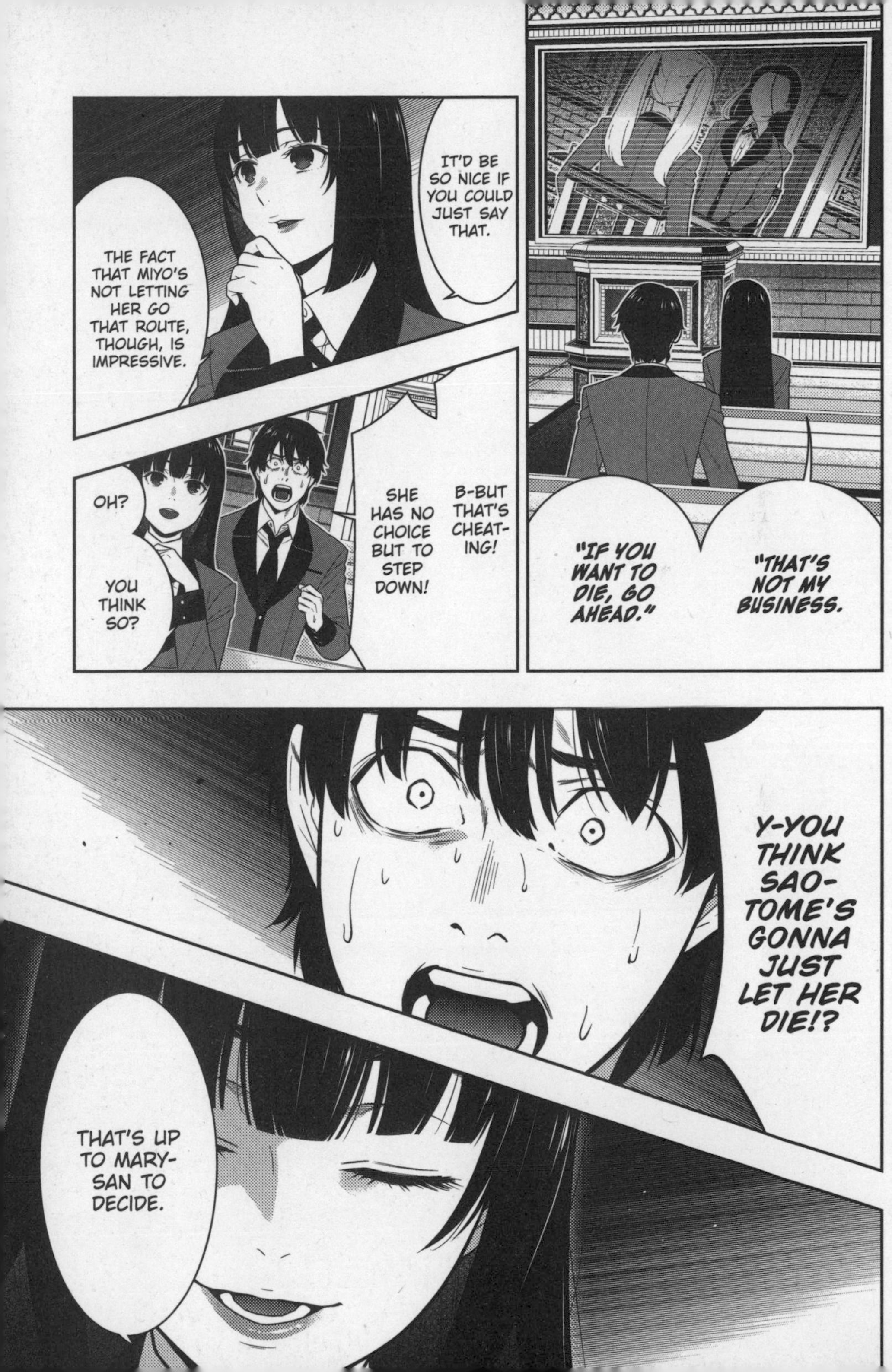
"THAT'S NOT MY BUSINESS.
"IF YOU WANT TO DIE, GO AHEAD."
IT'D BE SO NICE IF YOU COULD JUST SAY THAT.
THE FACT THAT MIYO'S NOT LETTING HER GO THAT ROUTE, THOUGH, IS IMPRESSIVE.
B-BUT THAT'S CHEAT-ING!
SHE HAS NO CHOICE BUT TO STEP DOWN!
OH?
YOU THINK SO?
Y-YOU THINK SAO-TOME'S GONNA JUST LET HER DIE!?
THAT'S UP TO MARY-SAN TO DECIDE.

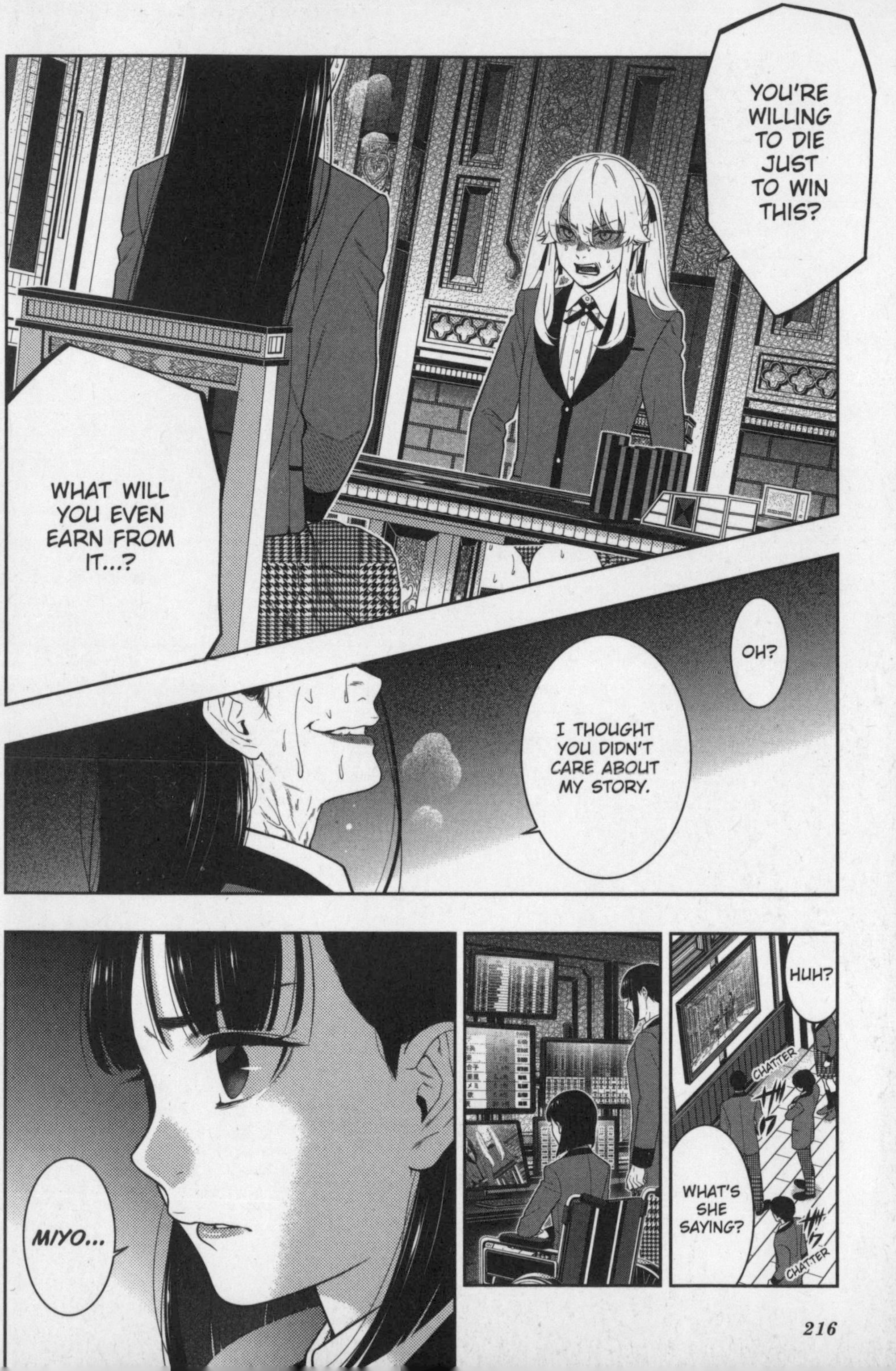
YOU'RE WILLING TO DIE JUST TO WIN THIS?
WHAT WILL YOU EVEN EARN FROM IT...?
OH?
I THOUGHT YOU DIDN'T CARE ABOUT MY STORY.
HUH?
CHATTER
WHAT'S SHE SAYING?
CHATTER
MIYO...

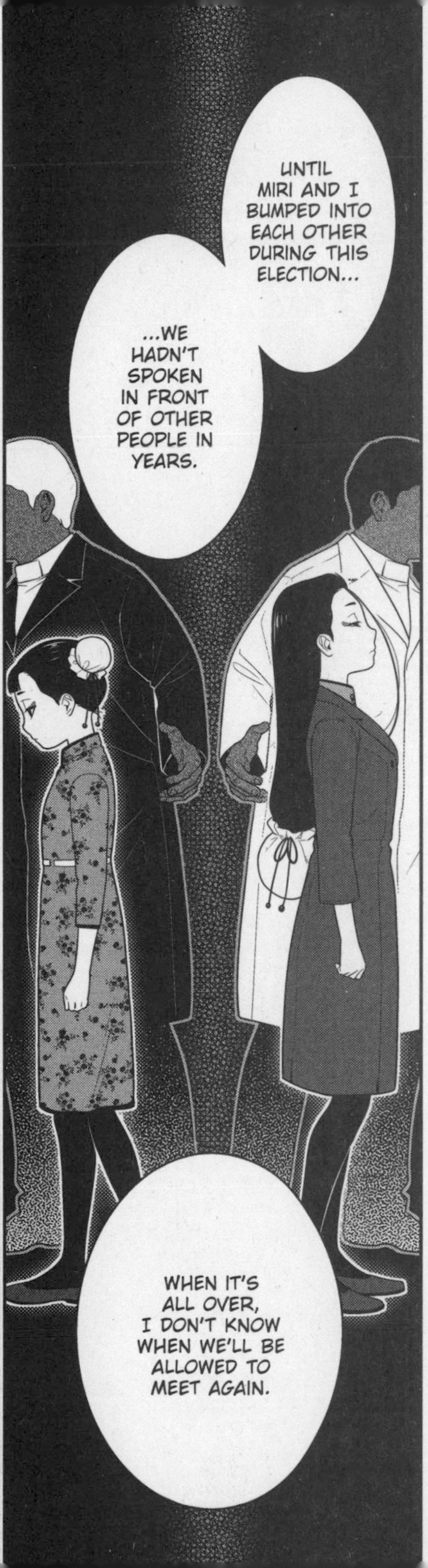
UNTIL MIRI AND I BUMPED INTO EACH OTHER DURING THIS ELECTION...
...WE HADN'T SPOKEN IN FRONT OF OTHER PEOPLE IN YEARS.
WHEN IT'S ALL OVER, I DON'T KNOW WHEN WE'LL BE ALLOWED TO MEET AGAIN.
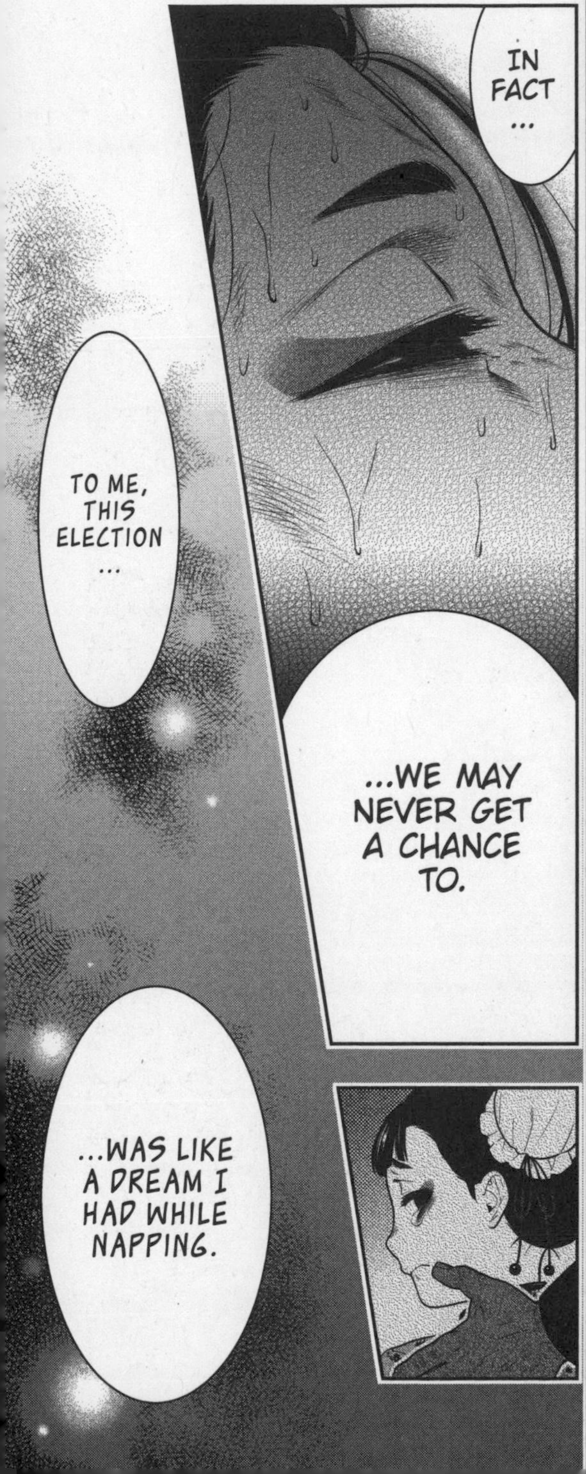
IN FACT ...
...WE MAY NEVER GET A CHANCE TO.
TO ME, THIS ELECTION ...
...WAS LIKE A DREAM I HAD WHILE NAPPING.

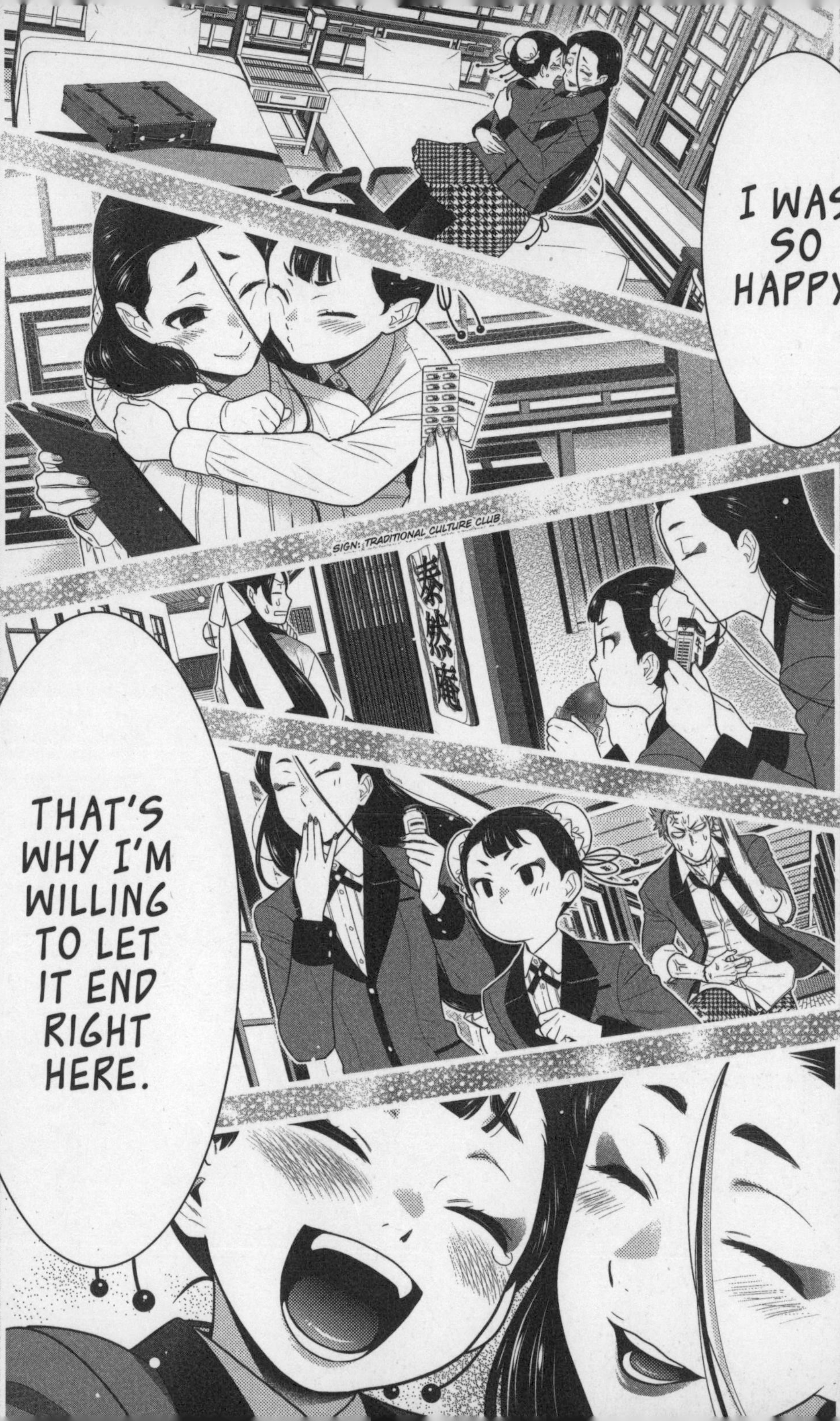
I WAS SO HAPPY.
SIGN: TRADITIONAL CULTURE CLUB
THAT'S WHY I'M WILLING TO LET IT END RIGHT HERE.

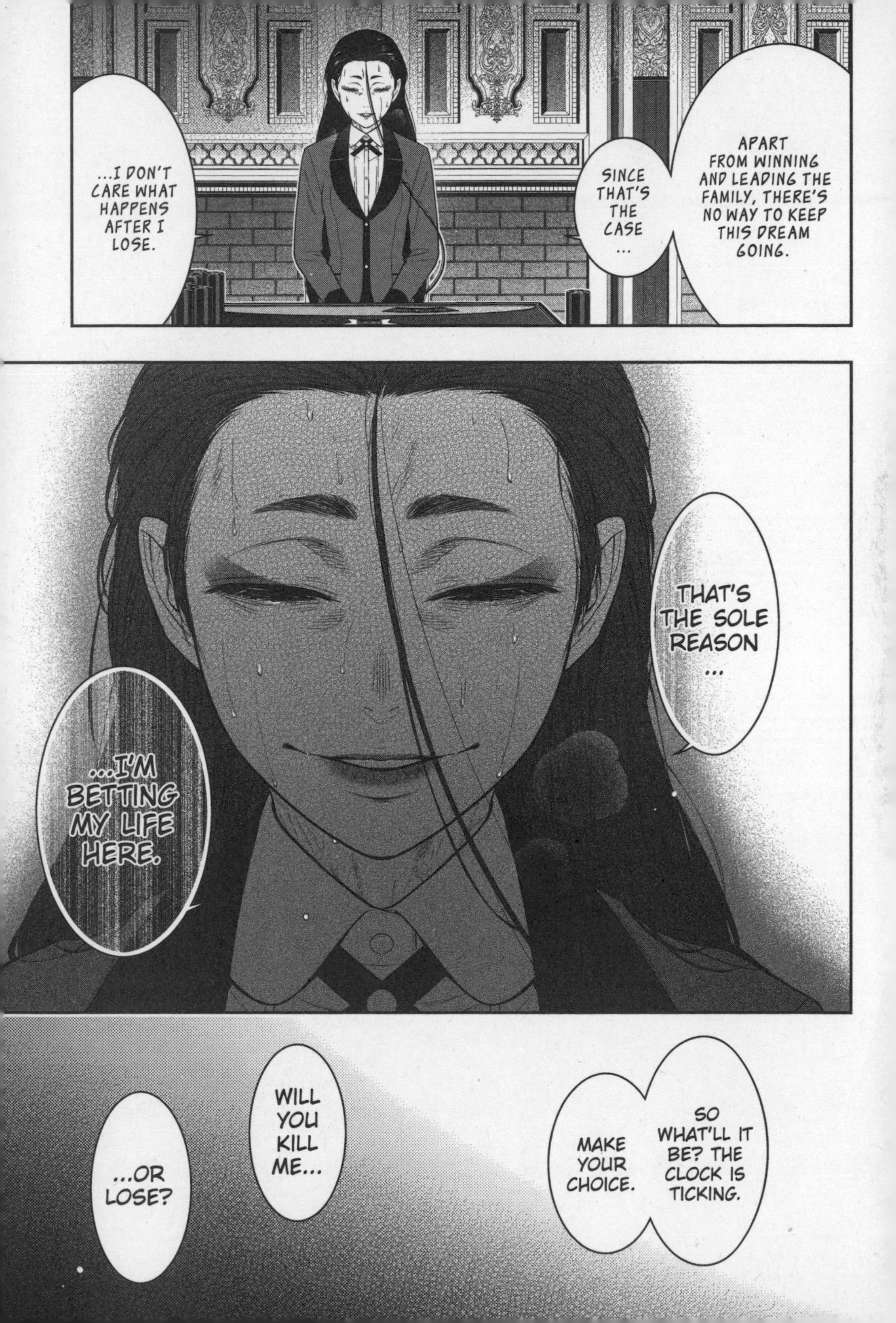
APART FROM WINNING AND LEADING THE FAMILY, THERE'S NO WAY TO KEEP THIS DREAM GOING.
SINCE THAT'S THE CASE...
...I DON'T CARE WHAT HAPPENS AFTER I LOSE.
THAT'S THE SOLE REASON...
...I'M BETTING MY LIFE HERE.
SO WHAT'LL IT BE? THE CLOCK IS TICKING.
MAKE YOUR CHOICE.
WILL YOU KILL ME...
...OR LOSE?

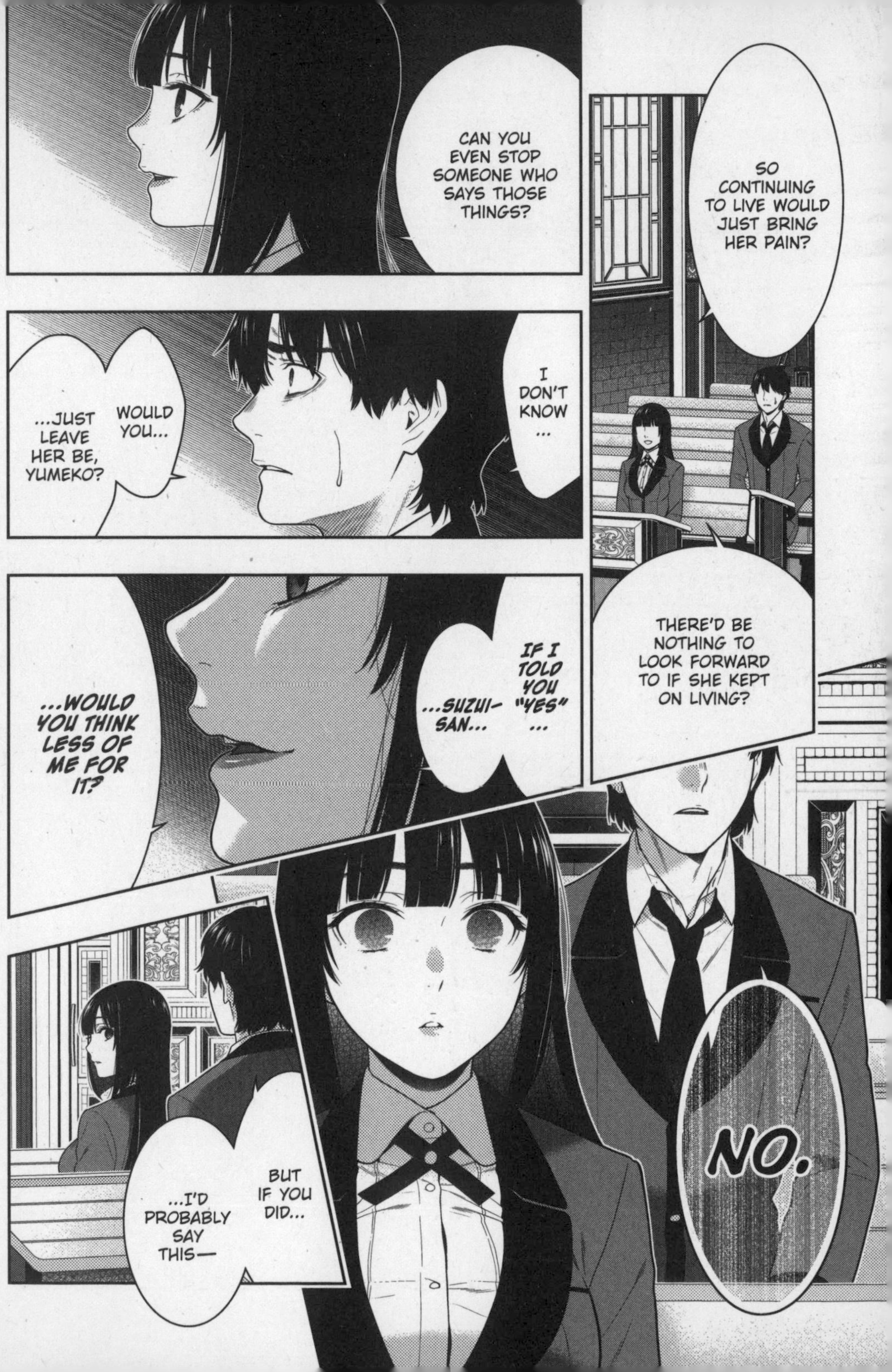
SO CONTINUING TO LIVE WOULD JUST BRING HER PAIN?
THERE'D BE NOTHING TO LOOK FORWARD TO IF SHE KEPT ON LIVING?
CAN YOU EVEN STOP SOMEONE WHO SAYS THOSE THINGS?
I DON'T KNOW ...
WOULD YOU...
...JUST LEAVE HER BE, YUMEKO?
IF I TOLD YOU "YES" ...
...SUZUI-SAN...
...WOULD YOU THINK LESS OF ME FOR IT?
NO.
BUT IF YOU DID...
...I'D PROBABLY SAY THIS—

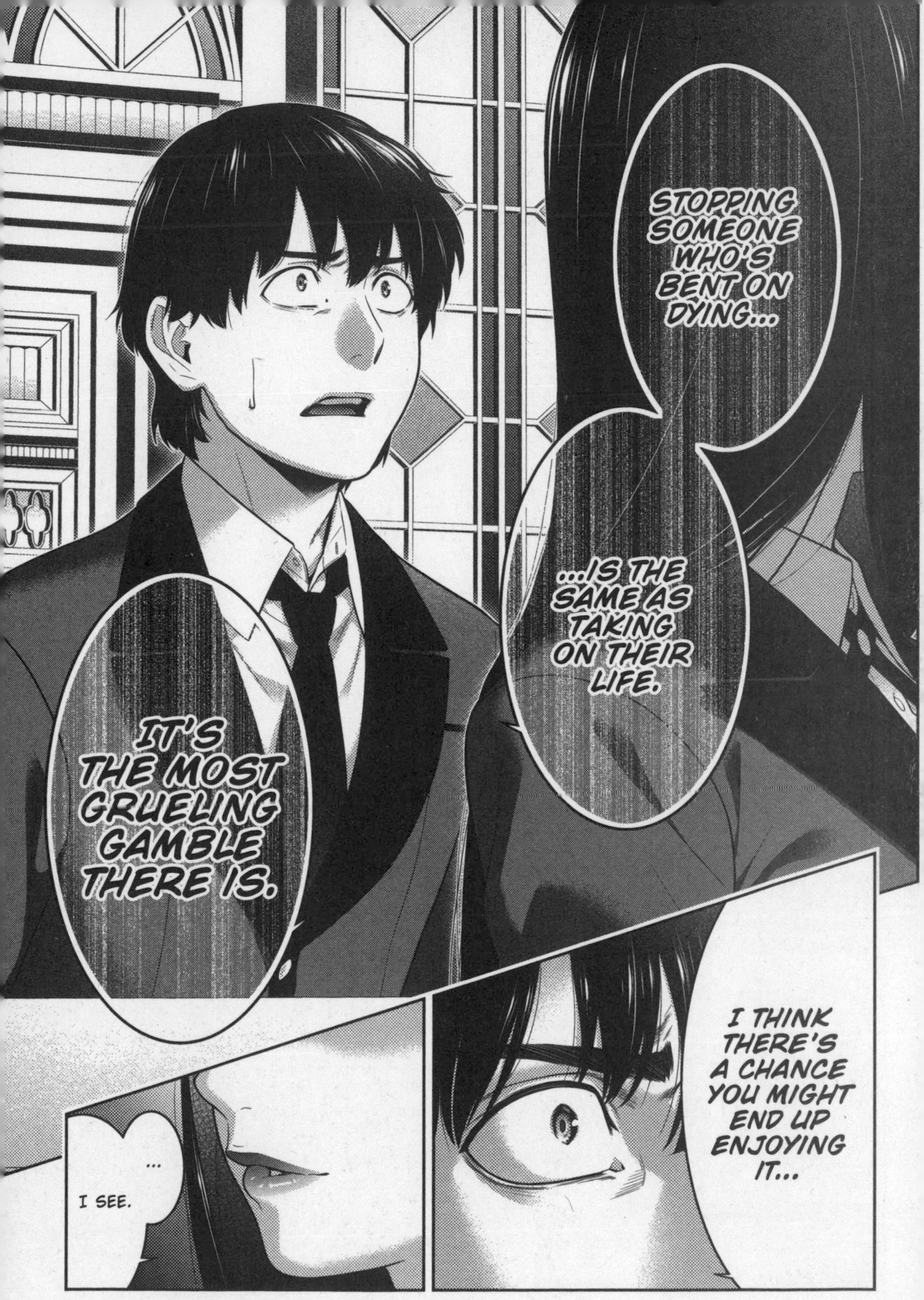
STOPPING SOMEONE WHO'S BENT ON DYING...
...IS THE SAME AS TAKING ON THEIR LIFE.
IT'S THE MOST GRUELING GAMBLE THERE IS.
I THINK THERE'S A CHANCE YOU MIGHT END UP ENJOYING IT...
...
I SEE.

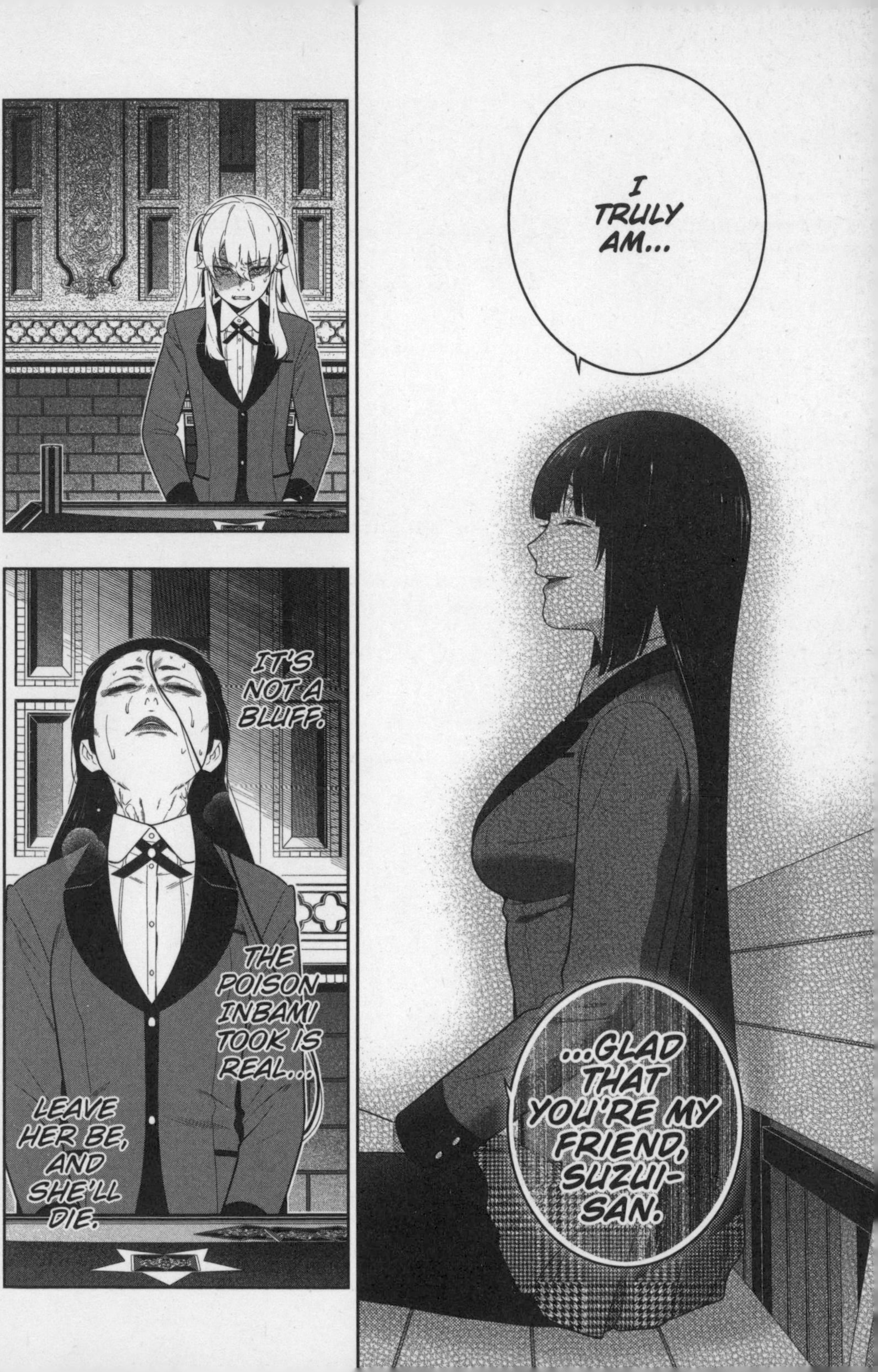
I TRULY AM...
...GLAD THAT YOU'RE MY FRIEND, SUZUI-SAN.
IT'S NOT A BLUFF.
THE POISON INBAMI TOOK IS REAL...
LEAVE HER BE, AND SHE'LL DIE.

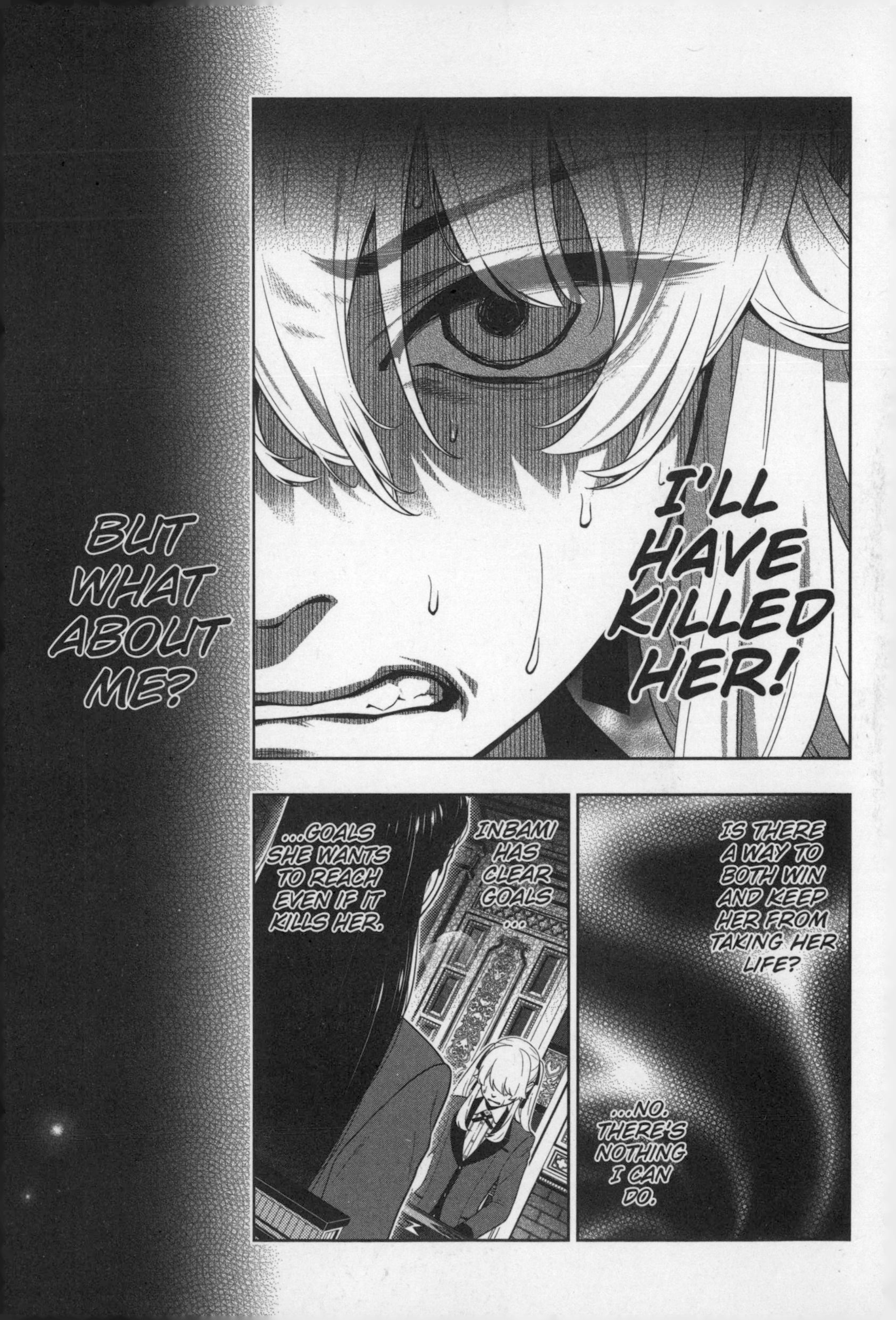
I'LL HAVE KILLED HER!
BUT WHAT ABOUT ME?
IS THERE A WAY TO BOTH WIN AND KEEP HER FROM TAKING HER LIFE?
...NO. THERE'S NOTHING I CAN DO.
INBAMI HAS CLEAR GOALS...
...GOALS SHE WANTS TO REACH EVEN IF IT KILLS HER.

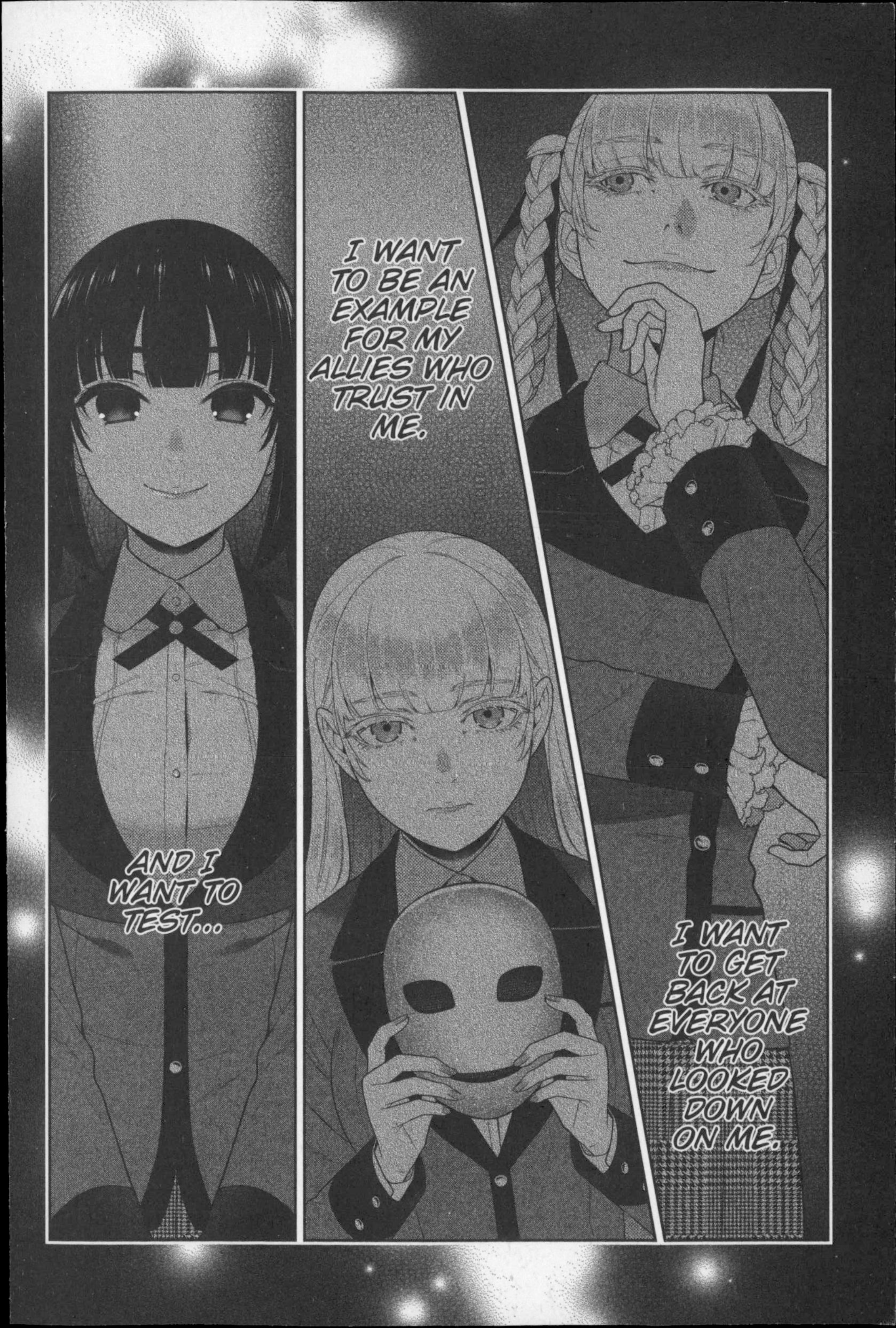
I WANT TO GET BACK AT EVERYONE WHO LOOKED DOWN ON ME.
I WANT TO BE AN EXAMPLE FOR MY ALLIES WHO TRUST IN ME.
AND I WANT TO TEST...

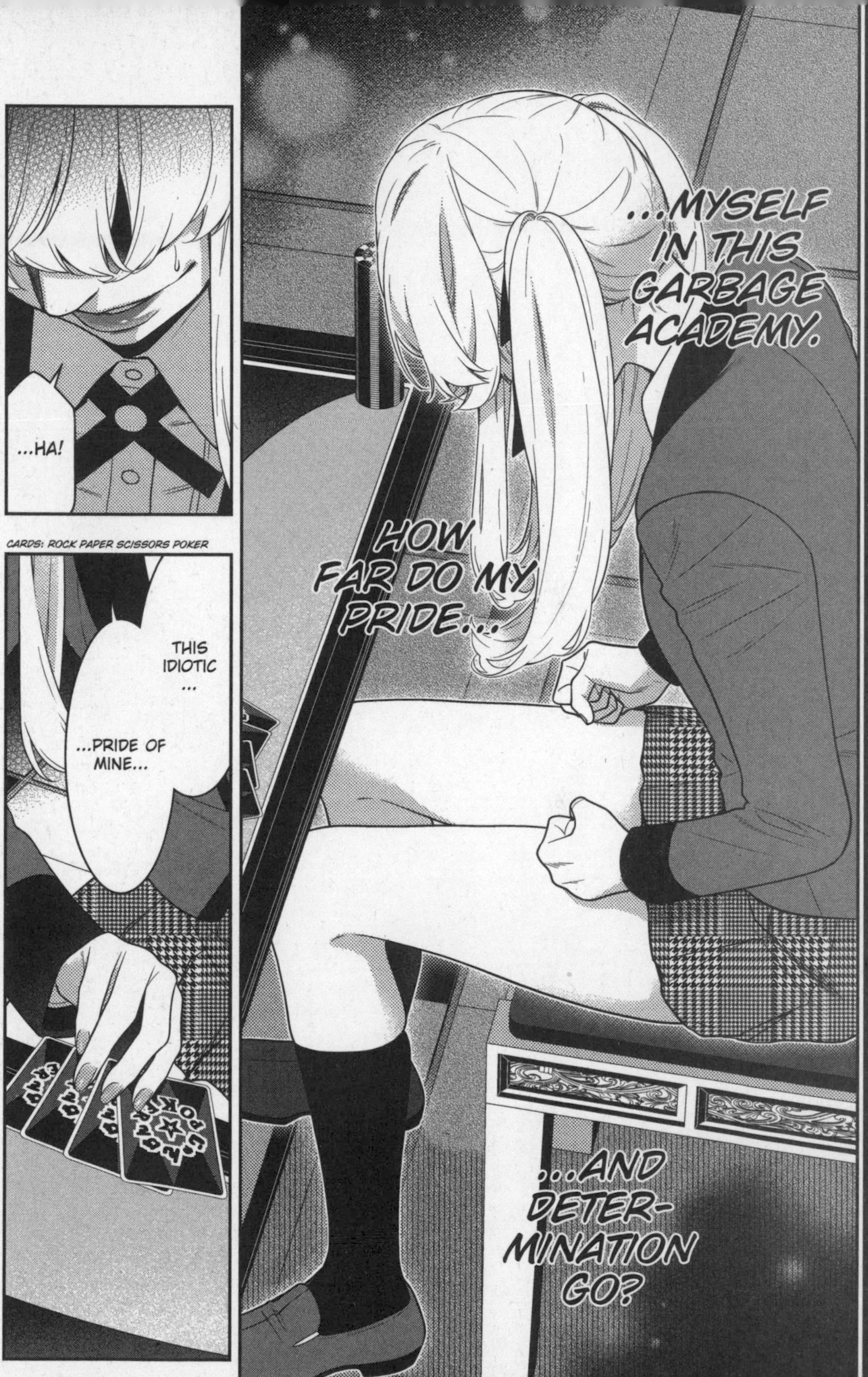
...MYSELF IN THIS GARBAGE ACADEMY.
HOW FAR DO MY PRIDE...
...AND DETER-MINATION GO?
...HA!
CARDS: ROCK PAPER SCISSORS POKER
THIS IDIOTIC ...
...PRIDE OF MINE...

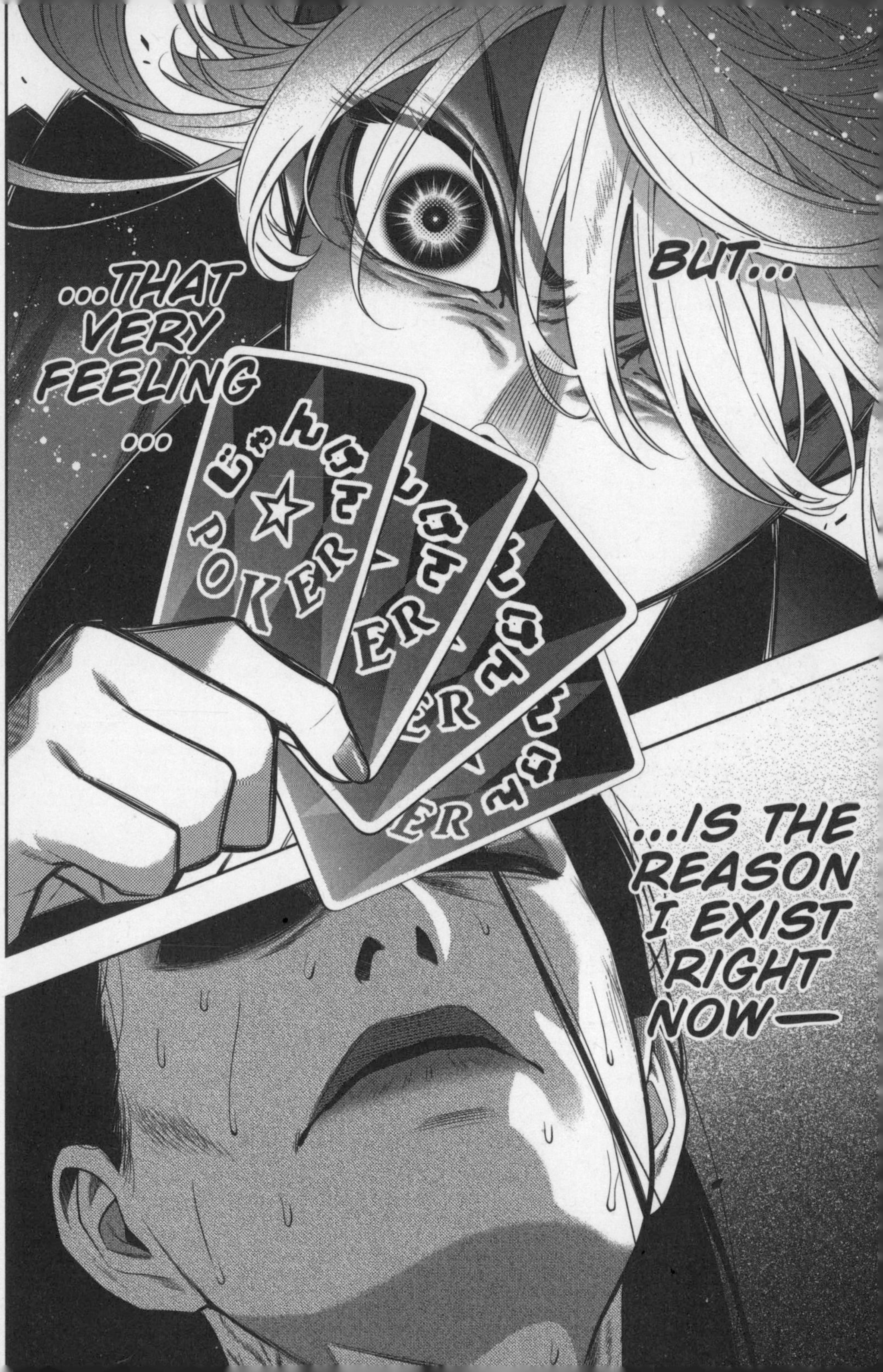
BUT...
...THAT VERY FEELING ...
POKER
...IS THE REASON I EXIST RIGHT NOW—

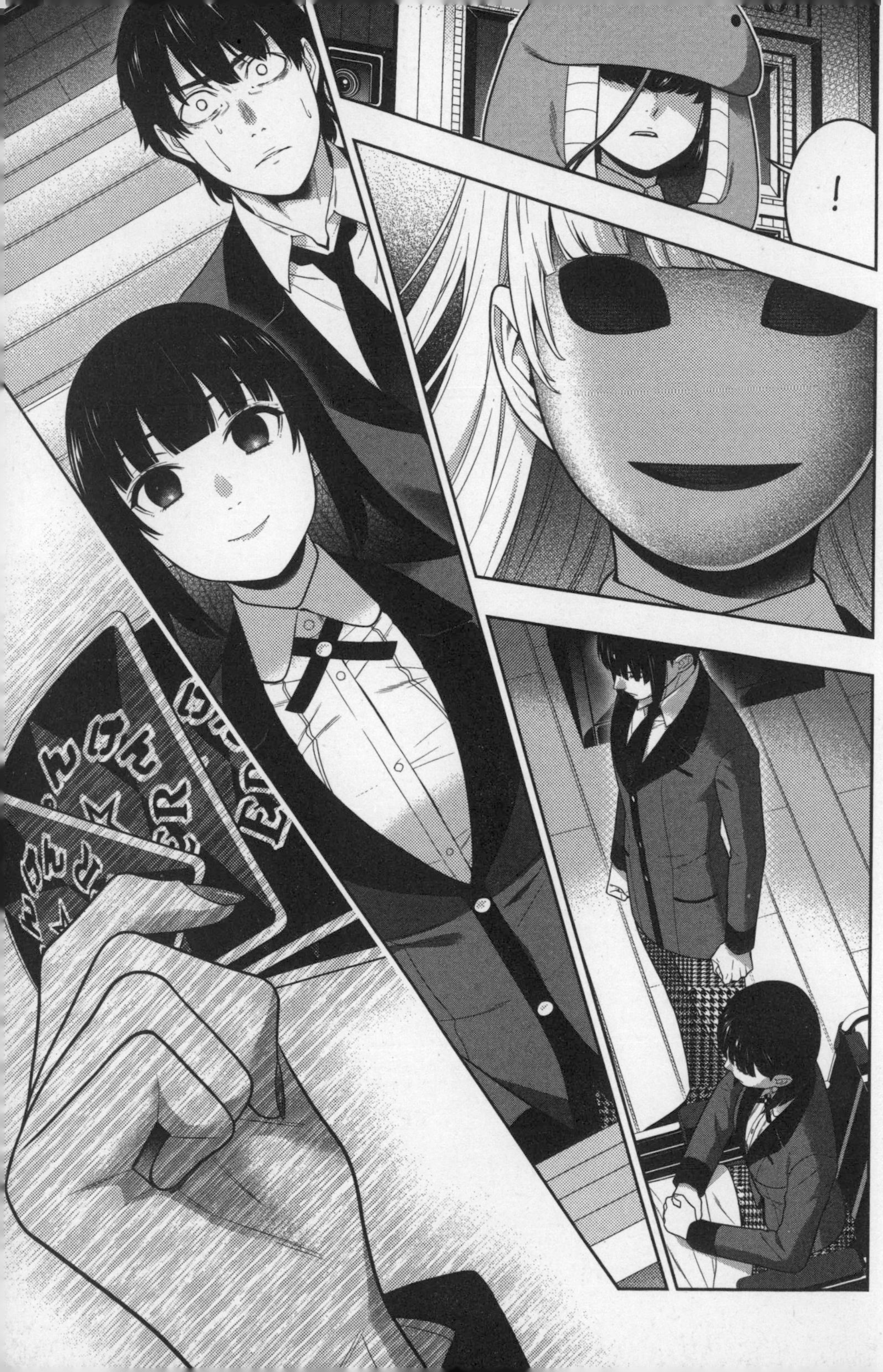
!

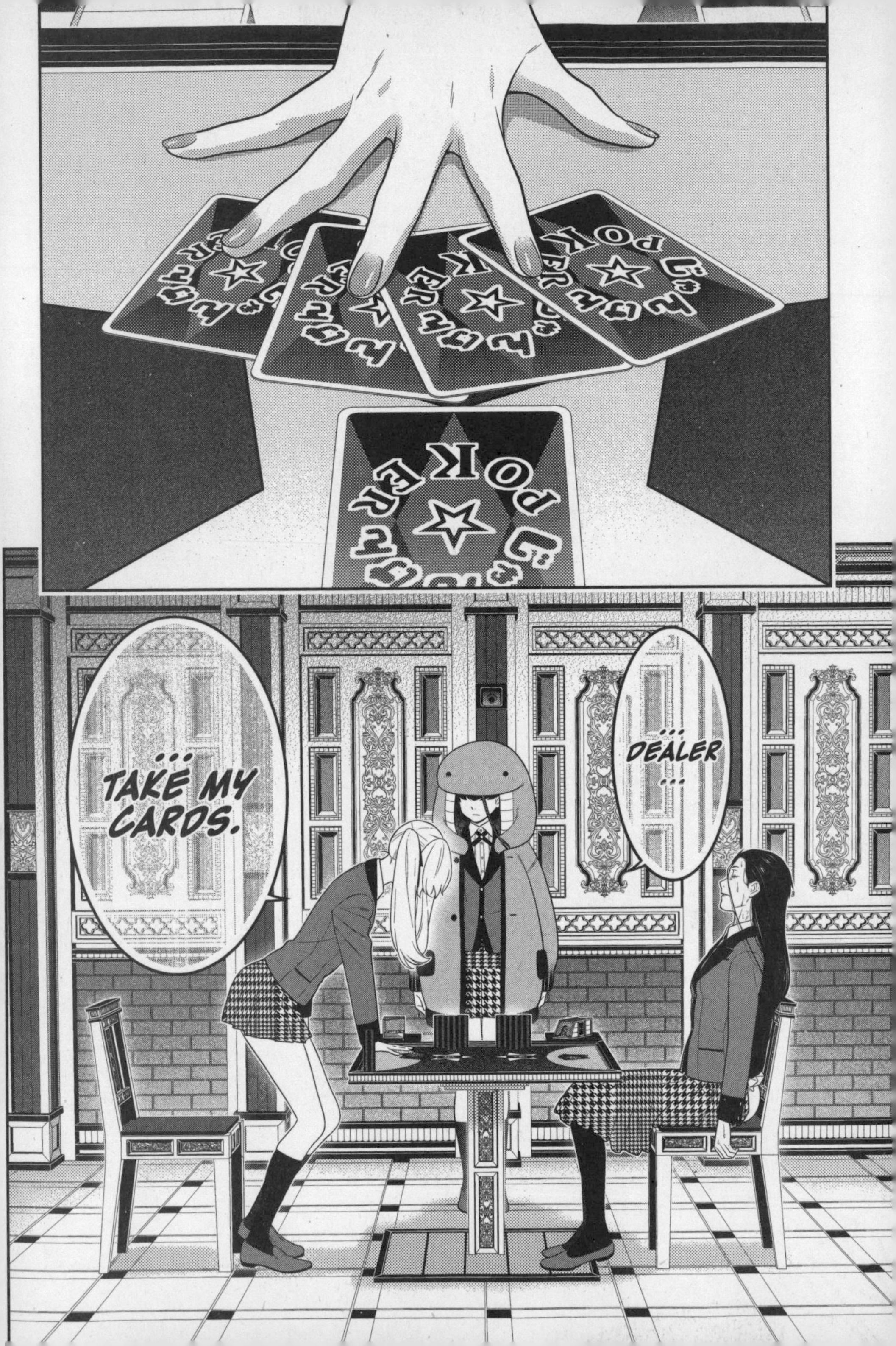
POKER
...DEALER...
...TAKE MY CARDS.

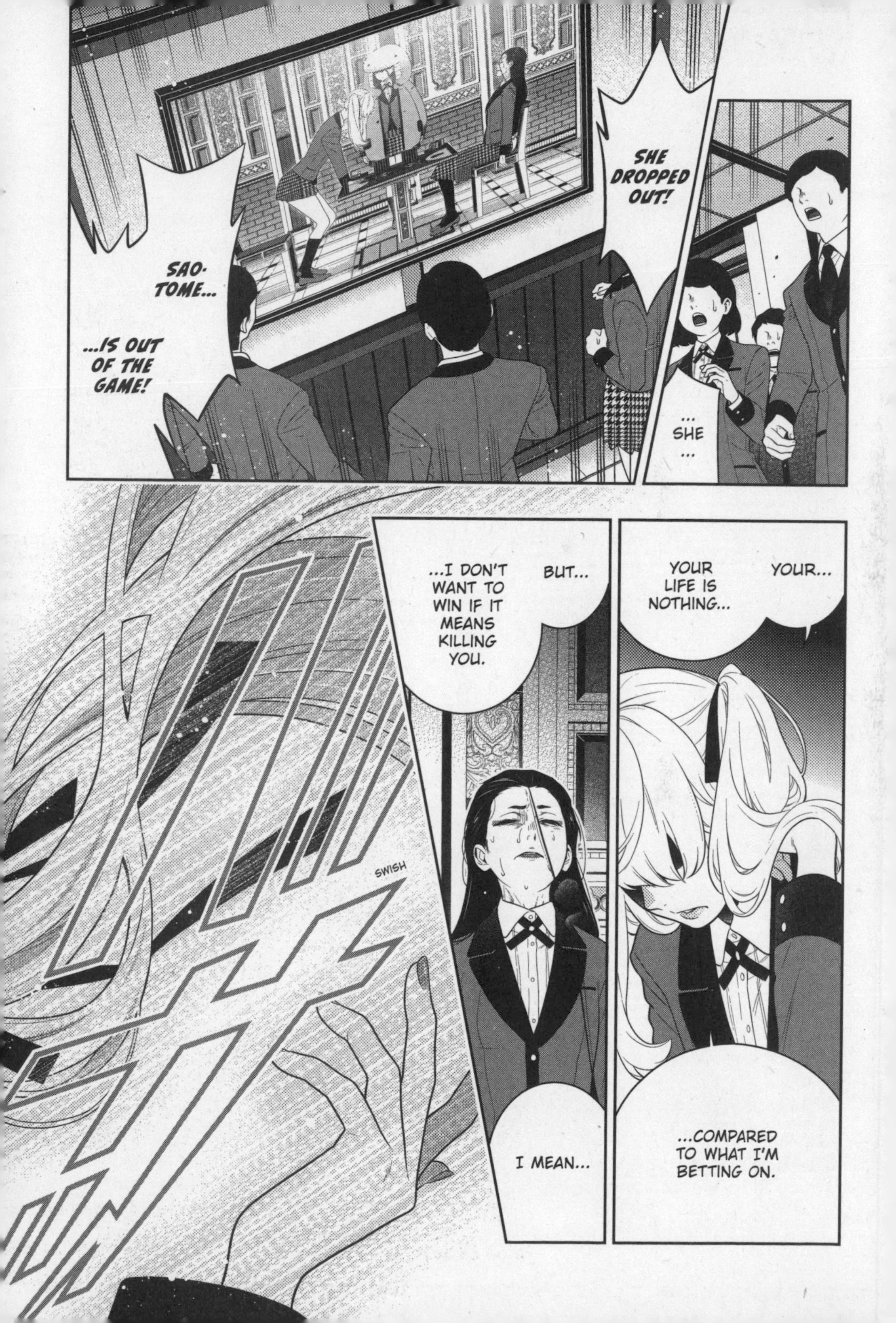
SHE DROPPED OUT!
... SHE ...
SAO-TOME...
...IS OUT OF THE GAME!
YOUR...
YOUR LIFE IS NOTHING...
...COMPARED TO WHAT I'M BETTING ON.
BUT...
...I DON'T WANT TO WIN IF IT MEANS KILLING YOU.
I MEAN...
SWISH

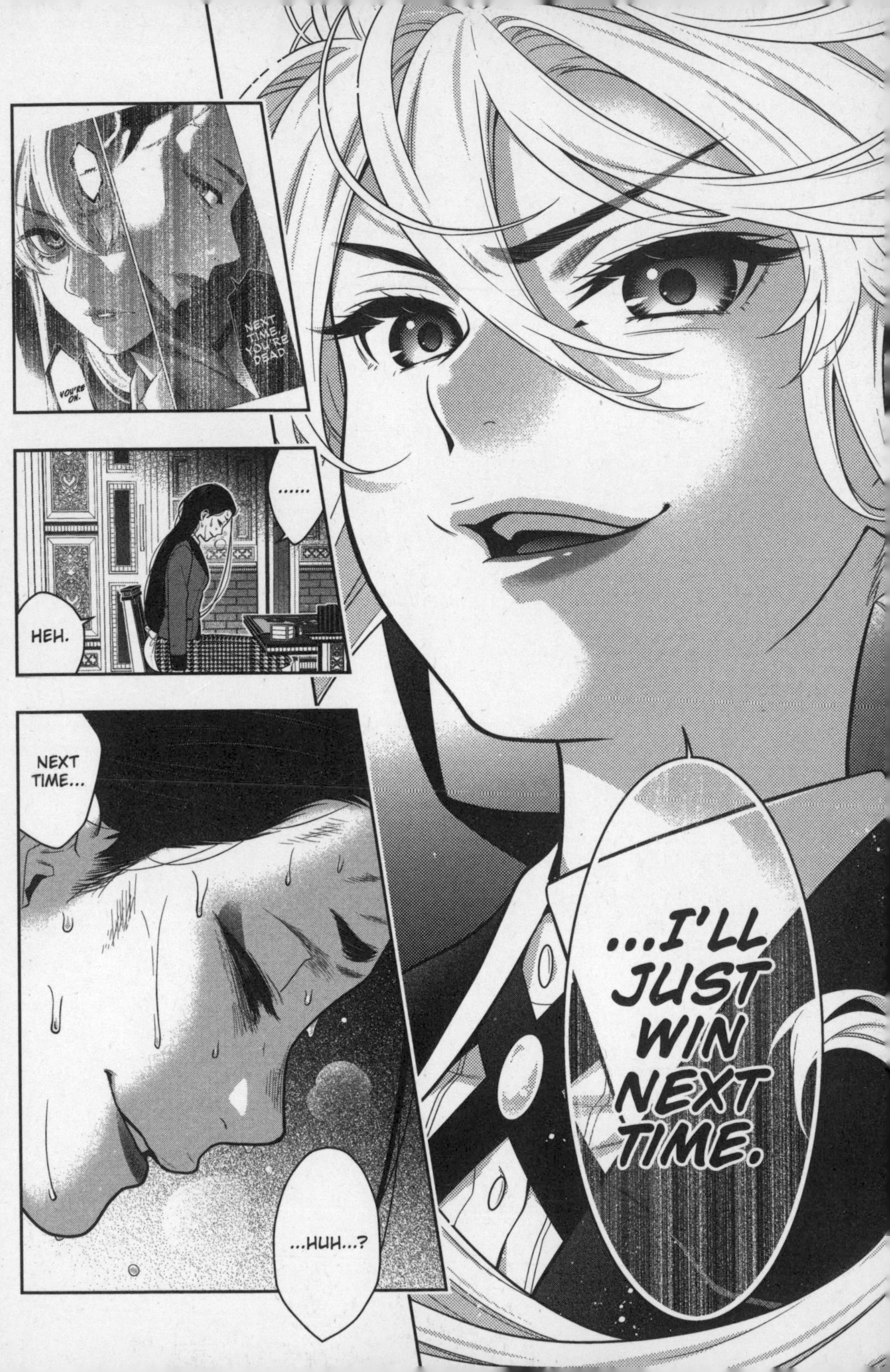
NEXT TIME, YOU'RE DEAD.
YOU'RE ON.
......
HEH.
NEXT TIME...
...I'LL JUST WIN NEXT TIME.
...HUH...?

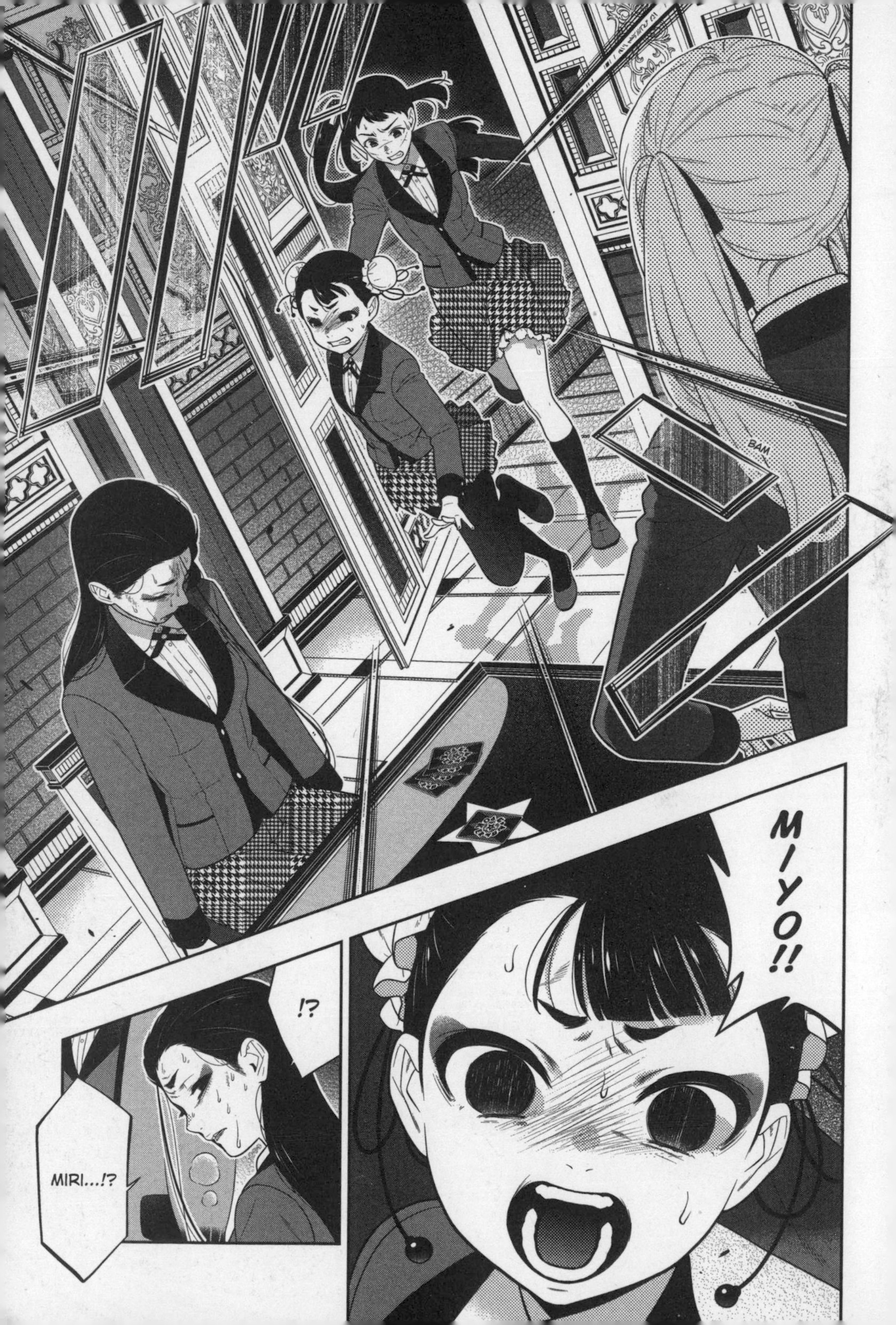
BAM
MIYO!!
!?
MIRI...!?

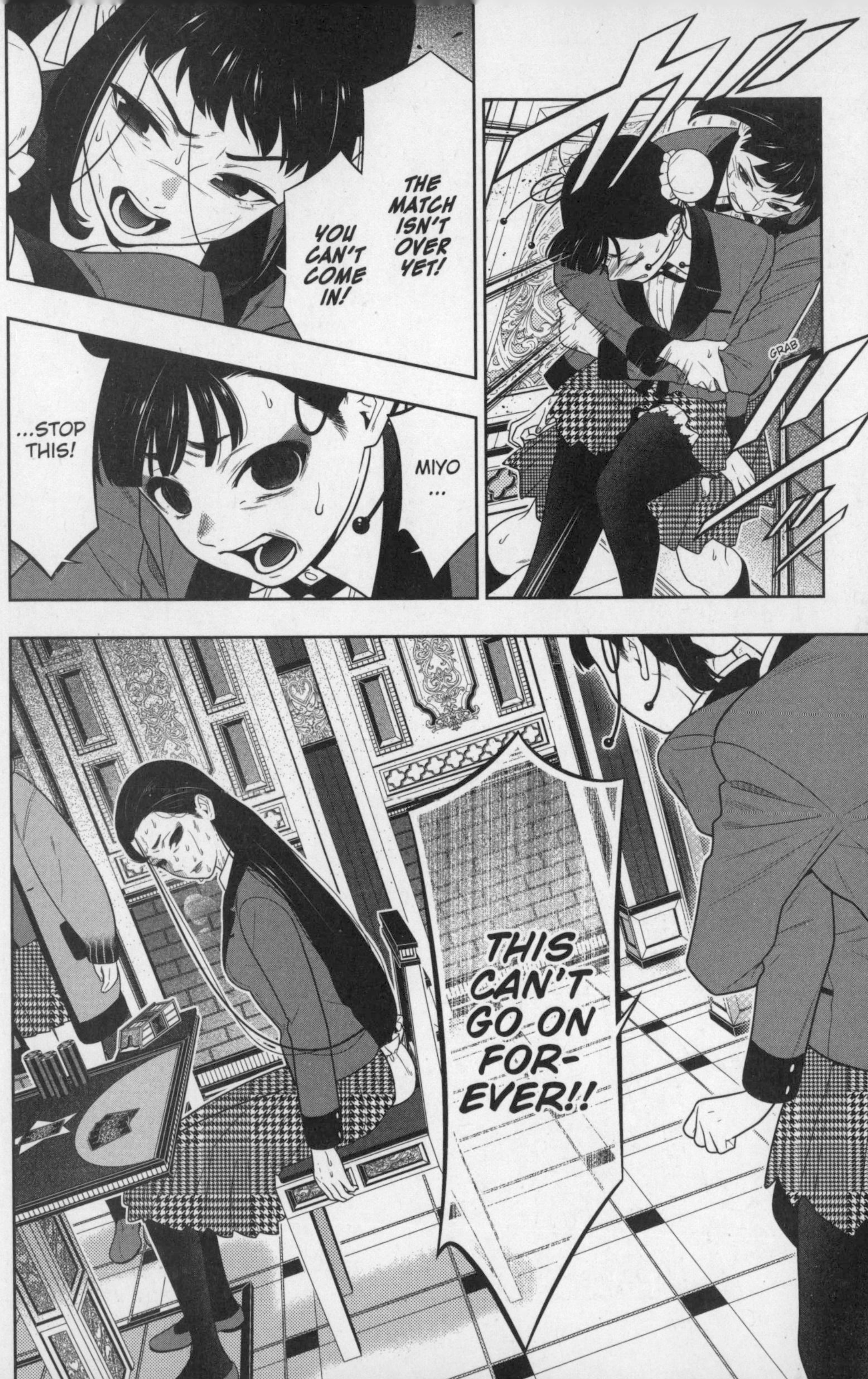
GRAB
THE MATCH ISN'T OVER YET!
YOU CAN'T COME IN!
MIYO ...
...STOP THIS!
THIS CAN'T GO ON FOR-EVER!!

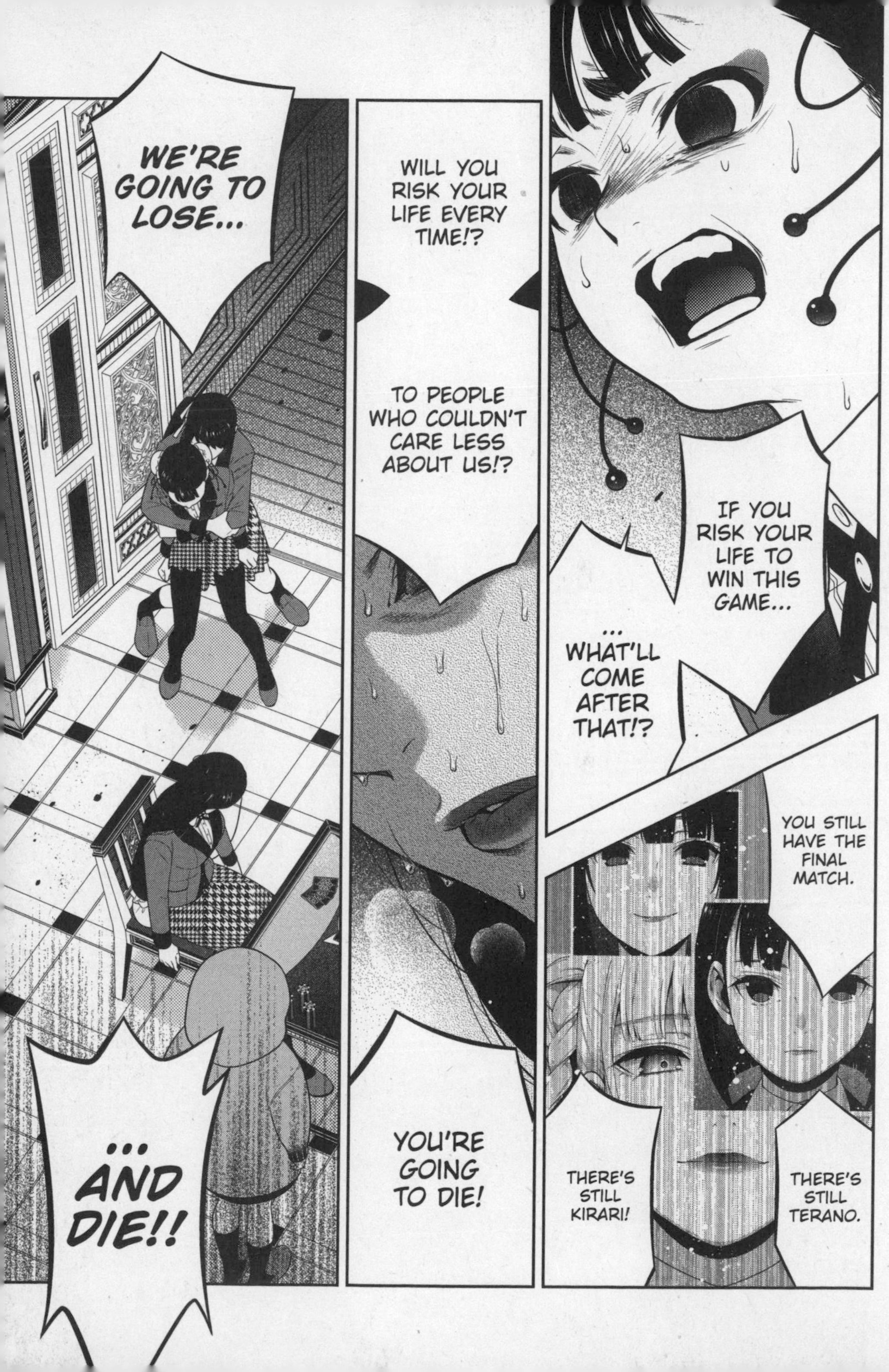
IF YOU RISK YOUR LIFE TO WIN THIS GAME...
...WHAT'LL COME AFTER THAT!?
YOU STILL HAVE THE FINAL MATCH.
THERE'S STILL TERANO.
THERE'S STILL KIRARI!
WILL YOU RISK YOUR LIFE EVERY TIME!?
TO PEOPLE WHO COULDN'T CARE LESS ABOUT US!?
YOU'RE GOING TO DIE!
WE'RE GOING TO LOSE...
...AND DIE!!

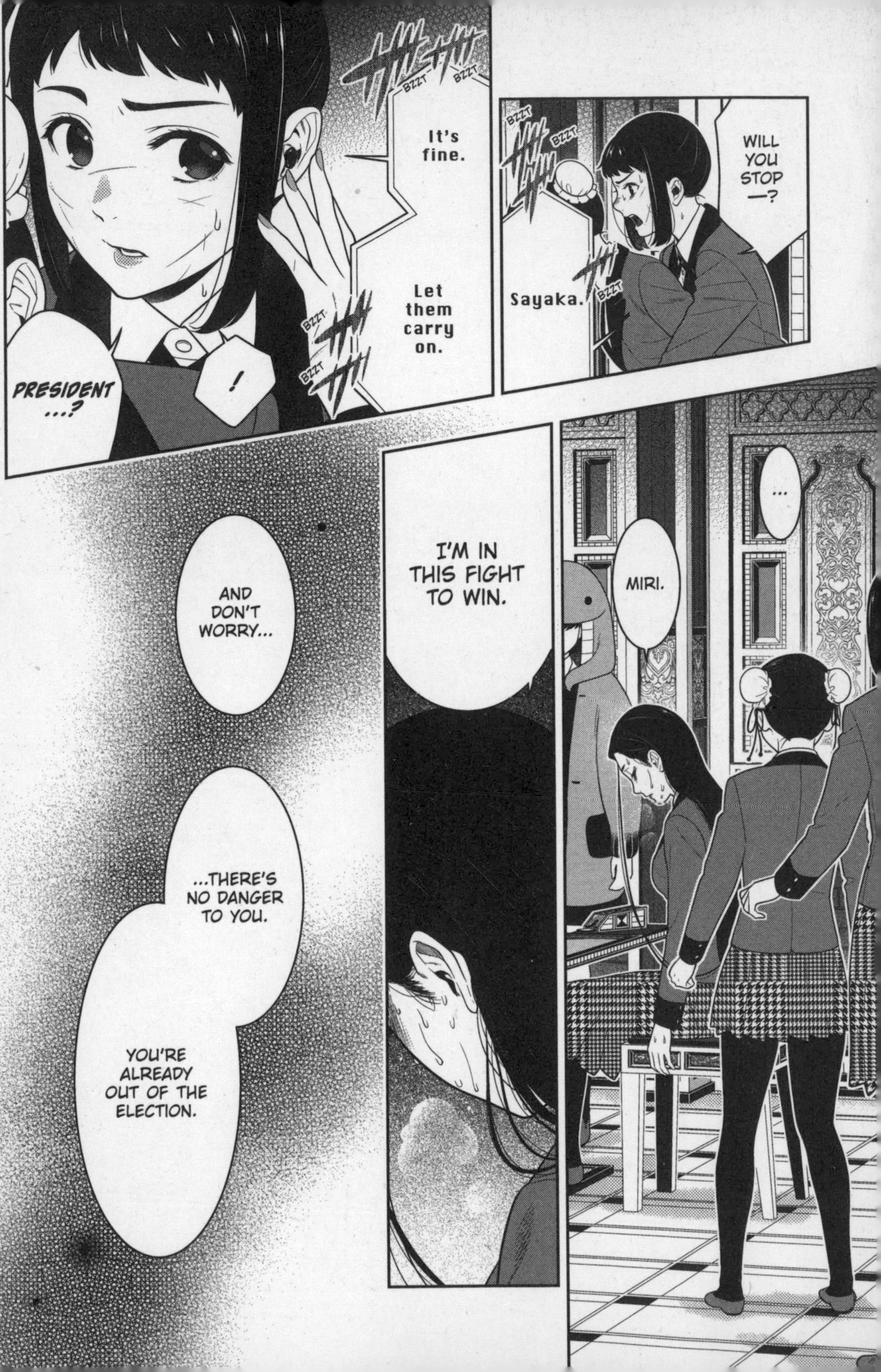
BZZT BZZT
WILL YOU STOP—?
Sayaka.
BZZT
BZZT BZZT
It's fine.
Let them carry on.
BZZT BZZT
!
PRESIDENT ...?
...
MIRI.
I'M IN THIS FIGHT TO WIN.
AND DON'T WORRY...
...THERE'S NO DANGER TO YOU.
YOU'RE ALREADY OUT OF THE ELECTION.

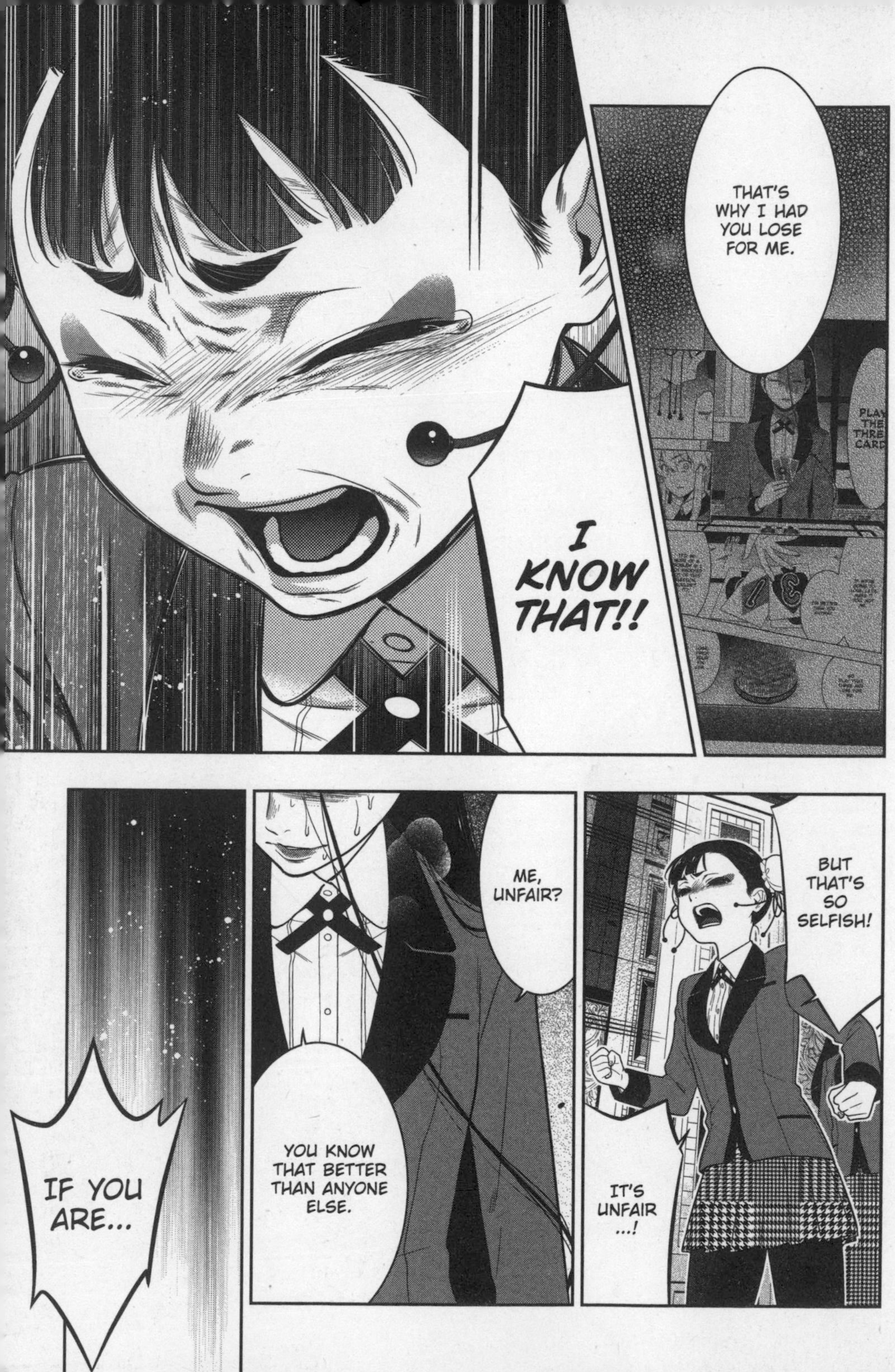
THAT'S WHY I HAD YOU LOSE FOR ME.
I KNOW THAT!!
BUT THAT'S SO SELFISH!
IT'S UNFAIR ...!
ME, UNFAIR?
YOU KNOW THAT BETTER THAN ANYONE ELSE.
IF YOU ARE...

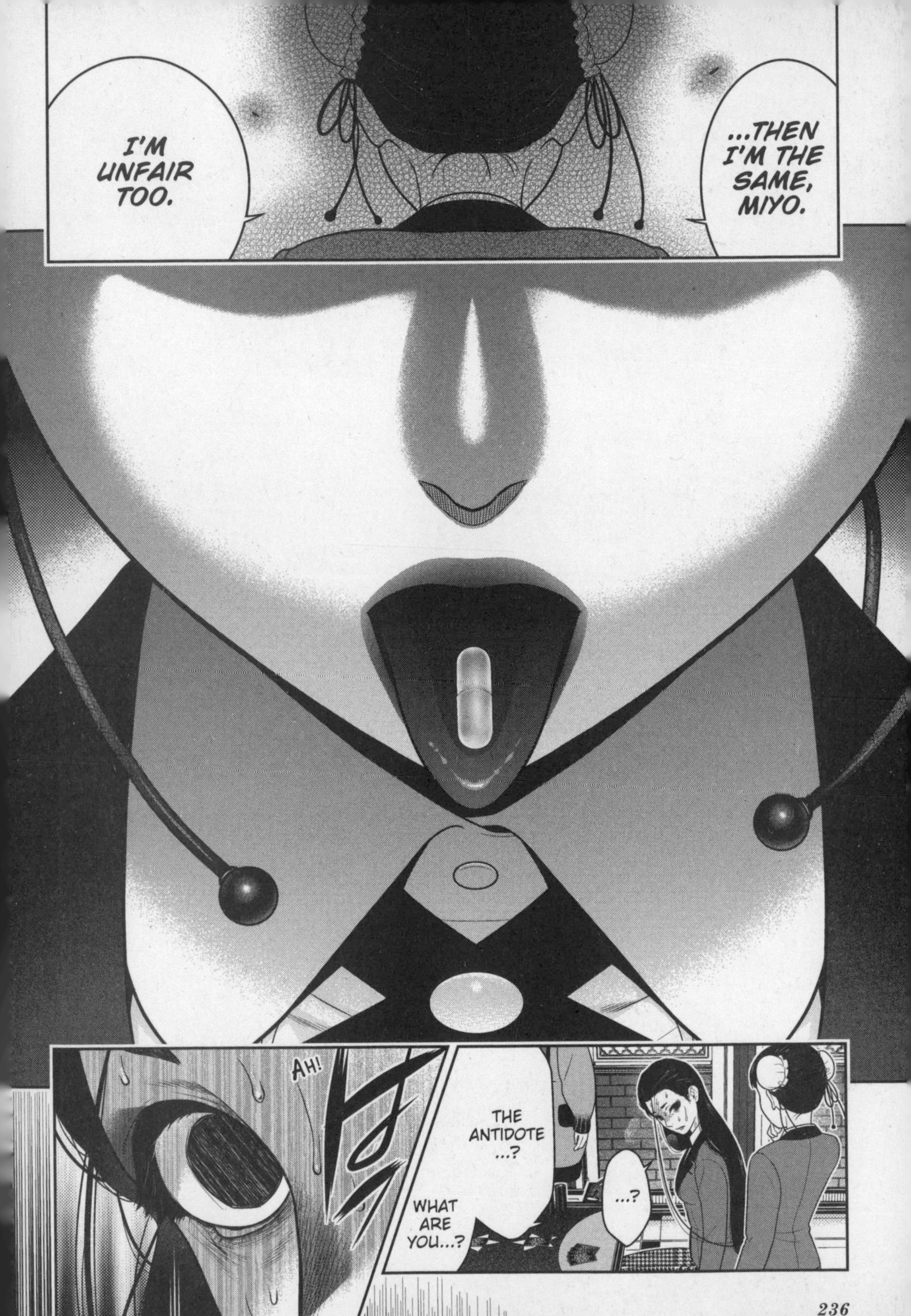
...THEN I'M THE SAME, MIYO.
I'M UNFAIR TOO.
THE ANTIDOTE ...?
...?
WHAT ARE YOU...?
AH!

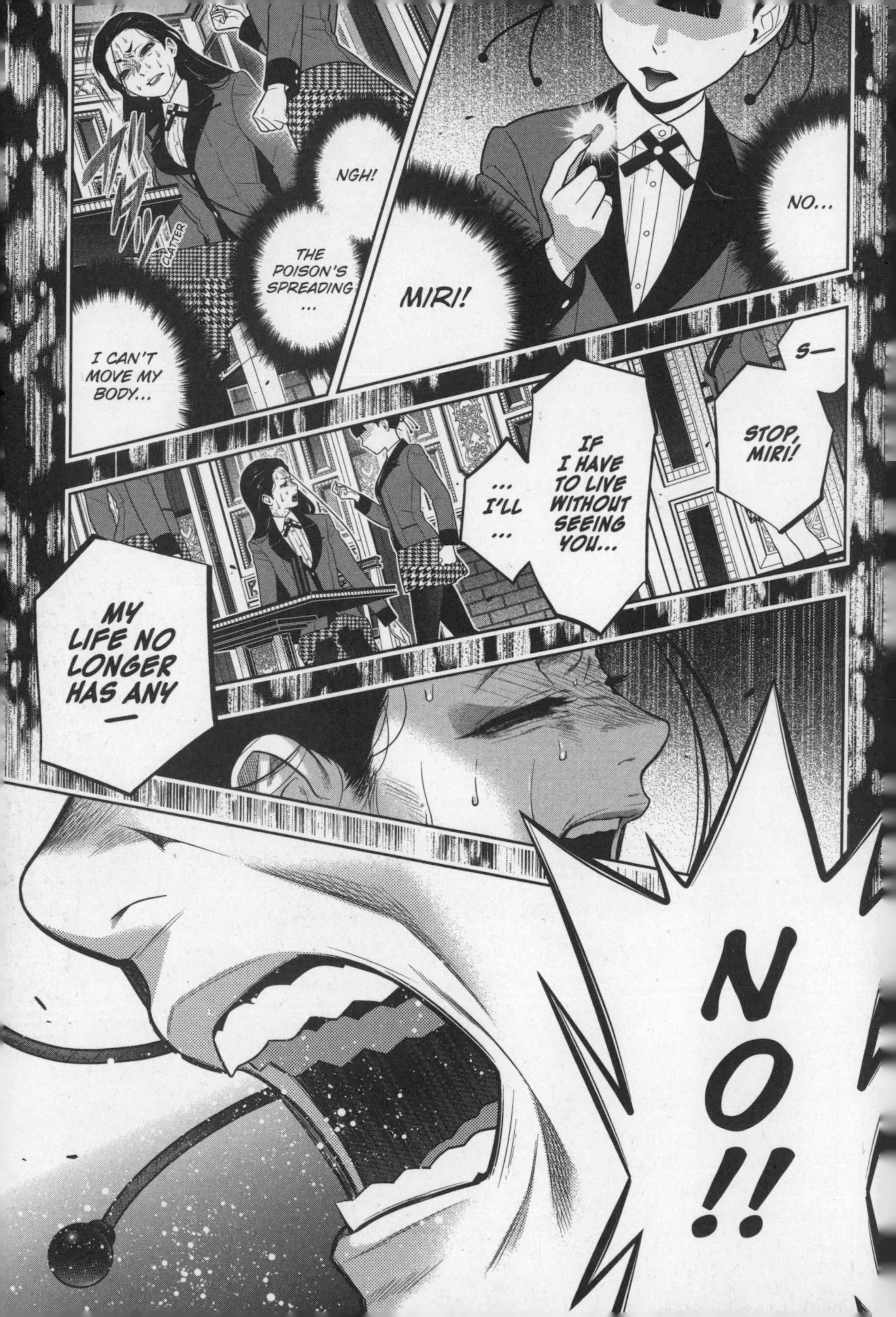
NO...
MIRI!
NGH!
CLATTER
THE POISON'S SPREADING ...
I CAN'T MOVE MY BODY...
S—
STOP, MIRI!
IF I HAVE TO LIVE WITHOUT SEEING YOU...
... I'LL ...
MY LIFE NO LONGER HAS ANY —
NO!!

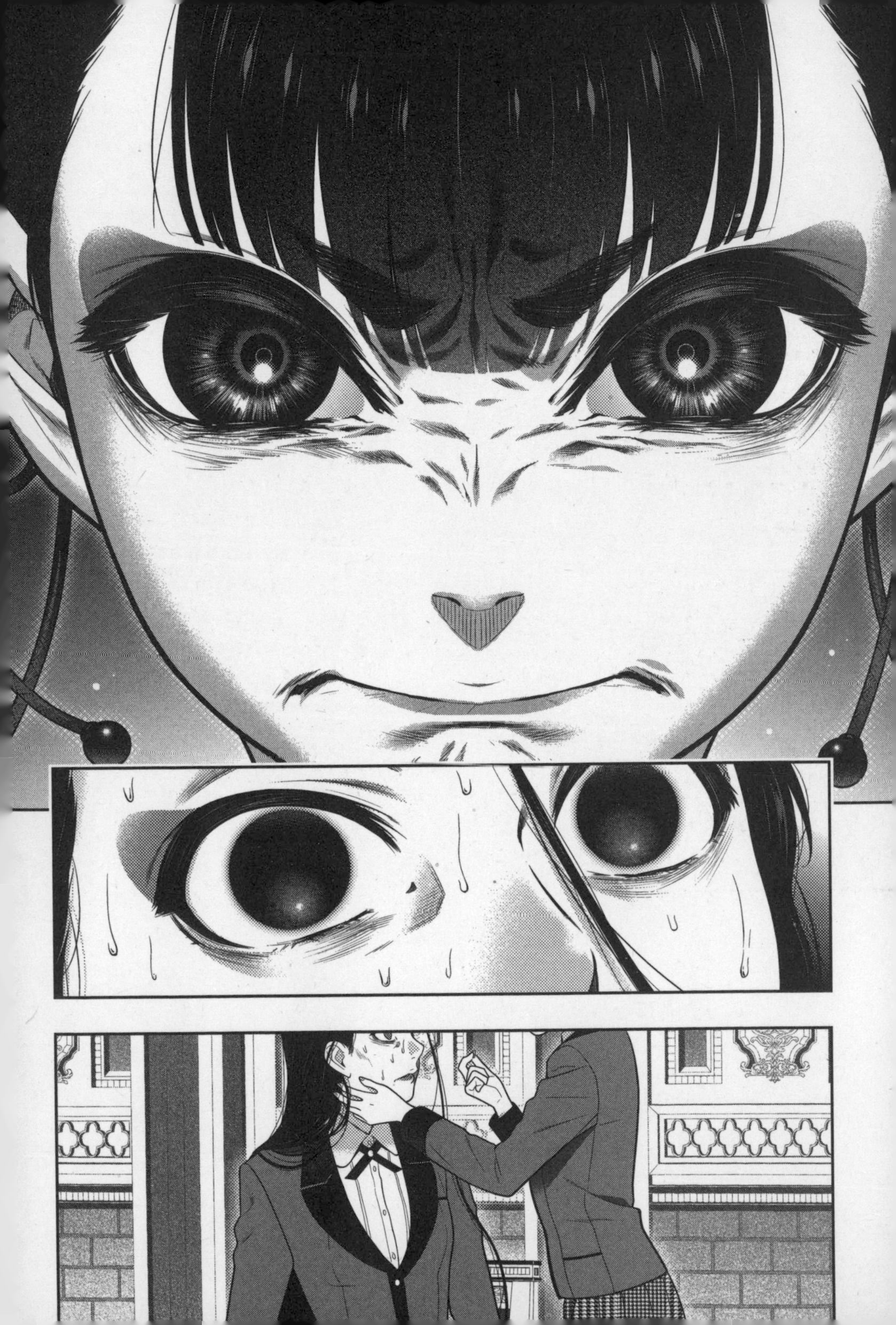

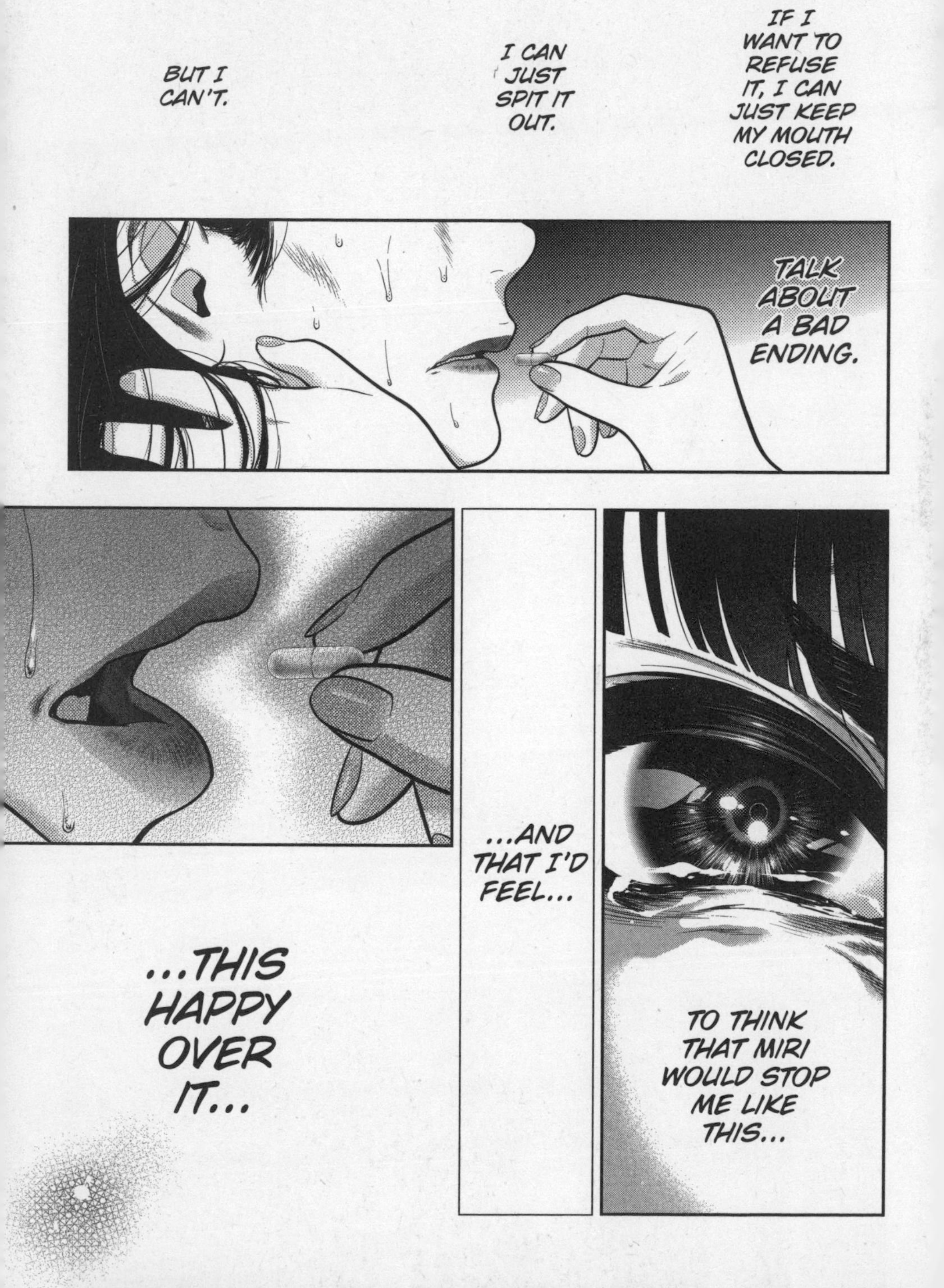
IF I WANT TO REFUSE IT, I CAN JUST KEEP MY MOUTH CLOSED.
I CAN JUST SPIT IT OUT.
BUT I CAN'T.
TALK ABOUT A BAD ENDING.
TO THINK THAT MIRI WOULD STOP ME LIKE THIS...
...AND THAT I'D FEEL...
...THIS HAPPY OVER IT...

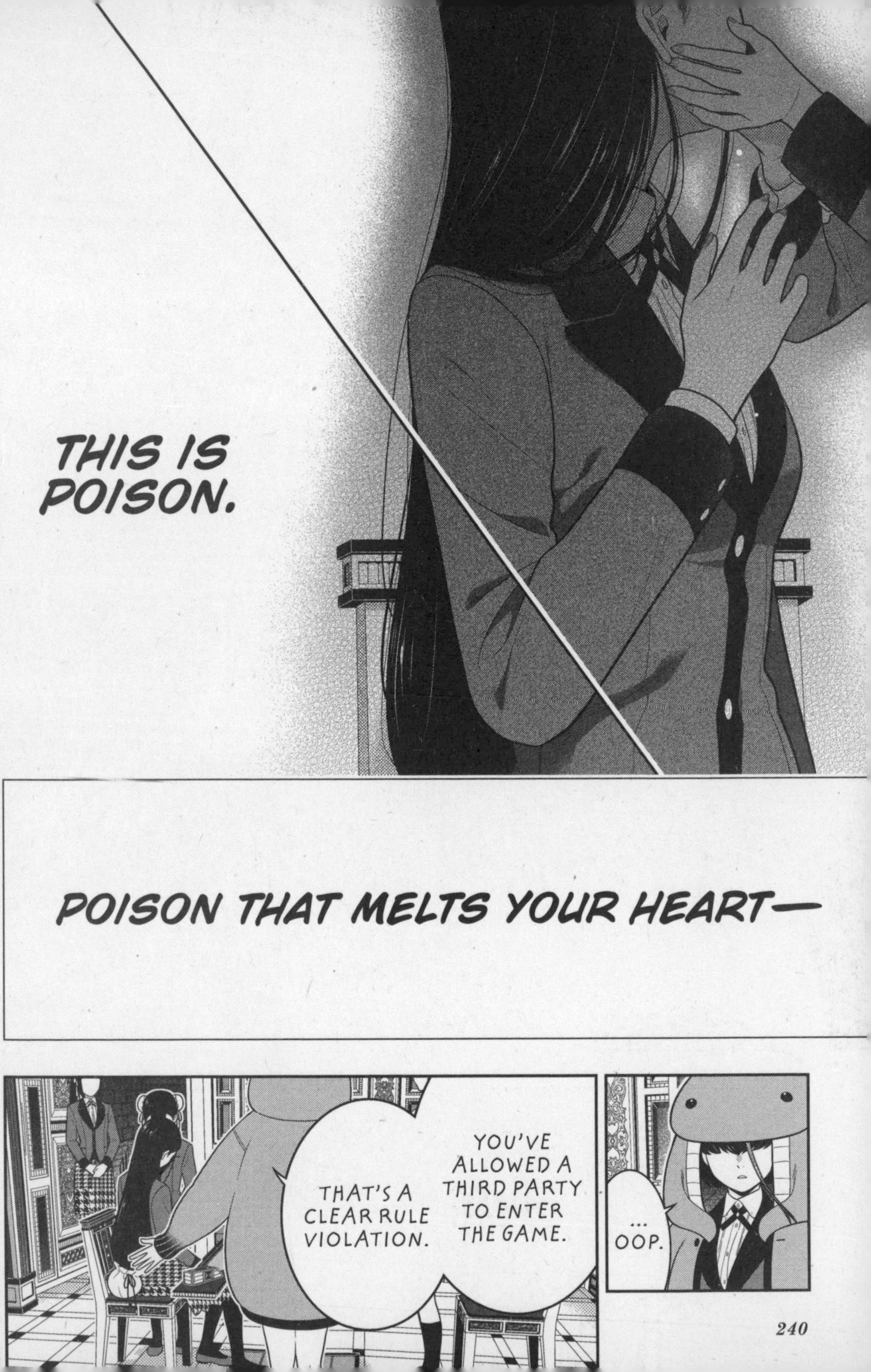
THIS IS POISON.
POISON THAT MELTS YOUR HEART—
... OOP.
YOU'VE ALLOWED A THIRD PARTY TO ENTER THE GAME.
THAT'S A CLEAR RULE VIOLATION.

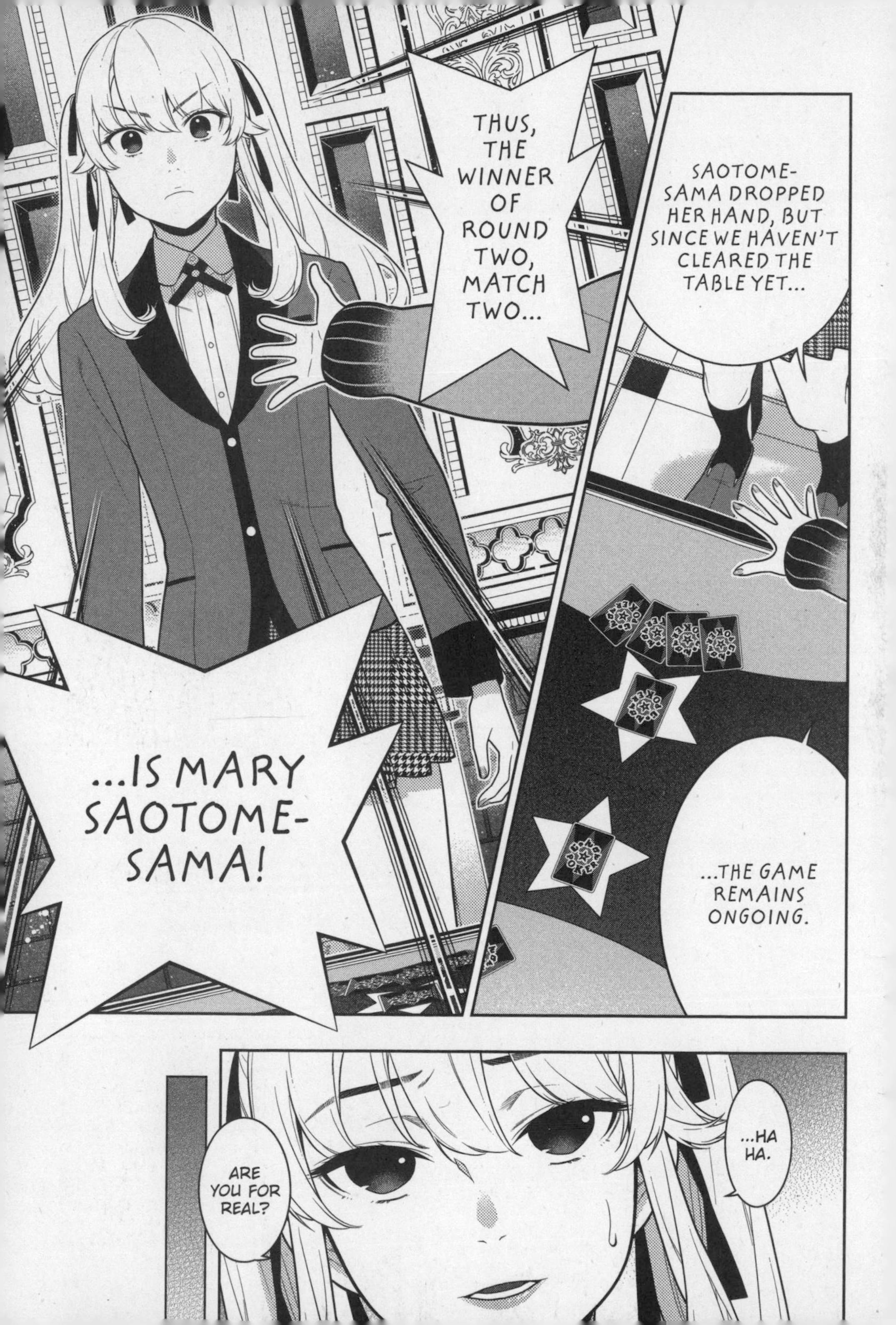
SAOTOME-SAMA DROPPED HER HAND, BUT SINCE WE HAVEN'T CLEARED THE TABLE YET...
...THE GAME REMAINS ONGOING.
THUS, THE WINNER OF ROUND TWO, MATCH TWO...
...IS MARY SAOTOME-SAMA!
...HA HA.
ARE YOU FOR REAL?

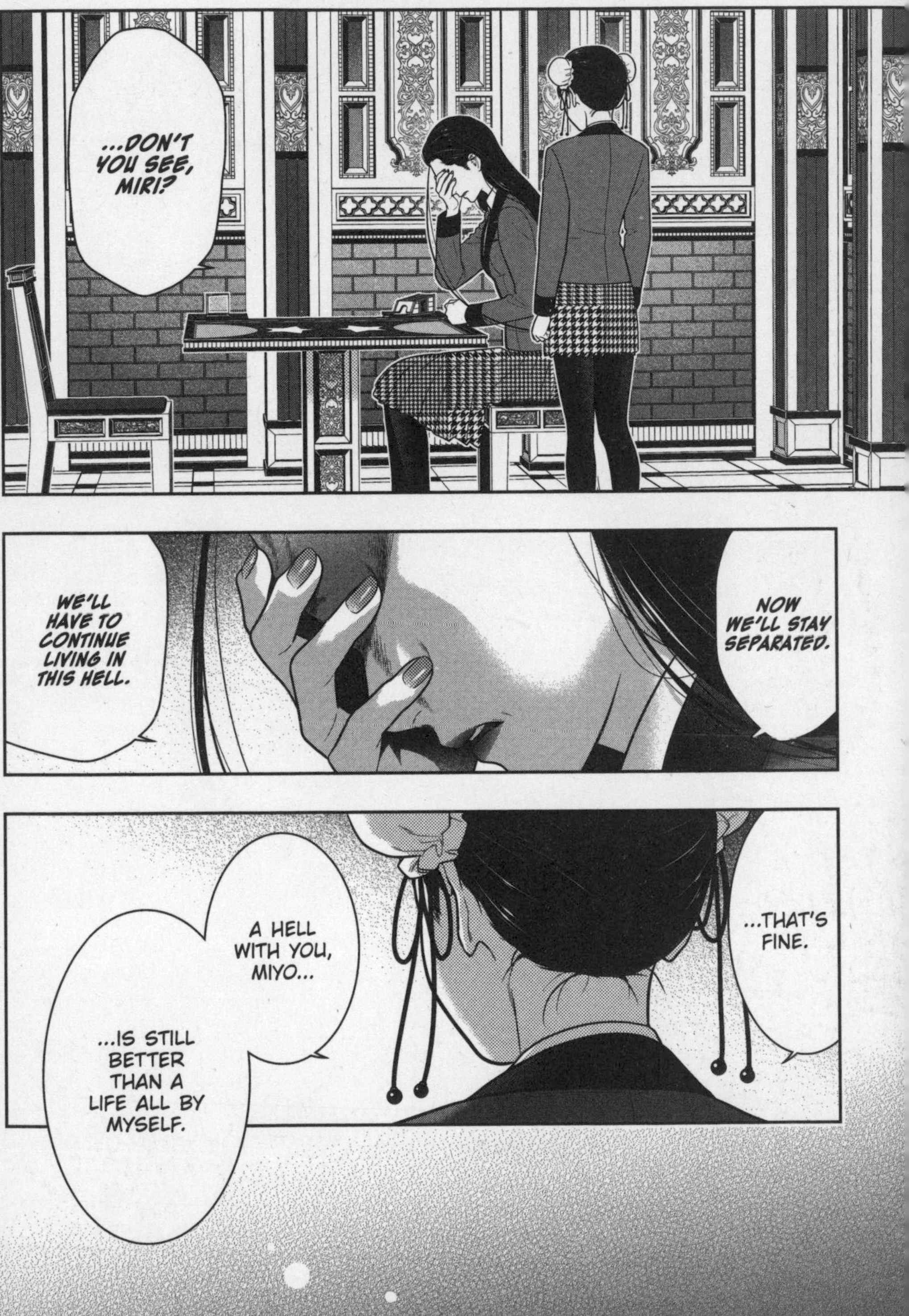
...DON'T YOU SEE, MIRI?
NOW WE'LL STAY SEPARATED.
WE'LL HAVE TO CONTINUE LIVING IN THIS HELL.
...THAT'S FINE.
A HELL WITH YOU, MIYO...
...IS STILL BETTER THAN A LIFE ALL BY MYSELF.

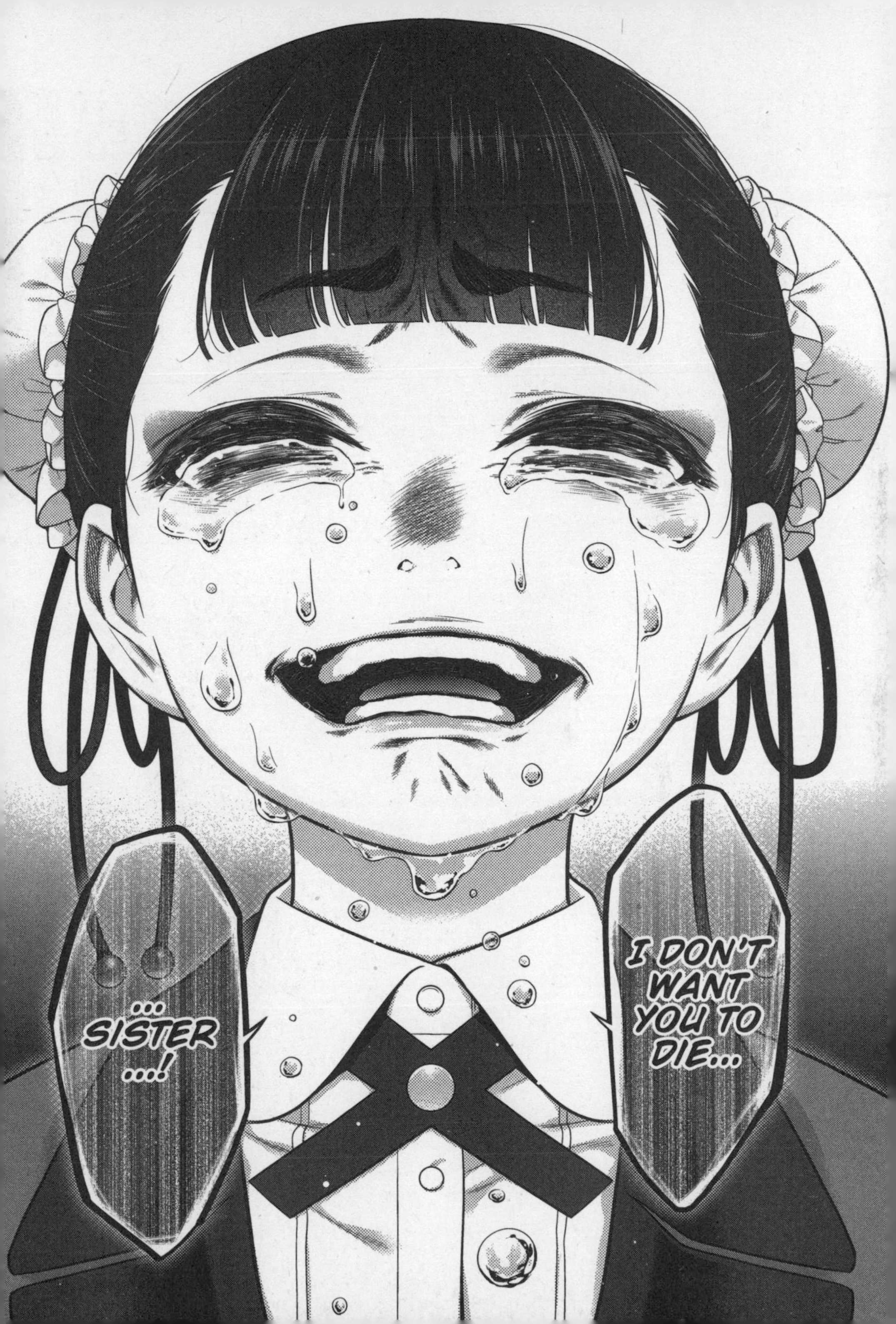
I DON'T WANT YOU TO DIE...
...SISTER ...!

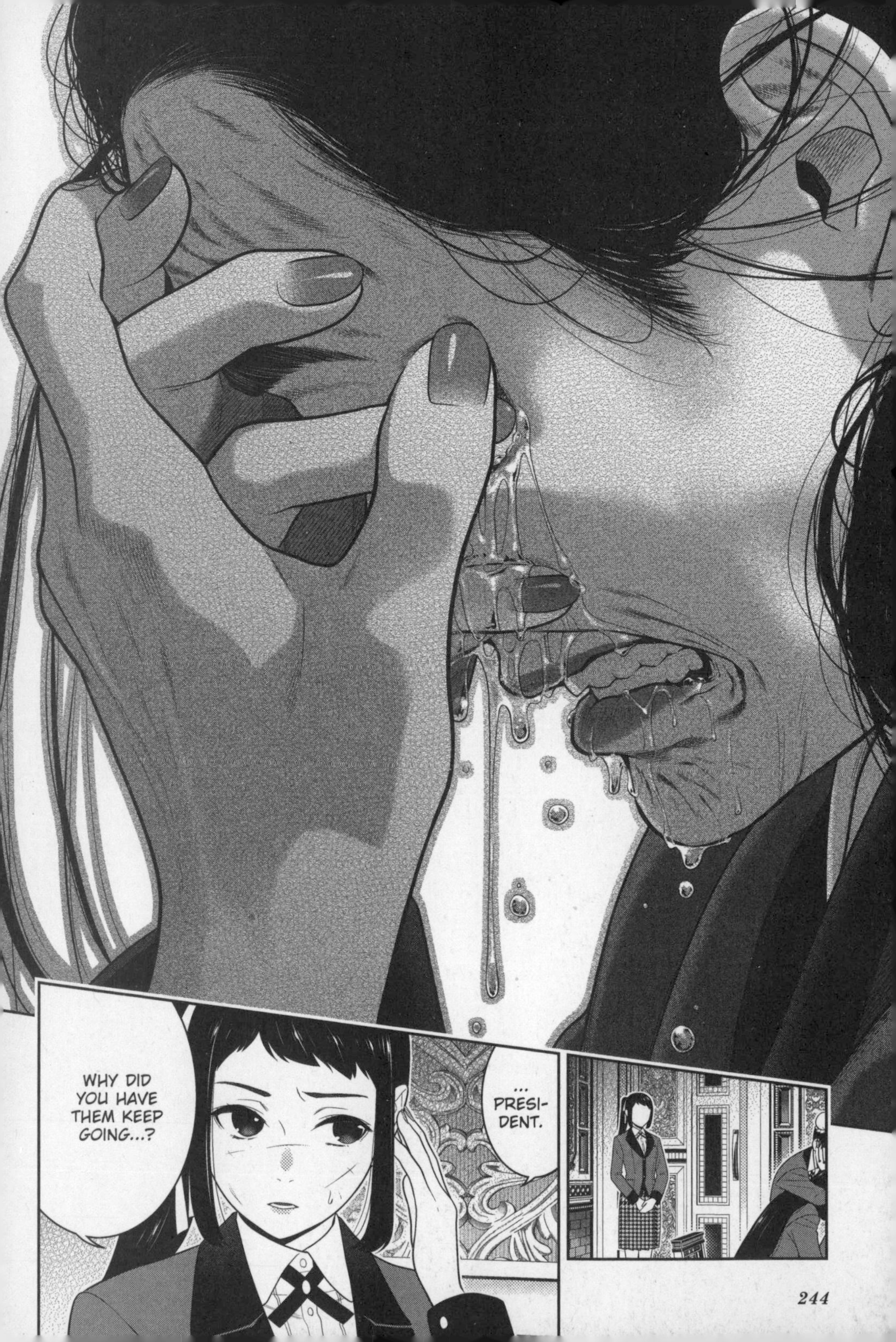

... PRESI- DENT.
WHY DID YOU HAVE THEM KEEP GOING...?

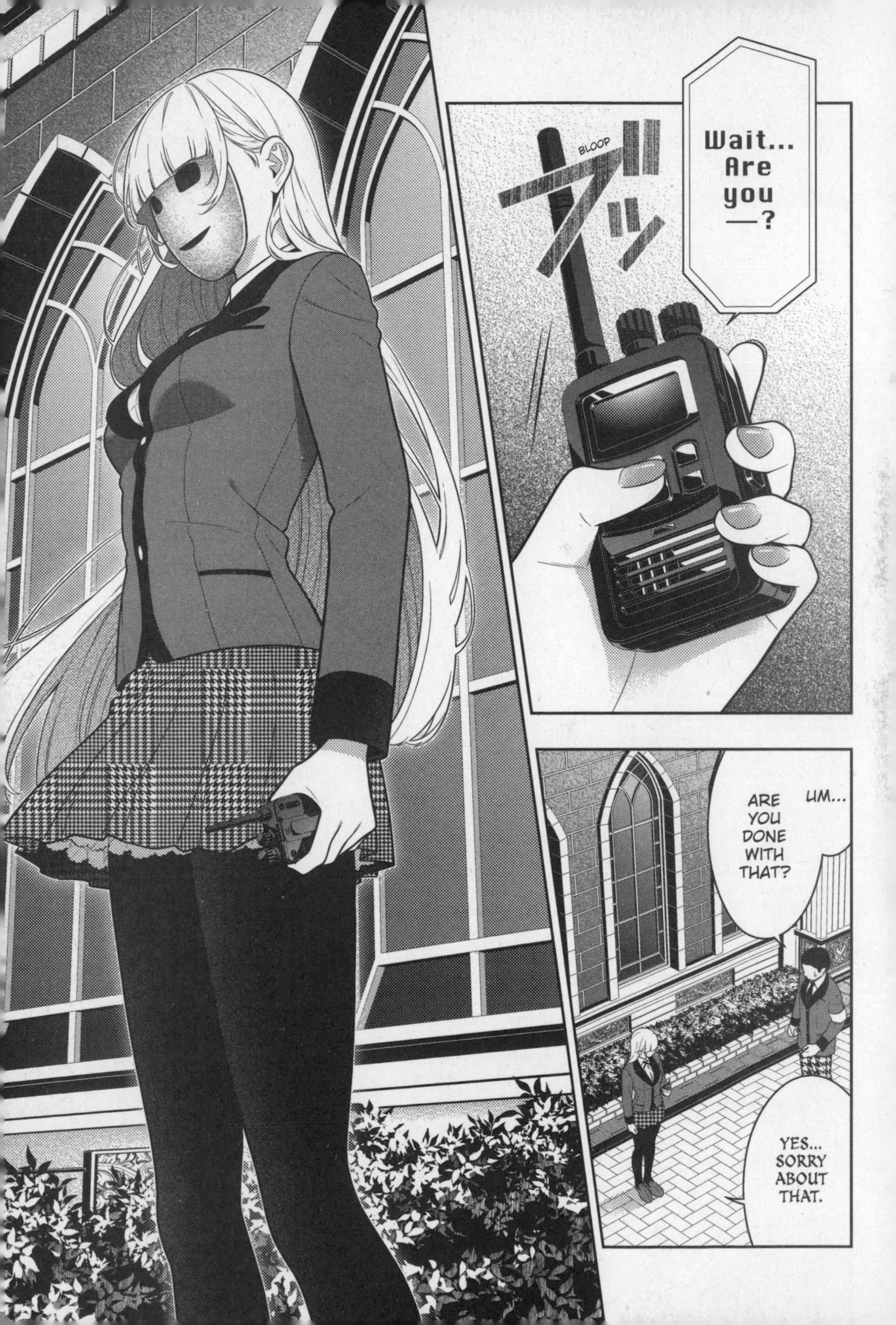
Wait... Are you —?
BLOOP
ブッ
UM...
ARE YOU DONE WITH THAT?
YES... SORRY ABOUT THAT.

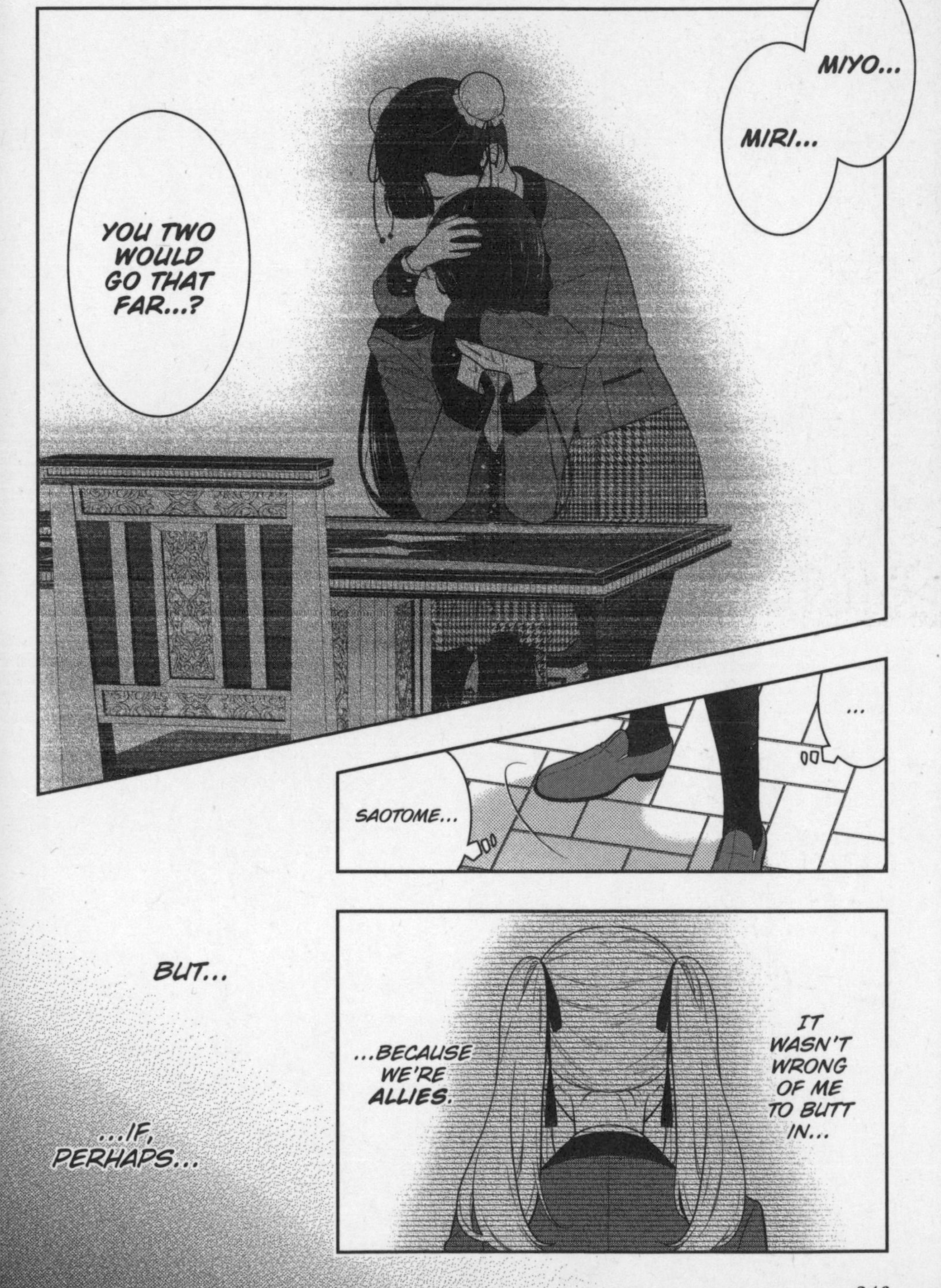
MIYO...
MIRI...
YOU TWO WOULD GO THAT FAR...?
...
SAOTOME...
IT WASN'T WRONG OF ME TO BUTT IN...
...BECAUSE WE'RE ALLIES.
BUT...
...IF, PERHAPS...

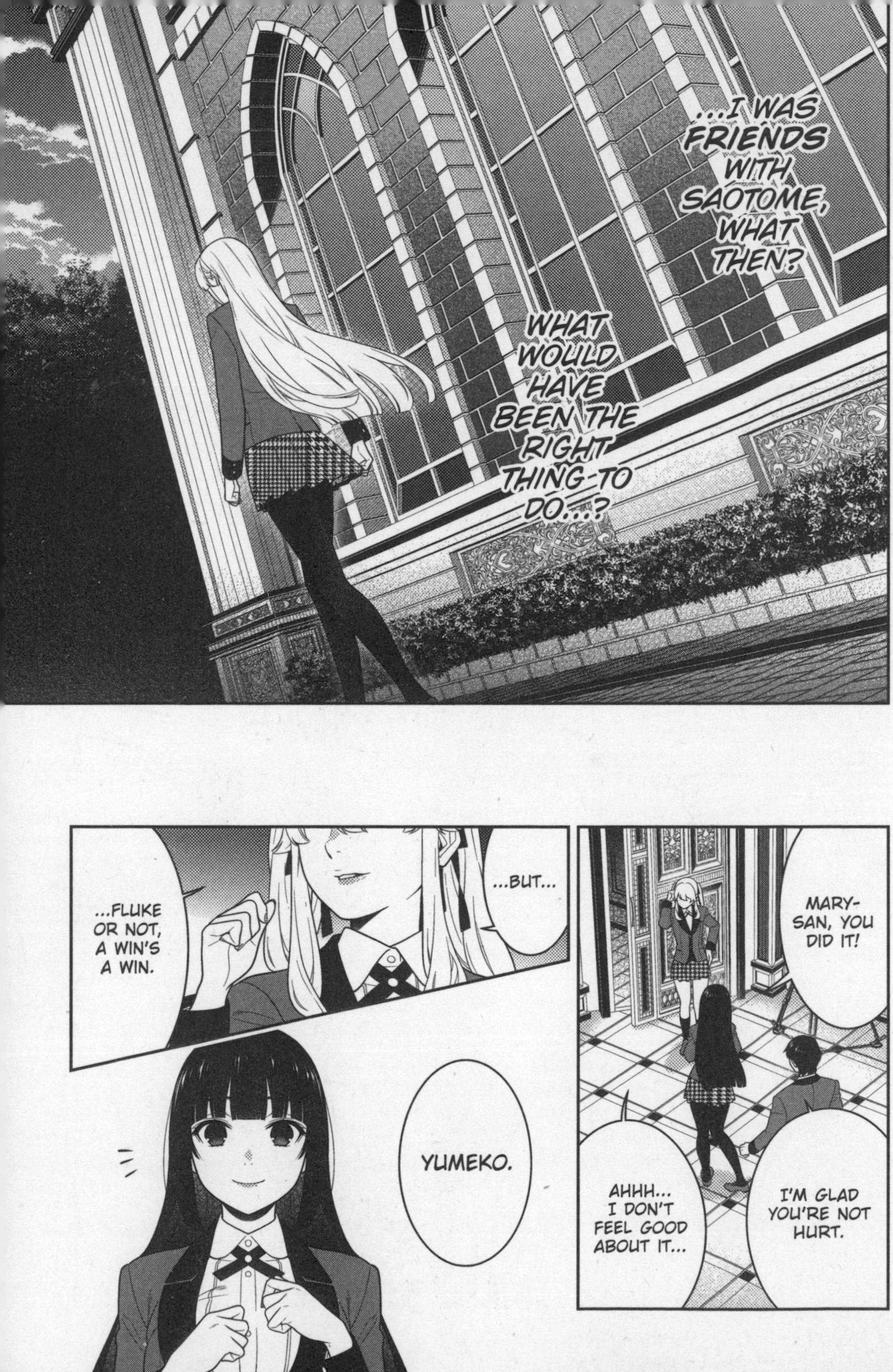
...I WAS FRIENDS WITH SAOTOME, WHAT THEN?
WHAT WOULD HAVE BEEN THE RIGHT THING TO DO...?
MARY-SAN, YOU DID IT!
I'M GLAD YOU'RE NOT HURT.
AHHH... I DON'T FEEL GOOD ABOUT IT...
...BUT...
...FLUKE OR NOT, A WIN'S A WIN.
YUMEKO.

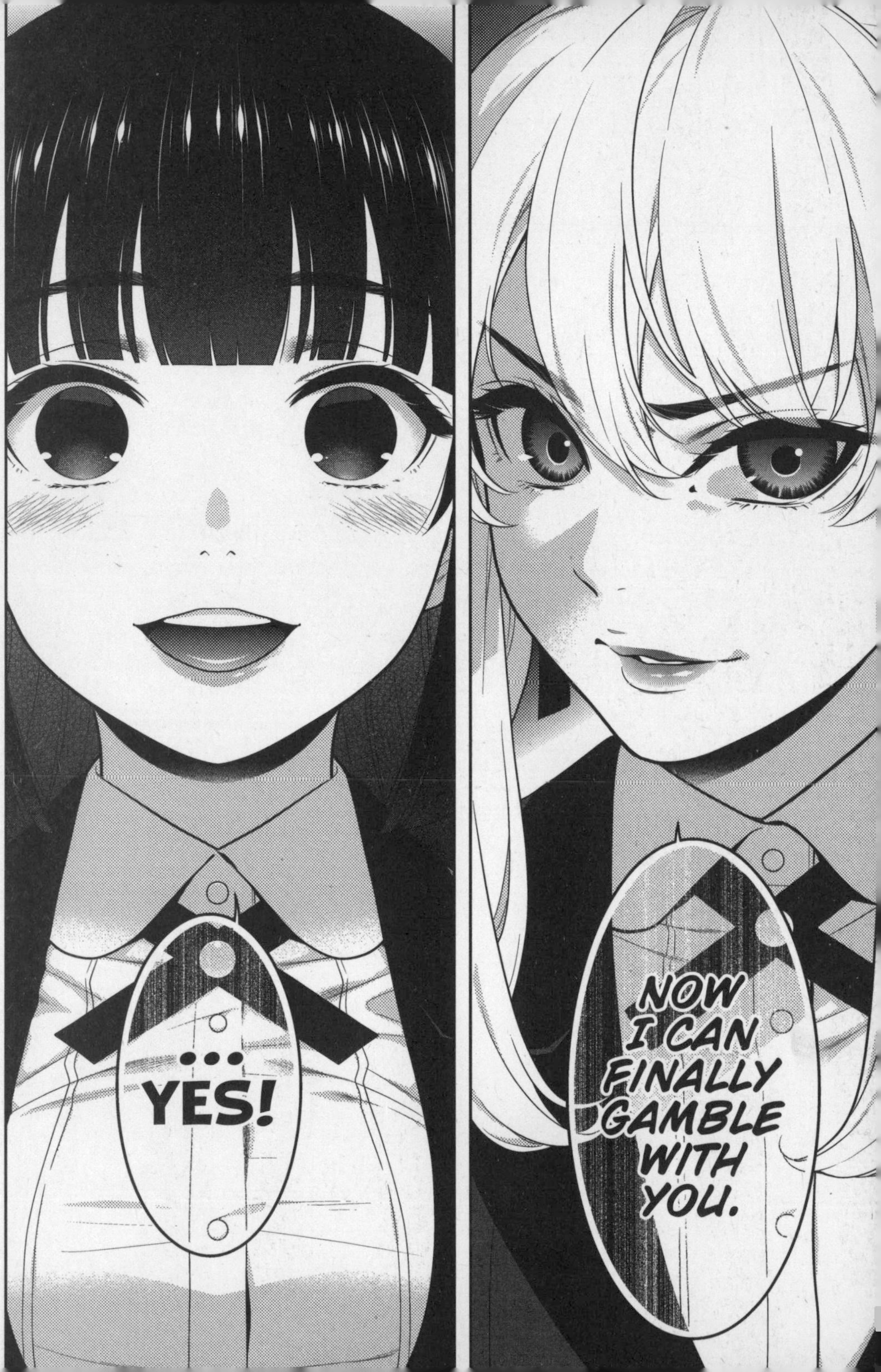
NOW I CAN FINALLY GAMBLE WITH YOU.
...YES!

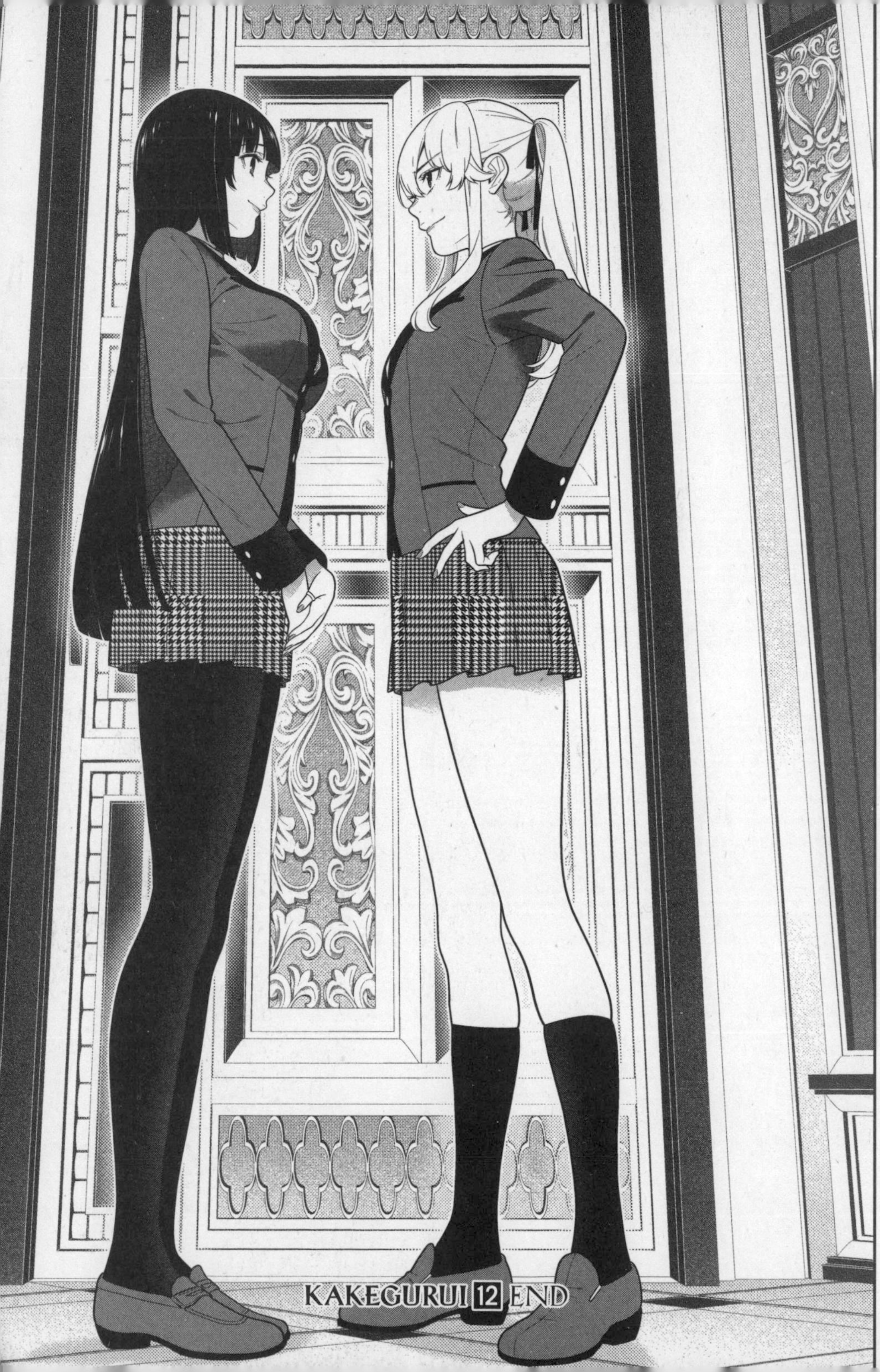
KAKEGURUI 12 END

THE 20XX ERIMI AUTUMN/WINTER COLLECTION

TIME FOR SOME END-OF-THE-VOLUME BONUS COMICS!

* THIS HAS NO RELATION TO THE ACTUAL STORY.

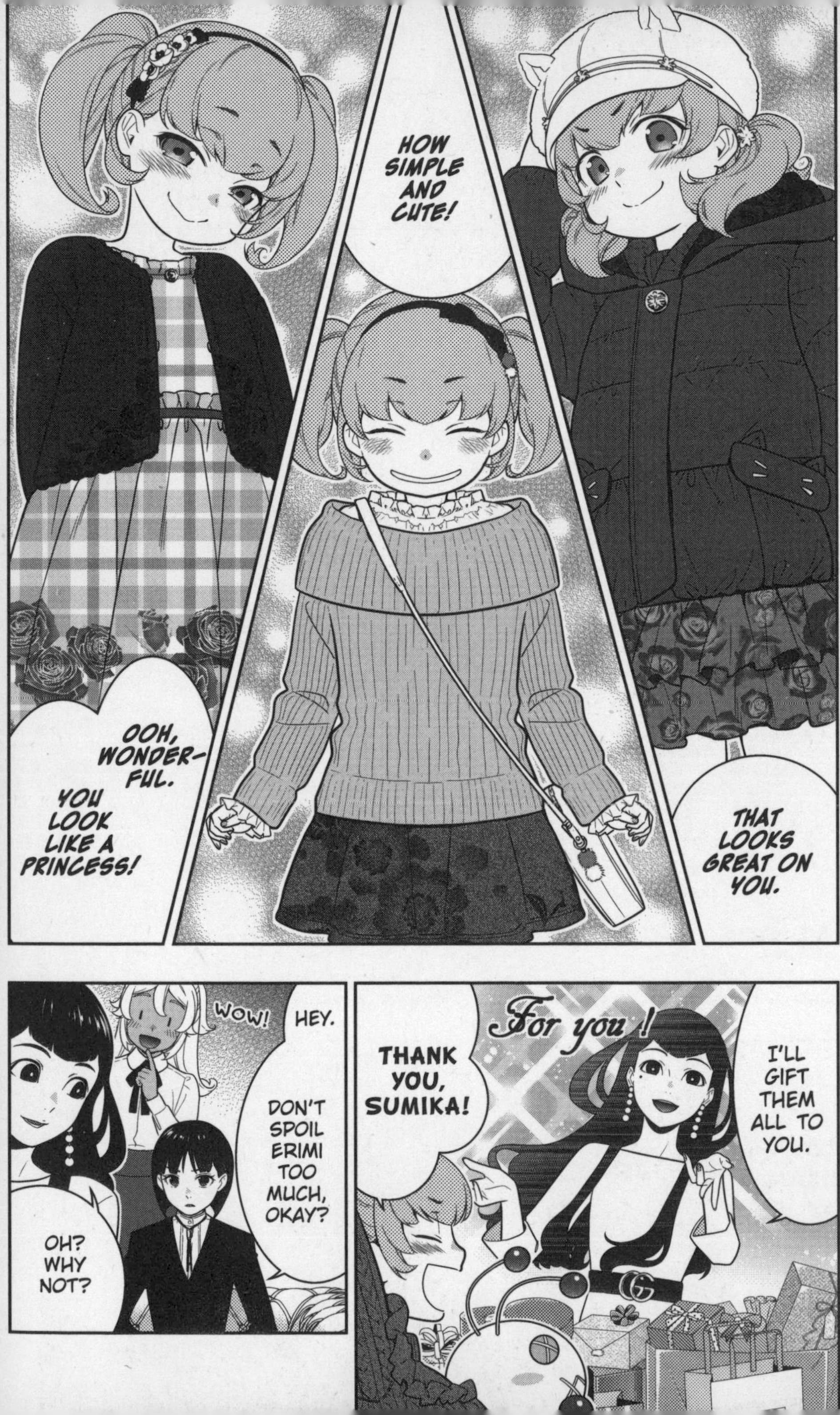
THAT LOOKS GREAT ON YOU.
HOW SIMPLE AND CUTE!
OOH, WONDERFUL.
YOU LOOK LIKE A PRINCESS!
I'LL GIFT THEM ALL TO YOU.
For you!
THANK YOU, SUMIKA!
HEY.
WOW!
DON'T SPOIL ERIMI TOO MUCH, OKAY?
OH? WHY NOT?

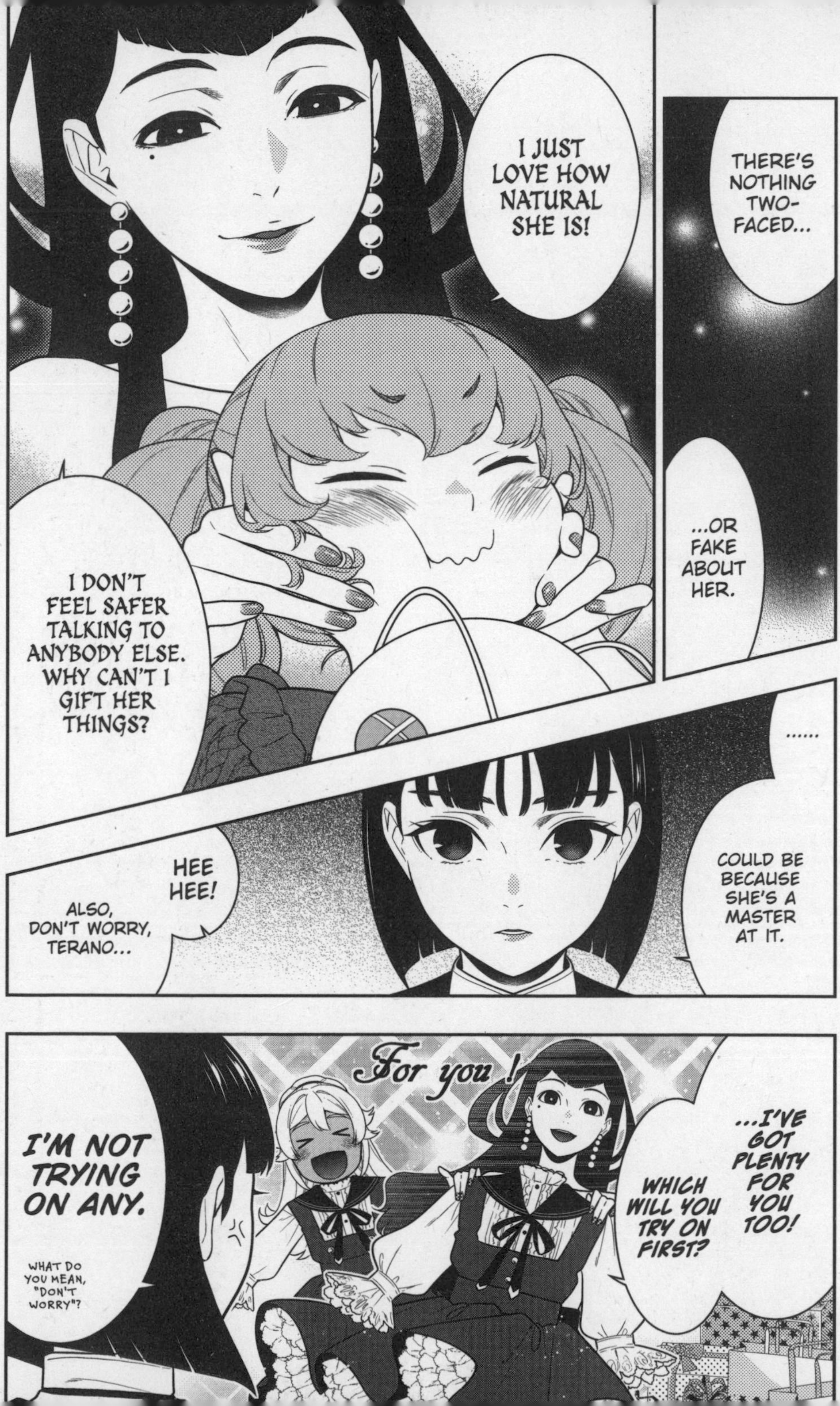
THERE'S NOTHING TWO-FACED...
...OR FAKE ABOUT HER.
I JUST LOVE HOW NATURAL SHE IS!
I DON'T FEEL SAFER TALKING TO ANYBODY ELSE. WHY CAN'T I GIFT HER THINGS?
......
COULD BE BECAUSE SHE'S A MASTER AT IT.
HEE HEE!
ALSO, DON'T WORRY, TERANO...
...I'VE GOT PLENTY FOR YOU TOO!
For you!
WHICH WILL YOU TRY ON FIRST?
I'M NOT TRYING ON ANY.
WHAT DO YOU MEAN, "DON'T WORRY"?

GAMBLING, THAT IS MY RAISON D'ÊTRE.

As the name suggests, this is a poker game that uses Rock Paper Scissors cards. It's different from "real" poker mainly because no matter how strong your hand is, you still have a 1-in-3 chance of losing every time. This naturally leads to some differing strategies when it comes to betting chips or bluffing. In the "Grand Meeting," each game is also played with the same deck. How will that affect the game? Read the story to find out.

ROCK

PAPER

SCISSORS

POKER

ROCK!

Thank you for picking up Volume 12 of *Kakegurui*! The "Grand Meeting" features the largest number of games and participants yet, which I think has made for a pretty lively volume. When we're plotting out a chapter with a main character in mind, we naturally want to have them do as much as possible, and due to page and story limitations, there are always parts we just can't fit in there. So it made me happy to dig deeper into each of the characters through the "Grand Meeting." I still have much more I want to say about them, but I'll do that when the next opportunity presents itself.

I'd like to thank Naomura-sensei and his assistants, as always, for not only keeping the cast looking beautiful but also expressing their pasts and complex expressions. I'd also like to thank my editors Sasaki-san and Yumoto-san, as well as everyone who gave their all to get this released. Finally, of course, I'd like to thank my readers. It was thanks to the support of many people that we've managed to get *Kakegurui*, Volume 12 out into the world.

Thank you all very much, and I hope I'll see all of you again in Volume 13 very soon.

Homura Kawamoto

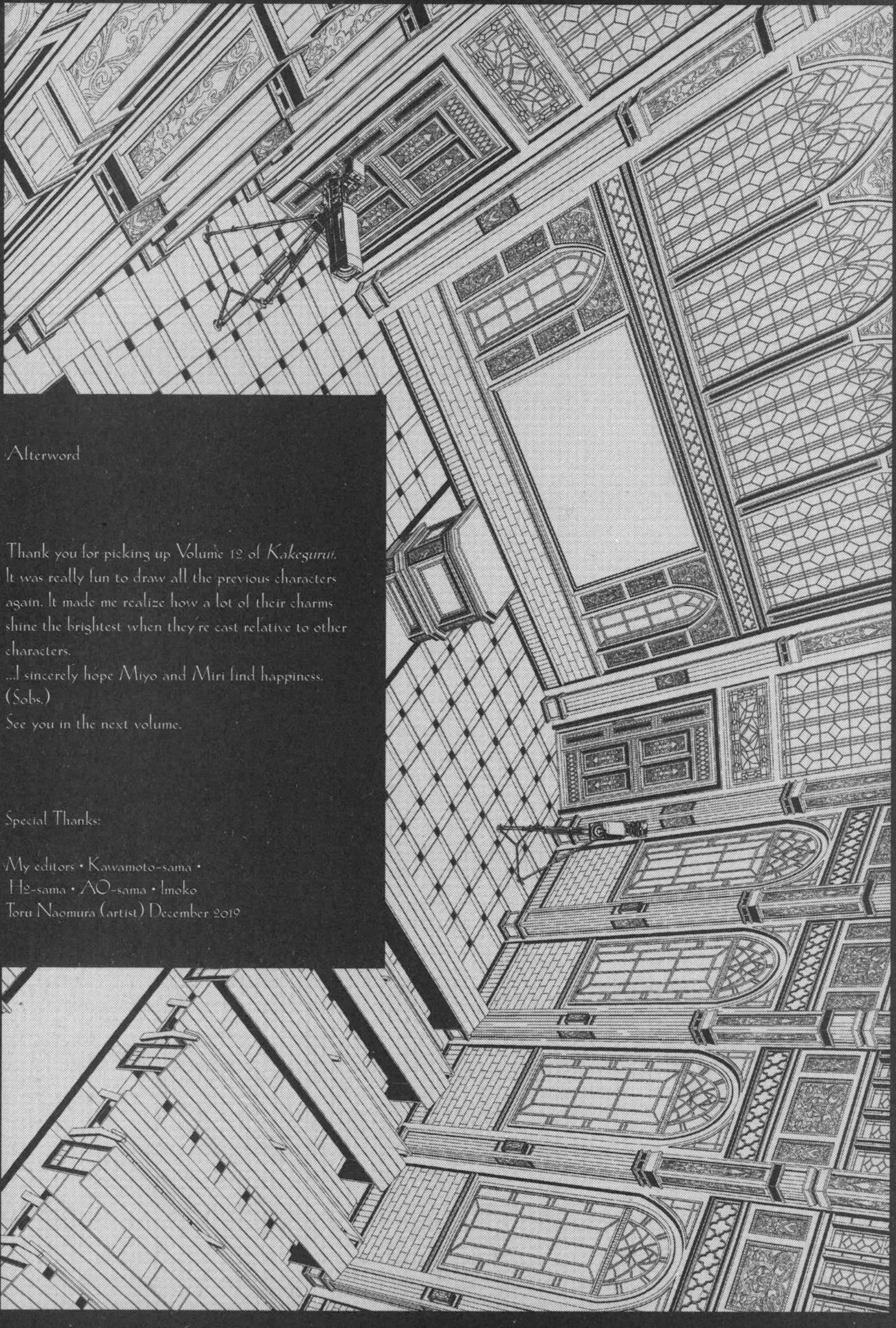

Afterword

Thank you for picking up Volume 12 of *Kakegurui*.
It was really fun to draw all the previous characters again. It made me realize how a lot of their charms shine the brightest when they're cast relative to other characters.
...I sincerely hope Miyo and Miri find happiness. (Sobs.)
See you in the next volume.

Special Thanks:

My editors • Kawamoto-sama •
H2-sama • AO-sama • Imoko
Toru Naomura (artist) December 2019

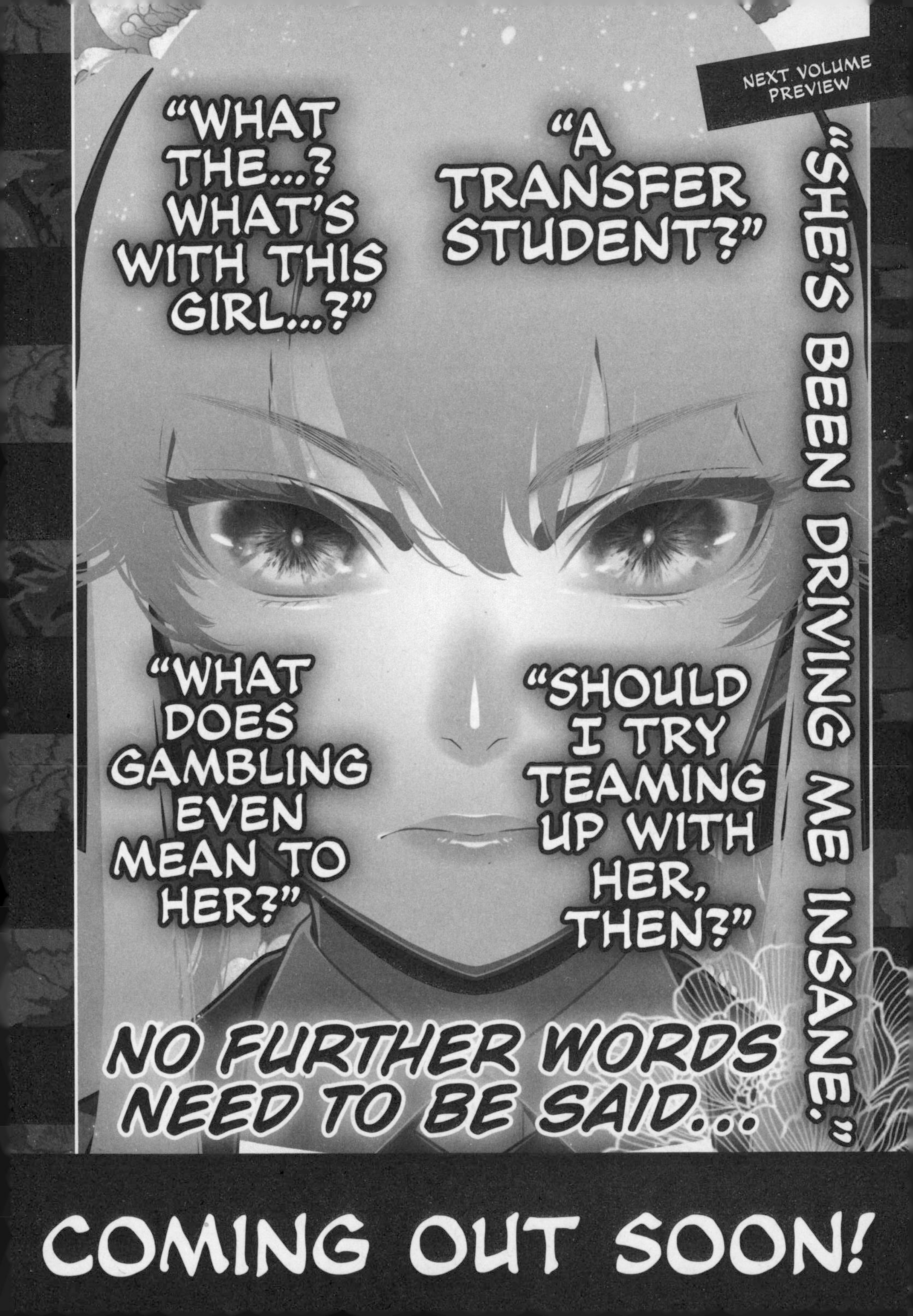
NEXT VOLUME PREVIEW
"WHAT THE...? WHAT'S WITH THIS GIRL...?"
"A TRANSFER STUDENT?"
"SHE'S BEEN DRIVING ME INSANE."
"WHAT DOES GAMBLING EVEN MEAN TO HER?"
"SHOULD I TRY TEAMING UP WITH HER, THEN?"
NO FURTHER WORDS NEED TO BE SAID...
COMING OUT SOON!

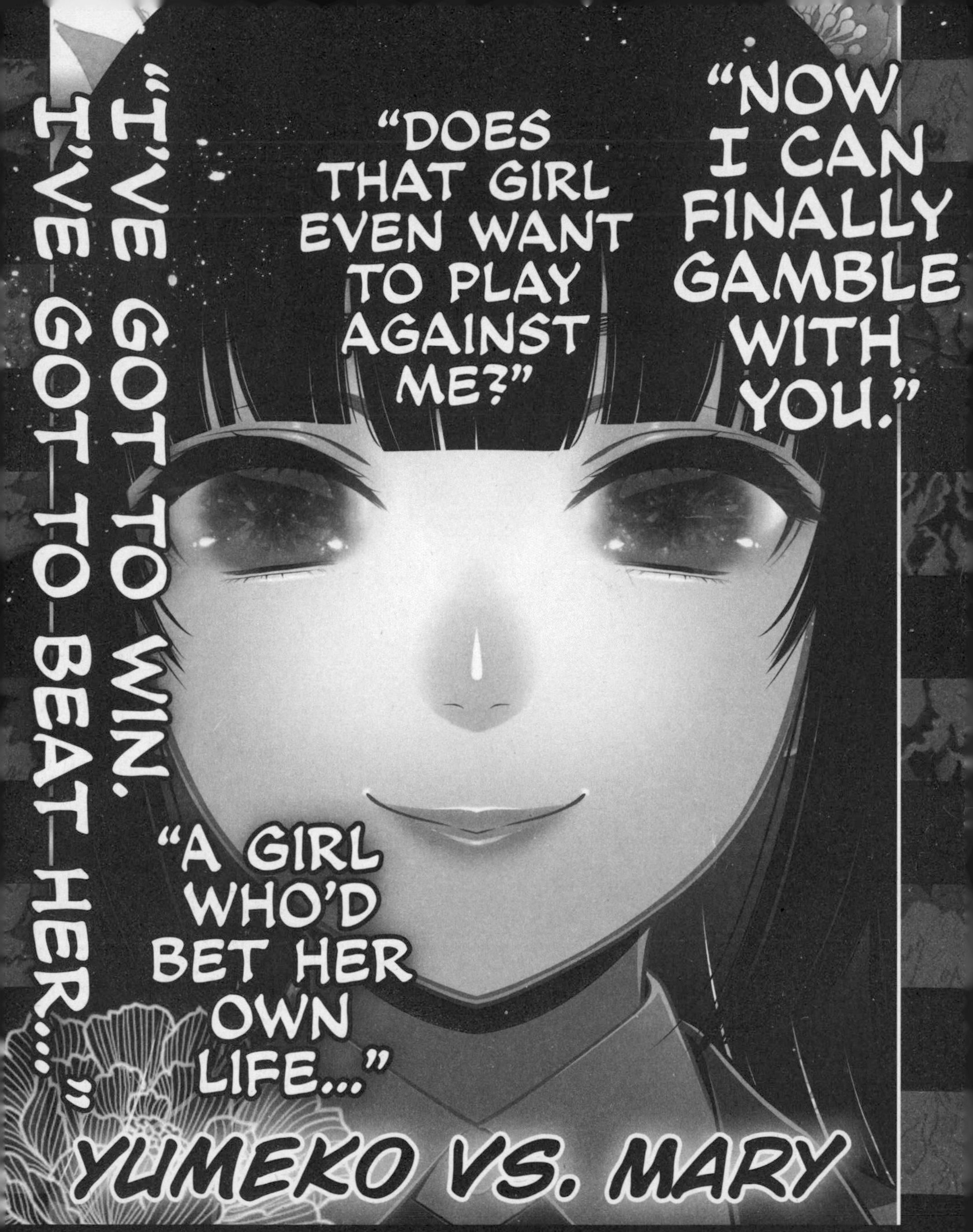
"NOW I CAN FINALLY GAMBLE WITH YOU."
"DOES THAT GIRL EVEN WANT TO PLAY AGAINST ME?"
"I'VE GOT TO WIN. I'VE GOT TO BEAT HER..."
"A GIRL WHO'D BET HER OWN LIFE..."
YUMEKO VS. MARY

KAKEGURUI VOLUME 13

MURDERER
IN THE STREETS, KILLER
IN THE SHEETS!

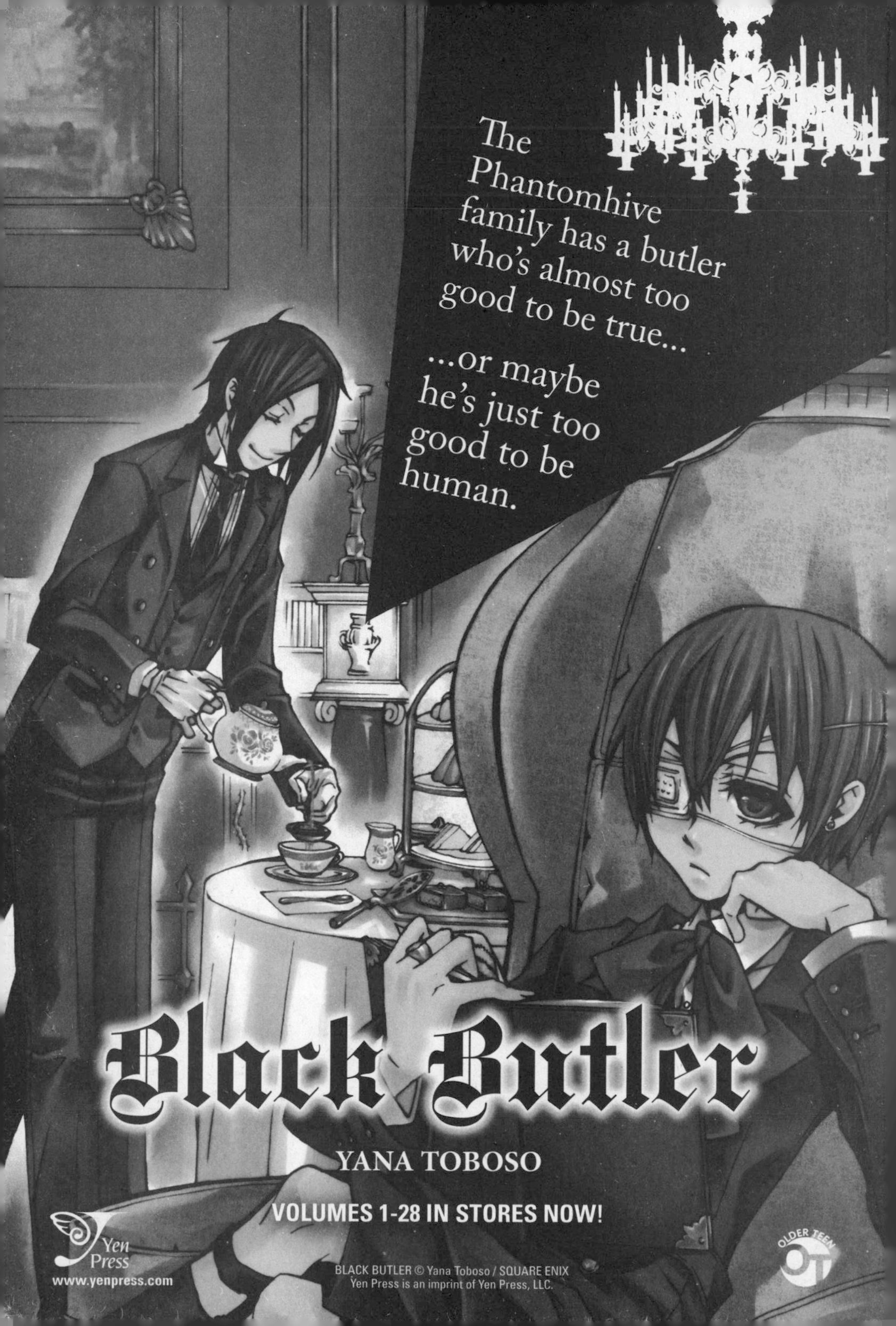

The Phantomhive family has a butler who's almost too good to be true...
...or maybe he's just too good to be human.
Black Butler
YANA TOBOSO
VOLUMES 1-28 IN STORES NOW!
Yen Press
www.yenpress.com
BLACK BUTLER © Yana Toboso / SQUARE ENIX
Yen Press is an imprint of Yen Press, LLC.
OLDER TEEN
OT

⑫

STORY: **Homura Kawamoto**
ART: **Toru Naomura**

Translation: Kevin Gifford
Lettering: Anthony Quintessenza

This book is a work of fiction. Names, characters, places, and incidents are the product of the author's imagination or are used fictitiously. Any resemblance to actual events, locales, or persons, living or dead, is coincidental.

KAKEGURUI Vol. 12 ©2019 Homura Kawamoto, Toru Naomura/SQUARE ENIX CO., LTD. First published in Japan in 2019 by SQUARE ENIX CO., LTD. English translation rights arranged with SQUARE ENIX CO., LTD. and Yen Press, LLC through Tuttle-Mori Agency, Inc.

English translation ©2019 by SQUARE ENIX CO., LTD.

Yen Press
150 West 30th Street, 19th Floor
New York, NY 10001

Visit us at yenpress.com
facebook.com/yenpress
twitter.com/yenpress
yenpress.tumblr.com
instagram.com/yenpress

First Yen Press Edition: August 2020
The chapters in this volume were originally published as ebooks by Yen Press.

Yen Press is an imprint of Yen Press, LLC.
The Yen Press name and logo are trademarks of Yen Press, LLC.

The publisher is not responsible for websites (or their content) that are not owned by the publisher.

Library of Congress Control Number: 2017939211

ISBNs: 978-1-9753-1519-1 (paperback)
         978-1-9753-1518-4 (ebook)

10 9 8 7 6 5 4 3 2 1

WOR

Printed in the United States of America